School Social Work

Practice, Policy, and Research

Also available from Lyceum Books, Inc.

THERAPEUTIC GAMES AND GUIDED IMAGERY: TOOLS FOR MENTAL HEALTH AND SCHOOL PROFESSIONALS WORKING WITH CHILDREN, ADOLESCENTS, AND THEIR FAMILIES, by Monit Cheung

EVIDENCE-BASED PRACTICES FOR SOCIAL WORKERS: AN INTERDISCIPLINARY APPROACH, by Thomas O'Hare

CLINICAL ASSESSMENT FOR SOCIAL WORKERS: QUANTITATIVE AND QUALITATIVE METHODS, 2E, by Catheleen Jordan and Cynthia Franklin

TEAMWORK IN MULTIPROFESSIONAL CARE, by Malcolm Payne, foreword by Thomas M. Meenaghan

HOW TO TEACH EFFECTIVELY, by Bruce D. Friedman

AN EXPERIENTIAL APPROACH TO GROUP WORK, by Richard Furman, Diana Rowan and Kim Bender

THE ETHICS OF PRACTICE WITH MINORS, by Kim Strom-Gottfried

CRITICAL MULTICULTURAL SOCIAL WORK, by Jose Sisneros, Catherine Stakeman, Mildred C. Joyner, and Cathryne L. Schmitz

DISABILITY: A DIVERSITY MODEL APPROACH IN HUMAN SERVICE PRACTICE, 2E, by Romel W. Mackelprang and Richard O. Salsgiver

SEVENTH EDITION

School Social Work

Practice, Policy, and Research

Carol Rippey MASSAT | Robert CONSTABLE | Shirley McDONALD | John P. FLYNN

LYCEUM
BOOKS, INC.
Chicago, Illinois

Published by

LYCEUM BOOKS, INC.
5758 S. Blackstone Ave.
Chicago, Illinois 60637
773+643-1903 (Fax)
773+643-1902 (Phone)
lyceum@lyceumbooks.com
http://www.lyceumbooks.com

10 9 8 7 6 5 4 3 2 1

ISBN 978-1-933478-02-9

Library of Congress Cataloging-in-Publication Data

School social work : practice, policy, and research / Robert Constable . . . [et al.].—7th ed.
p. cm.
Includes index.
ISBN 978-1-933478-02-9
1. School social work—United States. I. Constable, Robert.
LB3013.4.S365 2009
371.4′6—dc22

2008018286

Contents

Preface		ix
Section I	**History and General Perspectives in School Social Work**	**1**
Chapter 1	**The Role of the School Social Worker** *Robert Constable*	3
Chapter 2	**The Characteristic Focus of the Social Worker in the Public Schools** *Marjorie McQueen Monkman*	30
Chapter 3	**Evidence for the Effectiveness of School Social Work Practice** *Christine Anlauf Sabatino, Lynn Milgram Mayer, Elizabeth March Timberlake, and Theda Yolande Rose*	49
Chapter 4	**The Process of Ethical Decision Making in School Social Work: Confidentiality** *James C. Raines*	71
Chapter 5	**Ethical and Legal Complexities for School Social Workers with Confidentiality in Schools** *Sandra Kopels*	95
Chapter 6	**The Developing Social, Political, and Economic Context for School Social Work** *Carol Rippey Massat, Elizabeth Lehr Essex, Isadora Hare, and Sunny Harris Rome*	114
Chapter 7	**Evidence-Based Practice: Implications for School Social Work** *Carol Rippey Massat and Robert Constable*	140
Section II	**Policy Practice in School Social Work**	**153**
Chapter 8	**The School Social Worker as Policy Practitioner** *Carol Rippey Massat and Robert Constable*	155
Chapter 9	**School Social Work: Organizational Perspectives** *Edward J. Pawlak and Linwood Cousins*	176
Chapter 10	**School Policy Development and the School Social Worker** *John P. Flynn*	193
Chapter 11	**Needs Assessment: A Tool of Policy Practice in School Social Work** *Lyndell R. Bleyer and Kathryn Joiner*	217
Chapter 12	**Conducting and Using Research in the Schools: Practitioners as Agents for Change** *Nancy Farwell and Sung Sil Lee Sohng*	233

Chapter 13 **Educational Mandates for Children with Disabilities: School Policies, Case Law, and the School Social Worker** *Brooke R. Whitted, Malcolm C. Rich, Robert Constable, and Carol Rippey Massat* 254

Chapter 14 **Family-Centered Services to Infants and Toddlers with or at Risk for Disabilities: IDEA 2004, Part C** *Kathleen Kirk Bishop* 274

Chapter 15 **A History of the Education of African American Children** *Carol Rippey Massat and Cassandra McKay* 291

Chapter 16 **Policy and Law Affecting School Social Work with Vulnerable Populations** *Carol Rippey Massat and Cassandra McKay* 302

Section III Assessment, Consultation, and Planning in School Social Work **319**

Chapter 17 **Assessment, Multidisciplinary Teamwork, Consultation, and Planning in School Social Work** *Robert Constable and Galen Thomas* 321

Chapter 18 **A Framework for Cross-Cultural Practice in School Settings** *Frances Smalls Caple and Ramon M. Salcido* 339

Chapter 19 **Inclusive Education and the Least Restrictive Environment (LRE)** *Shirley McDonald and Robert Constable* 362

Chapter 20 **Collaboration and Consultation: Professional Partnerships for Serving Children, Youths, Families, and Schools** *Christine Anlauf Sabatino* 376

Chapter 21 **A Case Example of School and Mental Health Agency Collaboration** *Mary Constable Milne* 403

Chapter 22 **Assessment of the Learning Environment, Case Study Assessment, and Functional Behavior Analyses** *Galen Thomas, Marguerite Tiefenthal, Robert Constable, and Erin Gleason Leyba* 408

Chapter 23 **The Screening and Assessment of Adaptive Behavior** *James C. Raines and Richard Van Acker* 431

Chapter 24 **Classroom Observation** *Carol Rippey Massat and David Sanders* 452

Chapter 25 **Mental Health and School Social Work** *Michael S. Kelly, Helene Moses, Eric D. Ornstein, and Carol Rippey Massat* 464

Chapter 26 **Planning and Setting Goals: Behaviorial Intervention Plans, the Individualized Educational Program, and the Individualized Family Service Plan** *Robert Constable, Galen Thomas and Erin Gleason Leyba* 494

Chapter 27 **Response to Intervention and the School Social Worker** *Carol Rippey Massat, Robert Constable, and Galen Thomas* 522

Section IV Practice Approaches In Schools **533**

Chapter 28 **Developing and Defining the School Social Worker's Role** 535
Robert Constable and Helen Wolkow

Chapter 29 **School Social Work Practice with Families** 550
Robert Constable and Herbert J. Walberg

Chapter 30 **Case Management, Coordination of Services, and Resource Development** *Robert Constable and Richard S. Kordesh* 578

Chapter 31 **Working with Groups in Schools: Planning for and Working with Group Process** *Joan Letendre* 595

Chapter 32 **Working with Groups in Schools: Monitoring of Process and Evaluation of Outcomes** *Kendra J. Garrett* 610

Chapter 33 **Social Skills Training through Groups in Schools** 621
Craig Winston LeCroy

Chapter 34 **School-Based Crisis Intervention for Traumatic Events** 638
Jay Callahan

Section V School Social Work Practice Applications **663**

Chapter 35 **Tier 2 Behavioral Interventions for At-Risk Students** 665
Brenda Lindsey and Margaret White

Chapter 36 **School Social Work Collaboration with the Child Welfare System** *Sandra J. Altshuler* 674

Chapter 37 **Attendance and Truancy: Assessment, Prevention, and Intervention Strategies for School Social Workers** 692
Erin Gleason Leyba and Carol Rippey Massat

Chapter 38 **Bullying and Peer Sexual Harassment in Schools** 713
Susan Fineran, Shirley McDonald, and Robert Constable

Chapter 39 **Developing Safe, Responsive, and Respectful School Communities: Pathways to Intervention** *Shirley McDonald, Robert Constable, and Anthony Moriarity* 728

Appendices

Appendix A **School Social Workers and Confidentiality** 753
School Social Work Association of America

Appendix B **School Social Work Personal Safety Guidelines** 757
School Social Work Association of America

Index **763**

Preface to the Seventh Edition

The seventh edition of *School Social Work: Practice, Policy and Research* marks the further development of school social work as a specialization. The field has existed for over 100 years. Throughout the world it is becoming increasingly essential to education as families and communities strive to make schools safe and inclusive places for children to learn, to grow, and to flourish. Students growing up today face increasing complexity and risks. Parents and schools are equally concerned about these challenges.

School social workers, from their unique vantage point, have often been catalysts behind creative responses to societal and community changes. Over the past decades the substance and process of education has had to change, as has the practice of school social work. Legislative changes, shifts in society, and the welfare system have placed additional demands on educational institutions. Schools, which often find themselves in the middle of a political battleground, must respond to the mandates of law, as well as to the needs identified by families and communities.

The seventh edition of this book addresses key issues facing schools and school social workers today. It provides a model of social work role development in the complex and diverse world of services within the school community. The role model used in this book builds on the tasks which school social workers have always done well: assessment, consultation, planning, coordination, and individual, group, and family intervention. As education continues to develop, policy practice is also inherent to this role. This involves work with the whole school, the school community, and local, state and federal policy development. A policy practice model seeks to reconstruct the meaning of schools as safe places where families and schools can work together and manage risks to their children's best development. Infused throughout each chapter of the book are case examples and content that exemplify the practice of school social work in all its diversity with bilingual students, immigrant children, members of minority and oppressed groups, and female students, among others. New chapters, such as Milne's (chapter 21) illustrate the kind of innovative school-community–agency partnerships which are coming to be used in schools today. There is an enhanced focus on diversity, with two new chapters. The first addresses the history of education of African American children, and the second describes important policies relevant to work with members of vulnerable groups in the United States.

The field of school social work, its practice, policy and research, is being constructed by many different social workers interacting with their dynamic environments. Needs change and situations evolve, so that neither the future world of the school nor its students' needs can be typified or frozen in time. One of these changes has been the movement toward evidence based practice. This edition describes and critiques current applications of evidence-based practice in school social work. Principles of using evidence-based practice are described, and an evidence base for intervention is included throughout the book. Another change has been the development of a tier model for thinking about interventions by members of a school team to create change in broader or narrower segments of a school population according to need and potential effectiveness. Tier 1 interventions address issues that affect the risk of the general school population. Tier 2 interventions address groups of students who are at risk and who can be effectively served by group-oriented interventions. Tier 3 interventions address particular youths with even more serious risks and who need a more individualized approach. The tier model is used in Response to Intervention (RTI), which addresses primarily academic applications, as well as with social, emotional, and behavioral interventions, through such models as positive behavioral intervention supports (PBIS). In this edition, the tier approach is threaded throughout the book, with a special emphasis in chapter 17, a new chapter on RTI (chapter 27), and a new chapter on tier 2 interventions (chapter 35). The seventh edition reflects all of these practical changes while retaining its productive theoretical perspective.

This edition is a product of the work of forty-four authors who collectively provide ways to get a theoretical and methodological handle on the school social worker's role. With all of the diversity in roles, a remarkable unity in the material has always become apparent. Each author addresses different aspects of an emergent role. The authors also provide updated references to facilitate student's location of key source materials, Web sites and online resources to obtain materials and information not yet in print. As this edition was developed we sought to include the most recent developments in the field and, due to page limitations, we found it necessary to retire a number of excellent chapters that were found in earlier editions of this book. These chapters will be made available to the readers online through Lyceum Books, Inc. Please consult their website for details.

Section I, History and General Perspectives in School Social Work, traces the history and evolving role of the school social worker and provides a theoretical framework for school social work practice. Constable in chapter 1 outlines the content of school social work as a specialization and traces the history of the role. This is followed by a theoretical framework for practice in a classic chapter by Monkman. Chapters following discuss a school social work response to accountability movements in education. There is an increased focus on effectiveness and evaluation research throughout. More and more, school social workers are confronted by serious confidentiality concerns, given the presence of violence in schools, communities, and families; drugs in schools and the workplace; suicidal ideation of students; self-mutilation behavior; and other sensitive issues. Several chapters address these confidentiality issues.

School social workers and others continue to develop plans and programs to meet the particular needs of each school community. This vision of practice can be traced to the earliest days of school social work and to its continuation through periods of fundamental changes in society and in school policy. As a result of this developed role, dealing with the social dimensions and human needs inherent in the education process, schools in the present climate of enhanced expectations find they need the school social worker as never before. For education professionals, effectiveness has become critical. With an emphasis on outcomes, school systems are developing systems of accountability that demand school social workers show evidence for effectiveness of their interventions. The emphasis on effectiveness calls for high professional qualifications. It meshes with movements in school social work toward specialization. In accordance with the No Child Left Behind Act of 2001, states are setting standards for "highly qualified" school social workers. They are now introducing performance-based, post masters-degree mentorships for more permanent certification of school professionals.

Section II, Policy Practice in School Social Work, focuses on the framework, tools, and context for school policy development. Massat and Constable and frame this section with their discussion of the principles of policy practice and key policies that affect programs. The tools of policy change—research, organizational analysis, needs assessment and policy analysis—are presented in chapters 9 through 12. Whitted, Rich, Constable, and Massat (chapter 13) and Bishop (chapter 14) lay out the key elements of special education laws that profoundly affect social work practice in schools. Chapters 15 and 16 address history and policy relevant to school social work with vulnerable populations in the United States.

Section III, Assessment, Consultation, and Planning in School Social Work, centers on the school social work role in assessment, consultation, and planning for direct work with children and families, and with a broader school community. These tasks and skills are the basis for everything the school social worker does. To work with teachers, parents, and children is also to work with their school community context. The result is a broader assessment process that is crucial to the effectiveness of the school social worker in the development of programs and policies.

Cross-cultural practice, including, assessment, goal-setting and measurement, has become increasingly important for competent school social work practice. In Section III, both a broad framework and specific tools for practice are included to address these issues. Caple and Salcido provide a framework for cross-cultural practice. The movement toward inclusion of children with disabilities in regular education has strongly affected schools across the nation. McDonald and Constable address specific inclusion issues. Practice skills in consultation collaboration, classroom observation, adaptive behavior assessment, mental health, case study assessment, and goal setting are covered in chapters 20, 20, 21, 22, 23, 24, 25, and 26. A new chapter on response to intervention addresses this important topic.

Section IV, Practice Approaches in Schools, focuses on current approaches to practice in schools. In this section of the book, chapters cover: work with families, case management, an enhanced group work section, social skills training, and crisis intervention.

The final section of this edition, Section V, School Social Work Practice Applications, addresses school social work practice focused on specific issues and concerns. These include a new chapter on Tier 2 interventions, as well as updated chapters on child welfare and school social work, truancy issues, bullying and sexual harassment, and the development of safe and responsive school communities.

Acknowledgments

As the field of school social work continues to be constructed, we give special recognition to those whose vision has played a major part in this construction. Fondly missed, they remain with us in their writing and thought. Florence Poole envisioned a field of practice with practitioners guided by theory assisting the school to become a resource for children, and for children to use these school resources for their own growth. Carel Germain took a biological, ecological metaphor, a life model for social work practice, and used it to explain what social workers were doing. Marjorie Monkman, student of William E. Gordon, took Gordon's theories about building social work practice in new directions as she constructed ecological theory for school social work as a field of practice. These individuals live on in the theories they have woven, and they assist all of us in understanding the potential in the school social worker's role.

Each of us acknowledges the patience and forbearance of our spouses, children, grandchildren, friends, and colleagues, who made the endeavor possible. We wish to express warm thanks to David Follmer, our friend and publisher of all seven editions. We give thanks also to all of the helpful staff at Lyceum Books, most notably our copy editor Lyn Rosen. Our students' struggles with learning such a complex role continue to inspire us. They will take the field forward. Finally, to this we add the readers of the first, second, third, fourth, fifth, and sixth editions, now spanning over two decades, who supported us in the belief that the content is worthwhile and usable, and who urged us to further refine and develop these ideas in a seventh edition.

Carol Rippey Massat
Robert Constable
Shirley McDonald
John P. Flynn

About the Authors

Carol Rippey Massat is Associate Professor at the Jane Addams College of Social Work, University of Illinois at Chicago. She is currently editor of the *School Social Work Journal* and is the author of numerous social work publications. She serves on the Board of the Illinois Association of School Social Workers. She completed her AB (Rhetoric) at the University of Illinois at Urbana-Champaign, and her MSW at the University of Illinois at Urbana-Champaign, with a concentration in school social work. She also completed her PhD at the University of Illinois Urbana-Champaign School of Social Work. At the Jane Addams College of Social Work she chaired the school social work concentration for many years and has taught school social work practice, policy, and research over the past eighteen years. She worked as a social worker in Decatur, Illinois, for ten years.

Robert Constable is Professor Emeritus of social work at Loyola University Chicago. He completed his AB (Classical) at Georgetown University, his MSW degree at Loyola University, and DSW at the University of Pennsylvania with a focus on school social work. He has practiced as a school social worker in Gary, Indiana, Philadelphia, Pennsylvania, Evanston, Illinois, and in Project Head Start. Active in social work education, he has held faculty status at West Chester State University, the Jane Addams College of Social Work at the University of Illinois at Chicago, and Loyola University Chicago, and at several European universities. He organized graduate concentrations in school social work at the University of Illinois at Chicago and at Loyola University Chicago. He was co-director from 1992 through 1997 of the first social work graduate program in Lithuania at Vytautas Magnus University. Former editor of Social Work in Education, he is author of more than 100 publications in social work. He currently works as a social worker in private practice and continues his contribution to the literature of his profession.

Shirley McDonald is Vice President of the Park/Forest Chicago Heights, Illinois, School Board and chair of the Calumet District of the National Association of Social Workers. Former editor of the School Social Work Journal, she has long been a leader in the field of school social work. She is Past-President of the Illinois Association of School Workers and continued to serve on the Board of the Illinois Association of School Social Workers for many years. She has retired from service as a clinical associate professor at the Jane Addams College of Social Work, University of Illinois at Chicago, where she chaired the school social work concentration for many years and where she taught school social work practice to hundreds of students over her years of service. She has been a school social worker in special education cooperatives, serving children with low-incidence disabilities and their families. She also has taught elementary school for four years, first in Chicago and then in Flossmoor, Illinois.

John P. Flynn is Professor Emeritus at Western Michigan University. He earned his MSW from University of Michigan and PhD in social welfare policy and planning from the Graduate School of Social Work, University of Denver. He has taught social welfare policy, planning, and administration at both the graduate and undergraduate levels. In addition to the many social work articles he has published, he is author *of Social Agency Policy: Analysis and Presentation for Community Practice*, 2nd edition, Nelson-Hall, 1992.

Section One

History and General Perspectives in School Social Work

1

The Role of the School Social Worker

Robert Constable
Loyola University, Chicago

- The Intertwining Purposes of School Social Work and Education
- Stories of Practice: Models of School Social Work
- An Historical Analysis of School Social Work
- Whom Does the School Social Worker Serve?
- Where Does School Social Work Take Place?
- What Does the School Social Worker Do?
- Role Development

> *School social work is a specialized area of practice within the broad field of the social work profession. School social workers bring unique knowledge and skills to the school system and the student services team. School social workers are instrumental in furthering the purpose of the schools: to provide a setting for teaching, learning, and for the attainment of competence and confidence. School social workers are hired by school districts to enhance the district's ability to meet its academic mission, especially where home, school and community collaboration is the key to achieving that mission.* (School Social Work Association of America, 2005)

The family and the school are the central places for the development of children. Herein can be found the hopes for the next generation. There are often gaps in this relationship, within the school, within the family, and in their relationships to each other and to the needs of students. There are gaps between aspirations and realities, between manifest need and available programs. In the dynamic multicultural world of the child today, there are gaps between particular cultures and what education may offer. Everywhere it is a top public priority that children develop well and that schools support that development. Nevertheless, aspirations are unfulfilled, policies fail, and otherwise effective programs fail with certain students. School social workers practice in the space where children, families, schools, and communities encounter one another, where hopes can fail, where gaps exist, and where education can break down.

Throughout the world, schools are becoming the main public institution for social development. Schools are working to include those previously excluded from the opportunity of education. They are raising standards for educational outcomes to prepare citizens to participate in a multinational world, bound together by communication and by economic and social relations. The school social worker is becoming a useful professional to assist children who are marginalized—whether economically, socially, politically, or personally—to participate in this. Social workers work to make the education process effective. To do this, their central focus is working in partnership with parents on the pupil in transaction with a complex school and home environment. Education has become crucial, not only for each person to cope with the demands of modern living, but also for national economic survival (Friedman, 2005). It is very serious work. As a consequence of education's enhanced mission, an outcome-based education system is developing. This system is characterized by common standards, flexible notions of education to meet these standards, and higher standards for education professionals to deal differently with different levels of need. Because children begin school with different skills, abilities, and resources, they do not begin with a level playing field, and the imposition of uniform standards on all children logically leads to the need to shift resources to those who are more at risk for failure. While outcomes now drive all education law and policy, for children with disabilities in the United States outcome-driven, inclusive, and differentiated education has become established over thirty years.

The need for inclusion and differentiated assistance isn't just felt by children with disabilities. U.S. schools contain great diversity. Educators can no longer strive to teach to an imaginary grade norm at the middle of the class without taking into account the many different situations and capabilities of their students. The teacher's awareness of poverty and of differences in cultural understandings within the classroom sets the stage for a far more complex classroom reality. In Alabama, 43 percent of low-income students scored below basic, the lowest possible classification, on the 2007 National Assessment of Educational Progress math test, compared with 14 percent of students with family incomes above $36,000 (Jonsson, 2007). With current demographic and economic shifts—the closing of marginal industries, for example—46 percent of current public school students in the United States now come from families earning less than $36,000 per year, the cutoff point for eligibility for free or reduced-cost lunch and a useful defining point for low-income students. In thirteen states, 54 percent of public school students come from families that earn less than this amount (Jonsson, 2007). As of 2005, 42 percent of public school children were nonwhite or Hispanic (U.S. Census Bureau, 2007). In some urban areas it is common to have students from thirty-five different linguistic groups in one elementary school.

Mandated achievement testing has raised a national awareness of very many pupils falling far short of grade-level standards (Herbert, 2007; Schemo, 2007). While many educators believe that national standards should not be imposed on schools (they are generally locally governed), none question the fact that in many states only a minority of children come up to a recognized standard of proficiency. Rather they argue that the goals should be more realistic and achievable. In this regard, the state education agencies (SEAs) and school districts—which are closer to schools, teachers, and parents than the federal government—are more likely to be flexible and pragmatic about designing reforms to meet the needs of particular schools (Ravitch, 2007). Whatever balances ultimately emerge between federal, state, and local education policy making, no one disputes the need for school reforms. Because the individual situations of schoolchildren and their families must be taken into consideration in any successful reform, school social workers should expect their individualizing and family-centered roles to develop in general education in a manner similar to the development of their roles in regard to children with disabilities.

School social workers practice in the most vulnerable parts of the educational process, and so their roles can be as complex as the worlds they deal with. Practice rests on a wide range of skills that are defined and take shape through interactive teamwork. School social workers may work one-on-one with teachers, families, and children to address individual situations and needs. They become part of joint efforts to make schools safe for everyone. In preserving the dignity and respect due any one person, the school needs to become a community of belonging and respect. For example, social workers may work with a whole school on developing positive policies and educational programs dealing with harassment of students alleged to be gay or lesbian. When the school decides to implement a zero-tolerance policy, social workers are available to consult with teachers on implementation and to work with victims and perpetrators of harassment. They may help develop a crisis plan for the school with the principal, teachers' representatives, and the school nurse. They may work with that crisis team through a disturbing and violent incident, working in different ways with individual pupils and teachers experiencing crisis and with the broader school population. They may develop violence prevention programs in high schools experiencing confrontations between students. The list continues through many variations.

THE INTERTWINING PURPOSES OF SCHOOL SOCIAL WORK AND EDUCATION

School social workers have long been concerned about children who are not able to use what education has to offer. Gradually these concerns are coming to be shared by others. Over the span of a century, schools have broadened their mission and scope toward becoming more inclusive and toward ensuring respect for the individual differences of all children.

Consequently, social workers and many educators have come to share similar values. Each person possesses intrinsic worth. People have common needs. Schools and families are environments where children should develop, discover their own dignity and worth, and come to realize their potential. Unfortunately, the human potential of each person is often needlessly wasted. The worlds of young people, often so full of hope, can also be taken over by strange and distorted pictures of human worth and of social relations. School social workers work with young people and their school and family environments, assisting them to accomplish tasks associated with their learning, growth, and development, and thus to come to a fuller realization of their intrinsic dignity, capability, and potential. The school social work role is developed from this purpose and these values. It is not simply doing clinical social work in a school.

The basic focus of the school social worker is the constellation of teacher, parent, and child. The social worker must be able to relate to and work with all aspects of the child's situation, but the basic skill underlying all of this is *assessment*, a systematic way of understanding and communicating what is happening and what is possible. Building on assessment, the social worker develops a plan to assist the total constellation—teacher and students in the classroom, parents, and others—to work together to support the child in successfully completing the developmental steps that lie ahead. The basic questions are: What should the role of the school social worker be in a particular school community? and Where are the best places to intervene—the *units of attention*—in this particular situation? Guided by the purposes and needs of education and the learning process, an effective, focused, and comprehensive school social work role can be negotiated within a school community.

Role, the key to the understanding of what the school social worker does, is a set of expected behaviors constructed by school social workers together with their school communities. In each school, the school social worker's role is developed by social workers with others, such as the principal and the teachers. To do this, school social workers need to have a vision of what is possible, possess tools of analysis, be comfortable with the processes of negotiation, and coordinate their interventions with the life of the school. They can construct their role with others, assessing the needs and priorities of the school community and understanding what school social work can offer.

STORIES OF PRACTICE: MODELS OF SCHOOL SOCIAL WORK

A Classic Example of Clinical School Social Work

A child who speaks mainly Spanish in her family has her first experience of kindergarten in a predominantly Anglo school and hides behind the piano every school day. The more the teacher tries to move her from behind the piano, the more determined she becomes to remain hidden; it has now become a struggle of wills between child and teacher. The school social worker first assesses the situation in a consultation conference with the teacher, and they develop a few joint strategies focusing on the child's experience in the class. They might shorten the exposure of the youngster to the class or help the teacher modify the educational focus and expectations. The youngster might get started in school with a supportive person from her own community. The teacher might help the youngster work with another classmate who is less afraid and can be supportive. The teacher might invite the family to school to help them feel more comfortable. The family might convey that feeling of comfort to the child—the feeling that it's okay to be here. The social worker and teacher look for signs of the youngster's possible response. Chances are that the problem is at least partly one of language. Another possibility is that the youngster is not ready for kindergarten and should wait a bit. Or the youngster may need more detailed prekindergarten testing or a different placement in school that accommodates her special needs. The social worker will also assist the teacher in developing contacts with the parents, because in this case these contacts seem crucial.

So far the social worker has not seen the parents and may not need to. Perhaps with the social worker's consultation, the teacher can manage the situation. Consultation with the teacher is the first, most effective, least intrusive, and least costly use of the social worker's time. However, in many cases, and especially in the case of a child entering school, it may be necessary to confer with the parents. Parents, especially those from a different linguistic or cultural group, may be insecure and uncertain of their role in school. They may feel strange about being involved with the school. It is of course precisely these feelings that may be conveyed to the child, so that the child fears the school and can find no way to cope with it. The school social worker, aware of these fears, can take a normalizing approach toward them, with the intent of helping mother and father feel at ease. When the school social worker enters the home, he or she is entering the world of the family. In this story, the parents gradually feel comfortable and trusting enough to discuss their concerns. They are worried about letting their child go to school. They value education greatly but experience Anglo culture as distant, different, and threatening. Moreover, each parent has a different approach to discipline, and their difficulties with each other make them both feel helpless regarding some of the youngster's behavior. When the parents are in disagreement, the youngster always wins; this learned behavior is being carried into the school. The school social worker makes an assessment with the parents of how the child is responding, what the dynamics of the home are, and what type of agreement between parents, teacher, and child can be constructed. The school must support the child's first steps to adapt. The school social worker's work with the parents should parallel work already done with the child's teacher. In this case, the work between the teacher and the parents may suffice. In other cases, the social worker may opt to work with the child also, building on the work already done with the teacher and parents.

A School Crisis

Another school itself is in crisis. When too many things are taking place at once for the school to manage and remain a safe environment for children, or when children are having great difficulty processing a situation, a crisis happens in a school. In this story, the school is in turmoil because of the violent death in a school bus accident of one of the children, an 8-year-old Korean girl. The school has a general plan for dealing with crises, as well as a detailed crisis manual that the school social worker, as a key member of the crisis team, helped create. On hearing about the death, the social worker makes an immediate assessment of the points of vulnerability in the school and meets with the school crisis team. They agree on a division of work. The principal works with the news media and community and makes an announcement to teachers and students as soon as there is a clear picture of what happened. The social worker has been in touch with the girl's family to learn what their wishes are and to assess how they are managing the crisis. The social worker agrees to work with the family, staying in touch throughout the crisis. She cancels appointments, except those that cannot be changed, and opens her office as a crisis center for students and teachers who want to talk about what has happened. She consults with the teacher of the student who died, and they discuss how the class is to be told. Later, people who knew the student or who feel the need attend a small Buddhist memorial service, and still later, students, teachers, and the family preserve her memory in a more permanent way with a small peace garden in the school courtyard. The school and community deal with the aftershocks of the death in a healing process that takes place over the next several years.

A Child with Special Needs

A child with a disability needs to be moved from one class to another. In the first class she is more protected but achieves less than she is capable of. She is mostly friends with other children with disabilities. She is moving to a class with a wide range of children with different levels of ability, where, if she feels safe and accepted, it is hoped she might achieve more. However, she will experience greater stress, whatever her level of achievement. The decision to move her is based on tests that indicate that the student will be able to achieve in this class with some special help, and the move is carefully planned. The new teacher and the former teacher are fully involved in the process. The student is also fully involved, and the social worker has developed a supportive relationship with the student and with the parents. When the day for the move comes, the social worker is there in case of unforeseen difficulties. The social worker works with the teacher, parent, and child in the months following the move until it is clear that his services are no longer needed (Welsh & Goldberg, 1979).

Consultation and Placement of Students

The social worker at a junior high school develops an active prevention program. One problem the school faces is that children are coming to the junior high school (where classes are taught in different rooms by subject-oriented teachers) from self-contained sixth-grade classes in schools close to their homes. It is not unusual for such children to regress for a semester or more. Some never recover the level of achievement and feeling of safety they experienced when they had one teacher and knew the teacher and their classmates well. Through the classroom observation that is a normal part of her work in the school, the social worker gets to know the teaching styles of each of the teachers and the range of strengths each brings to his or her work with children. Before the four hundred new students from feeder schools come to the junior high school in September, she reviews their records from elementary school. She places each at-risk child with a homeroom teacher who fits well with that child's needs, making certain that there are only a few children with serious problems in each classroom, and a balance of children with positive social adjustment and learning skills. Referrals of children for help the following year amount to about half the normal rate, and children who need more intensive help are helped earlier.

Group Work in a School

In another school, seven 12-year-old boys decide in their discussions with each other that they all have problems with their fathers. They appear at the social worker's door, asking to form a group to discuss their concerns. The social worker, who is male, calls each of the parents for permission and invites them to come in to discuss the situation. The parents come in, some individually, some in a group, and the boys are seen in a group with some individual follow-up. The result in each boy is a lowering of tension in his relations with his father and a measurable academic and social improvement. No boy needs to be seen longer than three months.

Violence Prevention

A high school is experiencing a large number of fights between groups of students of different ethnicities over insulting language, opposite-sex relationships, and accusations of stealing, among other things. There is a particularly high level of tension around allegations of being gay or lesbian.

Fights have usually been handled through the intervention of the vice principal, but this has not been well accepted by the students and has resulted in escalations of punishment and students experiencing shame and wishing revenge on the students who have shamed them and on the vice principal. The school unites around the use of a violence prevention strategy to create a more positive school culture. Students, teachers, social workers, and administrators adopt the principles of recognizing others' contributions and successes, acting with respect toward others, sharing power to build community, and making peace (Peace Power, 2007). As a part of this they develop a voluntary mediation program. Some disputes between individual students are subject to mediation by a panel of specially trained students, who are selected by other students for their leadership ability. These programs lower tensions in the school as the entire school culture is improved and the dignity of each student is respected. The education program enables and encourages youngsters to deal with differences, including their own, by making peace with each other in a safe atmosphere. Different coalesced groups of Hispanic, white, and African American students adopt these principles and develop ways of expressing them.

Policy Practice

The school social worker in an urban high school becomes aware that the majority of parents in her school are native Spanish speakers. There is no translator available in the school, and communication with these parents has become very limited. The school social worker analyzes her school organization, using the framework for organizational analysis introduced in chapter 9. She learns from her analysis that power in the school tends to be highly centralized, and that certain key figures tend to be very important in both formal and informal power structures. These include the principal, the assistant principal, the school secretary, the head of the English department, the head of the physical education department, the custodian, the head of the student council, the head of the parent-teacher organization, the pastor of a local church, and the head of a community group that advocates on behalf of Latino families. The school social worker uses the policy practice skills described in chapter 10 to analyze the problem. She uses interactional skills to contact these power players in the school community to develop a coalition interested in addressing this issue. The group decides to carry out a needs assessment (see chapter 11). Surveys of parents, students, and teachers and existing school data overwhelmingly support the need for a translator on site. Using the framework for policy analysis discussed in chapter 10, the group develops a proposal for a new position of a part-time translator. Using their agenda-setting policy practice skills, the group works together to place this proposal on the school board agenda. Using their analytic policy practice skills, they anticipate that funding will be the primary obstacle, so they include plans for funding in their proposal. With widespread support, the proposal is passed by the school board.

The work of the social worker is the work of the school, and the effectiveness of the school social worker becomes the effectiveness of education. In each example of the role of the social worker, the social worker applies the basics of the school social work role to a different set of circumstances in concert with other members of the school team, finding collaborative ways for the school and its membership to solve problems.

AN HISTORICAL ANALYSIS OF SCHOOL SOCIAL WORK

The focus of school social work has followed the historic concerns of education. The problems confronted by the education institution over its long history have ranged from accommodating immigrant populations, discrimination against particular groups, truancy, and the tragic waste of human potential in emotional disturbances of childhood to problems regarding school disruption and safety, homelessness, drugs, and AIDS. The first social workers in schools were hired in recognition of the fact that conditions, whether in the family, the neighborhood, or the school itself, that prevent children from learning and the school from carrying out its mandate were the school's concern (Allen-Meares, Washington, & Welsh, 2000; Costin, 1978). School social work would draw its legitimacy and its function from its ability to make education work for groups of children who could not otherwise participate. Its history reflects the evolving awareness in education, and in society, of groups of children for whom education has not been effective: immigrants, the impoverished, the economically and socially oppressed, the delinquent, the disturbed, and those with disabilities. It drew its function from the needs and eventually the rights of these groups as they interfaced with the institution of education and confronted the expectation that they should achieve their fullest potential. In each situation, as school social workers defined their roles, there was a match of the social work perspective—its knowledge, values, and skills—with the missions and mandates of the school.

Inclusion of All Children. During the twentieth century, schools broadened their mission and scope toward greater inclusion and respect for the individual differences of all children. The passage of compulsory school attendance laws, roughly from 1895 through 1918, marked a major shift in philosophies and policies governing American education. This would eventually become a philosophy of inclusion. Education, no longer for the elite, was for everyone a necessary part of preparation for modern life. A half century later, the U.S. Supreme Court reaffirmed that education is a constitutional right, which, if available to any, must be available to all on an equal basis. The profundity of the change in access to education in our society is succinctly expressed in the landmark case of *Brown v. Board of Education of Topeka* (1954): "If education is a principal instrument in helping the child to adjust normally to this environment, it is doubtful that any child may reasonably be expected to succeed in life if he is denied the opportunity of an education. The opportunity of an education, where the state has undertaken to provide it to any, is a right, which must be made available to all on equal terms." This belief, inherent in the passage of compulsory attendance laws, has become the basis for an ever-growing extension of education to all children at risk, most recently to those with disabilities.

Respect for Individual Differences. The belief that education, if available to any, should be available equally to all was also energized by the emergent awareness of individual differences among students and the need, indeed the responsibility of the school, to adapt curricula to these differences. The initial thrust of education in a modernizing society would be to standardize curriculum, and thus the learning process, into one best way to learn and one set of subjects to be learned. The modern school was organized by a prescribed curriculum, standardized testing, and the grade system. Students had to fit into this prescribed curriculum and learning process. Their ability to do this was measured. The problem is that none of this standardization of learners, knowledge, and the learning process matches the real world. Learners are different. Learning is both an individual process and a relational process. Any curriculum is potentially diverse: it changes as knowledge changes. For students to learn optimally, the implications of these differences must be recognized. Testing and education research recognized these differences, but real change would come slowly. The system of learning within the norms of the grade system eventually became somewhat more individualized. Children with disabilities received individualized education programs with goals, expected learning processes, and educational resources tailored to their needs. The movement to individualize education for all children in the context of standards of achievement continues to be one of the central issues in education.

Philosophies of inclusion and respect for individual differences continue to shape profoundly the practice of education and provide the basis for the role of the school social worker. The correspondence between social work values, the emergent mission of education, and the role of the school social worker is illustrated by Allen-Meares (1999) in table 1.1. The mission of education, implicit in these values, became the basis for school social work as it emerged in the twentieth century.

The Beginnings of School Social Work

School social work began during the school year 1906–1907 simultaneously in New York, Boston, Hartford (Costin, 1969a), and Chicago (McCullagh, 2000). These workers were not hired by the school system but worked

TABLE 1.1 Social Work Values

Social Work Values	*Applications to Social Work in Schools*
1. Recognition of the worth and dignity of each human being	1. Each pupil is valued as an individual regardless of any unique characteristic.
2. The right to self-determination or self-realization	2. Each pupil should be allowed to share in the learning process.
3. Respect for individual potential and support for an individual's aspirations to attain it	3. Individual differences (including differences in rate of learning) should be recognized; intervention should be aimed at supporting pupils' education goals.
4. The right of each individual to be different from every other and to be accorded respect for those differences	4. Each child, regardless of race and socioeconomic characteristics, has a right to equal treatment in the school.

in the school under the sponsorship of other agencies and civic groups. In New York, it was a settlement house that sponsored the workers. Their purpose was to work in various projects between the school and communities of new immigrants, promoting understanding and communication (Lide, 1959). In Boston, the Women's Education Association sponsored "visiting teachers" who would work between the home and the school. In Hartford, Connecticut, a psychology clinic developed a program of visiting teachers to assist the psychologist in securing social histories of children and implementing the clinic's treatment plans and recommendations (Lide, 1959). In Chicago, Louise Montgomery developed a social settlement type of program at the Hamline School that offered a wide range of services to the Stockyards District community (McCullagh, 2000). This unheralded experiment anticipated the much later development of school-based services for the entire community. In many ways these diverse early programs contained in rough and in seminal form all the elements of later school social work practice. Over the following century, the concerns of inclusion and recognition of individual differences, the concept of education as a relational process, and the developing mission of the schools would shape the role of the school social worker.

The First Role Definition by a School System: The Rochester Schools

In 1913 in Rochester, New York, the Board of Education hired visiting teachers for the first time. The school's commitment to hire visiting teachers was an acknowledgment of both the broadening mission of education and the possibility that social workers could be part of that mission. In justifying the appointments, the Rochester Board of Education noted that in the child's environment outside the school there are forces that often thwart the school in its endeavors to educate. The school was now broadening and individualizing its mission, attempting to meet its responsibilities for the "whole welfare of the child," and maximizing "cooperation between the home and the school" (Julius Oppenheimer, qtd. in Lide, 1959).

Between School and Community: Jane Culbert

Only three years later in 1916 at the National Conference of Charities and Corrections, a definition of school social work emerged in the presentation of Jane Culbert. The definition would focus on the environment of the child and the school, rather than on the individual child. The school social worker's role was "interpreting to the school the child's out-of-school life; supplementing the teacher's knowledge of the child . . . so that she may be able to teach the whole child[;] . . . assisting the school to know the life of the neighborhood, in order that it may train the children to the life to which they look forward. Secondly the visiting teacher interprets to parents the demands of the school and explains the particular demands and needs of the child" (Culbert, 1916, p. 595). The definition is replete with concepts of education as a complex, relational process in the school community—a process school social workers could professionally support in the interests of children. Many of these concepts would find further development in education over the century: inclusion, respect for individual differences, and education as a process taking place in the classroom, in the family and in the community.

Culbert's statement of role would be developed and typified by Julius Oppenheimer in the school-family-community liaison (Lide, 1959). From his study of 300 case reports made by school social workers and visiting teachers, he drew thirty-two core functions that he considered to be primary to the role of the school social worker. School social workers would aid in the reorganization of school administration and practices by supplying evidence of unfavorable conditions underlying pupils' school difficulties and by pointing out where changes were needed (Allen-Meares, 2006; Allen-Meares et al., 2000).

From a Focus on the Environment to the "Maladjusted" Child: The Early Years

In 1920, the National Association of Visiting Teachers was organized and held its first meeting in New York City (McCullagh, 2000). Concern was expressed about the organization, administration, and role definition of visiting teachers (Allen-Meares, 2000). This organization, which later became the American Association of Visiting Teachers, would publish a journal, the

Bulletin, until 1955. In 1955 it was merged with the newly established National Association of Social Workers. The *Bulletin* was the place in which the writing and the thinking of this emergent field of practice appeared during these years. As a result of the influence of the mental hygiene movement of the day, there was a gradual shift in focus from the home and school environment to the individual schoolchild and that child's needs. Casework then became the preferred vehicle for working with the individual child. The shift toward casework is reflected in the Milford Conference Report in 1929 (American Association of Social Workers, 1929/1974). For the social work field as a whole, the shift was later crystallized by the work of Edith Abbott (1942) on social work and professional education.

Fields of Practice with Casework in Common: The Milford Conference

The basic issues in the maturation of social work practice and theory, and a possible future direction, were laid out in the Milford Conference Report. By the end of the 1920s, a wide range of fields of practice had organized themselves around the different settings of school, hospital, court, settlement house, child welfare agency, family service agency, and so forth. Social work education followed an apprenticeship model, in which students learned what were perceived to be highly specialized and segmented fields of practice. The question of what all these fields had in common became extremely important. In 1929, at the Milford Conference, the basic distinction between fields of practice, the specific practice that emerged from these fields, and the generic base for practice in these fields—that is, the knowledge, values, and skills of casework—was established. This distinction was extremely important for social work education and for the field of school social work in that it allowed each field of practice to flourish and develop on a common foundation of casework. The emergent profession of social work was indeed broad and diverse. Furthermore, no theory had emerged that could do more than offer a general orientation to helping. It still was up to the learner-practitioner and supervisor to find a way to relate theory to practice. This situation would remain the same, with various permutations, for more than a half century. The casework theory identified as generic would not refer to a concrete practice separable from its manifestation in different fields. There was no "generic" practice, but generic knowledge, values, and skills would be a foundation for a further differentiation of practice within fields of practice.

The Distinction between Generic and Specific Knowledge: Grace Marcus

The casework foundation of the 1920s and 1930s did not focus simply on individuals, as did later versions, but on individuals and family units together. It was much more than a simple methodological base because it included knowledge and values. It became a conceptual foundation for practice that was specific to a field. Practice differentiation took place in relation to specific identified fields, such as school social work, medical social work, psychiatric social work, child welfare, and family services. Grace Marcus (1938–1939) clarified the distinction between the concepts "generic" and "specific":

> The term generic does not apply to any actual, concrete practice of an agency or field but refers to an essential, common property of casework knowledge, ideas and skills which caseworkers of every field must command if they are to perform adequately their specific jobs. As for our other troublemaking word, "specific," it refers to the form casework takes within the particular administrative setting; it is the manifest use to which the generic store of knowledge has been put in meeting the particular purposes, problems, and conditions of the agency in dispensing its particular resources.

The distinction was important in that it allowed for professional differentiation on a common foundation and specified the relationship of method theory, such as casework, to its manifestation in fields of practice.

A Rationale for School Social Work Practice: Florence Poole

In 1949, Florence Poole described a more developed rationale for school social work practice derived from the right of every child to an education. Pupils who could not use what the school had to offer were "children who are being denied, obscure though the cause may be, nevertheless denied because they are unable to use fully their right to an education" (Poole, 1959, p. 357). It was the school's responsibility to offer them something that would help them to benefit from an education. Education would need to change to help children who were "having some particular difficulty in participating beneficially in a school experience" (Poole, 1959, p. 357). Her rationale would eventually mark a shift in the discussion of the school social work role. School social work would be essential to the schools' ability to accomplish their purpose: "At the present time we no longer see social work as a service appended to the schools. We see one of our most significant social institutions establishing social work as an integral part of its service, essential to the carrying out of its purpose. We recognize a clarity in the definition of the services as a social work service" (Poole, 1949, p. 454). She saw the clarity and uniqueness of social work service as coming from the societal function of the school. The worker "must be able to determine which needs within the school can be appropriately met through school social work service. She must be able to develop a method of offering the service which will fit in with the general organization and structure of the school, but which is identifiable as one requiring social work knowledge and skill. She must be able to define the service and her contribution in such a way that the school personnel can accept it as a service, which contributes to the major purpose of the school" (Poole, 1949, p. 455). Florence Poole's approach to practice was built on the parameters of the mission of the school, the knowledge and skill of social work, and the worker's professional responsibility to determine what needs to be done and to develop an appropriate program for doing it. Her conception, focused on the potentially rich interaction of social work methods and the mission of the school, was simultaneously freer to use a variety of methods to achieve complex personal, familial, and institutional goals. The effect of this shift in emphasis from casework to school social work, although unnoticed at the time, was enormous. A variety of social work methods, geared to the complex missions and societal functions of the school, was now possible. The ensuing discussion of theory for school social work would develop the relation of methods to the needs of children and schools in the education process. It would be the basis for an emergent theoretical literature and a diversified practice.

Poole ultimately shifted the focus from the problem pupil who could not adjust and adapt to the school to pupils and schools adapting to each other in the context of every child's right to an education. The conditions that interfere with the student's ability to connect with the educational system are diverse. Therefore, the functions of the school social worker would be flexible and wide ranging, developed in each school by encounters with the concrete problems and needs of the school community. The elements of this encounter have remained the same over many years, while the role has developed and school social workers have responded to changing conditions. New functions would emerge on the common parameters sketched out by Florence Poole's vision and contribution.

A Period of Professional Centralization

During the late 1950s and the 1960s, the major concern in the professional literature, in the profession, and in social work education had to do with what social workers from different fields of practice had in common, not what made them different. Considerable development of school social work as a field of practice had already taken place from the mid-1920s through 1955 and was the basis for the classic definitional work of Florence Poole. This growth trailed off by 1955 with the consolidation of the National Association of Social Workers (NASW). National organizations of social workers representing different fields of practice were merged into one single professional association. *The Bulletin* of the American Association of Visiting Teachers was merged into the new journal of the united social work profession, *Social Work*. With the loss of the *Bulletin*, school social work literature dropped off for a time.

The Transaction between Persons and Environments: Harriett Bartlett and William E. Gordon

During the late 1950s, and through the following decade, important work was done to clarify the common base of social work practice (Bartlett, 1971). The work of Harriett Bartlett and others built the foundation for a reorientation of methods and skills to a clarified professional perspective of the social worker. Bartlett (1959, 1971) worked with William E. Gordon (1969) to develop the concept of the transactions between individuals and their social environments into a common base and a fundamental beginning point for social work. As the focus shifted to the person-environment transaction, it was no longer assumed that the individual was the primary object of help. The development and diffusion of group and environmental interventions and the use of a range of helping modalities in richly differentiated areas of practice would make Gordon's and Bartlett's work useful. The best summary of this work appeared in the 1979 report of the Joint NASW-CSWE Task Force on Specialization, of which Gordon was a member:

> The fundamental zone of social work is where people and their environment are in exchange with each other. Social work historically has focused on the transaction zone where the exchange between people and the environment which impinge on them results in changes in both. Social work intervention aims at the coping capabilities of people and the demands and resources of their environment so that the transactions between them are helpful to both. Social work's concern extends to both the dysfunctional and deficient conditions at the juncture between people and their environment, and to the opportunities there for producing growth and improving the environment. It is the duality of focus on people and their environments that distinguishes social work from other professions. (Joint NASW-CSWE Task Force on Specialization, 1979)

The Beginnings of Specialization

During the late 1960s and following years there arose a renewed interest in developing theory and practice in areas such as school social work. The use of "generic" approaches to practice in each field was no longer an adequate base for the complex practice that was emerging. Various fields, such as education and health, were demanding accountability to their goals. The survival of social work in different fields would demand this accountability. There was a gradual redevelopment of literature, journals, and regional associations of social workers in different fields of practice.

The interest in specialization led to a profession-wide discussion of this issue and the report of the Joint Task Force in 1979. The Joint Task Force developed a classic formulation: fields of practice in social work grow from the need for mediation between persons and social institutions in order to meet common human needs. Practice within each field is defined by 1) a clientele, 2) a point of entry, 3) a social institution with its institutional purposes, and 4) the contribution of social work practice, its knowledge, values, and appropriateness to the institutional purpose and to common human needs. According to the Joint Task Force (1979), these needs and their respective institutions would include:

- The need for physical and mental well-being (health system)
- The need to know and to learn (education system)
- The need for justice (justice system)
- The need for economic security (work/public assistance systems)
- The need for self-realization, intimacy, and relationships (family and child welfare systems)

In each area, the social worker works as a professional and mediates a relationship between persons and institutions.

At this time, school social work was developing its own distinct identity, methodology, theory, and organization. It had large numbers of experienced practitioners, who were encouraged to remain in direct practice by the structure and incentives of the school field as it had developed. These were some of the first and strongest advocates of a movement in the mid- to late 1970s to develop practice and theory. With the development of state school social work associations, and then school social work journals, the search for some balance between what was common to all fields and what was specific to school social work began again. The issues were not always clear. Students would struggle with finding this balance in their attempts to match classroom theory with fieldwork.

Rethinking Casework in the Schools

During the 1960s, the school social work literature reflected a broadened use of helping methods in schools and a developing interest in broader concerns affecting particular populations of students in schools. At the same time, the social work profession experienced a renewed focus on social reform. The education literature, critical of the current organization of schooling and of the effectiveness of education, was preparing the way for school reform. Lela Costin (1969b) published a study of the importance school social workers attached to specific tasks, using a sample mainly derived from NASW members. Her findings showed a group of social workers whose descriptions of social work mainly reflected the clinical orientation of the social work literature of the 1940s and the 1950s. Reflecting on these findings, Costin (1972) showed disappointment at what she believed was an excessively narrow conception of role, given the changing mission of schools and the potential of practice to assist that mission. Her next step would be to develop a picture of what the school social work role should be.

Four Models for Practice: John Alderson

Following Costin's research, John Alderson used a similar instrument to study school social workers with a variety of levels of professional training in Florida. In his sampling, he found a much broader orientation than did Costin. The workers ranked leadership and policy making either first or second in importance. Subsequently, Alderson attempted a theoretical reconciliation of these findings with Costin's findings, and with the apparent clinical emphasis of many established school social work programs. He described four different models of school social work practice (Alderson, 1974). The first three of these were governed by particular intervention methods, whether by clinical theory, social change theory, or community school organization. In the first three models, one method would tend to exclude the others. The *clinical* model focused mainly on changing pupils identified as having social or emotional difficulties. The *school change* model focused on changing the environment and conditions of the school. The *community school* model focused on the relationship of the school with its community, particularly deprived and disadvantaged communities. His final model, the *social interaction* model, was of a very different order. This model utilized a more dynamic, flexible, and changing concept of role. The focus for practice based on systems theory would be on persons and environments, students (in families), and schools in reciprocal interactions. Social workers would adapt their roles to this interaction. Alderson's social interaction model followed two decades of the work of William E. Gordon, Harriett Bartlett, and the Committee on Social Work Practice, and the definition of a transactional systems perspective in social work.

Seven Clusters of School Social Work Functions: Lela Costin

At about the same time, Lela Costin (1973) developed the *school-community-pupil relations* model, which focused on "school and community deficiencies and specific system characteristics as these interact with characteristics of pupils at various stress points in their life cycles" (p. 137). She outlined seven broad groups of functions in the school social worker's role. School social workers do 1) direct counseling with individuals, groups, and families, 2) advocacy, 3) consultation, 4) community linkage, 5) interdisciplinary team coordination, 6) needs assessment, and 7) program and policy development (Costin, 1973). With its constant relation of a diverse professional methodology to a developing school purpose, the model harkened back to the beginnings of school social work.

Broadening Approaches to Practice

Later research in school social work (Allen-Meares, 1977) showed movement toward a model emphasizing home-school-community relations with a major focus still on problems faced by individual students. Other studies showed this broadening taking place as well (Anlauf-Sabatino, 1982; Chavkin, 1993; Constable, Kuzmickaite, Harrison, & Volkmann, 1999; Constable & Montgomery, 1985; Dennison, 1998; Lambert & Mullally, 1982; Timberlake, Sabatino, & Hooper, 1982). This finding can be characterized by Lambert and Mullally's (1982) pithy comment, "School social workers, at least in Ontario, do not place importance on one focus—individual change or systems change—to the exclusion of the other, but recognize the importance of both" (p. 81). The conceptual problem was not a question of individual change or systems change, but of how to organize the methodological diversity inherent in the role. Method theories taught outside the dynamic context of a field of practice often tended to focus either on individual change or systems change. Frey and Dupper (2005) developed a clinical quadrant (figure 1.1) to bring together clinical and environmental interventions in school social work. The most recent of a number of integrational methods approaches, their quadrant is an attempt to describe and encompass the method content of school social work practice, and in a very broad sense their interrelations.

In this context the ecological systems model became a useful theoretical model for understanding the school social worker's role. Ecology is the science of organism-environment interaction. A system is an organized holistic unit of interdependent, transacting, and mutually influencing parts (individuals or collectivities and their units) within an identifiable (social-ecological) environment (Siporin, 1975). The model leads to a view of person and environment as a unitary interacting system in which each constantly affects and

FIGURE 1.1 Clinical Quadrant

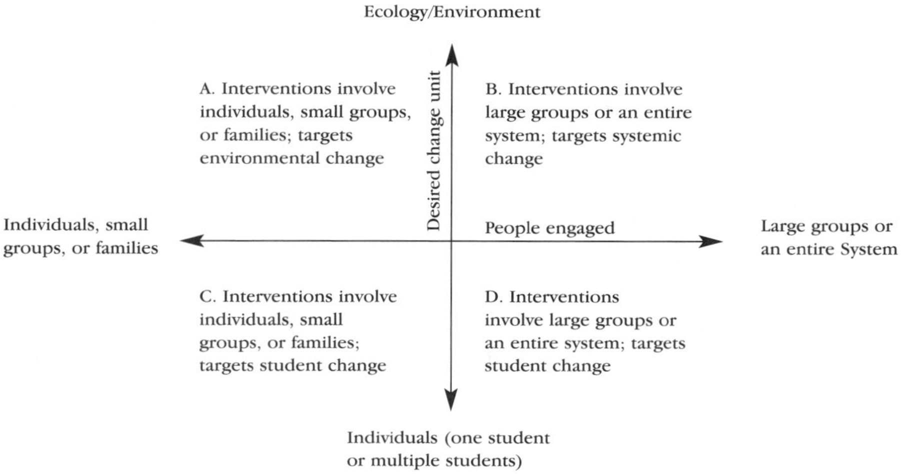

shapes the other. It allows for an understanding of the relationship between different methods of intervention and their theoretical bases. Behavior in the classroom may be understood better if one has an understanding of its context, its relations to other settings, and the relation of these settings to each other. As one learns to analyze the relations between systems, practice may build on this understanding. Choice of method(s) one may use depends on an understanding of the complex interaction of the systems involved. The model leads to clearer choices of where to intervene in a complex system and when an intervention may be most effective.

Germain (2006) uses ecological systems theory to clarify the dual function of social work: to "attend to the complexities of the environment, just as we attend to the complexities of the person" (p. 30). She moves to a health orientation from a medical-disease metaphor and to "engaging the progressive forces in people and situational assets, and effecting the removal of environmental obstacles to growth and adaptive functioning" (p. 30).

In the next chapter, Monkman offers a parsimonious analysis of school social work practice from the nature of schooling itself. Following the lead of her teacher, William E. Gordon, she defines a transaction as the relation between a person's coping behavior and the impinging environment. The social worker assists individuals and environments to cope with and become resources for each other. When this transaction is in danger of breakdown, the social worker intervenes with a wide range of situationally appropriate methods to create a better match. She defines this transaction, making it more operational, and more specific for both the purposes of practice and research.

These models provide a conceptual base for understanding and analyzing practice without allowing a narrowly preconceived method to dictate intervention. They allow for a set of dynamic relations in the school, with a clientele coping with maturational and educational goals and their integration. They are platforms or springboards for further development of school social work practice. Practice, policy, and research methodologies can be related to each other. They become more focused when they are applied to dynamic and complex transactions within the school community.

Emergent Issues and the Emergent Role

During the final three decades of the twentieth century, the inclusive and individualizing missions of the schools were expanded in response to the recognition of the right of children with disabilities to a free appropriate public education; the school reform movement; and recent concerns around violence, sexual harassment, and bullying in schools. Education is becoming outcome and evidence based (Kratochwill & Shernoff, 2003). There is a public policy emphasis on high professional qualifications that is meshing with movements toward specialization in school social work. In accordance with national legislation, states are setting standards for "highly qualified" school social workers and introducing post-masters mentorships for more permanent certification for highly qualified school professionals (Constable & Alvarez, 2006).

WHOM DOES THE SCHOOL SOCIAL WORKER SERVE?

Society places a heavy responsibility on schools and families. Schooling is not simply a process of teaching and learning, but of preparing children for the future. Schools are the vehicle for aspirations, not only for children who may conform easily to external expectations, but for every child. Responsibilities are placed on the school, on the parent, and on the child to make the educational process work so that each child who goes to school may fulfill his or her potential for growth. Schools need to be concerned for every child whose coping capacity is not well matched with the demands and resources of the educational institution. At one time or other, any person could be vulnerable. In addition, particular groups have borne certain burdens within society. Children come to school with messages from society, and sometimes from the school itself. Perhaps they feel that because of certain defining characteristics, such as gender, race, disability, ethnicity, or socioeconomic status, they cannot have the same aspirations as others, or that objective conditions, such as poverty, will surely prevent them from achieving their aspirations. The power of education, and many of the values that drive it, can refute these messages. School social workers with their central access to teachers, children and families in the school community can refute these messages as well.

WHERE DOES SCHOOL SOCIAL WORK TAKE PLACE?

The School Community Context

School is conceptualized as a community of families and school personnel engaged in the educational process. The educational process is dynamic and wide ranging and involves children, their families, and an institution called school. It is the context for school social work. School is no longer viewed as a building or a collection of classrooms in which teachers and pupils work together. The school community, no longer simply bounded by geography, comprises all those who engage in the educational process. As in any community, there are varied concrete roles. People fit into these communities in very different ways. Parents and families have membership through their children. Teachers and other school personnel are members with accountability to parents, children, and the broader community. Drawing on each person's capacities, the school social worker focuses on making the educational process work to the fullest extent. Therefore, school social workers work with parents, teachers, pupils, and administrators on behalf of vulnerable children or groups of children. The success of the process depends on the collective and individual involvement of everyone. The social worker helps the school community operate as a real community so that personal, familial, and community resources can be discovered and used to meet children's developmental needs.

The school is rapidly becoming the place of organization of all services to children and families. As long as it had been taken for granted that school would be isolated from the home, one part of the role of the school social worker has been to span the boundary between home and school. This has taken place since the origin of school social work in the early twentieth century (Litwak & Meyer, 1966). Schools have generally operated in relative isolation from their constituent families, each protecting its functioning from "interference" from the other. This isolation is, of course, counterproductive in situations of vulnerability or difficulty. There is a need for someone like the school social worker to span, and even challenge, these boundaries. The traditional approach of connecting children with networks of community services has been evident from the earliest years of social work in schools. Beginning in the late 1960s, the intensified parent involvement of Project Head Start and the war on poverty and, more recently, parent-sponsored schools have allowed for the development of models of empowerment and partnership.

The Societal Context

The connection of school social work to its school and community context is essential for the development of practice. The current legal and social policy context for school social work and the role of the school social worker in school policy development are discussed more fully in section II. In the United States and in certain Western European countries, there has been an erosion of state welfare systems and the supports they provide to families. As national government policies shift toward "market" approaches, it seems that the societal protections normally associated with childhood are declining. Many families are weakening while risks to children are increasing. High rates of suicide, addiction, violence toward and among children, teen pregnancy, AIDS, and early exposure to the job market through economic necessity are among these risks, to some extent created and in any case sustained by a laissez-faire attitude associated with the reigning free market philosophy.

Some of the risks generated by the market and the broader societal system may be buffered through strengthening institutions at the local level—through schools and homes that work and that respect human dignity and worth. In the face of these problems (or perhaps because of them) schools have continued their century-old quests, such as for greater inclusion in the educational mainstream of previously excluded groups of youngsters. The changes that have taken place in special education over the past thirty years are particularly important and reflect the possible relations between school policy and the school social worker's role. More recently, school reform experience in the United States has been bringing with it increased expectations for children. Yet no progress can be made on school reform if the problems that accompany poverty and socioeconomic class—that children are at risk and will not fulfill their potential without institutional, community, and family supports—are not dealt with (Mintzies & Hare, 1985). Impoverished school districts working with impoverished families generally achieve at rates considerably lower than their more privileged neighbors (Biddle, 1997).

WHAT DOES THE SCHOOL SOCIAL WORKER DO?

The school social worker's role is multifaceted. There is assessment and consultation within the school team. There is direct work with children and parents individually and in groups. There is program and policy development. In 1989 a group of nineteen nationally recognized experts in school social work was asked to develop a list of the tasks that entry-level school social workers perform in their day-to-day professional roles. The result was a list of 104 tasks, evidence of the complexity of school social work. These tasks fell along five job dimensions:

1. Relationships with and services to children and families
2. Relationships with and services to teachers and school staff
3. Services to other school personnel
4. Community services
5. Administrative and professional tasks (Nelson, 1990)

Further research on these roles, tasks, and skills found four areas of school social work to be both very important and frequently addressed:

1. Consultation with others in the school system and the teamwork relationships that make consultation possible
2. Assessment applied to a variety of different roles in direct service, in consultation, and in program development
3. Direct work with children and parents in individual, group, and family modalities
4. Assistance with program development in schools (Constable et al., 1999)

A key skill, the foundation of all other areas, is assessment. Assessment is a systematic way of understanding what is taking place in relationships in the classroom, within the family, and between the family and the school. The social worker looks for units of attention—places where intervention will be most effective. *Needs assessment*, a broader process, provides a basis for program development and policy formation in a school. It is often a more formal process that utilizes many of the tools of research and is geared toward the development of programs and policies that meet the needs of children in school.

ROLE DEVELOPMENT

Role development is the product of the interactions between what the school social worker brings to the situation, the perceptions of others, and the actual conditions of the school community. Role definitions are the joint and continuing construction of school social workers, education administrators, and others. They become reference points for practice, for policy, and for theory development, and they serve as a conceptual bridge between policy and practice. Where social workers are not the dominant profession, these conceptions interpret and validate their contributions. They regulate teamwork. General reference points for role can be found in the literature of school social work, in local education agency expectations, and state education agency standards. They can be found in standards developed by the NASW, the School Social Work Association of America (SSWAA), and other state and national associations. When these expectations are found repeatedly in practice, they set standards for professional performance. It is not usual for beginning school social workers to have a great deal of influence in the initial development of their roles. Indeed, the idea that they will ever influence the development of their roles in particular schools may seem foreign to their experience. Over a period of time, however, as they learn to respond in a more differentiated way to the needs of the school community, school social workers can influence the development of their roles in particular schools. People's perceptions of a role are tested and evaluated in relation to the needs, capabilities, and social networks of a particular school and the outcome—the product that results and its influence on students' experience of education.

It is important to understand the nature of education policy as it applies to school social work practice. The involvement with education and schooling creates a natural focus on research, policy, and program development as practice. From basic practice skills of assessment and consultation in the framework of ecological systems theory flow a wide range of possible interventions. These are developed with teachers, pupils, families, and groups. They involve clinical practice, consultation and teamwork, coordinating and integrating services, developing inclusion plans, dealing with crisis and safety issues in the school, and developing mediation and conflict resolution, each with its own sources of theory. These and other parts of the school social work role are developed systematically throughout this book.

References

Abbott, E. (1942). *Social welfare and professional education*. Chicago: University of Chicago Press.

Alderson, J. (1974). *Models of school social work practice*. In R. Sarri & F. Maple (Eds.), *The school in the community* (pp. 57–74). Washington, DC: National Association of Social Workers.

Allen-Meares, P. (1977). Analysis of tasks in school social work. *Social Work, 22*, 196–201.

Allen-Meares, P. (1999). The contributions of social workers to schooling—revisited. In R. Constable, S. McDonald, & J. Flynn (Eds.), *School social work: Practice, policy, and research perspectives* (4th ed., pp. 24–31). Chicago: Lyceum Books.

Allen-Meares, P. (2006). One hundred years: A historical analysis of social work services in the schools. *School Social Work Journal, 30*(3), 24–43.

Allen-Meares, P., Washington, R. O., & Welsh, B. L. (2000). *Social work services in schools*. Boston: Allyn & Bacon.

American Association of Social Workers. (1974). *Social casework: Generic and specific: A report on the Milford Conference.* Washington, DC: National Association of Social Workers. (Reprint of 1929 edition)

Anlauf-Sabatino, C. (1982). Consultation and school social work practice. In R. Constable & J. Flynn (Eds.), *School social work: Practice and research perspectives* (pp. 271–281). Homewood, IL: Dorsey.

Bartlett, H. (1959). The generic-specific concept in social work education and practice. In A. E. Kahn (Ed.), *Issues in American social work* (pp. 159–189). New York: Columbia University Press.

Bartlett, H. (1971). *The common base of social work practice*. New York: National Association of Social Workers.

Biddle, B. J. (1997). Foolishness, dangerous nonsense, and the real correlates of state differences in achievement. *Phi Delta Kappan, 79*(1), 8–13.

Brown v. Board of Education of Topeka, 347 U.S. 483 (1954).

Chavkin, N. (1993). *The use of research in social work practice*. Westport, CT: Praeger.

Constable, R., & Alvarez, M. (2006). Moving into specialization in school social work. *School Social Work Journal, 30*(3), 116–131.

Constable, R., Kuzmickaite, D., Harrison, W. D., & Volkmann, L. (1999). The emergent role of the school social worker in Indiana. *School Social Work Journal, 24*(1), 1–14.

Constable, R., & Montgomery, E. (1985). A study of role conceptions of the school social worker. *Social Work in Education, 7*(4), 244–257.

Costin, L. (1969a). A historical review of school social work. *Social Casework, 50*, 439–453.

Costin, L. (1969b). An analysis of the tasks in school social work. *Social Service Review, 43*, 274–285.

Costin, L. (1972). Adaptations in the delivery of school social work services. *Social Casework, 53*, 350.

Costin, L. (1973). School social work practice: A new model. *Social Work, 20*(2), 135–139.

Costin, L. (1978). *Social work services in schools: Historical perspectives and current directions* (Continuing Education Series # 8). Washington, DC: National Association of Social Workers.

Culbert, J. (1916). Visiting teachers and their activities. In *Proceedings of the National Conference on Charities and Corrections* (p. 595). Chicago: Heldman Printing.

Dennison, S. (1998). School social work roles and working conditions in a southern state. *School Social Work Journal, 23*(1), 44–54.

Frey, A. J., & Dupper, D. J. (2005). A broader conceptual approach to clinical practice for the 21st century. *Children & Schools, 27*(1), 33–44.

Friedman, T. L. (2005). It's a flat world, after all. *New York Times Magazine*. Retrieved April 3, 2005, from http://newyorktimes.com/magazine

Germain, C. (2006). An ecological perspective on social work in the schools. In R. Constable, C. R. Massat, S. McDonald, & J. P. Flynn (Eds.), *School social work: Practice, policy and research* (6th ed., pp. 28–39). Chicago: Lyceum Books.

Gordon, W. E. (1969). Basic constructs for an integrative and generative conception of social work. In G. Hearn (Ed.), *The general systems approach: Contributions toward an holistic conception of social work* (pp. 5–11). New York: Council on Social Work Education.

Herbert, B. (2007, October 2). Our schools must do better. *New York Times*. Retrieved October 2, 2007, from http://www.nytimes.com/2007/10/2/opinion/02herbert

Joint NASW-CSWE Task Force on Specialization. (1979). *Specialization in the social work profession* (NASW Document No. 79-310-08). Washington, DC: National Association of Social Workers.

Jonsson, P. (2007, November 1). South's schoolchildren now mostly low income. *Christian Science Monitor*, pp. 1, 10, 11.

Kratochwill, T. R., & Shernoff, E. S. (2003). *Evidence-based practice: Promoting evidence-based interventions in school psychology* (WCER Working Paper No. 2003-13). Madison: Wisconsin Center For Educational Research. Retrieved August 8, 2004, from http://www.wcer.wisc.edu/Publications/workingPapers/Working_Paper_No_2003_13.pdf

Lambert, C., & Mullally, R. (1982). School social work: The congruence of task importance and level of effort. In R. Constable & J. Flynn (Eds.), *School social work: Practice and research perspectives* (pp. 72–99). Homewood, IL: Dorsey.

Lide, P. (1959). A study of the historical influences of major importance in determining the present function of the school social worker. In G. Lee (Ed.), *Helping the troubled school child: Selected readings in school social work*. New York: National Association of Social Workers.

Litwak, E., & Meyer, H. (1966, June). A balance theory of coordination between bureaucratic organizations and community primary groups. *Administrative Science Quarterly, 11*, 31–58.

Marcus, G. (1938–1939). The generic and specific in social casework: Recent developments in our thinking. *American Association of Psychiatric Social Workers,* 3/4 [brochure].

McCullagh, J. (2000). School social work in Chicago: An unrecognized pioneer program. *School Social Work Journal, 25(*1),1–14.

Mintzies, P., & Hare, I. (1985). *The human factor: A key to excellence in education*. Silver Spring, MD: National Association of Social Workers.

Nelson, C. (1990). *A job analysis of school social workers.* Princeton, NJ: Educational Testing Service.

Peace Power. (2007). *Evidence-based tools for a culture of nonviolence.* Retrieved December 9, 2007, from http://www.peacepower.info/Home.html

Poole, F. (1949, December). An analysis of the characteristics of the school social worker. *Social Service Review, 23*, 454–459.

Poole, F. (1959). The social worker's contribution to the classroom teacher. In G. Lee (Ed.), *Helping the troubled school child: Selected readings in school social work*. New York: National Association of Social Workers.

Ravitch, D. (2007, October 3). Get Congress out of the classroom. *New York Times*. Retrieved October 3, 2007, from http://www.nytimes.com/2007/10/03/opinion/03ravitch

Schemo, D. J. (2007, October 16). Failing schools strain to meet U.S. standard. *New York Times*. Retrieved October 16, 2007, from http://www.nytimes.com/2007/10/16/education/16child

School Social Work Association of America. (2005). *SSWAA's organizational mission statement.* Retrieved April 1, 2008, from http://www.sswaa.org/

Siporin, M. (1975). *Introduction to social work practice*. New York: Macmillan.

Timberlake, E., Sabatino, C., & Hooper, S. (1982). School social work practice and PL 94-142. In R. Constable & J. Flynn (Eds.), *School social work: Practice and research perspectives* (pp. 49–72). Homewood, IL: Dorsey.

U.S. Census Bureau. (2007). *Children characteristics.* Retrieved June 12, 2007, from http://factfinder.census.gov/servlet/SSTable? *bm =y&-geo id=01000US&-qr name=ACS 2005EST G00*redoLog=false&state=st&format=

Welsh, B., & Goldberg, G. (1979). Insuring educational success for children-at-risk placed in new learning environments. *School Social Work Quarterly, 1*(4), 271–284.

2

The Characteristic Focus of the Social Worker in the Public Schools

Marjorie McQueen Monkman

- The Characteristic Focus of Social Work
- Ecological Perspective
- Social Work Knowledge
- The Purpose of Social Work Activity
- TIE Framework: Outcome Categories
- Concepts for Analyzing Resources
- Values
- Social Work Activities
- The Worker

Federal and state legislation and major legal decisions have given recognition to school social work services and provided opportunities to broaden these services. The recognition of school social work services in laws and policies creates greater expectations for the worker and challenges the profession. The purpose of this chapter is to conceptualize what the focus of school social work is and what the role of the individual worker is in utilizing this focus, in developing new techniques in practice, and in demonstrating desired change.

It is hard to overestimate the importance of the individual worker's contribution to change in the practice situation. Workers carry a heavy responsibility for what they bring to the practice situation. They bring a characteristic professional focus that is both broad and unique. The worker's focus makes it possible for him or her to identify knowledge needed for intervention. The worker uses activities and skills to bring about desired changes. The worker brings values that lead to the selection of perspective, knowledge, and action. The worker brings the contribution of charisma and personal style. It is through the social worker that professional focus, knowledge, values, and activities impinge on the practice situation. The role of the worker is formed from these attributes as they interact with the particular structure and expectations of the setting (see figure 2.1).

FIGURE 2.1 Contributions of the Worker

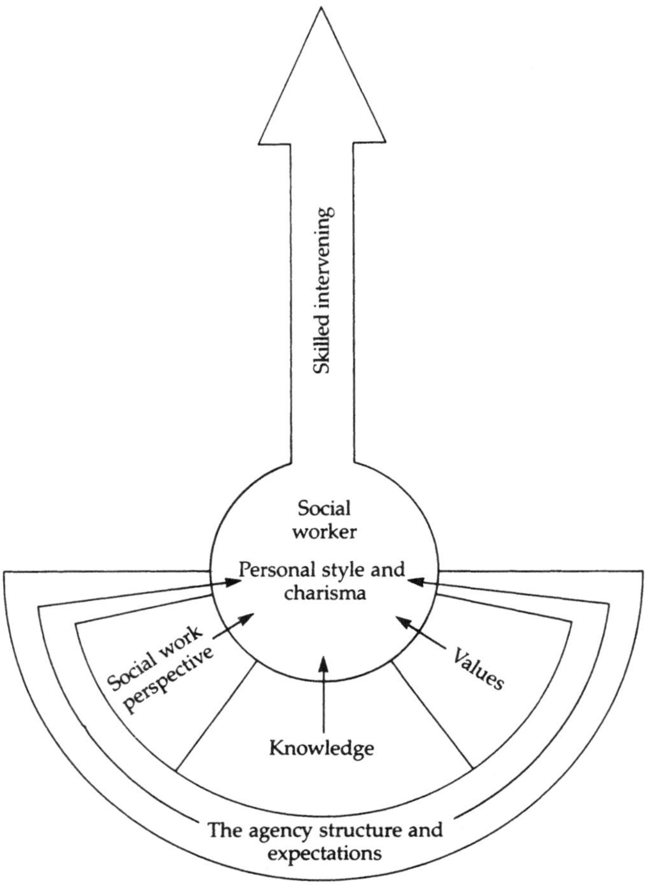

THE CHARACTERISTIC FOCUS OF SOCIAL WORK

From the beginning, the social work focus has been identified as resting on the person in the situation, a dual focus. As a result of this focus, social workers work with individuals in diverse aspects of life, perhaps more than practitioners of any other helping discipline. The conceptualization of the person in the situation was enhanced for social work by the work of Harriett Bartlett (1970), William E. Gordon (1969), and others (Germain & Gitterman, 1980; Gitterman & Germain, 1976; Monkman, 1976, 1978, 1981, 1983; Monkman & Meares, 1984; Pincus & Minahan, 1972; Schwartz, 1969). These theorists have conceptualized the traditional focus in a manner that reflects the roots and multiple avenues of practice. Their approach to defining the point of intervention in social work is to emphasize phenomena at the point where the person and the environment meet. Social work interventions take place in the transactions between the coping behavior of the person and the qualities of the impinging environment. The purpose of the intervention is to bring about a better match between the person and the environment in a manner that induces growth for the person and at the same time is remediating to the environment (Gordon, 1969).

In order to understand the characteristic focus of the social worker, one must understand the concepts of transactions, coping behavior, quality of the impinging environment, practice target, and outcomes of intervention.

Transactions

The activities at the interface may be termed transactions between the individual and the environment. Transactions embody exchanges in the context of action or activity. This action or activity is the combination of a person's activity and the impinging environmental activity; thus, exchange occurs only in the context of activity involving both person and environment. The transaction is created by the individual's coping behavior, on one hand, and the activity of the impinging environment on the other (Gordon, 1969).

Coping Behavior

Coping behavior is that behavior at the surface of the human organism that is capable of being consciously directed toward the management of transactions. The concept of coping behavior excludes the many activities that are governed by neural processes below the conscious level. It includes the broad repertoire of behavior that may be directed to the impinging environment and that can be brought under conscious control. Coping behaviors include not only behaviors directed at the environment, but also efforts of individuals to exert some control over their behaviors—to use themselves purposively.

Coping behaviors are learned behaviors, and once learned, they become established as coping patterns. Significant repetitions in coping behavior by individuals or groups of individuals suggest coping patterns that may at times become the focus of the interventive action. Looking for these patterns in what people are experiencing and how they are responding to a set of environmental conditions takes us beyond our traditional concern for the uniqueness and integrity of each individual. If we know something about these conditions and about human coping, we can say something in some detail and of substance about the response of a clientele to a social institution such as education, and from this we can develop the appropriate school social work response. In a relationship with any one individual, we respond to that person as a unique human being and as a part of a larger collectivity. We respect and encourage the effort of an individual with disabilities to overcome adversity and/or social discrimination, but we know that some of the experience of adversity and discrimination is shared by other people with disabilities. This knowledge is as much a base for action as is our knowledge of the person's unique response to adversity and discrimination.

People cope with themselves as well as with the environment, and this is also learned behavior. These behaviors, as they are developed over time, incorporate expectations and feedback from the environment. The ways individuals and groups cope are related to the information they have about themselves and their environment—how they perceive self and environment. This information is patterned into a cognitive structure that directs the coping behaviors and could even direct the perception of the environment in a manner that makes it difficult for the person to receive further information as feedback from the environment. There is a circular relation between what we usually do to cope with the environment and how we perceive things. An understanding of this relationship is the crucial assessment tool. If coping behaviors and patterns are not in keeping with the environment as we perceive it, we may then examine the information and the perceptions of the coping individual. We direct this assessment toward patterns of perception and action rather than seeking some type of single cause within the individual.

Coping is an active, creative behavior that constantly breaks the boundaries of the given. Adapting is seen as a passive concept that suggests that the person simply takes in the output from the environment. Some writers connect coping with stress in adapting and refer to coping as those behaviors emitted when there is stress in adapting. We would say that stress is inherent in any growing process, but that it is important to assess the degree of stress to understand the coping patterns adopted. The person is considered able to cope when he or she is dealing with the stress and "making a go of it" (Gordon, 1969).

Quality of the Impinging Environment

The other side of the transaction field is the environment. Social work practice has not confined its concern to the person in any particular situation—that is, at home, in the hospital, in school, or in any other situation. No other profession seems to follow people so extensively into their daily habitats. We are interested in how the qualities of any of these situations interact with the coping behaviors. As in the case of the coping behaviors, Gordon (1969) gave a way of partializing the qualities of a situation. He defined the qualities of the impinging environment as those qualities at the surface of the environmental system that the person is actually in contact with, rather than below-the-surface structures, which are assumed to be responsible for the nature of what the human organism actually confronts.

Although emphasis on the environmental side is on the impingements, it is recognized that it is a person's knowledge of what is behind the impingements that enables him or her to arrange for changes in those impingements in desired directions. It is often necessary to work for change on several levels. For example, a worker may be working with a truant child in an effort to get the child to return to school. At the same time, the worker may find that the teacher is happier with the child truant and that the administration is indifferent. Intervention may be needed at all three levels if the child is to return and remain in school (figure 2.2).

FIGURE 2.2 T.I.E. Framework: Transactions between Individuals and Environments

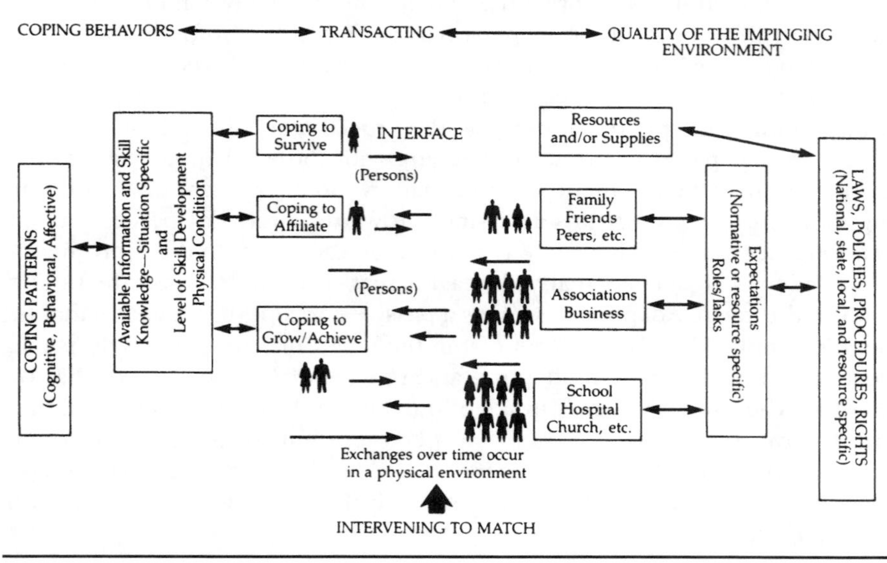

Practice Target

Transaction has been defined as activity that combines coping behaviors and the quality of the impinging environment. Through these transactions there is an exchange between the components of each side. The goal of social work practice is matching, that is, bringing about a fit that makes for positive outcomes for both the person and the environment. Professional intervention for bringing about a match may include efforts to change the coping behavior, the quality of the impinging environment, or both (Gordon, 1969).

Social work is concerned with what will happen to the coping behaviors and the quality of the impinging environment as a result of the exchanges between them. The relationship between coping and environment is reciprocal. Thus coping behavior and/or quality of the impinging environment could become what we are seeking to change, and thus our measures of outcome or dependent variables. To the degree that activity in the transaction changes, we may predict consequent changes in either the coping behavior or the environmental side, or both.

ECOLOGICAL PERSPECTIVE

We are essentially operating from an ecological perspective. Ecology seeks to understand the reciprocal relation between organisms and environment: how an organism shapes the environment to its needs and how this shaping enhances the life-supporting properties of the environment (Germain & Gitterman, 1980). The ecological perspective appears to fit social work's historical view much better than the medical or disease perspective that we seem to have adopted in past decades. The ecological perspective is essentially a perspective for relationships that take place in reality; it is a way of perceiving these relationships.

One of the reasons for the better fit of the ecological perspective to social work is that it is a multicausal rather than a linear causal perspective; that is, it makes possible a view of multifaceted relationships. From this perspective, our attention is called to the consequences of transactions between people and environment, but the metaphors, models, and theories we have previously borrowed have focused more on cause of action and have tended to be one-sided and unidirectional.

SOCIAL WORK KNOWLEDGE

A basic area of knowledge for social work is knowledge of the needs of people and how these needs are met. People individually and collectively have a need for physical well-being. These needs include food and shelter, which may be identified as needs for survival. People have a need for relationships, including intimacy and other forms of affiliating. People have a need for growth, which may include their need to know, to learn, to develop their talents, and to experience mental and emotional well-being.

A second major area of knowledge for social work is knowledge of the institutions or societal resources that have been established to meet these needs. We need knowledge of the major structures and processes involved in resource provision and development. This area is quite complex and involves expectations, policies, and procedures.

The third major area of knowledge is knowledge of the match between these institutions and the needs of the people. From the perspective of social work, this is knowledge of transactions and the result of these transactions for people and their environments. For example, the Individuals with Disabilities Education Act is an environmental policy change that changes societal expectations and resources for children with disabilities and, in turn, affects all children. The environmental impingements that individual children experience change as these policies change. The transactions between pupils and their teachers, peers, and even the physical structure of the school have become a part of the general experience of children. However, these children struggle to cope with change and new events brought on by these policies. These transactions are particularized and occur in time and space (at a particular time and in a particular place), as do all living transactions.

THE PURPOSE OF SOCIAL WORK ACTIVITY

The purpose of social work activity is to improve the match between coping behaviors and the quality of the impinging environment so that the stress in these transactions is not so great that it is destructive to the coping abilities of the individual or the environment. Changes are always occurring, and people are always coping or striving to manage change. Our purpose is to bring about not only a match that is not destructive but, if possible, one that makes the person better able to cope with further change and makes the environment less stressful to others.

As our focus becomes clear, we can make the knowledge we have of transactions more explicit for social workers and other disciplines. To do this we need to develop our focus in a way that makes what we aim to change—coping behavior and the impinging environment—more explicit. Figure 2.2 illustrates the concepts we will be discussing.

TIE FRAMEWORK: OUTCOME CATEGORIES

Coping Behaviors

Social workers basically deal with at least three categories of coping behaviors and three categories of the impinging environment (Monkman, 1978). This framework for dealing with the transactions between individuals and environments is called Transactions Individuals Environment (TIE). Surviving, affiliating, growing, and achieving form a continuum of coping.

There are then three categories of coping behaviors: coping behaviors for surviving, coping behaviors for affiliation, and coping behaviors for growing and achieving. These categories help us set priorities for practice intervention. Coping behaviors at any point in time are affected by information from past coping experience and build upon themselves over time. Our first consideration is whether the client has the capacity to obtain and use the necessities for surviving, and the second, whether he or she has the capacity to obtain and use the necessities for affiliating. Both surviving and affiliating skills seem to be prerequisites to growing and achieving.

Coping behaviors for surviving are those behaviors that enable the person to obtain and use resources that make it possible to continue life or activity. To survive we need to have the capacity to obtain food, shelter, clothing, and medical treatment, and to have access to these through locomotion.

Coping behaviors for affiliating are those behaviors that enable the person to unite in a close connection with others in the environment. Subcategories of affiliating behaviors are the capacity to obtain and use personal relationships and the ability to use organizations and organizational structure. Social workers would have great difficulty conceiving of a person apart from his or her social relations. Each individual experiences social relations through organizations and groups, families, schools, clubs, religious organizations, and so forth.

Coping behaviors for growing and achieving are those behaviors that enable the person to perform for, and to contribute to, him- or herself and others. Subcategories of coping behaviors for growing are the ability to develop and use cognitive capacities, physical capacities, economic capacities, and emotional capacities.

Quality of the Impinging Environment

The environment can be seen as comprising resources, expectations, and laws and policies. The categories of the environment do not have a priority of their own. Rather, because our major value is the person, their priority gets established in the match with coping behaviors.

Resources. Resources are supplies that can be drawn on or turned to for support when needed. Pincus and Minahan (1972) characterized resource systems as either informal, formal, or societal. Informal resource systems consist of family, neighbors, co-workers, and the like. Formal resource systems could be membership organizations or formal associations that promote the interest of members, such as AA and the Association for Retarded Citizens. Societal resource systems are structured services and service institutions, such as schools, hospitals, social security programs, courts, and police agencies. Resource systems may be adequate or inadequate and may provide opportunities, incentives, or limitations. In many situations, there are no resources to match the coping behaviors for surviving, affiliating, and growing.

Expectations. Expectations are the patterned performances and normative obligations that are grounded in established societal structures. Expectations can involve roles and tasks. Social workers recognize these structures and recognize that a positive role complementarity usually leads to greater mutual satisfaction and growth. However, it is not our purpose as social workers simply to help people adapt to societal roles or perform all expected tasks. Roles are the patterned, functional behaviors that are performed by a collection of individuals. Examples of roles are mother, father, social worker, and physician. Although these are normative patterns in our society, individuals do not always agree on the correct behaviors of a specific role. Roles do change because they are socially defined and functionally oriented. Sometimes this societal change is not acceptable to the individual and creates a mismatch between coping behaviors and the environment. A task is a way of describing the pressures placed on people by various life situations. These tasks "have to do with daily living, such as growing up in the family, and also with the common traumatic situations such as bereavement, separation, illness, or financial difficulties" (Bartlett, 1970). These tasks call for coping responses from the people involved in the situation.

Laws and Policies. Laws and policies are the binding customs or rules of conduct created by a controlling authority, such as legislation, legal decisions, and majority pressures. Subcategories of laws and policies are rights and responsibilities, procedures, sanctions, and inhibiting or restricting factors. As a category, laws and policies are seen as necessary and positive components of the environment. Yet it is also recognized that many single laws or policies have negative effects for groups of people. Some of our policies make survival more difficult. In some cases, particularly for welfare clients, receiving assistance from welfare agencies may make affiliation almost impossible.

Expectations, laws, policies, and procedures are communicated through resources. The quality of output from a resource, such as a school, is very much affected by the state and national policies that have been adopted. The ultimate test of these policies is the match they make with coping behaviors of those individuals with whom the school conducts transactions, namely children. Thus, if these transactions are destructive to the coping behaviors of children, the procedure for implementation or the policy itself is in need of change. This is another way of saying that policy is a legitimate target for change. Social workers are often in the best position for evaluating the match between policy and coping. The classroom is an example that may make the interrelationship of the environmental categories clearer. The expectations for tasks to be accomplished in the classroom come to the child through the teacher (and others). The teacher is a resource to the child, but unless he or she is able to bring the expectations in line with the coping behaviors of the child, there is no match. In some cases, the coping behaviors are so different from the expectations that other resources are necessary. Social workers might intervene in the environment and/or in the coping behaviors of schoolchildren, that is, in the resources, expectations, policies, and procedures, and/or in the coping. In some situations, however, change might be indicated in all six outcome categories.

Research Evidence

An exploratory study using a random sample of Illinois school social workers and utilizing the TIE framework described in this chapter lends provides evidence of the fit of this framework to practice (Monkman & Meares, 1984). The data show that coping behavior and environment outcome categories were selected in approximately equal amounts. A national study using a random sample of direct practice MSWs from a variety of practice settings gave additional evidence that social workers' outcomes are located in the categories described in this framework (Monkman, 1989).

Matching Person and Environment

The following discussion will be an oversimplification of the interrelation between transactions and the matching process, but it is a first step in utilizing the framework developed thus far. Two populations will be used as examples (figure 2.3).

FIGURE 2.3 The Characteristic Focus of School Social Work

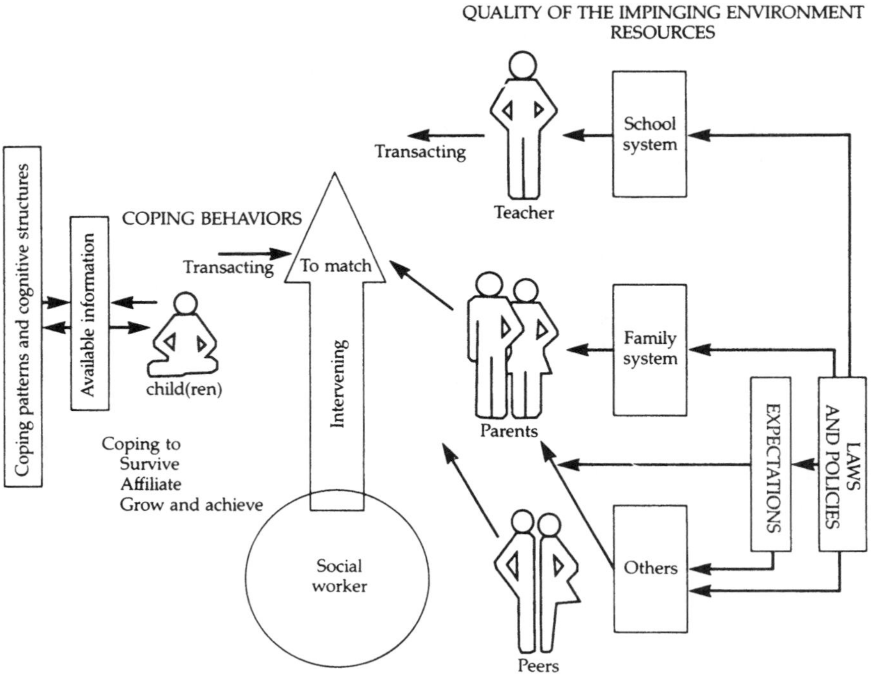

The first population to be considered comprises unmarried teenage parents. To be of help to this group, it is important for social workers to consider the match between behaviors for surviving, affiliating, and growing and each of the categories on the environmental side. For example, placing the teenage mother on homebound instruction may enhance cognitive achievement but may be destructive to affiliation in interpersonal relationships and affiliation with society and/or organizations. The student may not be aware of laws and policies that could affect her decision to have and keep her baby. Knowledge of the task of being a mother is important for both the mother and the child.

The second population we will consider is developmentally delayed children. Again, we are concerned with matching in all six categories. Many of the programs developed for developmentally delayed children are geared toward maximizing cognitive development—or, more specifically, academic achievement. Most of these programs do not develop affiliating or surviving skills. Very little energy is put into making a better match between the coping behaviors of the developmentally delayed child and the wide range of tasks for daily living.

It is important to remember that our outcome variables are both coping behaviors and the quality of the impinging environment. We may affect either or both. In the case of the teenage parent, the social worker may help to change her behavior in all three categories, as well as increasing resources. The worker may make information about expectations, laws, and policies available to her and may change some of the expectations emanating from her impinging environment. For example, the worker may change the demands for her to give up her baby or keep her baby. The developmentally delayed child may develop resources for increasing his or her affiliating behavior. He or she may even have measures of change in these behaviors. The worker may help his or her parents change their expectations so that they do not make impossible demands of the child.

Often, social work interventions involve teaming with other social workers and other helping individuals. For example, many interventions concerning growing and achieving behaviors for schoolchildren require social workers to team with the teachers of these children. Teachers spend many more hours with children than social workers do. They have more opportunities to help children develop coping behaviors and skills. By teaming with teachers, social workers can increase change possibilities for children. By bringing these two resources together, they can make a greater change in some aspect of the children's environment.

The point of these examples is to show that this framework makes it possible for us to partialize, generalize, and measure change in practice situations. It is possible to make each of these examples more explicit depending on the conditions of one's practice situation. To bring about these changes, a worker may, for instance, use knowledge of organizations, skills for working with groups, skills for data collection, and skills for communicating. The worker must also determine the major critical exchanges in the transaction.

CONCEPTS FOR ANALYZING RESOURCES

Resources have been identified as a major component of the environment. Resources such as family, school, and hospitals may be viewed as systems. Concepts from the general systems model are useful for conceptualizing and organizing data in the various resource systems. These concepts may be used to call attention to the skills necessary for the worker to get in and out of a resource system. This model calls to our attention such questions as: For what is the major energy in the system being used? Is tension in the system a productive or destructive force? What effect will change in one part of the system have on the other parts? Social workers become parts of systems. However, although the worker is a part of the system, the worker also intervenes in the system itself as a resource for children (Monkman, 1981).

Understanding Organizations

Workers need to understand what makes organizations operate if they want to use the school or other social agencies as a resource. For example, organizations have a managerial structure that is generally hierarchical. Organizational structure can be best understood in relation to organizational process. Workers need to understand the informal power that can be gained either from interpersonal relationships or from assuming responsibilities, as well as the power that comes from the formal structural arrangements.

A second but no less important process variable is communication. Communication serves a linkage function. It links various parts of the organization through information flow. This may be individual to individual, individual to group, unit to unit, or unit to the superstructure. Communication is often called the "life blood" of organizations or systems. Social workers have a particular responsibility for developing and maintaining channels of communication if they are to accomplish their own missions.

The climate of an organization has a major effect on its productivity. Climate describes expectations and incentives and is a property that is perceived directly or indirectly by individuals in the organization. Climate is made up of such phenomena as warmth, support, conflict, identity, reward, and risk. Social workers see climate as a major quality of resources and often as a target for change.

The earlier discussion makes clear that resources are dependent variables, or targets for change for social workers. Resources for clients may take a variety of meanings and may be the setting or place of employment of social workers. Thus, it is imperative for social workers to understand the systems or organizations of which they may be a part and to know and ask the essential questions for assessing resources.

Organizational systems have external environments. The exchange between an organization and its environment is essential to the growth of the organization. Organizational environment may be thought of in two categories: the general environment and the specific environment.

The general environment consists of conditions that must be of concern to all organizations. Examples of these include political, economic, demographic, cultural, technological, and legal conditions. The specific environment includes other organizations with which the organization interacts frequently or particular individuals who are crucial to the organization. Examples of the specific environment of a school system are the parents of the children enrolled in the school, the local mental health center, the local child welfare services, and the juvenile court.

Social Networks

Environments are made up of networks of resources. An important but sometimes neglected network is the client's informal social network—that is, peers, neighbors, friends, relatives, and so on. Each of these individuals is an important resource for the client, but the linkage and relationship between these individuals in the network are also important. Professionals are aware of the negative potential of peer influence on children. However, the positive aspects of these relationships are also useful to practice. Within these networks are members who serve as effective informal helpers. Knowledge of social networks and the ability to assess these in practice situations are becoming increasingly important as people become more mobile and lose contact with their own roots. Mobility weakens these linkages, increases isolation and loss, and simultaneously makes network relationships more important.

Networks of Service Organizations

Social workers are often in the position of developing networks of service organizations for clients. Many of our practice situations involve a service network such as the school, the family, the state child welfare agency, and the courts or judicial system. Social workers are particularly concerned about the relations between these resource systems. This is a domain of social work practice. Social workers may develop and use these interresource linkages, establish channels of communication between these resources, and develop new resources. Thus, school social workers are in the middle of a system, within an organizational structure, in an environment of social and environmental networks. In order to enhance the development of linkages between various human service organizations, they need to have knowledge of systems variables and organizational variables. Knowledge of the relations of change taking place in different parts of the system—of the tendency of systems to maintain themselves and to tighten their boundaries when threatened—can make the worker much more sensitive to the necessary steps in developing linkages between agencies.

We have reviewed concepts and knowledge applicable to the environmental aspects of school social work practice. Other areas of knowledge are equally applicable. These might be knowledge of normal growth and development of children and the stress in coping that accompanies different growth stages, knowledge of children with disabilities, knowledge of various learning processes, knowledge of specific resources, knowledge of major policies and policy issues affecting practices in the school setting, and knowledge of positive and negative transaction patterns. Certainly, the earlier discussion gives evidence of the breadth of knowledge that social workers need to bring to practice in the school setting. Although we borrow knowledge from psychology, sociology, economics, political science, and education, we borrow from them in relation to our perspectives and to accomplish the purposes of social work.

VALUES

Values guide the action of social work from the preferred perspective to the preferred action. A clarification of types of values is helpful in determining the role of a specific value in practice. Siporin (1975) has defined ten different types of values; five of these are particularly useful to social work:

1. Ultimate (conceived, or absolute) value is a general, abstract formulation, such as liberty, justice, progress, self-realization, and the worth of the individual.
2. Instrumental value is more specific and immediately applicable, such as acceptance of others, equality of opportunity for education, and safeguarding the confidentiality of client information. This is also termed a utility value when one is referring specifically to things being good or beneficial because of their usefulness to an end.
3. Personal value refers to what an individual considers good and right, or what is generally considered right or beneficial for an individual, such as individuality, self-respect, self-reliance, privacy, and self-realization.
4. Scientific value is one to which scientists commit themselves and that they believe should govern scientific behavior: rationality, objectivity, progress, and critical inquiry. Society is increasingly accepting these as general social values.
5. Professional value is one that professional people accept as a basis for professional behavior and to which they commit themselves, such as competence, impartiality, and placing a client's interest first.

The primary and ultimate value in social work seems to be that "It is good and desirable for man(kind) to fulfill his/her potential, to realize himself/herself, and to balance this with essentially equal efforts to help others fulfill their capacities and realize themselves" (Gordon, 1962). This value represents our dual focus on people and their environment, which has characterized social work practice from its beginning. From our ultimate values follow instrumental values that guide actions in practice. An example of an instrumental value is the right to self-determination. This instrumental value guides our practice unless it is in conflict with our ultimate value, that is, when the individual's self-determination is destructive to him or her or to others. Knowledge is usually required in order for a worker to make this determination. Thus, values and knowledge are different but interrelated in their application to practice. Values, however, give us purpose and ethical structure in social work.

While we accept professional values as a basis for our professional behavior, we are careful not to inflict our personal values on others. Hopefully, our personal values are not in conflict with the professional and ultimate values. Yet professional values may not encompass all our personal values. An example of this difference may be seen in relation to divorce. An individual worker may feel that divorce is wrong, but his or her professional values would enable the worker to help clients make this decision for themselves.

It is important to remember that social work has a philosophical base and requires judgment as to means and ends. The judgment, however, can be made with more explicit awareness of the knowledge and value implications.

Social workers must be able to understand the differences between knowledge and values and the relationship between the two. *Value* refers to what a person prefers or would want to be. This preference may involve all the devotion or sacrifice of which one is capable. *Knowledge* refers to the picture we have built up of the world as it is, not necessarily as we would like it to be. It is a picture derived from the most rigorous interpretation we are capable of giving to the most objective sense data we are able to obtain (Gordon, 1962). The future of social work may be dependent on this discrimination. That is, if a value is used as a guide in professional action when knowledge is called for, the resulting action is likely to be ineffective. If knowledge is called on when a value is needed as a guide to action, the resulting action may be destructive. Thus, "Both outcomes greatly reduce the potential for human welfare residing in the profession's heritage of both knowledge and values. Man's ability over time to bring some aspect of the world into conformity with his preferences (realize his values) seems to be directly proportional to his ability to bring his statements and perceptions into conformity with the world as it now is (develop the relevant science)" (Gordon, 1962).

SOCIAL WORK ACTIVITIES

Social work activities involve assessing, relating, communicating, planning, implementing, and evaluating. Assessing is the bridging concept between action and knowledge and values. This does not mean that assessing is a first step that occurs before any other activity. It is rather a continuous process that occurs as other data are gathered. The social work perspective makes explicit the view of the phenomena into which we intervene. Knowledge gives us the most accurate picture of these phenomena that we are able to obtain at any one point in time. Values lead in the choice of perspectives, in the desire to obtain knowledge, and in the choice of action approaches. The first step in any practice situation is to assess that situation from our perspective, with our knowledge, and in relation to our values. This step leads to change action.

In most practice situations, assessment occurs simultaneously with relating. The idea of establishing a relationship has been common in social work from the beginning. In recent years, it has been discussed as a process activity that leads to an end change, resulting in the phenomena into which we intervene. At times in the past, it has been confused with an end in itself or an outcome variable. Certainly, establishing a relationship may be seen as an interim goal, but not as an outcome in the practice situation. Social work places considerable importance on the skill required to relate to the major factors—whether client or resource—involved in any practice situation.

Communicating is an essential activity in practice. Most of our data are collected through communication. To a large extent the accuracy of our data is dependent on our ability to ask questions and clarify answers. It is through communicating that we express our desire and ability to relate and to help.

Planning activities lead to change goals and tasks for each party involved in a practice situation. Plans need to be based on the assessment of the practice situation, including the resources available to carry out these plans. Some plans include the development of other resources, as well as bringing about a match between individuals, coping behaviors, and existing resources. Planning involves time lines and criteria for assessing change, and contracts are the tools used to bridge planning and implementation.

Implementing a change plan is the activity used to accomplish these various tasks and goals. Implementation may involve linking people with resources, changing expectations of the client or of the resource, developing or changing policy, changing the procedures in a resource system, developing new or more effective coping behaviors in individuals, and so on.

Evaluating is part of the assessment process. In the beginning, we assess where the various parts of the practice situation are, and in the end, we evaluate or assess the changes in the various parts. We also evaluate activities that the change processes have accomplished. Evaluation is an assessment of both the outcome and the process. Assessment of outcomes is not possible without a perspective that makes our outcome measures clear. It is because this focus was not explicit in the past that we have been vague and inaccurate and/or have confused the relating process with an outcome measure. Assessing and evaluating are continuous processes that should be linked to our characteristic focus, knowledge, and values. Our assessing and planning processes need to be done in a manner that makes evaluation possible.

Each of these process activities involves many skills. They simply serve as a way of organizing our various skill areas. While there is a beginning and an ending to the change process, the steps in this process are not mutually exclusive or linear steps. They are rather interrelated and purposeful activities that together accomplish an end result.

THE WORKER

While workers may bring the characteristic focus, knowledge, values, and actions of the profession as resources to the change process, they also bring themselves. Workers, like clients, have experience, information, cognitive structures or preferred views of transactions, and predictions about the consequences of certain kinds of transactions. Each worker brings his or her own style of transacting. It is the responsibility of the worker to constantly change his or her perceptions in light of new knowledge, more accurate facts, new resources, and so on.

Workers often prefer particular practice activities. However, the worker's preferred skills should not blunt the awareness of what is needed in any particular situation. For example, some workers have knowledge of interventions to change coping behaviors of individuals. The specific knowledge, plus the worker's preference for particular activities, may lead to a limited practice. Various combinations of selected knowledge and individual preference may lead to a limited perspective for assessing and may lead workers to ignore important aspects of the practice situation. Workers may fail to develop skills for working with groups, the school system, or other community resources.

Many school social workers were trained at a time when methods of practice were the major divisions of training. Workers were trained to do either casework, group work, community organization, or intervention at the policy or administrative level. The major method for school social workers was casework. In more recent years, it has been recognized that there are many common activities in practice. It has also been recognized that change may be enhanced through collaboration and exchange with others who share common change goals. It is the responsibility of practitioners to keep up with changes in knowledge and to develop their skill level to incorporate new practice activities as they develop and are tested.

There is nothing, however, in the professional methodology or activities that can subordinate the unique personal artistic contributions that each worker brings to the helping process. Certainly, the individual's capacity to experience and express empathy and caring is valued among social workers. It is, however, the responsibility of the individual worker to evaluate the effects of his or her individual style on any change process. It is the worker's responsibility to recognize strengths and limitations. Workers must be self-conscious and disciplined in their use of unique qualities and personal style, just as discipline is inherent in the definition of art itself.

We have analyzed and specified the components, characteristic focus, knowledge, values, and skills that social workers contribute to the public schools. This contribution is significant and provides a response that can be useful to education in meeting the challenges of its changing mandate. In specifying the components of practice, we see the model developed as useful both for clarification of the contribution of the social worker and as a tool for building social work knowledge, and for research testing of theory. Because the construction of a model is the first step toward measurement and testing, we see the elements of the model as a first step toward the measurement and testing of components of social work practice. For each social worker, the task of participating in the development of new knowledge is just as important as application of the characteristic focus of the profession and its knowledge, values, and skills. There is much creative work to be done. The responsibility may seem heavy, but the challenge is exciting.

References

Bartlett, H. (1970). *The common base of social work practice*. New York: National Association of Social Workers.

Germain, C. B., & Gitterman, A. (1980). *The life model of social work practice*. New York: Columbia University Press.

Gitterman, A., & Germain, C. (1976). Social work practice: A life model. *Social Service Review, 50*, 601–610.

Gordon, W. E. (1962). A critique of the working definition. *Social Work, 7*(4), 3–13.

Gordon, W. E. (1969). Basic constructs for an integrative and generative conception of social work. In G. Hearn (Ed.), *The general systems approach: Contributions toward an holistic conception of social work* (pp. 5–11). New York: Council on Social Work Education.

Monkman, M. M. (1976). A framework for effective social work intervention in the public schools. *School Social Work Journal, 1*(1), 7–16.

Monkman, M. M. (1978). A broader, more comprehensive view of school social work practice. *School Social Work Journal, 2*(2), 89–96.

Monkman, M. M. (1981). An outcome focus for differential levels of school social work practice. In *Professional issues for social workers in schools* (pp. 138–150). Silver Spring, MD: National Association of Social Workers.

Monkman, M. M. (1983). The specialization of school social work and a model for differential levels of practice. In D. G. Miller (Ed.), *Differential levels of students support services: Including crisis remediation and prevention/developmental approaches*. Minneapolis, MN: Department of Education.

Monkman, M. M. (1989). *A national study of outcome objectives in social work practice: Person and environment*. Unpublished manuscript.

Monkman, M. M., & Allen-Meares, P. (1984). An exploratory study of school social work and its fit to the T.I.E. framework. *School Social Work Journal, 19*(1), 9–22.
Pincus, A., & Minahan, A. (1972). *Social work practice, model and method*. Itasca, IL: F. E. Peacock.
Schwartz, W. (1969). Private troubles and public issues: One social work job or two? In *Social welfare forum* (pp. 22–43). New York: Columbia University Press.
Siporin, M. (1975). *Introduction to social work practice*. New York: Macmillan.

3

Evidence for the Effectiveness of School Social Work Practice

Christine Anlauf Sabatino
Catholic University of America

Lynn Milgram Mayer
Catholic University of America

Elizabeth March Timberlake
Catholic University of America

Theda Yolande Rose
Catholic University of America

- Incorporating the Expanding Knowledge Base into Practice
- Defining Outcomes
- Intervention Effectiveness
- Intervention Findings
- Evidence-Based Intervention and School Social Work Practice
- Future Directions
- Internet Resources

The realities of school social work practice in the twenty-first century are creating new assumptions about practice models, goals, interventions, and documentation of outcomes and tasks as theory and practice are tested. Building on a review of a cumulative body of school social work research, this chapter examines the issue of practice effectiveness to:

1. Clarify expectations about practice evaluation in school social work;
2. Present criteria for locating, organizing, and assessing the information available to school social workers as a basis for developing effective school social work practice;
3. Review recent school social work outcome studies; and
4. Consider future directions for enhancing and evaluating school social work practice effectiveness.

School social workers are expected to embrace the value of science in their intervention methods and to use evaluation as a tool in directing and legitimizing these methods (Kratochwill, Albers, & Shernoff, 2004). As a specialization within social work, school social work practice takes place within the context of education. Recent school legislation (i.e., the No Child Left Behind Act of 2001) has promoted an outcome-based education system (Levine, 2004). School social work builds on professional social work values, ethics, functions, and theoretical bases (Constable & Alvarez, 2006) and uses applicable findings from social work research and from other professions. The demands for outcome-based practice and the realities of practice, however, do not automatically coincide. For example, even though school administrators expect school social workers to document program and practice outcomes, it is not likely that they would use these terms, and rarely do they include outcome evaluation in employment descriptions for school social work positions. They rarely ask school social workers to conduct policy analyses, program evaluations, or practice evaluations. In order to conduct valid and reliable program and practice evaluations, school social workers need financial resources provided by school systems and other funding sources. They also need opportunities and time for collaboration with research partners and access to the developing literature on evidence-based practice in social work (Roberts & Yaeger, 2004), Internet resources, professional associations, and state departments of education.

One must first of all acknowledge the complexity of the tasks involved. Given competing expectations and responsibilities and the diversity of a school social worker's role, it is not easy to evaluate the effectiveness of practice. Furthermore, understanding practice effectiveness in school social work is more complex than examining practice theory, methodology, and techniques. Indeed, much of the effectiveness of direct practice intervention comes from the many processes that underlie different theoretical orientations and developmental perspectives—for example, the therapeutic alliance or working relationship; the client-worker agreement on problem definition, tasks, and goals; and the client's hopes and expectations (Hubble, Duncan, & Miller, 1999; Okomoto & LeCroy, 2004; Snyder, Michael, & Cheavens, 1999). In addition, social workers use a variety of methods to deal with the multiple problems they encounter. Many of these methods involve working with and through others in consultation and teams in the school, in the community, and with parents (Allen-Meares, 1994; Constable, Kuzmickaite, Harrison, & Volkmann, 1999). Thus the effectiveness of the school social worker cannot easily be isolated from the effectiveness of the total team. In the face of this complexity, outcome-based program and practice evaluations inevitably identify only a portion of what school social workers actually do and how well they do it.

In addition to comprehending the complexity of their practice, school social workers need to understand the relationship between the *efficacy* standard for evaluating interventions in controlled experimental research and the *effectiveness* standard for evaluating interventions in a real-world practice context. Efficacy is the gold standard for evaluating intervention outcomes, and the translation of experimental research into effective day-to-day practice is a task undertaken by the entire field of professionals connected with schools: universities, professional organizations, state education agencies, school administrators, and direct practitioners (Kratochwill & Shernoff, 2003). One danger is that approaching this translation task with a narrowed focus on competing practice methodologies may inadvertently cause factors that research has shown to be very powerful to be overlooked. Examples of these factors include the therapeutic alliance, what clients bring to the intervention, team interaction or leadership, teacher consultations, classroom climate, peer interactions, community collaboration, the influence of policy, and the importance of system maintenance as well as system change. Another danger is that the essence of the profession's way of viewing, valuing, and thinking about children in the context of their schools, homes, and communities, as well as its simultaneous dual focus on person and environment (Gordon, 1969), is neither always visible nor easily captured by traditional research methods.

INCORPORATING THE EXPANDING KNOWLEDGE BASE INTO PRACTICE

This section reviews some of the questions behind an ongoing effort by school social workers and researchers to review the literature. How can an expanding knowledge base be incorporated into evidence-based practice? How might school social workers measure the impact of policies, programs, administrative actions, and service practices on children's educational and personal well-being? What can work in school social work?

Beginning to answer these questions involves three steps: collecting information about intervention outcomes from the literature, evaluating the information that has been collected, and organizing the material into a usable framework.

The first step involves the collection of information. Once the topic for the search is determined, computer technology can be used to assist in reviewing the literature. Raines (2004) has suggested several guidelines for searching *Social Work Abstracts* and other databases. These include accessing the relevant database; limiting the search; changing the display; learning new techniques for searching; combining search terms with the word "or"; investigating the evidence; looking for practice-related articles; narrowing the search with "and," and printing or saving findings or e-mailing them to oneself.

The advent of computer technology, particularly online databases and online journals, has both facilitated and hampered the accumulation and organization of professional literature. Easier access to information has increased the availability of evidence for practice and thus can have a positive impact. However, assessing the quality of the many available empirical studies, databases, and published practice guidelines is challenging (Gilgun, 2005), since not all the information found will be credible (Fonagy, Target, Cotrell, Philips, & Kurtz, 2002). Research needs to be evaluated by standards that match the complexity of what is being studied. Thus, the second step is evaluation of the literature, utilizing the lens of research methodology for soundness and credibility.

The process of evaluating research studies and findings is presented here as a series of open-ended evaluative questions. The first questions deal with whether the interventions work. Published articles describing randomized clinical trials with either control or routine treatment comparison groups are clearly the scientific ideal for deciding whether an intervention works. Next are questions on practice effectiveness: Which treatment model works better? For whom? In real school settings, reports describing qualitative studies and quasi-experimental designs with focal and comparison interventions are also important for building knowledge of practice effectiveness.

In any review of published research, the methodological rigor of each study is a primary concern (Brinberg & McGrath, 1982). The first evaluative questions may be: Is the research problem germane to school social work practice? Is the conceptual explanation of the problem clearly stated, parsimonious, feasible, and internally consistent? Internal validity involves the extent to which research findings can be attributed to the independent variables selected for study. This issue yields evaluative questions such as: Is the research method appropriate for answering the questions posed? Is the sample size adequate for answering the question? How representative is the sample? Are the variables measured by valid and reliable instruments appropriate for the research purpose? Is there a control or comparison group? These kinds of questions address threats to internal validity related to history, maturation, testing, instrumentation, regression to the mean, experimental morbidity, selection bias, and interaction (Campbell & Stanley, 1963). Additional questions assess whether the research design incorporates enough difference between the focal interventions and control (or comparison) interventions to allow variance in outcome effect: Did the experimental manipulation make a statistically significant difference and lead to clinically meaningful change?

In consideration of external validity, the focus is on the generalizability of the study. Evaluative questions include: Are the findings generalizable beyond the scope of the study? If the study is replicated, will the same findings occur? These questions reflect Campbell and Stanley's (1963) concerns about threats to external validity: multiple treatments, experimental conditions, interactive testing, and selection interaction.

For qualitative research, the evaluation criteria focus on authenticity and trustworthiness, including credibility, transferability, dependability, and confirmability. Thus, it is critical to assess threats to authenticity (reactivity, researcher bias, and respondent bias) and internal reliability (Rodwell, 1998). Evaluative questions include: Is the research question clear and congruent? Is the role of the researcher described? Are the paradigms and constructs specified? Was data collection done across a range of settings, times, and respondents? Are there comparable data collection protocols for all workers? Are coding and data quality checks done? Do the findings show parallelism across data sources?

Studies combining quantitative and qualitative approaches meet the standard of achieving a balance between rigor and relevance, precision and richness, elegance and applicability, and verification and discovery. Mixed-method or mixed-model designs increase the breadth and scope of the study by using triangulation, complementarity, initiation, development, and expansion (Tashakkori & Teddlie, 1998).

In addition to individual studies, the process of evaluating knowledge upon which to base interventions may involve reports of statistical meta-analyses of multiple intervention studies targeting a focal problem in order to aggregate the findings and determine best practices (Baker & Jansen, 2000; Gilgun, 2005; Raines, 2004). In meta-analyses, practice outcome findings can be sorted according to outcome content and/or research design. The goal is to compare the aggregated findings by using sophisticated statistical methodology to examine generalizability and the feasibility of replication. The results of meta-analyses, however, need to be interpreted and understood in the context of their practice applicability; one must distinguish what may be efficacious in a laboratory setting and what may be effective in a real practice context.

How then can state-of-the-art knowledge about practice efficacy be translated into usable knowledge for effective practice? The lens of theory can organize the collection of methodologically sound topical research that is relevant to school social work into a usable framework. From this framework, the literature can be synthesized into a conceptual narrative that focuses information and stimulates the development of practice models. We will review some of these theoretical frameworks that address the relation between large-scale and individual interventions in schools.

Adelman and Taylor (2000, 2006), for example, present an overarching conceptual framework for effective helping that focuses on barriers to student development, learning, and teaching. This framework encompasses a holistic developmental perspective that incorporates primary prevention and early intervention programs to address the root causes of the full range of problems, from adjustment difficulties to severe and chronic conditions. They posit that in order to overcome barriers to education, fundamental change in educational policies, school restructuring, and community collaboration are necessary. Their model highlights six interrelated areas: classroom-focused enabling, transition supports, student and family assistance, prevention and crisis response programs, parent and caregiver involvement, and community outreach.

Early and Vonk (2001) offer a different conceptual framework. In reviewing twenty-one outcome studies of school social work practice, they used the conceptual framework of risk and resilience, arguing that this framework is appropriate for school social work's preventive function. While *risk* refers to factors associated with the probability of a negative event or outcome, *resilience* refers to protective factors that promote capacity or coping abilities. On the environmental level, risk and protective factors exist in the larger environment as well as the environment of the school, neighborhood, and family. On the individual level, characteristics on the biological, psychological, social, and spiritual levels can be either risk or protective factors. The studies in this review reflect social work outcomes of decreased risk factors and augmented protective factors in youth development and psychosocial functioning. Thus, the presentation facilitates understanding what promotes resilience, or what lessens risk, and thereby clarifies target areas for setting goals and eliminating barriers to learning.

Kratochwill et al. (2004) offer a third conceptual framework with a three-tier model of prevention and intervention services based on developmental level and risk status. Services are categorized along a continuum of universal, selected, and indicated interventions. Tier 1 or universal interventions address the needs of an entire student group, independent of risk status, and have goals of enhancing protective factors and minimizing future difficulties. These interventions, such as violence prevention programs or school-wide behavioral expectations, reach approximately 80 percent of a student population. Tier 2 or selective interventions are designed to meet the needs of students who are non-responsive to universal interventions or who display significant risk factors, perhaps 10–15 percent of the student population. Examples are groups for children experiencing the divorce of their parents, early intervention, transition programs, social skills groups, classroom interventions, and consultation with teachers or parents. Finally, tier 3 or indicated interventions are designed to meet the needs of the estimated 1–5 percent of students whose failure to respond to universal and selected interventions indicates the need for more intensive, comprehensive, and expansive services implemented on a longer-term basis with coordinated efforts among teachers, parents, social workers, and community service providers. Examples might be students with distinguishing risk factors, delinquency, depression, or aggressive behavior.

DEFINING OUTCOMES

What is a good outcome? For whom is it good (Fonagy et al., 2002)? Which service programs and intervention processes are most effective in eliminating personal and environmental barriers to learning for which clients? Which children and youths need a different array of services? Do school social workers (or various team efforts) fulfill school system policy, program, and administrative directives? Which community partnerships provide the most effective service for children and families in the schools? What is the cost-effectiveness of service delivery (including adequacy and efficiency)? There are three broad approaches to conceptualizing outcomes. (1) Service outcomes document program impact and reflect the goals of the intervention, the process of the intervention delivered, and aggregate accomplishments. The measurement emphasis may be on different aspects of the service provided, including service availability, accessibility, and comprehensiveness; the intervention model itself and techniques selected; the processes, techniques, context, and quality of service delivery; the amount of intervention provided and the number of clients served; and the outcomes that reflect service mission and cost effectiveness. (2) Satisfaction outcomes document the user's contentment with the service delivered and the outcomes achieved. Satisfaction as a measure of success reflects service acceptability as well as the therapeutic relationship and is thought to correlate with client retention and change. (3) Practice outcomes document goal attainment or problem reduction as perceived by children, parents, teachers, school social workers, school personnel, the school system, and the community. As a measure of success, these outcomes reflect treatment processes and client changes occurring over the course of the intervention. Practice outcomes for children and parents may include in-session impact (awareness and insight, problem reduction, affect and behavior changes) and three types of post-session outcomes: immediate changes apparent at termination, such as symptom reduction, affect change, behavior change, and educational achievement; intermediate changes, which occur some months after termination, such as personal adaptation and changes in psychosocial functioning, interpersonal relationships, and coping with stressors; and long-term improvements that occur one year or more after termination, such as personality or other intrapsychic change. Practice outcomes reflecting goal attainment by school and community may include environmental barrier and resource changes as preludes to child and parent changes, concurrent environmental changes such as school-community collaboration patterns and teacher-child interactions, and program and policy changes occurring upon consideration of aggregated data.

INTERVENTION EFFECTIVENESS

There is a danger in focusing mainly on intervention models to the exclusion of other factors that also have profound effects on outcome. According to Hubble et al. (1999), it is likely that the beneficial effects of intervention, including school social work practice models, result largely from the combination of four therapeutic factors that research has identified as the principal elements accounting for client improvement:

1. Client extra-therapeutic factors (strengths and needs, risk and protective factors, intrapersonal resources and deficits, interpersonal social network involvement, and reflective skills the client brings) account for 40 percent of the outcome.
2. Relationship factors account for 30 percent of the outcome. These are the interpersonal connectedness and expressive attunement of the therapeutic alliance or working relationship. They include Rogers's (1957) classic core therapeutic conditions of a healing relationship—empathy, genuineness, and unconditional positive regard.
3. Placebo, hope, and expectancy factors—that is, the belief that change can occur, agreement with the rationale of a treatment approach, and "confidence in and mastery of a chosen method [that] ultimately works by enhancing the client's belief in the potential for healing" (Snyder et al. 1999, p. 183)—account for 15 percent of the outcome.
4. Model-specific factors (philosophical underpinnings, rationale, theory base, format, goals, tasks, techniques, treatment processes, and anticipated outcomes) account for 15 percent of the outcome.

Thus, a key question for future intervention is: How do these four therapeutic factors combine with the school setting to make school social work practice unique and effective?

Intervention Findings

In this era of accountability, mere descriptions of programs and practice models are no longer sufficient. Intervention processes and outcomes meaningful to the children, families, schools, and communities being served must be made explicitly clear (operationalized). Ideally, these school social work outcomes will grow out of the social work profession's orientation and values, target specialized school social work goals and functions, and incorporate language meaningful to the school setting's educational mission. In addition, the outcomes must reflect the reality and complexity of the interpersonal, intrapersonal, cognitive-behavioral, and empowerment theoretical frameworks used in the person-in-environment practice models in which school social work practice is based. Much of the time, the outcomes will also need to reflect multidisciplinary team contributions to the intervention, with attribution appropriately assigned to teamwork rather than to a sole practitioner.

At this point in time it is questionable whether sole reliance on school social work outcome studies that have been judged adequate by means of experimental research design criteria provides the best means of improving school social work practice. In reviewing the professional literature produced from the 1980s through the mid-1990s, two academic review teams identified sixty-four school social work outcome studies (Bailey-Dempsey & Reid, 1996) and 228 outcome studies of mental health practices in the schools (Hoagwood & Erwin, 1997). These academic reviewers, however, judged only five studies from the first set and twelve from the second as approaching best research practices for outcome studies. That is, 17 of 292 studies approached the ideal research design for lab experiments and yielded demonstrable results. A more recent literature review has directed attention to twenty-one controlled-outcome studies on the effectiveness of school social work interventions (Early & Vonk, 2001). This review highlighted the internal validity criteria ideally associated with outcome research and pointed toward a growing database from which social workers may draw to develop best intervention practices and policies for children.

Review of School Social Work Outcome Studies 1998–2007

To identify school social work outcome studies for this chapter, a computerized literature search of *Social Work Abstracts* from 1998 through April 2007 was conducted, using terms such as "education-school," "school social work outcomes," "school social work effectiveness," "school social work research," "school mental health outcomes," and "school social work interventions." This intervention-focused search yielded fifty peer-reviewed journal articles by social workers that described the outcomes of both school-based social work interventions and school-based multidisciplinary mental health interventions (see table 3.1). The majority of these studies used quantitative evaluative methodology. Although fewer than half of the total employed comparison group or control group designs, it is important to note that five of the seven studies published between 2003 and 2007 did use such designs. When the articles were analyzed by themes, patterns became apparent for the problems targeted, the models' conceptual pathways leading to change, the educational level of the targeted children, outcome goals, and goal attainment.

Thirty-six studies (72%) identified eight problem areas targeted for intervention: violence and aggressive behavior (10 studies), school behavior problems (3), academic achievement and attendance (10), drug use

TABLE 3.1 Summary of Fifty Selected School-Based Outcome Studies, 1998–2007

Problem	*Model's Conceptual Path*	*Education Level*	*Goals*	*Attained*	*Authors*	*Date*
Violence, aggressive behavior	Cognitive/behavioral	High school	• Increase students' sense of environmental safety • Improve attitudes toward violence • Increase skills and knowledge related to coping • Improve student behavior	Yes Yes Yes Yes	De Anda	1999
	Cognitive/behavioral	High school	• Decrease disruptive classroom behavior	Yes	Gerdtz	2000
	Cognitive/behavioral	High school	• Help students experience more positive management and expression of anger • Improve self-control Mixed	Mixed Mixed	Whitfield	1999
	Cognitive/behavioral	Middle school	• Increase internal locus of control	Mixed	Dupper	1998
	Information processing	Grade school	• Increase knowledge about sex abuse	Yes	Tutty	2000
	Interpersonal, mentoring	Middle school	• Reduce aggression of a small group	Mixed	Fast et al.	2003
	Ecological, mentoring	High school	• Evaluate the effectiveness of mentoring mothers and daughters in violent environments	Mixed	Cox	2001
	Ecological	High school	• Evaluate a school reform model's effects on violence	Mixed	Corbin	2001
	Ecological	High school	• Promote academic success in a disciplinary alternative program	Mixed	Carpenter-Aeby et al.	2001
	Solution/goal oriented	Grade school	• Achieve positive changes in behavior problems	Mixed	Franklin et al.	2001
School problems	Solution/goal oriented	High school	• Evaluate effectiveness of school social work as a means to solve adolescent problems in schools	Yes	Young & Jung	2002
	Information processing	High school	• Change stories into healthy narratives • Increase likelihood that students will reenter mainstream education by using narratives to promote strengths/solutions	Mixed Mixed	Carpenter-Aeby & Kurtz	2000
	Cognitive/behavioral	Grade school	• Improve teacher skills for coping with behavior problems in children	Mixed	Schiff & BarGil	2004
Academic achievement and attendance	Solution/goal oriented	Grade school	• Reduce absenteeism • Increase positive attitude toward school • Enhance self esteem	Yes Yes Yes	Baker & Jansen	2000
	Solution/goal oriented	Grade school	• Increase assignment completion	Mixed	Teall	2000
	Role modeling, mentoring	High school	• Increase school attendance • Increase achievement	Yes No	Brabazon	1999

	Role modeling, mentoring	Grade school	• Increase academic performance	Yes	Thompson & Kelly-Vance	2001
	Role modeling, mentoring	Grade school	• Increase attendance	No	Volkman & Bye	2006
	Interpersonal	Grade school	• Reduce absenteeism	Yes	Grooters & Faidley	2002
	Interpersonal, information processing	Grade school	• Improve students' psychosocial functioning • Increase understanding of learning disabilities	Yes Yes	Mishna & Muskat	2004
	Information processing	Grade school	• Assess the impact of an after-school program on academic performance	Yes	Zosky & Crawford	2003
	Interpersonal, activity oriented	Grade school	• Improve academic achievement • Improve behavior problems • Increase information exchange between home and school	Yes Yes Yes	Bowen	1999
	Behavioral	High school	• Increase AFDC teenagers' school attendance and completion	No	Harris et al.	2001
Drug use behavior	Role modeling, mentoring	High school	• Increase sense of well-being • Change reactions to situations involving drug use	Yes Yes	Taylor et al.	1999
	Information processing	School system	• Prevent substance abuse	Mixed	Marsiglia et al.	2000
	Ecological systems	Grade school High school	• Improve school climate by reducing theft and bullying • Improve school climate and teacher morale	Yes Yes	Bagley & Pritchard	1998
	Ecological, sociocultural	Middle school	• Decrease substance use	Mixed	Kulis et al.	2005
Peer relations	Interpersonal, activity oriented	Middle school	• Improve peer relationship skills	Mixed	Walsh-Bowers & Basso	1999
	Interpersonal, information processing	High school	• Increase communication and conflict resolution skills • Decrease aggressive responses	Yes Yes	Woody	2001
Sexual behavior	Information processing	Middle school	• Change knowledge and beliefs about sex practices	Yes	Arnold et al.	1999
	Information processing	High school	• Prevent pregnancy and STIs	Mixed	Smith et al.	2002
Family support Social support	Interpersonal	Grade school	• Strengthen parent involvement in child's academic life to prevent academic failure	Yes	Fischer	2003
	Interpersonal	Preschool	• Analyze IFSP eligibility and early intervention services for family-centeredness	Yes	Sabatino	2001
	Interpersonal	Middle school High	• Promote school attendance, success, and satisfaction/engagement/self-efficacy • Decreasing problem behavior	Yes Yes	Rosenfeld et al.	2000
	Interpersonal, activities, social networks	Grade school	• Increase parent engagement • Strengthen classroom functioning	Yes Yes	McDonald et al.	2006

TABLE 3.1 Summary of Fifty Selected School-Based Outcome Studies, 1998–2007—(*Continued*)

Problem	*Model's Conceptual Path*	*Education Level*	*Goals*	*Attained*	*Authors*	*Date*
Mental health	Interpersonal	School system	• Promote successful transitions	Yes	Walter & Petr	2004
Prosocial behavior	Role modeling, mentoring	Grade school	• Improve the functioning and empowerment of school-aged children	No	Itzhaky & Segal	2001
	Interpersonal, social support	Preschool	• Assess the effects of preschool programs on life success	Mixed	Caputo	2003
	Cognitive/behavioral	Grade school	• Change problem-causing behaviors	Yes	Openshaw	2004
	Cognitive/behavioral, task-centered skills building	High school	• Increase social problem solving • Strengthen problem-focused coping • Increase success in school	Yes Yes Yes	Harris & Franklin	2003
	Solution/goal oriented	High school	• Evaluate effectiveness of solution-focused therapy with Muslim students	Mixed	Al-Garni	2004
	Interpersonal	Middle school	• Articulate feelings through verbal expression using puppets and peers	Mixed	Romano	2001
	Interpersonal	Grade school	• Enhance social skills using classroom meetings	Mixed	Frey	2002
	Interpersonal	Middle school School system	• Achieve orderly classroom environments • Increase school-related self-esteem • Increase standardized test scores	Yes Yes No	Belcher et al.	2006
	Interpersonal	Preschool	• Assess social validity of classroom management intervention • Strengthen classroom environment	Yes Yes	Frey et al.	2006
	Interpersonal, activity oriented	Grade school	• Evaluate effectiveness of a social skills intervention on problem behaviors	Yes	Anderson-Butcher et al.	2003
	Interpersonal, activity oriented	High school	• Evaluate effectiveness of activity group therapy to advancing psychosocial growth	Yes	Troester	2002
	Interpersonal, behavioral	Grade school	• Decrease playground problem behaviors during recess • Decrease inappropriate use of equipment during recess	Yes Yes	Butcher	1999
	Information processing	Grade school High school School system	• Increase academic achievement and school self-esteem • Increase program satisfaction and school self-esteem	Yes Yes	Teasley & Lee	2006

behavior (4), peer relations (2), sexual behavior (2), family support and social support (4), and mental health (1). Fourteen studies (28%) identified interventions focused on increasing strengths such as pro-social behaviors and resilience.

The intervention models are framed in six conceptual pathways: cognitive behavioral (8 models), information processing (8), role modeling and mentoring (6), interpersonal and activity oriented (17), solution focused and goal oriented (5), and ecological systems (6).

Most of the studies targeted a particular age group: three articles targeted preschool, nineteen elementary school, six middle school, and sixteen high school. Two studies addressed two age groupings (one middle and high school, one elementary and high school). Four studies targeted a school system. Although some interventions targeted boys and some girls, only one intervention model was designed to address gender-specific issues or viewpoints.

These fifty studies identified seventy-three outcome goals. One-third (33%) of the goals were focused on problem resolution and involved decreasing behavior problems and interpersonal violence (16 goals) and increasing positive coping skills in dealing with alcohol, drugs, violence, and sex (8 goals). Almost half (48%) of the goals focused on developing strengths and involved increasing the repertoire of pro-social behaviors (17 goals) and increasing attendance and improving academic performance (18 goals). One-fifth (19%) of the goals were environmentally focused and involved increasing a sense of environmental safety and well-being (5 goals), instituting school programs and school reforms to influence academic performance (3 goals), strengthening teaching (2 goals), and enhancing parenting in relation to children's education (4 goals). Of the seventy-three outcome goals, two-thirds (66%) were clearly attained; one-fourth (27%) yielded mixed results. Some (7%) were not attained.

The National Institutes of Health Review

In January 2005, the National Institutes of Health published conference findings on preventing violence and adolescent behavioral health risks through its Evidence-Based Practice Center Program. Two programs met all the criteria for effectiveness, including the gold standard of randomized clinical trials, in work with the situations of high-risk youths: functional family therapy and multisystemic therapy (National Institutes of Health, 2005; Sexton & Alexander, 2003; Sheidow, Henggeler, & Schoenwald, 2003). Both programs used intensive family-oriented, multisystemic approaches that were more complex interventions than a sole focus on the youth. In many ways, the NIH report supports approaches that social work practice has worked with and generally taken for granted—complex multisystemic family interventions. Six programs addressing factors that were precursors to arrest or violence were classified as "effective with reservation"—that is, they had internal replicability but not external replicability. These programs included Big Brothers Big Sisters (reduction in hitting), Multidimensional Treatment Foster Care (reduction in incarceration), Nurse Family Partnership (reduction in arrest, crime), Promoting Alternative Thinking Strategies (reduction in peer aggression), and Brief Strategic Family Therapy (reduction in conduct disorder, socialized aggression) (National Institutes of Health, 2005). These successful programs have several characteristics in common:

- They have sound theoretical rationales.
- They utilize strong risk factors.
- They involve long-term treatments often lasting a year and sometimes much longer.
- They involve intensive work with those targeted for treatment, often using a clinical approach.
- The promote development of cognitive and behavioral skills.
- They are multimodal and multi-contextual.
- They focus on improving social competency and other skill development strategies for targeted youths and/or their families.
- They are developmentally appropriate.
- They are not delivered in coercive institutional settings.
- They are delivered with fidelity (National Institutes of Health, 2005).

Other effective interventions involved dramatically changing neighborhood environments, as in the Moving to Opportunity program. In addition, programs that increased educational attainment and decreased dropout rates were likely to yield the tangential benefit of reducing violence among those who were helped (National Institutes of Health, 2005). Further evidence suggested that get-tough programs and group detention centers do not work. Indeed, there is evidence they may make the problem worse by providing an opportunity for delinquent youths to amplify negative effects on each other (National Institutes of Health, 2005).

EVIDENCE-BASED INTERVENTION AND SCHOOL SOCIAL WORK PRACTICE

Research on effective models of practice provides general orientations to be adapted to the varied situations and multiple decision points of actual practice. Franklin, Harris, and Allen-Meares (2006) provide a 114-chapter evidence-based review of school services. Roberts and Yaeger (2004) have published a seminal text on evidence-based practice that includes 103 articles on intervention. Munson's article from this text develops general intervention guidelines for promoting evidence-based relationship-focused practice, and integrating scientific method into everyday practice. Such practice would ensure that:

- An intervention could be identified by the practitioner and understood by the client;
- An established connection between the intervention and the problem could be articulated by the practitioner in language comprehensible to the client;
- The practitioner and the client could implement the intervention with reasonable effort;
- The client would have an identifiable reason/motivation to comply with the effort;
- Along with the proposed intervention, an alternate intervention could be identified;
- Possible outcomes (intended and unintended, positive and negative) could be identified in advance of applying the intervention;
- The intervention could be observed and measured. (Munson, 2004, p. 255)

In this article, Munson attempted to relate the normal, finite realities of practice to the scientific method in a shared process with a client system. If evidence-based approaches truly were incorporated into practice, this sharing would result.

FUTURE DIRECTIONS

In the American educational system, highly skilled and committed professionals who are guided by the latest educational policy, practice, research, and technology provide educational and support services to millions of students. Yet it is evident that the system is marked by serious and pervasive deficiencies in outcome quality. These service deficiencies affect children and families, school systems and school personnel, and communities, resulting in increased family stress, school failure, and community predicaments that lower quality of life and consume unnecessary resources.

To address these service deficiencies, school social workers need to begin a national dialogue that focuses on building their capacity to develop progress measures, outcome measures, and reporting systems that document the quality of their practice; develop a range of universal, selective, and indicated practice models attentive to prevention and remediation; conceptually frame and operationalize their practice models before testing their effectiveness and facilitating replication; develop and test the effectiveness of new models with a simultaneous dual focus on both person and environment and risk and protective factors; and disseminate the findings of their research and development efforts. Supporting these points, the National Association of Social Workers' *Standards for School Social Work Services* (2002) states, "School social workers shall be able to evaluate their practice and disseminate the findings to consumers, the local education agency, the community and the profession" (standard 24). For this standard to begin to strengthen school social work practice today, a common approach to measuring the improvements in educational quality brought about by school social workers' services will be needed. An example of such a common approach is that of the National Quality Forum. The National Quality Forum (2004) is an association of health care professionals whose mission is to "provide meaningful information about whether care is safe, timely, beneficial, patient centered, equitable and efficient." Applying the National Quality Forum goals to school social work services, a group of school social workers concerned with development of the above capacities would:

1. Promote collaborative efforts to improve the quality of the nation's educational system through school social work performance measurement and public reporting;
2. Develop a national strategy for measuring and reporting school social work service quality;
3. Standardize school social work service performance measures so that comparable data is available across the nation (i.e., establish national voluntary consensus standards);
4. Promote home/school/community understanding and use of school social work service performance measures and other quality information; and
5. Promote and encourage the enhancement of school system capacity to evaluate and report on school social work service quality. (National Quality Forum, 2004)

Priority areas for improvement of school system quality through school social work services should be established by school social workers and be accompanied by appropriate and specific goals and objectives. An initial set of priority areas might include reducing school failure, ensuring the appropriate use of regular and special education services, increasing parent involvement, increasing community collaboration and service partnerships, and expanding outcome-based research and evidence of effectiveness.

Improvements in these priority areas would require greater investment in basic research, flexible school systems, greater collaboration among stakeholders, and investment in information systems and reporting mechanisms. Setting priority areas and implementing a common approach to defining constructs and measuring improved educational quality requires coordination among school social workers and other stakeholders. It is anticipated that this approach will increase not only educational quality but also the need for school social work services.

School social work roles, along with the roles of other school-based professionals, are now more clearly defined in relation to educational processes and goals than they once were. Further, they are more precisely defined by the expectations inherent in the explicit mandates of current national laws and policies for outcome-based education and in its implied corollary of evidence-based practice in schools. As a result, school social work is now developing an awareness of the practice and research that school psychology and counseling recognized earlier (Kratochwill et al., 2004). That is, they are beginning to develop practice models that specify theory, method, techniques, processes, and evidence-based outcomes and facilitate replication and comparison with other models. These models are using strengths promotion as well as problem reduction. Thus, a far more open, data-based, and functionally based system of practice is gradually emerging. As social work research begins to be recognized by others, increased opportunities for funded research are also becoming available to school social workers.

As shown in this chapter, there are a variety of frameworks with which to sort the literature, identify school-related problems, and assess effective intervention outcomes. Without systematic application of critical thinking and theory-driven research and implementation and documentation of evidence-based practice and policy, however, school social workers are at risk of failing to demonstrate their critical role in fulfilling the mission of American education and, more importantly, failing to fulfill their ethical obligation to clients.

INTERNET RESOURCES

Although school social work is only beginning to develop Internet resources, many professional organizations have ongoing commitments to maintain active Web sites about the use of evidence in practice. Web sites useful for school social work practitioners include the following.

American Academy of Child and Adolescent Psychiatry	www.aacap.org
American Psychological Association	www.apa.org
American Public Health Association	www.apha.org
Campbell Collaboration	www.campbellcollaboration.org
Center for Health and Health Care in Schools	www.healthinschools.org
Cochrane Collaboration	www.cochrane.org
Institute for the Advancement of Social Work Research	www.iaswresearch.org
National Association of School Psychologists	www.nasponline.org
National Association of Social Workers	www.socialworkers.org
School Social Work Association of America	www.sswaa.org
Society for Social Work and Research	www.sswr.org
Substance Abuse and Mental Health Services Administration	www.samhsa.gov
What Works Clearinghouse	http://ies.ed.gov/ncee/wwc/

In addition, Roberts and Yaeger (2004) provide a comprehensive list of Internet resources at the end of their *Evidence-Based Practice Manual.*

References

Adelman, H., & Taylor, L. (2000). Shaping the future of mental health in schools. *Psychology in the Schools, 37*, 49–60.

Adelman, H., & Taylor, L. (2006). *The implementation guide to student learning supports in the classroom and schoolwide: New directions for addressing barriers to learning.* Thousand Oaks, CA: Corwin Press.

Al-Garni, M. (2004). Solution focused therapy: Cross cultural application to school counseling in Saudi Arabia. *Journal of School Social Work, 13*, 40–58.

Allen-Meares, P. (1994). Social work in schools: A national study. *Social Work, 39*, 560–567.

Anderson-Butcher, D., Newsome, W., & Nay, S. (2003). Social skills intervention during elementary school recess: A visual analysis. *Children & Schools, 25*, 135–146.

Arnold, E., Smith, T., Harrison, D., & Springer, D. (1999). The effects of an abstinence-based sex education program on middle school students' knowledge and beliefs. *Research on Social Work Practice, 9*, 10–24.

Bagley, C., & Pritchard, C. (1998). The reduction of problem behaviors and school exclusion in at-risk youth: An experimental study of school social work with cost-benefit analyses. *Child and Family Social Work, 3*, 219–226.

Bailey-Dempsey, C., & Reid, W. (1996). Intervention design and development: A case study. *Research on Social Work Practice, 6*, 208–228.

Baker, D., & Jansen, J. (2000). Using groups to reduce elementary school absenteeism. *Social Work in Education, 22*, 46–53.

Belcher, C., Frey, A., & Yankeelov, P. (2006). The effects of single-sex classrooms on classroom environment, self-esteem, and standardized test scores. *School Social Work Journal, 31*, 61–75.

Bowen, N. (1999). A role for school social workers in promoting student success through school-family partnerships. *Social Work in Education, 21*, 34–47.

Brabazon, K. (1999). Student improvement in the intergenerational work/study program. *Child & Youth Services, 20*, 51–61.

Brinberg, D., & McGrath, J. (1982). A network of validity concepts within the research process. In D. Brinberg & L. Kidder (Eds.), *Forms of validity in research* (pp. 4–21). San Francisco: Jossey-Bass.

Butcher, D. (1999). Enhancing social skills through school social work interventions during recess: Gender differences. *Social Work in Education, 21,* 249–262.

Campbell, D., & Stanley, J. (1963). *Experimental and quasi-experimental designs for research.* Boston: Houghton Mifflin.

Caputo, R. (2003). Head Start, other preschool programs, and life success in a youth cohort. *Journal of Sociology and Social Welfare, 30*, 105–126.

Carpenter-Aeby, T., & Kurtz, P. (2000). The portfolio as a strengths-based intervention to empower chronically disruptive students in an alternative school. *Children & Schools, 22,* 217–231.

Carpenter-Aeby, T., Salloum, M., & Aeby, V. (2001). A process evaluation of school social work services in a disciplinary alternative educational program. *Children & Schools, 23*, 171–180.

Constable, R., & Alvarez, M. (2006). Moving into specialization in school social work: Issues in practice, policy, and education. *School Social Work Journal, 30*, 116–131.
Constable, R., Kuzmickaite, D., Harrison, W., & Volkmann, L. (1999). The emergent role of the school social worker in Indiana. *School Social Work Journal, 24*, 1–14.
Corbin, J. (2001). Addressing school violence: Using the framework of group psychotherapy to explore the impact of the school development program on school violence. *Smith College Studies in Social Work, 71*, 243–258.
Cox, A. (2001). Mentoring African American mothers and their daughters from violent environments: An approach for alternative schools. *Journal of School Social Work, 12*, 91–111.
De Anda, D. (1999). Project peace: The evaluation of a skill-based violence prevention program for high school adolescents. *Social Work in Education, 21*, 137–149.
Dupper, D. (1998). An alternative to suspension for middle school youths with behavior problems: Findings from a "school survival" group. *Research on Social Work Practice, 8*, 354–366.
Early, T., & Vonk, M. (2001). Effectiveness of school social work from a risk and resilience perspective. *Children & Schools, 23*, 9–31.
Fast, J., Fanelli, F., & Salen, L. (2003). How becoming mediators affects aggressive students. *Children & Schools, 25*, 161–171.
Fischer, R. (2003). School-based family support: Evidence from an exploratory field study. *Families in Society, 84*, 339–347.
Fonagy, P., Target, M., Cotrell, D., Philips, J., & Kurtz, Z. (2002). *What works for whom: A critical review of treatments for adolescents.* New York: Guilford Press.
Franklin, C., Biever, J., Moore, K., Clemons, D., & Scamardo, M. (2001). The effectiveness of solution-focused therapy with children in a school setting. *Research on Social Work Practice, 11*, 411–434.
Franklin, C., Harris, M. B., & Allen-Meares, P. (2006). *The school services sourcebook: A guide for school-based professionals*. New York: Oxford University Press.
Frey, A. (2002). Enhancing children's social skills through classroom meetings. *School Social Work Journal, 26*, 46–57.
Frey, A., Faith, T., Elliott, A., & Royer, B. (2006). A pilot study examining the social validity and effectiveness of a positive behavior support model in Head Start. *School Social Work Journal, 30*, 23–44.
Gerdtz, J. (2000). Evaluating behavioral treatment of disruptive classroom behaviors of an adolescent with autism. *Research on Social Work Practice, 10*, 98–110.
Gilgun, J. (2005). The four cornerstones of evidence-based practice in social work. *Research on Social Work Practice, 15*, 52–61.
Gordon, W. (1969). Basic concepts for an integrative and generative conception of social work. In G. Hearn (Ed.), *The general systems approach: Contributions toward an holistic conception of social work* (pp. 5–11). New York: Council on Social Work Education.
Grooters, L., & Faidley, B. (2002). Impacting early elementary school attendance: It can be done. *Journal of School Social Work, 13*, 70–90.
Harris, M., & Franklin, C. (2003). Effects of a cognitive-behavioral school-based, group intervention with Mexican American pregnant and parenting adolescents. *Social Work Research, 27*, 71–83.
Harris, R., Jones, L., & Finnegan, D. (2001). Using TANF sanctions to increase high school graduation. *Journal of Sociology and Social Welfare, 28*, 211–222.

Hoagwood, K., & Erwin, H. (1997). Effectiveness of school-based mental health services for children: A 10-year review. *Journal of Child and Family Studies, 6*, 435–451.

Hubble, D., Duncan, B., & Miller, S. (1999). *The heart and soul of change*. Washington, DC: American Psychological Association.

Itzhaky, H., & Segal, O. (2001). Model of after-school treatment programs as agents of empowerment. *Journal of Family Social Work, 5*, 51–68.

Kratochwill, T., Albers, C., & Shernoff, E. (2004). School-based interventions. *Child and Adolescent Psychiatric Clinics of North America, 13*, 885–903.

Kratochwill, T., & Shernoff, E. (2003). Evidence-based practice: Promoting evidence-based interventions in school psychology. *School Psychology Quarterly, 18*, 389–408.

Kulis, S., Marsiglia, F., Elek, E., Dustman, P., Wagstaff, D., & Hecht, M. (2005). Mexican/Mexican American adolescents and Keepin' It Real: An evidence-based substance use prevention program. *Children & Schools, 27*, 133–145.

Levine, A. (2004). *New roles, old responses.* Retrieved February 24, 2005, from http://www.tc.columbia.edu/news/article.htm

Marsiglia, F., Holleran, L., & Jackson, K. (2000). Assessing the effect of external resources on school-based substance abuse prevention programs. *Social Work in Education, 22*, 145–161.

McDonald, L., Moberg, D., Brown, R., Rodriguez-Espiricueta, I., Flores, N.,Burke, M., & Coover, G. (2006). After-school multifamily groups: A randomized controlled trial involving low-income, urban, Latino children. *Children & Schools, 28*, 25–34.

Mishna, F., & Muskat, B. (2004). School-based treatment for students with learning disabilities: A collaborative approach. *Children & Schools, 26*, 135–150.

Munson, C. (2004). Evidence-based treatment for traumatized and abused children. In A. Roberts & K. Yeager (Eds.), *Evidence-based practice manual: Research and outcome measures in health and human services* (pp. 252–262). New York: Oxford University Press.

National Association of Social Workers. (2002). *Standards for school social work services*. Washington, DC: National Association of Social Workers Press.

National Institutes of Health. (2005). *State of the science conference statement: Preventing violence and related health-risking social behaviors in adolescents.* Retrieved February 24, 2005, from http://concensus.nih.gov/ta/023/YouthViolenceFinalStatement011805.htm

National Quality Forum. (2004). *National Quality Forum mission.* Retrieved February 13, 2005, from http://www.qualityforum.org/mission/home.htm

No Child Left Behind Act of 2001. P.L. 107-110.

Okomoto, S., & LeCroy, C. (2004). Evidence-based practice and manualized treatment with children. In A. Roberts & K. Yeager (Eds.), *Evidence-based practice manual: Research and outcome measures in health and human services* (pp. 204–213). New York: Oxford University Press.

Openshaw, L. (2004). Achieving student goals by graphing student progress. *Journal of School Social Work, 13*, 9–19.

Raines, J. (2004). Evidence-based practice in school social work: A process in perspective. *Children & Schools, 26*, 71–85.

Roberts, A., & Yeager, K. (2004). *Evidence-based practice manual: Research and outcome measures in health and human services*. New York: Oxford University Press.

Rodwell, M. (1998). *Social work constructivist research.* New York: Garland.
Rogers, C. (1957). The necessary and sufficient conditions of therapeutic personality change. *Journal of Consulting Psychology, 21*, 95–103.
Romano, M. (2001). Puppets and peers in school social work. *Journal of School Social Work, 11*, 87–90.
Rosenfeld, L., Richman, J., & Bowen, G. (2000). Social support networks and school outcomes: The centrality of the teacher. *Child & Adolescent Social Work Journal, 17*, 205–226.
Sabatino, C. (2001). Family-centered sections of the IFSP and school social work participation. *Children & Schools, 23*, 241–252.
Schiff, M., & BarGil, B. (2004). Children with behavior problems: Improving elementary school teachers' skills to keep these children in class. *Children and Youth Services Review, 26*, 207–234.
Sexton, T., & Alexander, J. (2003). Functional family therapy: A mature clinical model for working with at-risk adolescents and their families. In T. Sexton, G. Weeks, & M. Robbins (Eds.), *Handbook of family therapy* (pp. 323–348). New York: Brunner-Routledge.
Sheidow, A., Henggeler, S., & Schoenwald, S. (2003). Multisystemic therapy. In T. Sexton, G. Weeks, & M. Robbins (Eds.), *Handbook of family therapy* (pp. 303–322). New York: Brunner-Routledge.
Smith, P., Buzi, R., & Weinman, M. (2002). Targeting males for teenage pregnancy prevention in a school setting. *School Social Work Journal, 27*, 23–36.
Snyder, C., Michael, S., & Cheavens, J. (1999). Hope as a psychotherapeutic foundation of common factors, placebos, and expectancies. In M. Hubble, B. Duncan, & S. Miller (Eds.), *The heart and soul of change* (pp. 179–200). Washington, DC: American Psychological Association.
Tashakkori, A., & Teddlie, C. (1998). *Mixed methodology: Combining qualitative and quantitative approaches.* Thousand Oaks, CA: Sage.
Taylor, A., Losciuto, L., Fox, M., Hilbert, S., & Sonkowsky, M. (1999). The mentoring factor: Evaluation of the Across Ages' intergenerational approach to drug abuse prevention. *Child & Youth Services, 20*, 77–99.
Teall, B. (2000). Using solution-oriented interventions in an ecological frame: A case illustration. *Social Work in Education, 22*, 54–61.
Teasley, M., & Lee, E. (2006). Examining the association between academic achievement and self-esteem in African American male youth in a community-outreach after-school program. *School Social Work Journal, 30*, 64–81.
Thompson, L., & Kelly-Vance, L. (2001). The impact of mentoring on academic achievement of at-risk youth. *Children & Youth Services Review, 23*, 227–242.
Troester, J. (2002). Working through family-based problem behavior through activity group therapy. *Clinical Social Work Journal, 30*, 419–428.
Tutty, L. (2000). What children learn from sexual abuse prevention programs: Difficult concepts and developmental issues. *Research on Social Work Practice, 10*, 275–300.
Volkmann, B., & Bye, L. (2006). Improved school attendance through adult volunteer reading partners. *Children & Schools, 28*, 145–152.
Walsh-Bowers, R., & Basso, R. (1999). Improving adolescents' peer relations through classroom creative drama: An integrated approach. *Social Work in Education, 21*, 23–32.

Walter, U., & Petr, C. (2004). Promoting successful transitions from day school to regular school environments for youths with serious emotional disorders. *Children & Schools, 26*, 175–180.

Whitfield, G. (1999). Validating school social work: An evaluation of a cognitive-behavioral approach to reduce school violence. *Research on Social Work Practice, 9*, 399–426.

Woody, D. (2001). A comprehensive school-based conflict-resolution model. *Children & Schools, 23*, 115–123.

Young, H., & Jung, K. (2002). A pilot project for school social work in Korea. *Journal of School Social Work, 12*, 35–46.

Zosky, D., & Crawford, L. (2003). No child left behind: An assessment of an after-school program on academic performance among low-income, at-risk students. *School Social Work Journal, 27*, 18–31.

4

The Process of Ethical Decision Making in School Social Work: Confidentiality

James C. Raines
Illinois State University

- Procedure and Principles
- Ethics and the Law
- Issues in Record Keeping

School social workers are constantly confronted with the conundrum of which student disclosures to keep confidential and which ones to divulge in the interest of school or student safety. Recent research indicates that students and parents often have vastly different expectations when it comes to confidentiality. McKee and his colleagues, for example, found that Latina and African American mothers believed that confidential gynecological services undermined their role as their daughters' protectors and saw no reason for their daughters to receive these services until after they became sexually active (McKee & Fletcher, 2006; McKee, O'Sullivan, & Weber, 2006). Their daughters, on the other hand, were loathe to discuss sexual behavior with their mothers and afraid of any breaches to their confidentiality. Lyren, Kodish, Lazebnik, and O'Riordan (2006) also found that African American parents felt that confidentiality simply did not apply to underage patients. Ninety-six percent expected doctors to tell them anything important, even if their teen children preferred otherwise. On the other hand, only 36 percent of their children expected this to happen. Indeed, the parents might be correct—Perez-Carceles, Pereniguez, Osuna, and Luna (2005) found that 95 percent of the physicians they surveyed provided confidential information to family members and 35 percent did so without patient consent. It is no wonder, then, that Lehrer, Pantell, Tebb, and Shafer (2007) found that many adolescents would rather forgo medical care than have their confidentiality broken. Males were less likely to seek help for depression, suicidal ideation, and suicide attempts if they thought confidentiality would be violated. Females were much less likely to seek help for sexual behavior, nonuse of birth control, and sexually transmitted infections as well as all the mental health concerns of the boys.

In spite of the evidence supporting the need for confidential care, there has been a growing number of attempts to curb the legal rights of adolescents to obtain such treatment (English & Ford, 2007). For example, according to the Guttmacher Institute (2007), the state of California gives all adolescents age twelve and older the right to seek contraceptive services, get treatment for sexually transmitted infections, obtain prenatal care, and give a baby up for adoption. Despite these legal rights, multiple school districts have denied teenagers the ability to leave school without parental permission to keep necessary medical appointments (Rosen, 2003, 2004).

If family physicians are caught between parents and adolescents regarding privacy issues, then school personnel are subject to the same dilemmas. Confidentiality issues permeate the school social worker's landscape. Consider the three scenarios below.

> A thirteen-year-old girl is sexually involved with a seventeen-year-old boy. Currently, they are "only" having oral sex, but he is pressuring her to "go all the way." She reports that she's the only virgin in her peer group and that the others make fun of her. She's scared to tell her very religious parents because she's afraid they'll send her to a strict parochial school. State laws prohibit sexual contact with minors under thirteen as well as with minors when the age difference is five years or more, so the law offers no guidance in this case.

> A fifteen-year-old boy reveals that he has been involved in "cutting." The wounds are all superficial and uninfected. He denies any suicidal thoughts or intent—it is merely his way of coping with feelings of numbness and existential angst about his future. He doesn't want to tell his single mother because the last time she found out, she sent him to an inpatient psychiatric program. Recent research clearly differentiates cutting from suicidal attempts, so the literature warns against overreacting in such cases.

> A twelve-year-old boy who is angry about his poor grades and disciplinary record threatens to blow up the school. He doesn't have any specific plans, nor does he possess any of the skills or materials needed to make a bomb. He doesn't want his foster parents to know because he's afraid they'll send him back to the group home, where he'd be the youngest and most vulnerable kid. Unfortunately, all the necessary bomb-making information is readily available on the Internet, so he could obtain it if he wanted to.

Other issues may concern alcohol and drug abuse, severe eating disorders, or mental health concerns (e.g., delusional thoughts). Each ethical dilemma is a practice problem as well. Thus the primary way to deal with such dilemmas is through good practice. In each case above, the youth is telling the school social worker of concerns and fears, attempting to come to terms with them. The radical solutions proposed by the students are expressions of concerns that the social worker might help redirect. The listening school social worker has already clarified confidentiality and its limitations in the youngster's language. He or she contracts around helping the student deal with an unacceptable situation. The social worker is a collaborator in the healing process. The student is the first place where the problem can be resolved. The social worker can help him or her in this by focusing simultaneously on the youth and the broader situation. That might involve helping the youngster get in contact with people who could be of help and opening some workable dialogue with parents. The social worker tells the youth that to continue, he or she needs to have some contact with parents. He or she tells the parents that the student has some concerns, and that the worker will not reveal those concerns unless there is some danger or unless the youngster asks the worker to do so. Contacts with others are first of all discussed with the student so that they can come to a joint approach. This process is part of the first session in one way or another and continues through the contact.

In the context of practice, the question of whether to reveal, what to reveal, and to whom is central to the work of the school social worker. The position statement of the School Social Work Association of America can be found in Appendix A. Taking these principles as a foundation, this chapter offers a procedure and principles for making decisions around some of the basic issues in school social work practice: whether or not to share information, how it should be shared, and how much should be shared. It also addresses the relationship between ethics and the law and provides a checklist for confidentiality.

PROCEDURE AND PRINCIPLES

There are seven steps that school social workers can use to work through the decision about whether or not to divulge confidential student material. Skipping or shortchanging any of these steps tends to reduce the quality of the decision.

Step 1: Know Yourself

Social workers must differentiate between their personal values and their professional values (Abramson, 1996). Sometimes these will coincide; sometimes they will conflict with each other. A helpful exercise is to list your values in a diagram with two overlapping circles. Social workers are bound by the National Association of Social Workers Code of Ethics (Jensen, 2002). There are six core social work values in the code that are ethical principles: service, social justice, the dignity and worth of the person, the importance of human relationships, integrity, and competence. These values are normative for all professional social workers regardless of their practice settings or roles, but individual practitioners facing specific situations must apply them judiciously. This requires what Manning (1997) has termed *moral citizenship*, "the responsibility to determine right and good behavior as part of the rights and privileges social workers have as members of a community" (p. 224).

Many ethical thinkers (deontologists) tend to approach problems on the basis of the belief that certain values and actions are intrinsically right or wrong. They may hold an absolute standard of truth telling with others. Others (consequentialists) may gauge their actions through an analysis of the goodness of their consequences. The latter, as relativists, would ultimately hold that the end justifies the means (Reamer, 2006). For example, they may think it is permissible to deceive the welfare system in order to obtain a livable income for clients. The most common form of the relativist approach is the utilitarian model, according to which one must weigh the costs and benefits of every decision. For example, those using a utilitarian approach may hold that both honesty and deception have risks and rewards that vary according to the situation.

A problem often comes from the way the issue is framed. The two positions reduce situations to less than what the practitioner needs to act on. They are stereotypical, somewhat oversimplistic, and ultimately radical. Social workers do need to act on the basis of principles and do need to weigh the costs and benefits of every decision. The question is how basic principles are translated into action within the complexity of any practice situation.

In the three practice cases above, each situation is already framed by differing values and consequences. By their nature, they demand a more complex system of analysis that takes in more variables, including the broader context and the subjective intentions and concerns of the individuals acting, and ultimately applies this complex measure to each case situation. There is no way to remove action from the context of norms and values. The practice relationship is governed by the expectations of society, of the profession, and of the client. The "fiduciary" relationship implies trust, which arises from vulnerability and initial inequality of power and strength, and mutual obligations (Levy, 1976). Pellegrino and Thomasma (1981) point out that the professional needs to be competent, respectful of the relationship, and protective of the moral agency of the client through the provision of information and the use of informed consent. The social worker becomes a coach, and thus a moral agent, to help clients find workable directions and relations with each other, to become themselves responsible agents and actors in a relational field (Constable, 1989). In the light of the inherent morality and complexity of the practice situation, deontological and consequentialist positions appear limited. Indeed, there is a necessary inexactness in application from theory to practice. Each situation, taken on its own, demands inherently complex and nuanced ethical thinking, discussed in the following parts of this article. For example, the obligation of the social worker to be truthful does not mean that the social worker is obliged to tell everything he or she knows about a situation or act as judge, jury, and police in any situation. Taking into account the developmental level of the client, the social worker may give the client truthful information in a way the client can use it.[1] In the above cases, the key is going to be to help the client understand and deal with the situation whenever possible. Taking into account the situation, the social worker has duties of protection from harm but is not obligated to enforce statutes outside his or her appropriate functions or to take responsibility for what others do when he or she has not been involved. The social worker and client are separate agents.

Loewenberg, Dolgoff, and Harrington (2000) recommend using an ethical principles screen by which values are rank ordered. They posit seven principles in the order in which they are listed in table 4.1.

TABLE 4.1 Ethical Principles Screen to Rank Values

Principles	*Definition*
1. Protection of life	Practitioners should seek to protect or prolong a person's biophysical life.
2. Equal treatment	Practitioners should treat persons in similar circumstances in a similar manner.
3. Autonomy/freedom	Practitioners should respect an individual's right to control or contribute to decisions that affect him or her.
4. Least harm	When faced with two negative outcomes, practitioners should choose the least harmful, least permanent, or most reversible option.
5. Quality of life	Practitioners should seek to promote the highest quality of life for both the individual and his or her environment.
6. Privacy & confidentiality	Practitioners should only seek to acquire relevant information and keep that material sacrosanct.
7. Truthfulness & full disclosure	Practitioners should be completely honest with their clients.

1. While there are special applications in social work, this is in fact a quite common virtue of ordinary life called tact, from the Latin word for silence.

Four caveats should be made about these principles. First, they may not be exhaustive. Social workers may decide that other values (e.g., the importance of the practitioner-client relationship) need to be integrated with the ones stated here. Second, these are one group of authors' ideas about the correct ordering of priorities. Individual practitioners may want to reorder these to suit their own consciences. A helpful exercise may be to look at these principles individually and wrestle with one's own ranking of them. Third, some of the principles suggest that social workers will be able to predict accurately the outcomes of their decisions. In actuality, we seldom possess twenty-twenty foresight. Finally, practitioners may disagree about how a particular principle is put into practice. For example, one person may feel that doing nothing accomplishes the least harm, while another may feel that inaction is a form of tacit consent to the client's questionable behavior.

Finally, workers must remember that self-awareness relates to countertransference. Each of us probably has a proclivity to tell or not to tell. Those with the tendency to tell may have experienced a foreseeable harm that could have been averted if only someone had had the courage to speak out. Perhaps we were bullied, sexually harassed or assaulted, abused, or neglected. We may have suffered quietly because we lacked a champion to protect us. Social workers with a secret wish to rescue or shield others from harm will need to think twice before breaking a confidence. Those with a tendency not to tell may subconsciously equate telling with "tattling." As an elementary school social worker, I always explained the difference like this: "Telling is about keeping people safe; tattling is about getting people in trouble." While this distinguishes a disclosure on the basis of its purpose, the end result may feel the same: you have "ratted out" your client or "squealed" on him or her (especially if those whom you've told have a different purpose in mind). Social workers who have a strong need to be liked by students will need to develop thick skin before they feel comfortable violating student confidences.

Step 2: Analyze the Dilemma

It is helpful to obtain the answers to several questions, some of which may be deceptively complex. There are four important issues to consider at this step. First, who are the stakeholders? Stakeholders are concerned parties with a vested interest in the outcome; they are not competing clients, as some have suggested (McWhinney, Haskins-Herkenham, & Hare, 1992; Prichard, 1999). Loewenberg et al. (2000) identify several participants in the social work process. Clients are people (or systems) who knowingly (but not always voluntarily) enter into a formal, contractual, and goal-driven relationship with the social worker. One of the flaws of the NASW Code of Ethics is that it does not fully address clinical practice dilemmas in host settings. Beyond the client system (individual, family, or group), there are three other important groups in school settings. First, there are colleagues (other social workers, psychologists, and teachers), who also provide professional services to students. Second, there are administrators (superintendents, special education coordinators, principals, and deans), who have responsibility for the educational community. Finally, there are relatives (parents, stepparents, or foster parents), who have legal responsibility for the student. Any of these may arguably have a right to know about dangerous or destructive conduct. If any of these groups feel disregarded, they have the potential to increase the cost of confidentiality to the practitioner. These costs may include professional ostracism by colleagues, loss of promotion or position by administrators, and litigation by relatives. Thus, it would be naive to underestimate the importance of other stakeholders in the process.

Second, a related question is: Who is the primary client? The NASW Code of Ethics is particularly unhelpful on this point. It states only that the term " 'clients' is used inclusively to refer to individuals, families, groups, organizations, and communities" (National Association of Social Workers, 1999, p. 1). There is no doubt that any of these can be a client, but this definition, unfortunately, does not answer the question of who actually is the client. Kopels and Lindsey (2006) rightly see this issue as the crux of many dilemmas about confidentiality. They argue that the alternative to dealing with the complexity of viewing school administrators, teachers, parents, and the community *equally* as clients, thus juggling "the competing interests of all these other stakeholders," is to view the student as the *only client* (p. 75). Somewhere between NASW's implied "everyone is a client" and Kopels and Lindsey's idea that only the student is the client is a view of the student as the *primary* client (Raines, 2008). This implies that a social worker's primary fiduciary responsibility is to the student, but that he or she may have secondary responsibilities to those who also have a responsibility to act in the student's best interests. Thus, parents and teachers (who often assume an in loco parentis role) may also be recipients of social work services and deserve some consideration in light of their special caretaking duties (Tan, Passerini, & Stewart, 2007).

Third, which values are in conflict? In the scenarios above, one applicable NASW value is the importance of human relationships. Berman-Rossi and Rossi (1990) note that confidentiality provides the basis for client self-disclosure and sharing of intimate details. On the other hand, another NASW value is social justice. A social worker has a duty to protect both the educational community and the student. One hopes that a commitment to a third value, integrity, will help balance conflicting demands.

Accordingly, when orienting a new child (and parents) to the social work process, I usually explain that there are two rules that govern my professional behavior. Rule 1 is "Everybody is safe." Rule 2 is "Everything is confidential." I then explain that sometimes these rules conflict (e.g., if students tell me someone is hurting them or that they may hurt others). When this occurs, rule 1 "wins." Thus, if I later feel compelled to break confidentiality, I can remind them of this discussion. This serves to keep the value of integrity intact.

Another set of potentially competing values is self-determination and paternalism. A superficial reading of the NASW Code of Ethics suggests that social workers should always choose client self-determination. This reveals a second flaw in the code: it presumes an adult-to-adult relationship that is mutual and egalitarian (Prichard, 1999). In schools, our clients (with the exception of some high school students) are legal minors who cannot give informed consent for themselves. Parents and other legal guardians must sign both informed consent to treatment as well as release of information forms (Jonson-Reid, 2000). While paternalism has a negative reputation, this is sometimes undeserved (Staller & Kirk, 1997). Children are both emotionally and intellectually dependent upon adults to make decisions in their best interests. Only gradually does society grant them greater control over decisions that affect them (e.g., child custody hearings, abortion, or driving privileges). What seems to be needed, especially for middle and high school students, is a procedure for informed assent. This differs from informed consent in that it is not legally binding but serves the clinical function of providing for some self-determination in the social work process. It is especially helpful in those cases where the child is not self-referred and may not initially see the value of social work services. When the child is an involuntary client, the parents may be the ones giving informed consent to the ultimate goals of treatment, but the child should still have some voice in the instrumental means about how to achieve these goals (Cone & Dalenberg, 2004).

When I receive referrals for social work services, I do not assume that students have been told why they have been sent to see me. I usually tell them what I have heard and ask for their perspective on the situation. If treatment has been mandated, I explain what I will routinely share with others, including parents and teachers. Routine disclosures typically involve three points. First, I usually provide the percentage of sessions attended out of the number scheduled—this decreases the possibility that a student will use counseling as an excuse to skip class. Second, I often provide the topics, not details, of what we've discussed—this is done primarily to help parents or teachers empathize with the student and increase their support for the student. Finally, I typically offer my opinion on whether the student is making progress—this helps parents to know if school-based counseling is working or whether they should try something different.

If these routine disclosures are acceptable, I ask students to give their assent to treatment. If these routine disclosures are unacceptable, I try to assess whether the child's problem may interfere with his or her capacity to assent to treatment. For example, students who are oppositional, anorexic, or addicted may be unable to admit they need help (Tan et al., 2007). When this is the case, parental consent must suffice. Occasionally, I have had students inquire if I would lie to authorities for them. My standard answer is "If I were to lie for you, you could never be sure that I would not lie to you." This stance serves to underscore the value placed on integrity.

Step 3: Identify the Courses of Action

For any ethical quandary, there are usually at least three different potential courses of action, and sometimes more. Given the examples that began this chapter, a social worker could decide (1) to keep all the material confidential to maintain the primacy of the therapeutic relationship and try to help clients resolve conflicting feelings about hiding such important issues from those who care for them, (2) to divulge the confidential material to protect the student or school's well-being and try to help the client understand why such a disclosure was important, or (3) to share the ethical dilemma with the client and try to empower him or her to disclose the problem to those who need to know.

In general, the more mature the student is, the more effort the social worker should make to share the ethical problem and empower the student to participate in the ethical solution. This has two benefits. First, it models the conscientious consideration of moral dilemmas. Second, it helps students avoid seeing solutions in an either-or fashion and find middle ground. An example will illustrate:

> Eric was a thirteen-year-old eighth grader with a serious marijuana problem that was affecting his schoolwork. He was the only son of two working parents who did not provide any supervision after school until they arrived home after 6:00 PM. He was very afraid of disappointing his parents and what measures they might take to curb his freedom. I reflected that it sounded as if he could not overcome this on his own and that he needed his family's help. I suggested that there were three ways we could handle it: (1) I could call his parents and share this with them directly while he listened; (2) I could meet with both him and his parents together to mediate; or (3) I could help him practice self-disclosure to his parents through role-playing. Eric worried aloud that his mother would "go ballistic" and wanted to tell his father alone first. I compromised on this point and Eric chose to go with the second option.

With the emphasis of the Individuals with Disabilities Education Act on students' self-determination when it comes to transition planning, there has been a renewed interest in helping them prepare for this responsibility by gradually giving them both the tools and the opportunities to apply their own critical thinking skills to real-life dilemmas (Karvonen, Test, Browder, & Algozzine, 2004). Sharing the steps of ethical decision making with middle school and high school students is one way to improve their capacity for good decision making later on.

Step 4: Seek Consultation

The fourth step in the decision process is to obtain outside expertise. One of the dangers of social work licensing laws is that they certify professionals for "independent practice." This tends to convey the notion that when practitioners have reached this level, they no longer need supervision or consultation from their colleagues—but nothing could be further from the truth. The NASW Code of Ethics makes it very clear that "social workers should seek the advice and counsel of colleagues whenever such consultation is in the best interests of clients" (National Association of Social Workers, 1999, p. 16). This consultation should be sought from colleagues with adequate expertise. There are two kinds of expertise that are important when it comes to ethical issues. The first type of expertise is clinical consultation. Secemsky and Ahlman (2003) provide a list of ten guidelines for choosing a supervisor, which could easily be extended to choosing consultants as well. Social workers do not need to breach confidentiality to obtain this advice. Social workers can seek counsel while keeping the client's identity anonymous by only sharing the most pertinent details of a case. An example will illumine this:

> A handsome young social worker had recently begun working at a high school when he sought consultation from me about an ethical dilemma. A senior girl he'd been seeing in treatment had become increasingly interested in his personal life and he had inadvertently shared more than was wise. She asked him if he'd ever like to hang out on the weekends. While he found the girl attractive, he had no intentions of violating any boundaries and told her so. She responded that this didn't matter because after graduation, they could "hook up" and no one would care. Flustered and frustrated, he was now considering transferring her to another worker but was worried about clinical abandonment issues and his own reputation within the workplace. I never knew the student's name and did not need to in order to provide consultation.

The clinical consultant also needs to be intimately familiar with the NASW Code of Ethics. Compared to psychologists and counselors, social workers have the highest hurdles to overcome before they can breach client confidentiality. The Code of Ethics makes it very clear that four conditions must be met before disclosure can occur without prior consent: "Social workers should protect the confidentiality of all information in the course of professional service, except for compelling professional reasons. The general expectation that social workers will keep information confidential does not apply when disclosure is necessary to prevent *serious, foreseeable, and imminent* harm to a client or other *identifiable* person" (section 1.07c, emphasis added).

Serious harm may be interpreted as aligning with the federal definition for serious bodily injury (Raines, 2006). These are defined as "injuries that involve substantial risk of death, extreme physical pain, protracted and obvious disfigurement, or protracted loss or impairment of the function of a bodily member, organ, or mental faculty" (18 U.S.C. 136(h)(3)). *Foreseeable* can be interpreted as referring to an event that can be reasonably predicted based on current knowledge of the person and the situation. *Imminent* refers to impending events in the near future or on a fixed date. Identifiable can mean that the person is either named or easily recognizable by title (e.g., principal) or physical description (e.g., the red-haired boy).

While these guidelines may help to decide when to disclose information, there is further guidance about how much to disclose. The Code of Ethics clarifies that the amount to be shared should be as little as possible: "In all instances, social workers should disclose the *least* amount of confidential information necessary to achieve the desired purpose for which the disclosure is made should be revealed" (National Association of Social Workers, 1999, section 1.07c). The code requires, however, that prior to doing so, "social workers should inform clients, to the extent possible, about the disclosure of confidential information and the potential consequences, when feasible *before* the disclosure is made" (section 1.07d). This requirement is one area where social workers are most vulnerable to charges of acting unethically. Whether it is due to fear of the client's (or parents') anger or sheer cowardice makes little difference. Treating others as we ourselves would prefer to be treated requires us to honestly tell clients that a disclosure is in the offing. In my experience, most clients are ultimately thankful for the forewarning.

The second type of expertise is legal advice. It is always wise for school social workers to have their own attorney and malpractice insurance since the district or co-op's lawyers and insurance company primarily serve the interests of those who pay their fees (Jensen, 2002). This does not mean that legal issues should be confused with ethical ones, but they do make a difference when one is considering the cost-benefit ratio. There are two main sources of legal guidance.

First, social workers need to understand what laws apply to the case. Laws that address the social worker–student relationship include the Family Educational Rights and Privacy Act (FERPA) of 1974 and the Health Insurance Portability and Accountability Act (HIPAA) of 1996.

FERPA should be familiar to all public school mental health professionals. This law allows for treatment records to be considered "sole possession" files that belong exclusively to mental health professionals or their substitutes (Raines & Ahlman, 2004). It also protects certain group records from inspection since revelation for one would entail a revelation for all. One particular sore spot in FERPA is the provision that allows for the nonconsensual release of information to a wide range of school personnel, including "other school officials, including teachers within the educational institution or local educational agency, who have been determined by such agency or institution to have *legitimate educational interests*, including the educational interests of the child for whom consent would otherwise be required" (section (b)(1)(A), emphasis added).

The phrase "legitimate educational interests" has become a point of contention between school-based mental health professionals and other school personnel, especially teachers and principals. Raines (2008) notes that since FERPA leaves this discretion up to the local education agency or school district (not the school principal), it may be wise for social workers to organize a task force made up of the vested constituency groups to establish district policy on this issue. Representatives of the task force should include parents, teachers, mental health professionals, district administrators, an attorney, and a student representative.

HIPAA is probably less familiar to many school-based social workers. According to Overcamp-Martini (2006), HIPAA pertains to social work practice whenever practitioners make medical claims for third-party reimbursement, such as Medicaid. This applies to both public and private school social workers who are involved in the electronic transmission of health care information. HIPAA protects "psychotherapy notes" from both parental and patient access. The federal definition of these records is: "Notes recorded (in any medium) by a health care provider who is a mental health professional documenting or analyzing the contents of a conversation during a private counseling session or a group, joint, or family counseling session and that are separated from the rest of the individual's medical record. Psychotherapy notes excludes medication prescription and monitoring, counseling session start and stop times, the modalities and frequencies of treatment furnished, results of clinical tests, and any summary of the following items: diagnosis, functional status, the treatment plan, symptoms, prognosis, and progress to date" (U.S. Department of Health and Human Services, 2003, p. 21). Both FERPA and HIPAA are federal laws, but states may decide to go beyond these statutes in their own laws. Therefore, school social workers should seek legal advice from someone familiar with both state and federal legislation.

Second, social workers need to understand what case law applies to the issue. Case law refers to judicial decisions that clarify vague portions of a law. They often provide rules of interpretation or precedents that other courts may follow. All social workers should be familiar with *Tarasoff v. Regents of the University of California* (1976). The plaintiffs were the parents of Tatiana Tarasoff, who was killed by a former boyfriend who had confided his intentions to his college therapist. The university psychologist notified campus police, but they merely questioned the boyfriend, who promised to stay away from Tatiana. The therapist's supervisor recommended that no further action be taken and ordered that the case notes be destroyed (Kopels & Kagle, 1993). The court determined that mental health professionals have a "duty to warn" when they know or should know that a client poses an immediate danger to a specific person or people. In the words of the court, "The protective privilege ends where the public peril begins" (*Tarasoff v. Regents of the University of California*, 1976). An example follows.

> Jose was an eight-year-old third grader who soiled his pants weekly while his estranged parents fought each other for sole custody. His mother was a recovering crack addict, and his father was a recovering alcoholic. His mother had temporary custody and his father refused to pay child support, so one night she met him in the dark with an imitation gun, demanding that he pay up. He did so only to find out later that she'd used one of Jose's toys to stage the threat. He confided to me that he was so enraged about this that he was thinking of paying a heroin addict $50 to kill her while he attended an AA meeting. Deciding that he had identified a specific person, a plausible plan, and an alibi, I consulted with my supervisor and we agreed to call the police and warn the intended victim. Later on, I testified in court that I doubted that he really meant to do it, but we couldn't take the chance given the level of his anger.

Contacting the police is not the only way to fulfill our duty to warn. Loewenberg et al. (2000) clarify that there are three other means as well: warning the intended victim directly; informing others who can alert the victim to danger; or taking "whatever other steps are reasonably necessary under the circumstances" (p. 104), such as hospitalization. Social workers should also determine the extent to which their state courts have affirmed the precedent set by *Tarasoff* or their state legislatures have codified the *Tarasoff* principles (Kopels & Lindsey, 2006).

Step 5: Manage the Clinical Concerns

There are three major clinical issues when one is considering whether or not to abridge client confidentiality: maintaining a standard of care, managing student reactions, and managing parental reactions.

First, it is essential that when making decisions about confidentiality, social workers demonstrate that they know and use the standard of care. A standard of care is simply what an ordinary, reasonable, and prudent professional with similar training would do under similar circumstances. For dangerous clients, it is imperative that practitioners never underestimate or minimize potential danger. This requires that we stay calm and carefully assess the client's level of risk for violent behavior. There are several areas that should be addressed. Cooper and Lesser (2002) recommend assessing (1) the frequency of the client's violent ideas (e.g., monthly, weekly, daily, obsessively), (2) the duration of those ideas (e.g., fleeting, episodic, or sustained), (3) the concreteness of the plan (i.e., its lethality, locality, imminence, and plausibility), and (4) the extent to which preparation has begun (i.e., gathering materials and knowledge/skill for its implementation). One might also add the client's degree of emotional dysregulation (Newhill, 2003). This includes clients' emotional sensitivity (how quickly they react), emotional intensity (on a scale of 1–10), and their ability to calm themselves back to a normal state. These inquiries should be considered in the context of the client's history of violence (e.g., previous attempts, fire setting, or cruelty to animals), level of impulse control, social support from family and friends, use of disinhibitants (alcohol or drugs), and immediate precipitating events (UCLA Center for Mental Health in Schools, 2003). An example will illustrate.

> Russell was a fifteen-year-old sophomore in high school with a lengthy involvement with the child welfare authorities. He had been reunited with his single father, who had been through therapy and parenting classes to get Russell back from foster care. Years of abuse, however, had left Russell bitter and vengeful. He had stolen his father's vehicle and crashed it into a tree in front of the school. He vowed that when his father was old, he would get even somehow. He didn't have a plan yet, but he was determined. When his father inquired about his son's progress, I reported that Russell came regularly and was discussing his resentment about his past abuse, and that progress was slow. While Russell had a violent history and a specific target, he lacked a specific plan and there was no imminent threat.

Second, practitioners should know that every student reacts differently to confrontation about a possible violation of privileged disclosure. Regardless of how well students are oriented to treatment and participate in giving informed assent, many will feel hurt, angry, and betrayed by the social worker. It is most important to protect the therapeutic relationship by remaining empathic and reflecting both the spoken and unspoken feelings of the client (Raines, 1990). It may also be appropriate for the social worker to disclose his or her own feelings of concern, worry, and sadness about the potential loss of trust (Raines, 1996). These two interventions work synergistically to maintain the human bond between worker and client. This bond enables practitioners to engage students in introspection about why they revealed the information. Did they have a secret desire to be stopped, to be caught, or to be punished? Did they mean to externalize an internal conflict? All of this must be grist for the therapeutic mill. Next, give the student as much choice as is developmentally appropriate. This does not mean, however, that social workers should shirk their ethical responsibilities. It does mean that students should be informed about what choices they have, as in Eric's case above. This gives the student a sense of ownership and control over the circumstances. One of the goals of treatment should be acceptance of responsibility for self and others (Yalom, 1980). Taking this responsibility completely out of a student's hands shortchanges this goal. Finally, involve students in decisions made in their best interests. The President's Commission on Excellence in Special Education (2002) found "that it is *always* appropriate for students with disabilities to be invited and present" at individualized education program meetings (p. 46). While this may hinder some of the freewheeling discussion, it also tends to hold negativity about students in check. It also provides an opportunity to address confidential concerns immediately rather than postpone their discussion.

Third, practitioners need to know that parents can react very strongly to the decision to preserve client confidentiality. Unlike their children, parents often have the ability to significantly increase the amount of pressure a social worker feels to disclose sensitive information by calling the principal, superintendent, and members of the school board. While state and federal laws have given adolescents increased rights over sexual health care as well as treatment for alcohol and drugs (Guttmacher Institute, 2007; Ward, 2002), parents still feel strongly that they should be consulted. It helps to have a clear policy from the start, as mentioned in step 2, because it allows the social worker to remind parents of the initial agreement. Mitchell, Disque, and Robertson (2002) recommend some further clinical approaches. First, school social workers should listen empathically to the parents' concerns, validate their feelings, and join with them in wanting what is best for the student. This helps allay fears of alienation from their child or feelings of jealousy toward the social worker. Second, it can help to coach the parents in how to listen nonreactively to their child's concerns. Workers can accomplish this by inquiring whether there have been some disclosures at home that have them worried and how they might facilitate parent-child discussion of the issues. Third, it may help to point out that an important part of adolescence is a growing independence that involves talking with trusted adults about private issues. Workers can do this by asking the parents if they had significant nonparental relationships when they were growing up with another relative, family friend, or professional, and exploring what this relationship meant to them at the time. Finally, it may help to offer a family session to address the issues. This helps to take the social worker out of the middle and facilitate good family communication skills on the part of the parents and the student.

Step 6: Enact the Decision

Once the dilemma has been analyzed, courses of action identified, consultation obtained, and clinical concerns managed, it would seem like the time to implement the resolution, but Loewenberg et al. (2000) recommend one final series of questions before action is taken. First, are you acting impartially? In other words, would you want someone to take this action if this were your child? Second, can you generalize this decision to similar cases? Finally, can you justify your decision in ways that make sense to others, including the student? If the answer to all of these is yes, then you are ready to act. If the answer to any of these is no, then more consultation should be sought.

Implementation may work as expected, but more often than not there are consequences that could not have been predicted (Robison & Reeser, 2000). Some participants (e.g., administrators) may be angry that they were not told about the problem sooner or want to punish the student for a crime he or she has not (yet) committed. Some participants (e.g., relatives) will feel embarrassed or envious that the student trusted the social worker with intimacies when they have known the child longer. Emphasize that the primary purpose is to protect people now, and applaud the student for having told anyone. This will help to keep the discussion focused on protection, the present, and the positives.

Step 7: Reflect on the Process

Mattison (2000) recommends that after the issue has been resolved, it is helpful to reexamine the process. Ask yourself the following questions: To what degree did my personal values influence this decision? To what extent did other participants influence my decisions? Were there courses of action that I failed to consider? Should I have consulted other people? Were there clinical concerns that I missed or underestimated? In hindsight did I make the right decision? What precautions (e.g., ethical orientation or informed assent) should I take to prevent problems in the future?

There have been a number of research studies that demonstrate that adolescents may choose to forgo mental health care if there is a chance that their privacy will be violated (Lehrer et al., 2007; McKee & Fletcher, 2006). This seems especially true for the most vulnerable youths, such as those who are sexually active, have poor family support, and suffer from depression or low self-esteem. Social workers would be wise to consistently evaluate the outcomes of their ethical decision making in order to identify prejudicial patterns of disclosure or iatrogenic effects related to disclosure (Raines, 2008).

ETHICS AND THE LAW

Too often social workers confuse the boundary between their ethical and legal obligations (Reamer, 2005). Lawsuits and subpoenas are insufficient reasons to breach confidentiality (Dickson, 1998). Another court case with which all practitioners should become familiar is *Jaffee v. Redmond* (1996). This case involved Illinois clinical social worker Karen Beyer, who refused to hand over records about her client's state of mind after her client, a police officer, killed someone in the line of duty (Booth, 1996). Beyer was held in contempt of court and the case was appealed to the U.S. Supreme Court, where NASW filed an amicus curiae (friend of the court) brief in her defense. In a 7–2 decision, the court established that client privilege extended to psychotherapists and that mental health was a public good that should be protected under the law (Lens, 2000). Social workers should not simply view themselves as agents of the state, nor should they feel compelled to report a client's past crimes. The exception to this rule is when the crime is especially heinous because it involves vulnerable victims who are both defenseless and dependent upon others (e.g., children and the elderly).

Most states where there is licensing of social workers recognize the protection of privileged communication. This generally means that matters communicated by clients to social workers in their official capacity are privileged. The social worker is obligated not to disclose them, except under certain narrowly defined circumstances. For example, a communication revealing an intent to commit a serious harmful act would be among these exceptions. It is important to know the privileged communication statute that governs your practice. A social worker served with a subpoena in a child custody case would inform the law office issuing the subpoena of this protection, citing the appropriate statutes. The attorney who filed the subpoena may not be aware of the protection afforded social workers. Clarifying one's obligation to observe the law makes it then incumbent on the issuers of the subpoena to demonstrate that their request falls within the area of exceptions in the state statute. On the other hand, providing information without invoking this privilege may leave the social worker unprotected and potentially obligated to provide further information, since the information is now subject to discovery. Even when social workers are obligated to respond to a subpoena, they can request that the court limit the order as narrowly as possible, ask for an "in camera" (in chambers) review, insist that the records remain under seal, and require that all records be returned at the end of the trial.

In 1999, the NASW Delegate Assembly narrowly voted (155–133) to amend the Code of Ethics just three years after its approval and publication. The passage in questions read: "Social workers should protect the confidentiality of all information obtained in the course of professional service, except for compelling professional reasons. The general expectation that social workers will keep information confidential does not apply when disclosure is necessary to prevent serious, foreseeable, and imminent harm to a client or other identifiable person, *or when laws or regulations require disclosure without a client's consent*" (National Association of Social Workers, 1999, p. 10, emphasis added). The revised code omitted the italicized portion from the 1996 version, thus clearly differentiating between ethical reasons for breaching confidentiality and legal reasons for doing so. This revision was prompted by a tidal wave of state legislatures' and political agencies' creation of laws and regulations restricting the rights of gays and lesbians to adopt children; women's reproductive rights; and the rights of immigrants to obtain education, health care, and social services ("Ethics and Reporting," 1999). The implication of this change appears to be that while social workers are mandated to report an imminent threat to self or others, they should not feel obligated to report someone who is merely guilty of a "status" offense, such as being a member of a sexual minority, being single and pregnant, or being an undocumented immigrant. In these cases, social workers should carefully weigh their legal mandates against their ethical obligations (Loewenberg et al., 2000).

Moral conundrums, then, could be placed on a typology consisting of two dimensions: ethical issues and legal issues (figure 4.1). Such a schema results in four categories of quandaries. First, some questions are neither ethical nor legal issues. An example is whether social workers should disclose their feelings to clients. In general, practitioners are on safer ground when disclosing current feelings about the therapeutic process than when disclosing personal details on their extra-therapeutic life (Raines, 1996), but this is primarily a clinical issue rather than a moral one. Second, some quandaries, such as the ethical orientation of clients, are only ethical issues, not legal ones. It is wise to inform all clients (even those transferred from other workers) about one's own approach to confidentiality, but this is not a legal mandate. Third, other controversies, such as one's duty to warn others of a client's potential for violence, are both ethical and legal issues (Kopels & Kagle, 1993). When we accept a student as a client, we embark on a fiduciary relationship (Kutchins, 1991). We can violate a client's privilege only for compelling reasons. Finally, some questions, such as whether school social workers should obtain clinical licensure, are mainly legal issues.

> Millard was a sixteen-year-old who had been raised by his single mother in Brooklyn before she died from diabetes. He was then reunited with his absentee father, who lived in the Bronx. Even though I worked in Millard's old therapeutic day school, my supervisor asked me to check up on him, since his previous worker had left the agency. I scheduled a home visit and found that Millard's father was a crack addict, there was no food in the apartment, and Millard had not been attending school. Millard, however, had the presence of mind to ask his father for a note explaining that he could not care for his son. Armed with the note and a compelling case for neglect, I brought Millard back to Brooklyn and placed him in one of the agency's emergency shelters. Child welfare authorities were outraged because in New York, separate boroughs are

FIGURE 4.1 Ethical-Legal Typology

Ethical but not legal issue	Both an ethical and a legal issue
Neither an ethical nor a legal issue	Legal but not ethical issue

> often separate counties and I had broken the law by crossing county lines with a minor. Fortunately, my agency stood behind my decision to remove Millard and bring him back to his old neighborhood. I successfully avoided both arrest and criminal prosecution for kidnapping.

ISSUES IN RECORD KEEPING

All social workers should be familiar with the requirements of the Family Educational Rights and Privacy Act, which guarantees parents both access to and control over the dissemination of school records (Jonson-Reid, 2000). In light of this legislation, it is important for social workers to know which files are official education records and which are not. Social workers' private notes are not part of the school record, nor are sole possession files stored on a computer (School Social Work Association of America, 2001). These documents should be stored under lock and key, or protected by a password if they are on a computer. Social developmental histories, case progress notes, functional behavioral assessments, behavior intervention plans, and individualized education program documents, however, are official school records. Case progress notes should contain dates of meetings, general topics discussed, and interventions employed. They should not contain intimate details, process recordings, or clinical impressions. Thus, social workers would be wise to write these documents in a way that does not offend or obfuscate the issues for clients and their parents. Finally, there are times when practitioners may have to take extreme measures to protect their client's privacy, as the following example shows.

> Maria was a recently divorced mother with whom I had weekly contact about how the domestic violence she had experienced influenced her two boys. She was looking for work when the position of the head of the school cafeteria opened up. Since she had extensive restaurant experience, she inquired if I thought it might be appropriate for her to apply for the job. I agreed but cautioned that if she was hired I may want to take extra precautions to preserve her privacy. She concurred and was offered the position. A week later I was called into the principal's office because he wanted to know why he couldn't find my social work files on this family. I replied honestly that I had put the files with my private notes under lock and key to protect both my client and the school. I used the occasion to clarify the nature of confidentiality with the principal. He was obdurate that he had to have the key as long as I worked in his school. With Maria's permission, I discussed this issue with my supervisor and my colleagues. They recounted similar stories and agreed to support me in bringing the issue to the superintendent and ultimately to the board of education. In the ensuing investigation, the principal repeated his position and was fired.

The question of what information should be shared with teachers and other members of the team is an important one. The sharing of information, often necessary for team functioning, is first of all limited to what the individual team member needs to know to carry out his or her function. A teacher concerned about a particular child who is sleeping in class may simply need to know that the child is very upset about things happening in the home, without the details. The consultation with the teacher can be geared to suggesting strategies to help her enable the child to become a part of the class learning process, with the social worker working individually with the child, the family, and possibly other agencies. School social workers should inform students and parents that information gathered under the individualized education program process is generally shared with all members of the individualized education program team. It is, however, up to the social worker, in collaboration with parents and the student, to reveal only what is necessary for the team's functioning. Another vignette describes this type of collaborative discretion.

> One of my routine interview questions for parents was "Is this the first marriage (or partnership) for you and your spouse (partner)?" One mother surprised me by replying, "No, it's not my first marriage, but my husband doesn't know." She must have noticed my puzzlement at why someone would want to conceal this fact from a spouse and explained that she was only nineteen when she got married the first time and the marriage only lasted a few months and produced no children. She looked back at that marriage as an impetuous mistake that bore no lingering implications for her current family. We jointly decided to omit this potentially embarrassing information from my social developmental history.

Deliberate concealment and omission demand a good deal of judgment on the school social worker's part, and the ability to do so is a highly developed skill. It is very important in beginning in a school that the social worker clarify with the team the nature and limits of confidentiality, and the procedures that will be used to ensure confidentiality. In this way, situations such as the principal wanting access to the social worker's private notes can be avoided.

The ethics of social work has evolved considerably over the past one hundred years (Reamer, 1998). Hopefully, in its next incarnation the NASW Code of Ethics will pay more attention to practice conundrums with minors and involving social workers in host settings, such as schools. The process outlined in this chapter is one practitioner's viewpoint based on a review of the literature and accumulated practice wisdom. Good social workers can disagree and still be good social workers (e.g., Kopels, 1992 versus Kardon, 1993). Reamer (2000) suggests that one of the ways that social workers can protect themselves is to diligently document their decision-making process. The decision-making process may ultimately be more important than the product of the decision because it demonstrates the decision was made carefully and with great deliberation (Reamer, 2005). For this reason, I have not provided any solutions to the dilemmas presented in this chapter, but I offer them as discussion fodder to which this process can be applied.

Confidentiality Checklist

- I have clarified my own personal and professional values.
- I have identified the primary stakeholders in the ethical issue.
- I have identified the primary competing values.
- I regularly provide an ethical orientation to new clients.
- I have obtained informed consent (and informed assent) for assessment.
- I have obtained informed consent (and informed assent) to treatment.
- I have identified several courses of action.
- I obtain clinical consultation about difficult issues.
- I obtain legal advice about difficult issues.
- I am familiar with the laws regarding the treatment and rights of minors.
- I carefully consider the clinical implications.
- I make sure the decision is impartial, generalizable, and justifiable.
- I review and document the process of decision making.
- I always keep my personal written notes in a locked file cabinet.
- I always use a computer password to protect private electronic files.
- I always write public documents in clear, inoffensive language.

References

Abramson, M. (1996). Reflections on knowing oneself ethically: Toward a working framework for social work practice. *Families in Society, 77*(4), 195–202.

Berman-Rossi, T., & Rossi, P. (1990). Confidentiality and informed consent in school social work. *Social Work in Education, 12*(3), 195–207.

Booth, R. (1996). *Clinical social work wins big in Supreme Court decision*. American Board of Clinical Examiners in Social Work. Retrieved December 30, 2007, from http://www.abecsw.org/images/news/JaffeevRedmond1996.pdf

Cone, J. D., & Dalenberg, C. J. (2004). Ethics concerns in outcome assessment. In M. E. Maruish (Ed.), *The use of psychological testing for treatment planning and outcomes assessment: Vol. 1. General considerations* (3rd ed., pp. 335–365). Mahwah, NJ: Lawrence Erlbaum.

Constable, R. T. (1989). Relations and membership: Foundations for ethical thinking in social work [Special issue on ethics]. *Social Thought, 15*(3–4), 53–66.

Cooper, M. G., & Lesser, J. G. (2002). *Clinical social work practice: An integrated approach*. Boston: Allyn & Bacon.

Dickson, D. T. (1998). *Confidentiality and privacy in social work*. New York: Free Press.

English, A., & Ford, C. A. (2007). More evidence supports the need to protect confidentiality in adolescent health care. *Journal of Adolescent Health, 40*(3), 199–200.

Ethics and reporting eyed after assembly: Left unchanged is language that requires reporting of certain acts and threats of violence. (1999, November). *NASW News, 44*(10), 5.

Family Educational Rights and Privacy Act, P.L. 93-380, 88 Stat. 571 (1974).

Guttmacher Institute. (2007, July 1). *State policies in brief: An overview of minors' consent law*. Retrieved August 3, 2007, from http://www.guttmacher.org

Health Insurance Portability and Accountability Act of 1996, P.L. 104-191, 110 Stat. 1998 (1996).

Individuals with Disabilities Education Improvement Act, P.L. 108-446, 118 Stat. 2647 (2004).

Jaffee v. Redmond, 116 S. Ct. 1923 (1996).

Jensen, G. (2002, November 15). *Ethically and practically speaking: Managing your malpractice liability*. Workshop presented at Illinois State University, Normal.

Jonson-Reid, M. (2000). Understanding confidentiality in school-based interagency projects. *Social Work in Education, 22*(1), 33–45.

Kardon, S. (1993). Confidentiality: A different perspective. *Social Work in Education, 15*(4), 247–249.

Karvonen, M., Test, D. W., Browder, D., & Algozzine, B. (2004). Putting self-determination into practice. *Exceptional Children, 71*(1), 23–41.

Kopels, S. (1992). Confidentiality and the school social worker. *Social Work in Education, 14*(4), 203–204.

Kopels, S., & Kagle, J. D. (1993). Do social workers have a duty to warn? *Social Service Review, 67*(1), 10–26.

Kopels, S., & Lindsey, B. (2006, Summer). The complexity of confidentiality in schools today: The school social worker context. *School Social Work Journal*, Special 100th Anniversary Issue, 61–78.

Kutchins, H. (1991). The fiduciary relationship: The legal basis for social work responsibility to clients. *Social Work, 36*(2), 106–113.

Lehrer, J. A., Pantell, R., Tebb, K., & Shafer, M. A. (2007). Forgone health care among U.S. adolescents: Associations between risk characteristics and confidentiality concern. *Journal of Adolescent Health, 40*(3), 218–226.

Lens, V. (2000). Protecting the confidentiality of the therapeutic relationship: *Jaffee v. Redmond*. *Social Work, 45*(3), 273–276.

Levy, C. S. (1976). *Social work ethics*. New York: Human Sciences Press.

Loewenberg, F., Dolgoff, R., & Harrington, D. (2000). *Ethical decisions for social work practice* (6th ed.). Itasca, IL: F. E. Peacock.

Lyren, A., Kodish, E., Lazebnik, R., & O'Riordan, M. A. (2006). Understanding confidentiality: Perspectives of African American adolescents and their parents. *Journal of Adolescent Health Care, 39*(2), 261–265.

Manning, S. S. (1997). The social worker as moral citizen: Ethics in action. *Social Work, 42*(3), 223–230.

Mattison, M. (2000). Ethical decision making: The person in the process. *Social Work, 45*(3), 201–212.

McKee, M. D., & Fletcher, J. (2006). Primary care for urban adolescent girls from ethnically diverse populations: Forgone care and access to confidential care. *Journal of Health Care for the Poor and Underserved, 17,* 759–774.

McKee, M. D., O'Sullivan, L. F., & Weber, C. M. (2006). Perspectives on confidential care for adolescent girls. *Annals of Family Medicine, 4*(6), 519–526.

McWhinney, M., Haskins-Herkenham, D., & Hare, I. (1992). NASW Commission on Education position statement: The school social worker and confidentiality. *School Social Work Journal, 17*(1), 38–46.

Mitchell, C. W., Disque, J. G., & Robertson, P. (2002). When parents want to know: Responding to parental demands for confidential information. *Professional School Counseling, 6*(2), 156–161.

National Association of Social Workers. (1999). *Code of ethics of the National Association of Social Workers*. Washington, DC: Author.

Newhill, C. (2003). *Client violence in social work practice*. New York: Guilford Press.

Overcamp-Martini, M. A. (2006). HIPAA and the electronic transfer of student information. In C. Franklin, M. B. Harris, & P. Allen-Meares (Eds.), *School social work and mental health worker's training and resource manual* (pp. 905–912). New York: Oxford University Press.

Pellegrino, E. D., & Thomasma, D. T. (1981). *A philosophical basis of medical practice*. New York: Oxford University Press.

Perez-Carceles, M. D., Pereniguez, J. E., Osuna, E., & Luna, A. (2005). Balancing confidentiality and the information provided to families of patients in primary care. *Journal of Medical Ethics, 31*(9), 531–535.

President's Commission on Excellence in Special Education. (2002). *A new era: Revitalizing special education for children and their families*. Washington, DC: U.S. Department of Education, Office of Special Education and Rehabilitative Services. Retrieved May 19, 2005, from http:www.ed.gov/inits/commissionsboards/whspecial education/reports/images/Pres_Rep.pdf

Prichard, D. C. (1999). Breaking confidence: When silence kills. *Reflections, 5*(2), 43–51.

Raines, J. C. (1990). Empathy in clinical social work. *Clinical Social Work Journal, 18*(1), 57–72.

Raines, J. C. (1996). Self-disclosure in clinical social work. *Clinical Social Work Journal, 24*(4), 357–375.

Raines, J. C. (2006). The new IDEA: Reflections on the reauthorization for social workers. *School Social Work Journal, 31*(1), 1–18.

Raines, J. C. (2008). *Evidence-based practice in school mental health*. New York: Oxford University Press.

Raines, J. C., & Ahlman, C. (2004). No substitute for competence: How to survive and thrive as a substitute school social worker. *School Social Work Journal, 28*(2), 37–52.

Reamer, F. G. (1998). The evolution of social work ethics. *Social Work, 43*(6), 488–500.

Reamer, F. G. (2000). The social work ethics audit: A risk-management strategy. *Social Work, 45*(4), 355–366.

Reamer, F. G. (2005). Ethical and legal standards in social work: Consistency and conflict. *Families in Society, 86*(2), 163–169.

Reamer, F. G. (2006). *Social work values and ethics* (3rd ed.). New York: Columbia University Press.

Robison, W., & Reeser, L. C. (2000). *Ethical decision making in social work*. Boston: Allyn & Bacon.

Rosen, L. (2003, October 26). Students' privacy vs. adult rights. *Sacramento Bee,* Metro/regional news.

Rosen, L. (2004, September 16). Rocklin schools ban confidential medical release. *Sacramento Bee*, Metro/regional news.

School Social Work Association of America. (2001). *Position statement: School social workers and confidentiality.* Northlake, IL: Author. Retrieved April 7, 2003, from http://www.sswaa.org

Secemsky, V. O., & Ahlman, C. (2003). Proposed guidelines for school social workers seeking clinical supervision: How to choose a supervisor. *School Social Work Journal, 27*(2), 79–88.

Staller, K. M., & Kirk, S. A. (1997). Unjust freedom: The ethics of client self-determination in runaway youth shelters. *Child and Adolescent Social Work Journal, 14*(3), 223–242.

Tan, J. O. A., Passerini, G. E., & Stewart, A. (2007). Consent and confidentiality in clinical work with young people. *Clinical Child Psychology & Psychiatry, 12*(2), 191–210.

Tarasoff v. Regents of the University of California, 551 P. 2d 334 (1976).

UCLA Center for Mental Health in Schools. (2003). *A technical assistance sampler on school interventions to prevent youth suicide*. Los Angeles, CA: Author. Retrieved May 19, 2003, from http://smhp.psych.ucla.edu

U.S. Department of Health and Human Services. (2003, May). *OCR privacy brief: Summary of the HIPAA privacy rule*. Washington, DC: Author. Retrieved August 15, 2007, from http://www.hhs.gov/ocr/privacysummary.pdf

Ward, K. (2002). Confidentiality in substance abuse counseling. *Journal of Social Work Practice in the Addictions, 2*(2), 39–52.

Yalom, I. D. (1980). *Existential psychotherapy*. New York: Basic Books.

5

Ethical and Legal Complexities for School Social Workers with Confidentiality in Schools

Sandra Kopels
University of Illinois at Urbana-Champaign

- Ethical Issues Related to Confidentiality in School Social Work Practice
- Legal Issues Related to Confidentiality in School Social Work Practice
- Other Factors that Influence Confidentiality

School social workers assist students to be successful in the school environment. School social workers accomplish this by providing or arranging for services to meet the needs of children. In addition to providing individual, group, and other services directly to children and their parents, school social workers frequently team with other members of the school environment. School social workers also work with a wide variety of individuals and organizations based outside the school, such as mental health agencies, child welfare services, probation officers, and health care providers.

This chapter focuses on under what circumstances, with whom, and how much information can be revealed. Whether school social workers work individually with children and their families, are part of a school-based team, or work with providers outside the school environment, the sharing of information with others is a concern common to all school social work roles and functions. In the course of providing services to children and families, school social workers are asked to discuss children and their needs with people both within and outside the school environment. School social workers face dilemmas when they are asked to disclose to others the confidential information they learned in the course of providing services to children and families. Consider these examples:

> A high school English teacher refers a student to the school social worker because of her concerns that the student may be depressed. The school social worker meets with the student to assess for symptoms of depression and determines that the student is depressed and would benefit from individual counseling. A short time later, the student gets into a fight at school and is referred to the principal for disciplinary action. The student tells the principal that he has been receiving counseling from the school social worker. The principal is considering expelling the student from school and wants to know why the student is seeing the social worker and what information the social worker may have that explains the student's behavior. Should the social worker give the principal details regarding the student's depression? How much information should the social worker provide to persuade the principal not to expel the student?
>
> The mother of a student contacts the school social worker because she and her husband have decided to divorce after years of constant fighting. She asks the social worker to meet with her child to help her adjust to the divorce and to the fact that her father has moved out of their home. The school social worker meets with the student and invites her to join a school-based group for children of divorce. The student agrees and attends regularly for one semester, sharing her feelings about her parents, their conflict, and their divorce. The school social worker later receives a phone call from the student's father, who inquires about his child's progress and wants to know what his daughter has said about him and her mother. If the father has the right to about know his child's progress, does he also have the right to learn the details of the sessions so he can use them as evidence in the upcoming divorce?
>
> A school social worker learns that a family in the school district has become homeless. The social worker wants to refer them to a local shelter. When the social worker calls the shelter, he learns that the shelter only has space for one additional family; the shelter has received inquiries from other agencies, and the shelter will make its own determination about who gets the vacancy, based on the severity of the needs. The shelter wants to know what the relevant family issues are and what is so urgent about their situation. Can the social worker disclose the family's situation to the shelter and share intimate details about the family so that the shelter will take them in?
>
> A school social worker attends a discharge-planning meeting for a high school student with whom the social worker worked during the previous academic year. The student has been hospitalized in a psychiatric facility because of a suicide attempt made over the summer. The psychiatrist stresses to the social worker that the student is extremely embarrassed about his hospitalization and

does not want anyone to know what happened. The therapeutic team expresses concern that if others learn about his suicide attempt, the student may try again. The psychiatrist and the other team members want to know the school social worker's perceptions of the student's needs and whether anyone in the school needs to know of the student's hospitalization and suicide attempt. Should the social worker share her views of the student's needs? Should she honor the therapeutic team's concerns and keep the information confidential? If she tells others in the school, with whom can she share the information, and how much information can she disclose?

ETHICAL ISSUES RELATED TO CONFIDENTIALITY IN SCHOOL SOCIAL WORK PRACTICE

Unfortunately, there are no easy answers to any of the above questions. Each question involves many factors that require judgment on the part of the school social worker. School social workers must learn to balance other individuals' desires for information about children and families against their ethical obligations to maintain the confidentiality of their clients' communications. Additionally, they must understand how legal concepts further complicate decision-making processes regarding disclosure of information about their clients.

National Association of Social Workers Code of Ethics

The starting point for all social workers in understanding their ethical obligations to their clients is the NASW Code of Ethics. Whether or not a social worker belongs to NASW, the NASW Code of Ethics serves as the basis for his or her ethical duties to maintain the confidentiality of client information. The current NASW Code of Ethics, approved in 1996 and updated in 1999, contains eighteen specific provisions pertaining to privacy and confidentiality. The confidentiality provisions range from topics such as the ethical principles related to client consent to the handling and disposal of written and electronic records. The most pertinent provision related to protecting client confidentiality is found in section 1.07c: "Social workers should protect the confidentiality of all information obtained in the course of professional service, except for compelling professional reasons. The general expectation that social workers will keep information confidential does not apply when disclosure is necessary to prevent serious, foreseeable, and imminent harm to a client or other identifiable person. In all instances, social workers should disclose the least amount of confidential information necessary to achieve the desired purpose; only information that is directly relevant to the purpose for which the disclosure is made should be revealed" (National Association of Social Workers, 1999).

To distill this ethical provision to its most basic form, the code states that social workers should keep all client information confidential, except when there are compelling professional reasons to disclose such information.

Social workers must maintain confidentiality except when the disclosure is necessary to prevent serious harm or injury to a client or another person. While seemingly simple, applying the confidentiality provisions of the NASW Code of Ethics to the school environment is quite complex. Complexities arise for a variety of reasons that will be addressed in this chapter. One such reason is the confusion that surrounds the question of to whom school social workers have an ethical obligation.

Position Statements on Confidentiality and the School Social Worker

The NASW Commission on Education and other professional organizations specializing in the interests of school social workers have issued position statements to assist school social workers in handling the difficult confidentiality issues that arise for social workers in the school setting. These statements do not attempt to provide instructions for school social workers regarding when confidentiality should be maintained and when information should be disclosed. Instead, the statements offer general principles to guide conduct in situations involving school social workers and confidentiality.

In 1991, the NASW Commission on Education issued a position statement entitled "The School Social Worker and Confidentiality." The position statement begins by recognizing the interplay between law and ethics and offers "general principles to . . . assist social workers with difficult decision-making." It provides confidentiality guidelines for specific topics such as informed consent, interviewing children, child abuse and neglect, substance abuse, and intended harm to self and others. It concludes by noting that school social workers must be thoroughly familiar with applicable legal regulations and employ ethical decision making when making difficult and sensitive judgments relating to confidentiality.

The School Social Work Association of America (SSWAA) also adopted its own position statement on confidentiality in the schools entitled "School Social Workers and Confidentiality" in 1991. The SSWAA statement expresses the belief that confidentiality is an underlying principle of school social work and is essential to establishing an atmosphere of confidence and trust between school social workers and the individuals they serve. It notes that a careful balance between ethical and legal responsibilities is a requirement of the provision of services to students in the school setting and that school social workers must weigh the consequences of sharing information and assume responsibility for their decisions. The SSWAA statement concludes that the best interests of students should serve as a guide in decisions regarding confidential information.

The position statements share a number of common themes. Each notes that ethics and law play a part in the decision making surrounding the release of client information. Each statement recognizes that the laws governing information disclosure are complicated and often conflicting. Each statement makes clear that social workers should be familiar with federal, state, and local laws that govern responsibilities related to confidentiality in specific situations. However, the position statements differ regarding whom school social workers are responsible to and how they should balance these duties.

The NASW position statement asserts that the school social worker has ethical obligations to more than one client in any given situation and views the student, parents, school personnel, and community as clients of the school social worker. The NASW position statement acknowledges that "the multiplicity" of clients contributes to the complexities of decision making for school social workers about confidentiality. The NASW position statement also explains that the responsibility of the school social worker to maintain student confidentiality needs to be balanced with the social worker's responsibility to parents and school administrators.

The SSWAA position statement differs in that it observes that information is communicated to school social workers by students and families with the expectation that the information will remain confidential. The statement acknowledges that school social workers may be members of teams and may be confronted by situations where the disclosure of information is critical to providing assistance to students and families. Thus the SSWAA position statement reasons that information should be shared with other school personnel only on a need-to-know basis and only for professional reasons. The statement further points out that the school social worker's responsibility to maintain confidentiality must be weighed against his or her responsibility to the family and school community. The statement concluded by recognizing that the school social worker's focus must always remain on what is in the best interests of students.

Who Is the Client?

Kopels (1992) challenged the stance of the NASW Commission on Education position statement that school social workers have a multiplicity of clients to whom they have an ethical obligation. She argued that viewing parents, school personnel, and the community as clients of the school social worker gives them equal status with students. She considered them to be stakeholders who may have genuine concern and legitimate reasons to want information about children, yet their interests do not give them the status of clients. If they were considered to be clients, there would be no logical or systematic way to resolve confidentiality conflicts. Kardon (1993) objected to Kopels's position. While he agreed that labeling all school personnel and the community clients of the school social worker was overly expansive, he disagreed with the view of students as clients. Kardon wrote that adhering to the standard of confidentiality interferes with school social workers' ability to work successfully in schools. Kopels (1993) countered that the ethical obligation to safeguard client confidentiality is owed to the student as client, and that decisions regarding information disclosure must be balanced against the primacy of the school social worker's obligation to the student.

Other authors have written about ethical issues that school social workers face in schools (e.g., Garrett, 1994; Jonson-Reid, 2000). Still others have created ethical decision-making models to assist social workers in their decisions regarding which student disclosures to keep confidential and which to reveal for the best interest of the student or the school (e.g., Dibble, 2006; Raines, 2004; Reamer, 2005). However, while acknowledging that school social workers need to consider certain ethical and legal issues and their own personal values when deciding to maintain or release confidential information, these authors do not directly address the question of who the client of the school social worker is.

When school social workers believe that they owe duties to more than one client, their decision making about confidentiality becomes confused and more complicated than it needs to be. When school social workers view students, school administrators, teachers, parents, and the community as clients, it becomes almost impossible to sort out who is entitled to information about a student. Having a multiplicity of clients creates ethical conflicts where none really exist. When school social workers elevate all interested individuals to the status of clients and then attempt to balance the interests of these multiple "clients," they self-impose unnecessary complications.

In school social work practice, the student is typically the client of the school social worker. When school social workers do not view the student as their only client, then the worker is forced to juggle the competing interests of other stakeholders for information access. Parents, school administrators, teachers, and the broader community are interested stakeholders in the life and functioning of the child. They need information about children to fulfill their own responsibilities to them.

Parents have legal responsibility for their children and usually have deep love for them and the desire that they develop into healthy, functioning individuals. Teachers and other professionals in the school are colleagues of the social worker and typically share the social workers' responsibility and concern for children's educational development. School principals and other administrators have supervisory authority over the social worker and are concerned for the overall educational condition and safety of the school for all students. They care about how a particular child may help or hinder their responsibilities. The broader community has more expansive interests. Community members may be concerned about the safety of their neighborhoods as well as the overall performance of their school systems.

All these vested interests—parents, teachers, school administrators, the community—become stakeholders who may request or demand information about students. However, their concern or interest about a child is different from their right to know such information. School social workers should maintain the confidentiality of the student unless there are compelling professional reasons to disclose the information to stakeholders. When social workers provide services to family members in addition to the student, the family members may also be considered to be school social work clients. School social workers incur a similar obligation to protect the confidentiality of family members' information absent compelling reasons for disclosure.

COMPELLING PROFESSIONAL REASONS

Provision 1.07c of the current NASW Code of Ethics states that "Social workers should protect the confidentiality of all information obtained in the course of professional service, except for compelling professional reasons. The general expectation that social workers will keep information confidential does not apply when disclosure is necessary to prevent serious, foreseeable, and imminent harm to a client or other identifiable person" (National Association of Social Workers, 1999). Provision H(1) of the 1979 version of the Code of Ethics stated that "The social worker should share with others confidences revealed by clients, without their consent, only for compelling professional reasons" (National Association of Social Workers, 1979). Each of these versions of the code requires social workers to protect confidentiality unless there are compelling professional reasons for not doing so. However, neither version of the code defines the phrase "compelling professional reasons."

The current code adds a statement that releases social workers from the expectation of maintaining confidentiality in certain situations, namely when "disclosure is necessary to prevent serious, foreseeable, and imminent harm to a client or other identifiable person" (National Association of Social Workers, 1999). This statement was added to allow social workers to disclose confidential information in situations involving client violence to themselves or others, in accordance with the duties imposed by case law (discussed later in this chapter).

Social workers who have compelling professional reasons for disclosing client information are allowed to do so as an exception to the general rule of protecting client confidences. The phrase "compelling professional reasons," although not defined, is generally understood to cover situations where the law requires social workers to disclose information (such as child abuse or elder abuse) or situations where the social worker believes disclosure may prevent serious physical harm. Social workers retain discretion and can rely on their professional judgment to disclose information in these limited circumstances. When school social workers learn something that causes them serious concern about the physical safety of students in their school, they have compelling professional reasons to disclose the information.

Some school social workers use "compelling professional reasons" as their justification for disclosing information to parents, school personnel, or others. They may feel that when they learn about something that they view as harmful to a child, they have compelling professional reasons to disclose it, as appropriate, to parents, colleagues, administrators, or others. For example, if a school social worker learns that a student is shoplifting, he or she may feel it is important to tell the parents so that the parents can correct the child's actions and so that the student does not get caught and face legal troubles. Arguably, social workers who act to protect a child may be able to ethically justify their decision to disclose, especially if they rely on an ethical decision-making model. Other social workers may not consider telling parents about a child's shoplifting a compelling enough reason to violate the student's confidentiality.

Other school social workers use "compelling professional reasons" as a justification to disclose almost any information they learn about a child to others. For example, a school social worker tells the classroom teacher that the affair a child's mother is having with a neighbor is the source of discord in the home and the child's difficulties in school. In this situation, while the social worker may believe that she has compelling professional reasons (the child's school success) to reveal the information to the teacher, most professionals would not consider a child's school success to be a compelling professional reason. Unfortunately, the Code of Ethics does not provide more direction to social workers on which reasons should be considered compelling.

Professionalism versus Confidentiality

The preceding discussion may leave the reader with the mistaken impression that school social workers have no obligation to maintain the confidentiality of anyone other than students or their family members. That is not the case. Rather, the preceding sections discuss who should be considered the client of the school social worker to whom the duty of confidentiality is owed.

School social workers do have responsibilities pertaining to multiple entities, including their colleagues, administrators, and the broader community. School social workers have the obligation to act professionally in their jobs. As professionals, school social workers should operate in ways that demonstrate respect to their colleagues and their employers. In some situations, colleagues may share personal information about themselves with the school social worker in the course of their professional relationships. For example, a teacher may tell the social worker about her own drinking or drug use. The social worker should keep that information to him- or herself unless the teacher's drinking interferes with her classroom performance. In other situations, administrators may seek out the social worker's advice about sensitive matters. For example, a principal may ask the school social worker how to handle talking to an employee who is suspected of using the school's computers to view pornography. In both of these situations, the school social worker would maintain the confidentiality of the communication, not because the teacher or the principal is the client of the social worker but because the social worker has a professional and ethical responsibility to act in ways that show respect for the dignity of others. Similarly, school social workers should not gossip to others about the daily happenings at their schools or about their colleagues or the parents of schoolchildren. The school social worker would not share this information, not because these individuals are their clients, but because the social worker should always act in a professional manner.

LEGAL ISSUES RELATED TO CONFIDENTIALITY IN SCHOOL SOCIAL WORK PRACTICE

School social workers can consult the NASW Code of Ethics, professional position statements, and scholarly literature on confidentiality to determine best practice principles regarding how to handle situations that concern disclosure of information regarding children or their families. These sources all share the recognition of the complexities pertaining to maintaining confidentiality in schools. These sources also share an emphasis on the role ethics plays in professional practice and attempt to provide school social workers with a way to think about resolving their ethical conflicts. However, the NASW Code of Ethics, position statements, and the literature on confidentiality have not provided school social workers with sufficient guidance on the legal issues that further complicate confidentiality. The information that follows may assist school social workers in recognizing the impact of certain legal issues on ethical school social work practice and confidentiality.

Disclosing Confidences in Dangerous Situations

One of the most problematic issues for school social workers is deciding when information should be disclosed for the protection of the student and others. The lack of understanding of the "duty to report," the "duty to warn," and the "duty to protect" leads to mistaken understandings of social workers' duties to disclose client confidences to protect clients and others (Kopels & Kagle, 1993). Social workers confuse their discretionary ability to disclose certain information with the requirement that they must release such information. This confusion stems from two sources: child abuse reporting and the court case that established a "duty to warn."

In 1974, Congress enacted the Child Abuse Prevention and Treatment Act (CAPTA). CAPTA provides federal funding to states in support of prevention, assessment, investigation, prosecution, and treatment activities related to child abuse and neglect. To receive CAPTA funding, states must have a system for the reporting of child abuse and neglect. Laws in all states set out which professionals are mandated to report child abuse and neglect: all states make social workers "mandated reporters" (Kopels, 2006). Therefore, when social workers suspect that a child with whom they are working may be abused or neglected, they need to report their suspicions. It should be remembered that until the early 1970s, social workers had no duty to intervene when children with whom they worked experienced child abuse.

Since the enactment of mandatory reporting, however, school social workers who learn of or suspect child abuse or neglect must make a report, regardless of whether the source of the knowledge is the student, the parent, other school personnel, or outside sources. Child abuse is considered to be a compelling professional reason to disclose confidential information. Additionally, most states have written into the laws governing confidentiality in various settings, such as mental health care settings and substance abuse treatment, an exception for child abuse and neglect reporting that allows the reporter to disclose such information without fear of being sued for the breach of his or her duty to maintain confidentiality. Because child abuse reporting is mandatory, social workers routinely act to protect children when they suspect a child is being harmed. In effect, there is almost no discretion on the part of school social workers to report child abuse if they have a reasonable belief that it has occurred. Because school social workers must report child abuse, they often believe that they are responsible for reporting any situation in which they feel a child is endangered. They mistakenly expand their duty to report child abuse or neglect to any situation in which a child may be at risk.

The second source of confusion about duties to disclose information for the protection of clients and others stems from the landmark case of *Tarasoff v. Regents of the University of California* (1974). The case involved a graduate student, Prosenjit Poddar, who told his psychologist that he intended to kill an unnamed but identifiable woman, Tatiana Tarasoff. Although the psychologist took steps to have the campus police detain him, Poddar later killed Tarasoff. Tarasoff's parents sued the psychologist and others for their failure to warn them of the harm posed to Tarasoff by Poddar. The California Supreme Court issued a ruling that established that "when a doctor or a psychotherapist, in the exercise of his professional skill and knowledge, determines, or should determine, that a warning is essential to avert danger arising from the medical or psychological condition of his patient, he incurs a legal obligation to give that warning" (*Tarasoff v. Regents of the University of California,* 1974). On its own, the California Supreme Court later amended its ruling and broadened the duty to warn to a duty to protect. The court stated that the discharge of the duty to protect can occur in a variety of ways, including warning the intended victim or others likely to apprise the victim of the danger, to notify the police, or to take whatever other steps are reasonably necessary under the circumstances.

The *Tarasoff* case established court-made precedent in California. However, courts in certain states (e.g., Illinois) have never adopted the duty to warn. Some states have enacted legislation that limits therapist liability to particular circumstances, while other states only place an obligation to protect third parties on delineated professionals. Most states have amended their confidentiality laws to allow an exception to maintaining confidentiality when disclosure of client information is necessary to warn or protect third parties. Clearly, different states do not consistently establish a duty to warn. Yet many social workers mistakenly believe that they have a duty to warn of violence and routinely disclose information that should be withheld (Kopels & Kagle, 1993). Most often, the duty to warn is not mandatory; instead, social workers must use their professional discretion. Unlike situations involving child abuse and neglect, in which social workers are required to act and report their suspicions of abuse or neglect, the duty to warn or protect relies on the social workers' use of clinical judgment to assess the degree of danger or harm to the individual or others and to take action, if warranted.

Physical Violence versus Harmful Acts

Another misunderstanding that arose as a result of the *Tarasoff* case concerns the fact that the duty to warn or the duty to protect applies only to situations where actual violence has been threatened. Under *Tarasoff*, when a therapist determines or should have determined that the client poses danger to another person, then the therapist is obligated to take action to protect others. The *Tarasoff* case, cases from other states, and most of the legislation created to balance when therapists should be responsible for taking action to protect others only create a responsibility to act when clients threaten serious *physical* harm or violence to themselves or others. For the school social worker, the potential for physical harm to a student or others in the school environment (classmates, teachers, administrators, or other personnel) is apparent in situations involving threats of suicide, self-mutilation, bullying, weapons in schools, gang behavior, and other violence directed toward others.

However, social workers often incorrectly expand their perceived responsibilities to situations other than those involving physical violence. School social workers often believe that they have a duty to warn or protect when they learn that students are engaging in behaviors that are illegal for children to do (e.g., drinking alcohol) or that may be harmful to them (e.g., having unprotected sex). A school social worker who learns that a student is engaging in unprotected sexual intercourse, is pregnant, or is using alcohol or drugs may view the situation as potentially dangerous to the student. The social worker may feel the need to disclose the information to protect the student from the danger caused by the student's condition. From a legal perspective, however, the fact that no physical violence is involved may not create any obligation to act.

While the school social worker may have no legal obligation to take action, the social worker may believe that he or she has an ethical obligation to do something. For example, a student's disclosure that he is smoking marijuana daily clearly creates a dilemma for the school social worker who wants to protect the student from himself. Some school social workers would talk to the student, assess the situation, discourage drug use, and make a referral for treatment but maintain the confidentiality of the student's disclosure. Other school social workers may feel the need to disclose the information. If so, the social worker should consider the level of the student's impairment, whether the student's grades have been stable or have dropped, whether the student drives while under the influence, the positive and negative consequences to the student as a result of the disclosure, to whom the disclosure should be made, and the likely benefit to the student before making a decision about revealing the information. If a twelve-year-old tells her social worker that she is seven months pregnant and has not told her parents about the pregnancy or received any prenatal care, the school social worker has no legal duty to act. Instead, the social worker has a discretionary decision to make. The social worker must assess the dangers stemming from the lack of health care to the student and the fetus and the consequences of the disclosure to the student. While there may be no duty to warn because there is no physical violence, the social worker may be able to discretionarily disclose the information to protect the student from imminent harm. Unfortunately, there is no formula for deciding at what point the potential for harm to self or others triggers a responsibility to act.

Imminence of Violence

Related to social workers' misunderstanding of the duty to warn is the concept of the imminence of the potential violence. Under the *Tarasoff* ruling and most legislation created in response to the duty to warn, any duty a professional may have typically occurs only when actual danger is imminent. In other words, when a social worker discloses information about a client's harmful actions or threats, it should be to prevent the furtherance of physical harm to the client or others. If a student tells the social worker that he brought a gun to school today and is going to "get" the kids who pick on him, the social worker should immediately disclose this information to the administration. Not only is there a threat of physical violence to other students, but the harm is imminent. If students disclose that they formerly used drugs but no longer do, or that they have had sexual activities with their boyfriends but have now broken up, any harm is in the past. The students' disclosures do not suggest physical harm to others, nor is any harm to themselves imminent.

The strictly legalistic approach to the contours of the duty to warn does not always coincide with the ethical notion of maintaining confidentiality unless there is a compelling reason for disclosure. If a school social worker chooses to disclose to parents information about drug use or sexual experiences that occurred in the past, the social worker should do so only if he or she believes the student will reengage in this behavior soon (e.g., due to a relapse or because of a reunion with a boyfriend).

Often, social workers have difficulty maintaining the confidentiality of students when they believe the results of the disclosures will ultimately be beneficial to the students. If a sixteen-year-old girl tells her social worker that she is two months pregnant and has not told her parents about the pregnancy or received any prenatal care, the school social worker has time to determine how he or she should respond to the situation. As in the above example of the twelve-year-old pregnant girl, the social worker should still assess the dangers stemming from the lack of health care to the student and the fetus and the consequences of a disclosure to the student. However, in this example, the student is older and hopefully more mature, and it is much earlier in her pregnancy. The social worker has time to work with the student to encourage her to tell her parents about the pregnancy, so that the social worker does not have to be the one to reveal it.

This discussion should not leave the reader with the idea that school social workers should take no action unless they learn from students or others that physical violence is imminent. Instead, this discussion is meant to demonstrate the complexities of the school social worker's role in maintaining confidentiality. State and federal law as well as court decisions around the country also contribute to the complexities of deciding whether to share information with others.

Age of the Child

The very fact that children are minors complicates legal decision making related to the imminence of harm. School social workers may be more concerned about younger children who engage in the same activities as older children, viewing the same activity as more harmful for a younger child. For example, a student may disclose to the school social worker that she is having sexual intercourse with her eighteen-year-old boyfriend. While it may not be advisable for adolescents to have sexual relationships at any age, the social worker may view the behavior as more imminently harmful if the student is twelve years old, rather than eighteen. If the student is twelve years of age, the social worker may assess the sexual relationship as more exploitative and more dangerous for the student and choose to disclose the information. If the student were eighteen years old, the social worker would decide to keep the information confidential.

Ironically, in some situations, student behaviors are problematic for the school social worker solely because the student is a minor. Students who drink alcohol are engaging in behavior that would be considered legal if they were adults. It is their status as children that makes the drinking unlawful and creates a possible responsibility to disclose the behavior to parents. Social workers who work with adults have no similar legal responsibility to report their clients' drinking to anyone.

Another complication related to the age of minors is the inconsistent treatment of minors under the law. As a general rule, children are viewed as incompetent to make decisions until they reach the age of majority (as defined by each state). Exceptions to this general rule include situations where children are legally emancipated before they reach majority age. Additionally, specific laws specify situations in which the legislature has recognized that the child is mature enough to make his or her own decisions regarding particular topics. For example, in some states, children above a certain age (e.g., twelve or fourteen) can make treatment and health decisions concerning alcohol/drug use, their mental health, and use of birth control or abortion services. Under these laws, the minor is the person from whom social workers need to secure consent for treatment or release of information. In some states, minors who are parents may be able to make medical decisions for their children, but not for themselves. When the laws in the state give certain rights to the minor (e.g., the right to consent and receive alcohol counseling), then the social worker has much less justification for disclosing this information to the parents or others.

Clearly, social workers must be familiar with the laws of their own state that pertain to different aspects of school social work practice. School social workers should always have a working knowledge of federal and state laws that govern issues related to consent for treatment, access to and disclosure of records, and how the age of the child may affect these issues. State and federal laws may differentially affect how workers outside the school setting handle confidentiality concerns (e.g., alcohol treatment centers, mental health facilities) and the responsibilities of different professionals (e.g., social workers versus teachers). In addition, the type of presenting problem (e.g., sexual disease transmission, child abuse) may have some bearing on confidentiality concerns.

OTHER FACTORS THAT INFLUENCE CONFIDENTIALITY

There are additional factors that school social workers should keep in mind when considering whether to disclose client information. These include releases of information, the amount of information to be disclosed in cases where disclosure is necessary, and the consequences of wrongly disclosing information.

Release of Information Forms

It may seem obvious, but decisions about disclosing information are greatly simplified when social workers obtain signed releases of information or other consent forms from clients. A release of information form is a document that allows an authorized individual to consent to disclosure of his or her information to a person or agency. The Family Educational Rights and Privacy Act of 1974 (FERPA) is a federal law that pertains specifically to education records. Under FERPA, parents have the right to consent to disclosure of their children's information until the child reaches the age of eighteen. At age eighteen, all rights transfer to the student.

In cases where a school social worker needs to disclose information about a student to individuals and agencies outside the school environment, he or she should ask the child's parents to sign release of information forms, which allows the school social worker to do so. He or she can discuss with the parents the type of information that they need to disclose, the purpose of the disclosure, and to whom the disclosure would be made and obtain their consent. Release of information forms are not needed to disclose information from the school record to individuals within the school environment who have legitimate educational interests in having the information.

Seeking the consent of parents or children over the age of eighteen to release education records simplifies disclosure issues because the school social worker has permission to share information with others. Of course, it is necessary to understand that FERPA only applies to the education records of students, which includes information that is in written or recorded form. FERPA does not apply to the personal notes of school social workers, nor does it apply to written records that are not educational in nature, such as mental health, alcohol/drug, or medical records. School social workers must be familiar with all laws that cover the release of different kinds of information and who the individuals responsible for providing consent are. In some cases, social workers may need the parents' consent to the release of their own records to outside agencies. In other situations, social workers may need to ask students to consent to the release of records that are not educational in nature.

Necessary Disclosures and the Minimum Possible Information

As mentioned earlier, to do their jobs effectively, school social workers often team with other service providers both within and outside the school to ensure that students receive the services that are most appropriate to their needs. Working as a team member often requires the sharing of information. However, there are a number of ways that sharing information with team members can be handled to reduce concerns about confidentiality.

In some types of school teams, the school social worker does not have any clinical responsibility for a student but is simply a member of a team that convenes to address a specific mission. For example, if a social worker is a member of a positive behavior interventions and supports team, the social worker, like all other members of the team, looks at ways that consistent behavioral rules will increase positive behaviors throughout the school. In this particular role, the social worker is working on behalf of the school. Often, the discussions concern general behavioral expectations for all students and do not address the behaviors of particular students. When the social worker contributes his or her knowledge of behavioral techniques or the developmental needs of children, the social worker is talking generally about the subject, not about the therapeutic needs of any specific child. Confidentiality is not a concern because confidential communications are not involved. If the team discusses a particular student who is on the social worker's counseling caseload and whose behavior is not in line with school expectations, the social worker can contribute information about how the specific child might be successful without disclosing any other aspects of the student's confidential issues.

In other situations, school social workers are on teams in which they must share information that they have about specific children. For example, school social workers are often members of teams that create individualized education programs (IEPs) for children with disabilities who have special education needs. The development of an IEP requires the team to have detailed knowledge of a child's specific needs and functioning. For example, the team must understand the child's present levels of academic achievement and functional performance and how the disability affects the child's involvement and progress in the curriculum. The team must obtain this knowledge so that it can fashion goals that meet the child's needs. In generating an IEP that meets a specific child's individual needs, the school social worker, like all other team members, must share information about the child with other team members. In cases where school social work services are being contemplated, the social worker may have to reveal information about why the child requires the initiation or continuation of such services. In the special education context, sharing information with other team members is not a confidentiality concern. Under federal special education law, the regulations explicitly allow IEP team members to share information to produce a plan for the child.

Under all circumstances, school social workers must continually assess whether it is truly necessary to disclose confidential information about a student to someone else. If, after careful consideration, the social worker decides that compelling professional or legal reasons support disclosure, the next step is to ensure that the least amount of information necessary is disclosed. In order to protect the privacy of the student, the social worker should release the minimum information necessary for the purpose. For example, if the social worker believes it necessary to tell the teacher about marital discord in the home that is negatively affecting the child's behavior, it is not necessary to tell the teacher that the student's father gets drunk all the time, which angers the mother, who then goes out and has affairs. School social workers should always release the least amount of information they can even when they have client consent or determine that the disclosure is consistent with ethical or legal considerations.

The Consequences of Disclosure without Consent

School social workers may encounter practice situations where they are tempted to disclose confidential information because they believe it is in the best interest of their clients or third parties to do so. Sometimes the discomfort of learning delicate information leads social workers to want to share the information with someone else, a colleague, supervisor, intimate partner, or friend, so that they have a sounding board for their own feelings. In those cases, the social worker is placing his or her own needs above the interest of the client. Sometimes social workers can justify their actions if they know that they are acting in accordance with professional ethics or the law. In other situations, social workers know that they should not disclose information but do so anyway. Before disclosing information without legal or ethical justification, practitioners must ask themselves whether such disclosure is worth the risk.

From a practical perspective, disclosure of students' information against the wishes of students can greatly reduce a social worker's effectiveness. When a student tells a social worker something that the student considers a confidence, yet the social worker discloses it to the parents or others, the student will be angry. In some situations, the seriousness of the information outweighs the fact that the student is angry. In other situations, the student's anger may be justified. For example, a sixteen-year-old tells the social worker that he recently got his driver's license and drove his friends to a party, where they all got "really wasted." If the social worker discloses this to the parents, there may be consequences for the student; for example, the parents may watch the student's actions more closely or require the student to go for drug counseling and revoke his driving privileges. While the student may be upset, the social worker can defend his or her actions ethically and legally because of the student's dangerous behavior.

However, if a sixteen-year-old student tells the social worker that he believes he is homosexual, and the social worker informs the parents that their son is gay, the student will be angry. In this case, the social worker cannot justify his or her actions ethically or legally because there are no compelling reasons to permit the disclosure. The social worker would find it difficult to explain to the student why he or she chose to disclose. The student will undoubtedly talk to his friends and caution them not to talk to the social worker because he or she cannot be trusted. The distrust will spread throughout the school and have long-term consequences on the social worker's effectiveness with students.

In addition to practical concerns, social workers who fail to uphold confidentiality consistent with their professional ethics or legal obligations may face other consequences. When social workers violate the law or professional ethics, they may be subject to lawsuits for breach of confidentiality or malpractice. They may also find themselves sanctioned by social work regulatory boards or professional associations. In all situations, before information is disclosed, the social worker should analyze the issues, including the personal and professional costs and benefits to them and their clients.

The profession of school social work has evolved significantly from the early days, when social workers served as liaisons between immigrant children in settlement houses and schools. The ability of school social workers to maintain confidentiality has evolved as well, becoming increasingly complicated and reflecting the problems facing school social workers today. Social workers can seek guidance regarding confidentiality from the NASW Code of Ethics, the position statements of school social work professional organizations, and the professional literature. School social workers should act in accordance with their ethical codes and maintain the confidentiality of information shared with them. If they release confidential information, they should do so only if they have compelling professional reasons for disclosure. Additionally, school social workers must be cognizant of legal issues that affect confidentiality generally, as well as specific legal issues that arise in practice in their states. These factors only increase the ethical and legal complexities of dealing with confidentiality in schools.

References

Child Abuse Prevention and Treatment Act, P.L. 93-247; 42 U.S.C. § 5101 et seq. (1974).

Dibble, N. (2006). *Ethical issues and professional boundaries for school social workers*. Paper presented at the Midwest School Social Work Conference, Arlington Heights, IL.

Family Educational Rights and Privacy Act, 20 U.S.C. § 1232g (1974).

Garrett, K. R. (1994). Caught in a bind: Ethical decision making in schools. *Social Work in Education, 16*(2), 97–105.

Jonson-Reid, M. (2000). Understanding confidentiality in school-based interagency projects. *Social Work in Education, 22*(1), 33–45.

Kardon, S. (1993). Confidentiality: A different perspective. *Social Work in Education, 15*(4), 247–250.

Kopels, S. (1992). Confidentiality and the school social worker. *Social Work in Education, 14*(4), 203–205.

Kopels, S. (1993). Response to "Confidentiality: A Different Perspective." *Social Work in Education, 15*(4), 250–252.

Kopels, S. (2006). Laws and procedures for reporting child abuse: An overview. In C. Franklin, M. B. Harris, & P. Allen-Meares (Eds.), *The school services sourcebook* (pp. 369–375). New York: Oxford University Press.

Kopels, S., & Kagle, J. D. (1993). Do social workers have a duty to warn? *Social Service Review, 67*(1), 101–126.

NASW Commission on Education. (1991). The school social worker and confidentiality. *School Social Work Journal, 17*(2), 38–46.

National Association of Social Workers (1979). *Code of ethics of the National Association of Social Workers*. Washington, DC: Author.

National Association of Social Workers. (1999). *Code of ethics of the National Association of Social Workers*. Washington, DC: Author.

Raines, J. C. (2004). To tell or not to tell: Ethical issues regarding confidentiality. *School Social Work Journal, 28*(2), 62–78.

Reamer, F. G. (2005). Update on confidentiality issues in practice with children: Ethics risk management. *Children & Schools, 27*(2), 117–120.

School Social Work Association of America. (1991). *School social workers and confidentiality*. Retrieved March 23, 2006, from http://www.sswaa/org/about/confidentiality.html.

Tarasoff v. Regents of the University of California, 13 Cal. 3d 177; 529 P.2d 553 (1974).

6

The Developing Social, Political, and Economic Context for School Social Work

Carol Rippey Massat
University of Illinois at Chicago

Elizabeth Lehr Essex
Governor State University

Isadora Hare
Rockville, MD

Sunny Harris Rome
George Mason University

- Does the Education System Really Prepare Students?
- Demographic, Psychosocial, and Socioeconomic Factors Influencing Achievement and Schooling
- Federal, State, and Local Responses
- The State Education Agency and the Local Education Agency
- Local Initiatives in Education: Social Services and Health Care
- Factors Affecting School Social Work Today

Since its inception over a century ago, school social work's content and direction have been influenced by the social environment, conditions and events within society, and the educational system (Allen-Meares, 2006). Schools play an integral role in preparing our youths to become healthy, creative, and productive adults, workers, and citizens. Because public schools are designed to serve all children, they inevitably reflect events and trends in society at large. Schools are a microcosm of the larger society in which they function. The United States is a vast, complex, pluralistic society. In a free market democracy, economic success and citizen participation at all levels of government are prime national goals. The extent to which the education system prepares the upcoming generation to achieve these goals in the new global economy is a matter of deep concern. For the United States, this concern has been the source of almost a quarter century of school reform. The events of September 11, 2001, accelerated some of these trends, particularly school safety and awareness of the school community. Lela Costin (1987) wrote that the essential purpose of school is "to provide a setting for teaching and learning in which all children can prepare themselves for the world they now live in and the world they will face in the future" (p. 538). Reflecting all the realities of this dynamic environment, school social work is at the center of an intricate transactional field of forces (Germain, 2006). This field includes demographic, social, economic, and political forces, to which schools respond with both conservative and innovative strategies.

DOES THE EDUCATION SYSTEM REALLY PREPARE STUDENTS?

One of the most hotly debated questions in education is whether our system prepares the upcoming generation to achieve in the global economy. There has been an increased focus, now over several decades of discussion of school reform, on setting high standards for student achievement. Testing is now mandated by the No Child Left Behind Act of 2001 (NCLB) for all states, but it is difficult to compare the results, since each state is allowed to set its own standards and to develop its own testing system. Thus, the most commonly used national standards are performance on SAT and ACT exams, which are taken only by college-bound high school juniors and seniors. In 2006, 1.46 million students took the SAT and more than 1.2 million students took the ACT in the United States (ACT, 2007; College Board SAT, 2007). More than 90 percent of U.S. colleges and universities require the SAT or ACT, despite the low ability of these tests to predict college performance. The test is, however, used as a common measure to equalize the problem of different grading patterns in different schools (Black, 2005). SAT scores have stabilized after edging up for the past ten years.

The need for reform has been accentuated by the performance of U.S. students on international tests. The 2003 results of the Program for International Assessment indicated that the United States ranked twenty-fourth of twenty-nine member nations of the Organization for Economic Development based on performance of fifteen-year-olds in math. Since the last assessment three years earlier, student scores had fallen below those of

Hungary, Poland, and Spain. The Trends in International Mathematics and Science Study (TIMSS) evaluates students in fourth and eighth grade and tests half a million students in thirty languages in forty-one countries, including some chief U.S. trading partners and economic competitors, such as Canada, Germany, Hong Kong, Japan, Korea, and Singapore. Overall, U.S. students tested in 2003 improved over the previous four years; however, the TIMSS 2003 figures indicate that scores for U.S. fourth graders had remained stable since 1995, while several other countries advanced (Bybee & Stage, 2005). Bybee and Stage suggest that the nation continues to lag behind other countries because "U.S. schools emphasize the acquisition of information at the expense of problem-solving and the acquisition of knowledge" and "the United States, in its effort to close the achievement gap, has emphasized basic knowledge to help underachievers rather than ensuring that all students learn challenging material" (p. 4).

The achievement gap between minority students and non-Hispanic white students remains a troubling concern for U.S. schools. African American and Hispanic students continue to score lower than non-Hispanic white students on state, national, and international standardized tests. The gap in test scores is accompanied by lagging results on measures of educational achievement. According to Greene (2003), in 2001, 72 percent of non-Hispanic white students but just over half of black and Hispanic students graduated from high school on schedule. These disparities can be partially explained by income, since approximately 58 percent of black children and 62 percent of Hispanic children live in households whose income levels fall near or below the federal poverty line (Fellmeth, 2005). Poverty is associated with low access to high-quality preschools; poor nutrition; inadequate health care; and attendance at poorly funded schools, which are likely to provide fewer highly qualified teachers and fewer educational resources. Others concerned about the achievement gap have noted the role of school-related factors, such as biases on standardized tests, stereotyping of minority children, and peer pressure ("Achievement Gap," 2004). Recent positive developments include some narrowing of ethnic disparities in scores on the ACT, SAT, and TIMMS (Bybee & Stage, 2005; Rafferty, 2004). However, major discrepancies still exist and need to be more adequately addressed if schools are to prepare all students for a successful future.

DEMOGRAPHIC, PSYCHOSOCIAL, AND SOCIOECONOMIC FACTORS INFLUENCING ACHIEVEMENT AND SCHOOLING

Demographics

Current demographics reveal a dense, complex, diverse, and multicultural picture. In 2005, 25 percent of the population was under age eighteen (U.S. Census Bureau, 2007b). As of 2005, 42 percent of American children were nonwhite or Hispanic (U.S. Census Bureau, 2007c).

The extent and nature of population diversity are changing rapidly. The United States is currently experiencing its second great wave of immigration, this time not from Europe, but from the economically developing worlds of Asia and Latin America (U.S. Census Bureau, 2004). The foreign-born population in the United States has grown from a low of 10 million in 1970 to 35.7 million in 2005 (U.S. Census Bureau, 2007c). Educating the new wave of immigrants presents a number of challenges. These include resolving issues related to language acquisition for children from non-English-speaking families and cultural differences in learning styles. Altshuler and Schmautz (2006) point out that the more relational, interdependent worldview of Hispanic children, while in many ways a cultural strength, may make them less likely to succeed on the high-stakes testing currently emphasized in U.S. schools. Unfortunately, the needs of these children are often subsumed by political debates related to inclusion of newcomers to the United States.

Poverty

In spite of the enormous wealth in the United States, the child poverty rate is among the highest in the developed world. One study, which examined child poverty rates in sixteen developed countries, indicates that the child poverty rate in the United States is higher than that of any other of these developed nations, even after government programs are taken into account (Allegretto, 2006). Nearly 18 percent (17.6%) of U.S. children under age eighteen lived below the federally defined poverty line in 2005 (DeNavas-Walt, Proctor, & Lee, 2006). The rates are even more alarming for young children and for children who are members of minority groups: 20.5 percent of children under age five, 33.5 percent of African American children, and 28.3 percent of Latino children lived below or near the poverty line in 2005 (U.S. Census Bureau, 2007b). The Foundation for Child Development (2007) reports that significant income and quality of life disparities between ethnic minority and white children have worsened since 2002.

According to the U.S. Census Bureau (2007a), children tend to be more economically advantaged if they are born to parents with a college degree. Children living in households with parents who are married are far less likely to live in poverty than children living in female-headed families: 8.5 percent of children living in married-couple households were living in poverty in 2005, compared to 42.6 percent of children in female-headed households.

Childhood poverty has both immediate and lasting negative effects. Children who are poor are more likely to have difficulty in school, to become teen parents, and to earn less and be unemployed more as adults (Federal Interagency Forum on Child and Family Statistics, 1997). Poor children often go to school in districts that are impoverished and less able to provide highly qualified teachers and rich educational resources. The gap between children living in poverty and their counterparts is greatly accentuated by the enormous differences in the role government plays in alleviating child poverty. Education and welfare funding, for example, show dramatic inequalities across states, with the thirteen wealthiest states spending an average of $639 per capita on social welfare programs, and the twelve poorest states spending only $408 per capita on average from 1977 to 2000 (Lewin Group & Nelson A. Rockefeller Institute of Government, 2004).

Homeless Children and Youths

Burt (2007) reported in testimony before Congress that about 1.6–1.7 million youths between the ages of twelve and seventeen become homeless each year. Most youths in homeless shelters are homeless for the first time and have been homeless a short time. However, street youths may be homeless for several years or longer. Burt reports that sexual minority status is a strong risk factor for homelessness, and the proportion of homeless youths who are gay, lesbian, or bisexual ranges from 6 percent to 11–35 percent in street samples. Males and females are equally represented among homeless youths, and race/ethnicity is proportionate to that of the communities that have been studied. Homeless youths are "three times as likely as national samples of youth to be pregnant, to have impregnated someone, or to already be a parent" (Burt, 2007, p. 4). Burt reports that risk factors for homelessness include school difficulties, substance abuse (40% report alcohol problems and 40–50% report drug problems), mental health problems, family conflict, child maltreatment, out-of-home placement, and involvement with the juvenile justice system.

Child Health and Mental Health

According to the Foundation for Child Development's Child and Youth Well-Being Index (2007), the physical health of children in the United States is declining, and health care indicators have sunk to the lowest point since 1975, the year the foundation began to collect data. Much of this downward trend is related to a slowdown in reduction of child mortality rates and to the great increase in childhood obesity, which has been linked to numerous serious health problems. The Foundation for Child Development reports that overall child well-being measures have stalled since 2002, halting an upward trend in child well-being that took place from 1994 to 2002.

One important effort to address child health has been the State Children's Health Insurance Program (SCHIP), which has been in effect since 1997, when it was created to address the health needs of children whose families do not qualify for Medicaid but are unable to afford private health insurance. Federal funding supports 70 percent of the cost of this program to states up to a fixed state allotment. States have latitude in the design and administration of their children's insurance programs. SCHIP, along with increased enrollment in Medicaid, has been successful in reducing the number of uninsured children nationally from 22.3 percent to 14.9 percent. However, about 9 million children still lack health insurance in the United States (Lambrew, 2007). As the authorizing legislation approached its 2007 expiration date, President Bush and Democratic legislators debated over the future of SCHIP, with the president favoring program retraction and the Democrats proposing expansion to cover a greater number of uninsured children (Kaiser Family Foundation, 2007; Pear, 2007).

The Office of the Surgeon General (1999, 2001) and the President's New Freedom Commission on Mental Health (2003) have documented the prevalence of mental health disorders in children and challenges in addressing mental health needs. About one in five children in the United States experiences a mental disorder during the course of a year (Office of the Surgeon General, 1999), and about 5–9 percent of all children experience a serious emotional disturbance (President's New Freedom Commission on Mental Health, 2003). Access to quality mental health treatment, particularly for ethnic minorities, is impeded by a number of systemic barriers, including an inadequate and fragmented service delivery system and cultural insensitivity (Office of the Surgeon General, 2001; President's New Freedom Commission on Mental Health, 2003). The New Freedom Commission envisioned an increased role for schools in reducing barriers to mental health diagnosis and treatment (see chapter 25).

Substance Abuse

Illicit drug use among students has declined but remains a significant concern. As of 2006, 48 percent of twelfth graders had used an illicit drug at least once in their life (Johnston, O'Malley, Bachman, & Schulenberg, 2007). The Monitoring the Future project, conducted by the University of Michigan's Institute for Social Research, began in 1975 and monitors adolescent drug use. Findings indicate that overall use of illicit drugs among youths peaked in the 1970s, declined through the 1980s, increased from the early to mid-1990s, and has decreased since then. From 2005 to 2006, use of marijuana declined among tenth and twelfth graders and methamphetamine usage declined among tenth graders. Use of most other drugs remained steady. These include inhalants, LSD and other hallucinogens, crystal methampetamine, heroin and other narcotics, crack and powder cocaine, sedatives, so-called "club drugs.," and steroids. Temporal trends in binge drinking have followed patterns similar to those of illicit drug usage, but with a less steep increase in the 1990s (Johnston et al., 2007).

Teen Sex and Pregnancy

There is a close inverse relationship between teen parenthood and school achievement. The leading reported cause of high school dropout among adolescent females is childbirth. Only 40 percent of mothers who have a child before age eighteen complete high school, whereas the completion rate is about 70 percent for women who delay childbearing until age twenty or twenty-one. Only 2 percent of teen mothers complete a college degree before age thirty, as opposed to 9 percent of those who delay childbearing. Children of teen mothers are more likely to drop out of school and have lower levels of academic achievement than children born to older mothers (National Campaign to Prevent Teen Pregnancy, 2007). Child Trends Inc. (1997) identified four risk factors for teen births: (1) early school failure, (2) early behavior problems, (3) family dysfunction, and (4) poverty. In contrast, involvement in school activities after the birth of the first child and receipt of a high school diploma or even a GED were strongly associated with postponing a second birth.

Forty-six percent of American adolescents ages fifteen to nineteen have experienced sexual intercourse, and by age nineteen, 70 percent have had intercourse. Teens are waiting longer to have sex, as evidenced by a decline from 19 percent of females and 21 percent of males experiencing intercourse before age fifteen in 1995 to 13 percent of females and 15 percent of males in 2002 (Guttmacher Institute, 2007). The teen birth and pregnancy rates in the United States have declined steadily since the early 1990s. By 2004 the birthrate for women ages fifteen to nineteen was 41.1 per 1,000, down a third since peaking in 1991 (National Campaign to Prevent Teen Pregnancy, 2006). The pregnancy rate for this same age group, after reaching a high of 117 per 1,000 in 1990, had declined to 75 per 1,000 by 2002 (Guttmacher Institute, 2006). Twenty-nine percent of pregnancies among fifteen- to nineteen-year-olds ended in abortion in 2002 (Guttmacher Institute, 2007). Although birthrates for black and Hispanic teens fell by 42 percent and 20 percent respectively between 1991 and 2002, they remain higher than for other groups (National Campaign to Prevent Teen Pregnancy, 2005).

Child Abuse and Neglect

In 2005, child protective service agencies identified approximately 899,000 abused or neglected children. Nationwide, the rate of victimization of children was approximately 12.1 per 1,000 children under age eighteen. This has dropped from 13.4 children per 1,000 in 1990. Nearly two-thirds (62.8%) of these were victims of child neglect; 16.6 percent suffered from physical abuse, 9.3 percent from sexual abuse, 7.1 percent from emotional maltreatment, and 2 percent from medical neglect. About 14 percent were affected by other types of maltreatment, as defined by various state laws (U.S. Department of Health and Human Services, 2007). Children up to age three were most frequently the victims of child maltreatment. In 2005, an estimated 1,466 children died as a result of child abuse or neglect. Of those children who died, 42.2 percent had suffered neglect only, 24.1 percent suffered from physical abuse only, and 27.3 percent suffered multiple forms of maltreatment. Psychological maltreatment resulted in 3.7 percent of the deaths, medical neglect in 2.5 percent, and sexual abuse in 0.3 percent of the deaths (U.S. Department of Health and Human Services, 2007).

School Safety and Youth Violence

Although violent crime among youths is declining, violence continues to be a serious threat to child well-being and school functioning. Violent crime increased during the late 1980s. However, from 1994 to 2003, rates of victimization among adolescents fell by approximately 50 percent to 51.6 per 1,000 for youths ages twelve to fifteen, and 53 per 1,000 for youths ages sixteen to nineteen (Child Trends Data Bank, 2005). Among Americans ages fifteen to twenty-four, homicide is the second-leading cause of death, and suicide is the third-leading cause of death (U.S. Census Bureau, 2001). African American males are at particular risk of homicide. Homicide is the leading cause of death for African American men ages fifteen to twenty-four (Resnick, Bearman, Blum, Bauman, Harris, Jones, et al., 1997; U.S. Department of Health and Human Services, 1999). American Indians and Native Alaskans have the highest youth suicide rate in the United States; whites have the second-highest rate (Centers for Disease Control and Prevention, 2007; Snyder & Swahn, 2004). Among youth ages fifteen to nineteen in 2004, the suicide rate for males was approximately three-and-a-half times the rate for females (Centers for Disease Control and Prevention, 2007).

In 2001, 18 percent of youths reported that they had been threatened or injured at school during the previous year. According to a national study by Astor, Marachi, and Benbenishty (2007), the annual average rate of victimization for teachers between 1998 and 2003 was 51 incidents per 1,000 teachers, one-fourth lower than the average rate for 1992 to 1996. They also found that 35 percent of school social workers had been assaulted or threatened during the previous year; most of the experiences involved attacks by students (77%), parents (49%), or gang members (11%). Eighty-one percent of public schools reported experiencing one or more violent incidents during the 2003–2004 school year (Dinkes, Cataldi, Kena, & Baum, 2006). However, the violent crime rate has declined in public schools, with a 2004 rate of 22 per 1,000 students compared to the 1993 rate of 59 incidents per 1,000 students ages twelve to eighteen (Dinkes et al., 2006).

A Spectrum of Violent Behaviors in School. Despite widespread concerns about youth violence, most youth homicides occur away from school, with homicide of a school aged child being 50 times more likely to occur away from school than in school (Dinkes et al., 2006). Nevertheless, incidents of violence in schools have led children to question whether they can be safe. The concern with making schools safe has become a major policy goal at federal, state, and local levels. Schools have been working on safety and developing crisis plans now as a matter of course.

Examination of the roots of violence in schools and among young people in general reveals a spectrum of violent behaviors. Bullying and harassment, once taken for granted as part of growing up, are now seen as violent behaviors that are seriously hurtful and totally unacceptable. If left alone, they can lead to greater violence or to suicide. Schools and school personnel who are aware of the existence of such harmful conditions and fail to respond can be held liable (*Davis v. Monroe County Board of Education,* 1999; *Nabozny v. Podlesny,* 1996). Not only is this spectrum of violence dangerous and harmful to its victims and perpetrators, but the fact is that nothing can succeed in a school when members of the community feel unsafe. Hunter and Schaecher (1995), discussing lesbian and gay youths who experience harassment, pointed out that "teachers and administrators bear responsibility for [students'] lack of learning because students are forced to concentrate on surviving in the school system, rather than on their studies" (p. 1058). At this point social workers customarily work with others in the school community to create a safe school environment (see chapter 39), to develop conflict resolution and mediation programs (see chapter 39), and to assist in the provision of school-based crisis intervention for traumatic events (see chapter 34). The problem of the spectrum of violence is first of all a problem of the school community, of its policies and procedures, and of who is included and how differences are managed. Only then is it also a problem of victims, perpetrators, and their membership in the school community.

Bullying and Sexual Harassment. In Norway and Sweden, public concern about bullying was aroused when several student suicides followed experiences of chronic bullying. Other countries, such as Japan and Korea, have identified school bullying as one of their chief concerns. Studies done on bullying involving 150,000 Norwegian and Swedish students found rates of 15 percent of schoolchildren involved in bully-victim problems. When similar studies were done in the United States, the prevalence rates for bullying were at least as high or higher (Olweus, Limber, & Mihalic, 1999). The National Crime Victimization Survey for 2005 found that about 28 percent of students ages twelve to eighteen reported having been bullied in the past six months (Dinkes et al., 2006).

Peer sexual harassment is experienced by even larger numbers of young people, boys and girls alike. In a study published in 2001 by the American Association of University Women, high school students were asked whether they had experienced any of a list of things that would be considered sexual harassment. These might involve comments or actions demeaning to another's sexuality or sexual orientation, or some sort of unwanted sexual imposition, such as pulling clothing off or down. Eighty percent of students reported being sexually harassed. (American Association of University Women, 2001). In a similar study among 342 urban high school students, Fineran and Bennett (1999) found 84 percent of students were experiencing sexual harassment (87% of females and 79% of males). Seventy-five percent of students reported perpetrating sexual harassment, boys at twice the rate of girls.

Students who identify themselves as gay, lesbian, bisexual, or transgender often have the most difficult experience. GLBT students report higher rates of suicidal ideation and suicide attempts than heterosexual students (Silvenzio, Pena, Duberstein, Cerel, & Knox, 2007). This vulnerable population needs the full range of social services from policy and program development through individual intervention. However, most of all, every school must be made safe for each person in it.

Dropouts

In 2001, 86.5 percent of students completed high school. The completion rate has increased gradually since 1972, when it was 82.8 percent. However, across states there is considerable variability, ranging from 90.1 percent in North Dakota to 65 percent in Louisiana. Although gaps between white and black student completion rates narrowed in the 1970s and 1980s, no improvement has occurred since that time. In 2001, 91 percent of whites completed high school, 85.6 percent of black students who began high school eventually graduated, and 65.7 percent of Hispanic students graduated (Kaufman, Alt, & Chapman, 2004). The President's New Freedom Commission on Mental Health (2003) reported a 30 percent high school dropout rate for all students with disabilities, with the highest rate (50%) for students with serious emotional disturbance.

Parent Participation

Parent participation in promoting the social, emotional, and academic growth of children is an important factor in academic achievement. Schools cannot educate children, particularly vulnerable children, without the cooperation of families (Walberg & Lai, 1999). Research studies provide substantial evidence of the importance of "parental connectedness" in providing protection against a range of risk behaviors. Such "connectedness" involves activities of children with parents, perceived caring, and high expectations of school performance (Resnick et al., 1997). In this context, a low level of parental involvement is cause for concern. Parent participation is especially low at the secondary school level. In 2002, only 29 percent of secondary schools, compared to 70 percent of elementary schools, reported that more than half of all parents attended open houses or parent-teacher conferences. Overall, only 27 percent of schools at all levels had parent-school contracts with over half of all parents. Just 3.1 percent of schools reported that more than half of all parents were involved with instructional issues, and just 1.4 percent reported that over half of all parents participated in school governance (National Center for Education Statistics, 2002). Schools are finding that they need more active outreach to get this involvement, particularly among lower-income and vulnerable families.

FEDERAL, STATE, AND LOCAL RESPONSES

Historically the federal government has attempted to promote student achievement by addressing the needs of children challenged by adverse physical, social, and economic conditions. It has become more active in education by beginning to develop laws and standards and to fund some school reform efforts.

Head Start

Head Start provides learning activities for economically disadvantaged preschool children, comprehensive health care services, and social services such as community outreach, referrals, family needs assessments, and crisis intervention. It also promotes parental involvement in the educational process. The Head Start program, begun in 1965, is being implemented in approximately 20,050 community-based nonprofit organizations and school systems (Administration for Children and Families, 2005). Despite its acknowledged effectiveness and widespread bipartisan support, the program has never been funded at a high enough level to reach all eligible children (Barusch, 2002; Ginsburg, 1995). The 1994 amendments to Head Start established an Early Head Start program, expanding the program's benefits to families with children under age three and to pregnant women. Services include early education in and out of the home, home visits, parent education, comprehensive health and nutrition services, case management, and peer support for parents (Administration for Children and Families, 2005).

The Head Start funding stream goes directly from the federal government to local programs. At least 90 percent of children served by a Head Start program must come from families that are at or below the official federal poverty line, and 10 percent of program slots must be reserved for children with disabilities. By 2006, thirty-eight states had established state-subsidized preschool initiatives, most often for four-year-olds, that could serve low-income and other at-risk children with family incomes above the poverty line. Georgia and Oklahoma offer free prekindergarten programs to all families whose children meet the age criterion, and a number of other states are working toward full implementation of universal preschool (Barnett, Hustedt, Hawkinson, & Robin, 2006).

Individuals with Disabilities Education Improvement Act 2004

The Individuals with Disabilities Education Act, first entitled the Education for All Handicapped Children Act, and most recently reauthorized as IDEA 2004, defines the constitutional right of all children with disabilities to a free appropriate public education in the least restrictive environment. It provides a model for the relationship between policy development at the federal, state, and local school levels. It also provides a model for the possible relationship between policy development and the school social worker's role. IDEA 2004, which came into effect in July 2005, contains a number of changes from IDEA 1997. It strongly reflects the scientifically based philosophy of NCLB. It requires school personnel and special education teachers to be "highly qualified." Local education agencies (LEAs) are required to provide professional development for all school staff so that they may deliver "scientifically based academic instruction and behavioral interventions." "Adequate yearly progress," a key NCLB phrase, is one of the goals for the performance of children with disabilities. IDEA 2004 strongly emphasizes inclusion of all children in regular state and district-wide assessments and requires that alternate assessments be aligned with the state's "challenging academic content standards." IDEA 2004 states that to the extent possible, special education and related services provided to the child should be based on peer-reviewed research. IDEA 2004 stresses the importance of maintaining high academic achievement standards; clear definition of expected results in objective, measurable terms; coordination of services; and availability of qualified personnel.

IDEA 2004 also reflects a shift in attitude regarding parents. This is reflected in a broadening of the definition of parent to include foster parents, kinship caregivers, and surrogate parents. In addition, there is a stronger emphasis on requirements of school districts to provide special education services for children whose parents have placed them in private schools and on requiring states to provide Child Find and similar activities for children in parentally enrolled private schools. IDEA 2004 also takes a stand on requiring families to medicate children by prohibiting state education agencies (SEAs) and LEAs from requiring a child to obtain a prescription for substances covered by the Controlled Substances Act.

IDEA 2004 also made changes in procedures related to eligibility for special education, development of individualized education programs (IEPs), and reevaluations. It removes the requirement that tests be conducted in the child's native language. The wording of this requirement was changed to "Assessments . . . are provided and administered in the language and form most likely to yield accurate information about what the child knows and can do academically, developmentally and functionally, unless it is not feasible to do so" (Individuals with Disabilities Education Improvement Act, 2004). IDEA 2004 states that, when determining whether a child has a specific learning disability, LEAs do not have to take into consideration severe discrepancies between achievement and intellectual ability in oral expression, listening comprehension, written expression, basic reading skill, mathematical calculation, or mathematical reading. In the discussion of evaluation for eligibility for special education, the legislation also removed the language regarding "present levels of performance" (Individuals with Disabilities Education Act, 1997) and changed the wording to "present levels of academic achievement and related developmental needs of the child" (Individuals with Disabilities Education Improvement Act, 2004).

IDEA 2004 makes some changes that affect the development of IEPs. It removes the requirement for benchmarks and/or short-term objectives to be part of an IEP, except for children with disabilities who take alternate assessments aligned to alternate achievement standards. For all other children with an IEP, the requirement is for a statement of measurable annual academic and functional goals. For children who take alternate assessments, an explanation of why the alternate assessment is necessary and why the selected assessment is appropriate for the child is required. Mandatory attendance at IEP meetings may be somewhat altered by the provision that a member of the IEP team shall not be required to attend an IEP meeting if parents and the LEA agree it is unnecessary. Similarly, after an annual IEP meeting has been held, parents and the LEA may then agree not to convene a later IEP meeting to make changes. Instead, they may agree to develop a written document to amend the current IEP. IDEA 2004 also provides for alternative methods of carrying out IEP meetings, including conference calls and videoconferences. It provides for multiyear IEP demonstration projects to be made through grants to states that apply. A reevaluation must occur every three years unless the parents and the LEA agree it is unnecessary. This changes the requirement for reevaluation of a child every three years to reevaluation if the LEA determines such a need exists or if a child's parents or teachers request it. For potential due process proceedings, IDEA 2004 adds a mandatory resolution session that must occur within fifteen days of a complaint.

In IDEA 2004, when there is consideration of disciplinary actions, the school district's burden to prove that behavior was not a manifestation of a child's disability has been removed. Similarly, if parents refuse evaluation of a child for eligibility for special education, the LEA is not deemed to have knowledge of a disability.

Elementary and Secondary Education Act Reauthorization: No Child Left Behind Act

The Elementary and Secondary Education Act (ESEA) was originally enacted in 1965. Its primary aim, through Title I, was to assist states in providing compensatory education to low-income, educationally disadvantaged children. The Improving America's Schools Act of 1994 amended ESEA to emphasize the need for children in Title I programs to attain the same high standards of performance demanded of students in the general population. Services were extended to teen parents, migratory children, neglected or delinquent youths in state institutions, and children in community day programs. There were also new opportunities for schools to operate schoolwide programs (serving all children in high-poverty schools), participation of private school students, and coordination of education with health and social services.

The 2001 ESEA reauthorization, the No Child Left Behind Act, was signed into law on January 5, 2002, by President George W. Bush. Considered the most sweeping reform of ESEA since its enactment, the act embodied the four basic principles of President Bush's education reform plan: stronger accountability for results, expanded flexibility and local control, expanded options for parents, and an emphasis on teaching methods that have been proved to work, such as evidence based approaches to the teaching of reading and empirically based curricular changes in teacher training programs. It extended the Title I program and increased federal funding for education. The act mandated an annual assessment of student progress in reading and in math through testing of students in grades 3 through 8, beginning in the 2004–2005 school year. These results, when disaggregated by school, by district, by state, by race, and by gender, were expected to create an accountability system, an annual report card on school performance and on statewide progress. If a school is identified as failing over a number of years, parents are allowed to transfer their child to a different school. There is money available for supplemental services for children in failing schools, for reading programs, and for charter schools. Other parts of the law are geared to enhancing the flexibility of LEAs in developing their own programs and policies. For example, ESEA money can be transferred to different related programs without separate approval (House-Senate Education Conference Report, 2001). In contrast to strictly regulated categorical programs of previous ESEAs, the focus of NCLB is on outcomes and increased flexibility for SEAs and LEAs. Counseling and school social work services are supported. The act recommended a ratio of one school social worker to eight hundred students (Mandlawitz, 2002).

This legislation promised to make profound changes to the federal-state-local relations in American education. In some ways, the LEA and the school community behind it have become even more important. There is a delicate balancing act between the SEA and the federal government. With the emphasis on local innovation, school social workers might have an opportunity to help students and their families deal with some of the source conditions behind underachievement. The possible empowerment of parents and school communities and the development of community resources may be particularly important for school social workers in communities where schools are failing. On the other hand, without effective programs of assistance for students and their families, the development of high-stakes accountability systems may have negative results, addressing the symptoms rather than the underlying problems. The dangers of grade retention and dropout are now even greater for nonachieving youngsters. Some states have tended to shift nonachievers into special education, avoiding counting them with the general education population. Schools that have succeeded in these systems have done so through the promotion of intensive learning, professional development for teachers, and targeted supports for students.

They looked at how particular students were learning and supported them with adaptive education strategies (Darling-Hammond, 2002).

According to *Education Week*, state tests have demonstrated improvement in children's academic achievement since the implementation of NCLB (Hoff, 2007). Thirty-seven of forty-one states with three years of data reported gains in reading, and twenty-nine of forty-one states reported gains in mathematics.

THE STATE EDUCATION AGENCY AND THE LOCAL EDUCATION AGENCY

Devolution from the Federal to the State Level

The emergent federal-state relationship "devolves" a certain amount of discretion to SEAs. In the Individuals with Disabilities Education Act and the No Child Left Behind Act, the federal level remains active in setting general goals and standards, and to some extent in funding them. SEAs, in turn, set standards for achievement of pupils in the local school districts, and they develop statewide testing. They develop regulations and procedures to conform to national standards, such as in the area of education of children with disabilities. States have adopted a variety of strategies to improve local education, including developing statewide testing programs; increasing efforts to prepare students for jobs; recruiting better educators; promoting family, community, and business involvement; making schools safer; and increasing access to computers. States have adopted statewide standards for student learning and statewide testing systems (Darling-Hammond, 2002). As these and other innovations are implemented, state and local governments are facing additional challenges brought about by devolution. For example, the Personal Responsibility and Work Opportunity Reconciliation Act of 1996, which is known as the Welfare Reform Act, gives states the primary responsibility for meeting the needs of low-income children and families. This includes making key decisions about welfare benefit levels, eligibility criteria, work requirements, time limits on receipt of assistance, and exemptions. Some states have, in turn, passed this responsibility on to individual counties.

Despite the increased activism of the SEA, the LEA remains the point of origin for the actual policies governing pupils and school personnel. In the United States, education is locally controlled; there are 97,382 schools, all of which jealously guard their independence and decision-making power (National Center for Education Statistics, 2007b). Working hand in hand at both the LEA and the SEA levels, school social workers have learned that professional survival depends on their influence on school policies.

State Reform: School Finance

Another area of intense activity, intended to address one of the primary barriers to student achievement, has been the area of school finance. The exact nature of the relationship between educational spending and student achievement is a matter of some controversy. Yet it is undeniable that financial resources contribute in important ways to the ability of the educational system to maximize student success. Even more than family poverty, schools with high concentrations of poverty are associated with adverse student outcomes (Kennedy, Jung, & Orland, 1986, as cited in Terman & Behrman, 1997). High rates of poverty and low rates of school funding conspire to strongly affect student achievement (Dahl & Lochner, 2005). This is particularly acute in urban school districts, where the cost of educating children is highest. Resource discrepancies affect the entire educational climate, including the quality of buildings and facilities, equipment and technology, and curriculum materials; availability of gifted and talented or extended-day programs; teacher salaries; teacher training; and teacher-student ratios (Biddle, 1997). Teachers in high-poverty schools report more student misbehavior, disruption, weapons, and violence; more absenteeism; and less parental involvement in education. Racial and ethnic minority students are more likely to attend high-poverty schools and thus are particularly disadvantaged by resource discrepancies (Smith, Young, Bae, Choy, & Alsalam, 1997).

The major questions are whether this arrangement is fair to all students and whether there is an acceptable remedy. The U.S. Supreme Court rejected the notion of a constitutional right to equality of education (*San Antonio Independent School District v. Rodriguez,* 1973), passing the issue of equity over to states and to their constitutions. Courts in over forty states have reviewed the question of whether, in light of a school finance arrangement largely dependent on property taxes, their own educational systems are in accord with their state constitutions. The lawsuits have focused on the adequacy of educational opportunity or the equity of resource distribution. Many of these challenges have been successful. These lawsuits continue to serve as catalysts for states to examine, refine, and in some cases redesign their school financing schemes, but the results have been inevitably uneven.

Sources of Funds

Historically, education was financed almost exclusively by local property taxes. Over time, this system became increasingly inequitable, with wealthier districts enjoying the dual advantages of a larger tax base and fewer school-age children among whom the proceeds must be spread. After the Depression, state governments dramatically increased their contributions. Drawing on state income and sales taxes, they now match local government in their overall share of education spending (Howell & Miller, 1997). On average, schools receive 46 percent of their funding from state funds and 37 percent from local governments (CBIA Education Foundation, 2005).

The federal financial contribution to education, though well publicized, remains quite small at approximately 8.2 percent (CBIA Education Foundation, 2005). It primarily takes the form of categorical assistance to aid schools in meeting the needs of specific populations of children, such as those with disabilities or the economically disadvantaged (Howell & Miller, 1997). On a national average, elementary and secondary schools receive approximately half of all locally generated taxes. Yet individual states vary considerably in the degree to which they rely on federal, state, and local funding. Data from 1995–1996 show Hawaii, for example, drawing 8.1 percent of its educational budget from federal funds, 90 percent from state funds, and only about 2 percent from local funds. New Hampshire, on the other hand, uses 5.1 percent federal funds, 49 percent state funds, and 46 percent local funds. Mississippi shows the greatest reliance on federal funds, at 15 percent (U.S. Census Bureau, 2003). As a general rule, wealthier states and districts derive more of their educational budgets from local taxes, while poorer states and districts rely more heavily on state and federal funds. Some states are also turning to new sources of revenue, including proceeds from lotteries, private payments, contributions, and corporate sponsorships. The allocation of educational dollars is very similar across jurisdictions. Typically, 61.5 percent is spent on instruction; 34.3 percent goes to support services, including administration, school social workers, school nurse, and maintenance; and 4 percent is for non-instructional services, such as lunch programs (National Center for Education Statistics, 2004).

Discrepancies in Spending

Although overall spending per pupil has increased over time in the United States, discrepancies in school funding—between states, between districts within a state, and between schools within a single district—can be staggering. For example, although the average national per pupil expenditure in 2000–2001 was $8,589, New Jersey spent an average of $12,485 per pupil, while Utah spent an average of only $5,578 per pupil (National Center for Education Statistics, 2003).

The story told by these numbers is complicated by the fact that equity is a difficult concept to define. The nation's 14,000 school districts vary tremendously in both size and composition; some have concentrations of students who are considerably more costly to educate because of poverty, disability, mobility, or limited English proficiency. For example, the state of Washington has reported that it costs 18 percent more to educate a student with limited English proficiency than the average per pupil expenditure (Bergeson, Mayo, Wise, Gomez, Malagon, & Bylsma, 2000). In terms of students with disabilities, although some federal assistance is provided through IDEA, it covers only about 19 percent of the actual costs of educating these children (Samuels, 2005). Per pupil expenditures for students who receive special education services are 1.91 times greater than costs to educate students without disabilities. Costs are 3.1 times higher for students with multiple disabilities than for regular education students. When students are placed in nonpublic schools or other agencies, the cost rises to 3.9 times that of a regular education student (Chambers, Skolnik, & Perez, 2003). This has a particularly strong impact on schools with high concentrations of children living in poverty, because poor children are more likely to be diagnosed as having a disability (Terman & Behrman, 1997).

Legal Remedies

Since the mid-1960s, courts in many states have entertained lawsuits based on the inequitable distribution of resources across school districts. Arizona was the first state in which the court found the school finance system unconstitutional because it failed to provide equitably for the construction and maintenance of school buildings. Other states where the school financing scheme has been found in violation of the state constitution include Arkansas, California, Connecticut, New Jersey, Washington, West Virginia, Wyoming, Kentucky, Montana, New Jersey, Texas, Arizona, Massachusetts, and Tennessee. Litigation around school finance continues in Florida, Louisiana, New Hampshire, North Carolina, Pennsylvania, South Carolina, and Virginia. One case resulted in a single school district (Los Angeles Unified) agreeing to equalize spending across its 564 individual schools (Augenblick, Myers, & Anderson, 1997). In the vast majority of cases, states have attempted to remedy financing inequities by increasing their overall educational budgets and targeting the increased resources to low-spending districts. This way, they are able to avoid taking resources away from higher-spending districts. In most cases, budgets are being enlarged through increases to the state's contribution, and through requirements for increased local contributions or rewards to school districts that make a strong local tax effort.

LOCAL INITIATIVES IN EDUCATION: SOCIAL SERVICES AND HEALTH CARE

There have been a plethora of changes in the educational, health care, and social services sectors, and these are influencing the practice of school social work. Schools are experimenting with various innovations in pursuit of better educational outcomes. New models of delivering a variety of services to children and families are emerging, most of these at the local level. School systems at the state and local levels are introducing a variety of nontraditional measures in the hope that these will raise student standards of achievement. Charter schools and vouchers, for example, are both designed to increase parental choice. Other examples include contracting with private for-profit corporations and the use of single-sex classes and school uniforms.

Charter Schools

Finn (1994) defined charter schools as "independent public schools, often run by a group of teachers or parents, innovative or traditional in content, and free from most regulations and external controls" (p. 30). Most charter schools emphasize a particular academic philosophy ranging from back-to-basics to newer pedagogical approaches. Charter schools are regulated at the state level and face a number of complex financial, governance, regulatory, and management challenges (Koppich, 1997). Minnesota was the first state to enact charter school legislation in 1991. In March 1998, twenty-nine states and the District of Columbia had charter school laws. As of April 2008, there are 3,924 charter schools nationwide, with the largest number of charter schools in California (494), Arizona (492), Florida (299), Texas (295), Ohio (245), and Michigan (239) (National Center for Education Statistics, 2007a).

Voucher Programs

Koppich (1997) defines vouchers as "government payments to households, redeemable only for tuition payments at authorized private schools" (p. 105). Vouchers are extremely controversial because private schools can select which students they will accept, thereby potentially leaving only the most disadvantaged or disabled students in the public schools. The question of whether vouchers violate the constitutional requirement of separation of church and state was addressed in the 2002 Supreme Court case *Zelman v. Simmons-Harris*. The Court ruled that the Cleveland, Ohio, voucher plan was constitutional even though 96 percent of children in the program were enrolled in religiously affiliated schools. Eighty-two percent of private schools in the United States are religiously affiliated.

Contracting for Services and Privatization

This involves the use of public education funds to purchase services from for-profit or not-for-profit organizations in the private sector. The most controversial form involves hiring for-profit firms to manage entire public schools. A private Minnesota-based firm, Education Alternatives Incorporated, contracted with the city of Baltimore in 1992 to operate nine public schools, but the contract was canceled after three-and-a-half years of its expected five-year period. Education Alternatives Incorporated also operated schools in Hartford, Connecticut, and Dade County, Florida neither of which was effective in improving academic outcomes.. Another national for-profit firm, the Edison Project, is managing schools in twenty states and claims positive results (Edison Schools, n.d.).

School-Linked Services

The emergence of new models of delivering health and social services to children and families is also changing the context of school social work (Franklin & Gerlach, 2006). In January 1994 more than fifty national organizations concerned with the well-being of children, youths, and families gathered in Washington, D.C., and reached a consensus regarding principles for developing integrated service systems. The concluded that such systems should be community based, school linked, family centered, culturally competent, comprehensive, and prevention focused. They should also feature ongoing needs assessment and program evaluation and should be collaborative in nature, merging categorical funding streams for the most efficient service delivery to families and children. Usually called school-linked services, these models are discussed in some detail in chapter 8 and chapter 30. They were developed in response to two forces. First was the recognition that many students were at risk of educational failure because of complex economic, social, and psychological problems (National Commission on Children, 1991). Second was the concern that services delivered to children and families in general are insufficient. The delivery system is fragmented, difficult to access, confusing, and uncoordinated. In school-linked comprehensive strategies, schools are no longer isolated providers of a single-component education for children and youths. They are active partners in a broader effort. As partners, schools have increased cooperation, communication, and interaction with parents, community groups, service providers and agencies, local policy makers, and other stakeholders (U.S. Department of Education, 1996).

There are many models of school-linked services based at the local school level. Some are called full-service schools; others are called family resource centers, or one-stop shopping centers (Hare, 1995). Another model is the school-based health center. Once considered controversial, these centers, first established in Dallas, Texas, and St. Paul, Minnesota, in the 1970s, now total 1,500 in forty-five states and Washington, D.C. The centers provide comprehensive physical and mental health services to underserved youths in high schools (41%), middle schools (12%), combined middle-high schools (5%), elementary schools (30%), combined elementary and middle schools (7%), and combined K–12 schools (5%) (National Assembly on School-Based Health Care, 2000). These various models of school-linked services provide both an opportunity and a challenge to school social workers. Often they bring social workers and other professionals from community agencies, both public and private, into the schools. Ironically, problems of communication and coordination have arisen between practitioners hired by outside agencies and those employed by the school. School social workers must be proactive in overcoming such problems because they are "strategically placed to act as bridges connecting agencies and schools, to provide a glue factor in collaborative work" (Pennekamp, 1992, p. 126).

FACTORS AFFECTING SCHOOL SOCIAL WORK TODAY

A number of the societal changes affecting school social work today are leading to a need for specialization. Medicaid (Title XIX of the Social

Security Act) funding for students living in poverty is being used in many school systems to finance social work services covered under the early and periodic screening, diagnosis, and treatment or the targeted case management provisions of the law (Farrow & Joe, 1992). This requires that school social workers have clinical credentials enabling them to be recognized as providers of Medicaid-funded services. NCLB calls for "highly qualified" school personnel, including school social workers, and IDEA 2004 echoes the call for high qualifications. These developments suggest an increased need for concentrations in school social work at the graduate level and for post-MSW supervision, mentorship, licensure, and certification requirements for school social workers. While these elements are present in some states, national trends are pressing all states to move forward toward school social work specialization (Constable & Alvarez, 2006).

All the developments described above reflect a shift in school policy development to the local level, even a belief that "a substantial part of budgeting, decision making, and accountability should occur at the level of individual schools, rather than at the school district level" (Guthrie, 1997, p. 37). Whether school social work survives and flourishes in this environment will depend on whether school social workers can articulate the connection between the social, personal, and educational process.

School social workers are school employees who are paid for by educational dollars. They must project their image not only as providers of clinical services to individual students and their families, but also as informed change agents with contributions to make to crafting policies and programs in the LEA. They must be able to define their contribution to the educational mission of the school. They must assist in translating education policies emanating from various levels—federal, state, or local—into effective, outcome-oriented programs in individual schools. New service models require that they enhance their team-building skills, both with other school professionals and with other social workers and members of other disciplines entering the school from the community. They must learn the skills required for collaboration and services integration. They must learn to become experts in community and school needs assessments.

References

"Achievement gap." (2004, September 10). *Education Week.* Retrieved May 31, 2007, from http://www2.edweek.org/rc/issues/achievement-gap/?levelId=1000&

ACT. (2007). *Facts about the ACT.* Retrieved May 31, 2007, from http://www.act.org/news/aapfacts.html

Administration for Children and Families. (2005). *Head Start: Fact sheet.* Retrieved March 24, 2005, from http://www.acf.hhs.gov/programs/hsb/research/2005.htm

Allegretto, S. (2006). *U.S. government does relatively little to lessen child poverty rates.* Economic Snapshots. Washington, DC: Economic Policy Institute. Retrieved July 11, 2007, from http://www.epinet.org/content.cfm/webfeatures_snapshots_20060719

Allen-Meares, P. (2006). One hundred years: A historical analysis of social work services in schools. *School Social Work Journal, 30*(3), 24–43.

Altshuler, S. J., & Schmautz, T. (2006). No Hispanic student left behind. *Children & Schools, 28*(1), 5–12.

American Association of University Women Educational Foundation. (2001). *Hostile hallways:* Bullying, teasing, and sexual harassment in schools. Washington, DC: Author.

Astor, R. A., Marachi, R., & Benbenishty, R. (2007). Violence in schools. In P. Allen-Meares (Ed.), *Social work services in schools* (5th ed., pp. 145–181). Boston: Pearson/Allyn & Bacon.

Augenblick, J. G., Myers, J. L., & Anderson, A. B. (1997). Equity and adequacy in school funding. *Future of Children: Financing Schools, 7*(3), 63–78.

Barnett, W. S., Hustedt, J. T., Hawkinson, L. E., & Robin, K. B. (2006). *The state of preschool 2006: State preschool yearbook.* Rutgers, NJ: National Institute for Early Education Research.

Barusch, A. S. (2002). *Foundations of social policy: Social justice, public programs, and the social work profession*. Itasca, IL: F. E. Peacock.

Bergeson, T., Mayo, C. L., Wise, B. J., Gomez, R., Malagon, H., & Bylsma, P. (2000). *Educating limited English-proficient students in Washington State.* Olympia: Washington Office of the State Superintendent of Public Instruction. (Eric Document Reproduction Service No. Ed 451311).

Biddle, B. J. (1997). Foolishness, dangerous nonsense, and real correlates of state differences in achievement. *Ph Delta Kappan, 79*(1), 9–13.

Black, S. (2005). Acing the exam. *American School Board Journal, 192*, 35–39.

Bybee, R. W., & Stage, E. (2005). No country left behind. *Issues in Science & Technology, 21*(2), 69–76.

Burt, M. R. (2007, June 19). *Understanding homeless youth: Numbers, characteristics, multisystem involvement, and intervention options.* Testimony before the U.S. House Committee on Ways and Means Subcommittee on Income Security and Family Support.

CBIA Education Foundation. (2005). *10 facts about K–12 education funding*. Retrieved March 26, 2005, from http://www.cbia.com/ed/NCLB/10facts.htm

Centers for Disease Control and Prevention. (2007.) *Injury center*. Retrieved July 6, 2007, from http://www.cdc.gov/ncipc/wisqars/

Chambers, J. G., Skolnik, J., & Perez, M. (2003). *Total expenditures for students with disabilities, 1999–2000*. Palo Alto, CA: American Institute for Research in the Behavioral Sciences. (Eric Document No. Ed 481398).

Child Trends Data Bank. (2005). *Violent crime victimization*. Retrieved March 24, 2005, from http://www.childtrendsdatabank.org/indicators/71ViolentVictimization.cfm

Child Trends Inc. (1997). *Facts at a glance*. Washington, DC: Author.

College Board SAT. (2007). *Total group profile report*. Retrieved March 31, 2006, from http://www.collegeboard.com/prod_downloads/about/news_info/cbsenior/yr2006/national-report.pdf

Constable, R. C., & Alvarez, M. (2006). Moving into specialization in school social work: Issues in practice, policy, and education. *School Social Work Journal, 30*(3), 116–131.

Costin, L. B. (1987). School social work. In A. Minahan (Ed.), *Encyclopedia of social work* (18th ed., pp. 538–545). Silver Spring, MD: National Association of Social Workers.

Dahl, G. B., & Lochner, L. (2005). *The impact of family income on child achievement* (NBER Working Paper No. W11279). Cambridge: MA: National Bureau of Economic Research.

Darling-Hammond, L. (2002). What's at stake in high stakes testing? *Brown University Child and Adolescent Behavior Letter, 18*(1), 1, 3.

Davis v. Monroe County Board of Education, 526 U.S. 629 (1999).

DeNavas-Walt, C., Proctor, B. D., & Lee, C. H. (2006). *Income, poverty and health insurance in the United States*. Washington, DC: U.S. Bureau of the Census.

Dinkes, T., Cataldi, E. F., Kena, G., & Baum, K. (2006). *Indicators of school crime and safety: 2006* (NCES 2007-003/NCJ214262). Washington, DC: U.S. Departments of Education and Justice.

Dwyer, K., Osher, D., & Hoffman, C. C. (2000). Creating responsive schools: Contextualizing early warning, timely response. *Exceptional Children, 66*(3), 347–365.

Edison Schools. (n.d). Retrieved March 28, 2005, from http://www.edisonproject.com

Elementary and Secondary Education Act of 1965. 20 U.S.C. 6301-6304.

Farrow, F., & Joe, T. (1992). Financing school-linked integrate services. *Future of Children: School-Linked Services, 2*(1), 56–57.

Federal Interagency Forum on Child and Family Statistics. (1997). *America's children: Key national indicators of well-being*. Washington, DC: Author.

Fellmeth, R. (2005). Child poverty in the United States. Human rights. *Journal of the Section of Individual Rights and Responsibilities, 32*(1), 2–5.

Fineran, S., & Bennett, L. (1999). Peer sexual harassment and the social worker's response. In R. T. Constable, S. McDonald, & J. Flynn. (Eds.), *School social work: Practice, policy and research perspectives* (4th ed., pp. 459–477). Chicago: Lyceum Books.

Finn, C. E. (1994, October). What to do about education 2: The schools. *Commentary*, 30–37.

Foundation for Child Development. (2007). *The Foundation for Child Development child and youth well-being index (CWI), 1975–2005, with projections for 2006.* Retrieved June 29, 2007, from http://www.fcd-us.org/usr_doc/2007CWIReport-Embargoed.pdf

Franklin, C., & Gerlach, B. (2006). One hundred years of linking schools with communities. *School Social Work Journal, 31*(3), 44–62.

Germain, C. B. (2006) An ecological perspective on social work in the public schools. In R. Constable, C. R. Massat, S. McDonald, & J. P. Flynn (Eds.), *School social work: Practice, policy and research* (6th ed., pp. 28–39). Chicago: Lyceum Books.

Ginsburg, L. (1995). *Social work almanac* (2nd ed.). Washington, DC: National Association of Social Workers Press.

Greene, J. P. (2003). *Public high school graduation and college readiness rates in the United States*. New York: Manhattan Institute for Policy Research.

Guthrie, J. W. (1997). School finance: Fifty years of expansion. *Future of Children: Financing Schools, 7*(3), 24–38.

Guttmacher Institute. (2006). *U.S. teenage pregnancy statistics national and state trends and trends by race and ethnicity*. New York: Author. Retrieved July 3, 2007, from http://www.guttmacher.org/pubs/2006/09/12/USTPstats.pdf

Guttmacher Institute. (2007). *Facts on American teens' sexual and reproductive health.* Retrieved June 16, 2007, from http://www.guttmacher.org/pubs/fb_ATSRH.html

Hare, I. (1995). School-linked, integrated services. In R. L. Edwards & J. G. Hopps (Eds.), *Encyclopedia of social work* (19th ed., vol. 3, pp. 2100–2109). Washington, DC: National Association of Social Workers Press.

Hershberger, S. L., Pilkington, N. W., & D'Augelli, A. R. (1997). Predictors of suicide attempts among gay, lesbian and bisexual youth. *Journal of Adolescent Research, 12*(4), 477–497.

Hoff, D. J. (2007, June 6). "State tests show gains since NCLB." *Education Week, 26,* 1.

House-Senate Education Conference Report. (2001, December 11). *No child left behind.* Washington, DC: U.S. Department of Education.

Howell, P. L., & Miller, B. B. (1997). Sources of funding for schools. *Future of Children: Financing Schools*, 7(3), 39–50.

Hunter, J., & Schaecher, R. (1995). Gay and lesbian adolescents. In R. L. Edwards (Ed.), *Encyclopedia of social work* (19th ed., pp. 1055–1063). Washington, DC: National Association of Social Workers Press.

Individuals with Disabilities Education Act, P.L. 105-17. U.S.C. 11401 et seq. (1997).

Individuals with Disabilities Education Improvement Act. P.L. 108-446 (2004).

Improving America's Schools Act of 1994, P.L. 103-382.

Johnston, L. D., O'Malley, P. M., Bachman, J. G., & Schulenberg, J. E. (2007). *Monitoring the future national results on adolescent drug use: Overview of key findings, 2006* (NIH Publication No. 07-6202). Bethesda, MD: National Institute on Drug Abuse.

Kaiser Family Foundation. (2007, April). *President's FY 2008 budget and the State Children's Health Insurance Program (SCHIP)* (Publication No. 7635). Menlo Park, CA: Author.

Kaufman, P., Alt, M. N., & Chapman, C. (2004). *Dropout rates in the United States: 2001* (NCES 2005-046). Washington, DC: National Center for Education Statistics.

Kennedy, M. M., Jung, R. K., & Orland, M. E. (1986). Poverty, achievement and the distribution of compensatory education services (an interim report from the National Assessment of Chapter I, Office of Educational Research and Improvement, U.S. Department of Education. Washington, D.C.: U.S. Government Printing Office.

Koppich, J. E. (1997). Considering non-traditional alternatives: Charters, private contracts, and vouchers. *Future of Children: Financing Schools,* 7(3), 96–111.

Lambrew, J. M. (2007). *The State Children's Health Insurance Program: Past, present and future.* Washington, DC: Commonwealth Fund. Retrieved June 29, 2007, from http://www.commonwealthfund.org/usr_doc/991_Lambrew_SCHIP_past_present_future.pdf?section=4039.

Lewin Group & Nelson A. Rockefeller Institute of Government. (2004). *Spending on social welfare programs in rich and poor states: Key findings.* Retrieved June 1, 2007, from http://aspe.hhs.gov/hsp/social-welfare-spending04/summary.htm

Lock, J., & Steiner, H. (1999). Gay lesbian and bisexual youth risks for emotional physical and social problems: Results from a community-based survey. *Journal of the American Academy of Child and Adolescent Psychiatry, 38*(3), 297–304.

Mandlawitz, M. (2002). Government relations report. *School Social Workers Association of America Mini Bell,* 1–3.

Nabozny v. Podlesny, 92 F.3d 446 (7th Cir. 1996).

National Assembly on School-Based Health Care. (2000). *Creating access to care for children and youth: School-based health center census 1998–99.* Washington DC: Author.

National Campaign to Prevent Teenage Pregnancy. (2005). *Teen birth rates in the United States, 1940–2003*. Retrieved March 24, 2005, from http://www.Teenpregnancy.org

National Campaign to Prevent Teen Pregnancy. (2006). *Teen pregnancy and birth rates in the United States.* Retrieved July 3, 2007, from http://www.teenpregnancy.org/resources/data/pdf/STBYST06.pdf

National Campaign to Prevent Teenage Pregnancy. (2007). *Teen pregnancy and education.* Retrieved June 16, 2007, from http://www.teenpregnancy.org/wim/pdf/education.pdf

National Center for Education Statistics. (2002). *Digest of education statistics tables and numbers*. Retrieved June 17, 2007, from http://nces.ed.gov/programs/digest/d02/dt101.asp

National Center for Education Statistics. (2003). *Total and current expenditures per pupil in fall enrollment in public elementary and secondary education, by function and state or jurisdiction: 2000–01*. Retrieved March 26, 2005, from http://nces.ed.gov/programs/digest/d03/tables/dt168.asp

National Center for Education Statistics. (2004). *Revenues and expenditures for public elementary and secondary education: School year 200–2001*. Washington, DC: Author. Retrieved July 11, 2007, from http://nces.ed.gov/pubs2004/rev_exp_02/index.asp

National Center for Education Statistics. (2007a). *Number of public elementary and secondary schools in the United States and other jurisdictions with membership, by type of school and state or jurisdiction, and number and percentage of students in charter, magnet, Title I eligible, and Title I schoolwide schools, by state or jurisdiction: School year 2004–05.* Retrieved July 11, 2007, from http://nces.ed.gov/pubs2007/overview04/tables/table_2.asp?referer=list

National Center for Education Statistics. (2007b). *Numbers and types of public elementary and secondary schools from the common core of data: 2005–2006.* Washington, DC: Author.

National Commission on Children. (1991). *Beyond rhetoric: A new American agenda for children and families.* Washington, DC: Author.

No Child Left Behind Act of 2001, P.L. 107-110.

Office of the Surgeon General. (1999). *Mental health: A report of the surgeon general.* Rockville, MD: Department of Health and Human Services, U.S. Public Health Service.

Office of the Surgeon General. (2001). *Mental health: Culture, race, and ethnicity: A supplement to mental health: A report of the surgeon general.* Rockville, MD: Department of Health and Human Services, U.S. Public Health Service.

Olweus, D., Limber, S., & Mihalic, S. F. (1999). *Blueprints for violence prevention. Book nine: Bullying prevention program*. Boulder, CO: Center for the Study and Prevention of Violence.

Pear, R. (2007, July 9). Battle takes shape over expansion of insurance program. *New York Times,* p. A13.

Pennekamp, M. (1992). Toward school-linked and school-based human services for children and families. *Social Work in Education, 14,* 125–130.

Personal Responsibility and Work Opportunity Reconciliation Act of 1996, P.L. 104-193.

President's New Freedom Commission on Mental Health. (2003). *Achieving the promise: Transforming mental health care in America* (DHHS Pub. No. SMA-03-382). Rockville, MD: Author.

Rafferty, I. (2004). ACT and SAT scores remain stable in 2004. *Chronicle of Higher Education, 51*(3), A36.

Resnick, M. D., Bearman, P. S., Blum, R. W., Bauman, K. E., Harris, K. M., Jones, J., et al. (1997). Protecting adolescents from harm: Findings from the National Longitudinal Study of Adolescent Health. *Journal of the American Medical Association, 278*, 823–832.

Samuels, C. A. (2005). District "bills" government on special education costs. *Education Week, 24*, 31.

San Antonio Independent School District v. Rodriguez, 411 U.S. 1 (1973).

Silenzio, V. M., Pena, J. B., Duberstein, P. R., Cerel, J., & Knox, K. L. (2007). Sexual orientation and risk factors for suicidal ideation and suicide attempts among adolescents and young adults. *American Journal of Public Health, 97* (11), 2017-2019.

Smith, T. M., Young, B. A., Bae, Y., Choy, S. P., & Alsalam, N. (1997). *The condition of education 1997* (NCES 97-3888). Washington, DC: National Center for Education Statistics.

Snyder, H. N., & Swahn, M. H. (2004). *Juvenile suicides: 1991–1998*. Washington, DC: Office of Juvenile Justice and Delinquency Prevention. Retrieved June 3, 2005, from http://ncjrs.org/html/ojjdp/196978/contents.html

Terman, D. L., & Behrman, R. E. (1997). Financing schools: Analysis and recommendations. *Future of Children: Financing Schools,* 7(3), 4–23.

U.S. Census Bureau. (2001). *Deaths and death rates by leading cause of death: 2001*. Retrieved March 24, 2005, from http://www.census.gov/prod/2004pubs/04statab/vitstat.pdf

U.S. Census Bureau. (2003). *Public education finances*. Washington DC: Author.

U.S. Census Bureau. (2004). *Foreign-born population of the United States current population survey—March 2004 detailed tables (PPL-176)*. Retrieved June 1, 2007, from http://www.census.gov/population/www/socdemo/foreign/ppl-176.html

U.S. Census Bureau. (2007a). *Children characteristics*. Retrieved June 12, 2007 from http://factfinder.census.gov/servlet/STTable?_bm=y&-geo_id=01000US&-qr_name=ACS_2005_EST_G00_S0901&-ds_name=ACS_2005_EST_G00_&-redoLog=false&-state=st&-format=

U.S. Census Bureau. (2007b). *Population and housing narrative profile: 2005*. Retrieved June 12, 2007, from http://factfinder.census.gov/servlet/NPTable?_bm=y&-qr_name=ACS_2005_EST_G00_NP01&-geo_id=01000US&-gc_url=null&-ds_name=&-_lang=en

U.S. Census Bureau. (2007c). *Selected characteristics of the native and foreign born populations*. Retrieved June 12, 2007 at http://factfinder.census.gov/servlet/STTable?_bm=y&-geo_id=01000US&-qr_name=ACS_2005_EST_G00_S0602&-ds_name=ACS_2005_EST_G00_

U.S. Department of Education (1996). Putting the pieces together: Comprehensive, school-linked strategies for children and families. Washington D.C.: Author.

U.S. Department of Education. (1998). *Early warning, timely response: A guide to safe schools. Press report: Frequently asked questions*. Washington, DC: Author. (ERIC Document Reproduction Service No. ED418372)

U.S. Department of Health and Human Services. (1999). *The surgeon general's call to action to prevent suicide, 1999*. Washington, DC: Author.

U.S. Department of Health and Human Services. (2007). *Child maltreatment, 2005*. Washington DC: U.S. Government Printing Office.

Walberg, H. J., & Lai, J. (1999). Meta-analytic effects for policy. In G. J. Cizek (Ed.), *Handbook of educational policy* (pp. 418–454). San Diego, CA: Academic Press.

Zelman v. Simmons-Harris, 536 U.S. 639 (2002).

7

Evidence-Based Practice: Implications for School Social Work

Robert Constable
Loyola University, Chicago

Carol Rippey Massat
University of Illinois at Chicago

- Evidence-Based Practice in School Social Work
- Using Evidence of Practice Effectiveness
- The Continuing Dialogue between Research and Practice
- Theory Development in School Social Work

In light of the national requirement that school interventions reflect effective practices, an evidence-based understanding of effective programs and practice is essential. This requirement, reflected in federal policies such as the No Child Left Behind Act of 2001 and IDEA 2004, mandates an approach to decision making that is transparent, accountable, and based on consideration of current best practices concerning effects of particular interventions on the welfare of individuals, groups, and communities. It relates to the decisions of both individual practitioners and policy makers (McDonald, 2000; Soydan, 2004). Evidence-based practice (EBP) consists of (1) an individualized assessment, with a search for the best available external evidence related to the presenting concerns; (2) a decision about the extent to which the available evidence may apply to a particular individual or situation; and (3) consideration of the values and preferences of the individuals involved (Sackett et al., cited in McNeill, 2006). EBP can guide the practitioner to consider the most promising ways to intervene in a given situation, taking into consideration tasks, resources, problems, and functions. Online reviews, such as the Campbell Collaboration, for social welfare data and the Cochrane Collaboration for health care, are very useful for following ongoing development and application of research from other areas to school situations.

The ethical foundation for evidence-based practice lies in the importance of providing services for which effectiveness has been documented. Help or harm can result from intervention. "Do no harm"—that is, the avoidance of harm and the search for the greatest possibility for help—governs practice. The development of this evidence-based understanding of effective programs and practice calls for continuing dialogue between practitioners and researchers and lifelong learning.

EVIDENCE-BASED PRACTICE IN SCHOOL SOCIAL WORK

There is no question that evidence is useful for praxis; the question is how it may be used. EBP has been widely accepted across many fields of professional practice. The school social worker, while not a researcher as such, needs to understand the language, findings, and methodology of research to communicate with others in school, to develop programs, to intervene effectively, and to evaluate interventions. However, certain challenges are significant when EBP from other areas is applied to the practice of school social work. These challenges demand a nuanced approach to the translation of research findings into practice.

Development of this evidence-based understanding is particularly challenging for the field of school social work, first of all because of the complexity of the school social work role. This role integrates practice, policy, and research and requires advanced preparation. Practice is rarely one simple intervention, but a combination of interventions and a response to an unfolding process. School social work practice is carried out at the intersection of the individual with the environment. Interventions occur at multiple points of this transaction. They involve community interventions, schoolwide change, teacher consultation, groups, and one-on-one work with children and usually families. There are multiple interveners, and parents are members of the team. Well-established practice experience suggests four basic principles governing the practitioner's response to a complex change process:

1. Keep clients in charge of their changes.
2. Continue to look for the inevitable and often unexpected changes in the situation.
3. Respond to these changes, based on your ongoing assessment.
4. Respond by maintaining a steady state in pursuit of the jointly agreed-upon goals or modifying your approach and intervention.

The school is a host setting for social workers. While the school's mission is student learning, social emotional development and the learning environment profoundly influence this process. The work done by school social workers encompasses complex, multifaceted interventions that are unlikely to have been evaluated. Also, the evidence base used most for school social work practice relies heavily on the mental health field. School social workers are likely to work with mental health issues but do not limit their work to mental health. In the mental health field the evidence base is mainly related to the *DSM-IV-TR* (American Psychiatric Association, 2000) diagnoses or *ICD* (Medical Management Institute, 2008) diagnoses. Although these typologies are presented as scientific fact, a careful analysis reveals a more complex picture. Diagnoses can overlap, and distinctions between diagnoses are often unclear. Insurance reimbursement issues, based on medical necessity, may affect what diagnosis is applied. Thus, these widely accepted categories may supply a shakier foundation than it would appear and can subtly distort social work intervention. Participants in clinical trials may or may not share uniform presenting concerns. In addition, there has historically been little social work input into these typologies, and many question whether it is ethical for social workers to use them.

Two bodies of evidence guide school social work practice. First of all, there is a gradually developing body of fundamental, knowledge-building evidence based on large experimental research studies using random controls and producing quantitative data. These studies point the practitioner in general directions. And there is the evidence that emerges from the practice situation. This general evidence—these directions—has to be translated into practice in the context of education. The evidence is necessarily incomplete, and practice necessarily becomes exploratory, collaborative, and pragmatic. A danger would be limiting practice to current research-based evidence (Bensdorf, 2006; Cournoyer & Powers, 2002; see Gibbs, 2003) strongly reflecting health care effectiveness issues. In any case this would privilege the aims of basic research over therapeutic responsiveness. Both are obviously important. Practitioners step into an ever-changing, swiftly flowing stream and must respond to these changes and this unpredictability. New problems emerge as society and technology change. For example, cyberbullying was not an issue before the ready availability of cell phones, instant messaging, and text messaging. As new problems emerge, new interventions need to be developed and tested. The practitioner is a major part of this ongoing process of winnowing research findings and developing more effective methodology.

In schools, the expected outcomes, not the diagnosis, organize evidence and activity. Methods then become a set of holistic and somewhat pragmatic responses to a changing situation, assisting subjects to take charge of their realities. The sources of evidence are complex, and the energies for change demand complex alliances. For social workers, that complexity distinguishes an art, a science, and a profession from a craft.

The field of school social work has developed a wealth of clinical expertise and anecdotal evidence, a routine evaluation of practice, a body of literature relating to school social work effectiveness, and an understanding of common factors of helping. All of these can assist in the task of applying evidence of effective practice derived from other areas. Ultimately the field continues in the process of developing clearer research-based practice principles, and practitioners work to translate these principles into practice.

Outcome-Oriented Practice

Evaluation of practice is an integral part of ethical practice and complements the use of evidence-based practice. Such practice is based on a shared understanding of outcome, and outcome becomes the proximate evidence of effectiveness. Outcome-oriented practice begins with mutual goal setting by the school social worker, others on the team, pupils, and parents. These goals govern evaluation, the measurement of outcomes, and examination of their work together. The setting of shared goals makes it possible to work together despite differences, to change course when necessary, and to evaluate what has been done. Outcomes become evidence of the degree of effectiveness of the interventions undertaken. The model developed in this book is intended to allow the practitioner to work flexibly with others in a changing situation, often venturing into unknown territory and using evidence as much as possible to assist decision making.

An outcome is the expected result of an intervention. It is measurable in behaviors or attitudes, and as such, it would be the primary evidence used to evaluate any particular intervention. Defining possible outcomes is the first step in evaluative research, and in the cumulative development of evidence toward the eventual development of practice guidelines. Based on some systematic assessment of what is possible, this definition is also the necessary first step in any practice intervention. When teachers, parents, the student, the school social worker, and others in the school agree to work toward a goal, this goal legitimizes and organizes the work to be done and the roles each takes in this common effort. The team comes to agreement on what range of behaviors need to be developed, agrees to work together on them, and then sets objectives (milestones) toward the accomplishment of more general goals, together with target dates for their accomplishment. Outcomes have to be limited to what is possible, and to what members of the group, especially the student of concern, agree on and want to accomplish. They may change as the situation changes, or as a particular set of outcomes appears less possible. Once there is agreement, outcomes are converted into specific tasks, which can be evaluated at different stages of the process formatively (milestones), and then summatively at the end (chapter 26). The process keeps everyone in control of his or her part of the situation.

Goals and objectives concentrate group and individual efforts on their accomplishment. They are shared with every person involved in a group effort, and they concentrate the support needed from teacher, parents, and social worker.

Outcome-oriented practice empowers people to begin to take action on their situations. Rather than being energized by a problem, deficit or diagnosis alone, it moves away from an individual deficit model toward a more normalized, strengths-based model of education. One might focus on remedying deficits: a student's depression or anger or the teacher's anxiety. Or one might start with methodology, shaping interventions to fit a given theoretical orientation or methodology. This would exemplify Abraham Kaplan's (1964) "law of the hammer" (give a small boy a hammer, and he will find that everything he encounters needs hammering).

The alternative is to treat practice in schools as part of the larger learning situation having inherent student tasks, which can be constructed to fit the student's development and build on strengths. Outcomes and tasks give people something to work on in their own way and provide some accountability to others (chapters 17 and 22). This approach to practice, utilized over thirty years with children with disabilities in school (chapter 8), fits into the normalizing mission of education. Such practice brings together personal change processes with potential support systems. It can use all sorts of methods in pursuit of its goals. It can change and adapt them when a particular approach does not quite seem to work. Many interventions and their theoretical bases (e.g., cognitive-behavioral, learning, interactional, systems theory, consultation theory, mentoring) are possible, as long as they are appropriate to social work and could comfortably lead to the goals and objectives. Other team members, with their own orientations, would effectively broaden the interventive effort, and agencies outside the school also broaden the effort. Assessment evidence, that an intervention has worked in other situations is most important in the initial decision-making and planning processes and continues to be important through the process. Outcome-oriented practice makes a connection between a general body of evidence associated with a set of methods or problems and the more individual processes of practice. Carleton Munson (2004) makes this connection, outlining general principles governing transparent evidence-based practice:

1. An intervention should be identified by the practitioner and understood by the client.
2. An established connection between the intervention and the problem should be articulated by the practitioner (depending on developmental level, some children can make the connection).
3. The practitioner and the client should implement the intervention with reasonable effort.
4. The client should have an identifiable reason/motivation to comply with the effort.

5. Along with the proposed intervention, an alternate intervention should be identified by the practitioner.
6. Possible outcomes (intended and unintended, positive and negative) of the intervention should be identified before the intervention is applied.
7. The intervention should be observed and measured (p. 255).

Evidence of School Social Work Effectiveness

The school social work field has documentation of effectiveness to the extent that its complex and varied interventions have been studied. In chapter 3, Sabatino, Mayer, Timberlake, and Rose review the contributions school social workers make to effective schooling. They find that, across a wide array of potential outcomes, school social workers do help schools to be effective. School social workers deal with a wide range of outcomes, such as developing skills and competence in individual students, preventing dropout, improving school performance, reducing abuse, helping students resolve interpersonal conflict and develop social skills, and effecting systemic changes (e.g., building school community, promoting use of services, reduction of bullying and fighting). The methodologies tested (e.g., cognitive-behavioral methods, group skill development, assertiveness training, psycho-education, case management) are varied. Overall, despite the diversity of problem and method, Sabatino et al. show generally positive outcomes with a few mixed findings. Early and Vonk (2001), in a similar review of the effectiveness literature, also found that the field currently makes a contribution to effective schooling.

There is also evidence of effectiveness of group interventions. Groups are powerful instruments for certain types of change. The group forms a supportive bond and helps members develop self-esteem, learn to expand student thinking, and experiment with more functional behaviors. Groups can accommodate an endless variation of problems and responses to specific conditions, such as students dealing with a particular disability, adolescents exploring dating relationships, parents new to a community, and children of divorce. However, for more individual issues, groups may lack needed flexibility or response, and thus school social workers also need to do individual interventions, consultation, and case management. Group work research in schools has focused on acquisition of social skills, assertiveness training, reduction of interpersonal conflict, sexual issues and drugs, and teaching students to solve problems. Outcomes are specific, relatively easily measurable, and comparable, since the goals of the group are clearly stated in the beginning and there is a fairly standard program (chapter 33). Group outcomes are measured as a matter of course. It is not surprising that they comprise the majority of research studies published in school social work (chapter 3; Early & Vonk, 2001; Staudt, Cherry, & Watson, 2005). Problem areas that have been successfully treated with group work in a school setting include poor relationships with peers, emotional reactions in adolescence (e.g., anger, depression), substance abuse, posttraumatic stress, and delinquency (Garvin, 2006). Studies of social skills groups, which predominantly use learning theory and/or cognitive-behavioral methods, have addressed aggressive behavior, depression, anxiety and withdrawal, isolation, substance abuse prevention, teen pregnancy prevention, peer mediation for interpersonal conflict, and the needs of children with cognitive and other disabilities (see chapter 33). Short-term results of such groups have been generally positive, although there is some question of whether the very specific results achieved over the life of the group (perhaps six weeks) generalize to other behaviors or last over time.

The literature on effective schools also supports the use of school social work. School social workers are expected to help make education effective for children, and the existing literature has asked, "What factors make education effective?" These factors could not be reduced to one single intervention method or actor. Furthermore, most of the factors that make schools effective go beyond teaching methods or school resources. These include the student's motivation and capacity, the classroom learning environment, peers, and family. In any case, despite differences in family income level or the educational philosophy of the school, effective schools have certain common characteristics. They have traditionally been the focus of school social workers. Students have better achievement where there is strong instructional leadership, a safe and orderly climate, a school-wide emphasis on basic skills, high teacher expectations for student achievement, and continuous assessment of student progress (Finn,1984; Purkey & Smith, 1983).

Parents have a powerful influence on the effectiveness of schooling (chapter 29; Paik & Walberg, 2007; Walberg, 1984; Walberg & Lai, 1999). Recent research suggests that parents interact with their children along at least seven dimensions: they nurture them; they manage the home and provide a climate of language and communication; they set standards and expectations and practice discipline; they provide materials that children can use for learning and development; they monitor the child's behavior; and finally, they teach skills that allow children to survive and flourish in their environment (Kreider, 2004–2005). The climate of language, materials in the home, and direct teaching of skills are aspects of learning most linked with the child's school success. Reflecting on these seven dimensions, Jeanne Brooks-Gunn estimates that one-third to one-half of the variation in school outcomes between poor and not-poor children can be accounted for by differences in parenting (Kreider, 2004–2005). Since school social workers have traditionally been the link between schools and families, these findings reinforce the importance of school social work practice.

The economics of research currently prevents a rigorous study of the multi-method and multisystemic family-focused practice usually done by social workers. In chapter 3 one such study done by the National Institutes of Health (2005) using functional family therapy and multisystemic therapy in problems of youth violence. Both programs used an array of methods geared to the particular situations, and mainly derived from a mixture of structural family therapy and behavioral intervention. And they were quite effective, using the "gold standard" of random clinical trials, something single-method approaches are generally unable to do. In these cases there was not one method, but a variety of methods, used as appropriate responses to developments in the situations. There was intensity, a family as well as individual focus (even for adolescents), and a focus on skills and social competence. Within these broad parameters, there was no attempt to limit interventions to one method, but there were attempts to deliver their approaches with fidelity.

Common Factors of Helping

There are common factors in effective helping processes that apply across methodologies and across presenting concerns, especially the underlying factors in the client-helper relationship. These include the relational bond, the core conditions of a helping relationships (empathy, genuineness, and unconditional positive regard), clients' active work on a problem; therapists' active and positive behavior in relation to tasks, and high and positive expectancy of change. These can more powerfully explain change than a particular theoretical orientation, methodology, or technique. One can conclude that a helping *process*, as much as a particular theoretical orientation, methodology, or technique, explains outcome. Hubble, Duncan, and Miller (1999) put these findings into perspective. They found that relationship factors account for roughly 30 percent of outcomes; environmental factors account for 40 percent of outcomes; and placebo, hope, and expectancy account for 15 percent of outcomes. Factors specific to a particular intervention model account for only 15 percent of outcomes. This should not be a surprising finding, given the power of the environment (which social workers target for change) and the long-established fact that if personal change is to be successful, the client, not the therapist, needs to take charge of change. Effective practice is helping clients to take charge in an appropriate manner (Garfield, 1994; Lambert & Bergin, 1994; Orlinsky, Grawe, & Parks, 1994).

THE CONTINUING DIALOGUE BETWEEN RESEARCH AND PRACTICE

Even though we have many tools for effective practice, including the use of an existing evidence base, evaluation of practice, a body of literature on school social work effectiveness across modalities, and the power of common factors of helping, the dialogue between research and practice must continue. One important area of study has focused on the range of the school social worker's role. How can and should the school social worker be used in a school? This is an important question for school social work practitioners, for school policy makers, and for university faculty. Studies of the role of the school social worker have accumulated sufficient evidence to guide practitioners and to develop credentials and policies. For example, in response to the No Child Left Behind Act's requirements for "highly qualified" education personnel, state departments of education have been able to develop criteria for the role of the social worker to set expectations for school social work certification and licensing (Constable & Alvarez, 2006). These stated criteria will eventually have a profound effect on the preparation of practitioners for school social work as a specialization.

Effectiveness research is reviewed at different places in this book. The basic questions can be developed as follows: What evidence will be useful to social workers? How can evidence important to decision making, methodology, and the helping relationship be brought together? What social work theoretical orientations would allow the necessary evidence base to be developed and used? What factors underlying the client-helper relationship are associated with good outcomes? What approaches to practice or intervention models are associated with good outcomes for particular client groups with particular problems or needs?

Practice guidelines would eventually emerge from cumulative and systematic research on outcomes (Procter & Rosen, 2003, 2004). Intervention for children with disabilities is outcome oriented, and these outcomes govern service. Outcomes are routinely being specified and evaluated in annual reviews with the school team, the parents, and often the student. However, school services are not yet at the point where outcomes can be easily and systematically classified and compared. Research comparing these outcomes and generating practice guidelines is still to be developed.

ISSUES IN THEORY DEVELOPMENT FOR SCHOOL SOCIAL WORK

While it is critical for the dialogue between research and practice to continue, paradoxically, the major challenge of EBP is social work theory development. What is the relationship between theory and practice in school social work? What criteria would distinguish between methods appropriate for school social work practice and those clearly inappropriate for it? How would school social workers use effective methodologies drawn from other areas? The issues demand further development of theory as well as the further development of practice. Few practitioners have the time and few school systems have the resources to do this type of research by themselves. Outcome research is already important, so in each situation there should be some formative evaluations and a summative evaluation as to whether the outcome has been achieved. In this sense, school social workers are not different from teachers, school counselors, and school psychologists. Certain assumptions are just taken for granted when teams operate effectively. They operate as team members and don't assume that one member's intervention alone has made the difference. When something doesn't work, they try something else. They know that any measurement is crude. They use methods they believe to be effective, and they test outcomes according to some acceptable criteria. More than that would demand a broader involvement of the research, practice, and policy communities working together.

Clearly there are some inappropriate, although potentially beneficial, methods. The school social worker is not responsible for prescribing drugs. Nor is the worker fully responsible for outside risks. And when the worker shares responsibility with others on the team, the solo practitioner model is not appropriate. Basic criteria for practice come from the fundamental focus of school social work, intervention in the "zone where persons and environments are in transaction with each other" (Joint NASW-CSWE Task Force on Specialization, 1979), and interaction with the developed mission of education (chapter 1; Poole, 1949). We are concerned about individuals and groups of children who, for social and/or emotional reasons, are having difficulty using or benefiting from education to grow, to flourish, and to achieve their potential as relational human beings. Shifting from a deficit perspective to a strengths model, we generate tasks and outcomes. These tasks are the key to what methods are used with what units of attention—whether teachers, students, or parents—and at what point of the process. Here theory, methodology, and technique yield to art. The art of the professional is to bring together methodology and technique in relation to goals and objectives (outcomes), then in relation to a particular process and to a particular situation.

References

American Psychiatric Association. (2000). *Diagnostic and statistical manual of mental disorders* (4th ed.). Washington, DC: Author.

Bensdorf, J. W. (2006). Mental health forum: Evidence-based social work practice. *Social Work Networker, 43*(2), 6.

Constable, R., & Alvarez, M. (2006). Moving into specialization in school social work. *School Social Work Journal, 30*(3), 116–131.

Cournoyer, B. R., & Powers, G. T. (2002). Evidence-based social work: The quiet revolution continues. In A. R. Roberts & G. Greene (Eds.), *Social worker's desk reference* (pp. 798–806). Oxford: Oxford University Press.

Early, T. J., & Vonk, M. E. (2001). Effectiveness of school social work from a risk and resilience perspective. *Children & Schools, 23*, 9–31.

Elementary and Secondary Education Act of 1965, 20 U.S.C. 6301-6304.

Garfield, S. L. (1994). Research on client variables in psychotherapy. In A. E. Bergin & S. L. Garfield (Eds.), *Handbook of psychotherapy and behavior change* (pp. 190–228). New York: John Wiley.

Garvin, C. D. (2006). Designing and facilitating support groups and therapy groups for adolescents. In C. Franklin, M. B. Harris, & P. Allen-Meares (Eds.), *The school services sourcebook: A guide for school-based professionals* (pp. 587–594). New York: Oxford University Press.

Gibbs, L. E. (2003). *Evidence-based practice for the helping professions*. Pacific Grove, CA: Thomson.

Hubble, D., Duncan, B., & Miller, S. (1999). *The heart and soul of change*. Washington, DC: American Psychological Association.

Joint NASW-CSWE Task Force on Specialization. (1979). *Specialization in the social work profession* (NASW Document No. 79-310-08). Washington, DC: National Association of Social Workers.

Kaplan, A. (1964). *The conduct of inquiry: Methodology for behavioral science.* San Francisco: Chandler.

Kreider, H. (2004–2005). A conversation with Jeanne Brooks-Gunn. *Evaluation Exchange, 10*(4). Retrieved February 1, 2005, from http://www.gse.harvard.edu/hfrp/eval/issue28/qanda.html

Lambert, M. J., & Bergin, A. J. (1994). The effectiveness of psychotherapy. In A. E. Bergin & S. L. Garfield (Eds.), *Handbook of psychotherapy and behavior change* (pp. 143–190). New York: John Wiley.

McDonald, G. (2000). Evidence-based practice. In M. Davies (Ed.), *Blackwell encyclopedia of social work* (p. 123). Oxford: Blackwell.

McNeill, T. (2006). Evidence-based practice in an age of relativism: Toward a model for practice. *Social Work, 51*(2), 147–156.

Medical Management Institute. (2008). *International statistical classification of diseases and related health problems* (9th ed.). Salt Lake City, UT: Author.

Munson, C. E. (2004). Evidence-based treatment for traumatized and abused children. In A. Roberts & K. Yeager (Eds.), *Evidence-based practice manual: Research and outcome measures in health and human services* (pp. 252–262). New York: Oxford University Press.

No Child Left Behind Act of 2001, P.L. 107-110

Orlinsky, D. E., Grawe, K., & Parks, B. (1994). Process and outcome in psychotherapy—noch einmal. In A. E. Bergin & S. L. Garfield (Eds.), *Handbook of psychotherapy and behavior change* (pp. 270–378). New York: John Wiley.

Paik, S. J., & Walberg, H. J. (Eds.). (2007). *Narrowing the achievement gap: Strategies for educating Latino, black, and Asian students.* New York: Springer.

Poole, F. (1949). An analysis of the characteristics of the school social worker. *Social Service Review, 23*, 454–459.

Procter, E. K., & Rosen, A. (2003). The structure and function of social work practice guidelines. In A. Rosen & E. K. Procter (Eds.), *Developing practice guidelines for social work intervention* (pp. 108–127) New York: Columbia University Press.

Procter, E. K., & Rosen, A. (2004). Concise standards for developing evidence-based practice guidelines. In A. Roberts & K. Yeager (Eds.), *Evidence-based practice manual: Research and outcome measures in health and human services* (pp. 193–199). New York: Oxford University Press.

Purkey, S. C., & Smith, M. S. (1983). Effective schools: A review. *Elementary School Journal, 83*(4), 427–452.

Sackett, D. L., Rosenberg, W. M. C., Gray, J. A. M., Haynes, W.S., & Richardson, W. S. (1996). Evidence based medicine: What it is and what it isn't. It's about integrating individual clinical expertise and the best external evidence. British Medical Journal, 312 (7023), 71–72.

Soydan, H. (2004). [Review of the book *International perspectives on evidence-based practice in social work*]. *European Journal of Social Work*, 7(3), 385–387.

Staudt, M., Cherry, D. J., & Watson, M. (2005). Practice guidelines for school social workers: A modified replication and extension of a prototype. *Children & Schools*, *27*(2), 71–80.

Walberg, H. J. (1984). Improving the productivity of America's schools. *Educational Leadership*, *41*(8), 19–27.

Walberg, H. J., & Lai, J. (1999). Meta-analytic effects for policy. In G. J. Cizek (Ed.), *Handbook of educational policy* (pp. 418–454). San Diego, CA: Academic Press.

Section Two

Policy Practice in School Social Work

8

The School Social Worker as Policy Practitioner[1]

Carol Rippey Massat
University of Illinois at Chicago

Robert Constable
Loyola University Chicago

- The School Social Worker's Role in Policy Practice
- What are the Skills of Policy Practice?
- Policy Practice in Action
- Acting as a Change Agent
- School Reforms
- The Educational Rights of Children with Disabilities
- Models of Responsive Family-Centered School Community Services
- Implications of Reform Movements for School Social Workers

In a rural midwestern community, a large, impoverished farm family had a daughter, Sarah,[2] who had differences from other children. As she grew, her walking was delayed, and her movements stiff. Her speech development was slow and hard to understand, yet her family delighted in the bright intelligence shining in her eyes. When Sarah was six, her mother carefully dressed her in a freshly ironed school dress and sent her to school with the other children, excited about the first day of school. Within a few days, this little girl returned home with a note pinned to her dress that read, "This child cannot learn. Do

1. Richard Kordesh was a coauthor of a similar chapter in the previous edition.
2. Identifying information changed to protect confidentiality.

> not send her to school." Saddened and disappointed, the family kept Sarah at home, loving her, caring for her, and helping her to learn what she could at home. After a few years, the first teacher left the one-room school, and a new teacher was appointed. She came to visit all the families and asked, "What about this little girl? Why isn't she in school?" The mother explained about the note, and the new teacher said, "Send her to school." Despite her cerebral palsy, Sarah eventually went to college and became a special education teacher, destined to help hundreds of children with disabilities.

This true story occurred before the passage of the 1975 Education for All Handicapped Children Act (P.L. 94-142). The 1975 legislation meant that never again could children like Sarah be denied an education. The power of policy worked and continues to work to assist children with disabilities to reach their potential and to contribute to society. The *Brown v. Board of Education* (1954) Supreme Court decision had a similar sweeping impact on education, with the determination that separate education was inherently unequal. Policy in all its forms has the power to change lives, for good or for ill. Schools as social institutions are inherently linked to public policy. There is little that the school social worker does that would be unconnected with policy. This fact is basic to social work practice within the school community.

It is an ethical requirement of the profession that social workers promote social justice and social change on behalf of clients and work to end discrimination, oppression, poverty, and social injustice—to involve themselves in policy and to participate in implementing policy. The preamble to the National Association of Social Workers (1999) Code of Ethics reads, in part:

> Social workers promote social justice and social change with and on behalf of clients. "Clients" is used inclusively to refer to individuals, families, groups, organizations, and communities. Social workers are sensitive to cultural and ethnic diversity and strive to end discrimination, oppression, poverty, and other forms of social injustice. These activities may be in the form of direct practice, community organizing, supervision, consultation, administration, advocacy, social and political action, policy development and implementation, education, and research and evaluation. Social workers seek to enhance the capacity of people to address their own needs. Social workers also seek to promote the responsiveness of organizations, communities, and other social institutions to individuals' needs and social problems.

No other professionals working in schools have this professional mandate. This focus is absent in the codes of ethics of teachers, nurses, psychologists, school counselors, and school administrators.

This ethical mandate may be carried out in different forms and at different levels of the environment. It may take place through advocacy on behalf of individuals and families, through organizational change, through community development, through research, or through policy development at the school, community, state, or federal level. In school social work these methods come to fruition in the mission of making the educational process effective for children who are having difficulty using what schools offer.

There are two narratives that interact and shape school social work policy practice. First is the narrative of social work, with its professional purposes, its values, its paradigm of the transactions of persons with their environments, and its methods developed over a century of practice, theory, and research development. Second, there is the narrative of schools: developing greater inclusiveness, and beginning to adapt themselves to individual differences, yet seeking to meet the demands of a multinational economy for high levels of education for individual and national survival. While progress is being made toward universal basic education, there are obstacles that prevent many children from having access to education and from using it well. School social work, which is developing throughout the world because the demands on education have amplified, seeks to deal with these obstacles (Huxtable & Blyth, 2002). Internationally, there is an increasingly level playing field provided by information technologies, and in every country economic survival is related to education (Friedman, 2005). Education has become the key to social development (Midgeley, 1997). With greater demands for educational achievement, American school reform is shifting toward outcome-based education, implementation of higher standards for school personnel, and greater accountability for effective practice. For school social workers, state education agencies (SEAs) are beginning to require specialized preparation prior to employment and a period of performance assessment for school social workers afterward (Constable & Alvarez, 2006). There is also a movement toward national certification of school social workers (Alvarez & Harrington, 2004).

THE SCHOOL SOCIAL WORKER'S ROLE IN POLICY PRACTICE

Schools and families hold the keys to the participation of future generations in society. Schools face social injustice in the form of economic inequality, inequitable school funding, racial and ethnic school segregation, gender inequities, sexual harassment, and oppression of marginalized groups. Chapters 15 and 16 expand upon the historic struggle in the United States to rectify inequities in education for racial and ethnic minorities, women, and sexual minorities. These two chapters also describe the policies that have attempted to address these issues. Through law, policy, and case law (court decisions), groups have engaged in a long struggle to eradicate social injustice in schools. Recognizing the power of policy and law, those forces seeking to limit others' potential have created policy and legislation to prohibit the education of minorities, to limit the right to vote to the favored few, and to limit funding for the education of minority or impoverished students. Others, also recognizing the power of policy, have crafted policies to combat segregation, to eliminate discrimination, and to provide opportunities to those who have been denied them.

A school social worker's inherent possibilities for involvement in the creation and implementation of policy at the school, community, local, state, and federal levels permit client group advocacy and engagement in this historic struggle. This section of the book is intended to give school social workers the background and tools to be policy practitioners. We describe skills and information needed to carry out policy practice. We define the context for policy practice by school social workers, the role of the school social worker in policy practice, and the skills and competencies for policy practice, with examples of policy reform. In the following chapters, we seek to provide the reader with an understanding of the steps of policy practice. First, the policy practitioner seeks information on the existing situation. Chapter 9 applies organizational analysis to school change processes. Chapter 10 provides an analytic framework for the analysis of educational policy. Chapter 11 describes the use of needs assessments to learn about the needs of schools and communities. Chapter 12 describes the use of research as a tool of change. The final four chapters in this section provide information on the history of relevant policy development and existing policies that affect our most vulnerable clients in schools, including children with disabilities and members of oppressed populations.

The role of the school social worker includes participation in program and policy development at the local school and community levels. This broad (Essex & Massat, 2006) role demands a deep understanding of the school as an organization, of policy analysis, and of research geared to program development and evaluation. For school social workers, policy development needs to take place in the SEA as well as in the school community. However, social policy has traditionally been pictured as national policy, far from the vital areas where much of school social work policy is developed, and so there can be a disconnect between theory and practice. Traditionally, policies are pictured as developing through federal, state, and local statutory, regulatory, and case law that are implemented from the top down. But this is only one part of policy and program development in school social work. At the federal and state levels, laws and policies may prescribe and suggest common goals and means. However, it is up to the grassroots level; the level of implementation; and the level of the school community, the local education agency (LEA), and each school to develop ways to carry out policies and develop programs.

Although policy is always embedded in practice, practice theory usually has been pictured as developing in a separate orbit. Where this connection is not acknowledged, there would appear to be little basis for a real practitioner role in policy development. Where there is no possibility of changing the contexts that shape it, practice becomes less effective. Furthermore, the limits of policies that prescribe but do not implement are becoming all too clear. Any such policy's success depends on the real environment of service and the capabilities of those implementing it. Some policies exist mainly on paper because no one has found a way to implement them successfully. Others may even work against their initial purposes. For example, a national dress code for schools would not likely be helpful to local schools. Regional variation, local and school commitment to school colors, and other factors would render such a policy useless. However, many schools have developed dress codes that meet their specific needs in addressing gang control, issues of class, and school solidarity.

School social workers do participate in policy and program development, particularly in the school community. Indeed, practice itself often creates policy. There are thus two necessary directions of policy development—from the top down, often expressed as public policy, and from the bottom up, often expressed as locality development. The inherently complex organization of each school makes room for policy practice, even at the local school level. Policies may originate from grassroots programs that resonate with needs and empower consumers to take action on those needs. Initiatives may develop as experiments from points where need and service are defined. In developing programs to meet the needs of the school community, school social workers are both developing and implementing policies. School social workers are well situated to have access to both levels.

For school social workers, the common thread in all of this is a need to understand the language and theory of policy as well as of practice. For example, it is part of the school social worker's role to help develop and implement crisis plans as a member of the school crisis team. A crisis plan is both policy and practice. Social workers work with teachers, parents, and pupils to create solutions to include youngsters with disabilities in general education classes. In all these areas, school social workers and the school team develop programs that make the implementation of policy possible. Since social workers work in the most difficult areas of education, their role can become an innovative one that goes beyond the givens of the institution or the situation. The distance from such innovation to policy and program development is not great. The two directions of policy, from the top down and from the bottom up, are beginning to mesh, particularly in recent legislation and school reform initiatives. It is important that school social workers see policy and program development as their participation in the school's active response in its own community context to societal conditions and to mandates. When school social workers have the freedom to develop their role, the school can become more responsive to societal and community conditions, as these inevitably affect the educational process (Meenaghan & Gibbons, 2000; Meenaghan & Kilty, 1994).

WHAT ARE THE SKILLS OF POLICY PRACTICE?

Bruce Jansson (2003) spells out an action framework for policy analysis and development of tasks and skills necessary for effective policy practice.

There are six components in his framework, applied here to school social work policy practice and developed further in this section. One component that must be included in a policy framework for practice must be the *context* of the policy. John Flynn describes a framework that includes careful analysis of policy context in chapter 10. The context includes the location of the policy and its bases for legitimacy. Is it a local, school, community, state, or federal policy? Is it based on legislation, case law, or regulations? What is the state of communication, and what are the boundaries of the system in which this policy occurs? What authority is needed to carry out this policy? Second, what is the *perspective* of stakeholders and policy advocates? Stakeholders, or those with a "vested interest in a specific policy or issue being contested" (Jansson, 2003, p. 70), can include members of interest groups, advocacy groups, administrators, and consumers. Their interests are further outlined in chapter 10. The third element of Jansson's framework is the patterns of participation in a given policy. The fourth is the identification of key tasks that policy advocates undertake. The fifth is identification of the fundamental skills of policy advocates, and the sixth is the identification of key competencies of policy advocates.

There are six tasks that are necessary in policy practice. Several of these tasks may occur at the same time rather than in a step-by-step progression.

1. In the *agenda setting task* practitioners gauge whether the context is favorable for a policy initiative, and they develop early strategies to place it on agendas of policy makers.
2. In the *problem-analyzing task*, practitioners analyze the causes, nature, and prevalence of specific problems.
3. In the *proposal-writing task*, practitioners develop solutions to specific problems. Proposals may be relatively ambitious, such as a piece of legislation, or relative modest, such as incremental change in existing policies.
4. In the *policy enacting task*, practitioners try to have policies approved or enacted. . . . Policy practitioners continue to work even after policy enactment when they undertake the *policy implementing task* in which they try to carry out enacted policies. . . . Policy practitioners evaluate programs when they undertake the *policy-assessing task* by obtaining data about the implemented policy's performance. (Jansson, 2003, p. 73)

In chapters 9, 10, and 11, several tools for policy analysis are described: organizational analyses, use of a policy analysis framework, and needs assessment. In chapters 13, 14, 15, and 16, information on existing policies is given as part of the policy context for practice. In chapter 12 the use of research as part of the role of the change agent is described. Research skills assist in the analysis of the needs of groups and organizations, and in carrying out ongoing evaluations of programs and policies and in carrying out outcome studies.

There are four skills school social workers need for policy practice.

1. They need *analytic skills* to evaluate social problems and develop policy proposals, to analyze the severity of specific problems, to identify the barriers to policy implementation and to develop strategies for assessing programs.
2. They need *political skills* to gain and use power and to develop and implement political strategy.
3. They need *interactional skills* to participate in task groups, such as committees and coalitions, and to persuade other people to support specific policies
4. And they need *value clarifying skills* to identify and rank relevant principles. (Jansson, 2003, p. 74)

Skills needed for policy analysis are described in chapters 9, 10, 11, and 12. The political and interactional skills needed for policy practice by school social workers are inherent in the tasks of collaboration by members of a school team. No school social worker is able to bring about policy change alone. Fortunately, these skills are comfortable ones for school social workers, who develop strong communication and interactional skills as part of their foundation and specialized training.

Competencies needed for policy practice include political competencies, analytic competencies, interactional competencies, and value clarifying competencies (Jansson, 2003). *Political competencies* include the ability to use mass media, take personal positions, seek positions of power, empower others, orchestrate pressure on decision makers, find funding, use personal power, donate time and resources, advocate for clients, participate in demonstrations, initiate litigation, and work on political change. Most of these activities can be carried out by school social workers as part of their professional role. However, some of them must be carried out during a school social worker's personal time. For example, working on a political campaign during working hours would be considered unethical for public school employees. Initiating litigation is also unlikely to be appropriate for a school social worker.

Analytic competencies include developing proposals, calculating tradeoffs, using existing research, using the Internet, budgeting, finding funding, designing presentations, diagnosing implementation barriers, developing political strategies, analyzing policy contexts, and designing policy assessments (Jansson, 2003). *Interactional competencies* include coalition building, making presentations, building personal power, forming task groups, and managing conflict. The competency of *value clarification* involves ethical reasoning to determine the identity and relative importance of values driving policy development and implementation.

A most important skill in policy development is the ability to work with others who may have different beliefs and investments in the policy development process. No policies are ever developed by one person. Policy development is often a matter of having the right connections with possible allies in a common effort. This political process means that none of the participants in change efforts will get all that they want. Policy development is often a matter of the right timing, the right place, the right network, and the will to overcome inevitable obstacles, to compromise, and to get things done. Social workers can apply all the skills they learn from other sectors of their practice to the development of a vision of how things might be, the will to get things accomplished with others, and the flexibility to develop a workable common proposition and then develop fallback positions when these initially fail. Here the work they could do in the school and in the school community is analogous to what they could do in larger forums, such as helping to develop state educational policy in relation to a particular issue.

POLICY PRACTICE IN ACTION

The school social worker can carry out policy practice as an individual, or as a change agent in an organization. As individuals, school social workers should maintain memberships in professional and advocacy organizations, such as state school social work organizations, the School Social Work Association of America, the National Association of Social Workers, and other relevant groups. Such organizations maintain websites and offer publications that include information on legislative updates and policy issues of concern to social workers so that pending legislation, policy changes, and court cases of interest can be easily accessed. Such groups also maintain easy-to-use links to respond to these issues through e-mail or phone calls to legislators. Subscriptions to Internet sites such as edweek.org also provide rapid notification of issues relevant to school social work. It is critical that school social workers know the identity and contact information for their state and federal representatives and senators, as well as local government and school board members. As a citizen, a school social worker may also choose to run for public office, run for a seat on a local school board, or participate directly in forums for policy development.

As citizens with an ethical responsibility to advocate social justice, school social workers should be prepared to write letters to newspapers, legislators, and other policy makers; to make phone calls supporting or rejecting policy initiatives; and to meet with policy makers.

Haynes and Mickelson (2003) have written an excellent guide for social work advocacy and policy practice. The reader may want to consult their book to learn more about how to carry out a wide range of policy practice activities. The following discussion will touch upon a number of options available to the school social worker.

A carefully crafted letter to a policy maker is an important tool of policy advocacy. A letter or e-mail written about a policy should be legible and no longer than one page. The writer should identify him- or herself and state the subject in the first paragraph. Only one issue should be addressed per letter. The specific issue or bill number should be clearly identified. In the second paragraph, an opinion should be clearly stated, as well as reasons for that opinion and relevant personal experiences or examples. In the third paragraph, specific action should be requested, such as a vote for or against a bill. The writer should include contact information, including an address. Some legislators will only respond to constituents. Others may wish to contact you for further information (Haynes & Mickelson, 2003).

Sending an e-mail to a policy maker is also a useful expression of opinion. Many organizational Web sites have links to legislators and make it easy to send e-mails on important issues. Such e-mails must also be carefully done. If the letter is sent as an e-mail, a clear and descriptive subject line should be used. For example, one might say, "Vote yes on HB 123." As in a letter, one's street address should be included. If you are e-mailing legislators, send your message only to those who represent your state or district. If you e-mail the chair of a committee who is not your representative, send a copy to your representative. Don't send attachments with your e-mail. As a potential source of viruses, an attachment will rarely be opened and can overload an e-mail system (Haynes & Mickelson, 2003).

Telephone calls to legislators can also be helpful. When making a call, do not expect to speak with a legislator. The call will likely be taken by a staff member. Call about forty-eight hours before a specific vote. Have your position on the issue ready to present in a concise format. Be ready to give identifying information, as legislators particularly want to know if you are a constituent (Haynes & Mickelson, 2003).

As professionals, school social workers may also be called to present testimony regarding proposed legislation affecting schools and children. In these cases, written testimony should be provided in addition to the oral statement given. Such written testimony ensures that the record will be accurate and professional (Haynes & Mickelson, 2003).

ACTING AS A CHANGE AGENT

In a number of states, state legislatures have not required the presence of school social workers in all public schools. This is disappointing since the presence of a school social worker in a school, with our distinctive code of ethics and unique professional perspective, can in and of itself influence the climate and policies of a school. In the roles of consultant, team member, and collaborator, the school social worker constantly has the opportunity to influence others in the school. It is also possible to take deliberate action to bring about organizational change that will benefit the students, teachers, and administration. Such change begins with an organizational analysis, discussed in chapter 9. A needs assessment, discussed in chapter 11, may be done to gather data regarding the needs of the school. Existing research may be reviewed, or new data collected, as discussed in chapter 12. When analysis has occurred and information has been gathered, the process of organizational change has begun.

No school social worker or other member of the team will bring about such change alone. Even if one were to grant the school social worker the authority to create a change, implementation of that change would require the cooperation of all the stakeholders. In this sense, the power of relationship is essential in creating a climate for needed change, and in building coalitions of interested individuals to work for change. Often change is derailed more by apathy or lack of time than by active opposition. Finding others who care and are willing and able to commit time and energy to a project may be the primary task needed. Such coalitions are time limited and focused on specific goals. Haynes and Mickelson (2003) state, "The more diversified the groups in a coalition, the more powerful the coalition becomes. Conversely, the greater the diversity, the more vulnerable it is to being splintered by outside and opposing groups" (p. 123).

Chapter 11 gives an example of the development of a school breakfast program as the goal of policy change. Such a program is easy to support and may well be embraced by almost everyone who is part of the school community. Other desired programs could include after-school programs, tutoring, violence prevention programs, and other initiatives to benefit the school and community.

SCHOOL REFORMS

Problems of social fragmentation, increased risks, and "savage inequalities" (Kozol, 1992) in education have energized a variety of efforts at social and educational reform converging on the schools and on families. The consequent changes in public policy reflect a strikingly consistent reform agenda reshaping diverse arenas, including education, child welfare, juvenile delinquency prevention, and community development. These have heightened the need for new working models of service coordination in schools and are combining with local forces to create an expanding new frontier for human service delivery. These reforms often break down in their implementation. For many children, the education process is fragmented and ineffective. A host of data identify many family structures that interfere with the effective socialization of children. Youngsters coming from difficult family and social situations seem hardly ready for the challenge of the more rigorous curriculum imagined by school reform movements.

The reforms in policy that are leading to the development of human services in schools emanate from a variety of legislative and administrative sources. A major current vehicle for school reform at the national level is the reauthorization of the Elementary and Secondary Education Act, now the No Child Left Behind Act of 2001. The act, coming out of concerns for student achievement from international comparisons, makes schools and students accountable for outcomes. Specific student outcomes to be attained by the schools and their students are now mandated by states. Statewide tests have been implemented to assess whether students are meeting those standards. Although some evidence suggests that high-stakes testing will lead to better performance (Carnoy & Loeb, 2002), leaders in general education and in special education are pointing out the need for further data and midcourse corrections to ensure that the law's promise is fulfilled (Hess & Finn, 2004; Sharpe & Hawes, 2003; Ysseldyke, Nelson, Christenson, Johnson, Dennison, Triezenberg, et al., 2004). To make this work there will be a need for shifts in funding according to what children need to meet state standards (Levine, 2004) and supplemental services for students having difficulty (Hess & Finn, 2004). Furthermore, developing the "highly qualified" teachers and education personnel needed to implement a system of individual assessment and flexible educational methods to reach these common goals would require SEAs to raise the bar for certification of teachers and other education personnel. These changes will have a profound effect on school social work. According to a widely quoted essay by Art Levine (2004) from Teachers College, Columbia University, the implications of these revolutionary changes for U.S. education are only beginning to be felt:

- Education has become one of the most powerful engines driving economies and determining individual and national success (Friedman, 2005).
- The schools have been told to raise achievement and intellectual skills for all students to the highest levels in history. The states mandated this by adopting higher standards for promotion and graduation, outcomes, testing, and certification accountability.
- Schooling needed to be redesigned, and to shift its focus from process to outcomes. The historically standardized processes would need to become variable, and the traditionally variable outcomes would have to become standardized. The emphasis would have to shift from teaching to learning. The focus would have to change from the teacher to the student.
- The teaching and administrative preparation and workforces have had to be redeveloped. The country needed millions of new teachers and administrators to quickly replace most of the current teacher and administrator corps, and it needed more able teachers and administrators to achieve the higher standards (Levine, 2004, Para. 19).

Although it is schools that are being held accountable for achieving outcomes, these outcomes can only be generated by families, communities, and schools together. The school social worker can serve as an anchor for a strong family and community perspective in a school, even as professional educators and school boards must focus on the educational process, on their outcomes, and on preparation of their staff.

Locally based school reform often follows this movement. Similar to human services, schools seek to improve their culturally appropriate practices. Many methods for involving families in schools are being tried out. More schools are experimenting with programs that keep them open into the evenings, on weekends, and during the summer, allowing them to function as community centers with a wide range of services for a wide range of populations, rather than simply as sites for classroom-based teaching. In short, schools and human services are seeking many of the same goals. These shared aspirations call for new institutional models for school-based services.

These ideas have been very much at the heart of school social work practice from the beginning. In 1906, the University of Chicago settlement house and the Chicago public schools sponsored the work of Louise Montgomery at Hamline School in the Back of the Yards neighborhood (McCullagh, 2000). As a social worker, Montgomery had a triple focus. Her project would reach out to parents of Hamline's schoolchildren, alumni, and others. It would develop social, cultural, and recreational activities for children and adults. Men, women, and children of all ages participated in lectures, travel talks, and social gatherings, and plays and musical performances were given by the schoolchildren. After-school clubs for children offered opportunities for cooking, sewing, music, stories, books, pictures, gardening, and school dramas. Throughout 1906, Montgomery made assessments of and worked to improve the health and social circumstances of 208 children performing below grade level. Assembling and reporting these data with an eye to the promotion of social change, Montgomery detailed their social and medical conditions. She proposed that the school had an obligation to know the living conditions of each schoolchild. She demonstrated that poverty and wage insufficiency were the primary problem that led to inadequate nutrition and inadequate housing, and in turn to large numbers of children performing below grade level for their age (McCullagh, 2000).

THE EDUCATIONAL RIGHTS OF CHILDREN WITH DISABILITIES

One powerful example of policy development related to school social work has been the educational rights of children with disabilities. The Education for All Handicapped Children Act (P.L. 94-142) marked the beginning of over thirty years of laws and policy development for children with disabilities, moving from the federal level to the SEA to the LEA. Responsible for profound changes in schools, these laws and policies, powered by a civil right, have become a model for an activist federal role in education (Turnbull & Turnbull, 1998).

From the beginning, school social work found itself at the center of the decision making and procedural safeguards for children with disabilities. The extension of the rights of children with disabilities to receive a free and appropriate public education to the area of early childhood in 1986 further opened the opportunity for early intervention with families as well as with children. Finally, the Regular Education Initiative encouraged youngsters with mild disabilities to receive some or all of their education in regular classrooms. Although the focus of this legislation has been on children with special needs, the thrust toward involvement with regular education is a trend that inevitably involves all children and the school as a whole.

In 1970–1972, two court decisions were made that were destined to revolutionize the delivery of services to children with disabilities in schools. The effects of these decisions would reverberate for many years, and they would change the fundamental nature of social services delivered to children in schools. These decisions, *Pennsylvania Association of Retarded Children (PARC) v. Commonwealth of Pennsylvania* (1971) and *Mills v. Board of Education of the District of Columbia* (1972), each contributed to the revolution by defining the concept of the right of individuals with disabilities to an appropriate education and to the same opportunities enjoyed in our society by children without disabilities. These court decisions acknowledged a set of civil rights for individuals with disabilities and sketched out boundaries that would give shape to those rights. With these constitutional rights now defined by court decisions, statutory laws had to catch up with the definitions coming from those decisions. The lawsuit in the *PARC* case was filed on behalf of thirteen school-age children with developmental disabilities who were placed in state institutions and the class of all other children with developmental disabilities in the state. These children had been denied the right to free access to public education, as expressed in law, policies, and the practices of the state education agency and school districts throughout the state. These laws, policies, and practices would postpone, terminate, or deny the access of children with developmental disabilities to a publicly supported education, including enrollment in a public school program, provision of tuition or tuition maintenance, and homebound instruction. The court order in the *PARC* case struck down sections of the state school code and set dates by which the plaintiff children and all other children with developmental disabilities in the state were to be reevaluated and provided a publicly supported education. Local districts that provided programs of preschool education were required to provide the same for children with developmental disabilities. Furthermore, the court urged that these children be educated in programs most like those provided to children without disabilities.

Mills v. Board of Education followed *PARC* by several months and was similar except that a wider range of disabilities was represented by the plaintiffs, and some of the children were residing at home. As in *PARC*, the court ordered that the plaintiffs and all others of the class receive a publicly supported education; the decision also specified that the plaintiffs were entitled to due process of law prior to any change in educational program. The District of Columbia Board of Education failed to comply with the court order, stating that it did not have the necessary financial resources, and that to divert money from regular education programs would deprive children without disabilities of their rights. The court was not persuaded by that contention. The school has an obligation to provide a free public education to children with disabilities. Failure to provide this education could not be excused by the claim that there were insufficient funds. "The inadequacies of the District of Columbia public school system cannot be permitted to bear more heavily on the 'exceptional' or disabled child than on the normal child" (*Mills v. Board of Education,* 1972). The resultant court order, which was quite comprehensive, could be summarized under two basic sections: a declaration of the constitutional right of all children, regardless of any exceptional condition or disability, to a publicly supported education, and a declaration that the defendant's rules, policies, and practices—which excluded children without providing for adequate and immediate alternative educational services—and the absence of prior hearing and review of placement procedures denied the plaintiffs and class rights of due process and equal protection of the law.

In the years following those decisions, laws such as the Vocational Rehabilitation Act of 1973 and the Education for All Handicapped Children Act (its current incarnations being the Individuals with Disabilities Education Act of 1997 and the Individuals with Disabilities Education Improvement Act of 2004) were passed (see Butler, 2005, for a line-by-line comparison of the two versions of IDEA). These laws defined these rights more precisely and set down the mechanisms for enforcement. Without the precision of definition provided by laws and regulations, education would have been chaotic in the decade following the court decisions.

Section 504 of the Vocational Rehabilitation Act of 1973 prohibits discrimination based on disability in programs and activities receiving federal financial assistance. The Education for All Handicapped Children Act further defined the right to a free and appropriate public education for all children with disabilities from kindergarten to age twenty-one. It also provided for education in the least restrictive environment (LRE) and spelled out the accountability and procedural safeguards that would ensure this right. Clarification of these rights can be found in the Individuals with Disabilities Education Act of 1997 and IDEA 2004. States that request funding under this law must file a state plan that ensures that the state will comply with the requirements set forth in the legislation. The Office of Special Education and Rehabilitative Services reviews these state plans and conducts on-site visits to determine whether educational programs comply with the law. Furthermore, all states that accept federal funds for any educational purpose must comply with Section 504 of the Vocational Rehabilitation Act of 1973. Section 504 is somewhat broader in its coverage than the various versions of IDEA, covering students who are physically ill and have a disability but do not have an educational disability. They may need special accommodations, aids, and services, but not "special education and related services" as specified in

IDEA. A state may decide to reject funding under IDEA but must still comply with Section 504 unless the state decides to reject all federal educational funds (this has not yet occurred). The Office of Civil Rights enforces Section 504 by investigating complaints and coordinating compliance reviews.

By the end of the decade and the beginning of the 1980s, a refined body of court decisions, laws and ensuing regulations, Office of Special Education policies, and Office of Civil Rights findings had begun to emerge. These have defined what is now an irreversible direction toward the enforcement of the rights of people with disabilities. The right to a free and appropriate education (FAPE) was to consist of more than equal access to education or even compensatory education. For people with disabilities, neither opportunities nor objectives could be the same as for students without disabilities. The new concept of the right to an education was to encompass, as Weintraub and Abeson (1976) clarified, "equal access to differing resources for differing objectives" (pp. 7–13).

The Individuals with Disabilities Education Improvement Act of 2004 (IDEA, 2004) retains much of the FAPE framework discussed above and aligns IDEA with the No Child Left Behind Act (NCLB). The civil right to FAPE continues to be built on a nondiscriminatory evaluation, defined in an individualized educational program (IEP), and protected by procedural safeguards. However, whenever possible and appropriate, the same academic achievement goals that govern general education should be applied to the more individualized goals and processes of special education. The civil right is secured by adherence to procedural safeguards, but also in a substantive way to the same academic expectations governing general education, whenever appropriate. Parental involvement is strengthened considerably. The relationship of national policy making to the SEA is clarified. The national level sets firm guidelines for SEAs to develop specific plans to meet the criteria. Finally, the No Child Left Behind Act expects the SEA to develop a system that defines and assesses the (high) qualifications of every education professional, including school social workers, and this system is extended to special education. These final provisions, when connected with state teacher certification, will have profound effects on school social work (Constable & Alvarez, 2006).

MODELS OF RESPONSIVE FAMILY-CENTERED SCHOOL COMMUNITY SERVICES

In the face of growing societal complexity and fragmentation, family and community structures can deteriorate and become less capable of providing a good socializing context for children. When family or community structures deteriorate, there can be a tendency for social institutions such as schools to take over family functions, prompting further deterioration. The solution to this dilemma lies in family-school relationships that preserve the integrity of both and build a community of care.

Barriers between categorical programs can be broken down; formal service systems can become more responsive to families, communities, and different cultures (Karger & Stoesz, 2005; Nelson & Adam, 1995). Such themes have reverberated through local, state, and national dialogues. Social work practitioners will find the following principles familiar:

1. Services should be designed and delivered with respect for the different cultures of clients, or, to use a predominant term in reform language, "customers." Culturally competent practices are required by policies to ensure that human services help recipients utilize the strengths in their cultural traditions and institutions.
2. Services should empower families to take active roles in the design, implementation, and evaluation of programs that serve them.
3. Services should prevent problems from occurring rather than only respond to problems after the fact.
4. Services should be accessible to people in the neighborhoods in which they live.
5. Services should be linked in comprehensive strategies, drawing on multifaceted resources from the fields of mental health, health care, economic development, and delinquency prevention, and other traditionally separate fields.
6. Services should assess and intervene in ways that address the problems and resources of whole families, rather than individuals only.
7. Services should emphasize the strengths, or assets, of the communities in which they are located, rather than stressing the deviance and deficiencies that might be present.

Among the more widely used models for creating school-based services are family centers, complex prevention initiatives, and brokered service networks. Increasingly, community leaders see the utilization of such models as a step toward the eventual establishment of full-service schools (Dryfoos, Quinn, & Barkin, 2005). Family centers create places in schools for whole families to receive services, to deliver mutual support to one another, and to deepen the involvement of parents in the school itself (Dupper & Poertner, 1997; Pennsylvania Department of Public Welfare, 2006; Southern Regional Education Board, 2001). Complex prevention initiatives take advantage of the fact that the school provides the best setting in which to reach the greatest numbers of children who are at risk of failure or have serious health or social problems (Developmental Research and Programs, 1995; Hawkins & Catalano, 1992). Brokered service networks, such as those established over thirty years by Communities in Schools (2007), reposition human services in schools in order to keep children in school and to allow teachers to focus on basic education.

Many family centers offer outreach to parents of young children. Most of the centers operate as a core program a family-visiting service structured on the Parents as Teachers model for parenting education (Parents as Teachers National Center, 2007). Participation in the center is often triggered by family visiting or by families meeting other families who participate at the center. They might request that the center become involved in community crime prevention or community development, activities for which funding might not normally be earmarked for family centers. The centers' philosophy requires them to respond to such preferences, even when doing so challenges them to undertake initiatives with organizations, such as an economic development corporation, with which they are not accustomed to working. It might lead staff members to stretch their job descriptions to the point where they need to learn skills they do not initially possess. They might get involved in community organizing or public advocacy.

The philosophy of the full-service school goes well beyond family centers, prevention initiatives, and brokered service networks to fully transform the school into a comprehensive service center. Throughout the country, community agencies are locating programs in schools, mainly in low-income urban and rural areas. Close to 1,500 comprehensive school-based clinics have been identified, and many more are in the planning stage. Hundreds of family resource centers provide other support services, including parent education, Head Start, after-school child care, case management, meals, crisis intervention, and whatever else is needed by parents and young children (Dryfoos et al., 2005). In 1994, Joy G. Dryfoos proposed a model for the full-service school. Her vision of the full-service school put the best of school reform together with all other services that children, youths, and families need. Most of these can be located in a school building. The educational mandate placed responsibility on the school system to reorganize and innovate. The charge to community agencies would be to bring the following into the school: health care, mental health care, and employment services; child care; parent education; case management; recreation; cultural events;public assistance programs; community policing; and whatever else may fit into the picture. The result is a new seamless institution, a community-oriented school with a joint governance structure that allows maximum responsiveness to the community, as well as accessibility and continuity for those most in need of services (Dryfoos et al., 2005).

Community schools seek to serve as the nerve centers for locality development and comprehensive neighborhood revitalization. Community schools and full-service schools exhibit the distance the movement can go to integrate human services, community development, and education.

IMPLICATIONS OF REFORM MOVEMENTS FOR SCHOOL SOCIAL WORKERS

The inclusion of children with disabilities in education is an example of effective top-down reform that has been successful because it is a civil right and because there has been some level of support at the SEA and LEA levels. Whether educational policy is made through regulations or through the courts, the effects of such policies and the direction the courts have taken in interpreting IDEA and Section 504 are becoming fairly clear. The major question is still one of implementation. How might schools absorb the changes in their traditional mission? How may the current service delivery system adapt to the current reality of entitlement to services through the schools? What models of school social work practice emerge from these mandates, which cover areas that school social workers have been serving for nearly a century? What role might school social work play in the implementation of services to children based on educational rights?

The development of school-based services is a reform that comes from the school community and state levels. The first implication of these developments for social workers is the creation of a changing boundary between the school and the community. When the school is a service center for the community, its traditional boundaries shift to include the entire community with a very different range of ages and needs. Education inevitably becomes redefined. Although the school is the natural place for such a center of services, this is still a radical change. The history of American education has demonstrated that it will take schooling a considerable amount of time to absorb these changes. The school social worker, who is familiar with the broader community and its concerns, is in a most important position to make the concept work. Given this broadening of the school's identity into a community-wide service institution, school social workers, with their generalist practice perspectives, might be best positioned among school-based professionals to play leading roles in implementation of these reforms. Such leadership might entail school community needs assessments, the monitoring of policy changes in human services that would support new school-based services, the facilitation of planning groups to establish new school-based collaboratives, or the use of increased supports in policies to expand the generalist approaches in their own practice.

Along with the changing boundaries, the school also must deal with the inherent diversity of the communities it may encompass. Schools have often been the places where ethnic and class differences found some resolution. The increased importance of school as a central resource for families may also make the potential for conflict greater.

The key to effectiveness of the programs will rest on whether they successfully assist and empower families. Such programs should be resources to help families develop the internal capacities needed to carry out their roles effectively. However, as history and experience attest, in the face of a weakened family structure, a program might further weaken families by attempting to manage their problems. The language and theory of practice and policy need to address these issues so that families remain in charge of their domains and partner with schools in a broadened education mission.

School reforms and human service reforms are creating considerable diversification in the roles families can play in schools. School social workers seeking to empower families to play more meaningful and productive roles in their children's education as well as in service delivery will find new opportunities to do so. Family centers constitute new institutional bases for parents in schools, allowing for better communication with school-based professionals as well as with one another. They make it easier to carry out family-centered, as opposed to merely student-centered, practice. They create a legitimate base from which families can support one another, a process that the group practice skills of social work can help facilitate.

Changes in the expectations of schools and in school structure are profoundly influencing the purposes and functions of school social work. Furthermore, as the school social worker becomes more deeply involved with consultation on issues that have implications not simply for single cases, but for entire school districts, an understanding of the roots of policy development in the schools is essential. Even now, in many locales, the knowledge and skills of school social work and its understanding of the school clientele are proving useful to the policy development process. Further development will depend on the commitment of school social workers to seeing policy development as a natural direction of practice and to preparing themselves for this role.

References

Alvarez, M. E., & Harrington, C. (2004). A pressing need for acceptance of an advanced national school social work certification. *School Social Work Journal, 29*(1), 18–27.

Brown v. Board of Education, 347 U.S. 483 (1954).

Butler, J. (2005). *P.L. 108-446. Individuals with Disabilities Education Improvement Act of 2004 compared to IDEA '97.* Retrieved March 31, 2008, from http://www.copaa.org/pdf/IDEACOMP-Titl%20II-III.pdf

Carnoy, M., & Loeb, S. (2002). Does external accountability affect student outcomes? A cross-state analysis. *Educational Evaluation and Policy Analysis, 24*(4), 305–331.

Communities in Schools. (2007). *Communities in schools: Helping kids stay in school and prepare for life*. Retrieved August 14, 2007, from http://www.cisnet.org/default.asp

Constable, R., & Alvarez, M. (2006). Moving into specialization in school social work: Issues in practice, policy, and education. *School Social Work Journal, 31*(3), 116–131.

Developmental Research and Programs. (1995). *Communities that care: A comprehensive prevention program-team handbook.* Seattle, WA: Author.

Dryfoos, J. G. (1994). *Full-service schools*. San Francisco: Jossey-Bass.

Dryfoos, J. G., Quinn, J., & Barkin, C. (Eds.). (2005). *Community schools in action: Lessons from a decade of practice.* New York: Oxford University Press.

Dupper, D. R., & Poertner, J. (1997). Public schools and the revitalization of impoverished communities: School-linked family resource centers. *Social Work, 42,* 415–422.

Education for All Handicapped Children Act, P.L. 94-142 (1975).

Essex, E. L., & Massat, C. R. (2005). Educating school social workers for their broader role: Policy as practice. *School Social Work Journal, 29* (2), 25-39

Friedman, T. L. (2005). It's a flat world, after all. *New York Times Magazine*. Retrieved April 3, 2005, from http://newyorktimes.com/magazine

Hawkins, J. D., & Catalano, R. E. (1992). *Communities that care*. San Francisco: Jossey-Bass.

Haynes, K. S., & Mickelson, J. S. (2003). *Affecting change: Social workers in the political arena*. Boston: Allyn & Bacon.

Hess, F. M., & Finn, C. E., Jr. (2004, September). Inflating the life rafts of NCLB: Making public school choice and supplemental services work for students in troubled schools. *Phi Delta Kappan, 86*(1), 34–40, 57–58.

Huxtable, M., & Blyth, E. (2002). *School social work worldwide*. Washington, DC: NASW Press.

Individuals with Disabilities Education Act, P.L. 105-17. U.S.C. 11401 et seq. (1997).

Individuals with Disabilities Education Improvement Act, P.L. 108-446 (2004).

Jansson, B. S. (2003). *Becoming an effective policy advocate: From policy practice to social justice*. Pacific Grove, CA: Brooks/Cole/Thomson Learning.

Karger, H. J., & Stoesz, K. (2005). *American social welfare policy: A pluralistic approach* (5th ed.). Boston: Allyn & Bacon.

Kozol, J. (1992). Savage inequalities. New York: Harper Collins.

Levine, A. (2004). *New rules, old responses*. Retrieved October 15, 2004, from http://www.tc.columbia.edu/news/article.htm?id=4741

McCullagh, J. G. (2000). School social work in Chicago: An unrecognized pioneer program. *School Social Work Journal, 25*(1), 1–5.

Meenaghan, T., & Gibbons, W. E. (2000). *Generalist practice in larger settings: Knowledge and skill concepts*. Chicago: Lyceum Books.

Meenaghan, T., & Kilty, K. (1994). *Policy analysis and research technology*. Chicago: Lyceum Books.

Midgely, J. (1997) Social welfare in global context. Thousand Oaks, CA: Sage.

Mills v. Board of Education of the District of Columbia, 458 G. Supp. 866 (DC, 1972).

National Association of Social Workers. (1999). *Code of ethics of the National Association of Social Workers.* Washington DC: Author. Retrieved July 15, 2007, from http://www.socialworkers.org/pubs/code/code.asp

Nelson, K., & Adam, P. (1995). *Reinventing human services: Community- and family-centered practice*. New York: Aldine de Gruyter.

No Child Left Behind Act of 2001, P.L. 107-110 (2001).

Parents as Teachers National Center. (2007). *Parents as teachers.* Retrieved August 14, 2007, from http://www.parentsasteachers.org/site/pp.asp?c=ekIRLcMZJxE&b=289386

Pennsylvania Association of Retarded Children (PARC) v. Commonwealth of Pennsylvania, 334 F. Supp. 1257 (E.D. Pa. 1971).

Pennsylvania Department of Public Welfare. (2006). *Pennsylvania 2006*. Retrieved August 14, 2007, from http://www.friendsnrc.org/download/fy06reports/fy06 pennsylvania.pdf

Sharpe, M. N., & Hawes, M. E. (2003, July). Collaboration between general and special education: Making it work. *NCSET Issue Brief, 2*(1), 1–6.

Southern Regional Education Board. (2001). *Helping families to help students: Kentucky's family resources and youth service centers*. Atlanta, GA: Author.

Turnbull, H. R., & Turnbull, A. P. (1998). *Free appropriate public education: The law and children with disabilities* (5th ed.). Denver: Love Publishing.

Vocational Rehabilitation Act of 1973, 29 U.S.C. 794 (1973).

Weintraub, F. J., & Abeson, A. (1976). New education policies for the handicapped: The quiet revolution. In F. J. Weintraub, A. Abeson, J. Ballard, & M. LaVor (Eds.), *Public policy and the education of exceptional children* (pp. 7–13). Washington, DC: Council for Exceptional Children.

Ysseldyke, J., Nelson, J. R., Christenson, S., Johnson, D. R., Dennison, A., Triezenberg, H., et al. (2004). What we know and need to know about the consequences of high-stakes testing for students with disabilities. *Exceptional Children, 71*(1), 75–94.

9

School Social Work: Organizational Perspectives

Edward J. Pawlak
Western Michigan University

Linwood Cousins
Longwood University

- People-Processing and People-Changing Perspectives
- Formal Organizational Structure
- Informal Structure and Relations
- The School as an Organizational Culture
- Understanding and Action
- Imaginization: Metaphorical Perspectives of Schools
- Managing Organizational Change

School social workers often feel like guests in schools. They may be unsure of themselves in the world of education. They may see their role in a narrower perspective than necessary—as simply that of a clinician, rather than as one who can make an essential contribution to the mission of education, work within the framework of a changing organization, help schools to meet the needs of students in their communities, and participate in policy and program development, as well as work directly with teachers, students, and families. To take a broader role, social workers need to understand the organizational structure of schools, and they need to develop a conceptual map of the system and its operations. This chapter is designed to get the school social worker started in the process of understanding how the school works as an organization, how social work services fit into that organization and its mission, and how to participate with others in shaping organizational policy and in the processes of program change.

Schools are organizational entities that have structures, processes, policies, and cultures. These factors affect school officials, teachers, staff, and students and their families. Accordingly, school social workers have a responsibility to understand and influence these factors—especially on behalf of students and families who are clients. School social workers cannot understand and influence what they cannot see. Therefore, they must use several organizational lenses—conceptual frameworks—to discern and manage or influence organizational structures, processes, policies, and culture (Netting & O'Connor, 2005). Rather than review all possible organizational frameworks, we have selected some that we believe are particularly useful to school social workers.

PEOPLE-PROCESSING AND PEOPLE-CHANGING PERSPECTIVES

Human services organizations are different from the profit-making enterprises that have been the focus of much organizational theory and research. They are entities that rely on *people-processing* and *people-changing* operations (Hasenfeld, 1983). This orientation points to several processing tasks for the school social worker: assessing and classifying student attributes, qualifications, and circumstances to decide eligibility for particular programs of study, special services and benefits, or participation in athletics and other extracurricular activities; exploring those attributes, qualifications, and circumstances to decide on appropriate program and benefit alternatives; selecting among the alternatives; and referring or placing students in a curriculum or program, or providing a benefit or a service (Lauffer, 1984). The key elements that a school social worker must address are organizational decision making, school modes of operation, and patterns of student processing and student change, and whether these patterns differ appropriately or inappropriately among students with particular attributes.

School social workers can use people-processing and people-changing perspectives to explore several questions. What are the rules and procedures used by school officials and faculty in transactions with students? Are these rules and procedures applied equitably among students who, for example, face discipline, suspension, or expulsion? What are the consequences experienced by students of decisions made or not made by school officials or teachers? Examples include a decision to refer or not to refer a student for testing or to special services, a decision to place a student on one academic track rather than another, or a decision not to sponsor Saturday school as a form of in-school suspension for students who are truant or have behavioral problems. Do students with particular characteristics experience different and less favorable school career paths than others (e.g., low-income versus upper-income students, girls versus boys, white students versus minority students)? Are students with particular characteristics screened in or out of particular programs (e.g., what kinds of students who exhibit what kinds of behavior in the primary grades are more likely to be screened into the early identification program)? Are some groups of students often inappropriately classified? Are students with particular characteristics or circumstances likely to have favorable or unfavorable labels? Do all students have equal access to school curricula, programs, and activities? Is stigma attached to participation in some school programs and activities? Which teachers or staff members are working with which students? These are some of the questions that can be raised about the school's processing operations and patterns of decision making by teachers and school officials.

The answers to these questions might lead school social workers to engage in one or more types of intervention (Jansson, 1994). There is *policy sensitive practice* (e.g., alerting a parent to his or her rights at an upcoming individual educational program [IEP] meeting), *policy-related practice* (e.g., informing a principal that a student who was qualified for a program was excluded), and *policy practice* (e.g., working with elementary school administrators to advocate termination of a disciplinary practice whereby some students with behavioral problems are removed from the classroom and are placed on the "bad kids" bench in the main office).

FORMAL ORGANIZATIONAL STRUCTURE

Formal structure refers to official established patterns in an organization. Several dimensions are used to describe the formal structure of organizations: formalization, standardization, centralization/decentralization, and horizontal and vertical complexity (Hall, 1996). These dimensions can be manipulated or altered such that aspects of the organization or its programs can be designed to be more or less formalized, standardized, centralized, or complex. Variations in organizational and program structure lead to variations in consequences (positive or negative) for school administrators, teachers, students, and parents. Although some school organizational and program structures are not accessible to and manipulatable by school social workers, some are. Practitioners have a responsibility to figure out which structures they can positively impact, and to try to do so. Some illustrations follow.

Formalization refers to the degree to which rules, policies, and procedures that govern behavior in the organization are officially codified and set forth in writing. Examples include rules governing how IEP meetings should be conducted, criteria governing disciplining of students, guidelines for conducting locker searches, and protocols for recording and reporting unexcused absences. Formalization prescribes behavior and usually reduces discretion (e.g., in a particular school district, principals may suspend students, but only the superintendent can expel students). However, formalization may legitimate discretion (e.g., in one school district a school social worker is charged to help children in their roles as students but may provide counseling to parents if such assistance will facilitate the child's school adjustment).

Standardization is a type of formalization in which organizations have uniform ways of dealing with various situations; rules or definitions are established that cover a particular set of circumstances and apply invariably. For example, schools have standardized forms and practices to record student absences and report them to parents, and school officials often follow a series of steps in which the frequency and intensity of interventions increase as absences increase.

These concepts can be used to analyze several aspects of a school's formal structure. Such analyses are useful for several reasons. Often people are comfortable with informal procedures. On the other hand, formalization and standardization can be functional if they reduce role ambiguity; document rights, duties, and expectations; and hold school officials, staff, teachers, students, or parents accountable. For example, formal structures that entitle students and parents to appeal a counselor's assigned program of study promote due process, fairness, and opportunities to negotiate and champion academic preferences, which may also ease strong feelings. In this sense, the lack of such formal procedures (due process) is likely to cast school administrators and teachers as authoritarian and arbitrary officials. Such perceptions among students and parents may contribute to strained relationships and may lead to student behavioral problems or parental defamation of the school in the community. Formalization and standardization may eliminate or constrain arbitrariness and may promote equitable treatment and equal opportunities for programs, services, or benefits. Standardization may promote consistency among staff members who have similar decision-making or processing tasks.

Formalization and standardization can be dysfunctional if they promote "bureaupathologies" such as red tape, inflexibility, and devotion to method and discourage innovation and appropriate discretion (Patti, 1982). When school rules and procedures are contested, a school social worker might ask if these have been formalized or if they are informal and a matter of convention (e.g., experienced teachers have probably heard a student or parent say: "Where does it say that students can't do that?"). Formalization and standardization may be dysfunctional when these lead to routinization or ritualistic behavior but the situation calls instead for the interpretation and implementation of a policy to be individualized. For example, some states have zero tolerance for weapons in schools, with severe penalties such as automatic expulsion from school for an academic year with no exceptions. A fourth-grade student in a small-town school brought a knife to school to cut brownies for her classmates. Her behavior came under the stipulations of the law, and she was barred from school. Some proponents were concerned that a precedent might be set if an exception were made, whereas others advocated that an exception does not drive out the rule. The student was suspended for a week after the superintendent and school board reviewed her case, and the incident was used to educate the school community about zero tolerance.

Centralization refers to the concentration of power, authority, and decision making at the top of the organization. As applied to a school district or system, centralization refers to the board, superintendent, or what is commonly known as the central office or central administration. As applied to a particular school, centralization refers to the principal, assistant principal, and office staff. *Decentralization* refers to the distribution of power, authority, and decision making throughout the organization. As applied to the school district or system, decentralization refers to arrangements such as regional offices or centers, or the delegation of some functions to school principals and faculty. As applied to a particular school, decentralization refers to the delegation of some functions to individual teachers, faculty committees, parent-teacher advisory councils, or teacher-student work groups. Within a particular school, the principal can make decisions about discipline, suspension, and access to services, or he or she can involve staff and parents in developing guidelines for such decisions or rely on a faculty advisory committee. Whatever the case may be, school social workers must first learn what is centralized or decentralized before they can engage in organizational change.

Centralized and decentralized structures can be functional or dysfunctional. For example, the centralization of decisions regarding expulsion in the superintendent's office is functional, because dismissal has profound consequences for the student and could lead to litigation; the decentralization of decisions to local school officials regarding which students should be referred for school social work services is functional, because the predominant needs of students vary from school to school. Generally speaking, centralization of authority, power, and decision making may be functional when schools have to manage boundary relationships with the external environment (e.g., the press, police, juvenile court, community advocacy groups), when scarce resources have to be rationed and carefully allocated, or when there are threats to the school (e.g., protests, litigation, complaints). Decentralization enables teachers, students, and parents to gain ownership of policies and programs and increases the likelihood that they will be successfully implemented and viewed as legitimate. For example, a decentralized decision-making structure such as a joint faculty-student committee on student conduct might promote student ownership of the code of conduct, whereas a centralized top-down imposition of the code might generate resistance. Decentralization also facilitates the management of change and uncertainty at the front lines of the organization, and bottom-up innovation and adaptation (Wagoner, 1994).

Horizontal complexity refers to the type and degree of organizational segmentation, such as departmentalization, and specialization of positions, roles, jobs, or duties. The degree of specialization and departmentalization can be functional or dysfunctional. High specialization sometimes leads to fragmented and uncoordinated delivery of services, but it also might contribute to efficiency and the availability of high levels of expertise. Sometimes school social workers have to run interference for students and parents who are overwhelmed with their problems and the bureaucratic maze of services.

Vertical complexity refers to the levels in the hierarchy from the top to the bottom of the organization. Vertical complexity may be functional or dysfunctional from the standpoint of a school social worker or parent interested in promoting change. If a change proposal has to traverse many hierarchical levels for approval, the structure may not be functional; if officials are accessible and there are few levels between the top and the bottom, organizational change may be more easily influenced.

Some aspects of formal structure are often depicted in pyramidal organizational charts and tables of organization that identify hierarchical relationships, preferred communication paths, and the complexity of the organization in terms of the different divisions, specializations, departments, or programs. However, these traditional organizational charts are being replaced by circle diagrams in which circles representing different organizational units partially overlap or are drawn to depict interdependencies, collaboration, and participation in decision making (Tropman, 1989). Linear, rational approaches to horizontal and vertical coordination in organizations are being supplanted by flatter organizations, negotiated political orders, fluid and dynamic structures, and combinations of loose and tight coupling among organizational units (Fennell, 1994). A variety of geometric shapes and diagrams are used to graphically depict these nontraditional organizational structures and relationships (Mintzberg, 1983).

As school social workers begin their assignments in a new school, they should devote time to comprehending the school's horizontal and vertical complexity, or its negotiated political order, often found in school manuals or handbooks. If such documentation is not available, school social workers are advised to be observant, check out the arrangements with opinion leaders, and map the structure or negotiated order for themselves. Such understanding is important because school social workers are required to integrate, coordinate, link, and communicate with different departments, units, positions, and roles in the school's structure. The role of a school social worker gives practitioners legitimate, unique access—in other words, structural mobility—to most, if not all, segments and roles within schools. Thus, school social workers must figure out their niche in the school, and which individuals in which positions might facilitate or hinder work with officials, teachers, students, and families.

INFORMAL STRUCTURE AND RELATIONS

People in schools—in fact, in all organizations—develop social relationships that are not prescribed by organizational officials. These social relationships evolve into patterned group processes and social structures that are known as the organization's informal organization, or informal structures and relations. These social relationships are informal in that they are unofficial, not mandated, and not planned. Informal structure is rarely, if ever, documented. (So don't ask your principal for a copy of the school's informal organization chart, because it doesn't exist. You can, however, draw one, as we will see shortly.)

There are four types of informal structures: affectional, communication, decision making, and power. These structures are not mutually exclusive, and the same participants may be involved in all structures but in different ways. *Affectional structure* refers to patterns of social relationships based on friendship, mutual attraction, similar interests, and common experiences—for whatever reason, people like each other and spend time together when it is not formally required by the organization. Affectional structure manifests itself in several ways: two or more staff members frequently have coffee breaks or lunch together, sit next to each other at meetings, attend professional conferences together, or socialize off the job. *Communication structure* refers to patterns of social interaction among staff members based on giving and getting information, opinions, viewpoints, or feelings (even when they are not within an affectional structure). Some common metaphors used to describe communication structures are the rumor mill, the grapevine, the talk on the street, leaks, and inside information or the inside track. You can detect the informal communication structure by observing who talks with whom after a controversy or a staff meeting. Who are the confidants, the listeners? Who do teachers depend on to figure out and report what's going on? *Decision-making structures* are patterns of social interaction among school personnel based on the solicitation or provision of analysis, insights, and advice leading up to a decision. You can observe decision-making structures by observing who consults with whom during deliberations (e.g., Is there a small group of experienced teachers who are often consulted on the side by the principal? Do particular teachers meet informally before a meeting in an attempt to sway opinion prior to a formal meeting?). *Power structure* refers to patterns of social interaction based on ability to influence. There are four types of power: referent, expertise, reward, and coercive (French & Raven, 1968). A teacher may have referent power because she is liked, and another may have expertise power because she is a respected English instructor. Some teachers have reward power because they support colleagues and praise them for their contributions, and others have coercive power because they have years of experience and can be abrasive, but colleagues are intimidated by them.

School social workers must strive to discern informal structure, because they will inevitably become a part of it, and they may have to work with or against it. School social workers must figure out who is included in which informal groups. Who is the "power behind the throne"? Who are the quiet movers and shakers? Who has the ear of the administration and who is "wired in"? Who really runs this place? Who are the insiders and outsiders? Is there an inner circle?

If mapping relevant informal structures and relations is essential or desirable, school social workers can easily do so with a formal organizational chart and highlighters of different colors. Let's assume that the school has an organizational chart in which each school official's, staff member's, and teacher's name and position are posted within a rectangular box. Let's assume that an assistant principal and two teachers are an affectional group, and the principal relies on the school secretary and head of the physical plant to keep their "ears to the ground" and keep her posted on goings-on. Different-colored highlighters can be used to visually map these two informal structures. Such mapping may help demystify the complex informal operational structure and relations within a school and their congruence with formal structure.

Several factors contribute to the development and maintenance of informal structure and relations. These are the characteristics or attributes of individuals, such as gender, race, age, and religion; common life experiences (e.g., parenthood, caring for an adult parent, attendance at the same university); shared values and interests (e.g., conservative orientation, quilting, or fishing); common memberships in organizations external to the school (e.g., a church, a political party); and sharing a common fate, such as working under an authoritarian, domineering principal. When informal structure is detected, school social workers should try to determine the factors that bond members together.

Informal structures not only involve administrators, teachers, and staff in varying combinations but may include students and parents. Teachers sometimes have favorites, both parents and students. Some students and parents are insiders because they have high participation rates in school activities; some students, teachers, and parent volunteers are involved in the ski club or play basketball together in the school gym on Sunday afternoon. Students can detect informal structures and have names for its variations—kids who think they're all that, jocks, band geeks, cheerleader-types, nerds, pocket-protectors, drama kids, brainiacs, suck-ups, grungies, preppies, queen bees, wannabees, oreos (black students who work for good grades and "act white"), wiggers (whites who "act black"), and emos (emotionals).

Informal structure serves several functions in organizations: it provides informal linkages between departments, positions, and roles (e.g., the school social worker and attendance officer worked together in another school district); it sometimes compensates for problems in the formal structure (e.g., when a principal was of little help to teachers who had to manage classroom behavior problems, they turned to an experienced tenured teacher for assistance); it socializes and orients new school personnel and students to life in the organization (what the dos and don'ts are); it provides a network for the circulation of information; it provides social support and alleviates stress and frustration; and it meets interpersonal and associational needs. In examining a school's informal structure, school social workers should try to figure out the functions that it serves and determine whether it supports or undermines the students served.

THE SCHOOL AS AN ORGANIZATIONAL CULTURE

The organizational culture of a school affects all school functions. This fact is particularly relevant to social workers who practice in schools where there is difficulty in understanding the mutual influence and effect on intraschool relationships of social and academic processes occurring between schools and society at large (see Perry, Steele, & Hilliard, 2003; McWhorter, 2001). Posing several questions brings the issues into focus: What is the nature of organizational culture in schools? Why is this information important to social workers? What do social workers need to know about organizational culture in schools to function effectively?

What is cultural about the organization of schools? Culture can be defined as the beliefs, values, traditions, and attitudes that are the basis of the frames of reference or meanings people use to organize reality and direct their behavioral actions. In deciphering the culture in how schools work as organizations, one must consider two important pathways.

Schools are transmitters of dominant cultural standards, norms, and values emanating from society at large. Dominant cultural norms are infused into schools through federal regulations, state and local boards of education, and universities as institutions for knowledge development and training. These institutions define, design, and organize academic materials that become a part of the educational and social activities that have to be administered in a school. For example, the selection and enforcement of reading, writing, and arithmetic curricula, as well as the methods to teach these subjects, are artifacts of Western cultural beliefs about learning and socialization, rather than a universal fact of human nature.

Interpersonal transactions occurring between students and teachers or staff provide another pathway for culture to permeate schools as organizations. Culture provides a blueprint for the meaning and interpretation of acceptable and unacceptable behavior, attitudes, emotions, and beliefs. For example, students generally understand that when they enter the classroom, the teacher is in charge. The teacher makes the rules and enforces them. He or she decides who can talk and when. When a student violates rules, the consequences generally fit the sanctioned norms in the school. As such, culture in schools manifests in an organized way various frames of reference or meanings associated with compliance and violations of official policies and regulations.

These two pathways of culture in the organization of schools are alike in that they reflect varying degrees of influence by dominant cultural norms in society at large. When there is a high degree of compatibility and homogeneity among students and school officials, there is likely to be less conflict within the organizational milieu of the school. However, such compatibility and homogeneity with a dominant culture in schools have never been fully the case for members of minority groups (e.g., African Americans, Native Americans, Hispanics) and are becoming even less common because of the increasing ethnic, religious, and economic diversity of groups residing in the United States.

School social workers must stay abreast of the influence and impact of organizational culture by being aware of the dominant beliefs, values, attitudes, and behaviors that are embedded in the customs, traditions, and notions of common sense forming the basis of administrative policy and regulations in schools. For example, social workers should examine disciplinary and evaluative activities occurring between social workers and students, between students and staff, and among parents, staff, and social workers. When observing disciplinary activities in school, social workers can ask themselves the following questions: Did the infractions of a rule or standard that led to disciplinary action reflect beliefs, values, and attitudes shared by the student and school official? When there is a lack of commonality, are the differences labeled as dysfunctional rather than being seen as variations in how people understand the multiple meanings of the rules and standards being enforced? These questions are especially important to consider when the outcomes are detrimental to the social, emotional, and academic well-being of students.

UNDERSTANDING AND ACTION

What do social workers need to know to understand and effectively engage in situations in which dominant cultural frames of reference that organize schools do not work? We refer to cases in which the organizational culture of a school is not held together by common frames of reference and therefore leaves students, teachers, and staff feeling incompatible and alienated and taking action based on these feelings. For example, many African Americans have experienced strain in relation to dominant cultural norms in school and have responded with resistance. Many African Americans have questioned the relevance of the subjects taught in school to their plight as a stigmatized group. Being able to read, write, and do arithmetic have not directly led to less racial discrimination and increased economic and political liberation. Mastery of these academic subjects can help, but not always.

In this context, when frames of reference operating in the organizational culture of a school are juxtaposed, compliance and noncompliance are better understood.

Another example is the kind of etiquette required in classroom interactions among students and between students and teachers. Many, but certainly not all, African Americans have been socialized in environments in which great value was placed on expressiveness and animation through language and the body in communicating with others. However, classroom etiquette generally requires that students sit still when speaking, stay in their seats, only address the teacher, and so forth. When students do not or cannot comply with these social and behavioral norms, they are punished or labeled dysfunctional.

Social workers must understand that organizational cultures contain meaningful processes manifested in terms of beliefs, values, attitudes, and behaviors that comprise frames of reference. Among minority and majority groups, meanings and frames are influenced by, among other things, historical and contemporary experiences in the United States and beyond. Members of minority groups often tend to experience school norms as extensions of the social, economic, and political inequality they experience in U.S. society. Many studies have documented this, and other studies have found that such relational strain between minorities and school staff influences the academic performance of the students and the evaluations of students by teachers and staff (Gibson & Ogbu, 1991; Spindler, 1997). Consider that school social workers tend to perform evaluations and assessments of students that serve as the basis of various forms of psychological, social, and educational interventions at school. These activities serve an important social and cultural function for schools and society at large. This function requires that social workers understand their own complicity, through their roles and activities, in enforcing dominant and often oppressive societal norms that function as part of the organizational culture in schools.

Social workers commonly interact with school staff who firmly believe that academic processes and contexts are free of culture or cultural bias. Noncompliance and low academic performance, in their view, reflect psychosocial dysfunction and cognitive or intellectual abnormality, respectively. School personnel and even some social workers may have difficulty seeing beyond the seemingly natural and just plain commonsense processes of most social and academic aspects of schooling. The fact that these processes are often taken for granted, however, is partially a product of the blinding nature of a dominant culture. These beliefs, traditions, and notions of common sense form parts of a frame of reference that maintains currently dominant organizational cultures in schools and widespread social, economic, and political inequality in society. This frame of reference has contributed to racism, or the belief that minorities fail in school because of their inferiority, and to beliefs that minority students simply need to persevere in their work and tolerate or overcome their feelings and perceptions of inequitable treatment by assimilation into the dominant culture or accommodating themselves to dominant cultural norms.

Social workers can do something about this. They can individually engage in accessible levels of the organizational culture of the school and collectively engage in advocacy, public education, and political action. Individual engagement begins with asking and answering the questions raised earlier: What are the beliefs, values, attitudes, and behaviors that form the basis of social and academic compliance and noncompliance by students? Answers to such questions can lead to interactions with students and staff in which one is guided not only by the surface or manifest understandings of disagreements between students and teachers, but also by the underlying or latent meanings that are the cultural foundation of such incompatibilities. The next step is to conduct educational, social, and psychological interventions that reach both levels of the problem and do not leave students and teachers limited to a traditional arsenal of labels, diagnoses, and other disciplinary actions and reactions.

The second application for social workers is a matter of scale. That is, the focus is on those legislative and academic policies and practices that provide unidimensional approaches to education in the first place. Activities in these domains require social workers to participate in advocacy and public education through community dialogues and political actions that directly or indirectly address official policy-making bodies. School staff meetings, board meetings, state education associations, and state legislatures are excellent sites for practice, and practitioners can also track federal bills in consort with the National Association of Social Workers' (NASW's) lobbying arm.

In conclusion, the understandings and actions regarding the organizational culture of schools proposed in this discussion offer a way in which school social workers can become transformative professionals. They can begin by understanding and rejecting the notion that academic and social functions in schools are neutral transactions in organizational cultures. Acting as such, social workers contribute to the realization of the overall interdependence between U.S. institutions such as schools and social, economic, political, and cultural processes in society at large.

IMAGINIZATION: METAPHORICAL PERSPECTIVES OF SCHOOLS

Imaginization is the name for organizational assessment and development created and practiced by Gareth Morgan (1993), an academician and consultant. Imaginization, the word, is the result of the fusion of the concepts of imagination and organization. Imaginization, the concept, refers to the creative use of similes and metaphors to interpret and shape organizational life and develop shared understandings of organizational structure, processes, roles, and culture. Similes and metaphors enable "new ways of thinking about management styles, organizational design, approaches to planning and change, and basic products and services" (Morgan, 1993, p. 265). One imaginizes by invoking similes and metaphorical images to frame and reframe organizational situations in new ways: "We don't teach in a school; we teach in a military organization with a principal who acts like General Patton." "Faculty and students are like an extended family." "The school is an oasis in a community beleaguered by gang fighting, drug dealing, and inadequate housing, with many single parents hanging on by their fingernails." Similes and metaphorical images are often used to characterize school cultures: "The teachers approach their work as if it were a calling, not just a job." "The only time you see those teachers move is when it's time to go home, and they usually beat the students out the door." Similes and metaphors send strong metamessages that influence student and parental attitudes and behavior toward the school.

These examples reveal how the process of imaginization begins—with similes and metaphorical images that serve as the points of departure for assessing the organization. Imaginization is not codified in behaviorally specific steps that one can mechanically follow. Metaphorical language is used to describe the basic protocol of imaginization: "Get inside." "Adopt the role of a learner." "Map the terrain." "Identify key themes and interpretations (to produce an evolving reading of the situation)." "Confirm, refute, and reformulate throughout." The method is exploratory yet deliberative; it is free-flowing yet anchored in organizational realities; it is directive yet participative; it is subjective yet objective. Nevertheless, there is sufficient structure and direction in the method for open, venturesome practitioners to begin imaginizing (Pawlak, 1994).

The fundamental processes of imaginization are not foreign to social workers. We intuitively rely on metaphor in our everyday organizational lives to read into and characterize what is going on. However, we seldom play out the readings in order to use them as heuristic devices to analyze and solve problems. School social workers will find imaginization congruent with their professional values and education. The process has a primacy of orientation toward organizational members' definition of the situation, ownership of organizational problems, and responsibility for change (Pawlak, 1994).

Images of schools through simile and metaphor development have been used to study school climate and environment. Grady, Fisher, and Fraser (1996) delineate four steps that can be adapted by school social workers to assess their schools:

1. Identify several most favored and least favored images of the school.
2. Identify positive and negative aspects of these favored and non-favored images.
3. Identify assumptions/beliefs/values/philosophies which underpin these favored and non-favored images.

4. Identify exemplars of language, rituals, ceremonies, stories, heroes, schedules, decision-making/delegating/accountability processes and so on which ought to be fostered in the school in light of the exercise. (p. 51)

As an exercise, formulate a simile or metaphor about your school. Run with it. Where does it take you? What does it reveal about the school as an organization? What corrective action or change is suggested by the metaphor? What are the factors that might facilitate or hinder change? This approach provides a refreshing counterpoint to traditional yet essential approaches to organizational analysis.

Thus far we have presented several conceptual frameworks that we believe are useful for understanding and analyzing schools as organizations: schools as people-processing and people-changing organizations, schools as formal and informal structures, schools as cultures, and schools viewed from metaphorical perspectives. Each framework enables school social workers to understand schools from different organizational viewpoints. We believe an eclectic approach is essential. No one perspective is adequate to penetrate the complexities of schools as organizations. If the application of one framework does not yield insight into organizational problems, then another should be tried.

School social workers are not interested in organizational analysis for its own sake. The results of organizational analysis must be transformed into change efforts. In the final section of this chapter, we offer some general guidelines for introducing and managing change. Detailed discussions of organizational change models, strategies, tactics, and development abound in the literature and on the Internet (Bailey, 1992; Burbach & Crockett, 1994; Flynn, 1995; Gottfredson, 1987; Mulkeen & Cooper, 1992; Netting, Kettner, & McMurtry, 1993; Netting & O'Connor, 2005; Pawlak, 1998; Smithmier, 1996).

MANAGING ORGANIZATIONAL CHANGE

Organizational analysis yields insights and findings about organizational conditions and problems, as well as the assets, strengths, and positive features of the school. These insights and findings are essential to the planning and implementation of change efforts. The following guide is offered as one way to approach changing schools from within.

1. Describe the organizational problem, condition, or opportunity for change. What are its features? How is the problem/condition distributed in the school? What are the key groups affected by the problem/condition, and what are the differentiating characteristics of the members of these groups? What are the consequences of the problem/condition? What is the magnitude of the problem/condition? (Pawlak & Vinter, 2004).

2. What factors contribute to or sustain the condition or problem? What factors brought about the change opportunity?
3. What is the desired outcome of the change you propose? What are the reasons for the proposed change?
4. Identify the key individuals, groups, roles, or units affected by the proposed change. How can they be involved in developing and implementing the change proposal? Identify organizational assets, strengths, and positive features that can be used to facilitate change.
5. What are the sunk costs in the status quo? There are two kinds of sunk costs—financial investments and psychological investments (e.g., the feeling that "this program is my baby"). What are the likely sources of resistance to change and the degree of resistance, and how might resistance be expressed?
6. Identify possible approaches to change and their advantages and disadvantages (see Packard, 2001; Robbins, 2003).
7. Think through the change that you want to introduce. Anticipate potential positive and negative scenarios, and how the former might be facilitated, and the latter overcome. (Don't make your chess moves one at a time.)
8. Anticipate the reactions of school officials, staff, teachers, students, or parents.
9. Explore these matters with trusted colleagues and ask for ideas.
10. What resources, time, support, or training are needed to implement change?
11. Develop a plan to influence change and a work plan to implement change. With such plans, influential individuals can envision the feasibility of change. Strive to develop shared ownership of the change proposal and process.

School social workers have a primacy of orientation toward helping students and their families through individual or group counseling, and often such approaches are appropriate. However, when organizational conditions contribute to or sustain student problems, helpful interventions on behalf of students must be directed at the school as an organization. The roles and status of school social workers, as well as their professional education, enable them to take holistic perspectives and to legitimately engage the structures, culture, units, roles, and personnel within schools. School social workers have more opportunities to leverage change than they might realize. Carpe diem.

References

Bailey, D. (1992). Organizational change in a public school system: The synergism of two approaches. *Social Work in Education, 14*(2), 94–105.

Burbach, H. J., & Crockett, M. (1994). The learning organization as a prototype for the next generation of schools. *Planning and Change, 25*(3–4), 173–179.

Fennell, H.-A. (1994). Organizational linkages: Expanding the existing metaphor. *Journal of Educational Administration, 32*(1), 23–33.

Flynn, J. P. (1995). Social justice in social agencies. In R. L. Edwards & J. G. Hopps (Eds.), *The encyclopedia of social work* (19th ed., pp. 2173–2179). New York: NASW Press.

French, J. R. P., & Raven, B. (1968). The bases of social power. In D. Cartwright & A. Zander (Eds.), *Group dynamics* (3rd ed., pp. 215–235). New York: Harper & Row.

Gibson, M., & Ogbu, J. (1991). *Minority status and schooling: A comparative study of immigrant and involuntary minorities*. New York: Garland.

Gottfredson, D. C. (1987). An evaluation of an organization development approach to reducing school disorder. *Evaluation Review, 11*(6), 739–763.

Grady, N. B., Fisher, D. L., & Fraser, B. J. (1996). Images of school through metaphor development and validation of a questionnaire. *Journal of Educational Administration, 34*(2), 41–53.

Hall, R. (1996). *Organizations: Structure, process, and outcomes* (6th ed.). Englewood Cliffs, NJ: Prentice Hall.

Hasenfeld, Y. (1983). *Human service organizations*. Englewood Cliffs, NJ: Prentice Hall.

Jansson, B. (1994). *Social welfare policy: From theory to practice* (2nd ed.). Belmont, CA: Brooks/Cole.

Lauffer, A. (1984). *Understanding your agency* (2nd ed.). Beverly Hills, CA: Sage.

McWhorter, J. (2001). *Losing the race: Self-sabotage in black America*. New York: Perennial.

Mintzberg, H. (1983). *Structure in fives: Designing effective organizations*. Englewood Cliffs, NJ: Prentice Hall.

Morgan, G. (1993). *Imaginization: The art of creative management*. New York: Sage.

Mulkeen, T. A., & Cooper, B. S. (1992). Implications of preparing school administrators for knowledge work organizations: A case study. *Journal of Educational Administration, 30*(1), 17–28.

Netting, F. E., Kettner, P. M., & McMurtry, S. L. (1993). *Social work macropractice*. New York: Longman.

Netting, F. E., & O'Connor, M. K. (2005). Teaching organization practice: A multi-paradigmatic approach. *Administration in Social Work, 29*(1), 25–43.

Packard, T. (2001). Enhancing site-based governance through organizational development: A new role for school social workers. *Children & Schools, 23*(2), 101–113.

Patti, R. (1982). Analyzing agency structures. In M. Austin & J. Hershey (Eds.), *Handbook on mental health administration* (pp. 137–162). San Francisco: Jossey-Bass.

Pawlak, E. J. (1994). [Review of the book *Imaginization: The art of creative management*.] *Administration in Social Work, 18*(4), 132–134.

Pawlak, E. J. (1998). Organizational tinkering. In B. Compton & B. Galaway (Eds.), *Social work processes* (4th ed.). New York: Allyn & Bacon.

Pawlak, E. J., & Vinter, R. D. (2004). *Designing and planning programs for nonprofit and government organizations*. San Francisco: Jossey-Bass.

Perry, T., Steele, C., & Hilliard, A. (2003). *Young, gifted, and black: Promoting high achievement among African-American students*. Boston: Beacon Press.

Robbins, S. (2003). *Organizational learning is no accident*. Retrieved April 5, 2008, from http://hbswk.hbs.edu/archive/3483.html

Smithmier, A. (1996). Schools and community-based collaboration: Multiple resistances and structural realities. *Planning and Change*, 27(1–2), 15–29.

Spindler, G. (Ed.). (1997). *Education and cultural process: Anthropological approaches*. Prospect Heights, IL: Waveland Press.

Tropman, J. E. (1989). The organizational circle: A new approach to drawing an organizational chart. *Administration in Social Work, 13*(1), 35–44.

Wagoner, R. V. (1994). Changing school governance: A case for decentralized management. *Planning and Change, 25*(3–4), 206–218.

10

School Policy Development and the School Social Worker

John P. Flynn
Western Michigan University

- Policy Defined
- Policy Analysis—Why Bother?
- Functioning in the Policy Space
- A Framework for Policy Analysis
- The Analysis of Existing Policy in a School System and Proposed Changes
- Fair Warning to Conscientious People
- A Few Final Words about Presentation of Policy Analyses

The responsibility for shaping educational policy is clearly shifting downward (hierarchically speaking) from the national to the state and local levels. There has been a shift in certain areas, such as matters concerning children with disabilities, away from closely regulated national standards and guidelines and toward encouragement of some state and local discretion in the design of programs and services for students and families. The school social worker is in a unique position to make valuable contributions to the opportunities afforded by this shift. The task of education is to draw on a range of competencies to facilitate the process and to minimize barriers to learning. The school social worker has an extensive repertoire of skills to contribute that comes from the profession's base in both clinical and direct services as well as its resources in policy, planning, and administration of human services. Social work's forte is the development and maintenance of functional linkages in human systems, a logical necessity for school systems aimed at educating the whole child and engaging families and community services. As education is being defined increasingly as engagement with the whole person-in-environment, social work experiences and skills bring unique perspectives and competencies to the team and to the school system.

The school social worker initiates, shapes, modifies, and applies organizational or school system policy in a number of ways. These opportunities lie in the ability to conceptualize, organize, and communicate systematic analysis of policies and the skill to know how and when to advocate a policy's implementation. This is true for existing policies, revision of a dysfunctional policy, and the proposal and effective communication of new policy options that meet student, family, and organizational needs. These policies can positively or negatively affect students,, particularly vulnerable or troubled students at risk. Depending on the content and implementation of such policies, opportunities and resources can be made available to or taken away from students.

POLICY DEFINED

Policy might be said to undergird all that is legitimate and sanctioned in organizations such as school systems. Dollars are not spent unless there is adequate authority in budget policy. Individuals are only free to act in ways that are commensurate with building policies. Teachers are free to improvise with instructional methods, so long as those approaches are within the bounds of curriculum policy. And so forth. These phrases are commonplace in schools, and their corollaries can be found in any organization. But what is policy?

First, policy, defined in its most general terms in the social welfare context, refers to those principles that give expression to valued ends and provide direction for appropriate action. That is, policy announces value preferences and provides a (verbal or nonverbal) statement of the broadest expectations and boundaries of intent and action. Some examples might be found in general institutional or organizational preambles, in mission statements, or in the annual performance objectives of a department such as a special education unit. These might be broad statements of intent that speak to equality, fair play and fair treatment, equal opportunity, or open enrollment, for example. Each of these concepts is a statement of principle, indicates valued ends, and suggests a range of actions to be taken to achieve desired ends. On the other hand, policy statements may be specific rather than general, as with requirements for eligibility, specification of parental rights or obligations, or expectations of staff performance.

Second, policy increases or reduces the number of probable outcomes that are possible in social interaction. Policy limits choices and opportunities and narrows the range of possible action. This is what is meant by the "stochastic nature" of social policy. When the expectations of behavior are not clear, the limits are boundless, and the environment becomes unpredictable and, at times, even chaotic. On the other hand, clarification through policy (assuming it is monitored and implemented) is a powerful way to communicate the values intended by the organization. Policy that is effectively implemented can make order out of chaos and increase the likelihood that behavior will be directed toward desired ends. Policy makes the outcomes of a social process much more predictable—people know (generally speaking) how to behave, what is expected of them, and what the likely outcome is to be when policies are clearly stated and implemented, and outcomes are monitored. Policy channels and influences human behavior. One example would be a school system's requirements on earliest age of entry into the school system. Others would be policy statements limiting the size and nature of any object that may be perceived as a weapon brought into a school building, or rules around who is welcome on school property, and under what conditions. These all limit the range and number of possible outcomes. Consequently, policy is a means whereby influence is exercised over the participants in the school system and over those in the school's significant environments.

Third, these policies may be embodied in formal policy statements or in the informal action of school staff. Common illustrations of formal policy might be rules and regulations, board resolutions, or administrative directives from a central office. Informal policy could be exemplified in the behavior or professional actions of school staff (such as a social worker's willingness to extend herself to do home visits, a teacher's availability to meet with parents after hours, or a principal's acceptance of certain errant behaviors and total rejection of others). The important point here is that these examples (i.e., both formal and informal manifestations of policy) are all illustrations of valued ends that give rise to desired actions as exemplified by school personnel.

Some would argue that policy is not really policy unless it is formally ratified by some legitimate body or office. However, that characterization applies only to formal policy that has been properly legitimated or sanctioned by those who have the right to take action. On the contrary, the fact cannot be denied that individuals and groups in social systems, schools included, establish policies by their own choices and behaviors within or in spite of formal policy boundaries. School personnel do this through their conscious and unconscious choices and preferences in interactions with each other, with students and their families, and with other organizations in the community.

Consequently, the school social worker must be aware of the power inherent in implementing or even creating policy within the school system. Policy is a tool that cannot be neglected and must be used appropriately.

This is why the school social worker should have facility in the use of that tool in conducting a systematic analysis of policy affecting everyday practice of the profession and be prepared to make that contribution to the team.

POLICY ANALYSIS—WHY BOTHER?

The ability to make or apply policy is the ability to influence the behavior of others. The ability to have power over another person or situation, to influence the probabilities of outcomes, carries no small ethical obligation. Consequently, it is absolutely essential for social workers in schools to be aware of this power, just as much as they are aware of the ethical obligation to be able to conduct a technically sound behavioral assessment or to assist a parent in making an informed decision. Development of skills in policy analysis can enable the social worker to examine the efficacy of a particular system-level or building-level policy, can assist in offering credible arguments for change, and can provide a framework for offering constructive or creative proposals for new policy. To appreciate the reality of this power, the school social worker must recognize what a particular policy is or could otherwise be, be aware of how policy does or could influence a situation, and understand the fact that policy is both formal and informal in its impact on stakeholders in the school environment. A clear understanding of these aspects of policy in a school system is fundamental to the social worker's ability to fulfill his or her membership in the professional team in the school.

FUNCTIONING IN THE POLICY SPACE

Social workers in schools have unique opportunities to function as both policy practitioners and policy analysts. That is, the social worker applies school policy in bringing services to the student and/or family or in bringing the student and/or family to the services. This role of providing linkage is an aspect of practice that makes the school social worker unique among team members. Social workers, given their assignment in schools, are in a position to observe and assess the utility or disutility of many policies (and their resultant procedures) from many sides due to that linkage position. In other words, the social worker in a school system or in a particular school has the opportunity to occupy a "policy space" in the course of providing services to students and/or families and in working within the school system. Consequently, direct practice and the delivery of services are intricately interwoven with opportunities for policy analysis. By way of illustration, perhaps a school system has particular guidelines on eligibility for special educational services. There is likely some latitude left to the discretion of school staff (i.e., the policy space) on how the criteria shall be met (such as what documents must be offered or available to determine eligibility) or how the eligibility data will be prepared and presented. The social worker has the opportunity to assist the classroom teacher and other ancillary personnel as well as the family to come to a productive decision for a child. At the same time, important information is generated concerning the adequacy of policies and procedures governing decision making on special education placements. On the clinical level, the nature and style of the social worker may color or shape the policy space. The social worker may or may not take an active or supportive role in developing the information for an eligibility claim or in monitoring any resultant plans agreed to by the parents and the school system. In other words, the school social worker has an opportunity to create his or her own "minipolicies" over time, as does the service team to which the social worker may be attached. Informed policy determines how and in what manner professional decisions are systematically or routinely carried out. Stated another way, school social workers and their team colleagues have tremendous discretionary power in many situations, and their decisions and their behaviors speak loudly of principles that give expression to valued ends and provide direction for appropriate action.

The school social worker has many opportunities to monitor, implement, modify, and promote school policy. In the first instance, it is essential for the analyst to realize the difference between policy that authorizes an action, program, or procedure and the actual implementation of that policy. The social worker as policy monitor is in a position to identify disparities between authorization and enactment of a policy. Any failures or shortcomings of policy implementation can be brought to light through thorough analysis and credible argument for change. The social worker can also use the analysis for other policy roles, such as acting as a policy expert on external policy mandates, acting as a constructive critic in voicing the policy options to be found in existing or proposed school policy, serving as a conduit or sounding board for students or families on the impact of school policies, or becoming a policy change agent within the school system itself or with the external environment (e.g., mental health agencies) regarding administrative or operational procedures in enacting school policy. Taken together, these roles provide a constellation of policy-relevant activities that compose the role of the social worker as a policy practitioner in the school. Nevertheless, whether one is fulfilling the role of policy monitor, expert, constructive critic, conduit/sounding board, or policy change agent, it is absolutely necessary that the role is supported by sound systematic analysis of the policy driving the professional activity. Such analysis supplies credibility to what is advocated by the social worker and lends to the power of any recommendations that might be accepted or implemented by others.

A FRAMEWORK FOR POLICY ANALYSIS

A disciplined and well-prepared professional person sets forth his or her theoretical perspective and plan of intervention prior to taking action. A true professional is aware of what theoretical model is to be used and what techniques are to be employed before taking action. This is obvious to the clinical practitioner, who can easily identify what theory or model he or she might be employing in working with a client. The need for conscious choice of assessment tools or policy analysis is no less important for those doing such analyses. This chapter will set forth suggested elements for the analysis of the content and process of policy and will provide illustrations by using examples relevant to social work services in the schools. This framework is an abridged version of one provided in detail in Flynn (1992), in which a number of examples and illustrations may be found. An additional approach may be found in Jansson (1999).

The elements for analysis are grouped into five categories and may generate different information depending on whether the policy under analysis is currently in place as a formal policy, is a proposed policy, is a proposed revision of an existing policy, or is an operational reality or informal policy.

The five categories are:

1. Identify the policy problem, the policy goals, and the policy statement (as written or published and/or as might be inferred from behavior).
2. Assess current and anticipated system functioning due to present policy or because of any proposed policy.
3. Determine the implications for selected values embedded or implied in the policy.
4. Establish the feasibility of the policy and resources needed for the desired outcomes of the policy.
5. Provide recommendations for wording and action of the new or revised policy.

These categories are relevant for examining the substantive content of a policy or the process by which a policy is implemented or has been developed. In real life, one may not need to examine every element of each category or all content and all processes. In all instances, however, it is necessary to examine the values implied in the policy as stated or as proposed.

THE ANALYSIS OF EXISTING POLICY IN A SCHOOL SYSTEM AND PROPOSED CHANGES

In the following pages of this chapter, a hypothetical policy statement will be used throughout to provide a basis for illustrating the elements of an analysis of policy. The reader could, of course, speculate about the use of these analytic elements on any particular existing policy or any policy that might be proposed for analysis or adoption. For heuristic purposes, we will assume that the Middleville School District has heard some concern in the community about the extent to which parents and guardians are properly involved in matters concerning their children. There is some question as to whether anyone other than school personnel is welcome in the schools.

A hallmark of any analytic framework is to set forth, in advance, the elements or characteristics of any phenomenon that will be studied or subjected to analysis. The reader will see that our first task is to identify the actual policy statement involving the policy under question, followed by groupings of explicitly stated elements that will be examined.

Identify the Policy Problem, the Policy Goals, and the Policy Statement: What Are the Problem and the Goals, and How Is the Policy Stated, or How Will It Be Stated?

Meaningful participation of parents in their own children's school experience and in the overall life of the school itself is often stated as a goal and a desirable condition in many school systems. This is often pursued through support for formal teacher-parent organizations, systematic use of volunteer parents in the classroom, augmentation of a school's technical/professional resources through the involvement of particularly talented parents, and so forth. The goal, in those instances, is generally to weld the interdependence of school and families, or school and community, in some instances. The goal may also be to maximize the use of resources in the school's environment. Other situations involve parents in making decisions, such as regarding the handling of disciplinary measures for a particular student or placement planning and individualized service plans for special educational services. Although there has been some feedback from the community that parents are not adequately represented, the Middleville School Board does have the following policy in place: "In all instances involving disciplinary action for a student and those events in which a placement in a special educational program is being considered for a student, the parents or legal guardian of such student will be informed and consulted and will actively participate in the decision process and any resultant determination (October 12, 2001)."

In this instance, the policy is formally stated, rather than being merely an informal but prevailing expectation, and is formally legitimated by the school board. As will be noted later in our analysis, formalization and legitimation may not necessarily mean that the policy is promulgated and enforced.

Bases of Legitimacy of the Policy and Source or Location. Is the location of the policy within or external to the school system? Who provides the right to take action, and where is that documented (i.e., in written form that can be accessed easily or in the repetitive or patterned behavior of significant actors observed in the system)? The policy has clearly been legitimated (i.e., the right to take action has been established) by the Middleville School Board. In fact, the documentation is available in writing and dated in board minutes. Furthermore, additional legitimacy is obtained in state and federal guidelines regarding parental participation in development of individualized service plan processes for special education evaluation and placement decisions. Parental notification (though not necessarily parental participation) is also required by state regulation in instances of a child's suspension or expulsion.

The Targets and/or Clients of Concern. Who is the object of change, and whose interests will be served by the policy? The target of a policy may be seen as that element (i.e., person or people) in whom desired behavior is being sought. In this sense, the target of the policy may be seen as all staff of the school system and the parents as well, since it is clear that the assurance of participation is both a right and a responsibility across the board. All parties are obligated to behave in ways such that parents are significantly involved.

On the face of it, every policy is presumed to benefit the client, and the client is widely assumed to be the customer, the guest, or the citizen, or in this case the student or the parent. However, if one assumes that the client is truly that element on whose behalf the goal is being sought, then the school system itself, or its staff, could also be seen as a beneficiary or a client in a number of ways. Assurance of parental participation allows the school system to satisfy state and federal requirements and, consequently, obtain outside funding, in order to serve the interests of the system as a whole. On the other hand, such a policy surely serves the interest of those parents who might otherwise find it difficult to participate in a meaningful way in key decisions affecting their children. This policy legitimates parental entry.

The Factors of Eligibility. Who is or what will be included or covered in the policy, and under what conditions? Any one claim to eligibility under this policy is rather vague. For example, the policy states that "In all instances . . . the parents or legal guardian . . . shall be informed." The policy gives no direction or suggestion as to whether "all instances" includes the first incident or first formal action or even the first informal discussion of the propriety of taking action. On the other hand, one could logically conclude that parental participation is mandated only when formal consideration of action is first considered or when final decisions are on the table. Some of the same vagueness can be found in the policy's wording regarding "will be informed and consulted and will actively participate in the decision." Consequently, the policy is vague and weak in this area and certainly provides a good example of the utility of having policy guidelines. Guidelines may be thought of as less formal, less restrictive signposts or suggested ways to operationalize policy so that the policy is consistently applied. Guidelines are not generally published in formal policy and are generally developed after a policy has been established. The analyst may need to determine whether such guidelines exist and whether they are adequate.

The Effect upon System Maintenance, Change, or Control. What is the intended and/or unintended effect upon issues of maintenance, change, or control within or for the school system? Who has vested interests in the policy's initiation or continuation? It would appear on the face of it that the intent of the policy is to bring about system change. The presumption is that parental participation has been inadequate and is desirable.

A question to ask here is whether parental/guardian participation is actually the norm in this school system or whether there is some misperception about the policy's implementation. One would have to examine the data on actual levels of participation of parents. For example, one needs to know the rate of participation at the present time in the various schools, grade levels, and neighborhoods in the entire school district to determine if there are any differential rates of participation. Moreover, those rates might have to be examined both before and after enactment of the policy so that any change in participation rates can be observed. Another aspect of examining change would also be to observe or document the behavior of school staff. Are various staff groups any more or less conscientious in fostering parental participation? Analysis of these data may offer some suggestion whether or not the policy serves the purpose of social control of staff or parents, or both, in bringing about desired participation within the system as a whole.

Explicit or Implicit Theories. What theoretical foundation gave rise to or supports the policy? The fundamental theoretical foundation of parental participation can be found in basic democratic theory that citizens have the right and responsibility to fully participate in decisions affecting their own (or their children's) lives. Furthermore, the policy is entirely in concert with common and case law regarding the primacy of parental responsibility for the welfare of children. Hence, this criterion is, generally speaking, unassailable as a policy feature.

There may be some significant actors within the school system who hold the theoretical or philosophical view that participation beyond the school's walls by others in the community (including members of the family) actually broadens and enriches the educational process and aids in individualized planning. On the other hand, some may view parental participation in professional affairs as an unnecessary burden. Those individuals should also be identified, and their positions and influence should be examined, and the resultant information may also have implications for the change or control questions raised above.

Topography of the Policy System. Can you map the terrain of who is involved in this system? What offices or units are or will be affected by this policy as it stands or by any changes that might be proposed? Who might constitute a viable "action system" to provide support for or opposition to such a policy? Who are some of the key participants? If one were to sketch out a conceptual map, there would be a number of relevant actors. The map would certainly include the school principal or principals, the classroom teachers involved, any special education personnel having professional knowledge of a particular situation, perhaps other community agencies also providing services relevant to a student, and the parent or guardian. It would be necessary, then, to examine the information on the actual range and variety of opportunities for participation. Are there potential advocacy groups involved? Are certain staff groupings or certain school principals especially interested in or opposed to investing in this issue?

Contemporary or Antecedent Issues. What are some of the issues embedded in this particular policy within or around the school system that should be considered? Are there other relevant past events that explain the existence of this policy or how the policy was developed or stated? It would be very important to identify any prior incidents related to the conditions covered by the policy (e.g., children bringing weapons to the school, controversial disciplinary actions, the general and actual practice—or lack of consistency, on the other hand—in involving parents/guardians in individualized service planning). There may be some historical baggage that gave rise to the policy's adoption. It may have been hastily crafted, or it may have been carefully considered and debated.

There may also be contemporary issues that place this issue on the system's agenda. For example, perhaps there are other issues in the community also involving matters of informed consent of parents or alleged arbitrary decisions being made by public officials in other arenas, such as adolescents gaining access to health care without parental knowledge or counseling services being provided to students without parental approval. These factors may suggest something about the potential for amending the policy or how firm a base of support the policy has in its present form.

Assessment of Current and Anticipated System Functioning

To some extent we have already moved into the domain of the second set of elements. In real life, it is impossible to deal with human systems in linear fashion. Real-life interaction is circular and iterative. However, this second set of the elements emphasizes an assessment of the current structural state of a system.

The State of Communication and System Boundaries. What is the nature of communication and interaction between key elements in the system as a result of this policy? For policy to be effective and to achieve power to bring about predictable behavior, policy must be clearly published and implemented. Do families actually have clear and frequent communication with and from the school? Do the boundaries between home and school, in general, seem permeable or impermeable? That is, is there generally a free flow of interaction or communication between home and school, or are the barriers and gates firm and protected? It is essential to determine the extent to which publication and implementation of this policy have actually occurred. Then, too, have divisional and departmental administrators and supervisors adequately monitored the implementation of this policy? Has the communication been unilateral by way of mere policy pronouncements from above? Rather, has communication been bilateral in that those who manage and supervise staff have engaged in practical discussions with the staff members implementing the policy in order to get corrective feedback?

From a practical point of view, have parents been informed sufficiently in advance so that their participation is reasonably convenient? Have professional staff appropriately assisted parents or guardians to be adequately prepared for whatever participation might be needed? In this particular policy, the parent would need to become familiar with the decision process and the range of options available in advance in coming to decisions about an individualized educational plan for a student, for example. Do staff assist them in meeting the spirit and intent of this policy? In the case of pending disciplinary action by the school, do staff assist parents in joining the school in productive problem solving or, instead, is the parent brought in only to be informed of decisions already made?

It is useful to examine the direction of the feedback by observing whether any difficulties encountered by staff in achieving full participation have been taken into account in the changes made to the policy or in the development of guidelines. This might have been done through examination of staff experience with the policy or in the allocation of more resources for achieving the policy goal. For example, have the boundaries between home and school been altered through increased funding for staff transportation for home visits or through publication of informational materials that familiarize parents with basic information on procedures?

It is sometimes instructive to identify key system points for communication. Are there various groups that have opportunity to influence one another concerning this policy? Are any particular bargaining, negotiating, or collaborative groups or coalitions likely to be forming because of this policy? Do psychologists, speech therapists, and social workers tend to have a position on informing and including parents that differs from that of most school principals, or do those groups work together on this?

Here it might be beneficial to see if any advocacy groups have communicated their interests in this matter, for example when the rate of expulsions or suspensions appears to weigh more heavily on a particular neighborhood or segment of the community. Do these groups tend to bring their concerns to staff who work at the implementation level, or do they tend to bring their concerns about the policy directly to the board at public meetings?

It could also be instructive to examine the school's general posture on parental participation at times other than special education procedures or disciplinary actions. Some examples might be the school's overall use of parent volunteers in the classroom, logistical support given by the school system for parent-teacher organizations, or other ways in which the school might give the metamessage that parents/guardians are welcome or unwelcome. In practical terms, how frequently do the home and the school come into interaction in this school system?

Authority, Influence, and Leadership. What authority, exercise of power, or leadership is given to or needed to effect this policy? Who holds power, and who actually can or does exercise that power? Assuming that the policy is functioning effectively, by whose or what authority and influence is the policy held to the line? Is the system's superintendent involved and aggressive? Is there monitoring by that office? On the other hand, is there actually little support but for the outreach initiatives of staff at the lowest levels? Could it be that the policy is failing due to lack of support at the departmental level or due to the lack of cooperation by many school principals? On the other hand, are principals generally advocates for meaningful parental involvement, but are service staff lax in taking initiatives to involve parents or guardians in any meaningful way? In any case, why is this happening? One might examine the extent or manner in which the system's administrative leaders (i.e., departmental directors, program heads, coordinators, or other significant actors) play roles in leadership in implementation of this policy.

Strains and Constraints. What effect does the policy have upon tension, variety, and entropy (i.e., the tendency toward disorder or the inability to do work in a system) within the system? Is it dysfunctional or functional? Some variety and variability in human systems is good. Groups and organizations—school systems included—thrive on sustainable variety. In fact, it might be argued that the greater the variety of inputs into the educational process, input from the home included, the stronger the overall educational process is. However, when tension is not managed and variety leads to chaos or a school's response is no longer predictable, then entropy sets in. That is, the system has less functional order and has less ability to do its work. Remember that the main purpose of policy is to give order and/or direction.

Some forms of tension are caused by strains in the system that (at least theoretically) can be corrected. Some examples in this instance might be inadequate numbers of service-level staff, overworked teachers with classes that are too large, principals having responsibility for too many buildings, and so forth. The greater variety of points of view provided by parents contributes more information for decisions about children, but it also adds to the quantum of information that staff have to deal with. In addition, when policy is published but not implemented, it may sometimes be because it lacks the support of guidelines giving direction to system personnel. A well-intended but unimplemented policy can be minimized or become practically nonexistent in this instance.

Other factors may be more in the form of constraints, defined here as those barriers that cannot be moved (except under unusual circumstances) because they are part of the nature of the phenomenon. In a school system, constraint may be found in the existence of labor agreements, such as a limiting definition on the length of the work day (though this factor is sometimes erroneously used as an excuse for inaction). Another example might be the lack of adequate physical facilities to accommodate some meetings, though this factor could be more of a short-term barrier, given newly assigned resources in the future.

Resistance to Change. How salient is this policy (i.e., how many groups or other issues does this policy affect)? What are the issues, forces, or factors that might give resistance to or mitigate against change as a result of the policy? A key question here is how many different groupings or categories this policy affects. The likely answer is that this is a very salient policy in that regard. The superintendent and the school board are very much in touch with a variety of publics that likely see themselves as stakeholders who should have a meaningful say in the system. There are currently nonprofit foundations interested in fostering family and community participation in local schools. State and federal statutory regulations require such participation in certain circumstances. In addition, some school personnel highly value broad participation, as suggested earlier. Consequently, there would appear to be very high probability of leverage here to promote a salient issue.

The next question to ask, then, is where any resistance or counter-resistance to policy implementation or change might exist within specific pockets or positions of school personnel. Is implementation of this policy in competition for financial resources with other needs in the system? Moreover, there should be some examination of whether particular segments of the community do not or cannot fully cooperate in seizing their opportunities to participate. Some examples of the latter grouping might be those who have been alienated by school experiences in the past, those who are limited by inadequate transportation, those who lack adequate substitute child care, and those who are limited by language barriers. Implementation of the policy may require allocation of new or altered resources to reach out to those parents.

In terms of bringing about system change for the policy, it is essential to determine where or to whom (i.e., what person or office) any informal and formal presentations of analysis and recommendations might best be brought forward. Might it be at the lowest level nearest the problem (i.e., using the principle of subsidiarity), such as the department having the most direct dealings with parents and families? Might it be in open discussions, such as at board meetings? Which point of entry is likely to have the greatest leverage, or the ability to engender meaningful discussion and change?

Feedback Devices. What channels exist that provide for information that guides the system toward corrective action based upon the policy's outputs? Good policy has built-in mechanisms for providing self-corrective feedback. Although we have had some discussion regarding feedback, this characteristic of policy needs additional attention. Some policy statements include a provision for assignment of monitoring to a particular position or office within the organization. Some sunset laws, those that purposely expire at a time specified before continuation legislation is considered, are an excellent example of a built-in feedback mechanism. Furthermore, both positive and negative feedback should be systematically sought. Middleville School's policy on participation is lacking in this regard. There is no suggestion in the policy statement itself that such feedback is desired or required. Hence, this policy analysis will likely recommend, in its summary analysis, that appropriate feedback devices must be established.

Impact upon the System's Dynamic Adaptation. To what extent does the policy enhance the system's ability to be more adaptive and self-corrective? Organizations must alter their forms over time in order to survive. This is what is meant by "dynamic adaptation." However, lacking the feedback mechanism just noted, there is nothing to suggest that the parental participation policy has any impact on the system's capacity for dynamic adaptation. Although the Middleville School District may be very dynamic in its forward movement, there is no evidence of that found in this particular policy.

Environmental Impact. What impact is there (or will there be) in the general educational climate as a result of the policy's existence? It is reasonable to assume that this policy would engender more positive feelings in the community, not only for parents and guardians of the system's students but for the broader community as well. After all, such a policy communicates the metamessage that this system is an open system. The school is open to the community, so to speak. Input is welcome. In fact, a parent's effort to be informed and fully participate could easily be interpreted as welcoming any of those individuals who might appropriately inform and advocate for a particular student, parent, guardian, or family in given problem-solving situations. Other community agencies might well perceive that there are open doors to this school system.

Determine Implications for Selected Values

The third category of elements involves an assessment of the congruence of the policy and its implementation with selected values. The word "selected" is carefully chosen here because who is to say what set of values should be brought to the analysis? First, since the values of adequacy, effectiveness, and efficiency are so much a part of U.S. folklore, it would be foolish not to include these values. Second, inasmuch as this text is for and about the practice of social work, the framework has drawn heavily on the Code of Ethics of the National Association of Social Workers (1999), hence the inclusion of the values of social justice, self-determination, identity, individualization, nonjudgmental attitude, and confidentiality. Consequently, the following elements and questions should be considered.

Adequacy. To what extent is the goal achieved when/if the policy is carried out, in terms of coverage both for individuals and for the system as a whole? The elements of adequacy, effectiveness, and efficiency are often uttered together in popular analysis as if the phrase provided a mantra for responsible citizenship. However, each of these elements differs in the sense of what is examined and expected. Adequacy is defined here in terms of the question given earlier: adequacy is the extent to which a goal is achieved if the policy is carried out. Furthermore, adequacy may be thought of as horizontal, or as the degree or extent to which all those who were meant to be covered are covered. In this instance, are all parents/guardians found to be included when it comes to participation in designated decisions? On the other hand, adequacy may be vertical, or the extent to which particular targets or clients or individuals are affected. Here, the question is whether only certain socioeconomic segments in the community receive different support in their participation, or whether only certain types of decisions receive differential parental attention by the school, such as placement for gifted children's planning or for special education, or only for participation in the parent-teacher organization. The issue with adequacy is coverage, who is covered, and how sufficient that coverage is.

Effectiveness. To what extent is there a logical connection, if any, between the means or techniques employed by the policy and the policy goal that is to be achieved? Effectiveness is related to what most people generally consider the outcome and its relation to what means were employed to obtain that outcome. In this instance, one must examine the means or methods whereby Middleville School personnel went about ensuring and obtaining full participation as mandated by the policy. As just noted, the presence and impact on specific target populations might be examined in this regard. Although pure cause-and-effect relationships are rarely documented in social phenomena, correlations between methods employed and participatory outcomes would likely be valid.

Efficiency. To what degree are the means employed in goal achievement maximized with the use of the minimum amount of necessary resources? The useful concept of efficiency has recently been clouded by the pervasive dialogue on managed care versus "managed cost." In that debate, the emphasis is either on efficiency in cost or on level of effort. Efficiency as an evaluative concept that refers to the degree to which the means employed in achieving the goal are maximized (i.e., used judiciously) and are employed while the minimum amount of necessary resources is being used. Put another way, did the job get done while the minimum amount of effort or cost was used?

This criterion suggests that the analyst should examine costs to both the parents/guardians and the school system as well as the benefits to both the parents/guardians and the school system. This analysis would likely be highly speculative in nature but worth the effort in determining how and to whom and to what extent any recommendations for action might be shaped. Furthermore, such analysis is likely to suggest both tangible and intangible costs and benefits that are likely to be difficult to concretize. Many of the costs could easily be psychological or social in nature. Nevertheless, this is a very important part of the analysis, and the analyst will have to be creative.

We would likely have to operationalize such concepts as time, effort, satisfaction, improvement, the quality of relationships, commitment, and sharing, and even the concept of participation itself.

Impact on Rights, Statuses, and Social Issues. What is the policy's impact on individual, group, or organizational rights and statuses, particularly in terms of equity, equality, and fairness? These elements are at the center of this analysis, because examination of these values and their presence or absence in the policy or its implementation are likely to shed light on much of the rest of the analysis. Policy can vitally affect a person's or a group's status and position in any social system, including a school system. Policy and its implementation can affirm proper rights and obligations, duties and responsibilities, prerogatives or privileges, or rewards or punishments. Aside from food and shelter, these are factors that heavily sustain life itself. This policy on parent/guardian participation surely assigns status and rights to some members of the community, whether the policy is operationalized adequately and whether or not it is enforced. A real test at the level of application may be found, however, in the extent to which people are treated equitably, equally, and fairly.

Equity may be defined as the extent to which people in similar circumstances are treated similarly. This is not to be confused with equality, in which people are treated the same in all circumstances. The policy analyst should try to determine whether all people were informed of the policy and that all parents and guardians were given the same opportunity to participate. That would be evidence of essential equal treatment. At the same time, it should be determined whether the principle of equity prevailed in that children and families in different situations needed differential treatment to achieve reasonably similar results as others. This would entail, for example, aggressive outreach to some; additional time before coming to joint decisions for others; possible inclusion of additional aides, advocates, or spokespersons for some; and so forth. Achievement of both equity and equality is most likely to give evidence that the policy was implemented with fairness.

Fairness is concerned with whether people or situations were dealt with in a manner that is reasonable and just as a result of application of the policy. Consequently, evidence of a carefully considered decision that is jointly arrived at in an open process without arbitrary rules is likely to promote just or fair treatment. The analyst should look for evidence of realization of this value or be prepared to provide rewording for the policy or a set of guidelines that would honor such outcomes.

Self-Determination. Does the policy honor the right of citizens to have a voice in the determination of those matters that vitally affect them? Surely self-determination is likely to be honored if the issues involved in justice and fairness are also to be achieved. Self-determination does not provide one with a unilateral right to establish the rules of conduct or the rights of choice beyond what is generally acceptable in a social contract. A central question here is whether the school system takes over for the family by unilaterally making decisions that should be made by or shared with the family.

Identity. What effect does this policy have on the self-image of the beneficiary (i.e., the client) or the target of the policy and on the need for and right to human dignity? This criterion speaks to the extent to which the policy or its application allows the receiver of the policy's intent to accept its impact with dignity. That is, human dignity should not be reduced by unreasonable and inappropriate policy directives. The purpose of policy is to support and enhance human interaction, not to demean any of its members. On the face of it, one might assume that the mere fact of inclusion in important decision-making processes would respect and enhance one's sense of identity. However, to gather data for this part of the task, the analyst will likely have to gather personal opinions from both past and current nonparticipating and participating parents and guardians. The views of third-party observers could also be of value.

Individualization and the Nonjudgmental Attitude. To what extent is the need for individuals (or groups or organizations) to be treated in terms of their unique nature, needs, and qualities recognized by the policy? This criterion is akin to the question of the policy's impact on identity. This criterion is focused more on the means and/or manner by which the system carries out its implementation of the policy, whereas identity speaks more to the outcome effect on the target person or people, who presumably are the beneficiaries of the policy.

Individualization speaks to the need for individuals and groups to be treated in terms of their unique nature, needs, and qualities. The nonjudgmental attitude speaks to the quality of behavior or demeanor of those who carry the policy out as representatives of the school system.

Here, one would want to examine whether the organization puts the policy into practice through person-to-person contact by informing families of the parents' or guardians' rights and opportunities or, instead, by merely informing families by memo or referring to school system policies in general. It could also be worthwhile to see how and whether participation as a concept is presented, such as whether it is characterized as a pro forma requirement or an inconvenience to the staff or whether it is viewed as a positive opportunity to share or collaborate in a child's school experience.

The GRADES Test. What are the implications of this policy for matters of gender, race, age, disability, ethnicity, and socioeconomic status? It can reasonably be said that most school personnel are not racist or sexist or guilty of a number of other isms, at least in terms of their conscious intentions and behaviors. Nevertheless, as patterns of behavior are established and routines set in, it is easy for the collective behavior of organizations and individuals to become institutionalized. Consequently, it is absolutely essential that the policy analyst consciously and explicitly press the analysis against a number of very similar questions. The question would go something like: "Given what has been observed, or given what might take place in the implementation of this policy, what implications are there for those of any particular gender or sexual orientation?" Or "for people of any particular racial identity or for people of color?" Or "for any particular age group?" Or "for any person with a disability?" Or "for people of any particular ethnic group?" Or "for those of any particular socioeconomic status?" Here is where you can do more than give lip service to advocating for those who might be disadvantaged by policy because of their GRADES identity.

In our fictitious policy in the imaginary Middleville School District, could it be that the task (and perhaps even burden) of participation will most likely fall on female caretakers? It is widely known that mothers, for example, are generally more active in relating to schools than fathers. An example would be mothers' attendance at conferences regarding their children. Could this mean that more aggressive efforts have to be made to involve males in the home-school collaboration, for example? Or how about the fact that there are increasing numbers of grandparents now raising their grandchildren? It is possible that grandparents may be less familiar with the culture of current school systems and even individual schools because it has been some time since they themselves were active in the schools? Perhaps different assumptions may have to be made regarding what needs to be communicated to grandparents or how the school might be perceived by families in those situations.

Then there are those families in which one person's disability is sometimes a limiting factor in the extent to which he or she can freely participate in a whole range of activities in the community, including the schools. Perhaps there are special needs for transportation for the person who might otherwise visit the school, or perhaps an inordinate number of visits to the home are needed as a substitute for some of the conferences on-site at the school. Perhaps the disability of a family member would require respite care to facilitate a family caregiver's visits to the school. These are just a few possibilities that could be considered in the policy analysis.

Then there is the question of any implications for the ethnic identity of the family. In carrying out the policy, are all staff adequately sensitive to unique cultural factors such as those family traditions in which only the male has authority to speak with those who might "intrude" on the family? Or how about those families who view any formal institution as a manifestation of authority to be feared or to be obeyed or to be revered?

Finally, what might seem the most obvious is often overlooked: the socioeconomic status of the family and what opportunities might have to be forgone due to lack of supports available to the "average" family. This would include considerations of the availability of a telephone and transportation, general good health, availability of clothing in which one feels comfortable in public, access to substitute child care, and so forth.

The main point of the GRADES test is that not all people have equal ability to enjoy what is offered to them, even with a sound and positively motivated social policy. Consequently, the professional person who is really committed to responding to the unique needs of individuals must consider that fact not only in professional clinical practice and service, but in any adequate policy analysis and policy implementation.

Establish Feasibility and Resources Needed for the Desired Outcomes

The fourth set of elements in the framework involves an assessment of the feasibility and availability of resources necessary to implement the policy. There are obviously a myriad of possible considerations but we will limit our framework to the following.

Technical Capacity. What particular technology, skills, and talents are available to the school system internally or externally to achieve the goal? Does that technology consist of people or equipment? Implementation of our sample policy would require very little hardware. Surely there could be some support needed in terms of distribution of newsletters, the use of advertising media, keeping mailing lists and phone lists up to date, and so forth. However, this policy is more likely to focus on considerations of people power.

People are resources in an organization. Foremost would be some assessment of the attitudes and commitment of administrators and service staff toward assertive implementation of this policy. If the assessment is positive or affirmative, then the need would be primarily to facilitate and provide support. If the assessment is negative or questionable, it may require in-service training or a different approach to supervision and performance evaluation of administrative and staff functioning. In situations in which it is particularly difficult to obtain cooperation of parents or guardians from certain groups or areas of the system, outside consultation may be needed from those who have also faced this problem but have experienced successful outcomes.

Finances. Are the financial resources available or likely to become available? Use of staff time, whether in training or retraining, or even in reallocation of staff resources devoted to the goals of most any set of policy priorities, can be seen as a financial cost. An obvious cost of aggressive outreach is a likely increase in reimbursable travel time for staff, or possibly a decrease in alternative reimbursable services provided by that same staff. It is important for the analyst to try to determine, if only speculatively, what the real cost might be to focus or refocus staff direction on implementing this policy. At the same time, one must try to also estimate the opportunity cost of not implementing the policy by not appropriately involving the targets of the policy. There may be long-term and broader systemic costs that have a financial price tag. Psychological costs must also be considered, such as impact on morale, stress, and/or community relations.

Time. To what extent is time a resource or a hindrance in achieving the policy goal? There appears to be no obvious implication for time as a factor in this policy in terms of any urgency for implementation. As just noted, there is an implication for the reallocation of use of staff time. If the school system has a history of excluding parental/guardian participation, the policy surely will demand more time of families. Time is a resource for families as well as for organizations. Consequently, there could be an increased demand on family resources in pursuit of a common mission, the adequate educational experience.

Rationality. In the final analysis, to what extent is or will the policy be perceived as being rational? Does the policy, as conceived, forge a link between the perceived problem and its logical solution? It is hard to think of an argument for not perceiving this policy as being rational, unless one has a narrow or erroneous view of what constitutes efficiency in use of staff time. As noted previously, the concept of encouraging full participation of people in affairs having implications for their lives is rooted in basic democratic theory. However, there might be those who would argue from a philosophical point of view that the purpose of the school is to teach, and that teaching is perceived only as a technical function performed only by those technically prepared in a particular way. However, this view is surely not prevalent today.

Power of the Policy. To what extent is the policy actually likely to shape or alter the behavior of those intended? Finally, one must question the extent to which this policy will actually have an impact on those for whom it is intended. This is the ultimate measure of the power of the policy. Will it actually shape the administration's or the staff's patterns of behavior in fostering and effectively using the benefits of more complete family participation? Will the policy actually do anything to increase or enhance the frequency and/or quality of participation by parents or guardians? Are there any sanctions related to compliance to bring about the desired outcomes?

On the face of it, "participation," "being informed," "being consulted," "decision process," and "determination" are words and phrases with a positive valence. Few people could be frightened or rejecting of the concepts and values generally implied. Put another way, who could argue with these concepts or the construct one might create by bringing these concepts together in a policy statement? On the other hand, participation of family members can be rewarded but surely not punished. Regarding staff, however, certain incentives and disincentives can be tied to their support for this policy.

Provide Recommendations

The fifth and final step of the analysis is, of course, to provide a clear and cogent statement of recommendations for wording of the policy and key action elements. This statement should focus on both strengths and weaknesses or any factors peculiar to the issue and those factors suggested by the data generated by the analysis. In this context, there are a number of considerations for communicating or conveying a policy analysis and any recommended action. As a reminder, the original policy is restated here: "In all instances involving disciplinary action for a student and those events in which a placement in a special educational program is being considered for a student, the parents or legal guardian of such student will be informed and consulted and will actively participate in the decision process and any resultant determination (October 12, 2001)." Any resistance to this policy would likely manifest as negative criticism of those portions of the policy statement that are vague or poorly operationalized. Some of the issues are discussed below.

The policy refers to "all instances" involving disciplinary action. One questions whether this is appropriate. Surely there could be classroom situations that are best handled within the classroom, and in some instances, those events could be shared with parents/guardians later, if appropriate. Perhaps there are some minor infractions of school rules that would best be handled more informally, given the opportunity to build positive rapport between, say, the principal and the student. Consequently, the analyst may suggest a rewording to something on the order of "all instances in which suspension, expulsion, or removal of a student's privileges" to replace "involving disciplinary action."

Perhaps the reference to "a special educational program" might not be interpreted the same by many in the community. This term serves as jargon for many within the system and most often refers to programs for those with learning and behavioral difficulties, but to others it might reference programs for gifted children. The analyst might suggest substitute language of "in programs other than the student's regular classroom or curriculum schedule" to replace the phrase "in a special educational program."

Presuming that the school board is committed to its goals of family participation, it is important to build a feedback mechanism directly into the policy statement rather than leaving this matter up to development of adequate guidelines or the good intentions of school personnel. Consequently, the policy statement could include: "Implementation of this policy shall be monitored regularly by the assistant superintendent for community affairs and progress reports will be provided quarterly to the Board of Education."

Perhaps the most difficult concepts to operationalize in the policy statement have to do with the phrase that reads: "will be informed and consulted and will actively participate in the decision process and any resultant determination." Experience would suggest that these policy provisions are not likely to be satisfied or clarified by a mere rewording. This is where development of more explicit policy guidelines would be appropriate. Guidelines are not part of the actual policy statement but are statements of intent and behavior that are necessary to achieve the intent of the policy. The following guidelines could be considered as suggestions for action elements and content:

1. "Drafting of any recommendations should clearly include active participation of parents and guardians of children currently enrolled in the school system. Special consideration should be given to soliciting input from both individuals who have been active in and may be assumed to represent any parent-teacher organization and any individuals who are not generally attached to any organized group associated with the school."
2. "The issue of 'informed' should include development of guidelines that will specify organizational behaviors that will give evidence of a person being informed. Such activities could include presenting parents/guardians with written procedures on review of a student's status and performance, specification of types of issues and procedures for appeal, participants' right to be accompanied by advocates of their choice, opportunity for dialogue with staff for purposes of clarification, and so forth. These alternatives should be considered in any drafting of guidelines."
3. "The question of operationalizing 'consulted' should speak to the manner and frequency with which contact should be initiated and pursued by school personnel. This would include fostering participation by both postal and telephone invitations and/or personal visits to the home, allowing sufficient advance notice, convenience in time and place of meetings, and the like."
4. "The extent and nature of 'actively participate' will, of course, be up to the participant to determine. However, the school could develop guidelines that communicate that family members' suggestions, comments, and statements of preference are valued. It should be noted in writing (not solely reliance on nonverbal behavior of staff) that family members' input is not only necessary but valued."
5. "Reference to 'resultant determination' could be clarified through guidelines and will be dependent on the type and nature of the decision or problem dealt with. For example, issues of disciplinary action may require reference to legal limitations or mandates of state law, as in the instance of weapons or drugs being brought into a school building. Such matters may require certain written commitments by both the school and the parent. In the case of special programming for a particular student's unique needs, some agreements may be informal, and a monitoring process agreed on. In other instances, there may need to be an official sign-off by both the school and the parent/guardian in order to satisfy mandatory regulations or funding and reimbursement considerations and to otherwise formalize agreements."
6. "Development and promulgation of guidelines should be mandated in the policy statement, and the office responsible for that task should be specified."

Given this analysis and the changes suggested, the modified policy to be recommended to the superintendent for ultimate consideration by the board would be:

> In all instances of suspension or expulsion of a student or removal of a student's privileges, and those events in which a student's placement in programs other than the student's regular classroom schedule is being considered, the parents or legal guardian of such student will be informed and consulted and will actively participate in the decision process and any resultant determination. Implementation of this policy shall be monitored regularly by the assistant superintendent for community affairs, and progress reports will be provided quarterly to the Board of Education. Guidelines necessary for implementation of this policy shall be developed and promulgated by December 1, 2010.

Other actions in support of our hypothetical Middleville School District example for support of the policy changes were introduced in the course of the analysis. To summarize, these action aspects (in additional to analytical tasks) should include:

1. Obtaining the endorsement of all key administrative or service departments within the school system, as appropriate, for the policy changes
2. Establishing relationships with community advisory and advocacy groups, such as the Association of Retarded Citizens, the Council for Exceptional Children, and the like
3. Offering in-service training for teachers and other ancillary service staff to prepare them and to prepare parents in advance for effective participation
4. Obtaining directives pertaining to the policy in writing
5. Reviewing such directives and policies, where possible, with new staff and new families as part of orientation routines.
6. Facilitating, supporting, initiating, and encouraging all those who embrace the policy and its purposes

FAIR WARNING TO CONSCIENTIOUS PEOPLE

The foregoing is merely an illustration of how an analytic framework might be used. It is not an instruction book. An analytic framework merely gives a list of possible considerations. This chapter has added a few possible brainteasers to those considerations to offer illustrations. In real life, the process is not so linear. It is, instead, circular with a lot of back-and-forth. In addition, in real life one is not able to gather information for each element, nor is it necessary to do so. Furthermore, any analytic framework should serve primarily as an instigator that merely stimulates further creative thought for the imaginative professional trying to take responsibility for constructive criticism.

A FEW FINAL WORDS ABOUT PRESENTATION OF POLICY ANALYSES

Effective analyses of policy are not hidden under a bushel basket. They need to see the light of day, of course, because they are done to be communicated. Such analyses are performed to teach, inform, or persuade. Consequently, policy analysis can be seen as fundamentally and honestly a political act, even under the most disciplined and objectively driven circumstances. Although the topic of how to communicate one's policy analysis is a topic in and of itself, there are a few generalities that can be stated to serve as reminders. These are provided here in the form of a list that will hopefully suggest further exploration:

1. The form and style, written or oral, should be comfortable and clearly not a repetition of the laborious manner presented here. The manner should be objective and not critical of any individual or group.
2. The content must be accurate and informative; the reader or listener must be assured that the analysis has contributed to his or her understanding and increased his or her confidence in understanding the issues.
3. The analysis should show working familiarity of all the relevant antecedent and contemporary issues impinging on the policy choice.
4. Argument must be balanced; the analysis should identify potential pros and cons or arguments for and against key choices to be made.
5. Speculation must be offered on the probable impact of key choices.
6. The presentation must use language that keeps the reader or listener target groups in mind and helps give those targets a clear mental picture of what is being communicated. The best way to do this is by clearly labeling sections, numbering key points or choices, and providing clear and concise summaries.
7. Lastly, the presentation must be consistent with professional values and ethics. Special emphasis must be given to accuracy of information and freedom from attempts at manipulation.

A comprehensive policy analysis communicated with these considerations in mind will add to the credibility of the analyst as well as to the analysis that is provided.

References

Flynn, J. (1992). *Social agency policy: Analysis and presentation for community practice* (2nd ed.). Chicago: Nelson-Hall.

Jansson, B. S. (1999). *Becoming an effective policy advocate: From policy practice to social justice*. Pacific Grove, CA: Brooks/Cole.

National Association of Social Workers. (1999). *Code of ethics of the National Association of Social Workers*. Washington, DC: Author.

11

Needs Assessment: A Tool of Policy Practice in School Social Work

Lyndell R. Bleyer
Western Michigan University

Kathryn Joiner
Western Michigan University

- What Is Needs Assessment?
- Why Conduct a Needs Assessment?
- Planning Your Needs Assessment
- Implementing the Assessment
- Analyzing Your Data
- Reporting Your Findings
- Sources for Data and Other Resources

WHAT IS NEEDS ASSESSMENT?

The ability to conduct a needs assessment is a crucial skill in school social work. It provides a systematic means of gathering data about a problem experienced by more than a few students in the school. It provides a broader context for the problems that students are experiencing. It provides a data-based means of communicating about this broader context in a way that school administrators, teachers, and community members can understand. It provides school social workers with a powerful data-based means of customizing their roles to fit the needs of a particular school or district.

A human need is any identifiable condition that limits a person in meeting his or her full potential. Human needs are usually expressed in social, economic, and health-related terms. From a research perspective, they are frequently qualitative statements. Needs of individuals may be aggregated to express similar needs in quantified terms (United Way of America, 1999).

A needs assessment is a data-gathering and planning activity for informing decision making. The data describe the characteristics, achievements, knowledge, behaviors, desires, needs, and/or opinions of a group of people or an entire community. Many have attempted to define human need in a more specific way. These attempts have ranged from Erikson's (1968) eight critical stages of development to Maslow's (1970) concept of motivation based on a hierarchy of needs. J. A. Ponsioen (1962) stated that every society's first duty is to take care of the basic survival needs of its citizens, which include biological, emotional, social, and spiritual needs. According to this view, each society must establish a level below which no person must fall. These levels vary from society to society and change over time within the same society. Thus need is a normative concept involving value judgments and is greatly influenced by social, political, and economic conditions. For example, in the early 1950s, a family was considered fortunate if it had a television. Today, a student whose family does not have a computer might be considered academically disadvantaged.

WHY CONDUCT A NEEDS ASSESSMENT?

The data obtained through a needs assessment process are used to:

- Help explain the nature of a problem, its characteristics, magnitude, or consequences;
- Provide clues about causes and possible interventions;
- Compare students with other students or other schools;
- Identify and monitor trends (academic achievement, graduation rates, etc.);
- Document a need to be included in the problem statement of a grant proposal;
- Convince school officials that a problem that warrants the allocation of resources exists;
- Demonstrate the need for programs threatened by budget cuts;
- Document the support for new programs or interventions;
- Determine if and where additional resources are needed;
- Provide information to assist with planning or developing new services/programs; and
- Influence legislation.

A needs assessment can be as simple as examining existing data. It can be as complex as a multiyear, multiphase study involving strategies to collect new data through questionnaires or community forums. Designing and administering surveys is time consuming and expensive. It is generally wise to explore and use existing data before considering any type of new data collection. Analyzing existing data can be very effective, and schools generally have a wealth of data on hand. Data are collected on attendance, test scores, demographic characteristics, free lunch eligibility, enrollment in specific programs, grades, results of standardized tests, and many other issues.

Data used in a needs assessment can include a range of types. These can include measurement of characteristics, counts and rates, knowledge, beliefs and opinions, behaviors, or desires.

Characteristics describe the group or population being studied and include ascribed features such as age, gender, race, and achieved characteristics like family income, poverty status, or highest grade completed.

Counts and rates provide data on the incidence and prevalence of conditions. For instance, the teen birthrate incidence is a measure of the number of births to teenage mothers compared to the number of female teenagers. Prevalence is the number of cases in a given population at a point in time, such as the number of teen suicides that occurred during a particular period in a community (Simons & Jablonski, 1990).

Knowledge might include math proficiency, reading comprehension levels, standardized test scores, or street smarts.

Beliefs and opinions range from thoughts about oneself, such as one's self-esteem, to views about behavior, such as moral or cultural values, and stereotypes about others, such as gender or ethnic stereotypes.

Behaviors might include frequency of talking out in class, the duration of study time, eating habits, use of alcohol, participation in sports, number of hours worked per week by full-time students, number of absences, and number of students suspended or expelled by reason. Normative behaviors fall within culturally expected/acceptable ranges.

Desires are what people want (or think they want) but don't have, whereas *needs* can encompass things that one (or others) thinks are missing. One can determine needs by directly asking the intended audience or through observation, or they can be inferred from available data, whereas desires and opinions are usually gathered directly from questions on a survey or through observation, interviews, focus groups, or community forums.

PLANNING YOUR NEEDS ASSESSMENT

Determine What You Need to Know

The first step is determining what you need to know, and then deciding what information is needed to make an informed decision. The second step is determining the best source by balancing accuracy and reliability against cost and time constraints. Often as you begin to explore doing a needs assessment, the list of questions to be answered keeps growing. To expedite the process, make a checklist and decide which data are critical to your goal, which data would be helpful to clarifying issues, which would be interesting to have, and which will not add any insight to the problem being studied. As part of your checklist, include a source column. This may help you narrow your choices. Remember to look at existing data first before gathering new data.

For example, a school district that wants to know if a school breakfast program is a worthwhile pursuit should be aware that extensive research indicating that behavior and academic performance of most students improve in school systems where breakfast programs have been established has already been done nationally. So what would be studied is not the relationship between breakfast and performance, but rather the need for a breakfast program in a particular school district.

The information needed is what percentage of students currently do not eat a nutritious breakfast; how many children would be eligible for a subsidized breakfast program; and, for those children who do not have a nutritious breakfast but are not eligible, how many parents would buy into a breakfast program. It might also be interesting to study other factors influencing academic performance, such as adequacy of sleep and parental involvement in study habits. Table 11.1 provides a grid to help frame the data needed, sources, methods of data collection, and level of usefulness.

TABLE 11.1 Types of Data or Questions and Associated Sources or Methods

Type of Data or Questions	*Source and Method*	*Essential*	*Helpful*	*Interesting*	*No Use*
Breakfast's impact on learning—does it make a difference?	Literature review, e.g., Nutrition & Learning www.nal.usda.gov/fnic/service/learnpub.htm	✓			
How many of our students eat a nutritious breakfast?	Students and/or parents via log, diary, or question	✓			
What are eligibility guidelines for subsidies?	U.S. Dept. of Health & Human Serv.; census		✓		
How many of our school's students are eligible?	School records: i.e., now eligible for free milk or lunch subsidy; census data on poverty		✓		
Are there any differences in achievement between:	*Grades and test scores plus:*				
Our students who do and don't eat breakfast?	students &/or parents, teacher observation	✓			
Our students who get <7 vs. >7 hours sleep?	students &/or parents log/diary, teacher observation			✓	
Our students with parental review of homework ?	parent signature on homework or not			✓	

To answer these questions, you might employ two tactics. First, have students keep a breakfast log or journal in which they record everything they eat for breakfast each morning for three weeks. To be effective, the students should update their journals as soon as possible after arriving at school (in homeroom or first class of the day). A nutritional guide would be used to analyze these journals to give positive points for healthy foods consumed. If a question at the end of the journal asked if the student was eligible for free or reduced-price lunches and/or Medicaid, that would answer the eligibility question. If a survey were developed for parents, it would also ask about eligibility and, for those not eligible, whether the parent would like nutritious breakfasts to be available for purchase. Don't forget to ask each family the grade level of the students in their family—just in case your school system can only phase in a new program a few schools at a time.

Once the data are summarized, the school district can then look at need (students not currently eating nutritious breakfasts) and examine the cost of starting a breakfast program (the number of students eligible for free and reduced-price meals and the number of students for whom parents are willing to pay). Eliminating barriers to participation is important too. Schools that use a prepaid meal card that does not distinguish between family-paid and subsidized meals have had the greatest success in getting eligible students to participate in meal programs, as these eliminate the stigma of being identified by peers as low income.

Your school may have other topics that need answers. Some examples of information that may be useful in planning school services or child-related programs are the following:

- the number of children living in your community and the percentage of the total population that those children represent
- the number of children living in poverty
- the number of homeless children (number using shelters and doubled-up with other families)
- mobility/transience, or the number and percentage of students who attend the same school in June that they attended in September
- the number of children with disabilities or special needs by type
- the number of children living in single-parent families or families in which both parents work outside the home
- the reported incidence of violent, serious, and misdemeanor juvenile crimes
- the services and resources already available to meet the specific need you are addressing

A thorough analysis could also look at other factors that might influence performance, such as amount of sleep; family income (access to reading materials, access to a home computer, educational toys, etc.); and parental involvement, such as regular parental review of homework and encouragement of reading in the home.

Build a Base of Support by Getting Others Involved

Discuss the project with school administrators, teachers, parents, and student representatives to develop a clear idea of the purpose of the needs assessment and what you hope to learn or achieve. One way to encourage cooperation among all the concerned parties is to form a small committee to help you formulate an action plan. In addition to promoting ownership of the project, involving others in the planning stage is a good way to make sure you haven't overlooked important details. Having the scope of the activity agreed on by the majority of those involved will reduce hurdles.

Write a Proposal or Plan

After you have determined the scope of the needs assessment, develop a written plan. In the proposal, include the following:

- methodology of the needs assessment
- tasks to be performed, and by whom
- projected time line
- budget for the project, which should be based on the activities and time needed to carry them out (in addition to personnel, there may be expenses for copying questionnaires and summary reports, computer time, phone calls, postage, and resource materials)

In writing your plan, be realistic about whether or not you have the time and the expertise to carry out all elements of the project. Don't set short deadlines. Give yourself enough time to collect data, review it, and produce a well-written summary. Keep in mind the impact school breaks will have on your project. It may be that you will want to perform certain tasks but will need to engage additional help from other professionals to perform certain functions. If there are colleges or universities close by, you may be able to work out a plan for a graduate-level or upper-level undergraduate class to take on all or portions of your study as their semester project. Many colleges and universities have research centers that provide technical assistance and consultation to nonprofit organizations at cost. Large corporations may have research staff that they are willing to loan for committee work or consultation. If you intend to carry out the needs assessment yourself, consider whether you will need or can get release time.

IMPLEMENTING THE ASSESSMENT

Accurate information is key to successful planning. Having reliable data can help you make your point and persuade others. Think of the group or groups that will be the beneficiaries of the needs assessment, and also think of the groups that will be potential funding sources or will make the decision to allocate resources to address the need. Gather data with both audiences in mind.

Consider the following scenario: You are concerned about the need for enhanced substance abuse prevention education. You provide a number of statistics from existing data regarding substance use and abuse. These could include such things as the age at which children begin to smoke and use drugs and alcohol, the number of teenagers and young adults who smoke or use alcohol, gender differences in who uses drugs, changes in use/abuse patterns over time, and the number of automobile crashes attributed to substance abuse by age of driver. Some data may only be readily available at state or national levels. You may cite the data as found, or you could provide a rough estimation of local incidence by applying state or national rates to local populations. In addition, you may gather local incidents and estimates from key observers. You might use an anonymous questionnaire, but be cautioned that the information could be under- or overstated.

Gathering Existing Data

Be sure to make use of your own organization. Most school districts have data on absences, suspensions, number of students repeating a grade, standardized test scores, student turnover (migration in and out of individual schools or the school district), immunization records, and so on. Also check with the regional or intermediate school district and the state department of education. Local libraries possess a wealth of data. If materials are not available at your library, the librarian may be able to assist with interlibrary loans, searches of other libraries' catalogs, and computer searches of various databases, including educational associations, census data, and federal and state resources. A local college or university library may provide access to the most current literature. The first step is to do a literature review or search to find out what other studies or data exist. Establish a profile of the student population affected by the problem, and describe your organizational structure, goals, and objectives. Finally, list programs, services, and resources currently in place to meet the need.

There are a number of federal, state, and local resources that you may consult in your search for data. Federal sources include the U.S. Census Bureau, the Department of Education, and the Department Of Health and Human Services. State sources include the Department of Education, the Department of Public Health, state data centers, state human service leagues, and special interest/lobby groups. Other sources include public, college, and university libraries; police and public safety departments; chambers of commerce; and school boards. In addition, the Internet is a useful resource, and many hospitals maintain medical libraries that may be open to the public, and you may want to pursue technical consulting with local universities. Other national organizations that may serve as useful sources of data include the Children's Defense Fund, Child Welfare League of America, and many other nonprofit foundations that fund programs and research about children and teens. Finally, potential sources of data from your own organization include teacher and guidance counselor records, evaluation forms and reports done for accreditation reviews, and standardized test scores. The list at the end of chapter provides additional ideas and resources.

Gathering New Data

Exhaust existing sources of data before determining if you need to collect new data. If you determine that you need additional data that can only be gathered firsthand, several methods are possible, including observation, focus groups, key informant interviews, and surveys.

Observation. The classroom observation methods outlined in chapter 24 can be adapted for your needs assessment. Observation involves counting the frequency of events and their duration, the context of schooling, or interactions between individuals. Observation of behavior is often the clearest method of measurement available. An example of gathering data through observation is counting the number of aggressive behaviors during passing periods in a high school. To do so, it would be necessary to clearly define aggressive behavior and to develop codes for behavior that are exhaustive and mutually exclusive. Piloting the coding scheme with more than one observer and then checking for interrater reliability is helpful as you develop your observation method.

Focus Groups. These small informal groups, led by a facilitator, gather information from audiences who fill out a questionnaire (e.g., teachers, students, parents, school administrators). You usually have a script or a short questionnaire to serve as a guide; however, the advantage of a focus group is that people build on the ideas of others, and therefore, the group may explore ideas that you or the committee never anticipated. The groups need to be audiotaped or transcribed, or careful notes should be made of responses.

Key Informant Interviews. Key informants are individuals in a position to know about or be aware of the problem you are studying. They may include the same people you would invite to a focus group (teachers, administrators, parents, other professionals, and/or students). A questionnaire is used, but the format enables the interviewer to follow up and clarify responses as well as explore areas that were not on the original questionnaire. This procedure is best when there are a limited number of issues to be discussed and a limited number of people to interview, and there are interviewers available who are trained not to be judgmental or to allow their own opinions to influence the outcome.

If an appropriate instrument or questionnaire already exists and has been tested, it may be the best use of time to obtain permission to use that instrument. Instruments may be found in the review of the literature or through searches of collections of measures. On the other hand, you may wish to design new survey/questionnaire instruments. Surveys may be used with in-person or phone interviews or can be distributed by mail or at meetings or other gatherings. If you decide to design a new instrument, develop your questions with data analysis and output in mind. Try to make it as easy as possible for respondents to answer. Keep in mind that a large number of open-ended questions requiring the person to write answers (rather than circle answers provided in a list) will add considerable time to your data analysis process, as you will have to categorize and then synthesize these responses. However, if you don't want to lead or limit the respondent by providing checklists or multiple-choice answers, an in-person or telephone interview, in which the interviewer reads the questions but does not provide a checklist of answers, is often a good compromise.

If time permits, pilot test your questionnaire on a small group (12–30 people) to help you anticipate the range of responses for checklists, and to see if some questions are too ambiguous or poorly worded. At the very least, have the person who will analyze the data look at the questionnaire from the perspective of data analysis. The ideal situation is to envision the type of data you want in a report then build a good questionnaire that addresses those topics.

Suggestions for Getting the Most out of Each Method

Focus Groups. In order to be as representative as possible and reduce bias or skewing, carefully identify those you want included. Schedule in advance. Hold the sessions at a location convenient for those who will be attending. Offer an incentive for attending (food, beverages, on-site child care for those with young children, a drawing for a prize or gift certificate). Have someone experienced lead the focus group. If possible, tape-record your sessions so you won't have to concentrate on note taking, and have a backup tape recorder.

Key Informant Interviews. Schedule the interviews in advance, and have your questions prepared. Let those being interviewed know how long the interview will take, and stick to that time frame.

Mailed Surveys. Allow adequate time for return mail, and possibly time to do follow-up if your initial response rate is low. Including a business-reply envelope or stamped self-addressed envelope will increase your response rate. This tends to be the least expensive method. However, response rates are lower in this method than in other methods, unless you offer an incentive or have a hot topic on which people want to express their opinion.

Phone Surveys. Try to schedule your phone calls at the time you think you will be most likely to reach the population you wish to survey. For example, schedule interviews during the day for stay-at-home moms or retirees, and evenings for working parents. This method tends to be expensive unless you have volunteers, such as PTA members, to make the calls. Phone interviewers must be trained so that they ask the questions and record answers in a standard format. You will need approximately ten phone numbers for every three surveys you hope to complete, and this is if you attempt each phone number at least three times on different days and at different times. It takes approximately six nights with twelve interviewers to complete 300 to 350 four-page questionnaires.

In-Person Surveys. Use interviewers who are friendly and outgoing. Keep the questions short so those being interviewed don't have to remember long sentences or lists. Use answer scales such as 1 = strongly agree, 5 = strongly disagree, on three-by-five cards, which can be handed to the person. Carry out the surveys at a time when those you want to reach aren't rushed. Pick your interview location carefully. For example, if you want to talk to students, a good place might be a quiet room located near a study hall or the library. Bad timing for students would be during midterm or final exams.

ANALYZING YOUR DATA

Unless your study is funded by a major foundation or a federal or state agency, which requires detailed documentation, you may be able to analyze your data by looking primarily at the frequency or prevalence of conditions. How many students are not eating a nutritional breakfast more than three times a week? How many students come from families with incomes below the poverty level? How many parents attend parent-teacher conferences? You may examine the frequency of opinions on questions such as: How many parents believe their children are receiving a strong foundation in the three Rs? How many parents feel it is important to review their child's homework?

If, however, you need to provide more extensive data analysis, many computerized software packages provide you with an assortment of statistical measures and tests that are appropriate for various types of data. If you feel your data analysis skills are rusty, consider using a consultant to provide this level of analysis for you. Remember, it's important for the consultant to review your data collection methodology, including the questionnaire, before you begin collecting data. Contact local colleges and universities for consultants in educational leadership, social work, statistics, and other disciplines that specialize in research.

Your data can be hand tabulated (under 50 respondents), entered into a spreadsheet such as Excel (50–500 respondents), or entered into and analyzed by a statistical analysis software package such as SPSS (Statistical Package for Social Sciences) or SAS (Statistical Analysis System). It depends on the size of the sample and the resources available to you.

Tips on Using Excel

For small sample sizes (50–500 respondents), you may manually enter the responses in Excel and calculate totals and percentages for each question or set of answers. The easiest way to get clean results is to enter each survey (subject, student, parent, or respondent) as a separate row. Enter each answer as a separate column. Then simply total each column to get the frequency or number who gave a particular answer (e.g., yes or no, strongly agree or strongly disagree) to each question. Table 11.2 shows the results of a few questions.

TABLE 11.2 Example Format for Data Entry and Analysis Using Excel Spreadsheet

	Eat Nutritious Breakfast 3x/Wk		*Eligible for Free Lunch*		*Important for me to review my child's homework*				
ID	*Yes*	*No*	*Yes*	*No*	*Strongly Agree*	*Agree Somewhat*	*Undecided*	*Disagree Somewhat*	*Strongly Disagree*
270	1		1		1				
271		1		1		1			
272	1			1			1		
273	1			1				1	
274		1	1				1		
275		1	1			1			
276		1		1	1				
277		1	1			1			
278	1			1		1			
279		1	1				1		
Total	**4**	**6**	**5**	**5**	**2**	**4**	**3**	**1**	**0**
%	40.0%	60.0%	50.0%	50.0%	20.0%	40.0%	30.0%	10.0%	0.0%

Another tip is to freeze the column headings. In that way, as you enter more and more rows of data, the headings will remain at the top of the page, helping ensure that you are entering the data for the matching question. To freeze columns in Excel, place your cursor in the first row that has data (not the row containing data labels) select Window from the menu and then click on Freeze Panes from the submenu (just under the heading and to the right of the first ID number). ID numbers are important for going back and finding data entry errors or tracing inconsistent answers back to a survey. Write the ID number on the survey as you begin to enter each questionnaire in the Excel file.

One drawback of using Excel is that you have to block or highlight all the data in your rows before sorting data. If you sort without highlighting all the data, just that column is sorted, and the tie or relationship to the rest of the questions for each individual is lost.

Optical Scanning

For larger samples (over 500 respondents), you may want to consider using an optical scan form for questionnaire responses. With this method, answer sheets are optically scanned instead of typed manually into a computer file. The optical scan format for data gathering and analysis generally saves time and money with large samples. Customized scan forms, which allow respondents to read the question and mark their answer next to each question, have the highest degree of accuracy. However, the minimum fee for printing customized forms is likely to be $1,000, which makes it more cost efficient only for surveys involving 500 or more respondents.

If your school has a software program that scans and produces results for teacher-designed student tests and quizzes, especially multiple-choice questions, you may be able to adapt your questionnaire to use that software. Make sure such use does not violate the software's purchase agreement.

REPORTING YOUR FINDINGS

This is a critical element to the success of your needs assessment. Present your results in a manner that is easy to understand. Do not lose sight of your audience. Focus your attention on the specific issue you have been studying, and use your data to show that the changes you are proposing will make a difference. If you want to convince your audience that there are programs or services that are effective, you should cite examples of successful programs or efforts.

Lengthy narratives are often not the best way to report your findings. You may find that a simple summary accompanied by charts, graphs, or tables showing your data in an easy-to-interpret format is the best way to present the results. Table 11.3 illustrates one method of displaying standardized test scores. The key statistic is the percentage of students with satisfactory test scores. School districts evaluate strengths and weaknesses in their curricula by looking at these data over time. Comparing your own school or school district with others in your county or state provides a measure of where your school or district stands in relation to others.

Sometimes it is easier to get a point across by providing the data in a graphic format (figure 11.1). For example, family income for two-parent

TABLE 11.3 Comparing Our School with State Proficiency Test Scores

Percentage of Students with Satisfactory Proficiency Test Scores: 2003–2004

Grade Level	*4th*		*7th*		*11th*	
Geographic Area	State	ZPS	State	ZPS	State	ZPS
Reading	47.5%	48.5%	44.2%	46.2%	43.5%	44.5%
Math	49.9%	50.2%	46.8%	48.4%	33.0%	32.7%
Science	70.0%	70.0%	61.9%	63.5%	58.1%	57.5%

State = State-wide average. ZPS = Average for our local public school
SOURCE: Fictitious Educational Assessment Program: 2003–2004

FIGURE 11.1 Impact of Family Type on Family Income

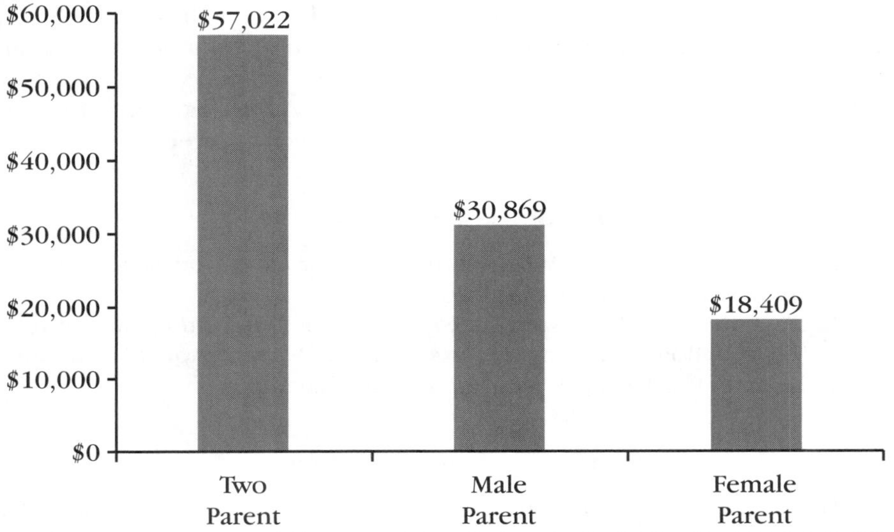

SOURCE: http://www.census.gov/hhes/income/histinc.html 8/9/2000

households is very different from that of single-parent households headed by a woman. Instead of wading through paragraphs of narrative, one can see from a table or graph how dramatically different economic circumstances can be for children living with two parents versus a single mother.

Needs assessment is a systematic data collection and analysis process. Its purposes are to discover and identify the resources the community is lacking in relation to generally accepted standards, and to transmit that information to those who make resource allocation decisions. The choice of data collection methods depends on several factors, including availability of existing data, the topic of need being explored, and time and cost constraints. Using existing data helps conserve time and funds. Using focus groups and/or key informants provides information on the level of support and allows you to rank needs by your audience's opinion of their importance. Questionnaires, although more costly and time intensive, enable you to directly measure the desires, beliefs, knowledge, and opinions of your intended beneficiaries and benefactors.

SOURCES FOR DATA AND OTHER RESOURCES

The Internet has a wealth of information, including results of studies, how-to guides, and data. Many reports are available on the World Wide Web, and some can be downloaded. Often the reports are in Adobe or PDF format. You can download the Adobe Reader software at the census.gov site and also at many of the sites that publish reports in the Adobe format. If you do not have a computer with a Web browser, try your school library or computer lab, your community's public library, or a local college or university computer center. Some federal, state, and private sources have data down to the local county level, as well as at the state and federal levels.

State Government Resources

The U.S. Department of Education has information on school demographics and enrollment. Web site:

To reach the Web site of your state government, type in the name of your state, followed by .gov. For example, the Web site for the state government of Michigan is http://www.michigan.gov.

Federal Government Resources

The official Web portal and starting point for any federal agency or department inquiry is http://usa.gov.

The National Contact Center (800-333-4636) is a centralized service that helps callers find any type of national data. Staff can answer your question or get you to someone who can. Recorded information on frequently requested subjects is available around the clock.

The U.S. Census Bureau Customer Services (301-457-4100) has phone numbers for 1,400 college and public libraries that have selected publications and some computer files on CD-ROM from the U.S. Government Printing Office and Census Bureau, as well as from state data centers, which are usually state government agencies (and assorted affiliates, often state universities) with data services. Centers receive Census Bureau data for their area and make them available to the public and are found in all states.

There are a number of U.S. Census Bureau publications. These include the Characteristics of the Population series ("General Social and Economic Characteristics"; "Detailed Population Characteristics"; "Living Arrangements of Children and Adults, Household & Family Characteristics"); "Income, Poverty and Health Insurance in the United States: 2003" (P60-226); the "Money, Income and Poverty Status in the United States," a population census that is conducted once every ten years; the *County and City Data Book,* which provides selected characteristics about counties and cities above 50,000 in population; and "Statistical Abstract of the United States: 2004–2005," available at http://www.census.gov/prod/www/statistical-abstract.html. In addition, demographic data from the Census Bureau is available at http://www.census.gov.

The Centers for Disease Control and Prevention's Youth Risk Behavior Surveillance System provides the national and state percentages of students by gender and grade level who report engaging in risk-taking behavior such as cigarette use; social drinking, binge drinking; use of drugs; seat-belt use; riding with a driver who is drunk; suicidal ideation and attempts; being the victim of bullying, intimidation, or violence at school; getting into physical fights; and carrying a weapon. Web site: http://www.cdc.gov/HealthyYouth/yrbs/index.htm

Indian Health Service. Web site: http://www.ihs.gov/

Library of Congress. Web site: http://www.loc.gov/

The National Center for Education Statistics brings together data from several NCES sources: the Condition of Education, Indicators of School Crime and Safety, Projections of Education Statistics, and Youth Indicators, as well as the Digest of Education Statistics (which gives per pupil expenditures). Web site: http://nces.ed.gov/edstats/

Office of Minority Health. Web site: http://www.omhrc.gov/

USA Services links to federal government sites, including Pueblo Publications. Web site: http://info.gov/

White House Social Statistics Briefing Room. Web site: http://www.whitehouse.gov/fsbr/ssbr.html

Private And Nonprofit Resources

The Center for Schools and Communities is committed to improving outcomes for children and families through training, technical assistance, program evaluation, research, and resource development. 275 Grandview Avenue, Suite 200, Camp Hill, PA 17011. Tel.: 717-763-1661. Web site: http://www.center-school.org/

The Center for the Future of Children is a collaboration of the Woodrow Wilson School of Public and International Affairs at Princeton University and the Brookings Institution that has produced such publications as *Children and Computer Technology, When School Is Out, Home Visiting: Program Evaluations, Protecting Children from Abuse and Neglect,* and *School Readiness: Closing Racial and Ethnic Gaps.* Web site: http://www.futureofchildren.org/

Children's Defense Fund, 25 E Street NW, Washington, DC 20001 Tel.: 202-662-3652. Web site: http://www.childrensdefense.org/

Council of Chief State School Officers, One Massachusetts Avenue, NW, Suite 700, Washington, DC 20001-1431. Tel.: 202-336-7000. Web site: http://www.ccsso.org/

Communities in Schools works to help students stay in school, learn, and prepare for a successful future. It sponsors a network that serves over 1,000 schools around the country. 277 South Washington Street, Suite 210, Alexandria, VA 22314. Tel.: 703-519-8999 or 800-CIS-4KIDS. Web site: http://www.cisnet.org/

Harvard Family Research Project. Harvard Graduate School of Education, 3 Garden Street, Cambridge, MA 02138. Tel.: 617-495-9108. Web site: http://www.gse.harvard.edu/hfrp/

Kids Count provides national statistics, updated annually by the Annie E. Casey Foundation, for all fifty states. There may also be a Kids Count data book for your state that provides more detailed county-level information on an annual basis. Web site: http://www.aecf.org/kidscount/

Michigan League for Human Services. 1115 S. Pennsylvania Avenue, Suite 202, Lansing, MI 48912. Tel.: 517-487-5436. Web site: http://www.milhs.org/

The National Association for the Education of Young Children leads and consolidates the efforts of individuals and groups working to achieve healthy development and constructive education for all young children. Primary attention is devoted to ensuring the provision of high-quality early childhood programs for young children. Web site: http://www.naeyc.org/

The National Campaign to Prevent Teen Pregnancy works to prevent teen pregnancy by supporting values and stimulating actions that are consistent with a pregnancy-free adolescence. Web site: http://www.teenpregnancy.org/

The National Dropout Prevention Network provides linkages to educators, communities, researchers, parents, and the private sector to find solutions to the common goal of preventing and recovering dropouts. Web site: http://www.dropoutprevention.org/

The National Foundation for the Improvement of Education. 1201 16th Street, NW, Washington, DC 20036. Tel.: 202-822-7840.

Practical Assessment, Research and Evaluation. Web site: http://pareonline.net/

United Way of America. 701 N. Fairfax Street, Alexandria, VA 22314. Tel.: 703-836-7100. Web site: http://national.unitedway.org

United Way of America Outcome Evaluation Measures. Web site: http://www.unitedway.org/outcomes/

Youth Crime Watch. Web site: http://www.ycwa.org/

References

Erikson, E. H. (1968). *Identity, youth and crisis*. New York: W. W. Norton.

Maslow, A. H. (1970). *Motivation and personality*. New York: Harper & Row.

Ponsioen, J. A. (1962). *Social welfare policy: Vol. 3. Contributions to theory*. The Hague: Mouton.

Simons, J., & Jablonski, D. (1990). *An advocate's guide to using data*. Washington, DC: Children's Defense Fund.

United Way of America. (1999). *Community status reports and targeted community interventions: Drawing a distinction*. Alexandria, VA: United Way of America.

12

Conducting and Using Research in the Schools: Practitioners as Agents for Change

Nancy Farwell
University of Washington

Sung Sil Lee Sohng
University of Washington

- Research in Schools
- Applications of School-Based Research
- Connecting to Unrecognized Constituencies
- Improving Home-School-Community Partnerships
- Promoting Inclusion and Involvement
- Beginning Your Research
- Low-Cost, Straightforward Methods

School-based practitioners seek practical knowledge to help students, schools, families, and communities improve educational experiences, processes, and outcomes in authentic ways. As schools become key public institutions fostering social and economic development, educational systems face increased demands to respond to the changing nature of a knowledge-based economy. New trends have brought profound changes for education, notably the increasing requirements that schools provide knowledge and skills linked to economic production needs. Entrepreneurial ideas concerned with profit and micro-focused knowledge could clash with broad and humanistic understandings of our world. Increasingly, school restructuring, accountability, testing, standardization, and measurement of educational activities have been framed as solutions to both social and educational problems (Lipman, 2004). Changes in the world economy require educational administrators and practitioners to examine closely the interlinked imperatives of productivity, accountability, and community in the processes and management of public education (Boyd, 1999). Under conditions of increasing social, economic, and political inequalities, inclusion has become ever more crucial to the mission of public education, ensuring that those who have been marginalized or excluded have the opportunity to participate fully. Practitioner-researchers are uniquely situated to work collaboratively within the interconnected networks of students, families, communities, and educational institutions to facilitate these changes.

These ideas are basic to the research process. As a practitioner-researcher, one views oneself as having the potential to build knowledge, an act of learning as well as a form of professional practice. Information is everywhere. One must learn to be attentive to information that sheds light on issues and processes that can promote creative and collaborative ways of identifying and addressing changing needs, challenges, and opportunities. Being a practitioner-researcher also means that one becomes disciplined—one learns to account for one's reasons for gathering information, for structuring questions in particular ways, and for how one gathers information and how one uses it.

This chapter demystifies a process generally considered the exclusive domain of professionally trained researchers. It suggests low-cost research approaches that can be carried out by school-based practitioners. Practitioner research is a unique genre of research. Experimental researchers strive for valid and reliable measures to ensure generalizability of their results; naturalistic researchers seek trustworthiness and authenticity to uncover the social rules for the situations they describe. In contrast, practitioner-researchers seek to understand the individuals, actions, policies, and events in their work environments to make professional decisions. As practitioner-researchers, school social workers participate in improving educational outcomes for students, restructuring schools and influencing curricula, developing on-site prevention programs, involving students in networks of community-based supports, and fostering social and political change to ensure that schools become more inclusive. Practitioner research reaches both within and beyond educational institutions to facilitate collaborative efforts with communities and families to support students' social development needs and contributes to the social work knowledge base.

A number of concurrent forces have advanced the growth and legitimacy of practitioner research. First, the conduct of research has been linked to the professionalization of social work practice. Second, following the postmodern challenge of objective truth, narratives, self-studies, cases, biographical methods, vignettes, and other writings as well as oral histories have been recognized as potentially significant sources for the knowledge base (Chamberlayne, Bornat, & Wengraf, 2000; Harold, Palmiter, Lynch, & Freedman-Doan, 1995; Holland, 1991; Josselson, 1996; Martin, 1995). Third, the interest in practitioner research has also increased in response to the movement to create reflective, critical practitioners (Altrichter, Posch, & Somekh, 1993; Jay, 2003; Pearlmutter, 2002). Fourth, educational reformers have recognized that the success of reform is dependent on an understanding of the context in which reform is to be implemented. Using inquiry processes such as action research, practitioners can bridge the gulf between policies and the actuality of everyday lives, adapting reforms to suit particular work situations (Armstrong & Moore, 2004). Emphases on the complex interrelated contextual factors that are the reality of students' lives as well as the interconnections of these with educational processes and outcomes have since the 1970s fueled a shift to qualitative research methods in education (Hammersley, 2000). Practitioner research can also underscore the importance of connective pedagogies that flexibly link individual learning styles and needs with the curriculum as well as with relationships, values, and experiences in the wider community (Corbett, 2001; Simpson, 2004). Finally, the work of Paolo Freire (1973) and others (Carr, 1995; Hick, 1997; Noffke & Stevenson, 1995; Sohng, 1996) has forged a link between practitioner research and critical pedagogical thought. Practitioner inquiry and other forms of action research are seen as emancipatory tools to help practitioners become aware of the often hidden hierarchical institutional structures that govern their work.

Following an introductory discussion of research in the schools, we consider a range of alternative applications and discuss their relevance for the school-based practitioner. We outline guidelines for initiating research, and we identify several low-cost methods for gathering data and using research.

RESEARCH IN SCHOOLS

The impact of the research explosion on local schools is well known to practitioners, showing itself in constantly growing paperwork requirements. School personnel at all levels spend much of their time completing forms and reports, usually providing data for research conducted elsewhere. The bulk of research, evaluation, and data-gathering efforts in the schools is a response to federal and state legislative mandates. Legislative bodies demand strict accounting for the funds they appropriate and impose heavy reporting and evaluation requirements. Legislation may also mandate regulations for what is viewed as legitimate research. For example, the No Child Left Behind Act of 2001 stipulates that the majority of research funded under federal law utilizes experimental designs and methods, randomized control groups, and models of causality (Lather, 2004).

Such methodological requirements could make research the domain of academics, whose specialized language and methods are assumed to be necessary conditions for scientific validity. In fact, the use of complex statistical methods often limits the communication of research results, shutting out practitioners and the public. All too often esoteric language and methods are worn as a badge of expertise and rationalized as necessary for scientific precision. Local school personnel, parents, and community members are rarely involved in designing the research, assessing research products, or suggesting applications. More often, these potential partners are considered instruments for achieving organizational objectives. They are, in this sense, passive receivers of information and objects of administrative control. Furthermore, even the most rigorous research designed from afar may yield statistically significant findings that have little practical application.

APPLICATIONS OF SCHOOL-BASED RESEARCH

If externally driven research is so often irrelevant to practice, as suggested above, then why should the practitioner be concerned with research at all? There are compelling reasons, both defensive and affirmative, for school social workers and others to conduct their own research. First of all, this is the age of accountability. Implementation of performance-based accountability systems can bring about complex reactions in school systems. Externally imposed performance-based accountability systems are rarely adequate for producing significant changes in program delivery at individual schools, beyond an emphasis on test performance (Elmore & Furman, 2001). Practitioner-based research can support a bottom-up change process, warding off top-down bureaucratic measures, and supporting a collegial form of accountability. Student engagement and learning are nested within complex contextual family and community networks that practitioner-based research can help illuminate. Educational reforms emphasize working toward institutionalization of cooperative principles as the focus of school renewal (Board on Children, Youth and Families, 2003; Holy, 1991). Studies of educational innovations suggest that involving the local school community in research helps mobilize the capacity for internal regeneration of policies and strategies for school-driven improvement (Broussard, 2003; Herr, 1995; Jones, 1991; Sirotnik, 1989). Rather than being passive consumers or clients, parents and community members can become active partners in the collaborative network (Armstrong & Moore, 2004).

Because school personnel spend their working lives with students, they are in an excellent position to identify educational issues firsthand. They are interested in what works and are sensitive to the practical constraints of school settings in ways that outside researchers may not be. The utilitarian, participatory, and localized nature of school-based research significantly reduces the gap between the discovery of what works and practical applications of this knowledge (deMarrais, 2004; Elliot, 1991; Hammersley, 2000). School-based research is the antithesis of externally generated and externally imposed change. Just as administrators and policy makers use research as a political resource, school social workers can do the same. Teachers, school social workers, psychologists, and others can use research to ward off new programs and requirements that are unfeasible, impractical, or harmful to students. On the other hand, they can use research in a positive way to gain support for new program initiatives, to demonstrate the effectiveness of their services, to obtain additional resources, or to find out what kinds of interventions work best. School social workers can use research to move beyond traditional clinical roles to enlarge the arena of practice. Research can be used as an adjunct to consultation and as a way of demonstrating the potential of a more ecological social work role.

Fostering Collaborative Practice

School social workers are in an especially advantageous position to develop collaborative school-based research. Collaborative interdisciplinary efforts highlight the social worker's expertise and the profession's unique competencies, moving the social worker from the periphery to a central role (Stevens, 1999). The profession has long been interested in effecting change through the empowerment, participation, and action of the people involved. The collaborative approach to research calls for interactive skills, cultural sensitivity, group decision making, and mediation and conflict management skills necessary for negotiation among diverse constituents and interests. This kind of collaborative research is characterized by participation in problem posing, practitioner participation in gathering data that answer questions relevant to his or her concerns, and collaboration among members of the school community as a "critical community." Here, research is aimed at generating data that can guide and direct planned change. It involves observation, assessment, interviewing, reading and analyzing reports and documents, and writing up findings. These skills are already within the behavioral repertoire of school social workers. We will review how to do this. However, first we examine some of the uses and potential benefits of practitioner-initiated school-based research.

Developing Multicultural Resources

Consciousness of multiple realities lies at the heart of postmodern thinking. Schools must incorporate diverse voices into their communities and their curricula, with particular attention to those who have been silenced (Banks, 1996; Sleeter, 1996). For example, a social worker at a predominantly white school noted that students of color were dropping out at a high rate. She formed a multiethnic team in collaboration with an administrator and a teacher to conduct an action research project examining the experiences of students of color at the school. The project helped focus attention on the larger institutional processes that silenced and privatized students' experiences of exclusion and alienation (Herr, 1995). The key concept in this endeavor is the deliberate, thoughtful development of research that illuminates the diversity of perspectives and interests. School-based research can offer a promising vehicle for assessing cultural diversity in curriculum, classroom, and school practices, and improving the campus climate for a diverse student body.

To make the case for new multicultural resources, you might begin by taking a look at how the composition of the student population at your school has changed over the years. To get an overall picture, you might examine student characteristics over the past ten years, comparing two different years for which you can get good demographic data. In considering diversity at your school, you should also familiarize yourself with both official and informal institutional policies and procedures, academic programs, and instructional support. Have these policies and programs kept pace with the changing student population? Are they being implemented fairly and effectively? A social worker in a large urban school district received many complaints from parents that their English-speaking children were placed in English-as-a-second-language classes for no apparent reason other than assumptions about their language abilities based on their Latino surnames. Similarly, bicultural instructional assistants in another district noted that East African children were being placed inappropriately in special education classes instead of in ESL classes. Social workers in these instances can collaborate with teachers, instructional aides, and assessment personnel in a self-study to investigate processes within the school, such as assessment and placement of students in remedial, special education, and ESL classes. Such processes may be affected by student ethnicity, immigration status, age, or gender. Combined with an analysis of changing demographics, policies, and available resources, this self-study can make the case for in-service training for staff and improved bilingual-bicultural resources such as student mentoring, tutoring, and support programs.

CONNECTING TO UNRECOGNIZED CONSTITUENCIES

The constituent base of multicultural education in this society consists of disenfranchised people, particularly children of color and/or of low-income backgrounds, refugees and other immigrants, children who are disabled, and youths who identify themselves as gay or lesbian, as well as their parents. However, in many arenas of multicultural activity, the professionals sometimes act as if they were the constituents. Professionals can certainly be allies, but they need to recognize their power and their self-interest, which may lead them to shape multicultural education to fit their own needs. A growing literature on multicultural education is directed toward professionals, often substituting for dialogue between school personnel and community people (Sleeter, 1996). Research redirected toward parents and community activists from different cultural groups can serve as an empowering resource for those who are often unheard and uninvolved. A community needs assessment (see chapter 11), for example, is an instrument whereby community members can make their educational needs known, expressing an action agenda for school change (Delgado-Gaitan, 1993; Williams, 1989).

IMPROVING HOME-SCHOOL-COMMUNITY PARTNERSHIPS

School social workers are in a good position to facilitate the involvement of family members in their children's education, a critical factor in student and family success (Broussard, 2003). Practitioner research can provide avenues for the involvement of immigrant and refugee parents and other marginalized families in the schools through parent support groups (Delgado-Gaitan, 2001), multicultural policy advocacy groups, and facilitation of direct parent-school communication, and in ensuring that the school provides a welcoming environment for families (Witherspoon, 2002). Practitioners concerned about community violence and the personal safety of students can use action research to assess the impact of local programs such as Neighborhood Watch in protecting youths from violence as they walk to and from school. Such research can identify methods of retaining students who live in potentially dangerous neighborhoods (Salcido, Ornelas, & Garcia, 2002). Collaboration with public housing and community-based youth programs can be an excellent means for the practitioner-researcher to understand and address student concerns regarding contradictions between their self-perceived strengths and obstacles in their real-life community contexts and the norms and missions of mainstream institutions such as the schools (Gran-O'Donnell, Farwell, Spigner, Nguyen, Ciske, Young, et al., 2001).

PROMOTING INCLUSION AND INVOLVEMENT

Creating and sustaining inclusive education involves the school social worker as cultural agent, one who understands the contradictions that exist in the transmission of a dominant culture in the schools (Blair, 2002). Practitioner research can be instrumental in promoting an agenda for inclusion, through the process itself, as well as by transforming school culture, curriculum, practices, and community relationships. Action research involving students of color or other marginalized populations, such as gay and lesbian youths, can be designed to educate the school community about diversity and homophobia, encouraging student engagement through activism and advocacy (Herr, 1995; Peters, 2003). For example, Native American students from West Seattle High School formed a community of inquiry to examine the use of Native American mascots, nicknames, and logos within the public school system and their impact on the cultural identities of Native American youths. Supported by the school social worker and the Native American community, they identified sixty-five schools in Washington State that have Native American mascots or logos. Their research indicated that Native American imagery in schools not only disrespects Native Americans by buying into historical stereotypes and caricatures but also perpetuates cultural ignorance and insensitivity within what is purported to be a supportive learning environment. The students who were originally interviewees became collaborators in a passionate change process, leading the campaign to change racist school practices and the school environment (Beeson, 2002). Another example is a community youth mapping project carried out by Latino and Southeast Asian students in Seattle. This project was supervised by one of the authors and a school social work intern in collaboration with key community-based social service agencies in 2003. Youth mapping provided a guided forum for youths to identify and critically examine assets and deficits in their community, find ways to build on the assets, and articulate actions to the deficits.

Demonstrating the Effectiveness of Services

As practitioners, we generally know, or think we know, the effectiveness of the services we provide. We sometimes assume that because we are professionals, others should take us at our word when we make claims about the need for and benefits of our services. However, in the absence of convincing evidence, such claims can be dismissed by others as self-serving. The following example demonstrates one school social worker's failure to document an important aspect of her work. In her case, the absence of data documenting her work led to lack of acknowledgment by administrators.

> A school social worker was valued by the principals and teachers of the schools she served for her effectiveness in handling crisis situations—episodes of students acting out, students' threatening violent and destructive behavior, and confrontations between students and teachers. She was frequently called on to handle emergencies. She felt that this disruption of her regular work schedule was well worth the price, because her availability to handle crises gave her the credibility she needed to get into the schools to do some of the more routine work. However, her crisis work was not officially recognized. It was not part of her job description, nor did her superiors know how much time it took or how much the principals appreciated it. Had she taken the time to document the number of such cases per month, to describe the circumstances and outcomes, and to record the feedback from the students and teachers, she could have used these data to gain official acknowledgment of an enlarged work role. She might also have gained greater insights into her work, recogni-

tion of her contribution, additional resources or decreased demands, or authorization for training school personnel in crisis intervention. As it stood, her work was appreciated by many but unacknowledged and unrewarded by administrators.

Fostering Collegial Accountability

School-based research conducted by practitioners on practical concerns can foster a greater congruence between research and practice and help to demystify the research process. It can also contribute to building greater collegial shared accountability. Let us assume, for example, that a social worker and a group of teachers have developed an alternative tutorial strategy, adding adult helpers to the classroom to work with a group of students rather than taking these students out of class for remedial instruction. The team wants to examine the effect of this experiment. The results would be measured by outcomes such as the students' progress, increase/decrease of tutoring time spent with each student, and the students' and teachers' assessment of the new procedures. Here, the purpose of research does not necessarily require rigorous research procedures but calls for collegial problem identification and problem solving.

The process of observing students and gathering data may also be an occasion for the team to examine and reflect on their interaction and behaviors with students. By having the opportunity to experience and experiment with the research process, the team members may gain an increased appreciation of research and come to demand more of themselves, for example, to be more parsimonious and specific in the data they collect, and more clear about learning objectives.

Establishing the Need for New Services

Arguments for the establishment of new services are all the more persuasive when supported by research data. Let us assume that a social worker and teachers feel that there is a need for a school breakfast program. School administrators resist this, concerned about the cost as well as the administrative problems of implementing a program for which there may be little constituent demand. In the absence of any other compelling reasons, administrators can easily deflect teachers' and social workers' requests for the program. When the request is accompanied by data showing the support from the students and parents, the number of children who come to school without breakfast, well-documented reports of behavioral problems and the lack of attentiveness of such children, information on the effects of nutritional deficits on learning, and data on the costs of the program, the request will be more seriously considered.

In another example, the social worker is concerned about reports of bullying across multiple age groups on and near the school grounds and advocates the implementation of an anti-bullying/conflict resolution curriculum. The principal discourages this due to lack of funds and concerns about workload. The social worker surveys parents, children, and teachers about the school climate and documents serious instances of bullying experienced by a significant percentage of children. This is then identified as a priority area for intervention, and the principal adopts a curriculum used in other district schools, with support from the PTA.

Establishing the Need for Additional Resources

School personnel are constantly seeking increased resources or reduced workloads to accomplish their work in keeping with professional standards. Administrators hear such requests so often that they are routinely dismissed. Administrators like to sidestep conflicts between professional standards or official policy requirements and the limited resources available to meet them. This forces the practitioner to reconcile conflicting demands as best he or she can. For example, with the requirements of the Individuals with Disabilities Education Act, school social workers, psychologists, special education teachers, and other educational specialists are often expected to carry out their regular work while accommodating time-consuming and cumbersome assessment and paperwork requirements for increased numbers of children. Administrators, themselves caught between federal and state requirements and limited resources, often thrust the problem downward, leaving it to school personnel to figure out how best to meet the new demands. School personnel work harder, take paperwork home with them, forgo planning and preparation time, or routinize work tasks. A more proactive approach would be to conduct team-based data gathering, documenting carefully the time required to perform specific tasks, thereby demonstrating the impossibility of completing them without sacrificing quality and deferring other responsibilities. Furthermore, the group involved in such data gathering and analysis can identify ways to reduce duplication and redundancy and can recommend new procedures more relevant to the school community.

Testing New Programs or Procedures

Often administrators develop new procedures in response to mandates from Congress, the state legislature, or the local school board. This top-down approach often results in new requirements being imposed with insufficient sensitivity to actual conditions within the schools. School personnel cope as best they can. However, it makes more sense to test new programs and procedures before they are implemented throughout the system. As an advocate of and participant in pilot tests, school social workers can expand their role while indirectly contributing to the empowerment of all school staff.

Illuminating Practices Normally Hidden from View

In all organizations, schools being no exception, there generally are some practices tacitly accepted but at variance with official policy that are not openly discussed. Research offers a way of bringing such practices out into the open by guaranteeing anonymity and confidentiality, thereby depersonalizing what may be very emotional issues. Examples include disciplinary practices, cultural sensitivity, discrimination, and concerns about student-to-student sexual harassment and harassment of gay and lesbian students. Teachers may be reluctant to discuss their own practices because they may violate official policy or because of the divisive nature of an issue. Such emotion-laden issues may be driven underground and beyond the scope of discussion. An anonymous survey might elicit responses that would never be brought out in open discussion and could serve to bring to the attention of administrators practices of which they might otherwise not know.

A favorite method of politicians to avoid taking action is to call for a study of the issues. Although outright opposition to an undesirable policy may be viewed by the administration as insubordination, proposing a study is a more constructive and conciliatory step that is harder for recalcitrant administrators to oppose. If, in fact, a study is undertaken, the results may help resolve differences about the implementation of a proposed policy.

BEGINNING YOUR RESEARCH

We have discussed a number of ways in which research can be used to enhance the role of the school social worker and to support organizational change initiated from below. We turn now to the more difficult question of how to do it. In this section, we offer guidelines for getting started and suggest ways to augment limited resources. The concluding section provides a discussion of readily available data sources and methods of conducting research that do not require special research training.

Questions for Focus

The most important part of research is your thinking process prior to doing something, and during the research process. Here are six questions to help you put your research process together. When you work through these questions, you end up with a research design.

- What do you want and need to know? Why do you want to know this? Right from the start you'll have to be clear about how you'll use the information you collect.

- What do you already know? Answering this question lets you make use of the information you already have, or that is available in the published literature.
- Where do you go to find out? Where are the answers to your questions? Are you going to ask people? Are you going to review reports and documents?
- Whom do you ask? If you're going to ask people to give you information, whom are you going to ask? If you need certain documents, where are you going to find them?
- What kind of information do you need? Do you need descriptive information? Do you need some numbers? Do you need stories? Do you need information that tells you what others think?
- Do you need help? What kind of help do you need? Advice about the topic? Help with research tools? Help in deciding whom to interview? Help with language translation or interpretation? Help from colleagues, students, parents, and supervisors?

Answering these questions will help you make decisions about what research tools to develop.

Be Clear about Objectives

The first step in contemplating any research is clarity of objectives, both political and substantive. What are the specific group or organizational goals to be accomplished by the research? Will these objectives be realized if the research is carried out? What are the costs in terms of both resources and possibly strained relations? If, for example, the objective is to encourage the implementation of a free breakfast program, would research findings in fact bring about that result?

It is important to distinguish between fairly broad goals and more specific objectives. A frequent error of practitioner-researchers is to undertake a study with only vague objectives, hoping to make some sense out of the findings later. This approach is time consuming and wasteful for researcher and participants alike. For example, in approaching the issue of discipline, one could try to find out about teacher, student, and parent attitudes as well as actual practices in the schools. However, if current practices are the focus of concern, that is what should be studied. If teachers' support for a particular policy is at issue, then their attitudes and opinions may be a more appropriate focus. The objectives, framed as precisely as possible, should determine the direction of the research, not vice versa.

Don't Try for Too Much

When one is thinking in research terms, everything becomes a potential subject of research. One must guard against being overly ambitious and be realistic about the adequacy of the resources available to do the job. If one is planning to do a study without additional help, how much time can realistically be spent? Will this be sufficient to complete the study? One should estimate the time needed to accomplish each specific step. Even if it can be done, are the results likely to be worth the effort? If the answer to these two questions is no, then the research should not be undertaken.

Involve Others at an Early Stage

There are two reasons to involve others at the early stage of a project. First, some might feel slighted, and justifiably so, if asked to join a project after the major directions have already been decided by others. Second, and more importantly, the contributions of others enlarge the scope of issues considered and provide an essential source of new ideas. On one hand, group process may complicate the orderly achievement of objectives, and groups are subject to groupthink, which may constrain the consideration of alternatives. On the other hand, research aimed at changing current practices should be undertaken with a view of building constituencies of support to help implement the findings.

Ask for Help

One way of extending available resources is to get additional help. This might mean seeking release time or volunteer assistance from colleagues and students. If the research objective is to bring about change, the greatest possible involvement of both colleagues and school community is desirable. Additional resources are available outside the school system. These include academics, student researchers, retired teacher associations, PTAs, community organizations, and advocacy groups. Advocacy groups have their own particular interest in practices within the schools, although their advocacy position may itself increase the suspicions of administrators. Academics are often interested in consulting on practical issues and may even be willing to undertake the research themselves if offered an interesting research issue and access to a site. University students are often available from a number of academic disciplines—social work, education, psychology, sociology, political science, and public administration—to carry out research that satisfies their practicum requirements under academic supervision.

LOW-COST, STRAIGHTFORWARD METHODS

Most social research is an extension of logical processes used in everyday life. In shopping for new clothes, getting estimates for car repair or home improvement, or planning a vacation, one's customary first step is to gather data on the reliability of the seller and the quality of the merchandise or service, its availability, and its price. Prior to the data-gathering stage, there may be some assessment of the need and ability to pay. Similarly, when contemplating research in the work setting, as a first step, one should specify the objectives of the research and then develop a research plan. This involves a determination of the information needed, its availability, and the methods required to obtain it, and the relative costs of time, materials, and other resources. At this point, you may also wish to review documents, data, and literature that are relevant to your research questions.

Use of Readily Available Data

There are several research approaches that require a minimum of time, some of which may be undertaken using readily available data. Although it is generally desirable to enlist the support of administrators and colleagues in undertaking research, there occasionally may be situations in which some administrators are threatened by the proposed research and withhold permission or seek in other ways to block it. In such instances, it is still possible to gather data by using records and documents that are public information. Perhaps the most straightforward kind of research involves the analysis of existing data. Schools are constantly compiling reams of data on every conceivable activity. Much of this information is funneled to state and federal agencies to meet reporting requirements but is not necessarily analyzed for local administrative purposes. Examples include aggregate data on pupil characteristics, family income, attendance, grades, achievement test scores, the number receiving free lunches, the incidence of visual or dental problems, the prevalence of handicapping conditions, the number in special classes or programs, and the incidence of problems requiring disciplinary action. Other data are available with respect to class size and caseloads of social workers and other educational specialists. Frequently, when caseload sizes are examined in relation to the performance requirements, a discrepancy between expectations and the reality of the workload is immediately apparent. The fact that a class for children with special needs contains fifteen children of differing ages and levels of ability and is taught by one teacher with no aide offers prima facie evidence of a resource deficiency.

Use of Public Documents

Another invaluable source of information is the school district's budget. The budget is a planning document that paints a good picture of what the district actually does and what its priorities are, as represented by the commitment of resources. An examination of the budget permits a comparison of the stated objectives with the actual allocation of resources to achieve those objectives. Other public documents that may shed light on local practices are federal and state laws, administrative codes and regulations, court decisions, state agency policy and procedural statements, and state and local education agency reports. (Such documents and data are becoming increasingly available on the World Wide Web. See chapter 11.) A reading of the state or federal requirements may reveal a discrepancy between these requirements and local practices. Some administrators intentionally keep information about the specific state and federal requirements from the school personnel who must implement them. Knowledge of deliberate violations of law can give school staff a powerful tool for advocating change. School practices with regard to discipline, suspensions, expulsions, and the notification and involvement of parents in placing children in special programs may be at variance with the law and/or district policy. If so, a range of interventions ranging all the way from judicious questioning to encouraging advocacy groups to file suit can encourage change.

Calculations of Costs and Procedural Practices

Another powerful kind of analysis is estimating the costs of procedures and practices. For example, it is a humbling exercise to calculate the cost of a single meeting in relation to its objectives and results. When one counts the dollar value of the participants' time, the costs can be quite substantial. Certain reporting requirements are costly, yet the costs are rarely calculated. In processing paperwork, one must consider the actual cost of completing the forms and reports as well as other hidden costs. These hidden costs include the costs of printing the forms, moving the paper through the organization, and handling and storing it, and the time of those who must read it and comment on and analyze it. Cost comparisons of alternative procedures can be used to support one alternative rather than another.

Seeking out Library, Web, and Other Resources, Records, and Research

Chances are good that most problems have been encountered elsewhere and subjected to some kind of analysis or research. Therefore, a good starting point in any research activity is the library and the Web. A review of the literature is a critical starting point for any research you plan to do. Reviewing the literature allows you to establish what is already known on the topic and is the basis for the research focus. The existing literature can suggest methods for carrying out the research. Published measures and questionnaires can make the job a lot easier by providing an established means of collecting data. The key is to familiarize oneself with the literature before finalizing any research questions or design. You may find that you can answer your question primarily by looking at existing studies, rather than by collecting original data.

When you review the literature, it is important to examine the most recent studies, especially since they will generally include summaries of earlier work in their review of the literature. However, classic studies must not be ignored. Often you can identify these classics by examining the reference lists of the articles you find when a particular author or study is repeatedly cited. This would indicate that their work is significant in the field and should be read. For example, someone who is interested in studying the role of the school social worker would not ignore the work of Lela Costin and Paula Allen-Meares in this area (see chapter 1).

University librarians are generally helpful in locating studies and reports. There are a number of excellent computerized reference files that can produce a list of titles and abstracts on specific subjects at nominal cost. Some excellent databases that can assist in a literature search are the *Educational Resources Information Center, PsycInfo,* and *EBSCO Host*, and others are available at libraries or through an Internet search engine. Many of these databases, which can be obtained through libraries, include online full-text copies of articles in major journals. Access may be limited to patrons of libraries that have purchased access to these resources. However, practitioners can gain access through a local university, or through their university alumni association. Partnering with a university faculty member or graduate student, or a professional association, can make these resources more accessible to the school social worker.

Academic specialists in schools of education and social work and departments of psychology and sociology may be familiar with specific bodies of literature and be willing to share their expertise with practitioners. For just about any problem that can occur in a public school setting, there are likely to be some interested specialists. In addition to academic departments of universities, educational specialists are found in the federal Department of Education, in state departments of education, in contract research firms, and on the staffs of interest groups such as state chapters of the Children's Defense Fund, Council for Exceptional Children, National Association of School Boards, Council of Chief State School Officers, National Association of Social Workers, and National Alliance for the Mentally Ill, as well as state school social work associations. A few phone calls or a visit to organizational Web sites are generally sufficient to access such networks and learn what work has already been done in a specific problem area. For example, if one is investigating student discipline, the Children's Defense Fund may be able to provide a number of references to completed studies, summaries of legal opinions and pertinent laws, and suggestions about model programs. The state teachers' union may maintain a research staff and have access to information on many school issues. Newspaper articles provide another source of data about school policies. In larger cities, local newspapers often have reporters who specialize in educational concerns and who develop expertise in particular educational areas. The papers themselves frequently maintain clipping files, as do school administrations. This is an important documentary record that should not be overlooked. School board minutes are available to the public and also supply a documentary record of actions taken and contemplated.

Methods for Gathering New Data

Other methods for gathering data about school activities include surveys, structured observation, interviews, action research, and online databases. Questionnaires are advantageous for gathering information that safeguards anonymity and providing a structured format for analysis of responses. The disadvantages are that they restrict the amount of data that can be gathered and analyzed, and questionnaire responses may be at variance with actual behavior. Face-to-face interviews offer an opportunity to gather information in greater depth. The interviewer can probe, ask additional questions, and clarify responses. Furthermore, some structure may be maintained through an interview schedule and a listing of topics or questions. Structured observations are those in which there is some purposeful gathering of data according to predetermined categories. Observational techniques such as the use of interaction scales to record information about who initiates interactions and who responds in a group meeting or in a class can become very sophisticated and complicated. More straightforward, simple observational methods usually suffice. For example, the methods described in chapter 24 for use in classroom observation are readily adaptable to research purposes. Very simple categorization and computations sometimes reveal profound meanings. Sometimes it is possible to enlist others in making observations. For example, all school social workers may agree to keep records of certain activities or to record observations of meetings in which they participate for subsequent analysis.

Letting the Facts Speak for Themselves: Compiling Data and Preparing Reports

A final stage in the process is the compilation of data and the preparation of a report or position paper. The format depends on the purpose of the research and the objectives. If one is attempting to block the initiation of a new policy or procedure, the report would necessarily differ from that used in an attempt to compare two alternative procedures, neither of which is particularly preferred. Those guidelines offered earlier for initiating the research can also serve in the planning of the report—one should be clear about objectives, avoid being overly ambitious, keep it simple, involve others, and seek the help of those with expert knowledge. In writing the report, one should avoid pejorative language, cast the findings in objective or neutral terms, and let the facts make the argument. Brevity and clarity are the watchwords. Graphic programs and materials, music, and multimedia sources enhance research presentations. Technology can make dry materials interesting, colorful, and appealing. Dissemination of research reports to the constituent communities through community centers and local organizations is important as a way to enlist their involvement with the school.

The following example illustrates a collaborative practitioner research effort utilizing a number of the methods and resources described above.

> A school social worker observed that communications between staff and the parents of incoming refugee and immigrant children were often strained and incomplete. Using existing school data and public documents, she noted the increasing diversity of the school population. She then initiated informal conversations with newcomer parents, who explained that although they were concerned about their children's education and well-being at school, there were many barriers to participation in parent-teacher conferences, and to discussing educational and disciplinary concerns. These barriers were linguistic, cultural, and logistical—for example, timing of appointments, adequate notification of activities at the school, differing cultural expectations on the parts of parents and teachers, need for language interpretation, and transportation. It was also apparent that even with the presence of bilingual classes, ESL teachers, and bilingual instructional aides, school personnel envisioned the concept of family within a narrow construction of mainstream, educated, middle-class English-speaking parents. The practitioner brought these concerns to a course on empowerment practice with refugees and immigrants taught by one of the authors. For her course project, the practitioner developed a participatory action research project in collaboration with staff at a local agency serving refugees and other immigrants, and with an intern who worked with school-age youths at a local multiethnic service organization. Through interviews with parents and school personnel, focus groups with parents and youths, and meetings with agency staff and parents, the research team developed a needs statement and designed a parent advocate project to help bridge the gap between newcomer families and schools. The research team further reviewed the educational and social work literature, searching for model interventions that had been effective in other school districts working on similar issues. They also sought the expertise of parents who had successfully involved themselves in the schools, and school personnel and staff at other refugee service agencies. They thus brought together multifaceted resources with which to facilitate the problem solving and creative work of the project participants. The team successfully submitted a proposal for funds for a three-year project to form and mentor parent advocate groups. The practitioner-researcher as an agent of change successfully mobilized family and community collaboration to improve children's educational experiences by building mutual cultural understanding and better school-family-community relationships.

Research is too important to be left entirely to researchers. This chapter shows some of the ways practitioners can conduct and use research and, in the process, enhance their practice roles. Perhaps the most difficult step is getting started, particularly in view of the widely held perception that the proper conduct of research requires expertise that comes only from years of specialized training and experience. Such a view rules out many of the relevant applications of research in schools. As shown in this chapter, school-based practitioners can rescue research from researchers and assume a more affirmative role in fostering collaboration, making space for diverse perspectives, and shaping school policy.

References

Altrichter, H., Posch, P., & Somekh, B. (1993). *Teachers investigate their work: An introduction to the methods of action research*. New York: Routledge.

Armstrong, F., & Moore, M. (2004). Action research: Developing inclusive practice and transforming cultures. In F. Armstrong & M. Moore (Eds.), *Action research for inclusive education: Changing places, changing practices, changing minds* (pp. 1–16). London: Routledge/Falmer.

Banks, J. (Ed.). (1996). *Multicultural education, transformative knowledge and action*. New York: Teachers College Press.

Beeson, J. (2002, May). We are not your mascot. *Colors North West*, 12–14.

Blair, K. (2002). School social work, the transmission of culture, and gender roles in schools. *Social Work, 21*(1), 21–33.

Board on Children, Youth and Families. (2003). *Engaging schools: Fostering high school students' motivation to learn*. Washington, DC: National Academies Press. Retrieved January 24, 2005, from http://www.nap.edu/books/0309084350/html/

Boyd, W. L. (1999). Environmental pressures, management imperatives, and competing paradigms in educational administration. *Educational Management & Administration, 27*(3), 283–298.

Broussard, C. A. (2003). Facilitating home-school partnerships for multiethnic families: School social workers collaborating for success. *Children & Schools, 25*(4), 211–222.

Carr, W. (1995). *For education: Towards critical educational inquiry*. Bristol, PA: Open University Press.

Chamberlayne, P., Bornat, J., & Wengraf, T. (2000). *The turn to biographical methods in social science: Comparative issues and examples*. London: Routledge.

Corbett, J. (2001). *Supporting inclusive education: A connective pedagogy*. London: Routledge/Falmer.

Delgado-Gaitan, C. (1993). Researching change and changing the researcher. *Harvard Educational Review, 63*(4), 389–411.

Delgado-Gaitan, C. (2001). *The power of community: Mobilizing for family and schooling*. Lanham, MD: Rowman & Littlefield.

deMarrais, K. (2004). Elegant communications: Sharing qualitative research with communities, colleagues, and critics. *Qualitative Inquiry, 10*(2), 281–297.

Elliott, J. (1991). *Action research for educational change*. Milton Keynes, UK: Open University Press.

Elmore, R. F., & Furman, S. H. (2001). Research finds the false assumption of accountability. *Education Digest, 67*(4), 9–14.

Freire, P. (1973). *Education for critical consciousness*. New York: Seabury Press.

Gran-O'Donnell, S., Farwell, N., Spigner, C., Nguyen, C., Ciske, S., Young, T., et al. (2001). *Perspectives of multicultural youth on community building: A participatory approach*. Unpublished manuscript.

Hammersley, M. (2000). Evidence-based practice in education and the contribution of educational research. In L. Trinder & S. Reynolds (Eds.), *Evidence-based practice: A critical appraisal* (pp. 163–183). London: Sage.

Harold, R. D., Palmiter, M. L., Lynch, S. A., & Freedman-Doan, C. R. (1995). Life stories: A practice-based research technique. *Journal of Sociology and Social Welfare, 22*, 23–44.

Herr, K. (1995). Action research as empowering practice. *Journal of Progressive Human Services, 6*(2), 45–58.

Hick, S. (1997). Participatory research: An approach for structural social workers. *Journal of Progressive Human Services, 8*(2), 63–78.

Holland, T. P. (1991). Narrative, knowledge and professional practice. *Social Thought, 17*(1), 32–40.

Holy, P. (1991). From action research to collaborative inquiry: The processing of an innovation. In O. Zuber-Skerritt (Ed.), *Action research for change and development* (pp. 36–56). Brookfield, VA: Gower Publishing.

Jay, J. (2003). *Quality teaching: Reflection as the heart of practice*. Lanham, MD: Scarecrow Press.

Jones, J. (1991). Action research in facilitating change in institutional practice. In O. Zuber-Skerritt (Ed.), *Action research for change and development* (pp. 207–223). Brookfield, VA: Gower Publishing.

Josselson, R. (1996). *Ethics and process in the narrative study of lives.* Thousand Oaks, CA: Sage.

Lather, P. (2004). This is your father's paradigm: Government intrusion and the case of qualitative research in education. *Qualitative Inquiry, 10*(1), 15–34.

Lipman, P. (2004). *High stakes education: Inequality, globalization, and urban school reform*. New York: Routledge/Falmer.

Martin, R. (1995). *Oral history in social work: Research, assessment, and intervention*. Thousand Oaks, CA: Sage.

No Child Left Behind Act of 2001, P.L. 107-110, 115 Stat.1425 (2002). Retrieved January 25, 2005, from http://www.ed.gov/policy/elsec/leg/esea02/107-110 pdf.

Noffke, S., & Stevenson, S. (1995). *Educational action research: Becoming practically critical*. New York: Teachers College Press.

Pearlmutter, S. (2002). Achieving political practice: Integrating individual need and social action. *Journal of Progressive Human Services, 13*(1), 31–51.

Peters, A. (2003). Isolation or inclusion: Creating safe spaces for lesbian and gay youth. *Families in Society, 84*(3), 331–337.

Salcido, R., Ornelas, V., & Garcia, J. (2002). A neighborhood watch program for inner-city school children. *Children & Schools, 24*(3), 175–187.

Simpson, L. (2004). Students who challenge: Reducing barriers to inclusion. In F. Armstrong & M. Moore (Eds.), *Action research for inclusive education: Changing places, changing practices, changing minds* (pp. 63–76). London: Routledge/Falmer.

Sirotnik, K. A. (1989). The school as the center of change. In T. J. Sergiovanni & J. H. Moore (Eds.), *Schooling for tomorrow: Directing reforms to issues that count* (pp. 89–113). Boston: Allyn & Bacon.

Sleeter, C. (1996). *Multicultural education as social activism.* Albany: State University of New York Press.

Sohng, S. (1996). Participatory research and community organizing. *Journal of Sociology and Social Welfare, 23(4)*, 77–97.

Stevens, J. (1999). Creating collaborative partnerships: Clinical intervention research in an inner-city school. *Social Work in Education, 21*(3), 151–162.

Williams, M. R. (1989). *Neighborhood organizing for urban school reform*. New York: Teachers College Press.

Witherspoon, R. (2002). The involvement of African American families and communities in education: Whose responsibility is it? In S. Denbo & L. Beaulieu (Eds.), *Improving schools for African American students: A reader for educational leaders* (pp. 181–191). Springfield, IL: Charles C. Thomas.

13

Educational Mandates for Children with Disabilities: School Policies, Case Law, and the School Social Worker

Brooke R. Whitted
Whitted and Cleary LLC

Malcolm C. Rich
Whitted and Cleary LLC

Robert Constable
Loyola University Chicago

Carol Rippey Massat
University of Illinois at Chicago

- What Are the Educational Rights of Children with Disabilities?
- How Does the Special Education System Work?
- What Is the Role of the Local School System?
- Who Is the Child with Disabilities?
- What Are Social Work Services in the Schools?
- What Is Special Education?
- What Are Related Services?
- What Is an Individualized Education Program?
- What Services Must the School Provide?
- What Is Placement in the Least Restrictive Environment?

- What Are Placement Procedures?
- Can Students with Disabilities Be Suspended or Expelled?
- What Are Provisions for a Resolution Session, for Mediation, and for an Impartial Due Process Hearing?
- What Are Due Process and Judicial Review?

This chapter is one of several in this book that focus on the implementation for school social workers of the mandate to provide a free and appropriate public education (FAPE) to children with disabilities. Here we provide an overview of the current law and its interpretation in court decisions. Chapter 8 discusses the court decisions that initially defined the right. Chapter 14 focuses on clinical and educational program development for preschool children with disabilities. Section III discusses the assessment process, the least restrictive environment and inclusion, the social developmental study, and the individualized education program.

The basis for all of this is a succession of federal laws and amendments together with their accompanying regulations, beginning in 1975 and continuing through the present. This succession of laws, beginning with the Education for All Handicapped Children Act and culminating in the Individuals with Disabilities Education Act (IDEA) and its amended versions, requires that every state and the District of Columbia ensure FAPE is available to all children with disabilities. The education of unserved or underserved children with disabilities has a clear priority over the education of children already receiving services. Such services must be provided to all qualifying children with disabilities. A student must generally be able to benefit from appropriate services. There is no financial needs test. The act is heavily parent/guardian oriented and requires states to maximize parental involvement in educational decision making every step of the way. Both parents of pupils with disabilities and the schools may invoke a formal administrative system for the resolution of disputes with *due process* procedural safeguards. Throughout this system, detailed steps of identification, evaluation, determination of eligibility, planning, service, and administrative appeals are set forth. The school social worker, as a school staff member, is an important figure throughout. School social workers, who inevitably work with children with disabilities and the special education system, need a working knowledge of the requirements of the act.

WHAT ARE THE EDUCATIONAL RIGHTS OF CHILDREN WITH DISABILITIES?

Over a period of twenty-five years a cumulative body of law, court decisions, and policies has developed in relation to the rights of children with disabilities to a FAPE. These became summarized in IDEA and its amendments, most recently IDEA 2004. When we refer to this cumulative body of law, we are referring to the legal principles codified in 20 *United States Code*, sections 1401–1468. When we refer to federal regulations, we are referring to 34 *Code of Federal Regulations* parts 300 and following. These are frequently updated, as the law and its regulations develop, and can be found in any law library or on the Internet. In reading this chapter, you may also wish to consult the footnotes for more detailed explanations of the law and case precedents. Each state department of education develops its own regulations following the federal ones, and these can generally be accessed from each state department of education's Web site. For the school social worker in the United States, the contents of this book furnish a general update on the most recent provisions of the law, including the Individuals with Disabilities Education Improvement Act of 2004. It is important for social workers in the United States to be familiar with this evolving body of law and its updates in order to design school social work roles that help the school respond to these mandates.

For the international reader practicing in a different legal orbit, it is important to see the relation of law to school policy, and from this to the school social worker's role. The difference in the U.S. legal tradition from that of other nations is the absence of a national education ministry that actively manages local schools. Instead, management of schools has historically been a state and local responsibility, while on the national level the emphasis is on law and policy development.

In the face of some neglect of children with disabilities prior to 1968, the rights of children to a FAPE have had considerable development in the United States. Turnbull and Turnbull summarize this tradition in the form of six rights:

1. The right to attend school—the principle of *zero reject*. Each school-age person with a disability has the right to be educated in a system of FAPE. Agencies and professionals may not expel or suspend students for certain behaviors or without following certain procedures; they may not exclude students on the basis that they are incapable of learning; and they may not limit the access of students to school on the basis of their having contagious diseases.
2. The right to a fair appraisal of their strengths and needs—the principle of *nondiscriminatory evaluation*. Socioeconomic status, language, and other factors need to be discounted and must not bias the student's evaluation; agencies and professionals must obtain an accurate, nonbiased portrait of each student. Decisions need to be based on facts, not simply categories: on what students are doing and are capable of doing, in relation to behavioral outcomes individualized for the student. The resulting education would remedy the student's impairments and build on strengths.

3. The right to a *beneficial experience* in school—the principle of free appropriate public education—means that schools must individualize each student's education, provide needed related services, engage in a fair process for determining what is appropriate for each student, and ensure that the student's education indeed confers a benefit. Education should have a positive outcome for each student. The emphasis of this discussion is not simply on provision of access to education but on adapting the system and on building capacities in the person with a disability so that certain results are attained.
4. The right to be *included* in the general education curriculum and other activities. The principle means that the schools must include the student in the general education program and may not remove a student from it unless the student cannot benefit from being in that program, even after the provision of supplementary aids and services and necessary related services.
5. The right to be treated fairly. The principle of *procedural due process* means that the school must provide certain kinds of information (notice and access to records) to students, special protection when natural parents are unavailable (surrogate parents), and access to a fair hearing process.
6. The right to be included in the decision-making process. The principle of *parent and student participation* means the schools must structure decision-making processes (including policy decisions on a statewide level) in such a way that parents and students have opportunities to affect meaningfully the education the students are receiving. A related principle of enhanced accountability to pupils and parents is moving in the direction of report cards related to individualized goals and educational programs.[1]

Although IDEA 2004 changed the standard for education services from "appropriate" to "maximum," the mandate to provide a free and appropriate public education remains the same. The phrase "free appropriate public education" means special education and related services that:

1. Have been provided at public expense, under public supervision and direction, and without charge;
2. Meet the standards of the state educational agency and secondary school educational agency;
3. Include an appropriate preschool, elementary, or secondary school education in the state involved; and
4. Are provided in conformity with a student's individualized education program. (20 U.S.C. 1401(8))

---

1. H. R. Turnbull & A. P. Turnbull. (1998). *Free appropriate public education: The law and children with disabilities* (5th ed., pp. 273–274). Denver, CO: Love Publishing.

HOW DOES THE SPECIAL EDUCATION SYSTEM WORK?

It is important to understand the impact of laws, court decisions, and policies on state and local educational systems. To respect the rights of children with disabilities to a FAPE and to qualify for federal financial assistance under IDEA, a state must demonstrate that it "has in effect a policy that assures all handicapped children the right to a free appropriate, public education" (26 U.S.C. 412(l)). That policy must be written in the form of a "state plan" and is subject to reapproval every three years by the U.S. Department of Education.[2] Children receiving no education are to have priority over those receiving some form of education (20 U.S.C. 1412(3)). Children with disabilities must be educated to the maximum extent appropriate with children who are not disabled. This is called the least restrictive environment mandate (20 U.S.C. 1412(5)). The FAPE required by IDEA must be tailored to the unique needs of each child through a document called an individualized education program (IEP), which is prepared at a formal meeting between a qualified representative of the local education agency (LEA), the child's teacher, the child's parents or guardian, and, where appropriate, the child.[3] In some cases, a team member may submit his or her input in writing, if the parent gives consent, and if a team member's area of curriculum is not being changed or discussed, that team member is not required to attend the IEP meeting (20 U.S.C. 1400, 614(d)(1), (ii), and (iii). Parental involvement and consultation in this process must be maximized.[4] IDEA also imposes on the states detailed procedural requirements—that is, a set of rules outlining exactly how the educational rights of children with disabilities are to be protected. The rights of parents to consent to the provision or termination of special education services, to question the decisions of educational personnel, and to invoke a highly specific administrative hearing process are all outlined in IDEA (20 U.S.C. 1415 et seq.). Both parents and

2. 20 U.S.C. 1412; 20 U.S.C. 1413. The state plan describes the goals, programs, and timetables under which the state intends to educate children with disabilities within its borders.

3. 20 U.S.C. 1401(18). The IEP must include at the minimum statements of present levels of educational performance, how the child's disability affects involvement and progress in the general curriculum, measurable annual goals, including academic and functional goals, specific services to be provided to the child, the extent to which the pupil will be able to be educated with nondisabled students, the projected date of initiation and anticipated duration of services, a statement of needed transition services, and various criteria for evaluating progress. 20 U.S.C. 1412(3), 1412(5), 1401(1). IDEA projects an alternate assessment for pupils who cannot participate in the regular (grade level) assessment. Short-term objectives are required only for pupils having an alternate assessment (H.R. 1350, 614(a)(2) A, B).

4. *Board of Education of the Hendrick Hudson Central School District, Westchester County, et al. v. Amy Rowley et al.*, U.S. 176, 73 L. Ed.2d 690, 102 S. Ct. 3034 (1982). Excluding parents from the process has, pursuant to *Rowley*, often been held by courts to be a "fatal flaw" committed by educators. *Spielberg v. Henrico County*, Education of the Handicapped Law Review (SEE http://www.wct-law.com/CM/Publications/publications17.asp) (hereafter EHLR) 441:178 (Washington, DC: CRR Publishing).

schools may request mediation or an impartial due process hearing to appeal virtually any educational decision.[5] Any party dissatisfied with the results of the initial due process hearing may request and receive an impartial review by the state agency[6] and, if not satisfied with that review, may then go to court.[7]

IDEA has long placed an affirmative duty upon school systems to seek out all children in need of special education, from birth to age twenty-one. This system, called Child Find, must be a part of every state plan. IDEA 2004 expanded the role of Child Find to require that school districts provide services for homeless children, wards of the state, and students in private schools (20 U.S.C. 1400, 612(a)(1)(C)).

Although IDEA leaves to the states many details concerning development and implementation of particular programs, it imposes substantial requirements to be followed in the discharge of the states' responsibilities. Noncompliance with federal procedural requirements may be sanctioned by the withholding of federal dollars flowing to the offending agency.[8] For example, a state's educational system might be investigated by the U.S. Department of Education for failing to educate children in the least restrictive environment. Such a failure would be evidenced by a pattern of educating children with physical disabilities in separate facilities even though the children in question have no problems other than the physical ones that challenge them. The federal law requires that education of children with disabilities be, to the maximum extent appropriate, with children without disabilities. The failure of a particular state to meet this requirement raises a risk of sanctions.

WHAT IS THE ROLE OF THE LOCAL SCHOOL SYSTEM?

The law ultimately obligates the LEA to provide a FAPE with related services to all children with disabilities. The federal legal mandate requires the local school district to be the "agency of last resort" for the provision of specialized services to this population of children. Other child-serving agencies might engage in interagency squabbles concerning who should pay for or

---

5. 20 U.S.C. 1415(b)(1)(D) and (E). Complaints can be brought "about any matter relating to" the child's evaluation and education.

6. *Mayson v. Teague*, 749 F.2d 652 (1984).

7. 20 U.S.C. 1415(b)(2) and (c), 20 U.S.C. 11415(e)(2). A party may go to either state or federal court. Recently, plaintiffs filing in state court have been "removed" by the school district to the federal district court. This is only a good strategy where a state board of education seeks removal, as these entities are protected by Eleventh Amendment sovereign immunity, while local school districts are not protected. *Dellmuth v. Muth*, 109 S. Ct. 2397 (1989), *Gary A. v. New Trier High School District and the Illinois State Board of Education*, 796 F.2d 940 (1986).

8. 20 U.S.C. 1414(b)(2)(A). Noncompliance may also be sanctioned by judicial review. U.S.C. 1416.

provide services. LEAs and the respective state boards of education are not able to engage in such finger-pointing.[9] Under the Illinois school code, for example, special education services not provided by another agency must be provided by the LEA or the state board of education.[10] Thus the educational sector—even in a time of shrinking resources—is and has been a consistent source of dollars for children's services.

WHO IS THE CHILD WITH DISABILITIES?

IDEA defines a child with a disability "as a child evaluated . . . as having mental retardation, a hearing impairment including deafness, speech or language impairment, a visual impairment including blindness, a serious emotional disturbance, . . . an orthopedic impairment, autism, traumatic brain injury, other health impairment, a specific learning disability, deaf-blindness, or multiple disabilities, and who because of these impairments needs special education and related services" (34 C.F.R. 300.7). Eligibility runs from birth to age twenty-one. The key to eligibility is having a listed disability and needing special education and related services. Having a disability implies difficulty in dealing with one's environment and indeed with the very programs and supports intended to help. The purpose of IDEA cannot be achieved without a profession, such as school social work, that focuses on child, family, and learning environment, each in relation to the other, and that views the child as a whole.

WHAT ARE SOCIAL WORK SERVICES IN THE SCHOOLS?

Social work services in schools include:

1. Preparing a social or developmental history on a child identified as possibly having disabilities,
2. Group and individual counseling with the child and family,
3. Working with those problems in a child's living situation (home, school, and community) that affect the child's adjustment in school,
4. Mobilizing school and community resources to enable the child to learn as effectively as possible in his or her educational program, and
5. Assisting in developing positive behavioral intervention strategies. (34 C.F.R. 300.24(13); 20 U.S.C. 1402(29))

Social work addresses the fit between schooling and the needs of children with disabilities and their parents. A particular group of children who

---

9. *Parks v. Pavkovic*, 753 F.2d 1397 (7th. Cir. 1985). In the district court opinion, Judge Prentice Marshall said that such finger-pointing was one of the most heinous violations of federal law he could imagine.

10. Ill. Rev. State. Ch. 122 (14-8.02).

experience difficulties in school and usually need social work assistance are those who are emotionally disturbed. Emotional disturbance is a condition exhibiting one or more of the following characteristics over a long period of time and to a marked degree that adversely affects educational performance:

> An inability to learn which cannot be explained by intellectual, sensory, or health factors;
> An inability to build or maintain satisfactory interpersonal relationships with peers and teachers;
> Inappropriate types of behavior or feelings under normal circumstances;
> A general pervasive mood of unhappiness or depression;
> A tendency to develop physical symptoms or fears associated with personal or school problems. (34 C.F.R. 300.7(9))

WHAT IS SPECIAL EDUCATION?

Special education and related services are defined individually for each pupil by a multidisciplinary team, that is, in each particular situation and for each child. The team, which must include the parents, prepares the resulting IEP. The need for special education and related services is a key to the definition of the child with a disability. Thus, because of that disability and based on a complete, multifaceted, nondiscriminatory assessment, there is a need for special education and related services. According to IDEA, "special education" means specially designed instruction, at no cost to the parent, to meet the unique needs of a child with a disability. This includes classroom instruction, instruction in physical education, home instruction, and instruction in hospitals and institutions (34 C.F.R. 300.26). IDEA 2004 mandated that all special education teachers must be "highly qualified" and meet the same standards as those outlined in the No Child Left Behind Act.

Special education is offered once a child has been found eligible for services through a formal case study evaluation. An initial case study evaluation must take place within sixty calendar days of the request for the evaluation, unless the state utilizes its own time line. Similarly, reevaluations for continuing eligibility for special education services must also take place within sixty calendar days.

WHAT ARE RELATED SERVICES?

Related services means transportation and such developmental, corrective, and other supportive services as are required to assist a child with a disability to benefit from special education. The term includes such services as transportation, speech pathology and audiology, psychological services, physical and occupational therapy, recreation, early identification and assessment of disabilities in children, counseling services, and medical services for diagnostic or evaluation purposes. It also includes school nurse services,[11] interpreting services, social work services in schools, and parent counseling and training (34 C.F.R. 300.24).

WHAT IS AN INDIVIDUALIZED EDUCATION PROGRAM?

The IEP is the blueprint for all that happens in the education of a child with disabilities. It is a series of guidelines for educators to follow in conferring educational benefits, and a useful document for parents to follow in determining whether those benefits are being made available. School districts must write an IEP before they can provide services (20 U.S.C. 1401(18)). IDEA is quite detailed in its specification of the contents of this document (20 U.S.C. 1401(19)). The IEP must include a "statement of measurable annual goals, including academic and functional goals" (20 U.S.C. 1400, 614(d)(1)(A)(i)(I)(cc)). Transition planning must be documented for students no later than the first IEP in effect when a child turns age sixteen, and such planning must include appropriate, measurable postsecondary school goals and a listing of transition services needed to help students reach these goals.

Parental participation is key to IEP development. IDEA broadens the definition of parent to include natural or adoptive parents; guardians; a person acting in place of a parent, such as a grandparent or stepparent; or duly appointed surrogate parents. Foster parents may serve as surrogate parents if the natural parents do not have the authority to make educational decisions, according to state law, and the foster parents have a parental relationship with the child and are willing, and there is no conflict of interest (20 U.S.C. 1400(606)).

The role of the regular education teacher at IEP meetings was strengthened in IDEA 2004. Regular education teachers must help "determine the appropriate behavior interventions and strategies, and supplemental aids and services that are necessary for their classrooms" (20 U.S.C. 1414(d)(3)(C)).

All IEPs must be reviewed at least every year. A new IEP needs to be written at least every three years.[12] Parents and guardians are always entitled to

---

11. This was formerly "health services" and excluded nondiagnostic medical services, such as ongoing medical treatment. Medical services are defined by who must provide the services, not by the specific service. Thus IDEA designated the school nurse as a related service. If a particular nondiagnostic medical service can be provided only by a physician, the LEA need not cover it as a related service. 20 U.S.C. 1401(17); also see *Kelly McNair v. Oak Hills Local School District*, EHLR 441:381 (6th Cir. 1988–1989), in which the court held that special transportation need not be provided to a deaf child because the need for it was not related to her disabling condition. The statute specifically required a connection between the related service and the unique needs of the child.

12. IDEA recommends this take place at least once every three years "unless the parent and LEA agree that a reevaluation is unnecessary" (H.B. 1350 614(a)(2) A, B).

question IEPs through the due process procedures (20 U.S.C. 1414(a)(5)). Many state boards of education publish manuals on how to write an IEP, and all states have organizations and resource centers to assist parents and guardians in understanding the process of writing an IEP. The input of the social worker during the drafting of the IEP often has a substantial effect on the recommendations made, and social work services are often among the crucial "related services" in the IEP. School districts sometimes list their recommendations for the pupil prior to drafting an IEP. This is a significant procedural error. IDEA requires the assessment and then the IEP to be done first, on the logical assumption that recommendations for a particular educational setting and specific services cannot possibly be made until the needs of the child are determined. When recommendations are made before the IEP is drafted, this is sometimes a good indicator that school authorities are simply offering the program they have available rather than creating a customized program to meet all the needs of the child. It is legally improper and a violation of IDEA for recommendations to be based on administrative convenience, costs, waiting lists, or any factor other than the needs of the child with disabilities in question.[13]

The parent or guardian of a child covered by IDEA must be given prior notice whenever the school district proposes a change in the educational placement of a child, or a change in its provision of a FAPE for the child (20 U.S.C. 1415(b)(1)(c)). This notice must contain an official explanation for the change being proposed, and the reasons why less restrictive options were rejected (20 U.S.C. 1415(b)(1)(d)). The consent of a parent or guardian is required for the initiation or termination of educational benefits (34 C.F.R. 300.505). It is good practice to secure this consent for a reevaluation and/or change of the program. The parent has the right to ask for revisions in the child's IEP (34 C.F.R. 300.350). Notification of proposed changes, regardless of their magnitude, is required in all instances under IDEA, because the right to demand a hearing is always vested in the parent or guardian who disagrees with the changes (20 U.S.C. 1415(b)(1)(E)–(d)). Once a year, at the minimum, the parent should be given a complete description of available procedural safeguards (20 U.S.C. 1400 615(f)(3)(D)). Changes to an IEP may be made by amendment without a redrafting of the entire IEP. A school district and a parent may agree not to convene an IEP team meeting for the purposes of modifying an IEP and instead "may develop a written document to amend or modify the child's current IEP" (34 CFR 300.324(a)(4)(i)). The child's IEP team needs to be informed of these changes, and the parents need to receive a revised copy of the IEP with the amendments incorporated. "Complete failure" to implement an IEP has been held to constitute a change in the child's educational placement, as

13. *Timothy W. and Cynthia v. Rochester, N.H., School District*, EHLR 441:393. 875 F.2d 954 (1989).

well as a failure to provide a FAPE.[14] An IEP is not, however, a contract, nor is it a guarantee that the child will achieve the results contemplated.

WHAT SERVICES MUST THE SCHOOL PROVIDE?

The LEA is obligated to provide the special education and related services (or, for certain children, the "supplementary aids and services") required so that the pupil can attain the objectives stated in the IEP. The components of an IEP are special education, related services, supplementary aids and services, program modifications, and personal support. These are to benefit the student so that he or she can advance appropriately toward attaining the annual goals, be involved and progress in the general curriculum and participate in extracurricular activities and other nonacademic activities, and be educated and participate with other children with disabilities and nondisabled children in those extracurricular and nonacademic activities (20 U.S.C. 1414(d)(1)(a)(3)). The mandate for use of related services is broad, going beyond special education to include what is necessary for the child to participate in general education and extracurricular activities.

Social Work Services

Under IDEA the educational sector is required to pay for related services, which would include any services required to assist a child to benefit from special education. A key issue has been what level of related services is necessary for a child to "benefit" from special education. The *Rowley* case involved a hearing-impaired girl who understood only about half of what was occurring in class. Nevertheless, Amy Rowley received As and Bs because of her high intelligence.[15] Her parents wanted the school to provide a full-time sign language interpreter to attend class with her, but the Supreme Court held that the student was not so entitled, as she was already receiving an "educational benefit" without the interpreter.

Rowley generally is used by schools to back up the argument that they are not required to provide the best education—only an education that is minimally appropriate and available. Social workers should likewise be aware that the recommendations contained in their reports should address the minimum services necessary to enable the child to benefit from educational programming. For instance, some depressed students may need non-medical psychotherapy to attend to instructional tasks. In some cases such psychotherapy has been held to be a related service that must be provided

14. *Lunceford v. District of Columbia Board of Education*, 7455 F.2d 157, 1582 (D.C. Cir. 1984).

15. *Rowley*, 458 U.S. at 184.

by the schools.[16] The distinction between a fundable service and a nonfundable service turns on whether mental health services, psychotherapy, or social work services (as they were defined earlier) would assist a particular student to benefit from special education. In a number of decisions the courts further defined a "service-benefit" standard.[17] The standard involves evaluating two criteria: (1) whether the program is designed to improve the student's educational performance and (2) whether the program is based on the student's classification (e.g., challenged with emotional disturbance).[18]

Psychotherapy

On the other hand, in another decision, it was held that the service-benefit standard for determining whether psychotherapy is a related service is overly broad and inordinately encompassing. When the justification for the services is only psychological improvement, the LEA is not responsible for providing mental health services to the student.[19] It must be clearly demonstrated that social work services would assist students to benefit from special education. In school social work, the general language for demonstrating this is found in the previous definition of school social work services. For many years, school social workers have defined their practice in relation to education, as this book will attest. Further court decisions will clarify these boundaries.

Children Unable to Benefit from Education

There are several thousand children in the United States so lacking in brain capacity that they are unable to benefit from any educational services.[20]

---

16. *Max M. v. Thompson*, 592 F. Supp. 1450 (1984). This student's neurotic anxieties prevented him from attending school, and the school social worker, among others, recommended psychotherapy. The school district did not provide the therapy. The parents paid for two years of treatment and then asked for reimbursement from the district. The court held that the school was responsible for the services to the extent that a nonphysician could provide them. The district, then, had to reimburse parents for the equivalent of psychologist-provided therapy, a lower amount than the actual cost, since a psychiatrist had been the therapist. See also *In the Matter of "A" Family*, 602 P.2d 157 (S.C. Mont.), which held family therapy to be a related service, and *Gary B. v. Cronin*, 625 F.2d 563, n. 15: "While psychotherapy may be related to mental health, it may also be required before a child can derive any benefit from education."

17. See *Papacoda v. Connecticut*, 528 F. Supp. 68 (D. Conn. 1981). *Vander Malle v. Ambach*, 673 F.2d 49 (2nd Cir. 1982), further proceedings 667 F. Supp. 1015 (S.D.N.Y. 1987). *Mrs. B. v. Milford Board of Education*, 103 F.3d 1114 (2nd Cir. 1997).

18. See also the discussion of these points in Turnbull and Turnbull, pp. 161–164.

19. *Clovis Unified School District v. California Office of Admin. Hearings*, 903 F.2d 635 (9th Cir. 1990).

20. R. Rothstein. (1982). Educational rights of severely and profoundly handicapped children. *Nebraska Law Review*, 61, 586. See also *Parks v. Pavkovic*, 753 F.2d at 1405, in which the Court speculated about what type of child might not ever be able to benefit and concluded that such a child would have to be in a coma.

The U.S. Supreme Court has declined to review a hotly contested case in which a child "lacking any cortex" was held to be entitled to related services even though he was unlikely to benefit from services.[21] The *Timothy W.* case originated in Rochester, New Hampshire, where the school district argued that providing any services to such a hopelessly disabled child would be a waste of tax dollars better spent on less disabled children.[22] In their pleadings to the Court, the attorneys for the schools, astonished by the decision of the appellate court, said that such decisions requiring school personnel to provide services to children who cannot benefit from any services "may have unfortunate consequences for families of uneducable children because [they] raise false hopes, which in turn often lead to bitterness and disillusionment" and ultimately to intensive family therapy or marital counseling.[23] The U.S. Supreme Court would not, however, read in any exceptions to IDEA that are not present—and no exception was drawn for so-called uneducable children with disabilities.[24]

If a child needs a residential setting in order to benefit from education, the school must pay for such a setting, and there can be no charges to the parents or guardian.[25] If other agencies are active and are able to pay part of the cost, such payments are allowed as long as such agencies do not charge the parent.[26] When a school district writes an IEP stating that another agency is to provide some of the services, the school district is still the "agency of last resort," and parents may rightfully turn to the schools for recompense.[27]

A well-known U.S. Supreme Court case has held that clean intermittent catheterization (CIC) is a related service.[28] Amber Tatro needed CIC several times daily in order to stay in class and to benefit from educational services.

---

21. EHLR 441:393; *Timothy W. and Cynthia W. v. Rochester, N.H., School District*, EHLR Summary and Analysis, pp. 265–266 (December 1989). Federal appellate court citation: 875 F.2d 954 (1989); U.S. District Court citation: EHLR 509:141 (1987). See also B. R. Whitted. (1990, Winter). Educational benefits after *Timothy W.*: Where do we go from here? *Illinois Administrators of Special Education Newsletter*.

22. 875 F.2d at 954.

23. *Petition for Writ of Certiorari to the United States Supreme Court of Rochester, N.H., School District v. Timothy W. and Cynthia W.*, EHLR Summary and Analysis, 226 (November 1989).

24. *Honig v. Doe*, 484 U.S. 305, 108 S. Ct. 592 (1988). Note that the Supreme Court, in refusing to review a decision, does not in the process issue an opinion covering its reasons. The citation in this note refers to the Court's tendency to read IDEA rigidly, and in *Honig*, it refused to read in a dangerousness exception to the principle that restricts exclusion of pupils with disabilities from school.

25. *Parks v. Pavkovic*, 753 F.2d 11397 (7th Cir. 1985), cert. denied at 473 U.S. 906 (1985). Interprets 34 C.F.R. 300.302, among other regulatory provisions.

26. See the Disabled Children's Program of the Social Security Act, 42 U.S.C. 1382 et seq.

27. *Kattan v. District of Columbia*, EHLR 441:207.

28. *Amber Tatro et al. v. Irving (Tx.) Independent School District et al.*, 4568 U.S. 883 (1984).

In *Tatro* the schools argued that CIC was a medical service and therefore not a related service. The U.S. Supreme Court did not agree, noting that CIC was not exclusively within the province of physicians and could be administered easily by the school nurse. The school district was required to provide this service.

WHAT IS PLACEMENT IN THE LEAST RESTRICTIVE ENVIRONMENT?

One further principle, that of least restrictive environment, governs the all-important placement process. This principle is defined in the law as follows: "To the maximum extent appropriate, children with disabilities . . . are educated with children who are nondisabled, and . . . special classes, separate schooling, or other removal of children with disabilities from the regular education environment occurs only if the nature or severity of the disability is such that education in regular classes with the use of supplementary aids and services cannot be achieved satisfactorily" (20 U.S.C. 1412(a)(5)(A)). This principle is extremely important to achieving the general purposes of IDEA. Related services in the IEP (including the school social worker's contribution) are intended to assist the pupil to advance appropriately toward attaining his or her annual goals, to be involved and progress in the general curriculum, to participate in extracurricular and other nonacademic activities, and to be educated and to participate with other children with disabilities and nondisabled children in the general curriculum. The principle of inclusion presumes that the child with disabilities should participate in the general curriculum. It requires the IEP to explain the extent, if any, to which the child will not participate with children without disabilities in regular classes and in extracurricular and other nonacademic activities (20 U.S.C. 1414).

However, the term "inclusion" is not to be found anywhere in the IDEA legal mandate. In recent years, some advocates have said that the special education system is not working, and that to benefit from educational services, students must be "fully included" in the mainstream. Many have gone so far as to present this concept as a part of the law and to tell parents this new law says they must cooperate in the full mainstreaming of their children. Nothing could be further from the truth. The law governing the least restrictive environment has not changed and merely requires that to the maximum extent appropriate, children with disabilities should be educated with children without disabilities. Although there is a presumption that the child with disabilities should participate in the general curriculum when appropriate, no federal law has ever mandated "full inclusion" without consideration of educational needs. Inclusion as such, discussed in chapter 19, is often a matter of state policy. Federal law requires all school districts to make available a full continuum of alternatives from the least restrictive (such as complete mainstreaming with one resource period per day) to the most restrictive (private residential placement). Part of the school social worker's role in these cases is to work with pupil, parents, and the school to construct this environment.

WHAT ARE PLACEMENT PROCEDURES?

Placement procedures make the connection between the assessment and the IEP. Disabilities are inevitably connected with social functioning in one way or another. If assessments are to be complete, multifaceted, and nondiscriminatory, as the law prescribes, the school social worker should participate in most assessments. In some school districts the social worker is the person responsible for the social developmental study of the child. The social worker's understanding of the child's current adaptation to home and school environments, the child's previous developmental steps, and the culture and functioning of the family is essential to any assessment. In the same vein, the annual goals for the child, the corresponding education program, and related services, as developed in the IEP, often explicitly involve tasks for the social worker with the child, with the family, and with education professionals. In the process of interpreting evaluation data and planning an IEP, the multidisciplinary team needs to

"Draw on information from a variety of sources, including adaptive and achievement tests, teacher recommendations, physical condition, social or cultural background, and adaptive behavior" and "Ensure that information obtained from all of these sources is documented and carefully considered." In addition, "If a child needs special education and related services, an IEP must be developed for the child" (34 C.F.R. 300.535).

CAN STUDENTS WITH DISABILITIES BE SUSPENDED OR EXPELLED?

On January 20, 1988, the U.S. Supreme Court issued its opinion in *Honig v. Doe*.[29] This strongly worded case set forth guidelines that educators have actively and hotly debated ever since. Two California cases related to *Honig* involved violent, acting-out pupils who were suspended "indefinitely" and later expelled under the California statute that allowed indefinite suspensions. The school district's attorneys argued, when the cases finally reached the judicial level, that Congress could not possibly have intended that the schools be required to keep serving dangerous emotionally disturbed pupils when staff members and other students were in peril. The

29. *Honig v. Doe*, 484 U.S. 305, 108 S. Ct. 592 (1988), interpreted the stay-put provision of the Education of the Handicapped Act, 20 U.S.C. 1415(e)(3). The authors strongly recommend that social work students read this case in its entirety. *Honig* is a powerful tool for advocates of special education, and a thorough knowledge of the procedures set forth by the Supreme Court is crucial.

Court held that Congress "very much meant to strip schools of the unilateral authority they had traditionally employed to exclude disabled students, particularly emotionally disturbed students, from schools."[30] The U.S. Supreme Court, in this case, demonstrated clearly its reluctance to read into IDEA meanings never expressed by Congress.

The net effect of this case is that a school may not remove a pupil with a disability from school for behavior that is a manifestation of the disabling condition without the consent of the parents.[31] To determine whether the behavior was or was not a manifestation of the disability, the IEP team must consider whether (1) the conduct in question was caused by or had a direct and substantial relationship to the child's disability and (2) whether the conduct in question was a direct result of the school district's failure to implement the IEP (20 U.S.C. 1400 615(k)(1)(E)). If a district does find a child's behavior to be related to his or her disability, then it is required to (1) create a functional behavior assessment and a behavior intervention plan for the child (see section III of this book) or revise the child's functional behavior assessment and behavior intervention plan if one was already completed and (2) return the child to his or her previous educational placement.[32] The Supreme Court has clearly expressed its feeling that allowing schools to suspend pupils who are dangerous to themselves and others for up to ten days cumulatively per school year gives educational authorities sufficient time to seek parental consent, negotiate alternatives, or go to court to obtain permission of a judge for the removal. Additionally, IDEA law has created certain circumstances (students bringing guns to school, or knowingly possessing, using, or selling dangerous drugs or inflicting serious bodily injury on another person in school) where the school may go beyond the ten-day limit, possibly up to forty-five school (not calendar) days (20 U.S.C. 1400, 615(k)(1)(G) and (k)(1)(H)(2)).[33] In any case a change of placement occurs if removal is more than ten consecutive school days, or there is a series of

30. 484 U.S. at 321.

31. IDEA requires that if the LEA, the parent, and relevant members of the IEP team determine that the conduct was a manifestation of the child's disability, the child must be provided a FAPE and that the IEP team conduct a functional behavioral assessment and implement a behavioral intervention plan (see section III). Except under special circumstances outlined in the text, the child is returned to the original placement (H.R. 1350, 615(k)(1)(F)).

32. M. L. Yell. (1989). *Honig v. Doe*: The Suspension and expulsion of handicapped students. *Exceptional Children, 56,* 60-69; M. L. Yell. (1990). The use of corporal punishment, suspension, expulsion, and time out with behavioral disordered students in public schools; legal considerations, *Journal of Behavior Disorders*, *15*(2), 100–109.

33. If a student with a disability brings guns to school; knowingly possesses, uses, or sells dangerous drugs; or inflicts serious bodily injury on another person in school, the school can place the student in an alternative education setting for up to forty-five days. In these cases, during a parental appeals process the child would remain at the alternative placement during the pendency of the dispute (20 U.S.C. 1400, 615(k)(1)(G) and (k)(1)(H)(2)).

removals totaling more than ten days in one academic year. The child must be provided FAPE and receive a functional behavior assessment and a behavior intervention plan. Modifications of the original program may be needed (20 U.S.C. 1400, 615(k)(1)(D)).

IDEA 2004 also provides some protections for children not yet eligible for special education if a school district has knowledge that a child has a disability. The school district is considered to have knowledge of the disability if the parent has expressed concern about a possible disability to the school in writing, if the parent has requested a case study evaluation, or if a teacher or other school district employee has expressed specific concerns about a pattern of behavior to the director of special education or other supervisory personnel (20 U.S.C. 1400, 615(k)(5)(C)).

Social workers should become familiar with the basic law of suspension and expulsion of pupils with disabilities, because they may find themselves in the position of mediating disputes between schools and families of disabled students.[34] Moreover, social workers are commonly called as experts in due process hearings for the purpose of establishing whether the behavior in question is or is not related to the pupil's disabling condition. Finally, current law relating to suspension and expulsion is a powerful tool for families of the disabled to persuade school authorities to consider more restrictive alternatives for the child, such as private extended-day school programs or residential placement, when appropriate.

WHAT ARE PROVISIONS FOR A RESOLUTION SESSION, FOR MEDIATION, AND FOR AN IMPARTIAL DUE PROCESS HEARING?

It is not surprising that there can be differences between parents and others on the multidisciplinary team over a possible recommended placement for a child. In these circumstances, the due process protection of the Fifth and the Fourteenth amendments to the United States Constitution demands more formal procedures. After all, a civil right is being defined. It was the intent of the framers of IDEA that parents and educators be encouraged to "work out their differences by using nonadversarial means."[35] IDEA provides for a resolution session to encourage resolution of complaints without the need for involvement of attorneys or hearing officers. Under 20 U.S.C. 1400 section 615(f)(1)(B)(ii), after a school district receives a request for a due process hearing, it is mandated to convene an IEP meeting to try

34. For further information on mediation, see C. B. Gallant. (1980). Mediation: A unique due process procedure which utilizes social skills. In R. J. Anderson, M. Freeman, & R. L. Edwards (Eds.), *School social work and PL 94-142: The Education for All Handicapped Act*. Washington, DC: National Association of Social Workers. Frequently, social workers are called upon to act as impartial mediators as well as to utilize their skills in facilitating communication between the school and family.

35. *Congressional Record,* May 12, 1997, p. S4298.

to resolve the complaint within fifteen days unless both parties agree to waive the meeting. If the parent attends the meeting without an attorney, the school district must be unrepresented as well. The parties may agree to use state mediation procedures instead of a resolution session. The next step would be an impartial due process hearing. In most cases, it is only after these steps have been taken, and the issue is still unresolved, that the case would go to court.

Mediation is a voluntary process conducted by a "qualified and impartial mediator who is trained in effective mediation techniques" (20 U.S.C. 1415(e)). Mediation cannot be used to deny or delay a parent's right to an impartial due process hearing. The state education agency usually has a list of approved mediators and carries the cost of the mediation process. Any agreement reached by the parties to the dispute is set forth in a written mediation agreement. Discussions in the mediation process are confidential and cannot be used as evidence in subsequent due process hearings or civil proceedings. Both parties may be required to sign a confidentiality pledge prior to the mediation process (20 U.S.C. 1415(e)(A–G)).

The impartial due process hearing is conducted by either the state education agency or the LEA, although not by an employee involved with the education of the child. It is a somewhat more formal process than mediation. Any evaluation completed in relation to the pupil must be disclosed at least five days prior to the hearing. There are procedural safeguards: parents have the right to be accompanied or advised by counsel and by experts, the right to present evidence and confront and cross-examine and compel the attendance of witnesses, the right to a verbatim record, and the right to written findings of fact and decisions. If the hearing is conducted by the LEA, its outcome may be appealed to the state education agency, where another hearing may take place. If the problem is not resolved at this point, it may be brought to court (20 U.S.C. 1415(f)(g)). During due process hearings, the child's placement remains the same unless he or she has not been admitted to public school. In such a case, the child would be, with the parents' permission, placed in the public school until the completion of the proceedings.

Several recent court decisions have clarified some of the procedures for due process hearings. In a recent court decision, *Schaffer v. Weast,* the Supreme Court determined that the side to go first in a due process hearing is the party that requested the hearing.[36] They held that the "burden of persuasion" fell on the party that initiated the process. In a second case, *Arlington Central School District Board of Education v. Pearl Murphy*, the Supreme Court held that even if parents prevail in a due process case, they are not entitled to reimbursement for any expert witnesses that they hire as part of their case.[37] Should they prevail, the parents are still entitled to reim-

36. *Schaffer v. Weast* (04-698) 546 U.S. 49 (2005) 377 F.3d 449

37. *Arlington Central School District Board of Education v. Murphy* (No. 05-18) 402 F.3d 332.

bursement of reasonable attorney fees, however. Finally, in *Winkelman v. Parma City School District*, the Supreme Court held that parents can represent themselves and their child in a due process hearing.[38] The appellate court had dismissed the parents' claim because they had no attorney. The Supreme Court held that this would leave some parents, such as those who could not afford an attorney, without a remedy in the courts under IDEA. In these cases, the Supreme Court has demonstrated a consistent reluctance to interpret into the act any provisions that are not specifically mentioned in the law.

WHAT ARE DUE PROCESS AND JUDICIAL REVIEW?

Once the second review is completed, any party dissatisfied with the result may appeal it to either state or federal court (20 U.S.C. 1415(e)(2)) by filing a lawsuit requesting appropriate relief against the other party.[39] It is important to note that the stay-put provision operates while all proceedings are taking place (20 U.S.C. 1415(e)(3)). This provision requires that the child remain in his or her current placement while due process proceedings are pending. During this time, the district must pay for all educational services in the current placement. When certain behaviors occur, the school may place the student in an alternative education setting for up to forty-five calendar days. In these instances, the stay-put placement is this alternative setting.

The *Burlington* case clearly provides that even if the parent loses at each stage of the process, the district cannot obtain reimbursement from the

---

38. *Winkelman v. Parma City School District,* 550 U.S. ___ (2007).

39. A practical note: If the district loses, there is a fair degree of reluctance on the part of the school boards to proceed with a lawsuit. One reason is that the child usually has to be sued as a "necessary party." Another reason is expense. Insurance carriers for districts resist providing coverage for these matters, so a school board must vote to proceed knowing that the district will expend precious local dollars with no hope of recoupment if the district loses. Finally, even if the district wins on the administrative level, if it is sued by the parents, the insurance carrier will resist coverage for any reimbursement costs or Protection Act attorney fees, since these are not "damages." *Tonya K. v. Chicago Public Schools et al.,* 551 F. Supp. 1107 (1988). The greatest pressure on a district for settlement, then, is at the end point of the administrative proceedings. IDEA allows a prevailing school district to recover reasonable attorney's fees if a court determines that the parents' action in filing a due process action is "frivolous, unreasonable or without foundation." Courts can also levy a fee against the parents if their action is deemed to have been brought for an improper purpose, such as "to harass, to cause unnecessary delay, or to needlessly increase the cost of litigation." When parents prevail, they may be able to recover their attorney's fees, but some federal courts have ruled that parents who prevail through private settlement agreements with school districts are not entitled to attorney's fees. On the other hand, the prevailing party, whether parent or school district, will be able to collect the cost of attorney's fees (H.R. 1350, 615(I)(3)(B)).

parent.[40] The stay-put provision is thus a powerful tool for parents if proceedings commence when the pupil is in an educational setting that satisfies the parents. Most commonly, the child is in a school-funded residential placement, while the district seeks to return him or her to a less restrictive setting. If the parents request due process at this point, the child must remain in the residential setting at district expense during the pendency of all proceedings, through and including appellate court review.

Conversely, when the current placement is one that the parents feel is not appropriate, the stay-put provision operates to the benefit of the school district. In this instance, the parents' goal is to effect an alternative placement that they and their experts feel is more appropriate than the current setting, whereas the school district usually seeks to maintain the status quo. The school district continues to pay the cost of the child's educational placement, regardless of who requests due process.[41] For younger pupils entering school for the first time, the "current" placement is interpreted by most states to be the setting in which the child would be placed in the absence of any disability. For a student with disabilities transferring from one school district to another, the current placement is determined by the student's most recent IEP.

Legislation and case law on the civil right to a FAPE for children with disabilities have created new structures of service for these children. The social worker's services are framed in a developing body of law. It is important to understand that this law is not simply a set of procedures. It places a mandate on the school district and on the social worker to provide services that will enable children with disabilities and their families to survive in an initially unequal struggle. Here the language of the law can be translated into the language of service. The more familiar social workers are with both languages, the more able they will be to translate them into services that can redress this inequality.

---

40. See *Burlington School Committee v. Department of Education*, 471 U.S. 359 (1985). There have been instances, however, where school districts have sought reimbursement. In November 2003, for example, a federal district court in Illinois ruled in favor of the parents in an action in which the school district was seeking to be reimbursed for transportation costs under stay-put (*Aaron M. v. Yomtoob*, 38 EHLR 122 [2003]). In the court's ruling, allowing school districts reimbursement of monies during stay-put periods would have a chilling effect on parents exercising their rights under the school law.

41. Note that it is not just parents who can request due process. Schools sometimes seek to provide a service that the parents oppose. For instance, the district may want to place the child in a classroom for the mentally retarded (MR), while the parents may feel that their child is not retarded, but learning disabled. The parents' refusal to consent to the "MR" placement may be met by the district's request for due process. From a liability point of view, this is the only alternative for districts in such a position. Parents are frequently unable to accept that their child is so low functioning. The social worker may be called upon to assist the parents in working through their shame and guilt, among other feelings.

14

Family-Centered Services to Infants and Toddlers with or at Risk for Disabilities: IDEA 2004, Part C

Kathleen Kirk Bishop
Wheelock College

- Historical Perspective
- Mandate versus Choice of Services
- Analyses of Selected Aspects of the Law
- Requirements for a Statewide System
- Developing Best Practice Models
- Part C's Continuing Impact
- Discussion Listservs

This chapter on Part C of the Individuals with Disabilities Education Improvement Act of 2004 (IDEA 2004) has a threefold purpose. It presents a brief summary of key parts of the law with the greatest relevance for social work education and practice; it suggests areas where social workers can assume practice and leadership roles in the continued interpretation and implementation of the law, and it seeks to describe and highlight best social work practice with infants, toddlers, and their families.

HISTORICAL PERSPECTIVE

Part C continues to pose challenges to professionals and families to go beyond their traditional roles and to work collaboratively with one another in health care, education, social services, mental health, and other public and private agencies (Bishop, 1987). The precursor to IDEA 2004's Part C was signed into law by Congress in 1986 as P.L. 99-457, Part H. Part H signaled a new concern for the health and well-being of infants and young children with and at risk for disabilities and their families. It created a discretionary program to help states plan and implement statewide, comprehensive, coordinated, multidisciplinary interagency systems of early intervention services for all eligible infants and toddlers from birth to three years old and their families.

Perhaps the most unique and groundbreaking aspect of this legislation was the initiation of a paradigm shift in the way professionals would provide services to families. This paradigm shift is represented most clearly by the requirement that an individualized family service plan (IFSP), rather than the more traditional individualized educational program (IEP), be developed. The requirement for an IFSP recognizes that families are essential partners in all aspects of the care of their children. Thus any IFSP that is developed requires professionals to collaborate with families in the planning, design, and implementation of service systems. The requirement encourages interprofessional and collaborative practices, recognizes and supports the strengths of families, and encourages the delivery of services in the natural environments of infants and toddlers. All social workers who work with children up to three years of age and their families are essential partners in the implementation of this legislation, whether they are in hospitals, early intervention programs, schools, child care and after-school programs, or public and private child welfare agencies.

It is important to distinguish between early intervention services described in Part C of IDEA (services for infants and children up to age three) and Part B services, which are for children and young adults ages three to twenty-one. Early childhood programs offered to preschoolers ages three and over are offered through Part B. States have the option to create a policy that would allow parents to choose to continue early intervention (Part C) services "until such children enter kindergarten" (20 U.S.C. 1400 635(c)) rather than transitioning them into preschool services offered through Part B at age three (20 U.S.C. 1400 638(4)). If a state chooses to create such a policy, then parents who choose these services will not be afforded the FAPE protections offered under IDEA for special education students prior to their placement in kindergarten. They may have to pay for all or part of these services, and it is possible that the services are provided by less specialized personnel. Such parents must give written consent to continue early intervention services once their child reaches age three. Some parents may choose to keep a child in the same services he or she received from infancy to age two if they feel satisfied and comfortable with the early intervention service providers or do not wish their child to transition to new services, but they need to be quite sophisticated about their choices and/or have a good, unbiased case manager to help them. Thus a child may continue to have an IFSP until entering kindergarten, or until he or she is eligible by state law to enter kindergarten (20 U.S.C. 1400 635(c)(1)).

MANDATE VERSUS CHOICE OF SERVICES

IDEA 2004 provides formula funding on a voluntary basis for all states to fully implement a comprehensive, multidisciplinary statewide interagency system of early intervention services for infants and toddlers with disabilities and their families. States are not required to participate in the program. In addition, they are not required to include infants and toddlers at risk for developmental delays in the state definition of whom they will serve. What this means is that some states may, and have, excluded at-risk groups from their definition of the population to be served, and some states may choose not to accept the funds and implement the program.

For social workers, Part C is a moral mandate. It is legislation that can be used to leverage services to historically underrepresented populations, particularly minority, low-income, inner-city, and rural populations. It is also legislation that can be used to support states that have higher-than-average populations of infants and toddlers, high infant mortality rates, and high rates of children living in poverty. There is a major emphasis on prevention. Thus, social workers must use their advocacy skills to implement Part C and to make sure that infants and toddlers who live in poverty or with disabilities have the same opportunities for health and well-being as all other infants and toddlers.

ANALYSES OF SELECTED ASPECTS OF THE LAW

This discussion is limited to selected aspects of IDEA 2004 in relation to infants and toddlers at risk of disabilities. It explores several key components of the law and the regulations: who will be served, early intervention services, requirements for a statewide system, procedural safeguards, the IFSP, and service coordination. These components of the law have major implications for social work practice.

It is important to understand the philosophy of this act as it was originally authorized and subsequently revised. Perhaps the philosophy is best reflected by the fact that the word "families" is mentioned at least thirty-one times in the original 1986 legislation. The family focus continues to be present in subsequent versions. The opening policy statement of the current law sets a major focus on families and on prevention:

> Congress finds that there is an urgent and substantial need—
>
> to enhance the development of infants and toddlers with disabilities, to minimize their potential for developmental delay, and to recognize the significant brain development that occurs during a child's first 3 years of life;
>
> to reduce the educational costs to our society, including our nation's schools, by minimizing the need for special education and related services after infants and toddlers with disabilities reach school age;
>
> to maximize the potential for individuals with disabilities to live independently in society;
>
> to enhance the capacity of families to meet the special needs of their infants and toddlers with disabilities; and
>
> To enhance the capacity of State and local agencies and service providers to identify, evaluate, and meet the needs of all children, particularly minority, low-income, inner city, and rural children, and infants and toddlers in foster care.[1]

The focus on families signals a change in early childhood intervention services from a child-centered philosophy to one that is family centered. Services to infants and toddlers with disabilities are to be provided within the context of their families and other natural environments.

This family-centered philosophy recognizes the family as the central presence and support in the child's life, while service systems and personnel change. It suggests recognition, respect, and support for the crucial role that family members play in the daily care and nurturing of their children. It directs professionals to work as partners with families in securing the best possible early intervention services for their children. The principles of family-centered services and family-professional collaboration guide social workers as they participate in the implementation of all aspects of Part C services, whether one is working directly with children and families or developing policy, programs, practice guidelines, and/or evaluation strategies. In whatever arena social workers participate, families' voices and experience are to be central in all aspects of the provision of services, resources, and supports.

Who Will Be Served?

In the context of the law, infants and toddlers with disabilities are defined as children under three years of age who need early intervention services because they are experiencing delays in cognitive, physical, communication, social, emotional, or adaptive development or have a diagnosed physical or mental condition that has a high probability of resulting in developmental delay. Beyond this, "developmental delay" takes the meaning given by the state. Each state is required to adopt a definition of developmental

---

1. Quotes from the law have adapted its technical language to the needs of the text. For exact quotes, see 20 U.S.C. 1400 et seq.

delay; this definition can be as comprehensive or as restrictive as it wishes. An at-risk infant or toddler is an individual less than three years of age who would be at risk of experiencing a substantial developmental delay if early intervention services were not provided to him or her (section 632(1)). Defining "risk" and "developmental delay" remains a pressing challenge for each state and for children and their families. Children who are eligible in such categories could include children who are biologically, socially, emotionally, medically, or environmentally at risk. IDEA 2004 added Child Find criteria that specifically focus on certain populations: infants and toddlers in foster care, homeless children, premature infants, infants with physical risk factors associated with developmental delay, children who have been abused or neglected, substance-exposed infants, and children exposed to family violence. This emphasis on underserved populations is also present in IDEA 2004 changes in requirements for state applications for Part C grants. Such grants must now include assurances that policies and procedures have been adopted to ensure the involvement of such underserved groups as homeless families, rural families, and wards of the state (637(a) and (b)(71)).

Early Intervention Services

The term "early intervention services" means developmental services that are designed to meet the developmental needs of an infant or toddler with a disability as identified by the IFSP team (section 632(4)(C)) in any of the above areas, as defined by the state. These services need to meet the standards of the state in which the services are provided. Services are diverse, reflecting the complex needs at this age level. They include family training, counseling, and home visits; special instruction; speech pathology and audiology services and sign language and cued language services; occupational therapy; physical therapy; psychological services; service coordination services; medical services only for diagnostic and evaluation purposes; early identification, screening, and assessment services; health services necessary to enable the infant or toddler to benefit from other early intervention services; social work services; vision services; assistive technology devices and assistive technology services; and transportation and related costs that are necessary to enable an infant or toddler and the infant or toddler's family to receive services (section 632(4)(C–E)). These services need to conform with the IFSP. They need to be provided in natural environments, including the home and community settings in which children without disabilities participate (section 632(4)(E)).

REQUIREMENTS FOR A STATEWIDE SYSTEM

It is up to each state to develop the early intervention system that best suits its needs. In general, a statewide system of coordinated, comprehensive, multidisciplinary interagency programs providing appropriate early intervention services to these children would include the following components:

1. A rigorous definition of the term "developmental delay" that will be used by the state in carrying out programs
2. A state policy that ensures that appropriate early intervention services based on scientifically based research, to the extent practicable, are available to all infants and toddlers with disabilities and their families, including Native American infants and toddlers with disabilities and their families residing on a reservation geographically located in the state and infants and toddlers with disabilities who are homeless and their families
3. A timely, comprehensive multidisciplinary evaluation of the functioning of each infant or toddler with a disability in the state, and a family-directed identification of the needs of each family of such an infant or toddler, to assist appropriately in the development of the infant or toddler
4. For each infant or toddler with a disability in the state, an individualized family service plan
5. A comprehensive Child Find system, including a system for making referrals to service providers that ensures rigorous standards for appropriately identifying infants and toddlers with disabilities
6. A public awareness program focusing on early identification of infants and toddlers with disabilities—including dissemination of information to primary referral sources, especially hospitals and physicians, and information for parents, especially those with premature infants—and other physical risk factors
7. A central directory that includes information on early intervention services, resources, and experts available in the state and research and demonstration projects being conducted in the state
8. A comprehensive system of personnel development, including the training of paraprofessionals and the primary referral sources, that includes innovative strategies and activities for recruitment and retention of early education service providers, preparation of early intervention providers who are fully qualified, and training personnel to coordinate transition services for infants and toddlers to appropriate preschool programs (such training may also include preparation for work in rural and inner-city areas and training in the emotional and social development of children and young children)
9. Policies and procedures that establish and maintain personnel qualifications to ensure that they are appropriately and adequately prepared and trained, including the establishment and maintenance of qualifications that are consistent with any state-approved or recognized certification, licensing, registration, or other comparable

requirements that apply to the area in which such personnel are providing early intervention services

10. A single line of responsibility in a lead agency designated or established by the governor to carry out administration, supervision, and monitoring of programs; assignment of financial responsibility; development of procedures to ensure that services are provided in a timely manner; and resolution of intra- and interagency disputes
11. Procedural safeguards
12. A system for compiling data
13. A state interagency coordinating council
14. Early intervention services that are, to the maximum extent appropriate, provided in natural environments and that are provided in a setting other than a natural environment that is most appropriate, as determined by the parent and the individualized family service plan team, only when early intervention cannot be achieved satisfactorily for the infant or toddler in a natural environment (section 635(a)(1–16))

Members of the state interagency coordinating council are appointed by the governor. In making these appointments, the governor should ensure that the membership reasonably represents the population of the state. The composition of the council should be at least 20 percent parents of infants and toddlers with disabilities, and at least 20 percent providers of early intervention services. In addition, representatives of the state Medicaid program, the state coordinator of services for education of homeless children and youths, the state child welfare agency, the state mental health agency, Head Start, the state legislature, and professional education must be involved.

The law delegates an important policy agenda to the council. It advises and assists the lead agency (determined in each state) in the identification of sources of support for early intervention programs. It deals with the assignment of financial responsibility to the appropriate agency, and the promotion of interagency agreements. It assists the lead agency in the preparation of applications and amendments to policies. It advises and assists the state education agency regarding the transitions of toddlers with disabilities to preschool and other appropriate services. It prepares and submits an annual report to the governor on the status of early intervention programs within the state (section 641 (a–e)).

The Individualized Family Service Plan

The IFSP is the key document governing provision and evaluation of services to individual children and their families. As such, it models family involvement in planning and in family-centered and collaborative practice. Revolutionary in its conception, it addresses in a single plan the child and family as a unit, regardless of who delivers and who pays for the services. It reflects family-professional collaboration that honors the wishes of the family. It is first of all a family-directed assessment of the resources, priorities, and concerns of the family. Building on this, it identifies the resources, supports, and services necessary to enhance the family's capacity to meet the developmental needs of the infant or toddler. The IFSP requires collaboration with the family on the identification of major outcomes expected for the child and family and, building on that, a clear and specific statement of the services to be provided to the infant or toddler and the family. Although there may be a tendency to see the IFSP as another form of an IEP, it is important to conceptualize the IFSP differently. The IFSP is not an IEP with a couple of family goals added, nor is it a group of plans from a variety of agencies located in a single folder labeled "IFSP."

There is a strong emphasis in the IFSP on the empirical foundation for practice. This reflects a national commitment to services that are supported by evaluative research, and for which outcomes can be measured. For example, statewide systems must have a policy that ensures that early intervention services are based on scientifically based research. The IFSP must contain a description of early intervention services that are based on peer-reviewed research, and the IFSP must include a statement of measurable goals and outcomes (635(a)(2), 636(a)(3), and 636(d)(3–4)).

A major goal of the IFSP is to ensure that the family is an integral part of the plan from the beginning of its development to the end of its implementation. For school social workers, whose orientation would put them in a leadership position in this process, these requirements translate into the need for family-centered communication and interventions. There is a considerable body of literature pertaining to the value of family-centered approaches to children and families. Many programs emphasize the importance of being family centered. However, families and professionals continue to report difficulties in translating the family-centered philosophy into concrete actions. Some concrete examples of best practices in constructing the IFSP are collaborative agenda development for IFSP meetings; openness to holding meetings in places and at times that are convenient for the family; and use of language that is strengths based, respectful of families, and easily understandable by all participants.

Service Coordination

Service coordination is an active, ongoing process and requires the coordinator to carry out the following responsibilities:

- Assisting parents of eligible children in gaining access to early intervention services and other services identified in the IFSP
- Coordinating the provision of early intervention services, such as ongoing pediatric care
- Facilitating the timely delivery of services
- Continuously seeking appropriate services and situations necessary to benefit the development of the child

The law states that the IFSP must identify the service coordinator from the profession most immediately relevant to the infant or toddler's and family's needs (or the person who is otherwise qualified to carry out all applicable responsibilities) (section 636(d)(7)). This person is responsible for the implementation of the plan and coordination of services with other agencies and persons. The kinds of specific service coordination activities involved are activities that are very familiar to social workers. These would be coordinating evaluations and assessments; ensuring the development, review, and evaluation of the IFSP; assisting families in finding service providers; ensuring that services are delivered in the natural environments for infants and toddlers and as close to home as possible; helping families access advocacy services; and, finally, facilitating the development of a transition plan to preschool services.

These service coordination activities recognize the multidisciplinary, collaborative interagency nature of the services that are required for this population of children and families. They emphasize the importance of the coordination function necessary to integrate and implement the services effectively. Although the law suggests that the service coordinator come from the profession most immediately relevant to the infant or toddler's and family's needs, in reality several factors are of critical importance in the choice of a service coordinator. She will need to be responsible for the implementation of the IFSP. She should be someone with whom families are comfortable working. She should believe in and support families as experts on the care of their child. She should have experience using a collaborative process with families and other professionals. She should see families as full members of the team. She should have the skills and experience to coordinate services with other agencies and providers.

School social workers have long experience in liaison with other agencies, and with case management and coordination of services (see chapter 30). They are a natural choice to assist families with service coordination activities. For social workers, the service coordination functions and activities described in the laws and regulations are natural and expected components of social work services (Kisthardt, 1997; Rose, 1992). Social work as a profession traditionally has supported the values of client self-determination and participation in the development of plans for service, privileging the voice of families and advocating structural and systemic change. They are recognized in many settings as the link between clients and community services and resources

Procedural Safeguards

Inclusion of a program or service in a statewide system demands procedural safeguards. The following are minimal procedural safeguards expected by the law. Infants, toddlers, and families have:

1. The right to timely administrative resolution of complaints (any party, aggrieved by the outcome of an administrative complaint, has the right to bring a civil action relating to the complaint in any state court of competent jurisdiction or in federal district court);
2. The right to confidentiality of personally identifiable information, including the right of parents to written notice of and consent to the exchange of such information among agencies consistent with federal and state law;
3. The right to accept or decline any particular early intervention service without jeopardizing other services;
4. The opportunity to examine records relating to assessment, screening, eligibility determinations, and the development and implementation of the IFSP;
5. Access to procedures to protect the rights of wards of the state, including the assignment of an individual to act as a surrogate for the parents;
6. The right to written prior notice when changes in the identification, evaluation, or placement of the infant or toddler are contemplated;
7. The right to be fully informed in the parents' native language of any contemplated changes unless it clearly is not feasible to do so; and
8. The right to use mediation for some exceptions to policies or procedures (section 639(a)(1–8)).

In the course of any proceedings or action regarding the placement, the infant or toddler would continue to receive the appropriate early intervention services currently being provided, unless the state agency and the parents otherwise agree (section 639(a)(8)(b)).

Practice Implications for Social Workers

Before discussing particular approaches to practice, social workers who are practicing with infants and toddlers with or at risk for disabilities and their families must first examine their own values, biases, culture, attitudes, and beliefs about families. This examination must extend to their own family of origin, extended family history, and practice history. The examination and work on self must be continuous throughout one's practice life.

As we move toward identifying best practice in the twenty-first century, it is imperative that we develop practice models that are responsive to the rapidly increasing number of children from racial minorities in the U.S. population. By the year 2010, one of every four children will be a child of color (Chan, 1991). These children are the largest at-risk group for disabilities associated with poverty. Lack of maternal prenatal care, poor prenatal nutrition, and inadequate health care for poor children (Schorr, 1989) all contribute to risk of disability.

Social workers have a long history of concern for families (Germain, 1968; Hartman & Laird, 1983; Richmond, 1917) and the environments in which they live and work. Family-centered practice is a model of social work practice that locates the family in the center of the unit of attention or field of action (Germain, 1968). As conceptualized within the life model of social work practice (Germain & Gitterman, 1980), the domain of family-centered social work practice is in the transactions between families and their environments. Over the past twenty years, new theories and new ways of conceptualizing and contextualizing the issues and challenges for children and families within their social environments have emerged. These approaches include empowerment (Cochran, 1992; Pinderhughes, 1995), strengths-based practice (Weick & Saleebey, 1995), social constructionism (Laird, 1995), narrative therapy (White, 1995), collaboration with families (Bishop, Woll, & Arango, 1993), and partnership with communities (Bishop, Taylor, & Arango, 1997; Delgado, 2000; Ewalt, Freeman, & Poole, 1998) and with multiple organizations and systems (Gray, 1989). Services should be developed and delivered in a culturally appropriate and responsive manner (Fong & Furato, 2001; Rounds, Weil, & Bishop, 1994). The intent of the law dovetails with social work's concern to secure social justice and human rights for those families most oppressed and marginalized by issues of poverty, racism, and ableism. Newer expectations provide new opportunities to apply these emerging approaches to early intervention services for infants and toddlers most at risk for or with a disability.

DEVELOPING BEST PRACTICE MODELS

The following social work practice approaches lend themselves to the spirit and the requirements of the legislation to provide early intervention services to infants, toddlers, and their families. Families have reported that these are the approaches that are most respectful to their children and themselves (Bishop et al., 1993). It is within a partnership with social workers and other professionals that they can work most effectively to achieve their goals for their children and for their family (Bishop et al., 1997). Helping families identify their priorities and connecting them to appropriate services will increase the likelihood that they and their children will receive the early intervention services they want and need. These practice approaches are all family centered, community based, culturally competent, interprofessional, and coordinated.

A social worker who uses family-centered practice approaches views the family and its members as people with strengths, honors the expertise and experience of the family, and works with the family as a full partner and decision maker. The social worker should not be making assumptions about what the family wants and needs to care for their child with a disability. Instead, the social worker should explore with each family their priorities and concerns, what resources and supports they have, and what the family wants and needs in order to provide the best care to their child. Such approaches and questions, which transfer power and decision making to the family, will require new ways of doing business for schools, child care centers, after-school programs, and all agencies serving young children and their families. If such agencies value families and aspire to deliver services in a family-centered manner, it will require changes such as flexible service hours and examination of the agency menu of services and asking families to help define what is missing and what is unnecessary. Where teams are in place to do evaluations of infants and young children, family members must be welcomed as part of the team and integral to all aspects of the assessment, intervention, and evaluation processes. Such practice approaches move us away from viewing families as dysfunctional, from blaming families for their children's problems, and from rescuing children from their families. They move us toward strengths- and empowerment-based models that view family members as people with strengths and resources, as people with expert knowledge about their children, and as crucial partners in all aspects of their child's care.

A social worker who uses community-based practice approaches works with families to understand the natural environments in which they live, work, and play as a family. Using an ecological approach and the ecomap tool, the social worker needs to work with the family to understand where their sources of strength and support are, and what community resources they are currently using with their child. This exploration includes natural systems of support for the family, such as extended family, relationships in religious communities, local storekeepers, neighborhood social networks at playgrounds, and child care centers. Most families want their services delivered as close to home as possible, and in the context of a community of support. (For a fuller discussion of community-based practice, see Delgado, 2000; Ewalt et al., 1998.)

Social workers who use culturally appropriate practice approaches (Lum, 2003) need to ask families to be their teachers and/or to suggest other community members who might be willing to help social workers and other members of the team understand the cultural norms and values associated with providing help. Families need to be given opportunities to teach team members about their particular culture and what are acceptable cultural practices in relation to the disability. In addition, the role of religion and spirituality in relation to cultural practices may also need to be explored. Team recommendations need to be adapted to fit the family's unique notions of supports, services, and resources.

The social worker providing services to very young children and their families is often working with many providers from a variety of disciplines, as well as paraprofessionals, and needs to be skilled at interprofessional collaborative practice approaches. No single provider, no single agency, and very few communities can provide all the services families with infants and toddlers with disabilities need. "Collaboration with families and other(s) is a necessity and an obligation of professional leadership" (Corrigan & Bishop, 1997, p. 149). Families face a confusing array of services, troubled child services, and family health insurance programs. They want and need professionals who can work together, overcome turf battles, share resources, and use team-building and collaboration skills to help their child and family. Social workers have these skills and can forge partnerships between families and the professionals who provide their services, so that they are offered in the most family-friendly and effective manner.

A social worker must be skilled in service coordination practice approaches. Service coordination involves using family-centered, community-based, and interprofessional collaborative approaches as an active and ongoing process to meet the infant or toddler's and the family's needs and priorities. It is the service coordination element that translates the individual family service plan from a paper document to a series of services and activities that are focused on providing the early intervention services that the child needs and involves supporting the family to achieve their goals for their child. Social workers have a special responsibility to this population of children and families. Infancy and toddlerhood are critical and vulnerable times in the lives of children, times of rapid growth and change. They are critical and vulnerable times for families too. Families who have infants and toddlers with disabilities face the additional challenges of responding to the unique needs of their children with a disability. Social workers are skilled at providing the appropriate services and supports that the family and their child require.

The following suggestions provide some examples of how social workers can fulfill their responsibilities as providers and advocates of early intervention services that reflect a family-centered, community-based, culturally responsive, and coordinated approach. Such practice needs to develop and model family-professional partnerships (Bishop et al., 1993) in all aspects of service provision, especially in the development of an IFSP and the provision of case management services. It needs to ensure that family support services are available to all families who desire them, including such services as respite care, sibling support, grandparents' support, family-to-family support, and fathers' groups. It needs to provide services to families that reflect the principle of normalization and are as close to home as possible and in the families' natural environments. It needs to support a family's participation in all meetings that concern their child and family, using planning instruments, such as IFSPs, in partnership with families and other service providers. It needs to advocate services that are accessible, flexible, culturally sensitive, and responsive to the diversity of family desires and styles (Rounds et al., 1994). It needs to assist other professionals in understanding the cultural and social experience of the child in the family and community (Clark, 1989) and facilitate collaboration between and among service providers and agencies in the family's local community.

In order to support this type of practice, state- and community-wide models for practice with infants and toddlers and their families need to be developed. School social workers need to connect with the contact person at the designated lead agency in the state and collaborate in statewide efforts to develop best practices. The following tasks are particularly important as these models are developed and implemented:

- Working on confidentiality procedures that will ensure maximum protection of families while facilitating information sharing that will benefit families and protect them from duplicative procedures and services
- Developing collaborative training programs in which families and professionals have opportunities to educate each other
- Advocating the necessary financial resources to facilitate full implementation of the law, particularly including serving at-risk infants and toddlers

PART C'S CONTINUING IMPACT

Since 1986, service systems in education, social services, health, and mental health have become more complex. They have grown and expanded in a manner that makes it increasingly difficult to provide family-centered, community-based, culturally responsive services in a coordinated and seamless manner. New parents of an infant or toddler with a disability face this complexity and disarray in services at a point when they may have the least time and energy to find services for their child and themselves.

With Part C acting as a catalyst for change, there has been considerable leadership from federal agencies, particularly the Maternal and Child Health Bureau's Programs for Children with Special Health Care Needs (Brewer, McPherson, Magrab, & Hutchins, 1989). In January 1994, more than fifty national organizations concerned with the well-being of children, youths, and families, including the National Association of Social Workers, American Academy of Pediatrics, and National Education Association, developed a set of principles that would pave the way for unprecedented collaboration among essential services at the local, state, and federal levels (American Academy of Pediatrics, 1994). The Federal Interagency Coordinating Council has also provided leadership by using family-professional collaborative processes and developing materials that describe and encourage family-centered, community-based, culturally appropriate early intervention services. At about the same time, the National Commission on Leadership in Interprofessional Education was founded to promote interprofessional collaborative practices and training. Its mission statement states: "Through a family/professional partnership, the Commission will support the preparation of a new generation of interprofessionally oriented leaders in health education and practice, who possess the knowledge, skills, and values to practice in new community-based integrated service delivery systems" (National Commission on Leadership in Interprofessional Education, 1995). More recently, the social work accrediting body, the Council on Social Work Education, has begun to study issues of certification, licensing, and accreditation for interprofessional practice. The accreditation standards passed by the council's Commission on Accreditation in 2001 include interprofessional practice as part of the content for social work practice. In December 2001, the Maternal and Child Health Bureau, Division of Programs for Children with Special Health Needs and Their Families, in concert with the 2010 Goals for the Nation, launched a ten-year Action Plan to Achieve Community-Based Service Systems for Children and Youth with Special Health Care Needs and Their Families. This ten-year action plan reaffirms the need to work in partnership with families in their local communities to achieve appropriate care and to support all children with or at risk for a disability and their families. Families have been active leaders and participants in all these developments. Through organizations such as Family Voices and Parent-to-Parent, they influence Congress and federal, state, and community agencies. Their object is to fulfill the promise of Part C and encourage full funding for the family-directed provision of early intervention services.

Although much of this emphasis on interprofessional education and practice (Kane, 1975, 1982) is not new to social work education and practice, the emphasis on a family-professional partnership in the planning, implementation, and evaluation of services is new (Bishop et al., 1993). Families are now recognized as having critical knowledge about and experience caring for their children and are viewed as equal partners on the team. Part C has been instrumental in the implementation of this philosophy of care.

The emphasis on the provision of services in the natural environments of infants and toddlers coincides with a rededication to the concept of community as an important source of supports and resources for children and their families. This new era of community renewal has dramatically changed the role of social workers in community practice. Social workers once again have assumed the role of change agent. Today, greater emphasis is placed on encouraging community members to participate and assume leadership roles in all phases of community capacity development (Ewalt et al., 1998).

In summary, social workers have a leadership role and need to make a major contribution to this process. They collaborate with families in the development and implementation of early intervention services that reflect families' concerns and desires for their children with disabilities as well as the needs of the children. They can advocate systemic changes that support families' efforts to be successful with their children, regardless of their social, cultural, political, and economic status in society. In addition, social workers have a role to play in assisting other professionals in understanding the values, knowledge, and skills needed to work with families in a family-centered manner. The social worker's responsibility requires action in four areas: (1) family-centered services and supports to infants, toddlers, and their families; (2) service coordination activities in partnership with families, providers, agencies, and communities; (3) service system change activities; and (4) legislative advocacy.

Social workers should be actively engaged in partnership with parent/family leaders and parent/family organizations; with local and state legislators; with federal and state health, educational, social services; and with mental health service systems to develop family-oriented services for this population and best practices at state and community levels. At stake is the possibility that all infants and toddlers at risk for or with disabilities may be supported to grow, develop, and learn to their full potential. It is the right thing to do, and it helps ensure human rights and social justice for these young children and their families (Finn & Jacobson, 2003).

DISCUSSION LISTSERVS

The following Listservs will allow the interested reader to follow conversations among family and parents' groups as they monitor the changes in the law, their projected responses, and other areas of interest. Some of these Listservs are not limited to Part C but are useful for understanding the current issues for families.

Fv-talk@yahoogroups.com
Groups@yahoo.com/group/FV-talk/
Familypartners@yahoogroups.com

References

American Academy of Pediatrics. (1994). *Principles to link by: Integrating education, health and human services for children, youth, and families: Systems that are community-based and school-linked*. Available from the American Academy of Pediatrics, 601 Thirteenth Street, NW, Suite 400 North, Washington, DC 20005.

Bishop, K. K. (1987). The new law and the role of social workers. *Early Childhood, 3*(2), 6–7.

Bishop, K. K., Taylor, M. S., & Arango, P. (Eds.). (1997). *Partnerships at work: Lessons learned from programs and practices of families, professionals and communities*. Burlington: University of Vermont, Department of Social Work.

Bishop, K. K., Woll, J., & Arango, P. (1993). *Family/professional collaboration for children with special health needs and their families*. Burlington: University of Vermont, Department of Social Work.

Brewer, E. J., McPherson, M., Magrab, P. R., & Hutchins, V. L. (1989). Family-centered, community-based, coordinated care for children with special health care needs. *Pediatrics, 83*(6), 1055–1060.

Chan, K. (1991). Social work with ethnic minorities: Practice issues and potentials. *Journal of Multicultural Social Work, 1*(1), 29–39.

Clark, J. (1989, January 17). *Proposed roles and mission for professionals working with handicapped infants and their families*. Unpublished manuscript, Iowa State Board of Education.

Cochran, M. (1992). Parent empowerment: Developing a conceptual framework. *Family Sciences Review, 5*, 3–21.

Corrigan, D., & Bishop, K. K. (1997). Creating family-centered integrated service systems and interprofessional educational programs to implement them. *Social Work in Education, 19*(3), 149–163.

Delgado, M. (2000). *Community social work practice in an urban context*. New York: Oxford University Press.

Ewalt, P. L., Freeman, E. M., & Poole, D. L. (Eds.). (1998). *Community building: Renewal, well-being, and shared responsibility*. Washington, DC: NASW Press.

Finn, J. L., & Jacobson, M. (2003). *Just practice: A social justice approach to social work*. Peosta, IA: Eddie Bowers.

Fong, R., & Furato, S. (Eds.). (2001). *Culturally competent practice: Skills, interventions and evaluations.* Boston: Allyn & Bacon.

Germain, C. B. (1968). Social study: Past and future. *Social Casework, 49*, 403–409.

Germain, C. B., & Gitterman, A. (1980). *The life model of social work practice*. New York: Columbia University Press.

Gray, B. (1989). *Collaborating: Finding common ground for multiparty problems*. San Francisco: Jossey-Bass.

Hartman, A., & Laird, J. (1983). *Family-centered social work practice*. New York: Free Press.

Individuals with Disabilities Education Improvement Act, P.L. 108-446 (2004).

Kane, R. A. (1975). *Interprofessional teamwork*. Syracuse, NY: Syracuse University School of Social Work.

Kane, R. A. (1982). Lessons for social work from the medical model: A viewpoint for practice. *Social Work, 27*(4), 315–321.

Kisthardt, W. (1997). The strengths model of case management: Principles and helping functions. In D. Saleebey (Ed.), *The strengths perspective in social work practice* (2nd ed., pp. 97–113). New York: Longman.

Laird, J. (1995). Family-centered practice in the postmodern era. *Families in Society, 76*(1), 150–162.

Lum, D. (Ed). (2003). *Culturally competent practice: A framework for understanding diverse groups and justice issues* (2nd ed.). Pacific Grove, CA: Brooks/Cole.

National Commission on Leadership in Interprofessional Education. (1995). Executive board minutes.

Pinderhughes, E. (1995). Empowering diverse populations: Family practice in the 21st century. *Families in Society, 76*(3), 131–140.

Richmond, M. (1917). *Social diagnosis*. New York: Russell Sage Foundation.

Rose, S. (1992). *Case management and social work practice*. New York: Longman.

Rounds, K., Weil, M. O., & Bishop, K. K. (1994). Practice with culturally diverse families of infants and toddlers with handicapping conditions. *Families in Society, 75*(1), 3–15.

Schorr, L. B. (1989). *Within our reach: Breaking the cycle of disadvantage*. New York: Anchor Books.

Weick, A., & Saleebey, D. (1995). Supporting family strengths: Orienting policy and practice toward the 21st century. *Families in Society, 75*(1), 141–149.

White, M. (1995). *Reauthoring lives: Interviews and essays*. Adelaide, Australia: Dulwich Centre Publications.

15

A History of the Education of African American Children

Carol Rippey Massat
Cassandra McKay
University of Illinois at Chicago

- Pre–Civil War Schooling of African American Children
- Post–Civil War
- Constitutional Amendments
- Racial Discrimination and Segregation

The history of African American education involves a centuries-long struggle in the United States to achieve equal educational opportunities. At times in U.S. history, education of African Americans has been outlawed, and at other points in time, schools have been a means of social control through education for assimilation. *Education for assimilation* refers to efforts to use education as a tool to encourage members of different cultural groups to adopt the characteristics and norms of a dominant group while relinquishing their own traditions and cultures. Education, as the traditional key to opportunity, is a valued right for all citizens, but equal education has yet to be achieved for many members of minority groups. This fact is rooted in the history of African American schooling. History lives today, and a shadow of bigotry and racism continues to fall on American schools across the nation.

PRE–CIVIL WAR SCHOOLING OF AFRICAN AMERICAN CHILDREN

Pre–Civil War schooling of African Americans involved an extended struggle that is detailed in Carter Woodson's 1919 book *The Education of the*

Negro Prior to 1861. When education was first beginning to be offered to African American slaves, Protestants and Quakers followed the example of Catholics in providing education. From the inception of slavery until 1835, religious groups were the primary educators of African Americans. Initially, both Protestants and Catholics who were proponents of slavery believed that by teaching Christianity to slaves, they would be conferring a benefit to them that justified the institution of slavery (Woodson, 1919). The Anglican Church of London established a school led by the Reverend Thomas Goose in South Carolina in 1695. A second school was opened in 1704 in New York. In the early 1700s, education of African Americans was established in Virginia, and later in North Carolina, also under Christian auspices.

About 1700, the institution of slavery began to be attacked by a number of different Christian groups. No longer seeing slavery as a beneficial path to salvation, Christians of various denominations began to voice the opinion that slavery was in direct opposition to their faith. The abolitionist movement also advocated education of African Americans as right for both individuals and society (Woodson, 1919).

Yet literacy laws prohibiting slaves from learning to read English were enacted for fear of insurrection. South Carolina prohibited the teaching of slaves in 1740, and in 1800 prohibited the education of all African Americans. Virginia and Georgia also made education of Negroes illegal, and North Carolina, Delaware, and Maryland passed laws requiring strict inspection and regulation of places where African Americans might gather, such as schools (Woodson, 1919). Nevertheless, slaves did participate in numerous rebellious acts and insurrections during this time (see *A History of Negro Revolt* by C. L. R. James, 1969, for more information). Only with the end of the Civil War were African Americans officially declared free to read. Major events such as the establishment of the Freedmen's Bureau and the passing of the Thirteenth, Fourteenth, and Fifteenth amendments to the Constitution aided in this declaration.

POST–CIVIL WAR

The Freedmen's Bureau was initially established to aid refugees of the Civil War but was primarily known for its aid to newly freed slaves. One of the most widely recognized achievements of the Freedmen's Bureau was its establishment of public schools for newly freed slaves. The Freedmen's Bureau was abolished in 1872. At the end of 1870, 150,000 African American children were attending school. In addition, at the culmination of five years of effort, nearly six million dollars had been expended to establish schools of higher learning (Du Bois, 1901). Many of these institutions, such as Fisk, Clark Atlanta, Howard, and Hampton universities, remain in operation today.

An important educator involved in this initiative was Brigadier General Samuel Chapman Armstrong. An agent of the bureau, Armstrong created and led Hampton Normal and Agriculture Institute (later Hampton University) in

1868. Armstrong provided the educational architecture to acculturate and assimilate the newly freed slave. Through promotion of education for assimilation, he sought to "train and civilize" freed slaves in order to maintain a stratified social order, but this mission was shrouded in a cloak of humanitarianism. Girded by a moral conviction to save those flagrantly referred to as "inferior Negroes" from themselves, the Hampton Institute sought to provide former slaves a means of survival in a changed world. Hampton prepared African American teachers in the Hampton Institute philosophy. These teachers furthered the promotion of Armstrong's educational ideology. Booker T. Washington was a firm believer in and advocate of the Hampton experiment. His influence would have deep and sustained implications for education for assimilation of African Americans (Watkins, 2001).

The racially tense climate that surrounded the establishment of Tuskegee Normal and Industrial Institute in 1881 convinced Booker T. Washington that education must dignify common labor for the African American. Washington believed that African Americans could achieve economic self-sufficiency through mass industrial education and vocational training, which he considered the best tactic in negotiating survival (Ogbu, 2004).

Washington, however, did not challenge the historical inequalities of wealth and power and avoided confrontation between the races. His avoidance of confrontation was criticized, and some have viewed Washington as someone who helped to legitimize the status quo, and whose actions supported the repressive tenets of education for assimilation. Such education for assimilation contributed to the creation of a subjugated workforce that was disconnected from real political power (Potts, 2002). Further, Washington's rhetoric of subservience to the old slave master brought more criticism. Washington (1900/1972) posited, "The wisest among my race understand that the agitation of questions of social equality is the extremest folly, and that progress in the enjoyment of all the privileges that will come to us must be the result of severe and constant struggle rather than of artificial forcing" (p. 76). This philosophy diminished progress toward a politically vital African American citizenry and was critiqued by W. E. B. Du Bois (1901/1994), who asserted: "Mr. Washington's programme practically accepts the alleged inferiority of the Negro races" (p. 30) and later, Carter G. Woodson (1933/1998), who stated: "In our so-called democracy we are accustomed to give the majority what they want rather than educate them to understand what is best for them. We do not show the Negro how to overcome segregation; but we teach him how to accept it as final and just" (p. 101).

CONSTITUTIONAL AMENDMENTS

Three key amendments to the Constitution were passed soon after the end of the Civil War. The Thirteenth Amendment ended slavery. The Fourteenth Amendment made black people citizens of the United States and prohibited state laws limiting their rights. The Fifteenth Amendment prohibited racial discrimination in voting. The Thirteenth Amendment was declared ratified on December 18, 1865. Delaware did not ratify the amendment until 1901, and Kentucky did not ratify it until 1976. The amendment was never ratified by Mississippi.

The Fourteenth Amendment to the Constitution provides equal protection to all male citizens of the United States and prohibits states from passing laws that would restrict U.S. citizens' rights to life or liberty, or to hold property or vote. This amendment was declared ratified July 28, 1868. Delaware did not ratify the amendment until 1901, Maryland waited until 1959, and Kentucky did not ratify the amendment until 1976, over one hundred years after it was proposed.

The Fifteenth Amendment to the Constitution of the United States asserts that the "right of citizens of the United States to vote shall not be denied or abridged by the United States or by any state on account of race, color, or previous condition of servitude." It was ratified February 3, 1870, but southern states circumvented the law to prevent African Americans from voting through the use of poll taxes, literacy tests, and other restrictions. The Voting Rights Act of 1965 finally led to the majority of African Americans in the South registering to vote. Temporary provisions in the act are still subject to debate for reauthorization by members of Congress. The Voting Rights Act was up for reauthorization in 2007.

RACIAL DISCRIMINATION AND SEGREGATION

Racial discrimination was a part of federal law and case law before the Civil War. Before the Civil War, black men were not allowed to join militias, the U.S. Army, or the navy. The federal government would not provide passports to free black individuals.

After the Civil War, de jure segregation—that is, segregation that is a matter of formal policy or law—spread across the United States. Black codes, or Jim Crow laws, which limited the rights of African Americans, treating them as second-class citizens, were passed. In many states including California, North Carolina, Alabama, Indiana, and Mississippi, separate and unequal accommodations were maintained. Integration of educational facilities, lunch counters and restaurants, buses, trains, hotels, and prisons was prohibited, and interracial marriages were outlawed. Those who defied the laws were subject to fines, arrest, and violent retaliation.

In the southern states, sharecropping became a means to continue economic exploitation of African Americans. With the emancipation of slaves, plantation owners lost their labor force. In order to recoup their losses, they rented plots of land primarily to African Americans to plant and harvest crops. All supplies to till the land had to be purchased, mostly on credit from the landowner at exorbitant prices. At harvest time, the landowner would decide what percentage of the crops' profit settled the debt. The sharecropper rarely saw a profit after paying rent and was usually more indebted to the landowner than he had been the previous year (Ochiltree, 2004).

Congress rebelled against the South during Reconstruction, when the Republican Party took control of southern state governments. During this period, black people were first elected to public office in the South, and much discriminatory state legislation was repealed. The Civil Rights Act of 1866 was passed, and the 1875 Civil Rights Act was designed to prohibit segregation in public places.

The Democrats took control of the South by 1877, and the gains made during Reconstruction were lost. Systematic efforts to stop African Americans from voting became routine, and a segregated society, including separate schools and separate public facilities, was created. The Supreme Court, in the *Civil Rights Cases* (1883), decided that African Americans had no right to be "special favorites" as citizens. This allowed more and more discriminatory legislation to be passed. In the Supreme Court case of *Plessy v. Ferguson* in 1896, the famous decision was made that "separate but equal" facilities were acceptable. The Supreme Court decision in *Williams v. Mississippi* in 1898 allowed a plan in Mississippi that would disenfranchise almost all black people in the state and keep black people from serving on juries. De jure segregation grew as Kentucky prohibited white children's use of any textbook ever used by a black child, and Alabama prohibited integrated checkers games. Segregation was supported both by the law and by terrorist organizations such as the Ku Klux Klan and the Knights of the White Camellia. These groups killed both blacks and whites who favored reform.

Historical accounts testify that the Thirteenth, Fourteenth, and Fifteenth amendments did not succeed in ending racial discrimination and segregation. Segregation is a problem that has affected both African Americans and other ethnic minorities, particularly Hispanic children. However, much of the case law has been established around issues of racial segregation of white and African American students.

For African Americans, schools began as segregated education. Woodson (1919) reports that this was the result of the views of both white people attempting to organize such schools and African Americans themselves. The state of New York in 1864 included a provision in the state code that communities could offer separate schools for white children and "children of African descent" (Woodson, 1919, p. 121) as long as they were funded in the same manner. In 1900, the state of New York passed legislation stating that no one could be denied admittance to any public school regardless of race, color, or previous condition of servitude.

The case of *Roberts v. City of Boston* was the first challenge to segregated schooling. Roberts lost the challenge, but the state of Massachusetts prohibited racial segregation of schools in 1855. The solidification of racial segregation of schools in federal policy did not formally end, however, until the Supreme Court decision *Brown v. Board of Education of Topeka* in

1954. This landmark case marked the change from federal policy that accepted a "separate but equal" doctrine to one that acknowledged that to be separate is to be inherently unequal.

Because of the great variability of local schools and conditions, the Supreme Court ordered schools to desegregate "with all deliberate speed." Schools were to develop desegregation plans under the supervision of local courts. This meant that states and communities had considerable latitude in the pace and timing of desegregation.

Individual schools tried to delay or defeat the Brown decision through "freedom of choice" plans and even the closing of public schools. Freedom of choice plans did not explicitly require segregation but allowed parents to select the school their children would attend (Fischer & Sorenson, 1996). Freedom of choice plans were not totally rejected by the Supreme Court, but in *Green v. County School Board of New Kent County* (1968), the Court stated that freedom of choice plans were unacceptable if other reasonable means to desegregate were available. The closing of public schools was tried in Virginia, which resulted in the repeal of compulsory attendance laws so that school attendance became controlled by local decisions. Prince Edward County closed the public schools and instituted private whites-only schools that received governmental assistance. This effort to sustain de jure segregation of schools was struck down as unconstitutional by the Supreme Court in 1964 in *Griffin v. County School Board of Prince Edward County* (La Morte, 2005).

The South was the initial target of desegregation efforts. The documentary *Eyes on the Prize: The Fighting Back Years* (Public Broadcasting Service, 1987) vividly chronicles the struggle to desegregate southern schools. A notorious example is that of Little Rock, Arkansas, where the local school system attempted to desegregate but the governor of the state ordered the National Guard to prevent black students from entering their assigned schools (La Morte, 2005). The schools then sought to delay desegregation with the argument that the delay was necessary to preserve public peace. However, in *Cooper v. Aaron* (1958), the Court declared that desegregation could not be postponed.

In Mississippi, once called the "the closed society," the Council of Federated Organizations, a consortium of civil rights organizations including the Congress of Racial Equality, the Southern Christian Leadership Council, the National Association for the Advancement of Colored People, and the Student Nonviolent Coordinating Committee, spearheaded the 1964 Freedom Summer Project. The 1964 Freedom Summer Project was a social action endeavor established to challenge the unjust and unequal treatment of African American citizens in Mississippi primarily by attempting to register as many black voters as possible. The Freedom Summer Project brought national attention to the violation of human rights, particularly the voting rights, of African American citizens in Mississippi, where they were unfairly subjected to literacy laws that prohibited them from voting. If an individual could not read to the satisfaction of a registrar, he or she was not allowed to register to vote. Although Mississippi was the last state of the union to enact compulsory education in 1918, education was still used as a means to perpetuate the myth of African American inferiority. In 1962, Mississippi paid schools $81.86 for each white student and $21.77 for each black student, and in many districts the discrepancies were much worse. In Yazoo County, which had a 59.4 percent black population, white schools received $245.55 per student, and black schools received $2.92 per student (Rothschild, 1982).

In order to address the problem of inferior schools for African American children, freedom schools were established during the 1964 Freedom Summer Project. The freedom schools were set in motion by a letter from Charlie Cobb, a Howard University student, to Bob Moses, director of the Summer Project. He wrote: "If we are concerned about breaking the power structure, then we have to be concerned about building our own institutions to replace the old, unjust, decadent ones which make up the existing power structure. Education in Mississippi is an institution, which must be reconstructed from the ground up" (qtd. in Chilcoat & Ligon, 2004, p. 4). The prospectus of the curriculum for the freedom schools stated that volunteers, many of whom were white northern college students, were to:

1. promote equality and basic democratic rights among marginalized adult African Americans;
2. dramatize the need for change in Mississippi;
3. participate in the process of bringing . . . social justice to a portion of the population which had been denied them throughout American history;
4. teach them about the political life of the state and encourage them to participate in it, and to contribute to the body of knowledge about their condition in Mississippi, so that more can be done to alleviate it. (Chilcoat & Ligon, 1999)

The freedom schools offered tools to African Americans to challenge discrimination. The freedom school approach had three bases: problem-posing education, teaching for social justice, and affirmation of African American identity (Aaronsohn, Cobb, Lynd, Garrett, Lauter, O'Connell, et al., 1991; Chilcoat & Ligon, 1999; Perlstein, 1990; Rothschild, 1982). They gave African American students tools of critical literacy, and skills to advocate for themselves and others. By the end of the summer of 1964, forty-one freedom schools had been established across the state of Mississippi.

On a national scale, fourteen years after *Brown*, American citizens could no longer tolerate separate and unequal education for children of color. In *Alexander v. Holmes County Board of Education* (1969) the Supreme Court decided that no further delay was permissible and that all school districts were to end dual school systems immediately and to operate as unitary school districts.

In 1971 the Supreme Court made a definitive and detailed desegregation decision. In *Swann v. Charlotte-Mecklenburg Board of Education* (1971), the Court ordered that teachers be assigned in a manner that would achieve faculty desegregation, that future school construction or school closings not support a dual system of education, that single-race schools be examined to make sure that current or past discrimination had not caused a lack of diversity, that attendance zones be changed to undo segregation, and that children be bused to school, if needed, to dismantle dual systems of education (La Morte, 2005).

The Equal Educational Opportunities Act of 1974 solidified the federal commitment to educational equality and spelled out steps to be taken when desegregation was ordered by the courts owing to a finding of denial of equal educational opportunity.

Busing as a Desegregation Tool

Busing of children from one part of a district to another to achieve racial integration has been a controversial tool. Given the long history of local control of schools and commitment to neighborhood schools, busing raised a number of issues. In *Swann v. Charlotte-Mecklenburg Board of Education* (1971), the Court ruled that busing was acceptable, since, in that case, assigning children to neighborhood schools would not result in the dismantling of the dual system of education. In a related case, *North Carolina Board of Education v. Swann* (1971), the Supreme Court affirmed an order that declared a North Carolina law prohibiting both racial assignment of students and busing based on racial assignment unconstitutional. This ruling was based on the court's view that racial assignment was an essential tool of desegregation.

Desegregation in the North

Racial segregation was also occurring in the North, and illegal segregation has been found in many northern cities. For example, statutes requiring separate but equal schools were present in New York until 1938, in Indiana until 1959, and in Wyoming until 1954 (La Morte, 2005). Fischer and Sorenson (1996) write: "A key difference existed between southern and northern segregated schooling. Whereas it was done blatantly and through open official action in the South, it was usually accomplished in the North through complex and not-so-open arrangements between public officials and leaders in business and industry to control housing, real estate development, and finance as well as through the location of business, industry, and schools. Courts, however, ruled that such actions violate the Fourteenth Amendment just as the more open official actions of the South had done" (p. 279).

De jure segregation, which is segregation mandated by law, differs from de facto segregation. De facto segregation occurs when people choose to live in different neighborhoods and then send their children to neighborhood schools (Fischer & Sorenson, 1996). Only de jure segregation is illegal. Because the Fourteenth Amendment prohibited only de jure segregation, it has been difficult to address segregation outside the South, which often occurred through what appeared to be de facto segregation.

Interdistrict Integration

In the midst of "white flight" from urban schools, the problem of desegregation has become one that crosses school district boundaries. Large urban school districts have often become almost all black/Hispanic. In a challenge to this situation, a federal district court ordered that fifty-three independent school districts surrounding Detroit be consolidated with the Detroit public schools. Parents who had moved to suburbs to attain greater educational opportunities for their children opposed this decision. The Supreme Court decided in *Milliken v. Bradley* (1974) that there was evidence of de jure segregation only in the Detroit public schools and that the fifty-three other districts had no violations. Therefore, they failed to uphold the district court's order. La Morte (2005) states: "Many observers consider Milliken I as marking an end to the United States Supreme Court's unwavering support of desegregation efforts. Subsequent to this decision, the Court has been viewed decreasingly as a friendly and receptive forum for achieving school desegregation" (p. 307).

In another decision in 1996 (*Sheff v. O'Neill*), the Connecticut Supreme Court ruled that the state's means of establishing school districts and attendance statutes were unconstitutional, since they produced segregation of minority students in Hartford schools and thus limited equal educational opportunities. In this case, the court determined that the state legislature was required to remedy segregation in public schools in Connecticut regardless of whether the segregation occurred because of de jure or de facto segregation. Since then, another Connecticut decision (*Sheff v. O'Neill,* 1999) laid out details of remedies to correct the educational inequity caused by racial segregation of minority students in the city of Hartford and white flight to suburban non-minority school districts (La Morte, 2005). Such decisions by a state court may provide a model for addressing the seemingly intractable problem of segregation as it exists today.

On June 28, 2007, the Supreme Court took a significant step backward in its decision regarding plans by Seattle and Louisville to desegregate their schools. In response to the verdicts in *Parents Involved v. Seattle School District* and *Meredith v. Jefferson County Board of Education,* the *New York Times* (2007) wrote:

> The nation is getting more diverse, but by many measures public schools are becoming more segregated. More than one in six black children now attend schools that are 99 to 100 percent minority. This resegregation is likely to get appreciably worse as a result of the court's ruling.
>
> There should be no mistaking just how radical this decision is. In dissent, Justice John Paul Stevens said it was his "firm conviction that no Member of the Court that I joined in 1975 would have agreed with today's decision." He also noted the "cruel irony" of the court relying on Brown v. Board of Education while robbing that landmark ruling of much of its force and spirit. The citizens of Louisville and Seattle, and the rest of the nation, can ponder the majority's kind words about Brown as they get to work today making their schools, and their cities, more segregated.

As we begin to examine the current status of law and policy relating to minority children in the next chapter, we must understand the historical context of schooling for African American children in this country. The struggle for education has been part of the historic struggle in the United States of African American citizens to gain the rights and privileges that all our citizens need and deserve. Only by understanding this historic struggle can we fully understand the issues today.

References

Aaronsohn, L., Cobb, C., Lynd, S., Garrett, J., Lauter, P., O'Connell, B., et al. (1991). Mississippi freedom school curriculum 1964. *Radical Teacher, 40*, 19–22.

Alexander v. Holmes County Board of Education, 396 U.S. 19 (1969).

Brown v. Board of Education of Topeka, 347 U.S. 483 (1954).

Chilcoat, G., & Ligon, J. (2004, September). *Developing participatory democracy (and other wonderful "things"): Those "bothersome" educational organizations (?) and their "Great Potential Curriculumers" at the New York Curriculum Conference for the Mississippi freedom schools*. Proceedings of the Freedom Summer Conference, Miami University, Oxford, OH.

Chilcoat, G., & Ligon, J. (1999). Helping to make democracy a living reality: The curriculum conference of the Mississippi freedom schools. *Journal of Curriculum and Supervision, 15*, 43–68.

Civil Rights Act of 1866, 14 Stat. 27 (1866).

Civil Rights Act of 1875, 18 Stat. 335 (1875).

Civil Rights Cases, 109 U.S. 3 (1883).

Cooper v. Aaron, 358 U.S. 1 (1958).

Du Bois, W. E. B. (1994). *The souls of black folk*. New York: Dover. (Originally published 1903)

Du Bois, W. E. B. (1901). The Freedmen's Bureau. *Atlantic Monthly, 87*, 354–365.

Equal Educational Opportunities Act of 1974, U.S.C. 1203(f).

Fischer, L., & Sorenson, G. P. (1996). *School law for counselors, psychologists, and social workers* (3rd ed.). White Plains, NY: Longman.

Green v. County School Board of New Kent County, 391 U.S. 430 (1968).

Griffin v. County School Board of Prince Edward County, 377 U.S. 218 (1964).

James, C. L. R. (1969). *A history of the Negro revolt*. New York: Haskell House.

La Morte, M. W. (2005). *School law: Cases and concepts*. Boston: Allyn & Bacon.
Meredith v. Jefferson County Board of Education, 551 U.S. ____ (2007).
Milliken v. Bradley, 418 U.S. 717 (1974).
North Carolina Board of Education v. Swann, 402 U.S. 43 (1971).
Ochiltree, I. (2004). Mastering the sharecroppers: Land, labor, and the search for independence in the U.S. and South Africa. *Journal of Southern African Studies, 30*(1), 41–61.
Ogbu, J. (2004). Collective identity and the burden of "acting white" in black history, community and education. *State Review,* 35
Parents Involved v. Seattle School District, 551 U.S.____ (2007).
Perlstein, D. (1990). Teaching freedom: SNCC and the creation of the Mississippi freedom schools. *History of Education Quarterly*, 30, 297–324.
Plessy v. Ferguson, 163 U.S. 537 (1896).
Potts, E. (2002). The DuBois-Washington debate: Conflicting strategies. In E. Peterson (Ed.), *Freedom road: Adult education for African Americans* (pp. 27–40). Malabar, FL: Krieger.
Public Broadcasting Service. (1987). *Eyes on the prize: America's Civil Rights years 1954–1965*.
Resegregation now. (2007, June 29). *New York Times.* Retrieved July 3, 2007, from http://www.nytimes.com/2007/06/29/opinion/29fri1.html
Roberts v. City of Boston, 59 Mass. (5 Cush.) (1850).
Rothschild, M. A. (1982). The volunteers and the freedom schools: Education for social change in Mississippi. *History of Education Quarterly*, *22*, 401–420.
Sheff v. O'Neill, 238 Conn. 1, 678 A.2d 1267 (1996).
Sheff v. O'Neill, 45 Conn. Sup. 630, 657 (1999).
Swann v. Charlotte-Mecklenburg Board of Education, 402 U.S. 1 (1971).
Washington, B. T. (1972). The story of my life and work. In L. Harlan & J. Blassingame (Eds.), *The Booker T. Washington papers* (Vol. 1, pp. 1–206). Urbana: University of Illinois Press. (Originally published 1900)
Watkins, W. (2001). *The white architects of black education: Ideology and power in America, 1865–1954*. New York: Teachers College.
Williams v. Mississippi, 170 U.S. 213 (1898).
Woodson, C. G. (1919). *The education of the Negro prior to 1861: A history of the education of colored people of the United States from the beginning of slavery until the Civil War*. Retrieved June 23, 2007, from http://andromeda.rutgers.edu/~natalieb/The_Education_Of_The_Negro_P.pdf
Woodson, C. G. (1998). *Miseducation of the Negro*. Trenton, NJ: Africa World Press. (Originally published 1933)

16

Policy and Law Affecting School Social Work with Vulnerable Populations

Carol Rippey Massat
Cassandra McKay
University of Illinois at Chicago

- Current Policy Issues Affecting Minority Children
- Native American Children and Educational Policy
- Gender and Educational Policy
- Homeless Children and Schools
- Policy Issues in Bilingual Education

In order to carry out effective policy practice, school social workers in every country must understand the history and policies that affect vulnerable groups in schools. In the United States, this would include African American and other ethnic minority students, bilingual students, students with limited English proficiency, girls and women, GLBT students, and homeless children. All these groups have experienced discrimination in schools and in society. This history of discrimination has led to legislation and case law intended to protect members of such groups from additional oppression.

Good schools are crucial for the survival of any vulnerable group. The educational process itself has at times served as an oppressive force for members of vulnerable groups, and some theorists posit that schooling remains a pervasive and effective form of social control. For example, textbooks have often presented only European American male history, and the writings and histories of ethnic and racial minorities and women have been excluded (Apple, 1998). Some educational curricula have implicitly focused on the development of a low-income workforce that is likely to produce exploitative work conditions (Kliebard, 1998). Consumer-driven classroom media can also target the unsuspecting consumer (Kenway & Bullen, 2005). Education for assimilation, as discussed in chapter 15, is the use of schooling to teach members of oppressed groups to take on the characteristics of a dominant group and abandon their own cultures. Ferdman (1990) asserts that an "assimilation perspective emphasizes the dysfunctionality of differences and the maintenance of the dominant culture, and so demands that subordinate groups acculturate" (p. 183). This perspective was realized in the historical origins of African American education, and in the education of Native American children and other vulnerable groups.

Education was seen as such a powerful tool in the hands of African Americans that it was prohibited in many places and times during the 246 years of slavery in America. After the passage of the Thirteenth Amendment to the Constitution in 1865, education benefiting African Americans adopted an assimilationist stance, which is still in effect today. Gerald Pine and Asa Hilliard (1990), proponents of integrating African themes into educational curricula, confront this assimilationist perspective because it does not address the history of Africans before slavery, the struggle against slavery, colonialism, segregation, apartheid, and domination, and common aspects of historic systemic oppression (Hilliard, Payton-Stewart, & Williams, 1995).

CURRENT POLICY ISSUES AFFECTING MINORITY CHILDREN

There are several current trends and policy issues that adversely affect many minority children. These include racism, resegregation, the persistent achievement gap between minority students and non-minority students, overrepresentation of minority children in special education, potentially biased tests, and issues around bilingual education.

Racism

African Americans have historically been treated as inherently inferior to white Americans. However, even those holding this racist view often believed that African Americans could still be important in advancing the economic prosperity of the United States. They sought racial cooperation by minorities within an unequal society, which gave birth to the Hampton Normal and Agriculture Institute, Tuskegee Normal and Industrial Institute, and a myriad of other missionary schools for the people then called Negroes. This influence lingers today.

Some members of American society assert that anti-black racism is a thing of the past and has no bearing on contemporary society. However, in schooling, income, arrests, employment, housing, education, entertainment, advertising, and private and public discourse, racism persists, and the color line continues to be the problem of the century (Du Bois, 1903/1998), with racially tinged public debates over issues that guide public policy such as affirmative action, crime, and the prison industrial complex (Giroux, 2003). One manifestation of this problem in schools lies in the negative pathological labels such as "at risk," and "disadvantaged" often bestowed on African American children, and views of these children as possessing "cultural deficits." Ramona Edelin (1995) challenges these labels that have become grounds for educational policy making (Watkins, 1993).

Some assert that color blindness is the ideal for social policy makers and for society. While not denying the existence of race construction, color blindness denies that racial discrimination is responsible for injustices that support white privilege, replicate group inequalities, and negatively affect the economic mobility and the acquisition of political power of marginalized people (Giroux, 2003). Moreover, the logic of color blindness negates race as "a marker of identity or power when factored into the social vocabulary of everyday life and the capacity for exercising individual and social agency" (Giroux, 2003, p. 198).

Resegregation

Despite years of vigorous federal efforts, many school districts are almost entirely made up of minority students, and other districts have little racial or ethnic diversity. Kopels (2007) describes the "radical return toward resegregation" (p. 277) by the Supreme Court, citing several Supreme Court decisions of the 1990s, including *Board of Education of Oklahoma City v. Dowell* (1991), in which a school district was given unitary status upon a finding that past discriminatory practices had been redressed. She writes, "After a declaration of unitary status, the courts presume any government action creating racially segregated schools to be innocent, unless a plaintiff proves that the school district intentionally decided to discriminate" (p. 277). When new segregation problems emerged, the Court ruled that court supervision had been effectively ended when it was found that past discrimination had been eliminated to the extent possible. In *Missouri v. Jenkins* (1995), the Supreme Court ruled that the comprehensive plan ordered by a federal district court to integrate schools and improve student achievement in Kansas City schools went beyond the scope of constitutional limitations on court interventions. The Kansas City plan, which involved magnet schools and capital improvements to attract students from outside the district and from private schools, was ambitious, expensive, and ultimately not supported by the state of Missouri or the Supreme Court. Kopels summarizes these decisions and notes that they demonstrate a philosophy of decreasing judicial involvement in education and a move away from desegregation. A recent decision of the Supreme Court on June 28, 2007 (*Parents Involved v. Seattle School District* and *Meredith v. Jefferson County Board of Education*), continues the trend toward resegregation.

Achievement Gap

Despite many years of effort to desegregate schools, there are indicators that minority children have not been receiving adequate educational opportunities. This is reflected in a persistent achievement gap on standardized measures of achievement, high school graduation rates, and college attendance rates (Bybee & Stage, 2005; Fellmeth, 2005; Greene, 2003). Many attribute this problem to the strong association between minority status and poverty.

Some research evidence suggests that curricula vary by social class. Jean Anyon's (1980) critical ethnography of four Boston area elementary schools unveiled differing kinds of curricula and different functions of schooling for children of various socioeconomic classes. Curricula can be categorized in various ways (Anyon, 1980; Eisner, 1979; Schubert, 1981, 1986): taught curriculum (overtly communicated by instruction and materials), learned curriculum (what is internalized by the student about self and his or her world), null curriculum (absence of a particular curriculum, e.g., advanced mathematics, leading to the lack of its use in the future by the learner), hidden curriculum (often implicit instruction that stratifies learners for future labor), and outside curriculum (ad hoc instruction experienced in the learner's home via peers, media, and formal organizations). In Anyon's study, class instead of race was the noted factor that determined the structure of taught, learned, null, and hidden curricula:

- Children of working-class parents were taught to follow the steps of a procedure, usually mechanical, involving rote behavior, with very little decision making or choice. Academic success was based on whether students followed the rules, not whether answers were right or wrong.
- Children of middle-class parents were encouraged to get the right answer. If one accumulated enough right answers, one got a good grade. It was important to follow the directions in order to get the right answers; however, there was allowance for some choices and decision making.
- Children of professional parents received more opportunity to be creative in their work. Students were encouraged to work independently, engaging in critical thought and expressiveness; expand and illustrate ideas; and obtain the freedom to choose appropriate methods and materials to complete their work.

- Children of executive/ruling-class parents were expected to develop their own analytical intellectual powers. Children were continually asked to reason through a problem, and to produce intellectual products that were both logically sound and of top academic quality. A primary goal was to conceptualize rules by which elements may fit together in systems and then to apply these rules in solving a problem.

With its emphasis on high-stakes testing, the No Child Left Behind Act of 2001 (NCLB), as implemented, seems to subscribe to a working-class and middle-class standard of academic success. Creative programming goes unfunded for many schools in diverse communities, and children have limited opportunity to develop decision-making skills relevant to their future aspirations. Academic failure is attributed to the students' inability to perform well on standardized exams that are often disconnected from the students' daily lives.

The No Child Left Behind Act can label a school a failing school if any one of the demographic subgroups is not achieving at the level identified by each state as adequate. Thus NCLB tends to have less impact on schools with small numbers of minority children or children with disabilities, since if there are fewer than forty students of an identified group in a school or members of a group that attend that school for fewer than 140 days, that group is not considered in the determination of annual yearly progress. Identified groups are the school as a whole; whites, blacks, Hispanics, Native Americans, Asians, multiracial individuals, the economically disadvantaged, those who have limited English proficiency (LEP), and students with disabilities.

Overrepresentation of Minority Children in Special Education

Minority children continue to be overrepresented in special education classes across the country. In one recent study of this issue, the investigators found that different and non-standard procedures were being followed in the assessment of minority students for special education (Ebersole & Kapp, 2007). Others have speculated that this is the result of bias in testing (discussed below) or due to the relationship between minority status and poverty. In 1959 the American Association on Mental Retardation decided that too many individuals were being inaccurately categorized as mentally retarded owing to an overreliance on IQ tests. They then decided to add adaptive behavior to their definition of mental retardation in order to add consideration of daily functioning to the evaluation. Later the association reduced the cutoff score for mental retardation from one standard deviation below the mean to two standard deviations below the mean in order to address this continuing disparity (American Association on Mental Retardation, 2002).

Despite these changes in definition, minority students continue to be overrepresented in special education. The National Center for Culturally Responsive Educational Systems was formed to address these issues, and the center reports on data on overrepresentation of racial, ethnic, and cultural minority students across the nation. They report disproportionate placement of African American students in all states, with the lowest rates of disproportionate placement occurring in Georgia, Indiana, Michigan, Oklahoma, New Hampshire, North Dakota, Rhode Island, and West Virginia. The group of states with the second-lowest rates of disproportionate placement are Arkansas, Illinois, Kentucky, Maryland, Mississippi, New Jersey, New York, Pennsylvania, Maine, and Tennessee. The highest disproportion is occurring in Colorado, Idaho, Iowa, Minnesota, Montana, Nevada, Oregon, South Dakota, Washington, and Wisconsin. The second-highest group of states in terms of disproportion are Arizona, California, Kansas, Louisiana, Massachusetts, Nebraska, New Mexico, North Carolina, South Carolina, and Utah (National Center for Culturally Responsive Educational Systems, n.d.). There appears to be greater disproportion in the West and northwestern parts of the country and somewhat less in the East and states bordering the Mississippi River. See the center's data map at http://nccrest.eddata.net/maps/index.php to examine the pattern of disproportionate representation of African American, Hispanic, and other students by state. What is clear is that it is highly unlikely that students of various racial and cultural groups vary so widely from Indiana (lowest rate of disproportion), for example, to Iowa (highest rate of disproportion). These varying rates strongly suggest that state policies and procedures contribute to the rates of overrepresentation in special education of minority students in different states.

Potentially Biased Tests

Two important federal district court cases have examined the question as to whether standardized tests can be used to determine placement of minority students. In *Larry P. v. Wilson Riles* (1984), Judge Peckham acknowledged controversy over what such tests actually measured. He decided to assume that such tests were accurate in measuring the mental capacity of white students; he asked if they were also valid for black students. Expert testimony in that case demonstrated that the IQ tests being used had only been developed and standardized for use with white middle-class students. Fischer and Sorenson (1996) write: "Despite the knowledge that a pioneer in developing IQ tests in the United States had said they were not valid for black persons and that certain items were widely considered to be culturally biased, little effort had been made to investigate these issues. Furthermore, bias was not sought out; possible defects in the tests were not corrected; and there was little investigation of why black children consistently scored lower, as a group, than white children" (p. 116).

Judge Peckham stopped the use of IQ testing in the evaluation of black children for special education and ordered that all black children then in placement be reevaluated without such tests.

In the second case (*Parents in Action on Special Education v. Hannon*, 1980), Judge Grady, after listening to expert testimony, became convinced that the credibility and expertise of the "experts" were not convincing enough to base a decision on their testimony. Therefore, he decided to examine the standardized tests himself to determine whether the items were biased. He found in his examination of the Wechsler Intelligence Scale for Children–Revised and the Wechsler Intelligence Scale for Children that there were eight biased items. There was one biased item on the Stanford-Binet test. Judge Grady believed that, since tests were only one component of the evaluation process, these biased items would be overcome by the expertise of those administering the tests and the multidisciplinary nature of the assessment. While Judge Peckham viewed the impact of these tests as substantial and often the primary determinant in the decision regarding placement in special education, Judge Grady saw the tests as only one component of a broad multifaceted assessment. Judge Peckham, seeing the disproportionate number of minority children placed in special education and noting the failure to norm and validate such tests for minority children, put the burden of proof on the school system to show that the tests were not discriminatory. Judge Grady placed the burden of proof on the children's representatives to show that the tests were discriminatory (Fischer & Sorenson, 1996).

NATIVE AMERICAN CHILDREN AND EDUCATIONAL POLICY

American policy on the education of Native American children has historically shifted back and forth between assimilationist goals to those that respect and value Native American cultures. This history begins with the period from 1776 to 1926 that involved a policy of assimilation or education of Native American children into the white European culture and abandonment of their own cultures. Assimilationists used boarding schools as a mechanism to have Native American children adopt European values and beliefs. Colonel Henry Pratt established the most well known of such schools in Carlisle, Pennsylvania, in 1879 (American Indian Education Foundation, 2007). He sought to totally assimilate Native American students by mandating standard uniforms, the cutting of the long hair of the boys, and the imposition of new Anglo names; refusing to serve any traditional Native American foods; and prohibiting the use of Native languages.

In 1905, education of Native Americans took a new direction, with a decreased emphasis on assimilation and a move toward day schools rather than boarding schools. In the 1920s John Collier, the executive secretary for the Native American Defense Association, began reform efforts that led in 1926 to the Meriam Report, which recommended that younger Native American children attend a school close to home and that only older children attend boarding schools, that the "uniform course of study" involving only white values and traditions be abandoned, and that Indian children be given tools to work with both white and Native American cultures (National Center for Indian Education, n.d.). Charles Rhoades, Indian commissioner, began to follow these recommendations in 1929, and in 1933 John Collier was appointed commissioner of Indian affairs by Franklin Delano Roosevelt. Under Collier, federal policies moved away from assimilation. Collier helped to draft the Indian Reorganization Act of 1934 (National Center for Indian Education, n.d.). This period marked the beginning of policies that led to a valuing of Native American cultures and non-assimilationist education, and respect for Native American art and language. However, from the 1940s through the 1950s, this movement went backward. Funding was cut for services on reservations, and off-reservation boarding schools were again recommended. In the 1960s through the 1970s, this trend was reversed with substantial changes in public policy. For example, in 1965, the National Advisory Council on Indian Education was formed; in 1966, President Lyndon Johnson appointed Robert Lafollette Bennett, a Native American, commissioner of Indian affairs; and in 1968, President Johnson established the National Council on Indian Opportunity to facilitate Native American participation in federal decision making regarding Indian policy. In 1969, the Special Subcommittee on Indian Education, Senate Committee on Labor and Public Welfare, published the Kennedy Report. That report said: "the dominant policy of the federal government toward the Native American has been one of coercive assimilation" and the policy "has had disastrous effects on the education of Indian children" (U.S. Senate Committee on Labor and Public Welfare, 1969, p. 21).

The Indian Education Act of 1972, now known as Part A, Title IX of the Education Amendments of 1994, provides federal support for education of Native American and Native Alaskan children in public schools, as well as tribal schools and Bureau of Indian Affairs schools.

However, in the 1980s and 1990s the trend was less supportive of Native American cultures, and the Office of Indian Affairs was almost eliminated in 1995. President Clinton vetoed a budget that would have effectively eliminated the Office of Indian Affairs. The National Unity Task Force, a Native American political action committee, was formed and lobbied to change jurisdiction over the Office of Indian Affairs from the Department of the Interior to the Department of Education. This effort was successful.

GENDER AND EDUCATIONAL POLICY

Sex Discrimination

The primary federal legislation that relates to gender and schools is Title IX of the 1972 Education Amendments. This was the first major federal legislation to prohibit sex discrimination in schools that receive federal funds. This includes discrimination in employment as well as admission and treatment of students. Title IX applies to preschool through graduate-level education organizations that accept federal funds. Regulations for the legislation were published in 1975. This legislation also prohibits discrimination against pregnant students, who, in earlier years, may have been expelled or excluded from school on the basis of their pregnancy. According to Kopels (2007), most sex discrimination lawsuits based on Title IX have focused on athletic programs and admissions policies. She writes, "The very fact that public schools now have women's and girl's sports teams, like soccer or basketball, owes its origins to Title IX legislation" (p. 283). Title IX also has been used on behalf of those who are at risk or who have experienced sexual harassment in schools.

Women have made much progress. On August 26, 1920, the Nineteenth Amendment to the Constitution at last gave women in the United States the right to vote. Illinois, Wisconsin, and Michigan were the first states to approve this amendment, while Georgia and Alabama were the first to oppose it. Many occupations and professions once barred to women now admit women to their ranks, and in some traditionally male occupations, women have overtaken men in numbers. However, from 2003 to 2005, college-educated women's median income was an average of 74 percent of that of college-educated men, with college-educated men earning a median income of $61,603, while the median income of college-educated women was $45,684. The income disparity in women's earnings ranges from 64 percent of men's salaries in Louisiana to 89 percent in West Virginia. According to the U.S. Census Bureau (2007), this is true across all occupational categories that they list.

The Office for Civil Rights of the U.S. Department of Education is responsible for enforcing Title IX in approximately 16,000 local school districts; 3,200 colleges and universities, libraries, museums, vocational rehabilitation agencies, and state education agencies; and about 5,000 for-profit schools in the United States. Anyone who believes there has been discrimination on the basis of sex against a person or group in one of these programs may file a complaint with the Office for Civil Rights under Title IX. The person filing the complaint may complain on behalf of another person or group. Usually, complaints must be filed within 180 days of the date of the alleged discrimination, unless the office extends this time period. For filing procedures, see the Web site of the Office for Civil Rights. If discrimination is found, the case may be referred to the Department of Justice for court action, or federal funding to the school or program can be withdrawn after a hearing with an administrative law judge.

A second law that relates to gender and schools is the Civil Rights Act of 1964, Title VI. This act prohibits discrimination in the workplace based on race, color, religion, sex, or national origin. People over age forty are also a protected category in regards to employment owing to the Age Discrimination in Employment Act of 1967.

Sexual Minorities

Sexual minority students and personnel are not a protected class under federal legislation. Title IX has, however, been used as the foundation for case law that has established that schools cannot allow harassment of GLBT students (*Nabozny v. Podlesny,* 1996). Schools are nonetheless legally permitted to discriminate in employment against GLBT individuals, and it remains legal in many states to dismiss a school employee because he or she identifies as gay, lesbian, bisexual, or transgender. A New Jersey court upheld the dismissal of a transgender teacher because of "psychological harm to students" (*In re Grossman,* 1974). A federal court upheld the firing of a teacher for his failure to include on his application for employment the fact that he belonged to a group called Homophiles, a group that urged public acceptance of homosexuality (*Acanfora v. Board of Education*, 1974).

School districts have the right to include sexual minorities as a protected group in their nondiscrimination statements, and many school districts have chosen to do so.

HOMELESS CHILDREN AND SCHOOLS

All school social workers should be familiar with Title VII-B of the McKinney-Vento Homeless Assistance Act. This program was initially authorized in 1987 and was reauthorized with the No Child Left Behind Act of 2001.

The law defines homeless children and youths as individuals who lack a fixed, regular, and adequate nighttime residence, including those who 1) share housing with other individuals due to lack of housing, financial hardship, or a similar reason; 2) live in motels, hotels, trailer parks, or camping grounds due to a lack of alternative adequate accommodations; 3) live in emergency or transitional shelters; 4) were abandoned in hospitals; 5) are awaiting foster placement; 6) have a primary nighttime residence that is not designed or usually used as a regular sleeping accommodation for humans; and 7) live in cars, parks, public spaces, abandoned buildings, substandard housing, bus or train stations, or similar settings, as well as migratory children who are living in any of the circumstances described above (U.S. Department of Education, 2004). An *unaccompanied youth* is defined as a youth not in the physical custody of the parent or guardian, such as a youth living in runaway shelters, cars, parks, or other inadequate housing.

If a family becomes homeless, the local education agency (LEA) must make school placement decisions on the basis of the best interest of the child. The LEA must continue the child or youth's education in the school of origin for as long as the family is homeless, or the LEA must enroll the child in any public school that nonhomeless children living in the same attendance area as the homeless child are eligible to attend. To the extent possible, the LEA must keep the child in the school of origin unless this goes against the wishes of the parent or guardian.

No obstacles can legally be placed in the way of school enrollment of homeless children, even if the child is unable to produce documents usually required for enrollment, such as a birth certificate, immunization record, school records, or medical records. The LEA must provide transportation, if needed, to and from the school of origin if the child remains in that attendance area. If the child is staying in another area, the two LEAs must either share equally the costs of transporting the child or agree upon a method of apportioning financial responsibility. Further guidance on the implementation of the McKinney-Vento Homeless Assistance Act is available at the Web site of the U.S. Department of Education.

POLICY ISSUES IN BILINGUAL EDUCATION

Bilingual education has been a controversial issue, especially as immigration has emerged as a divisive political topic. Proposition 227, approved in California in 1998, was intended to dismantle California's bilingual education program. This law was upheld in the *Valeria v. Davis* (2002) decision, which determined that the law was constitutional (La Morte, 2005). Arizona followed suit in 2000.

While not all states have carried out such extreme measures, the federal Bilingual Education Act, Title VII of the Elementary and Secondary Education Act, was eliminated in 2002 as one of the changes in the No Child Left Behind Act (the most recent reauthorization of the Elementary and Secondary Education Act). It was reborn as the English Language Learners Act, with the goal of rapid acquisition of English by limited English proficiency (LEP) students. The word "bilingual" was expunged from the act, and funding would no longer be made through competitive grants. Instead, formula grants to states would be made, based on the number of English language learners (Crawford, 2002).

The federal Bilingual Education Act was first enacted in 1968 and provided strong support for bilingual learners. The first year, no funds were appropriated to carry out the law, but the following year, it was funded. The law provided funding to school districts to provide competitive grants directly to school districts that would be used to support the education of non-English-speaking students through 1) resources for educational programs, 2) training for teachers and teacher aides, 3) development and dissemination of materials, and 4) parent involvement projects. It did not require bilingual instruction or the use of students' native languages in the classroom. The act focused on low-income students. Some states had barriers such as English-only laws that created implementation problems.

The Supreme Court decision in the case of *Lau v. Nichols* (1974) provided important policy guidance for bilingual education. This act, on behalf of San Francisco students of Chinese descent, found that it was not enough to provide non-English-speaking students equal access to English-only classrooms and reading materials, because, if the students could not read or speak English, the provision of English-only classes and materials prevented them from receiving an education. The court did not require a specific remedy, leaving that decision to educators (Fischer & Sorenson, 1996).

The Equal Educational Opportunities Act of 1974 also affected bilingual education policy, stating states may not "deny equal educational opportunity to an individual" because of "the failure by an educational agency to take appropriate action to overcome language barriers that impeded equal participation by its students" (20 U.S.C. 1703f) (1982).

The Bilingual Education Act amendments of 1974 defined a bilingual education program as one that provided instruction both in the student's native language and in English. English-as-a-second-language programs alone were not enough. The amendments specified the goal of such a program as the preparation of LEP students to participate effectively in regular classrooms as soon as possible. The amendments included the removal of the low-income requirement of the 1968 act. The amendments also established regional support centers to provide guidance and support to schools, required a national clearinghouse for bilingual education, and provided funding for capacity building for bilingual programs (Stewner-Manzanares, 1988).

In 1975 and 1978, the law was amended again. The 1975 amendments were intended to assist schools in complying with the *Lau* court decision through what were called the "Lau remedies" or guidelines on implementing policy based on *Lau v. Nichols*. The Lau remedies described educational strategies for teaching students with limited English-speaking ability. Schools were mandated to develop compliance plans if they were found to be noncompliant with Title VI of the Civil Rights Act and if they had twenty or more students of the same language group who had been identified as having a primary or home language other than English. These twenty students did not all have to have limited English language ability (Stewner-Manzanares, 1988). The 1978 amendments expanded eligibility to LEP students and specified the goal of such programs as being the development of English skills as quickly as possible in order for students to be educated in English-only classrooms.

The Bilingual Education Act of 1984 amendments awarded several grants for programs for LEP students, including:

1. transitional bilingual education programs, in which structured English-language instruction is combined with a native-language component and up to 40 percent of the class may be non-LEP students;
2. developmental bilingual education programs, in which full-time instruction is given in both English and a second language with the goal of achieving competence in both English and a second language;
3. special alternative instructional programs in which the native language need not be used, but English-language instruction and special instructional services are given to facilitate achievement of English competency. (Stewner-Manzanares, 1988)

The 1988 Bilingual Education Act changed the formula for grants to schools to increase the percent that could go to special alternative educational programs. This gave more flexibility to schools that found that transitional bilingual education programs were not feasible for them. The act set a three-year limit on student participation in transitional bilingual programs unless special circumstances existed, which would justify up to an additional two years. Family English literacy programs were to include provisions for instruction in English, U.S. history, and U.S. government for noncitizens eligible for temporary resident status under the Immigration and Naturalization Act. Information provided to parents or guardians was required to be in a language that they could understand. The 1988 legislation emphasized the training of qualified personnel.

In 1994 the Bilingual Education Act was reauthorized as Title VII of the Improving America's Schools Act. The law cited numerous obstacles to education of LEP children. They included a shortage of qualified educators, overrepresentation in special education, the limited English skills of their parents, and segregation. This act was positive regarding use of a child's native language in the classroom.

The elimination of the Bilingual Education Act and the creation of the English Language Learners Act set high standards for the educational achievement of LEP children but seriously backed off from support for bilingual education. This is a manifestation of the English-only trends that have been growing since the 1980s. Proponents of English-only classrooms believe that, in the past, immigrant groups had to learn English and to abandon their native languages and that this continues to be essential to the maintenance of a unified American language and culture. Thirty states have passed legislation declaring English their states' official language.

School social workers have a duty unique among school personnel: to advocate for individuals and groups who belong to populations that have suffered historic discrimination and oppression. These groups include African Americans, Native Americans, bilingual students, girls and women, sexual minorities, and homeless children. The first step is to understand the current issues and how they are rooted in history and policy related to these vulnerable populations. These have been broadly outlined in this chapter, but the histories and contexts of groups are unique to each school and community, and specific community change involves learning about specific schools and communities and applying that knowledge in working with others to support students, families, and educators.

References

Acanfora v. Board of Education, 491F.2d 498 (4th Circ. 1974).

American Indian Education Foundation. (2007). *1776–1926: Indian education means "assimilation."* Retrieved July 5, 2007, from http://www.nrcprograms.org/site/PageServer?pagename=aief_hist_1776

American Association on Mental Retardation. (2002). *Mental retardation: Definition, classification, and systems of support* (10th ed.). Washington, DC: Author.

Anyon, J. (1980). Social class and the hidden curriculum of work. *Journal of Education 162*, 67–92.

Apple, M. (1998). The culture and commerce of the textbook. In L. Beyer & M. Apple (Eds.), *The curriculum: Problems, politics, and possibilities* (pp. 157–176). New York: SUNY Press.

Bilingual Education Act, P.L. 90-247, 81 Stat. 816 (1968).

Bilingual Education Act, P.L. 103-382 (1994).

Board of Education of Oklahoma City v. Dowell, 498 U.S. 237 (1991).

Bybee, R. W., & Stage, E. (2005). No country left behind. *Issues in Science & Technology, 21*(2), 69–76.

Civil Rights Act of 1964 (.L. 88-352, 78 Stat. 241).

Crawford, J. (2002). *Obituary: The Bilingual Education Act*, 1968–2002. *Rethinking schools online, 16*(4). Retrieved March 23, 2008, from http://www.rethinkingschools.org/archive/16_04/Bil164.shtml

Du Bois, W. E. B. (1998). *The souls of black folk*. New York: Dover. (Originally published 1903)

Ebersole, J. L., & Kapp, S. A. (2007). Stemming the tide of overrepresentation: Ensuring accurate certification of African American students in programs for the mentally retarded. *School Social Work Journal, 31*(2), 1–16.

Edelin, R. (1995). Curriculum and cultural identity. In A. G. Hilliard, L. Payton-Stewart, & L. O. Williams (Eds.), *Infusion of African and African American content in the school curriculum: Proceedings of the first national conference* (pp. 37–50). Chicago: Third World Press.

Education Amendments of 1994, P.L. 103-382.

Eisner, E. W. (1979). *The educational imagination: On the design and evaluation of school programs*. New York: Macmillan.

Elementary and Secondary Education Act of 1965, 20 U.S.C. 2701 et seq.

English Language Learners Act. (2001). No Child Left Behind Title III: "Language Instruction for Limited English Proficient & Immigrant Students Program"

Equal Educational Opportunities Act of 1974. 20 U.S.C. Sec. 1703.

Fellmeth, R. (2005). Child poverty in the United States. *Human Rights: Journal of the Section of Individual Rights and Responsibilities, 32*(1), 2–5.

Ferdman, B. (1990). Literacy and cultural identity. *Harvard Educational Review, 60*, 181–182.

Fischer, L., & Sorenson, G. P. (1996). *School law for counselors, psychologists, and social workers* (3rd ed.). White Plains, NY: Longman.

Giroux, H. (2003). Spectacles of race and pedagogies of denial: Antiblack racist pedagogy under the reign of neoliberalism. *Community Education, 52*, 191–211.

Greene, J. P. (2003). *Public high school graduation and college readiness rates in the United States*. New York: Manhattan Institute for Policy Research.

Griffin v. County School Board of Prince Edward County, 377 U.S. 218 (1964).

Hilliard, A. G., Payton-Stewart, L., & Williams, L. O. (Eds.). (1995). *Infusion of African and African American content in the school curriculum: Proceedings of the first national conference*. Chicago: Third World Press.

Improving America's Schools Act of 1994, P.L. 103-382.

Indian Education Act of 1972, Title IV, P.L. 92-318.

In re Grossman, 316 A.2d 39 (N.J. 1974).

Kenway, J., & Bullen, E. (2005). Globalizing the young in the age of desire: Some educational policy issues. In M. Apple, J. Kenway, & M. Singh (Eds.). *Globalizing education: Policies, pedagogies and politics* (pp. 31–44). New York: Peter Lang.

Kliebard, H. M. (1998). *Schooled to work: Vocationalism and the American curriculum*. New York: Cambridge University Press.

Kopels, S. (2007). Securing equal educational opportunity. In P. Allen-Meares (Ed.), *Social work services in schools* (5th ed., pp. 262–292). Boston: Pearson Allyn & Bacon.

La Morte, M. W. (2005). *School law: Cases and concepts*. Boston: Allyn & Bacon.

Larry P. v. Wilson Riles United States Court of Appeals, 1984. 793 F.2d 969 (9th Cir.).

Lau v. Nichols, 414 U.S. 563 (1974).

McKinney-Vento Homeless Assistance Act of 1986, P.L. 100-77, 101 Stat. 482, 42 U.S.C. 11301 et seq.

Meredith v. Jefferson County Board of Education, 551 U.S. ____ (2007).

Missouri v. Jenkins, 515 U.S. 70 (1995).

Nabozny v. Podlesny, 92 F 3d 446 (7th Cir. 1996).

National Center for Culturally Responsive Educational Systems. (n.d.). *National data map*. Retrieved July 5, 2007, from http://nccrest.eddata.net/maps/index.php

National Center for Indian Education. (n.d.). *History of Indian education*. Retrieved April 11, 2008, from http://www.nrcprograms.org/site/PageServer?pagename=aief_hist_1960

No Child Left Behind Act of 2001. P. L. 107–110.

Parents in Action on Special Education v. Hannon. United States District Court, 1980. 506 F.Supp. 831 (N.D. Ill.)

Parents Involved v. Seattle School District, 551 U.S.____ (2007).

Pine, G. J., & Hilliard, A. G. (1990). Rx for racism: Imperatives for America's schools. *Phi Delta Kappan, 71*(8), 593–600.

Schubert, W. H. (1981). Knowledge about out of school curriculum. *Educational Forum, 45*, 185–199.

Schubert, W. H. (1986). *Curriculum: Perspective, paradigm, and possibility*. New York: Macmillan.

Stewner-Manzanares, G. (1988). *The Bilingual Education Act: Twenty years later*. Focus, 6. National Clearinghouse on Bilingual Education. Retrieved July 8, 2007, from http://www.ncela.gwu.edu/pubs/classics/focus/06bea.htm

Title IX, Education Amendments of 1972. (Title 20 U.S.C. 1681–1688).

U.S. Census Bureau. (2007). *Occupation by sex and earnings in the past twelve months*. Retrieved July 10, 2007, from http://factfinder.census.gov/servlet/STTable?_bm=y&-geo_id=01000US&-qr_name=ACS_2005_EST_G00_S2401&-ds_name=ACS_2005_EST_G00_

U.S. Department of Education. (2004). *Education for homeless children and youth programs: Title VII-B of the McKinney Vento Homeless Assistance Act*. Washington, DC: Author. Retrieved July 6, 2007, from http://www.ed.gov/programs/homeless/guidance.pdf

U.S. Senate Committee on Labor and Public Welfare. (1969). Indian education: A national tragedy—a national challenge (Kennedy Report). Washington, DC: U.S. Government Printing Office. Eric Document #ED 034625.

Valeria v. Davis d, 307 F3d 1036 (9th Cir. 2002).

Watkins, W. (1993). Black curriculum orientations: A preliminary inquiry. *Harvard Educational Review, 63*(3), 321–338.

Section Three

Assessment, Consultation, and Planning in School Social Work

17

Assessment, Multidisciplinary Teamwork, Consultation, and Planning in School Social Work

Robert Constable
Loyola University Chicago

Galen Thomas
Southern Illinois University

- Assessment in School Social Work
- Needs Assessment of a School Community
- Multidisciplinary Teamwork
- Consultation
- How Do Assessment, Teamwork, and Consultation Work? (And How Do They Work Together?)
- New Developments in General and Special Education: An Outcome-Oriented, Strengths-Based Service Delivery Approach
- Positive Behavioral Interventions and Supports
- Response to Intervention (RTI)

This section of the book is focused on the related processes of assessment, multidisciplinary teamwork, and consultation. These processes deal with decision making, which often takes place as a process within the multidisciplinary team and with the principal. The process of needs assessment, discussed earlier in chapter 11, can affect both policy practice and clinical practice. By assessing school and community needs, school social workers can tailor their role to meet the emergent and particular needs of the school. The nature of a student's situation and of the team also demands multiple perspectives. Assessment of the classroom learning environment and its dynamics is linked to consultation with teachers and other team members, to functional behavior assessments, to positive behavioral interventions and support, and to the social worker's work with particular students and their families. Finally, there is a comprehensive case study assessment of a particular student's situation.

ASSESSMENT IN SCHOOL SOCIAL WORK

At one time education was predominantly defined by standard curricula at each grade level. Some students fit into this system, but many did not. In special education this changed with the development of public policy demanding individualized curricula geared to the student's individual needs. When education is driven by the goals of each student, methods of education become flexible, individualized, and dependent on individualized assessment. The concept of education broadens to include social-emotional learning and developmental tasks. Such an assessment process demands more of the multidisciplinary team, and the school social worker has an important role in this process. In general education, the development of outcome-based education and the movement toward common standards for students could have similar consequences. Testing each student's response to educational interventions, teachers become diagnosticians of student learning styles, prescriptors of the best means for each student to master the skills and knowledge that constitute common standards, and assessors of student progress (Levine, 2004). The school social worker would assist in these assessments, working between the team, the student, and the family to individualize these processes to meet students' needs.

For school social workers *assessment* is a systematic way of understanding and communicating what is happening in the pupil's relations within the classroom, within the family, and between family and school. It provides a basis for deciding the places where interventions will be most effective. The school social worker has access to major sectors of life activity of individual pupils, teachers, and parents. This access allows for a practice approach that emphasizes interaction with the individual and with these important sectors. The ecological systems perspective is a holistic approach to practice, which allows the social worker to understand transactions with the environment, to make institutional and psychosocial assessments that address the complex transactions of persons with their environments, and to draw upon a wide range of knowledge in this process. The relation of education to the psychosocial tasks of child and family gives focus and definition to assessment, clarifies the possible unit(s) of attention, and develops the consequent role of the school social worker.

The focus of assessment is on strengths as well as concerns. The social worker looks for strengths and resources in the situation and in its participants in the face of processes, which without intervention can lead to deterioration and deficit. What are the possibilities for changes in the relations, tasks, and expectations in the classroom, in the home, and in the child's patterns of learning to cope? From this unique vantage point, the worker assists teachers and parents to discover their own personal repertoire of ways to assist the child's coping. Assessment focuses on conditions in the person, the environment, and in their transactions that may be causing difficulty or can help them to cope with difficulties they face. What support systems or services might make it possible for persons to survive, to cope, to form satisfactory interpersonal relationships, and to experience an increased level of success in the community and family environment? The answers will depend on these individuals' needs and capacities, how they are coping with their environment, and how their environment responds to them.

Assessment and intervention have their own logical sequences. Strengths-based and rooted in systems theory, they are all about possibilities for change. They move from the outside in, from the environment to the person interacting and coping. Assuming learning is a natural process—with the relational connections inherent and necessary to this process—the social worker helps it take place and helps pupils, teachers, and parents to deal with obstacles. In different circumstances and with a better understanding of the pupil's needs, teachers and parents might tailor their own educational approaches and expectations to the pupil's needs. When important adults change their approach, pupils may respond without further intervention. Directly or indirectly, the social worker helps pupils to respond differently to what are often small changes in the classroom and the family. At the same time, the social worker assists parents and teachers to respond to the pupil's efforts at coping.

NEEDS ASSESSMENT OF A SCHOOL COMMUNITY

The broadest assessment of the school and its community is *needs assessment*. This type of assessment, described in greater detail in chapter 11, is an assessment of the context for the problems individual students and groups are experiencing in school. Needs assessments provide a systematic means of gathering data about a problem experienced by more than one student. A needs assessment focuses on relationships among the school, the community, the family, and student needs. It should be the basis for the social worker's role, his or her participation in the development of policies, programs, or services for schools. Needs assessments provide data that parents, teachers, administrators, and community members can understand. With these data, social workers can tailor their roles to fit the needs of their particular school and community. A good example of this is the need to develop a safety plan in every school. This process, discussed in greater detail in chapters 34 and 39, involves the social worker in the school's and the community's attempt to develop a rapid and appropriate response to a situation where children are potentially at risk and to develop longer-term supports for grieving and healing processes.

In the following example a social worker did a needs assessment as she started her new job:

> As the first school social worker in a school district, my responsibilities were to be focused in a new elementary school (grades 2–5) enrolling more than 700 children. The new school had consolidated several old smaller schools. The children were from diverse communities and backgrounds. Additional pressure was presented by new families moving in from outside the region because of the availability of jobs at a new industrial plant. One of my first challenges was to determine what my role would be in this situation and how I would set priorities. I decided I did not have enough information to set priorities. I needed information on the perspectives of other members of the school community, especially the teachers. With administrative approval I developed a brief needs assessment form and distributed it to the teachers. This one-page form offered some possible areas of concern from which they could indicate priorities and concerns as well as space to identify specific issues not listed. This questionnaire was based on listening to teachers in the teachers' lounge as well as initial conversations with the principal and some key informant teachers. The feedback I received told me that teachers were concerned about several issues: 1) there was a general lack of civility among pupils, resulting in frequent fights on the playground and in the lunchroom; 2) there was a lack of parent involvement, especially with parents who were new to the district; and 3) some students appeared particularly in need of individual help. After the initial needs assessment, I discussed priorities with the principal. My first goals emerged: to help restore civility in the school; to develop special services for specific pupils who were out of control; and to get parents involved. None of these could be accomplished outside of a team approach. I started by assuming responsibility for a supervised recess program for students who were referred by their teachers. Here I showed social skills videos, had pupils role play appropriate behaviors, and focused on skill-development activities. I kept data on the number of repeat offenders. The school would punish repeat offenders by preventing them from socializing with peers. I was able to demonstrate that there were relatively low numbers of students who were abusing the fact that I used the time of supervised recess to teach skills. Later we developed a peer mediation program and a student assistance program (SAP). Students could voluntarily

request peer mediation for interpersonal conflicts. Teachers could refer pupils who were having difficulty for consultation with the SAP team before deciding whether a referral to special education was necessary.

On the basis of the needs assessment information, which I continued to collect, I initiated several new programs over the year. This included a peer mediation program—a local law school provided training for student peer mediators. I developed a parent survey, distributed to all parents with children in the school. Then I developed three parent workshops during the year based on the parent survey; a student assistance program to provide early prevention and interventions for students experiencing problems; whole classroom lessons for topics such as conflict resolution, offered to teachers at their request; and a mini-grant for family-centered services that funded parent workshops, bought materials, and supported students attending an after-school tutorial program.

I have been continually assessing the impact of these programs through data collection as well as informal feedback from teachers and students. This information keeps administrators informed and helps us to make adjustments in services offered. It was important to document the impact of the programs, because there were some skeptics who preferred more punitive interventions with students. Later I provided consultation with the district, so that the SAP approach and peer mediation programs have been expanded through the high school level. Most recently the superintendent told me of her plans to add another social work position, now at the high school level to develop these and other programs.

Comprehensive Assessment and Individual Situations

A comprehensive school social work assessment of a pupil's situation differs from assessment done by the school psychologist to establish intelligence and academic achievement. A school social work assessment has a broader focus. With the social work focus on the transactions of persons with environments extended to the student in multiple environments, it draws upon qualitative and quantitative data. The assessment aspires to a depth and personalized understanding that goes beyond comparison of the person's attributes to a larger population of individuals. Qualitative assessments rely on credibility (validity) and dependability (reliability) of the information presented, rather than being normed by comparison to a broader population. Credibility and dependability are strengthened by the confirmation of multiple sources of information gathered from multiple settings inside and outside of school. There are multiple respondents (parent, teacher, and student). There are multiple methodologies to gather information: interviews with parents, teachers, and the student; observations in various settings (classes, playground, the home, and the community); formal instruments; and records from school and community providers can be used as well. With all these methodologies, the focus is always on the dynamics of relationships, and not simply on the particular individual, seeking areas of strengths for the student, family, and school personnel rather than focusing on areas of deficit (see Jordan & Franklin, 1995).

Assessment of a Classroom Learning Environment and Its Dynamics

In a school, the classroom learning environment is a central context for assessment. Teaching is a challenging and intense job. Since the pupil's need is also to some extent the teacher's need, assisting the teacher is always central to this process. It is the first step in intervention. The school social worker responds to concerns expressed by a teacher by gathering information, often observing the class, providing consultation, and developing a plan with the teacher. The goal is to help the teacher to find a perspective and a way to deal with the challenging situation and to review other possibilities for intervention when necessary. These may be direct work with the parents or the pupil. When there is a possibility for a special education referral, *prereferral intervention* with the teacher by the team is recommended. This is a team-based, preventive problem-solving approach with the teacher prior to taking the step of a formal referral. Together with the teacher, they review the situation, hypothesize causes to explain the student's difficulties, and develop strategies to remediate those difficulties (Buck, Polloway, Smith-Thomas, & Cook, 2003). Assessment of the classroom learning environment is expanded upon in this section of the book. For children with special needs, teamwork and consultation are expected and prescribed by law and regulations. These processes are described in greater detail in all of the chapters of this section.

MULTIDISCIPLINARY TEAMWORK

Schools are increasingly oriented to teamwork as their responsibilities become more complex. Teamwork involves working through other persons and other persons working through you. Good teamwork is an antidote for inevitable dysfunctionality in the often stressful and sometimes competitive world of school professionals. Teams balance their common goals with differences in expertise. As schools deal with increasingly complex expectations, collaborative teams and teaming processes gradually have come to be seen as the means to define problems and develop solutions through face-to-face interaction. Skills can be exchanged. Thinking processes can change, and more novel solutions can be generated. Interdependent decision making and problem solving rest on small-group interpersonal skills of trust building, communication, leadership, creative problem solving, decision making, and conflict management (Thousand & Villa, 1992).

A *multidisciplinary problem-solving team* comprises a number of individual members of the school community, each of whom possesses particular knowledge and skills, who come together to share their expertise with one another for a common purpose (cf. Toseland, Palmer-Ganeles, & Chapman, 1986). Teams don't just happen; they are constructed by their members in the context of particular expectations. Collaborative teams and teamwork processes are major instruments of substantive school change. Collaborative decision making implies shared ownership of problems and solutions, the sharing of skills, a different level of thinking processes, and the ability to persist in working at difficult tasks. It opens the way toward attainment of group goals (Thousand & Villa, 1992). Five assumptions about a team's decision making and actions are critical to its success. Members of the collaborative team agree to:

1. Coordinate their work to pursue common, publicly agreed upon goals,
2. Believe that all team members have unique and needed expertise,
3. Value each member's input equally,
4. Distribute leadership among all the members of the group, and
5. Collaborate with others, using face-to-face interaction on a frequent basis assuming interdependence and individual accountability. (Thousand & Villa, 1992)

An observational study of school teams done in California over the course of five months came up with five clusters of team tasks and activities:

1. Teams most frequently engaged in *needs identification, program development, and planning*. A key activity here was the identification of intervention needs and the development of interventions, both individual and systemic (or programmatic).
2. A second cluster of activities had to do with *intrateam communication*. This involved coordination of the work different team members did with students and sorting out the systemic impacts of possible interventions.
3. A third cluster was *case identification and construction*. Here the team engaged in collective case identification and problem identification, "layering" multiple interpretations and perspectives and clarifying different possible points of intervention.
4. Teams engaged in *mutual support and training*. This would be informal professional development, perhaps about special education procedures, suspected-abuse reporting, mental health diagnoses, truancy procedures, or district policies.
5. Teams made *accountability checks*. They would verify that procedures were done and hold each other accountable for team-related work (Phillippo & Stone, 2006).

There can be a number of problems experienced when teams attempt to share expertise for a common purpose. The team needs to find a way to balance the power and perspectives of its members, encouraging a genuine sharing of resources (Tiefenthal, 1980). It also needs to maintain its objectives or change them systematically when necessary. It needs to maintain its appropriate authority structure. The problem of professional differences and territory is complicated by some overlap of responsibilities and functions among the roles of the social worker, psychologist, and counselor on the school team (Agresta, 2004; Radin & Welsh, 1984). Each has particular strengths to contribute. At the local school level, teams define their roles differently according to the district policy, the perceived needs of clientele, and the capabilities of their members. School social workers need to negotiate aspects of their roles with the team and with the school principal. Other team members may have a very limited understanding of social work training and expertise.

The roles and relations of team members are also defined at the state education agency (SEA) level. This definition of roles has become particularly important. Each state must define certification or licensing criteria for the "highly qualified" school personnel expected by the No Child Left Behind Act (NCLB) to work in a school (Constable & Alvarez, 2006). At the SEA level the stakes are high. Social workers have learned that if they are not active in these deliberations at the state level, they can lose at the local level as well. There needs to be constant vigilance of professional associations over their territory. There is often conflict between the SEA's interest in defining and delimiting (or broadly expanding) certain pupil personnel functions and the local education agency's definitions and interests. Professional rivalries and political realities may mask and legitimize themselves as a concern for administrative efficiency.

Professional Boundaries and Distorted Power Arrangements

The team's effectiveness is built on its ability to utilize its members' differing perspectives and skills. There needs to be a shared understanding of team members' roles and ways of operating. Distorted power arrangements on the team can limit a team's potential effectiveness. Professional boundaries within the team can be too rigid. Members can spend considerable energy protecting their territory to the exclusion of their common purposes. In contrast, weak boundaries can lead to mediocrity and, at worst, to chaos. For example, if the social worker is limited to only gathering information from the family, this would severely restrict her ability to gain a full perspective on the interpersonal dynamics occurring at school. However, if team members do not take responsibility for reaching consensus on solutions, their work will be unproductive.

Teams are constantly working out their relational balances. Social workers can't do an assessment or even effectively enter the team without an understanding of the capabilities and skills of each team member, and an understanding of the agreements team members have arrived at to regulate their contributions. Often team members have difficulty translating their specialty into something the team (or the pupil and family) can use. The social worker, as a functional generalist, works across the multispecialty and multicultural worlds of schools, agencies, and homes. In states where school social work is well developed and defined, this skill often results in the social worker assuming a leadership role, such as serving as the coordinator of the team.

In special education, with its more prescriptive legal framework, the team process is more formalized. The minimum team composition is governed by regulation. This core team could be expanded upon, with various other experts called in as needed (Thousand & Villa, 1992). For example, the federal Code of Regulations mandates that parents (or parent surrogates) of children with disabilities be invited to take part in team deliberations for their child (34 CFR 300 121(a)). Assessment is then developed in the context of the multidisciplinary team's efforts to assist pupils in the educational process and individualize plans based on what the school can offer.

CONSULTATION

Research has shown that consultation is perhaps the most important tool of the school social worker (Allen-Meares, 1994; Anlauf-Sabatino, 1982; Constable, Kuzmickaite, Harrison, & Volkmann, 1999; Nelson, 1990). If teamwork involves the art of sharing perspectives and skills in the interests of a common purpose, consultation is the art of assisting others to become more effective in dealing with complex problems. Consultation, discussed in greater detail in chapter 20, presumes good teamwork. Team membership is the best path to the development of a trusting consultative relationship. Assessment is a key component of consultation and teamwork. Applied to the pupil, the family, the classroom, and the resources of the team, assessment is done as a joint and shared problem-solving process.

HOW DO ASSESSMENT, TEAMWORK, AND CONSULTATION WORK? (AND HOW DO THEY WORK TOGETHER?)

To see how assessment, teamwork, and consultation work, let us examine typical cases in general and special education.

> Hakim was a very sad first grader. He had few friends and seemed dazed in class. He would play with pencils and other supplies on his desk while the teacher talked. The teacher noticed him making "strange random noises, deliberate hums and grunts," in class as he did his work. When it came time for him to work independently, he had to ask the teacher to repeat the directions. His need for constant adult attention made the teacher, with a class of twenty-eight 6-year-olds, feel desperate. "Fix him please." On the other hand, he was

working at grade level. His art, which he loved, revealed close family connections, houses and yards, and his brothers playing soccer with him. The teacher had made no effort to contact the family. Hakim was the youngest of a large and close Assyrian family. His brothers, two uncles, two cousins, his grandmother, and his parents all lived together with him. His father worked long hours. The parents were bilingual, but Assyrian was spoken in the home. He was very bonded to his mother. His mother was shy, uncertain whether she should be involved with the school, and somewhat overprotective. She talked about her own difficulties in school and with the language. The social worker observed Hakim in class, contacted the family, and set up ongoing communication between the mother and the teacher. The assessment revealed a shy, somewhat immature first grader dealing with a different language and culture. His noises in class were Hakim talking to himself in Assyrian. The teacher felt helpless with his differences and what they seemed to mean. She had little information about the situation and was becoming impatient with him. Hakim perceived her impatience and was reacting to it. The mother, herself uncertain in a different culture, was reacting to Hakim's stories of school with her own defensiveness. Although the social worker contacted the mother and developed a relationship, much of her work was with the teacher. The social worker provided cultural information. Working with the strengths of the teacher, she helped her to be more confident with Hakim and his parents, to provide appropriate attention, and set appropriate goals with Hakim. When she did this and took a strengths-based approach to involve the family, Hakim responded positively, gradually becoming more confident with the teacher in class. He began to share his unique sense of humor with others.

Here the cultural situation reinforced Hakim's shyness, the mother's uncertainty, and the teacher's impatience and feelings of helplessness. As a team member, the social worker assessed the situation and worked through the teacher, provided information and support, and helped build a connection between the family and the school. Once contact had been made with the family, the teacher could handle the situation with the social worker's ongoing consultation and availability. To work apart from or in competition with the teacher in this case would have been dysfunctional and self-defeating.

Special Education

The right to a free appropriate public education for the child with disabilities demands a more formalized assessment process (a complete multifaceted nondiscriminatory evaluation) and an individualized education program (IEP) for educational placement. Multidisciplinary teamwork is mandated in special education as part of this process. The team should at least include the parents of the child, a regular education teacher, a school administrator, and a person to interpret the results of testing. The parents are expected to be equal participants along with school personnel in developing, reviewing, and revising the IEP for their child (34 CFR Appendix A, Question 5). School social workers are often members of this team. Their services are defined in the federal regulations to include:

1. Preparing a social or developmental history on a child with a disability;
2. Group and individual counseling with the child and family;
3. Working in partnership with parents and others on those problems in a child's living situation (home, school, and community) that affect the child's adjustment in school;
4. Mobilizing school and community resources to enable the child to learn as effectively as possible in his or her educational program; and
5. Assisting in developing positive behavioral intervention strategies. (34 CFR 300.24(b)(13))

The same principles in general education of respecting others' different competencies and functions apply to special education with the additional procedural safeguards meant to protect a constitutional right. Two somewhat typical case examples of social work assessment, teamwork, and consultation in special education follow:

> Steve was a 10-year-old African American boy who had received special education services since early childhood and was placed in a special classroom for children with behavior disorders/emotional disturbances. He had been in four schools before his father died three years ago. His mother's confusing and disruptive lifestyle finally brought his maternal grandmother to take permanent custody of him the year following his father's death. In the evaluation two years ago, he was reported to have serious learning problems. He appeared to be angry in school, easily frustrated, and distractible, and had very low self-esteem, but the assessment had not taken into account the turbulence and confusion of his living situation. His current teacher saw none of the previous problems. He was not a slow worker and was no longer easily frustrated. His grandmother, who came to school for the first time when invited by the social worker, confirmed a picture of a boy who, after a turbulent period in his other schools, was gradually adjusting to his new home and school, although he was shy in the neighborhood. The team noted that the previous, out-of-date, and narrowly focused assessment had taken on a life of its own but no longer reflected Steve's current situation. In any case, a reevaluation was essential. Based on the reevaluation, a plan for Steve's placement in a general education class with supports was developed. The social worker helped Steve manage the transition to general education, provided consultation to the new teacher, and continued to provide support to the grandmother and to Steve as needed.

> Brian was a 15-year-old placed in math and reading classes for youth with learning disabilities in his high school. He was neatly dressed and well groomed. Both parents saw him as truthful, neat, responsible, adultlike, and perfectionistic. He interacted well with his parents but tended to withdraw when faced with something unpleasant. His history was of mixed school

achievement. Sometimes he did very poorly, but in both seventh and eighth grades he made the junior high school honor roll. Nevertheless, there was no reevaluation of his situation or recommendations for changes. In his sophomore year Brian stopped working almost entirely and refused to participate in any activity, including taking tests. He was nondisruptive, but passively resistant in the classroom. He refused to engage with the social worker. Despite the implications of his learning disability, teachers took his lack of cooperation personally. There was a pervasive negative tone in their discussion of him and in correspondence sent home. Brian saw this as his power struggle with his teachers. They were thinking of punishing him by having him drop driver education. This was the only class he enjoyed and in which he demonstrated achievement. Brian's parents sensed the teachers' attitudes and felt alienated from them and from the school. They just hoped that he would pass sophomore year before he dropped out. If he did that, they would reward him with a pickup truck. Brian's father had himself dropped out in tenth grade. The social worker worked with his teachers to defuse their power struggle with Brian. He worked with the parents to develop more appropriate expectations and rewards. He developed a transition plan with Brian and the family in case Brian did drop out during the year, and he worked with Brian on Brian's own educational and vocational goals.

As in the case of Hakim in general education, and Steve and Brian in special education, the assessment, teamwork, and consultation processes are interrelated and crucial to success. In both special education cases, the earlier reviews appear to have been either missing or perfunctory, but the faulty assessment began to take on a life of its own. The team needed to rethink its approaches and make sense of both situations. There needed to be a broader strengths-based assessment. The social worker had to work with the student, the parents, and the team. As a prerequisite to working in special education, the social worker needed to translate terms such as "reevaluation," "complete, multifaceted nondiscriminatory assessment," "parent participation," and "transition planning" into skilled social work practice. The social worker was able to use an understanding of the regulations governing special education to assist the student. Further work with the student and family, discussed in the next section, is dependent on assessment and the decision-making processes within the team, as well as with the parents and with the student.

NEW DEVELOPMENTS IN GENERAL AND SPECIAL EDUCATION: AN OUTCOME-ORIENTED, STRENGTHS-BASED SERVICE DELIVERY APPROACH

The approaches prescribed in the laws of special education, detailed here and elsewhere in this book, have created profound changes in the entitlements of children with disabilities to a free appropriate public education. These changes in entitlements have been linked to overrepresentation (in relation to their expected frequency in a population) of students in certain categories, such as specific learning disability, and overrepresentation of minority students. A *deficit* approach to assessment leading inevitably to categorizing the pupil and to placement outside of general education has long received criticism. Based on their own research into educational outcomes, critics of the current system (Skrtic, 1991; Ysseldyke, Algozzine, & Thurlow, 2000) pointed out seven problems with the deficit approach:

- Eligibility for services is determined by identifying deviant characteristics that permit the labeling of disability.
- Services are delivered through categorical programs, such as those for learning disability and emotional disorder.
- The role of regular education personnel becomes to refer problem students to other experts; referral usually means removal, and so a perverse incentive is created to identify and refer problem students (Algozzine & Ysseldyke, 1981; Ysseldyke, 1983).
- Assessment and diagnosis use standard criteria for disability; the issue becomes not what may be affecting the behavior or what the student needs to do better (functional assessment), but whether he or she fits into a predetermined class.
- The least restrictive environment (often a stressful environment for the teacher and student) proves difficult to implement, and therefore students tend to be segregated in special classes or separate resource rooms.
- The special education system disproportionately enrolls minority students.
- The majority of students receiving special education services continue to receive separate instruction until they graduate or drop out of school.

In many ways the issues present in the cases of Steve and Brian exemplify some of limitations of a deficit approach. Students tend to be caught in categories. Strengths can be ignored because of this categorization. Power struggles develop. Members of the team might stay within their specialties and lose the student and the meaning of the situation. Students feel they are trapped in special education no matter what they do. Parents, particularly minority parents or parents of high school pupils, can be left out. These concerns have led to the gradual development of an approach that would focus on strengths, on outcomes, and on collaboration.

Assessment

Assessment in such an outcome-oriented, strengths-based, collaborative service delivery approach places a strong emphasis on direct observation in the natural environment (classroom, playground). Functional behavior assessments would often be made of the student's academic and behavioral performance. The key questions in functional behavior assessments are: How is the student currently performing? How does the student respond to interventions suggested by the problem-solving team? What is the relation between students, educational environments, and their behavior? Assessment of eligibility for special education services would be based on how the student responds to change efforts of the teacher, the student, and the parents.

Interventions

The assessment, teamwork, and consultation demanded by this approach have to be extremely sophisticated. The functions of the team (now the problem-solving team) shift from the older multidisciplinary team tasks—referral, testing, and placement—to an ongoing, dynamic, problem-solving focus. Instead of following a deficit model that focuses on dysfunction in the pupil alone, the team looks for combinations of factors, as in the previous social work assessment and intervention examples. It follows an interaction model, examining and responding to the combination of student curriculum/instructional/environment/family/community systems. This encourages a holistic focus, rather than just assessing/testing for student deficits. Interventions are identified based on needs in the student/school curriculum/instructional/family/peer group/community environment, rather than simply delivering services to the student after a disability label has been identified. The helping process is based on strengths-based problem solving. This builds on the resources of the teacher, the student, the parents, and the resources of other personnel in a manner similar to the social work theoretical models discussed in this book. Services are flexible in terms of who provides the services, where services are provided, and the amount of services provided. This approach is very compatible with the ecological systems model developed in this book, but without proper supports, it could fail or, if misused, become an excuse for limiting services, developing inexpensive services, or not delivering services at all. In a broader framework of services such assessment and intervention planning would fit well with the local area network wraparound planning approach, discussed in chapter 30.

POSITIVE BEHAVIORAL INTERVENTIONS AND SUPPORTS

The identification and implementation of positive behavior interventions with students who display behavior problems is clearly mandated by the Individuals with Disabilities Education Act (IDEA). The school social worker is specifically identified as one of the professionals expected to assist in this process. The regular education teacher is also identified as an important contributor to identifying positive interventions that may be effective in decreasing negative behaviors and/or increasing positive behaviors. Individual behavior intervention plans, building on a functional behavior analysis, for students who display behavior problems are developed further in chapters 22 and 26. Tier 2 interventions are described in chapter 35.

The development of school-wide systems of positive interventions has been encouraged through a variety of federal initiatives: safe and drug-free schools, IDEA, character education, and so on. At this point, there is an expectation in the law that positive behavioral interventions and supports (PBIS) should be a part of every general and special education teacher's repertoire of skills. The PBIS model proposes proactive strategies to define, teach, and support appropriate student behaviors. This emphasis has resulted in coordinated and research-supported efforts for all school personnel to participate in positively focused school-wide discipline models. The goal is to prevent school discipline problems through system-wide interventions that focus on increasing positive behavior of all students rather than using traditional punitive efforts directed toward students who engage in rule-breaking behavior.

> The school administrator, school social worker, and other members of the school planning team decided to adopt a PBIS model. After attending a training session, the school social worker began providing whole-class presentations on prosocial topics each month. The teachers were provided with possible activities to use during the month to reinforce the lesson presented. School-wide monitoring of specific behaviors permitted reinforcement of positive goals through recognition ceremonies and celebrations for class and individual accomplishments. Families were included through a variety of techniques: a newsletter explaining the goals of the program, things that families could do to encourage the positive behaviors to occur at home, and invitations to participate in some of the recognition ceremonies held at the school. All of these efforts contributed to a positive learning environment and promoted prosocial behaviors for all students, not just those with IEPs.

RESPONSE TO INTERVENTION (RTI)

In chapter 7, we defined evidence-based practice as follows:

> [Evidence-based practice (EBP)] mandates an approach to decision making that is transparent, accountable, and based on consideration of current best practices concerning effects of particular interventions on the welfare of individuals, groups and communities. It relates to the decisions of both individual practitioners and policy makers (McDonald, 2000; Soydan, 2004). Evidence-based practice consists of (1) an individualized assessment, with a search for the best available external evidence related to the presenting concerns; (2) a decision about the extent to which the available evidence may apply to a particular individual or situation; and (3) consideration of the values and preferences of the individuals involved. (Sackett et al., cited in McNeill, 2006)

Applied to teaching in general education, Response to Intervention (RtI) procedures envisage a continuum of evidence-based teaching responses to difficulties in learning and social behavior. This continuum of teacher responses would first of all comprise *universal interventions* (tier 1), which would apply to everyone in the class. These might be classroom management skills, such as consistently implementing an acknowledgment system to recognize appropriate behavior in class, minimizing transition time between activities, and/or providing multiple and varied opportunities for students to respond during instruction. *Targeted interventions* (tier 2) apply to groups of students who do not respond as expected to tier 1 interventions. The teacher might develop a "check-in and check-out" system to provide additional structure, prompts, instruction, feedback, and acknowledgment for students who are having difficulties with certain classroom tasks. Finally, *individualized interventions* (tier 3) would apply to persons who do not respond to tier 2 interventions. These would be specific and time-intensive assessments to determine individual gaps in skills. (Fairbanks, Sugai, Guardino, & Lathrop, 2007). It might be a functional behavior assessment. It might involve the prereferral team. It might ultimately be a referral for special education services. Thus RtI envisages a winnowing process, taking place in regular education. RtI is based on pragmatic, evidence-based ways of responding to students and testing students' responsiveness to teaching rather than, in the case of a pupil with learning disabilities, attempting to categorize the pupil through testing for a severe discrepancy between intellectual ability and achievement (Fuchs & Fuchs, 2005). Thus RtI becomes an alternative to a deficit approach.

IDEA 2004 provided that the states may not require the criterion of a severe discrepancy between intellectual ability and achievement to determine a specific learning disability. Instead it permitted the local education agency to consider a child's response to research-based interventions (as above) as part of the determination process for a specific learning disability (34 CFR 300.307, 300.309, 300.311). Thus it is encouraged that assessment be based on the child's response to research-based interventions (34 CFR 300.307(a)(2)). It also requires that children be observed in their learning environments to document academic performance and behavior (34 CFR 300.310). The school social worker has not been the person who would identify learning disability. On the other hand, understanding the language and concepts of the RtI process, developing prereferral assessments and consultation, working with the team, and conducting observations in the classroom are all part of the school social worker's role. Emotional disturbance is one of the factors to be ruled out in the identification of specific learning disability. To the extent RtI develops in general education, school social workers need to be familiar with its language and methodology and their role in it.

Research on the school social work role (Allen-Meares, 1994; Constable et al., 1999) has pointed out the overarching importance of assessment, multidisciplinary teamwork, and consultation. Because these affect how others in the school will work with children, they have a broader impact than the social worker's direct intervention with individuals and groups of students and their families. The emphases on teamwork and functional assessment, emerging from laws, policies, and regulations for children with disabilities, have long been a familiar part of school social work practice. Projected changes in general education will in the long run affect the school social worker's role. Section III develops these related themes of assessment, teamwork, and consultation as the foundations for policy, program development, and intervention with children and their families in the school community.

Resources

Zuna and McDougall (2004) recommend a number of resources that track this developing field, including the Web sites of the Office of Special Education Programs of the Department of Education, the National Information Center for Children and Youth with Disabilities, the Collaborative for Academic, Social and Emotional Learning at the University of Illinois at Chicago, the Beach Center on Disability, and the Association for Positive Behavior Support. Members of the Association for Positive Behavior Support receive newsletters and a subscription to the *Journal of Positive Behavior Interventions*. Several useful publications are the *Journal of Applied Behavior Analysis; Communication-Based Interventions for Problem Behavior: A User's Guide for Positive Change* by Carr, Levin, McConnachie, Carlson, Kemp, and Smith; *Positive Behavioral Support: Including People with Difficult Behavior in the Community* by Koegel, Koegel, and Dunlap; *Antecedent Control: Innovative Approaches to Behavioral Support* by Luiselli and Cameron; and *Functional Analysis of Problem Behavior: From Effective Assessment to Effective Support* by Repp and Horner.

References

Agresta, J. (2004). Professional role perceptions of school social workers, psychologists and counselors. *Children & Schools, 26*(3), 151–164.

Allen-Meares, P. (1994). Social work services in schools: A national study of entry-level tasks. *Social Work, 39*, 28–34.

Algozzine, B. A., & Ysseldyke, J. E. (1981). Special education services for normal students: Better safe than sorry? *Exceptional Children, 48*, 238–243.

Anlauf-Sabatino, C. (1982). Consultation and school social work practice. In R. T. Constable & J. P. Flynn (Eds.), *School social work: Practice and research perspectives* (pp. 271–281). Homewood, IL: Dorsey.

Buck, G. H., Polloway, E. A., Smith-Thomas, A., & Cook, K. W. (2003). Prereferral intervention processes: A survey of state practices. *Exceptional Children, 69*(3), 349–360.

Constable, R., & Alvarez, M. (2006). Moving into specialization in school social work: Issues in practice, policy and education. *School Social Work Journal, 30*(3), 116–131.

Constable, R., Kuzmickaite, D., Harrison, W. D., & Volkmann, L. (1999). The emergent role of the school social worker in Indiana. *School Social Work Journal, 24*(1), 1–14.

Fairbanks, S., Sugai, G., Guardino, H., & Lathrop, M. (2007). Response to intervention: Examining classroom behavior support in second grade. *Exceptional Children, 73*(3), 288–310.

Fuchs, D., & Fuchs, L. S. (2005). Responsiveness-to-intervention: A blueprint for practitioners, policymakers, and parents. *Teaching Exceptional Children, 38*(1), 57–61.

Jordan, C., & Franklin, C. (1995). *Clinical assessment for social workers: Quantitative and qualitative methods*. Chicago: Lyceum Books.

Levine, A. (2004). *New rules, old responses.* Retrieved October 2004, from http://www.tc.columbia.edu/news/article/.htm?id=4741

McDonald, G. (2000). Evidence-based practice. In M. Davies (Ed.), *Blackwell encyclopedia of social work* (p. 123). Oxford: Blackwell.

Nelson, C. (1990). *A job analysis of school social workers*. Princeton, NJ: Educational Testing Service.

Phillippo, K., & Stone, S. (2006). School-based collaborative teams: An exploratory study of tasks and activities. *Children & Schools, 28*(4), 232–234.

Radin, N., & Welsh, B. (1984). Social work, psychology and counseling in the schools. *Social Work, 24*(1), 28–33.

Skrtic, T. M. (1991). *Behind special education: A critical analysis of professional culture and school organization*. Denver, CO: Love Publishing.

Soydan, H. (2004). [Review of *International perspectives on evidence-based practice in social work*.] *European Journal of Social Work, 7*(3), 385–387.

Thousand, J. S., & Villa, R. A. (1992). Collaborative teams: A powerful tool in school restructuring. In R. A. Villa, J. S. Thousand, W. Stainback, & S. Stainback (Eds.), *Restructuring for caring and effective education* (pp. 73–107). Baltimore: Paul H. Brookes.

Tiefenthal, M. (1980). Multidisciplinary teams. In R. T. Constable & M. Tiefenthal (Eds.), *The school social worker and the handicapped child: Making PL 94-142 work* (pp. 21–24). Dekalb, IL: Regional Resource Center.

Toseland, R. W., Palmer-Ganeles, J., & Chapman, D. (1986). Teamwork in psychiatric settings. *Social Work, 31*(4), 46–52.

Ysseldyke, J. E. (1983). Current practices in making psychoeducational decisions about learning disabled students. *Journal of Learning Disabilities, 16*, 226–233.

Ysseldyke, J. E., Algozzine, B. A., & Thurlow, M. L. (2000). *Critical issues in special education*. Boston: Houghton-Mifflin.

Zuna, N., & McDougall, D. (2004). Using positive behavioral support to manage avoidance of academic tasks. *Teaching Exceptional Children, 37*(1), 18–25.

18

A Framework for Cross-Cultural Practice in School Settings

Frances Smalls Caple
University of Southern California

Ramon M. Salcido
University of Southern California

- Culturally Competent Practice
- Understanding Culture through Perspective Building
- The Role of Social Worker-Learner
- Understanding Acculturation and Cultural Exchange
- A Framework for Culturally Competent Practice
- Systems Assessment
- Family Assessment and Engagement
- Skills of Cross-Cultural Practice
- Planning and Service Delivery

This chapter focuses on how school social workers might be better prepared for and therefore more effectively deliver culturally competent practice. Many young people and their families occupy subordinate positions in societies throughout the world, often dominated ("colonized") by the social and

Some material from this chapter is from Frances S. Caple, Ramon M. Salcido, and John di Cecco. "Engaging Effectively with Culturally Diverse Families and Children," in *Social Work in Education, 17*, 159–170. Used with permission of the National Association of Social Workers.

economic power, privilege, and prestige of other groups. Subordination of so-called minority populations (Longres, 1991; Taylor, 2001) arises most typically when powerful members of the dominant group hold in low esteem some characteristic such as race, gender, ethnicity, or religion (Taylor, 2001). When this attitude is translated into discriminatory or prejudicial actions, the subordinated persons are often placed at a distinct disadvantage in regard to the achievement of life goals. On the other hand, the importance of education for national and personal survival has led to the growth throughout the world of school policies that aspire to: 1) raise the quality of education to an international standard; 2) include previously marginalized populations, who never had equal access to a good education; and 3) individualize the educational process to accommodate disabilities, personal differences, and ways of learning. Women in Afghanistan, tribal groups in South Africa, Russian children in Lithuania, Gypsies in Romania, children of migrant workers, homeless families, families facing racial discrimination in the United States, and many others may continue to be marginalized throughout the world. For children who are members of such populations, school can become a battleground for personal survival.

CULTURALLY COMPETENT PRACTICE

Culturally competent school social work practice (National Association of Social Workers, 2001) has grown from the need to connect previously marginalized people to the education process, to develop just conditions in the school community, to assist in the individualization of education, and to counter negative beliefs about human capability (Huxtable & Blyth, 2002). Indeed, school social work derives its legitimacy from the fact that there is still a struggle and that special efforts need to be made to make education work for people who have experienced social marginalization. In this process the school social worker has multiple roles working with different systems: individual pupils, parents, and teachers (microsystems); the *nexus,* the connections between all of these in an educational process in a school community (the mesosystem); and the *mix* of laws, policies, and cultural beliefs and the broader systems that affect every school community (the macrosystem). Since these processes take place internationally, the examples given in this chapter have global contexts.

In the process of becoming a social worker, one needs to develop *cultural competence.* Social workers live in and are a part of society and are therefore subject to the class values, attitudes, and norms predominant within that society (Weaver, 1999). These norms may have also served to subordinate members of different cultural groups. A social worker's perspective for working with culturally diverse clients is drawn from values, beliefs, and specialized knowledge and skills. Without a way of organizing acquired knowledge into culturally competent practice, one's perspective may become biased.

Cultural competence refers to the process by which individuals and systems respond respectfully and effectively to people of diverse cultures, languages, classes, races, genders, sexual orientations, ethnic backgrounds, religions, and other areas of diversity. Culturally competent school social workers recognize, affirm, and value the worth of individuals, families, and communities and protect and preserve their dignity. Cultural competence is a lifelong process for school social workers, who will always encounter diverse clients and new situations in their practice (NASW, 2001). Social workers must recognize the strengths that exist in all cultures (NASW, 2001). True cultural competence goes far beyond the individual social worker. School social workers help school communities to develop capacities to become more culturally competent by: 1) valuing diversity; 2) developing the capacity for cultural self-assessment; 3) developing understanding of the dynamics inherent when cultures interact; 4) institutionalizing cultural knowledge; and 5) developing programs and services that reflect an understanding of diversity between and within cultures (NASW, 2001).

The school is a center of cultural development for children and the developing community. It must become safe for learning and development for all children and for their families. For this to succeed there must be a belief that there is real community ownership by everyone of the process of education. School communities all over the world are dealing with ethnic and cultural differences and the tensions and fears that often arise from these differences. School social workers need to join with educational administrators, teachers, and parents to build a school community that may be *different* from its surroundings in its norms of nonviolent resolution of differences, respect for others, their values and life ways, and the respect for self that accompanies this respect for others in a safe community.

School social workers have to be concerned about social justice in the school community. Thus, they engage in activity to correct and change unfair situations, discrimination, and actions that hurt others because of differences due to race, ethnicity, gender, sexuality, religion, or any other characteristics that may make people culturally different. One important problem in the United States and throughout the world is the issue of racial and ethnic tension in schools. This issue is addressed by school social workers in the following real-life examples:

> In the United States, Rita McGary, as a high school social worker in a suburb of Washington, D.C., worked with a multiethnic population of Native Americans, various Hispanic cultures, various Asian cultures, African Americans, and various white cultures. It was a situation of racial and ethnic tension. She developed mediation systems and conflict resolution and worked with six different cultural groups in separate forums to build group solidarity and resolve problems within and between groups in a context of respect (McGary, 1987).

> In post-Soviet Lithuania, Daiva Kuzmickaite, a school social worker, worked in a conflicted school. The school culture, reflecting Soviet times, was somewhat artificial and full of conflicts and hopelessness. There were serious problems

> experienced between and among majority Lithuanian students, and the Polish and Russian minority students. No one expected these groups to befriend each other. The school itself and its students felt disconnected from the realities of post-Soviet Lithuania and the economic competition of an emergent multinational world. Students were in a bubble prior to their entrance into very different economic and social realities; however, in some ways they knew the harsh world they lived in, and they reflected these realities in their relationships with each other. Teachers, trained to impose harsh discipline and to shame their students into submission, were uncertain in the face of an emergent Lithuania. The school social worker worked with others to guide a process of cultural change within the school community. She worked with the principal and with teachers to develop policies that fit the emergent Lithuanian cultural realities. She developed group programs for students to find different ways to work out problems themselves, with their own resources. She assisted teachers in finding new ways of relating to the needs of their students. She worked with diverse families and with children who were having difficulty with this process as well.[1]

Throughout the world, schools exist whose students are primarily from minority or vulnerable populations. In these cases, schools may serve both as places of safety and of transaction with the larger society. The following example illustrates this process:

> In South Africa, Miriam Mabetoa, a school social worker worked in a rural Black homeland. Although tribal differences have meaning, there are no other ethnic groups in the school. Students and residents of this homeland feel left out of an urban society. The painful national history of racism, together with rural-urban issues, is experienced through lowered expectations and hopelessness. The school, built by the labor of homeland residents and parents, tries to be a place of development and hope, and here the broader society is partially experienced. Truancy and dropouts are prevalent, however, and the combination of hopelessness and economic realities are behind these problems. The school social worker's model of practice focused on school-community development and then helping individuals and groups of students and parents find a part for themselves in this reconstructed community that offers hope (Mabetoa, 1996).

In each case the school social worker assisted in the building of a safe school community where differences are respected, resolved, and, indeed, the basis for growth and development of the whole school community.

UNDERSTANDING CULTURE THROUGH PERSPECTIVE BUILDING

Social workers seeking cultural competence soon realize the impossibility of acquiring specific knowledge about every racially, ethnically, or other-

1. The example is taken from Robert Constable's field liaison work in Lithuania in 1994.

wise diverse client. We have identified four principles as essential for developing a generic perspective for culturally competent practice in the United States and in many other countries in this developing multinational and multicultural world:

1. In a developing, multicultural world, cultures are complex; for example, there is no single American culture.
2. Diversity is to be acknowledged and valued.
3. Members of each cultural group are diverse.
4. Acculturation is a dynamic process.

Historical and Theoretical Views

The focus on cross-cultural practice appears to have been influenced by several historical developments within the United States as a whole, within the public schools in particular, and within the social work profession itself. Although these factors are varied and complex, some observational reflection on history can be important in assisting school social workers to think about their practice and follow through with effective assessment of needs and plans for change. In U.S. culture, the school has been both a center of development and of conflict throughout its multiethnic history. Over a century, schools have struggled to develop inclusive communities where there is respect for individual differences. For young families schools are becoming centers of development. Problems of violence experienced in the community, issues of harassment, intimidation, and bullying have brought about a needed focus on developing a culture of safety and respect for differences. Legislation and case law have mandated desegregation and thus the interaction of diverse groups in schools, but this may be far from the experienced reality.

The United States has always been culturally diverse, even though it has often functioned as if it were a single culture. Legislation, public policies, and procedures were drawn on the order of the dominant groups who held elected or appointed offices and who shaped those laws and policies. The country's indigenous Indian population was subjugated, and the land was gradually settled by peoples from all countries of the world, whether they came free and voluntarily, were enticed by the possibility of economic gains, or were enslaved or indentured and came involuntarily.

The earliest non-indigenous settlements in the northern colonies were voluntarily formed according to the country of origin of the residents. The ethnic communities of modern cities reflect a similar continuing pattern of members of groups tending to band together. One reason for such community and neighborhood formation is obvious: it allows for the greatest preservation of those things held dear and most familiar by the people who settle there—those things that help identify who they are as a people—the customs, values, and beliefs that comprise their culture. The pattern of community growth and development in the southern colonies was more racially oriented. The earliest settlement included black immigrants brought involuntarily as slaves. De jure segregation, or segregation mandated by law, spread following the end of the Reconstruction period in the South in the late 1800s.

In the period of the country's western expansion, new settlements were acquired by what some perceive as "expansionist wars": the Mexican-American War (1846–1848) and the Spanish-American War (1898). Through the greater part of United States history, most Mexican-American and Puerto Rican residents of the United States became Americans through the acquisition of new territory (Kilty & Vidal de Haymes, 2000). The settlements in the West also included immigrants from Asian Pacific islands and countries.

Native Americans were restricted to reservations established by treaties between the various Indian nations and the U.S. government. Altogether, these early patterns resulted in highly segregated communities, whether they were formed involuntarily or voluntarily. Chow (1999) noted, for example, that the "isolated, residentially segregated Chinatowns developed as mechanisms of self-protection against the racism, exclusion, and oppression experienced by early Chinese immigrants" (p. 71). With the advent of public education for all children, the highly valued neighborhood school was thus similarly segregated on racial and ethnic cultural lines. Southern schools were segregated by laws that prohibited the mixing of racial groups.

For the last half century, the country has struggled to keep up with rapid changes brought about by federal and state orders to desegregate public schools and public facilities, based on the historic Supreme Court decision *Brown v. Board of Education of Topeka* (1954). The nature of racially and ethnically isolated neighborhoods meant that school buses became one vehicle of desegregation. In the aftermath of all efforts, some U.S. schools became more racially mixed than they had ever been, while significant numbers of African-American and Latino students still attend schools that almost exclusively enroll one ethnic group. Immigrants seeking personal gain and refugees from war-torn countries continued to enter the United States to join what was then often referred to as the "melting pot." The relative ease and various means of transportation in this country enable constant migration within its borders, and the populations of many states reflect constant shifts in their demographic mix.

The United States is becoming more diverse (Weaver, 1999), largely through immigration and domestic migration. The Census Bureau reports that in 2006, minorities (persons of color) accounted for one-third of the nations' 300 million residents. If we define "persons of color" as a member of a racial minority group, four states and the District of Columbia now have more "minority" residents than white residents: Hawaii, which has a 75 percent minority population; the District of Columbia, which has a 68 percent minority population; New Mexico, where 57 percent of the population belongs to minority groups; California, where 57 percent of residents are members of minority groups; and Texas, which has a 52 percent minority population (U.S. Census Bureau, 2007).

The diversity in the United States is becoming more obvious with the efforts to eliminate barriers as to where residents live, work, and attend school. The 2006 Census Bureau's estimates confirm the country's increased diversity. Interestingly, the 2006 Census population estimates show increases from the year 2000 to the year 2006 in the U.S. Hispanic population of 3.4 percent, bringing their numbers to 44.3 million, with the largest representation in California, Texas, and Florida. The African American population increased by 1.3 percent to 40.2 million with the largest numbers in New York, Florida and Texas. The increased number of African Americans in Texas is largely due to resettlement as a result of Hurricane Katrina in Louisiana. The Asian-American population grew by 3.2 percent to reach 14.9 million, with the largest numbers living in California, New York, and Texas. The Census also estimated that 4.5 million Native Americans and Alaskan Natives and one million Native Hawaiian and other Pacific Islanders reside in the United States. The total White population grew only 0.3 percent during this time period, to reach 198.7 million. The White population is projected to be about 53 percent of the population in 2050. These trends clearly suggest a need for competence in cross-cultural practice by school social workers, who are themselves diverse in ethnicity.

These figures reflect a marked change from figures reported at the turn of the twentieth century. Between 1890 and 1920, there were approximately eighteen million immigrants, including Catholics and Jews, who came to the United States from Ireland, Germany, Italy, and Eastern Europe. This was the largest entry of immigrants in the country's history. The second wave of a large number of immigrants, occurring at the close of the twentieth century, included great numbers of persons from economically developing worlds of Asia and Latin America (Booth, 1998).

European immigration sparked the notion of America as "the 'melting pot,' a place where many cultures were blended to create a strong American identity" (Pryor, 1992, p. 153). Because the English language was one vehicle for binding people together, schools became the place for teaching the language as well as "transmitting the knowledge and values needed for successful social functioning" (Pryor, 1992, p. 153). The social work profession as a whole and school social work practice in particular emerged during this same time, "assisting in the process of assimilating and acculturating immigrants" (Pryor, 1992, p. 154) to become citizens. The development of a multicultural economy in the later years of the twentieth century made schooling even more important for personal and national survival.

The notion of a "melting pot"—a single American culture with a single set of common values, customs, and beliefs—was challenged during the 1960s when debate and demonstrations were carried out to affirm and actualize the civil rights of oppressed people, notably African American people (Pryor, 1992). Other countries have had different crucial periods when they had to confront the complexity and diversity of their cultures.

Despite challenges to the "melting pot" metaphor, there continue to be strong efforts to retain an expectation of conformity to a single American culture. A newer metaphor attempting to reflect a unified American culture refers to U.S. culture as a "salad bowl"—one in which diverse elements become a part of an integral whole while still retaining their special qualities. In this word picture, the entire "salad bowl" is the single U.S. culture that has a unifying set of meanings, purposes, and global values such as the beliefs that "all (people) are created equal" and there is "liberty and justice for all." Yet, there is visual confirmation and clear acknowledgment that each element can be able to have and retain its individual set of meanings and purposes (the places where it is *unlike* another culture) even as it participates in making the whole what it is. There may be no need for the melting pot or the salad bowl metaphors, when there is greater refinement of the knowledge, understanding, and acceptance of the existing cultural diversity. The distinct diversity of each person's system, and of the various groups to which people belong, can be acknowledged and valued as providing real and potential sources of strength for the person's overall functioning and well-being.

THE ROLE OF SOCIAL WORKER-LEARNER

The most direct and accurate source of data concerning cultural realities is the person one is working with, in the context of the school culture values. This itself becomes subject to change in the dynamic and personal context of a helping relationship. There is no single profile that fits all members of any specific cultural group. Reliance on the worker's general, acquired knowledge of how Americans behave or how the members of a given ethnic group behave is insufficient. The social worker must be willing to assume the role of *social worker-learner* (Green, 1998). Specifically, the social worker must be able to explore directly with members of the school community, and in the context of their cultural values and lifestyles, the meaning of life events and presenting problems, any history of past or current oppression, and the person's relative acculturation to the dominant culture. In the emerging transcultural world, assessment becomes a set of strategies such as those developed by Helen Brown Miller (personal communication, as cited in Constable & Lee, 2004, p. 107), which provide guideposts to discern both differences and commonalities across cultures.

- Consider all clients as individual people first, then as members of a specific ethnic group.
- Never assume that a person's ethnic identity tells you everything about his or her cultural values or patterns of behavior.
- Treat all "facts" you have heard or read about cultural values and traits as hypotheses, to be tested anew with each client; Turn facts into questions.
- Remember that all members of minority groups in this society are at least bicultural; they have had to integrate two value systems that are often in conflict, and these conflicts may override any specific cultural content.
- Some aspects of a client's cultural history, values, and lifestyle are relevant to your work with a client; others may simply be interesting to you as a professional. Do not prejudge what areas are relevant.
- Identify strengths in the client's cultural orientation that can be built upon. Assist the client in identifying areas that create social or psychological conflict related to biculturalism. Seek to reduce dissonance in those areas.
- Know your own attitudes about cultural pluralism, particularly whether you tend to promote assimilation into the dominant societal values or to stress the maintenance of traditional cultural beliefs and practices.
- Engage your client actively in the process of learning what cultural content should be considered.
- Keep in mind that there are no substitutes for good clinical skills, empathy, caring and a sense of humor.

UNDERSTANDING ACCULTURATION AND CULTURAL EXCHANGE

If there is no single American culture and little likelihood that there ever will be, and if there is diversity among members of each cultural group, what is to be acknowledged and valued? How do diverse members of a society coexist, and how can school social workers understand and incorporate their knowledge into effective cross-cultural practice? Some understanding of the dynamic process of acculturation as an ongoing process that occurs throughout the life span of individuals and groups can be helpful. *Acculturation* means a process in which either we are constantly "adapting to or borrowing traits from (other) cultures" or "cultures (are merging) as a result of prolonged contact" (Merriam-Webster's Collegiate Dictionary, 2000, p. 8). Changes occur as members of a multicultural society transact in extended contact or have extended exposure to other cultural groups, as through the media. This phenomenon is most easily seen in cross-cultural adoption of hairstyles, clothing, music, foods, and selected rituals. The understanding and appreciation of such cultural exchanges are vital for the promotion of professional competence in cross-cultural practice.

This life-span phenomenon is especially true for children throughout their school years. Although some family cultures are similar to that of the school, each child will make some adaptive shifts from one system to the other. Thus, it is common for families to report child behavior at home that is different from that reported by school personnel. In addition, immigrant children may be at a different level of acculturation to the dominant U.S. culture than their parents, and this fact may require special attention in the engagement and ongoing treatment process.

Most schoolchildren will make such shifts between family and school cultures without much difficulty; the child perceives the norms of the school and behaves accordingly. The greater the incongruity between the culture of the individual and the culture of the system in which interaction occurs, the more dynamic the process of acculturation becomes. The potential for conflicts is particularly high when the cultural imperatives of one group are ignored or openly dismissed as irrelevant in person-environment transactions. The social worker should be prepared to recognize, assess, and negotiate resolution of such conflicts. One approach to conflict resolution would include the facilitation of an accurate perception of cultural differences and the open sharing of cultural beliefs and norms by all parties engaged in the social work process.

The dynamic processes of acculturation may be even more keenly observed in situations where there are recent immigrants, migrants from other locales, or where there are specially designed plans for integration that bring students from diverse neighborhoods to a more distant school. The school social worker is well advised to anticipate cultural conflicts and to prepare some preventive planning and strategies to attenuate potential problems.

A FRAMEWORK FOR CULTURALLY COMPETENT PRACTICE

Overview

School social work, as specialized practice, brings together interventions at the micro, meso, and macro levels, and uses a variety of skills so that the entire school community strives to make education work for all children. This is especially important for children in danger of exclusion from effective participation in this process. In a variety of chapters dealing with direct and indirect intervention, practice, policy development, and research, this book develops an integration of theory, supporting the role as it is carried out in schools. At the microsystem level, the social worker focuses attention on the biopsychosocial-educational needs of the child and family. Those actions that take place within the school itself are considered mesosystem interventions because the social worker is typically a part of and working within that system. Macrosystem interventions are those undertaken on behalf of schoolchildren and their families with larger systems such as a neighborhood and community organizations and would include efforts to influence local, state, and national policy and budget developments.

There are a number of major issues that American schools face and that relate directly to their own diversity. One issue is a long-standing one of overrepresentation of minority children in special education (Hosp & Reschly, 2003). The second issue is the achievement gap on standardized tests between minority and non-minority students (Barton, 2003). These issues may have to do with difficult conditions many minority children face. They may also indicate that, from one small action to another, the system itself is sorting out children from kindergarten on, and is systematically failing to recognize inherent capabilities and ways of learning until it is too late. A third issue is that of racial tension in schools (Goldsmith, 2004; Hawley, 2004; Stearns, 2004). School social workers can address these problems through intervention at all levels, including school-wide interventions. In the previous example from a multiethnic high school in the United States a social worker combines group work and community development, working with different subgroups in conflict. She helps each to develop their internal supports, participate in their education, developing conflict resolution and mediation processes to manage intergroup tensions (McGary, 1987). Various chapters of this book present examples of theory and practice of school community needs assessment, consultation, collaboration, inclusive education, coordination of services, family involvement, social skills groups, development of mediation, school responsiveness to risks, and violence and safety programs: all of which can deal with aspects of conflict and racial/ethnic tension. However, the issue is often ignored. In the absence of a way to address the issue it becomes embedded in the fabric of the school, so that both students and staff experience aspects of racial/ethnic tension.

Basic Assumptions and Perspectives

Schools in the United States have always reflected some degree of diversity. Every person has some cultural uniqueness that places him or her in a category apart from everyone else. And so, all social work practice is multicultural (Thornton & Garrett, 1995). The basic knowledge, values, and skills of the profession provide a solid foundation for building a framework for such practice. (See, e.g., Compton, Galaway, & Cournoyer, 2004; Hepworth, Rooney, & Larsen, 2002; Woods & Hollis, 2000.) The social worker, armed with the paradigm of person in transaction with the environment, a concept broadened by practice theorists in the ecological perspective (Germain & Gitterman, 1996; Monkman's chapter 2 in this book), begins with a perspective of establishing a transactional relationship. With the open-system paradigm comes the expectation that clients have key expertise on their situations and that all participants in the service transaction will be influenced to some extent by the others. With a deemphasis on experts solving problems, the social worker now assists participants in finding workable solutions together. The social work relationship is marked by empathy and caring concern; social workers will demonstrate nonjudgmental acceptance and expectation; clients will be aided as far as possible to exercise their rights of self-determination (Compton, Galaway, & Cournoyer, 2004). When the social worker genuinely demonstrates a nonjudgmental attitude toward clients, the distinct diversity of each client system is also acknowledged. The acknowledgment of differences can provide real strength for the client's overall functioning and well being. Value dilemmas will arise, but the social worker would recognize and address these in ways that do not harm client systems.

Learning the nature and meaning of the client's or a group's life situation is of key importance. It is when the culture of the client system is markedly different from that most familiar to the social worker that social workers may have the greatest challenges meeting the ideals of the profession. Not only may the worker's own values, beliefs, and patterns of behavior be inherently different from those of the client, but the client's life experiences within society may not be sufficiently understood by the worker to allow real empathy. However, effective cross-cultural work is more than "skin deep." Within the United States, so much emphasis is placed on race and ethnicity that it is often believed that when the worker and the client are of the same race, all will be well. Even when the social worker and client system have great similarities, there are also inevitable differences. For example, during a consultation session with another social worker, a White school social worker openly expressed her concerns about her difficulty in understanding and working with poor White clients. In that instance, there were cultural issues other than race or ethnicity to consider, such as, perhaps, class, regional origins, neighborhood norms, and so on.

SYSTEMS ASSESSMENT

Practice in school settings makes an assessment of the entire ecosystem and intervenes at the most appropriate points in the system to effect desired change. The focus of treatment ultimately is to improve the goodness of fit between the client and others in the ecosystem, including the social worker. The effectiveness of problem solving depends as well on the worker's understanding of and sensitivity to the client's cultural beliefs, lifestyle, and social support systems. Assessments and interventions may be directed toward a variety of units of attention: the family, specific members of the family, the teacher, or others in the ecosystem. A primary emphasis of treatment is to empower client systems (pupils and their families) and to intervene in other parts of the ecosystem that create barriers to empowerment. And so, the worker who uses the ecosystems framework assumes various roles—enabler, facilitator, coordinator, mediator, and teacher—as he or she moves across system boundaries in dealing with the transactions between the client system and the school ecosystem.

The School Social Worker

One of the essential components of effective cross-cultural practice is each social worker's ongoing examination and assessment of one's own cultural beliefs and values, and how personal biases may impact the social work process (Weaver, 1999). Another part of this process would include working to understand and accept one's own cultural identity. Beginning to think about this activity can evoke surprising responses for the social worker who may not have thought about her racial or ethnic culture. In open forum in a university setting, white students have sometimes commented that they have no ethnicity; that they had given no thought to their "culture," per se. A part of the ensuing discussion included the observation that the white person had grown up in the United States and simply had not had to consider his race or ethnicity at any time in his life. In other discussion, there were notions expressed that "ethnicity" was a reference just to "people of color." Whatever the social worker's cultural identification, it is important that the self-assessment be open and honest. Therefore, it is vital to have a safe place to review attitudes and value conflicts that routinely arise. It could be helpful to begin by making lists, such as "I will/may have difficulty working with" (name: race, ethnicity, religion, sexual orientation), then identifying and reviewing the nature of the anticipated difficulty. The importance of this work is emphasized by Allen-Meares and Burman (1999), who noted that "with the development of self-awareness and cultural competency, biases and discriminatory practices shaped by socialization processes and erroneous beliefs can be recognized and altered, replaced with a focus on client strengths, abilities, and resources" (p. 50).

The School Site/System

Assessment also includes the manner and degree to which the school site and system as a whole demonstrates its attitudes about cultural diversity. In what ways are all children welcomed, their cultures acknowledged and valued? Are first-time enrollments facilitated or made difficult to a point where children are not permitted to attend until all records are in place? How are behavior problems handled? Are proportionately more or fewer children from certain racial or ethnic groups referred for suspension, or for special education evaluation? Are parents welcomed and treated with respect in nonstereotypical ways? A subtle but telling expression of stereotyped behavior from a school:

An African American family responded to their child's elementary school with resentment when a letter from the school regarding their child's academic performance was addressed to the mother only. The information card on file had contained the father's name as well, and a notation that both parents resided at the home. The family felt that the father had been totally ignored and that they had been stereotyped as a "black-single-mother household." Their feelings of resentment needed to be addressed before the real work of problem solving could begin.

The Community System

Cross-cultural knowledge and skill also include becoming familiar with the client community, a part of every needs assessment of a social worker coming into a new school and working out a service plan. One skill includes using available census data and other computerized sources to develop a community profile as to boundaries of the census tract served by the school, recent changes in and the current racial/ethnic characteristics of the community, and other information, such as poverty rates and housing ownership. Is the immediate school neighborhood the primary or only census tract for the students? Are students from other neighborhoods permitted or mandated to attend this particular school? How are such students transported? Can they easily participate in after-school activities? Are there culturally competent community support systems conveniently available in the school or home community to address identified needs?

The community profile enables the school social worker to prepare a cultural map. This can be a useful tool, especially if the social worker lives outside the school's boundaries. The cultural map serves to identify and record the cultural resources of a community (Green, 1998) and thereby link services with the community. Culturally sensitive organizations and services often have been developed within the ethnic community to meet the needs and promote the strengths of Latinos, African Americans, Asian Americans, and Native Americans (Chow, 1999; Gutierrez, Ortega, & Suarez, 1990). The information documented in the cultural map would include culturally sensitive organizations, such as: racial/ethnic service providers, faith-based organizations, volunteer networks, a full range of other community organizations, and small community businesses that provide information and referrals. The skills developed in cultural mapping replicate a small community study and facilitate gaining entry into the community.

School Policies in the Meso- and Macrosystem

Cross-cultural practice that focuses on social justice would encourage critical assessment of structural inequalities that create unjust and oppressive conditions. However, a recent study by Ornelas (2004) showed that most of the social work activities of both professionals and interns were for the benefit of the organization and not necessarily to correct unfair policies. There was little evidence of involvement in developing policy or organizational changes that might address issues such as the achievement gap or overrepresentation of minority students in special education. What is needed is an understanding and support for advocacy. Advocacy is practice that emphasizes policy development and that seeks to assist powerless groups to develop and improve their situations (Jansson, 2003). School social workers must consider diversity at more than just the cultural level, and should address environmental factors that place subgroup members at a disadvantage (Jansson, 2003). Advocates work with others to make school services and policies more responsive to children and their families, communities, and diverse cultures, emphasizing cultural strengths and assets in the development of services and programs.

Advocacy can begin with applied research and needs assessment. How are school policies and programs working to meet needs? There needs first of all to be an understanding of the legal and political systems, the federal, state, and local codes, policies and procedures governing both general and special education, which profoundly impact the state and local education systems. These are discussed in Section II of this book.

Some aspects of how the school community mesosystem actually operates can be addressed through research and evaluation as tools of change (Chapter 12), organizational analysis (Chapter 9) and needs assessment (Chapter 11). Among questions the school social worker might use to assess performance are: What are the numbers and nature of suspensions and expulsions at the school site? What is the demographic profile of students and staff in the school? Is there a match between race and ethnicity of teachers and students? Does racial/ethnic tension exist in the school? Are informal patterns of segregation occurring in the school, for example, in nonstructured settings? What are the numbers and nature of assignments to special education classes or special schools? Is there appropriate parental involvement in decision-making processes for such assignments? Is there a higher rate of problems for particular groups than is reflected among all pupils in the school? Are there appropriate processes and procedures to ensure the safety and equal educational opportunity for everyone?

These various levels of assessment of the entire school community ecosystem enable the school social worker to intervene at the most appropriate points in the system to effect desired change, and to enhance the potential cross-cultural work with and on behalf of the schoolchild and his or her family. Strategies to ensure social justice could include a range of advocacy activity, from regular reminders of stated policies in planning sessions, consultation, and workshops with teachers and administrators to more remedial measures designed to correct observed inequities. Given that the school social worker is a part of the school system, tactics and strategies must be carefully planned so as to maximize the likelihood of effective change.

FAMILY ASSESSMENT AND ENGAGEMENT

Cultural assessment of the child and family requires that the school social worker be open and willing to learn from the client, and to use that knowledge on the client's behalf. In every culture, there exist some expectations and codes of behavior around areas of discipline, time, health, and religious beliefs. A worker's understanding of what these values are, where they fall on a value continuum of traditional to modern, and how they interface with behavioral expectations of the education system regarding children's learning are key elements of cross-cultural practice in school settings.

People from diverse racial and ethnic groups have experienced different forms of oppression and racism in their interactions with the majority culture. Placing these concerns into a cross-cultural perspective involves exploring the client's historical experiences with the majority culture and, if applicable, with migration and immigration. This history may include movement both within the United States and across foreign borders. In this connection, there may be historical conflicts among or between certain cultural groups that will need to be explored, especially as settlement in new areas brings youth and their families in direct contact with other cultural groups they may have sought to avoid in their former communities.

Ethnography offers a useful set of principles to guide the process of cultural assessment of the child and family (Thornton & Garrett, 1995). Such an approach is critical in view of the fact that, because *all* practice has some cross-cultural elements, it would be impossible for a social worker to know everything about a particular culture. Furthermore, it is not sufficient to categorize a client as belonging to one or more cultural groups and assuming—or stereotyping—experiences, behaviors, and needs. The values and lifestyles of individuals are highly personal and are best known by the client. It is within that cultural context that the social worker comes to understand the meaning of life events and presenting problems, any history of past or current oppression, and the client's relative acculturation to the dominant culture. Thornton and Garrett (1995) described the application of ethnographic research to multicultural practice and noted three assessment tools: the open-ended interview, direct observations, and document analysis. The purpose of the open-ended interview is to understand clients and their points of view (Thornton & Garrett, 1995). Questions, which elicit a personal narrative and discussion, are used in this process. Whatever background information the school social worker has can be used to begin. Then, as responses come from the client, new open-ended questions may become obvious to continue and to broaden the social worker's understanding. For example, recent immigrants might be asked: How did you come to move to this place? What was life like in your original country (hometown)? In what ways is life different here? An interview with a family whose child has been referred because of frequent absences might be asked other global questions. Throughout this process, the social worker learns "to be slow to assess and cautious to generalize, understanding that information relevant to one client may not transfer to another" (Thornton & Garrett, 1995, p. 69).

The second skill from ethnography is observation, which can occur in home visits, at community events, or in interviews. These observations would be objectively documented and would particularly include foods, activities, communication patterns, interactions, relationships, schedules, dress, and roles (Thornton & Garrett, 1995). School social workers, whose clients are predominantly of a specific racial/ethnic or religious group, may seek immersion experiences, such as extended visits to the clients' country of origin or frequent visits to neighborhood restaurants or other eateries that cater to local residents, churches, synagogues or mosques, community centers, and community celebrations such as parades, ballgames and picnics. In some areas, local television stations devoted to ethnic/racial and religious broadcasting provide other less direct sources of observations.

Finally, the kinds of documents that can promote cultural understanding include popular and professional literature written about and/or by persons identified as part of the cultural group, as well as any available descriptive information generated by community and government groups (Thornton & Garrett, 1995). In addition, given the earlier patterns of settlement and resettlement of many culturally diverse groups, narrative history, such as that of African slaves in the United States, documents, such as the Emancipation Proclamation, treaties with Native American nations, and federal Indian policies can be helpful in understanding the landmarks in the memories of oppression and racism or liberation experienced by a particular group (Weaver, 1999).

SKILLS OF CROSS-CULTURAL PRACTICE

The social worker needs to understand and be able to:

- Take the perspective of the other in building relationships and coming to common ground, as well as valuing differences;
- Assist students and teachers to do this through both individual and group work;
- Assist particular groups and individuals to build their own identity in ways that also regard the identities and needs of others;
- Assist in the formulation, development, and implementation of respectful school policies and practices;
- Assist in building a school community of safety and respect, where conflicts and differences are resolved in a creative way; and

- Engage in multiple forms of practice, intervening at different system levels (microsystem, mesosystem, and macrosystem levels) to promote respect for cultural differences and address issues of a safe and civil community.

To do this the social worker must develop skills of assessment based on a transcultural perspective, alive to the different experiences of others and other groups. The transcultural perspective focuses on the possibility of developing connections between and among persons of diverse cultural experiences and socioeconomic backgrounds. It reaches out toward a vision of what is common to all cultures, what is different in each, and the communication necessary to manage differences. It assumes that people construct relationships with the hope of securing fulfillment of similar basic needs and relational goods, but may have different understandings and may interact with each other in somewhat different ways (Constable & Lee, 2004, p. 104). The social worker shares this perspective with others in the school—teachers and students and parents—as appropriate. Together, but with many difficulties along the way, they attempt to build a common school culture of respect, appreciation, and valuing of diversity. The development extends to school policies and procedures and of course to every aspect of the school social worker's role. In every society, each with its own inherent racism, with fears of others and fears of difference, this is a challenge. It is implicit in the expectation that the school be a center of cultural development for children and for the community. The school cannot simply reflect the attitudes of its surroundings. Even as it will inevitably reflect these tensions, it must aspire to something better.

Caple, Salcido, and di Cecco (1995) identified some common basic skills for cross-cultural practice in the engagement stage. Early in initial contacts, it is important to spend some time simply getting to know the client, making appropriate introductions, and exchanging small talk. In this activity, the school social worker begins to convey the empathic caring and concern so vital for establishing a trusting relationship in cross-cultural practice. The ethnographic interview process could be helpful in highlighting the importance the school social worker places on getting to know and understand who the client is as a person, notwithstanding the nature of the presenting problem. Obviously if the presenting problem involves a crisis or is heavily charged with conflict and expressions of anger from the client, the ethnographic questions would be postponed to a later, more appropriate time in the engagement process.

Interaction between practitioner and client may also be influenced by parents' perceptions of the role of the worker. In the countries of origin of some immigrant clients, the social work role is not known, and some of these clients may view the practitioner as a government agent. Therefore, the task of the practitioner is to explain his professional role and the function of the services he can provide (Caple et al., 1995). Other basic skills are:

1. *Relationship-Building Skills*. The building of the worker-client relationship is the next task after observing courtesy protocols. Our observation in working with parents is that minority parents often feel powerless to express their needs to professionals if they feel the practitioner will not "hear" them. The differences in attending behavior across cultures and individuals may cause culturally and racially diverse clients to terminate counseling earlier than those from White, European backgrounds (Ivey, D'Andrea, Ivey, & Simek-Morgan, 2007). Thus, an important part of establishing rapport is being an effective listener who is able to demonstrate attention and interest in the client's communications in a manner that the client understands. The practitioner's use of facilitation skills can demonstrate to clients a desire to truly listen. Chamberlain et al. (1985) defined facilitation as short utterances used by the practitioner to prompt the client to continue talking. Ivey and Authier (1978) suggested nodding the head, using phrases such as "m hmm" and "Tell me more," and repeating one or two words spoken by the client as approaches to promote a continuing conversation. These behaviors convey interest and acceptance.

2. *Communication Skills*. Effective cross-cultural practice requires effectiveness not only in listening and facilitation, but also in spoken communication. Ivey and Authier (1978) proposed that one way the effective practitioner can engage in culturally appropriate behavior is by generating a broad array of selective communication skills including open- and closed-ended questions, paraphrasing, reflection of feelings, and summarization. Ivey's (1977) work on cross-cultural skill development (microcounseling) set the groundwork for developing universal cross-cultural communication skills. After using paraphrasing, reflection of feelings, and summarization, the practitioner then repeats the information she has gathered and specifically asks the client if the information is accurate. In our model, we conceptualize this validation step as a "cultural check."

3. *Understanding the Client's Definition of the Problem*. Definitions of problems are culture specific and complex. Sue and Zane (1987) argued that defining a problem is a culturally bound activity. Members of a particular cultural group may not agree with the definition of a problem provided by members of the dominant culture (Gold & Bogo, 1992) or persons perceived by the client as representing the dominant culture. Green (1998) noted that it is critical to recognize how the client views the problem. Pedersen (2000) explained that each person perceives the world from his or her own cultural point of view, and one skill practitioners can use is to perceive the problem from the client's cultural point of view. The nature of the client's worldviews and values interacts with the behavioral norms that the client has adopted (Mokuau & Shimizu, 1991).

4. *Promoting Social Belonging; Without Belonging There Is No Survival*. People live, not simply in their own worlds, but in networks and in communities of belonging. There is a well-known Korean proverb: "As a fish must live in water, so people must live in a society where they find acceptance" (Constable & Lee, 2004, p. 115). Both an understanding of social connectedness and belonging and an ability to promote and develop it are crucial for every level of transcultural practice. In Rita McGary's example in a suburb of Washington, D.C., a large part of her work had to do with developing intergroup connections, so that the groups could communicate and work out problems with other groups and with the school community. In Miriam Mabetoa's example the students felt great solidarity with each other and with their teachers, but not with the national government and the prevailing economic necessities, which demanded migration and loss of this solidarity for economic survival. In Daiva Kuzmickaite's example students had to develop real solidarity with each other, parents with the school, and teachers with each other. They never had this solidarity in the previous system and had to learn it anew. In short, a whole school community had to be re-created, something her visionary principal did perceive as the essence of the school social worker's role in the emergent, new Lithuania.

The problems or issues discussed need to be well identified and conceptualized by the client. The school social worker should ask parents or family units what the problem means to them, their family, and their culture. Various cultures have developed their own indigenous models of service, help-seeking behaviors, and belief systems. The school social worker must have or seek knowledge of the array of culturally specific imperatives and responses available in a particular school's ecosystem to understand the client's cultural definition of the problem. These cultural perceptions may then lead to a decision to work with the entire extended family, respected community leaders, and other natural helpers (Morales & Salcido, 1995).

PLANNING AND SERVICE DELIVERY

Planning for effective service delivery is activated only after a broad-based assessment. There may be urgent needs arising from a crisis situation, however, in general, the plan is made and put into action after the cultural assessment is incorporated with other assessment of the presenting problem. Parents and, to the extent possible, the child are engaged as active members—partners—in the planning and service delivery process, as they were in the assessment phase. For example, no real purpose will be served by referring a client to a worker-determined resource that the client does not value or agree will be helpful. The design of the service plan is consistent with the ecosystems perspective where strengths are promoted and reinforced. The social worker assumes various roles—consultant, enabler, facilitator, advocate, broker, coordinator, mediator, collaborator, counselor, or case manager—as he or she engages any or all parts of the client's ecosystem (Caple et al., 1995; Gutierrez, Yeakley, & Ortega, 2000).

The social worker's role within the school is vitally important in promoting culturally appropriate attention to the needs of individual students as well as for groups of children. Through roles as consultant, collaborator, and teacher, the school social worker imparts information and translates to teachers and administrators the meaning of behaviors that may have cultural links or inferences. In-service training may be a contribution the social worker can make to enhance the cultural competence of the school as a whole. Parents may be asked to participate in all activities directed to improving the cultural competence of the system.

The social worker as advocate would use information gathered in the assessment of the school to promote systems changes that would be culturally responsive to identified needs.

Within the community, the social worker as cultural broker develops linkages with cultural community agencies that may be effective resources for the child and family. Included in the broker role are the skills of coordination and collaboration. Clients who have special language needs will require particular attention on referral to ensure effective outcomes. Linking non-English-speaking clients to bilingual professionals or bilingual services is another form of cultural brokering.

There are occasions in cross-cultural practice when the school social worker may need an interpreter to manage linguistic or cultural communication. Care should be taken in using members of the extended family or others in the client's social network for professional work of counseling and gathering sensitive information. In the general planning for cross-cultural practice in a school and community, the community profile and cultural maps drawn during the needs assessment phase should include notations of where cultural and language interpreters may be located. (For a fuller discussion of the use of interpreters in cross-cultural practice, see Caple et al., 1995, pp. 165–167.)

Competence in cross-cultural social work will only come through continued practice. The open learner who makes errors in calculations and processes can review these—ideally directly with the client or with one's supervisor or consultant, or at least in self-reflection—with a view to correcting those errors or refining one's skills for the next time. A sense of humor helps. Clients who observe the social worker as genuinely seeking to understand and meet the client when he or she is working with them are very likely to be willing to overlook errors of that kind. Like all practice, whether including a new set of principles and considerations or sharpening skills used before, there is a developmental continuum. For cross-cultural practice, it begins with awareness and sensitivity to the needs of others and emerges as beginning and growing competence. As values and knowledge are honed into effective practice these skills can be applied at micro, meso, and macro levels for effective interventions and social change.

References

Allen-Meares, P., & Burman, S. (1999). Cross-cultural therapeutic relationships: Entering the world of African Americans. *Journal of Social Work Practice, 13*(1), 49–57.

Barton, P. (2003). *Parsing the achievement gap: Baselines for tracking progress*. Princeton, NJ: Educational Testing Service. (ERIC document ED 482 932)

Booth, W. (1998, February). One nation, indivisible: Is it history? *The Washington Post*, pp. 18–19.

Brown v. Board of Education of Topeka, 347 U.S. 483 (1954).

Caple, F. S., Salcido, R. M., & di Cecco, J. (1995). Engaging effectively with culturally diverse families and children. *Social Work in Education, 17*, 159–170.

Chamberlain, P., Davis, J. P., Forgatch, M. S., Frey, J., Patterson, G. R., Ray J. et al. (1985). *The therapy process code: A multidimensional system for observing therapist and client interactions*. Eugene, OR: Oregon Social Learning Center.

Chow, J. (1999). Multiservice centers in Chinese American immigrant communities: Practice principles and challenges. *Social Work, 44*(1), 70–81.

Compton, B. R., Galaway, B., & Cournoyer, B. R. (2004). *Social work processes* (7th ed.). Pacific Grove, CA: Wadsworth.

Constable, R., & Lee, D. B. (2004). *Social work with families: Content and process.* Chicago: Lyceum Books.

Germain, C. B., & Gitterman, A. (1996). *The life model of social work practice: Advances in theory & practice* (2nd ed.). New York: Columbia University Press.

Gold, N., & Bogo, M. (1992). Social work research in a multicultural society: Challenges and approaches. *Journal of Multicultural Social Work, 2*(4), 7–22.

Goldsmith, P. A. (2004). Schools' role in shaping race relations: Evidence on friendliness and conflict. *Social Problems, 51*(4), 587–613.

Green, J. (1998). *Cultural awareness in the human services: A multi-ethnic approach* (3rd ed.). Boston: Allyn & Bacon.

Gutierrez, L., Ortega, R. M., & Suarez, Z. E. (1990). Self help and the Latino community. In T. Powell (Ed.), *Working with self-help* (pp. 221–236). Silver Spring, MD: National Association of Social Workers.

Gutierrez, L, Yeakley, A., & Ortega, R. (2000). Educating students for social work with Latinos: Issues for the new millennium. *Journal of Social Work Education, 36*(3), 541–555.

Hawley, W. D. (2004). Who knew? Integrated schools can benefit all students. *Education Week, 23*(34), 41.

Hepworth, D. H., Rooney, R. H., & Larsen, J. A. (2002). *Direct social work practice: Theory and skills* (6th ed.). Pacific Grove, CA: Brooks/Cole-Thomson Learning.

Hosp, J. L., & Reschly, D. J. (2003). Referral rates for intervention or assessment: A meta-analysis of racial differences. *Journal of Special Education, 37*(2), 67–80.

Huxtable, M., & Blyth, E. (2002). *School social work worldwide*. Washington, DC: NASW Press.

Ivey, A. (1977). Cultural expertise: Toward systematic outcome criteria in counseling and psychological education. *Personnel and Guidance Journal, 55*, 296–302.

Ivey, A., & Authier, J. (1978). *Micro counseling*. Springfield, IL: Charles C Thomas.

Ivey, A., D'Andrea, M. D., Ivey, M. B., Simek-Morgan, L. (2007). *Theories of counseling and psychotherapy: A multicultural perspective.* Boston: Pearson Education.

Jansson, B. S. (2003). *Becoming an effective policy advocate: From policy practice to social justice.* Belmont, CA: Brooks/Cole.

Kilty, K. M., & Vidal de Haymes, M. (2000). Racism, nativism, and exclusion: Public policy, immigration, and the Latino experience in the U.S. *Journal of Poverty, 4*(1–2), 1–25.

Longres, J. (1991). Toward a status model of ethnic-sensitive practice. *Journal of Multicultural Social Work, 1*(1), 41–56.

Mabetoa, M. (1996). *An indigenised school social work model for rural communities in Bophuthatswana*. Unpublished PhD dissertation, University of Witwatersrand.

McGary, R. (1987). Student forums: Addressing racial conflict in a high school. *Social Work in Education, 9*(3), 159–168.

Merriam-Webster's Collegiate Dictionary (10th ed.). (2000). Springfield, MA: Merriam-Webster.

Mokuau, N., & Shimizu, D. (1991). *Handbook of social services for Asian and Pacific Islanders*. New York: Greenwood Press.

Morales, A. T., & Salcido, R. (1995). Social work practice with Mexican Americans. In A. T. Morales & B. W. Sheafor (Eds.), *Social work: A profession of many faces* (7th ed., pp. 527–552). Boston: Allyn & Bacon.

National Association of Social Workers. (2001). *NASW standards for cultural competence in social work practice*. Retrieved February 9, 2004, from http://www.socialworkers.org/practice/standards/cultural_competence.asp

Ornelas, V. (2004). *Examining characteristics of school social work macro practice: The academic preparation of MSW students*. Unpublished dissertation. University of Southern California.

Pedersen, R. (2000). *A handbook for developing multicultural awareness* (3rd ed.). Alexandria, VA: American Association for Counseling and Development.

Pryor, C. B. (1992). Integrating immigrants into American schools. *Social Work, 14*(3), 153–159.

Stearns, E. (2004). Interracial friendliness and the social organization of schools. *Youth & Society, 35*(4), 395–420.

Sue, S., & Zane, N. (1987). The role of culture and cultural techniques in psychotherapy. *American Psychologist, 42*, 37–45.

Taylor, R. (2001). Minority families in America: An introduction. In R. L. Taylor (Ed.). *Minority families in the United States: A multicultural perspective* (3rd ed., pp. 1–16). Englewood Cliffs, NJ: Prentice-Hall.

Thornton, S., & Garrett, K. J. (1995). Ethnography as a bridge to multicultural practice. *Journal of Social Work Education, 31*(1), 67–74.

U.S. Census Bureau. (2007). Minority population tops 100 million. Retrieved May 20, 2007, from http://www.census.gov/Press-Release/www/releases/

Weaver, H. N. (1999). Indigenous people and social work profession: Defining culturally competent services. *Social Work, 44*(3), 217–225.

Woods, M. E., & Hollis, F. (2000). *Casework: A psychosocial therapy* (5th ed.). Boston: McGraw-Hill.

19

Inclusive Education and the Least Restrictive Environment (LRE)[1]

Shirley McDonald
University of Illinois at Chicago

Robert Constable
Loyola University Chicago

- The Least Restrictive Environment (LRE) and Inclusion
- A Continuum of Alternative Placements
- Types of Integration
- What Do General Education Teachers Need for LRE?
- Prereferral Consultation: The Problem-Solving Team
- The Process of Making Placement Decisions: The IEP Team
- Preparations for Inclusion of a New Student
- Transition Planning

The policy that, whenever appropriate, children with disabilities are to be educated with children without disabilities demands from the social worker a full range of skills: assessment, teamwork, consultation, planning, and intervention skills. Assessment for the least restrictive environment (LRE) demands an understanding, arrived at with the team, of the range of possibilities available to students. These questions become the focus of the assessment: What are the pupil's general needs? What are her learning needs?

1. William Holley was listed as coauthor of a similar chapter in the previous edition.

What educational resources can she deal with and use? What responsibilities fall to the team, the school, and the family? What joint planning needs to emerge from this discussion? What process should take place within and between all of these to maintain the pupil in the least restrictive environment? The least restrictive environment may be a general education classroom, but that may be more stressful than a more restrictive environment. Without appropriate supports it may be beyond the student's capabilities. The social worker consults with others and intervenes wherever it is necessary as a team member. The goal is for pupils to adapt over time to appropriate learning and socialization tasks through exposure to general education adapted to their learning needs.

THE LEAST RESTRICTIVE ENVIRONMENT AND INCLUSION

The law defines LRE as:

> (i) To the maximum extent appropriate, children with disabilities . . . are educated with children who are nondisabled, and (ii) Special classes, separate schooling, or other removal of children with disabilities from the regular education environment occurs only if the nature or severity of the disability is such that education in regular classes with the use of supplementary aids and services cannot be achieved satisfactorily. (20 U.S.C. 1412[a][5]; 34 C.F.R. 300.550)

The word *inclusion* is not to be found anywhere in the Individuals with Disabilities Education Act (IDEA) legal mandate. However, the principle of inclusion can be found in a presumption that the child with disabilities should participate, to the maximum extent appropriate, in the general education curriculum. Reflecting this presumption, IDEA requires the individualized educational program (IEP) to explain the extent, if any, to which the child will *not* participate with children without disabilities in regular classes and in extracurricular and other nonacademic activities (20 U.S.C. 1414). This principle is developed further in a classic statement by Turnbull and Turnbull (1998) that the schools must include the student in the general education program and may not remove a student from it unless the student cannot *benefit* from being in that program, even after the provision of supplementary aids and services and necessary related services.

The use of the term *benefit* can create a problem. A pupil may derive benefit from something that may not be most *appropriate* for him, that is, geared to his particular needs, including the need for social integration. He might derive more benefit from a more appropriate setting, or more appropriate objectives or learning tasks. This open-ended use of language creates the need for discussion among the team and with the parents and a systematic determination of what is most appropriate and of greatest benefit. This also can create confusion. The presumption of the law, however, is that, unless another environment can be justified as clearly more appropriate, the general education environment, with supplementary aids and services, if needed, is the preferred site of learning.

Research Findings

More students with disabilities are spending some time in general education. Recent research points out that over the last decade there has been an increase from 27.3 percent to 44.7 percent of students with mental retardation (MR) placed in general education classrooms for some or much of the school day. Placement in separate settings decreased from 72.7 percent to 55.3 percent. The proportion of students with MR placed in separate facilities decreased by 46 percent and these proportions were stabilizing (Williamson, Mcleskey, Hoppey, & Rentz, 2006).

Research has consistently pointed out that the decision-making process in development of an individualized education program carried with it a somewhat perverse incentive to place a student in a more restrictive environment. This was documented in a series of studies beginning in the early 1980s (Algozzine, Christenson, & Ysseldyke, 1982; Christenson, Ysseldyke, & Algozzine, 1982; Ysseldyke et al., 1983). By the time the team completed a more formal process, there was an investment in placement. The general education teacher would often have given up, and the prophecy of placement became self-fulfilling. Teachers could be intimidated by students who presented difficult problems and demanded time and energy and became persuaded that special class arrangements could meet a student's needs better.

On the other hand, a series of demonstration projects in adaptive education showed that many children with mild-to-moderate disabilities did better in regular education classes *adapted to their needs* (not simply geared to the middle of the class) than a control group of similar children who had been placed in smaller special education classes (Wang & Birch, 1984a,b). Research on the effectiveness of separate class placement for children with milder levels of mental retardation found that they generally did better academically in regular education (Freeman & Alkin, 2000). For students with more severe MR there were mixed results on academic outcomes, but there were improved social skills and competence (Freeman & Alkin, 2000).Recent studies suggest that even pupils with moderate to severe intellectual and developmental disabilities would have more access to the general education curriculum if educated with nondisabled peers (Soukup, Wehmeyer, Bashinski, & Bovaird, 2007; Wehninger, 2003).

At this point, discussion is shifting from questions of inclusion in a whole-group arrangement to more functional conceptions of disability, that is, what is the *fit* between the person's capacities and the educational context in which the person would function (Wehninger, 2003). While whole-group arrangements might take place 43 percent of the time in general education, other inclusion arrangements, such as one-to-one instruction, small group, and independent grouping might take up the remainder of time. In one study, students in the whole-class instructional grouping were engaged for only 23 percent of time observed, while engagement in other modalities ranged from 43 to 50 percent (Logan, Bakeman, & Keefe, 1997). Soukup et al. (2007) found similar results and concluded that adaptations from the whole-class learning format would be more effective.

These data, together with the fact of overrepresentation of minority children in special education, continue to support inclusion. However, parents of children with severe disabilities tend to favor a more protective (and restrictive) environment (Palmer, Fuller, Arora, & Nelson, 2001). Nor is inclusion always welcomed by regular education teachers, particularly if the teacher is unclear about how to handle the child with special needs or feels unsupported in what she tries to do. Research on teachers' attitudes toward integration/inclusion explains some of this. It is estimated that, although about two-thirds of teachers believe in the general concept of integration, only 40 percent believe that it would be a realistic policy for all children (Scruggs & Mastropieri, 1996). Teachers tend to be more negative about integrating the child with more severe disabilities (Forlin, 1995; Ward, Center, & Bochner, 1994). They also tend to be negative about the impact of children with emotional and behavioral problems on other children (Hastings & Oakford, 2003), but the actual experience of inclusion in their school made a difference (Villa, Thousand, Meyers, & Nevin, 1996) in their confidence that they could teach these students (Leroy & Simpson, 1996). These repeated findings may be stable indicators of teachers' concerns (Avramidis & Norwich, 2002), which are nevertheless subject to modification by experience and by supports within the school environment itself (Carrington: 1999; Janney, Snell, Beers, & Raynes, 1995).

A CONTINUUM OF ALTERNATIVE PLACEMENTS

The concept of a continuum of alternative placements provides language to differentiate levels of restrictiveness. Federal regulations have long mandated that a continuum of alternative placements be available to children with disabilities. The following continuum is drawn from the law (20 U.S.C.1412[a]5), federal regulations (34 C.F.R.300.26), and the Illinois Administrative Code (23 Ill. Admin. Code Ch.I, 226.300) as an example of state education agency (SEA) application of these principles. The alternative placements range on a continuum from the least to the most restrictive:

1. Instruction in regular classes. The child receives basic educational experience through instruction in regular classes. However, these experiences are modified through:
   a. Additional or specialized education from the teacher,
   b. Consultation to and with the teacher by specialists in the child's area of difficulty,

c. Provision of special equipment, materials, and accommodations,
d. Modification in the instructional program (e.g., multi-age placement, grading),
e. Modification of curriculum content or instructional methodology, and
f. Other supplementary services, such as itinerant or resource services (possibly outside the classroom) in conjunction with the regular class placement.

2. Instruction in special classes. The child receives specially designed instruction through a special education class; the child is included in those parts of regular classes that are appropriate.
3. Instruction in special schools. The child receives specially designed instruction in a special school; the child is included in those parts of regular classes that are appropriate.
4. Instruction in the home/hospital. The child receives services at home or in a hospital or other setting because he is unable to attend school elsewhere owing to a medical condition.
5. Instruction in state-operated or nonpublic programs. The child is served in a state-operated or nonpublic facility because her disabilities are so profound or complex that no services offered by the public schools can meet her educational needs.

Supplementary services to make education with less restriction possible may include itinerant instruction, or resource rooms for special instruction for children with learning disabilities, emotional disorders, or speech and language difficulties. School social work is listed as one of the supplementary aids and services or related services that would make LRE possible.

TYPES OF INTEGRATION

Another useful set of concepts in planning for LRE is that of types of integration. These concepts emerged in the early discussion of LRE, quickly became basic to the discussion, and have continued to be useful (Kaufman, Gottlieb, Agard, & Kucic, 1975). There are three types of possible integration of a pupil into the LRE: temporal integration, instructional integration, and social integration. Each expands possibilities and assists in planning to balance the LRE by providing the most appropriate education. Each rests on a careful assessment that includes the student's ability to move from one setting to another, and the support system available and in place to help the student.

Temporal Integration

Temporal integration refers to the amount of time the student with disabilities spends with peers who are not disabled. The underlying assumption is that the greater the amount of time spent by students with disabilities with peers without disabilities, the more socially adaptive will be their social and instructional growth experience. Time spent with peers without disabilities need not necessarily be formal instruction time. It may involve the lunchroom, recess, shared field trips, or other shared activities. Successful temporal integration involves an informed estimate of how the groups of students will interact in informal situations, preparation for both groups and some monitoring of the experience.

Instructional Integration

Instructional integration refers to the extent to which a student with special needs is integrated into the general education classroom or the extent to which the general education curriculum is taught in the special education classroom. Three conditions of compatibility must exist for instructional integration to occur: 1) compatibility between the student's needs and the learning opportunities available in the general classroom; 2) compatibility between the student with challenging physical or emotional needs, learning characteristics, and educational needs, and the general education classroom teacher's ability and willingness to modify instructional practices; and 3) provision by general and special education personnel of an appropriate, coordinated, and well-articulated educational program (Kaufman et al., 1975).

Social Integration

Social integration refers to the placement of children with disabilities in situations where informal relations and friendships with their peers without disabilities are possible. Social integration may involve psychological and physical closeness, interaction with peers, and assimilation or acceptance of students with disabilities in the general classroom (Kaufman et al., 1975). The social worker, having an understanding of group and interpersonal dynamics, has a particularly important role in assisting social integration.

The social worker would provide regular consultation with the general education teacher to facilitate a good fit between the pupil's essential needs and the learning environment. How might the teacher adapt the material and his teaching style to these needs? Perhaps a volunteer parent, a classmate, or an older student might work with the pupil. Perhaps a pupil needs a quiet place, requires an opportunity to talk, or could benefit from more direct interaction with classroom materials or classmates. Perhaps this student would work better in one of the alternate instructional arrangements discussed above.

WHAT DO GENERAL EDUCATION TEACHERS NEED FOR LRE?

What do general education teachers need to successfully include students with moderate to severe disabilities in their classes? Rachel Janney, a teacher, and her colleagues studied this question in an inclusion project in several Virginia school districts. All reported that inclusion was very difficult for them. Several factors appeared to be particularly significant for successful integration:

> 1. Teachers need top-down administrative support, guidelines, and technical support, as well as demonstrated appreciation for their efforts in implementing the guidelines.
>
> 2. Teachers need at the same time to be given freedom to individualize and create their own adaptations, to be allowed to take ownership of the process.
>
> 3. Teachers need hands-on support from "coaches" with personal experience in integrating disabled students in their classrooms. Getting to know these coaches, who would be available to provide hands-on support to them and the integrated students, is preferable as initial preparation than the more traditional, didactic type of presentation or workshop.
>
> 4. Once the students are integrated, the experience of working with and thus getting to know these students well is what makes the final overall response to the integrative experience universally positive. This is true even for teachers who feel that significant extra work is involved in making the inclusion or integration of these students successful. "It was more work, but worth it."
>
> 5. Finally, teachers need a sense that they are not alone in the endeavor, that they have supportive people to turn to, even to lean on. This helps teachers work through difficult adjustments, particularly the adjustment of sharing their classrooms with other professional personnel. (Janney et al., 1995, p. 437)

On the other hand, if these supports are withdrawn the process of accommodating differences can quickly go into reverse. The following case points out the complex of factors in the school community that sustains inclusion or any other large-scale innovation.

> Socrates Middle School in south Florida had been notably successful in its inclusion program. With consultation from the University of Florida, it developed a school culture characterized by shared decision making, collaboration, and teaming. Then a new principal, whose main experience was elementary education and who was less committed to inclusion, came on board. At the same time, the school population and the percentage of students with disabilities rose. Many new teachers arrived, with less experience of inclusion or commitment to it. The numbers of full-time and part-time co-teachers, who had supported the inclusion effort, dropped drastically. And the remaining co-teachers were given expanded responsibilities, including lunchroom duties. The teaching staff became more focused on meeting state grade-level tests. In this perfect storm, the evaluation results over four years concluded that inclusion had not been sustained. (Sindelar, Shearer, Yendol-Hoppey, & Liebert, 2006)

Consultation with the Teacher

The Janney et al. (1995) research points out that general education teachers can adapt to children with special needs when appropriate supports are provided. Social work consultation with teachers and other professionals is a direct and efficient intervention for adapting the classroom environment to better meet the special needs of students with disabilities. The social worker needs to take time to develop an empathic, supportive, and trusting relationship with the teacher, and to become knowledgeable about the problems between the student with disabilities and the students without disabilities. The social worker needs to listen to the teacher's perception of the situation, be aware of the strengths the teacher brings to the situation, and support those strengths. She needs to help the teacher deal with concerns about the pupil's needs and his ability to deal with the student and find a workable educational approach, while being aware of the total educational milieu within which the teacher is functioning.

Social workers must become knowledgeable about the educational process so that their unique skills and understanding of human interaction can be effectively applied in the context of each educational situation. School social workers are in a position to offer teachers additional skills and techniques that can assist them in classroom management and in dealing with individual problematic behavior.

PREREFERRAL CONSULTATION: THE PROBLEM-SOLVING TEAM

Including students with widely diverse needs in a single classroom is a big task. Teachers often cannot deal easily with the wide array of students' needs simultaneously. The social worker and other support personnel may help most effectively by becoming part of a teacher-assistance or problem-solving team. Problem-solving teams have the same multidisciplinary membership as a team conducting a more formal assessment for placement, except that more experienced teachers are usually available as resources or may be members of the team. The social worker is usually a member. The first use of such a team is a meeting prior to an actual referral, when a teacher is feeling the pressure of the needs of a particular pupil. Prereferral consultation (Graden, Casey, & Bonstrom, 1985; Graden, Casey, & Christenson, 1985) is a means of appropriately maintaining a student with mild to moderate disabilities in general education. Prereferral problem-solving teams, under various names, have developed in school districts and in many cases have been promoted by state policy.

Such teams may also provide a variety of other individual and group interventions. For example, the social worker and possibly a speech pathologist may conduct social skills groups. The psychologist, teacher, and social worker may offer role-playing exercises and include students as participants. Any of these specialists may enhance classroom integration of the student with disabilities by adapting his or her interventions to current lessons. The social worker may use playtime, or other less structured activities, as a social group-learning experience in the classroom. Through this team approach the social worker and other specialists can provide students with activities and experiences that they can share or model with peers in the general classroom. Such support personnel can share their expertise with a wide array of other professionals, and these in turn can share what they learn with others (Stainback, Stainback, Courtnage, & Jabel, 1986; Welsh & Goldberg, 1979).

THE PROCESS OF MAKING PLACEMENT DECISIONS: THE IEP TEAM

Once the IEP conference has generally determined which services the student will require to address the identified needs, the final decision of an individualized educational program (IEP) conference is where the student under consideration is to be placed. The placement decision must take into account two often opposing considerations: 1) Which setting can best meet the student's educational needs, and 2) which setting offers the least restrictive environment while giving adequate support to the student's identified educational needs? Unless the pupil has a severe or "low-incidence" disability, many decisions do become a compromise between these considerations. The team would want to maintain the child in as normal a setting as possible, and with as normal a routine as possible, and at the same time pay special attention to needs that require either additional support, or a different, possibly unique accommodation. Both the presumption toward the general education environment and the continuum of alternative placements are crucial to this decision process. If the student is to experience an interruption or a change in his general education program, the less restrictive options that were considered, but not agreed on, must be formally documented. The team must justify why each was insufficient to meet the student's educational needs.

PREPARATIONS FOR INCLUSION OF A NEW STUDENT

The school social worker may assist the teacher in planning the physical location of the students within the classroom. Using the social worker's knowledge of patterns of interaction, students may be regrouped to make the climate more conducive to learning for everyone. Co-teachers, if available, can divide the work, so that different norms for achievement can be matched with different levels of learning. The social worker may work directly with all of the children in the classroom to help them accept the student with disabilities and to assist in the integration of that student into the group. The three basic formats the social worker may use are: 1) an educational format: films, bibliotherapy, or discussion of the specific disability; 2) an affective education approach to help students know and understand one another better so that they can function more comfortably as a group; and 3) a problem-solving approach through formal classroom discussion of problems that affect students. The social worker can help teachers to develop the necessary skills to use these formats in the classroom by modeling and co-leading these groups with the teacher and then consulting regularly in a supportive educational role.

LRE implies a complex process of people working together to support the growth of a student and her best dynamic adaptation to education and learning tasks. The case of Terry is a good example of this process:

> Terry is a 15-year-old freshman student in a large, diverse high school. She has cognitive limitations and generally needs help in containing her high levels of anxiety. She has developed a variety of symptoms including rituals, phobias, panic reactions, and negativism. She is fearful of people looking at her. When things go particularly badly, she is capable of a temper tantrum. Although she is working and making improvements in feeling comfortable in social settings, she will withdraw and shut down in unfamiliar settings with unfamiliar people. She is isolated from peers and has no friends. She would benefit from getting involved, with support and careful planning, in extracurricular activities. She loves swimming and enjoys art. She is on medication, and is gradually learning to manage her anxiety. When she does get upset, she has learned how to cope by asking to take a break and then retreating to an isolated place in the room where she can cool off. She usually recoups within five minutes. Teachers and other students accept this. She needs help going from class to class. In the beginning, the social worker and teachers accompanied her unobtrusively. Gradually a few student aides have gotten involved with this. Later she may manage some of these passages on her own, but she is not there yet. With the exception of her general education social studies and art classes, she works in self-contained classrooms. There is a plan to expand her general education participation, as she feels more comfortable. The social worker works directly with her, coordinating with the family and her psychiatrist, and with her general and special education teachers. A large part of the work is a team effort to support her coping. This is gradually taking place. She is conscious of dealing with anxiety-producing situations in the halls and with other students and gradually getting better at it. Teachers and eventually students are becoming sensitive to her signals when she feels under unusual pressure and needs more time and support to compose herself. They are learning a great deal from Terry.

For the social worker, working with Terry's situation was a matter of consultation, planning, therapeutic intervention, solving problems, and keeping the process moving in a good direction. She worked directly with Terry so that Terry was able to process what she was doing and begin to take control. As Terry gradually developed abilities to cope with anxiety, the social worker helped her to generalize and take credit for her learning.

TRANSITION PLANNING

When a student requires a change to a different program, whether more or less restrictive, the social worker's task as a member of the special education team is to plan for a smooth transition to the new program, and to provide for the necessary resources during this process. Planning this transition includes collaborating with family, key administrators, and teachers. It is essential to explore the student's and her family's reactions and concerns. With this knowledge, the social worker works with other team members to identify alternative programs appropriate to the student's needs. Next, the social worker's support and understanding can be key factors in helping the student adjust satisfactorily to another educational setting. If a child is placed in a specialized setting, the social worker may continue to see her individually. Moreover, the social worker may work with new teachers to help them understand how a particular student functions and how to deal with the student's needs. It must be stressed frequently that follow-up services, sometimes referred to as bridging activities, are essential to the student, family, or teacher for a successful transition. Welsh and Goldberg (1979) developed an eight-step process for such transitions. Although each of the steps by itself is not new, their combined use is significant. If the transition is to be successful, all eight steps need to be incorporated. Only the order can be changed. Otherwise, the vulnerable child has a high probability of not succeeding in the program that she is entering.

1. Assess the pupil's psychosocial and educational gains, her strengths and weaknesses, and readiness for a new program.
2. Assess available educational programs that could meet the needs of the pupil.
3. Involve the pupil in the recognition of the need for change, in the assessment process, and in the preparation of the planned change.
4. Involve the parent in the assessment process and in the preparation for the change being considered.
5. Obtain the commitment on the part of the receiving program to take the pupil and prepare the school personnel who will be involved in the new educational plan.
6. Make arrangements with the new teacher to reach out to the pupil so that she can feel welcome.
7. Be there when the actual move is made, so that it goes according to plan.
8. Offer supportive consultation services to the pupil, family, and teacher after placement. (Welsh & Goldberg, 1979)

All children are unique and have special needs and their own ways of learning. The ultimate payoff for creating more flexible programming often is a more effective educational environment for everyone. The problem is that this new emphasis, together with larger class sizes, can also awaken confusion, uncertainty, fear, and anxiety among school personnel. The school social worker, who has traditionally dealt with socio-emotional factors that hinder or promote the process of education, has much to offer in helping educators learn to understand and adapt to this challenge. The social worker may consult with teachers and other team members about instructional adaptations, reassuring them of the positive payoffs inherent in creating more opportunities for all students through the increased diversity.

Without teamwork that supports pupils and teachers in complex arrangements, LRE is not possible. Supportive planning and teamwork are the keys to success or failure. Students who are reentering the general education system with little or no support are at great risk of dropping out after falling far behind both academically and socially. Transitions into different settings and systems with the school are, of course, crucial tasks for school social work service delivery.

The students most at risk for failure are those with "invisible disabilities," such as learning disabilities, emotional disorders, communication deficits, or mild motor dysfunctions. Such students have previously experienced significant difficulties in the general education setting. These have led to their being evaluated and identified as needing special assistance. The students are understandably anxious about reentering the system where they experienced those difficulties. Such students, without visible signs of their disability, are at greater risk of being misunderstood and thus may be held to different standards than a student with a limp or hearing aid, which signals that they have an identifiable challenge.

As the social worker assesses a student's total milieu, it may become apparent that environmental factors cannot be restructured sufficiently in a given general education setting to meet the needs of a particular student. If the available resources of the general education classroom and teacher cannot be restructured sufficiently to meet the student's needs, continuing to retain the student in that general education classroom, though it would be the least restrictive environment, might adversely affect the student. An example might be a student with a hearing impairment. For this student in a general education classroom, the environment might not be sufficiently stimulating. Perhaps there is insufficient social interaction because there are too few pupils who are skilled in signing. An appropriate recommendation may be to provide an environment with more students with hearing impairments with whom, through signing, the target student can experience more social interaction. On the other hand, to have a mix of experiences through different classes, some with students with hearing impairments, some without students with hearing impairments, might be most helpful.

School social workers have a special opportunity to make the educational process more beneficial to students as awareness of the meaning of the least restrictive environment and school social work practice continues to evolve. School social workers have the skills. The challenge for school social workers is to contribute creatively and positively to the changes in general education that serve the best educational interests of all students. The rights of all students are served by including those with identified disabilities into the general education setting whenever possible.

References

Algozzine, B., Christenson, S., & Ysseldyke, J. E. (1982). Probabilities associated with the referral to placement process. *Teacher Education and Special Education, 5*(3), 19–23.

Avramidis, E., & Norwich, B. (2002). Teachers' attitudes toward integration/inclusion: A review of the literature. *European Journal of Special Needs Education, 17*(2), 129–147.

Carrington, S. (1999). Inclusion needs a different school culture. *Inclusive Education, 3*(3), 257–268.

Christenson, S., Ysseldyke, J., & Algozzine, B. (1982). Institutional constraints and external pressures affecting placement decisions. *Psychology in the Schools, 19*, 341–345.

Forlin, C. (1995). Educators' beliefs about inclusive practices in Western Australia. *British Journal of Special Education, 22*, 179–185.

Freeman, S. F. N., & Alkin, M. C. (2000). Academic and social attainments of children with mental retardation in general and special education settings. *Remedial and Special Education, 21*(2), 2–18.

Graden, J. L., Casey, A., & Bonstrom, O. (1985). Implementing a prereferral intervention system: Part II. The model. *Exceptional Children, 51*(6), 487–496.

Graden, J. L., Casey, A., & Christenson, S. (1985). Implementing a prereferral intervention system: Part I. The model. *Exceptional Children, 51*(5), 377–384.

Hastings, R. P., & Oakford, S. (2003). Student teachers' attitudes toward the inclusion of children with special needs. *Educational Psychology, 23*(1), 87–95.

Illinois Administrative Code 23 Ill. Admin. Code Ch.I, 226.300

Individuals with Disabilities Education Act, PL 105-17. U.S.C. 11401 et seq.

Individuals with Disabilities Education Improvement Act (IDEA 2004). Public Law 108-446.

Janney, R. E., Snell, M. E., Beers, M. K., & Raynes, M. (1995). Integrating students with moderate and severe disabilities into the general education classes. *Exceptional Children, 61*(5), 425–439.

Kaufman, M. J., Gottlieb, J., Agard, J., & Kucic, M. B. (1975). Mainstreaming: Toward an explication of the construct. *Focus on Exceptional Children, 7*, 4.

Leroy, B., & Simpson, C. (1996). Improving student outcomes through inclusive education. *Support for Learning, 11*, 32–36.

Logan, K., Bakeman, R., & Keefe, E. (1997). Effects of instructional variables on engaged behavior of students with disabilities in the general education classroom. *Exceptional Children, 64*, 481–497.

No Child Left Behind Act of 2001, PL 107-110

Palmer, D. S., Fuller, K., Arora, T., & Nelson, M. (2001). Taking sides: Parent views on inclusion for their children with severe disabilities. *Exceptional Children, 67*(4), 467–484.

Scruggs, T. E., & Mastropieri, M. A. (1996). Teacher perceptions of mainstreaming/inclusion, 1958–1995: A research synthesis. *Exceptional Children, 63*, 59–74.

Sindelar, P. T., Shearer, D. K., Yendol-Hoppey, D., & Liebert, T. W. (2006). The sustainability of inclusive school reform. *Exceptional Children*, *72*(3) 317–331.

Soukup, J. H., Wehmeyer, M. L., Bashinski, S. M., & Bovaird, J. A. (2007). Classroom variables and access to the general curriculum for students with disabilities. *Exceptional Children, 74* (1), 101–120.

Stainback, W., Stainback, S., Courtnage, L., & Jabel, T. (1986). Facilitating mainstreaming by modifying the mainstream. *Exceptional Children, 52*(2), 144–152.

Turnbull, H. R., & Turnbull, A. P. (1998). *Free appropriate public education: The law and children with disabilities*. Denver, CO: Love Publishing.

Villa, R., Thousand, J., Meyers, H., & Nevin, A. (1996). Teacher and administrator perceptions of heterogeneous education. *Exceptional Children, 63*, 29–45.

Wang, M., & Birch, J. (1984a). Comparison of a full time mainstreaming program and a resource room approach. *Exceptional Children, 51*, 33–40.

Wang, M., & Birch, J. (1984b). Effective special education in regular class. *Exceptional Children, 50*, 390–399.

Ward, J., Center, Y., & Bochner, S. (1994). A question of attitudes: Integrating children with disabilities into regular classrooms? *British Journal of Special Education, 21*, 34–39.

Wehninger, M. L. (2003). Defining mental retardation and ensuring access to the general curriculum. *Education and training in developmental disabilities*, *37*, 223–234.

Welsh, B., & Goldberg, G. (1979). Insuring educational success for children-at-risk placed in new learning environments. *School Social Work Quarterly, 1*(4), 271–284.

Williamson, P., McKlesky, J., Hoppey, D., & Rentz, T. (2006). Educating students with mental retardation in general education classrooms. *Exceptional Children, 72*(3), 347–61.

Ysseldyke, J. E., Thurlow, M., Graden, J., Wesson, C., Algozzine, B., & Deno, S. (1983). Generalizations from five years of research on assessment and decision-making: The University of Minnesota Institute. *Exceptional Children, 4*, 75–93.

20

Collaboration and Consultation: Professional Partnerships for Serving Children, Youth, Families, and Schools

Christine Anlauf Sabatino
The Catholic University of America

- Collaboration: Integration of Expertise and Services across Professional Boundaries
- The Knowledge Base of Consultation
- Models: Goals, Objectives, Skills, and Techniques
- Phases of Consultation
- Challenges for School Social Work Consultants
- A Mental Health Consultation Model For School Social Workers
- A Case Example for Multiple Consultation Models

Collaboration and consultation are two practice methods that incorporate the professional insights of multiple school personnel and community agencies to improve the quality of school-based student support services. These methods create multi-disciplinary partnerships as well as community linkages with other human services experts, professional teams, and agencies to meet the needs of at-risk student populations. The objective of this chapter is to provide school social workers with conceptual frameworks to guide their collaboration and consultation practice using classical and emerging theories and concepts. First, collaboration principles and practices are identified and discussed, including several typologies of collaboration practice relevant to schools and communities. Second, consultation literature is synthesized in relation to theory, practice, and research from a variety of professions. Six models of consultation are discussed, including the major goals, objectives, skills, and techniques for each. One consultation model is presented in greater detail, because it provides the school social worker with an empirically derived and theoretically derived framework for sorting, understanding, and addressing classroom teacher concerns about students. Finally, the chapter offers a case example for consultation knowledge building and skill development that captures real-life school problems.

COLLABORATION: INTEGRATION OF EXPERTISE AND SERVICES ACROSS PROFESSIONAL BOUNDARIES

Collaboration is a broad term that carries a variety of meanings including teamwork, partnership, group effort, association, alliance, and cooperation. It is not consistently linked with any particular theoretical framework or specific concepts for assessment or intervention. Rather, the term is used as a descriptor in conjunction with work across various fields of practice, populations, problems, and therapeutic methods (See Roberts & Greene, 2002).

Barker (2003) defines professional social work collaboration as the procedure in which two or more professionals work together to serve a given client. In other words, collaboration is a course of action in which various participants work together to achieve a common goal by pooling their knowledge, skills, and resources (Abramson & Rosenthal, 1995). In the schools, it is based on the premise that no one discipline can meet the diverse needs of today's student body because countless factors contribute to students' school success. Indeed, the school system by itself is often unable to meet the needs of some students, but through collaboration it accomplishes collectively what cannot be achieved separately (Graham & Barter, 1999). Pooling school staff expertise and promoting community partnerships is emerging as a highly effective service strategy in pupil services (Dryfoos & McQuire, 2002).

Collaboration challenges isolated professional and organizational work efforts and shifts multidisciplinary work from discrete policies and procedures to holistic student well-being. It requires service delivery systems that create inclusive and flexible processes that break through categorical program approaches (Mizrahi & Rosenthal, 2001). Collaboration challenges professionals to go beyond their traditional roles. It also contributes to the growth and well-being of the participants. The process enhances professional capabilities because collaborators understand that the world is more complex than the one that lies within their own professional boundaries and functions. Participants have more opportunities to deal with the entire context and process of a problem. The problem-solving efforts undertaken and the service delivery systems implemented capture these understandings and act in response to them.

Bridging traditional professional and organizational boundaries for collaboration is a complex process. Successful interdisciplinary and interorganizational work does not magically emerge because collaborators gather around an issue. Collaboration, if it is to succeed, requires that the participants develop relationships of trust. It requires a common view of what is in the best interest of the student, family, and community.

Collaborative decision making means the team shares ownership of problems and solutions, shares skills, uses different thinking processes, and has the flexibility to work on different aspects of a complex task. It opens the way toward attainment of group goals (Thousand & Villa, 1992). Gallessich (1982) and Lopez, Torres, and Norwood (1998) offer the following guidelines, which may be applied to build effective collaboration among school teams and community stakeholders.

1. *Structure*. Each member brings professional knowledge, values, and skills to the team. Efforts to blend multi-disciplinary strategies may give rise to fear that one's own profession will be disregarded, or worse, that there will be turf battles. The underlying philosophy of collaboration calls for various disciplines to plan and act together. In some instances this requires revisions in policy, job descriptions, leadership structure, and accountability requirements. Roles and assignments must be determined. Goals and methods must be clarified. Unresolved conflicts in these areas may result in high tension. These changes, successfully navigated, can bring about a different work culture.

2. *Openness*. A culture of trust between collaborators is necessary. This trust requires recognizing each other's competencies, trusting each other's communications, and relying on each other's work. Mutual respect and understanding of each other's professional values and service orientation are preconditions to successful work and help maintain flexible working relationships.

3. *Self-examination*. Collaborators must commit to systematic reviewing and study of their own processes. Successes and failures both require review and exploration. These efforts ensure group accountability; it is one thing to plan collaboration and another to implement it.

4. *Heterogeneity*. The inclusion of different professions with different styles and perspectives strengthens collaboration through joint planning,

and shared decision making. It supports the school's mission, maximizes resources, and generates new paradigms for assessment, service, referral, and follow-up. The heterogeneity of a collaborative work group must not be so great that it interferes with the structure, openness, and group processes. Merging different professional values and philosophies, however, guards against excessive specialization and fragmentation.

Lopez, Torres, and Norwood (1998) use these same principles but delineate them as three levels of collaborative competencies. *Intrapersonal competence* consists of reflection and self-awareness wherein one acknowledges personal beliefs, values, and thoughts in relation to professional collaboration. *Interpersonal competence* is the development, maintenance, and nurturing of mutual respect and appreciation as the central features of the collaborative relationship (Kapp, 2000). *Interprofessional competence* draws upon groupwork skills to develop a shared vision, awareness of professional differences, and respect for collective power (Bronstein, 2003). Anderson-Butcher and Ashton (2004) describe a variety of collaborative frameworks that are employed to address different types of student needs. *Intra-organizational* collaboration refers to the interactions and communications among school personnel in a specific school setting. These efforts provide direction and strategies to promote positive student outcomes. Familiar examples include school-wide prevention and intervention programs, prereferral services, special education teamwork, Section 504 support services, and alternative language teams (Mishna & Muskat, 2004). *Interagency collaboration* occurs when multiple agencies with various mission statements develop formal agreements to work toward a common purpose or goal. These collaborations usually consist of the school working with local public and private social service, health, mental health, and early intervention programs. Interagency councils developed in conjunction with early intervention programs are an example of interagency collaboration (Mizrahi & Rosenthal, 2001). *Interprofessional collaboration* involves two or more professionals working together to help a particular student and his/her family. This usually takes place when there are co-occurring conditions that might bring about school failure. The co-morbid conditions require comprehensive, integrated, individualized, and supportive services for school success. Examples of interprofessional collaboration include full-service schools, school-linked services, after-school youth development programs, and collaborative partnerships between universities and school systems (Dryfoos & McQuire, 2002; Jozefowicz-Simbeni & Allen-Meares, 2002). *Family-centered collaboration* is born out of the belief that parents are full-time partners with school professionals in determining what types of services meets their priorities, resources, and concerns. Parents have the capacity to implement case management components of service plans and to serve as liaison between the school and community agencies. Family-centered collaboration is strengths-based and empowering (Lynn & McKay, 2001; Sabatino, 2001). *Community collaboration* involves all stakeholders in improving children's learning. It is inclusive and diverse, providing the opportunity for all stakeholders to learn from one another. Sometimes community collaboration takes the form of *locality development* to bring about overall citizen participation in issues; other times it takes the form of *social planning,* wherein problem analysis and problem solving are data driven. In both cases, the overarching goal is to strengthen the community to overcome barriers to youth development and school success (Altshuler, 2003).

As collaboration becomes more important for school social work practice, it is increasingly easier to search electronic journals and search engines to study the professional literature on collaboration. Important scholarship is being developed in relation to graduate education (Sessions & Fanolis, 2006; Tourse, Mooney, Kline & Davoren, 2005), conceptual frameworks (Weist, Ambrose, & Lewis, 2006), empirical research (Jonson-Reid & Kim, 2007; Strand & Badger, 2007), role analysis (Agresta, 2006, 2004), and textbooks (Tourse & Mooney, 1999).

THE KNOWLEDGE BASE OF CONSULTATION

History and Definition

Consultation is an indirect method of professional social work that assists others to become more effective in dealing with their complex work-related problems. Consultation has evolved into one of the most significant forms of intervention in school social work practice. Its scope has widened from providing traditional expert clinical assessment of a child's psychosocial functioning for special education evaluations to strengthening the broader social environments of the classroom, the school, and the community, that promote student well-being and supportive school environments. This has been accomplished by offering a range of consultation services that include education and training, behavioral and mental health consultation, and programmatic and organizational development consultation.

The historical relationship between school social work practice and consultation services has been traced back as far as the turn of the twentieth century (Oppenheimer, 1925). It has been traditionally identified in the literature as an enduring and valued school social work task (Allen-Meares, 1994; Allen-Meares, Washington, & Welsh, 2000; Boyle-Del Rio, Carlson, & Hailbeck, 2000; Carr, 1976; Constable, Kuzmickaite, Harrison, & Volkmann, 1999; Costin, 1969; Meares, 1977; Meares, 1982; Timberlake, Sabatino, & Hooper, 1982). Unfortunately, school social work texts and reference books rarely incorporate scholarship related to the theory, research, and application of school social work consultation services (Bye & Alvarez, 2007; Franklin, Harris, & Allen-Meares, 2006; Openshaw, 2008).

Consultation is defined as an interactional process that takes place between a help-giver and a help-seeker. The help-seeker is experiencing difficulties in performing professional functions with a client, group, or organization. The various approaches to consultation agree that consultation: 1) is a problem-solving process; 2) takes place between a professional consultant and a consultee, who has responsibility for service delivery; 3) is a voluntary relationship; 4) has the objective of solving a work-related problem of the consultee; 5) is a relationship in which the consultant and the consultee share in solving the problem; 6) and helps the consultee become better prepared to deal with similar problems in the future (Caplan & Caplan, 1993, 1999; Kadushin, 1977; Meyers, Parsons, & Martin, 1979; Zischka & Fox, 1985).

Another way to define consultation is to contrast it with supervision and education. In a supervisory relationship, the supervisor holds a position of authority in the hierarchical institutional structure, which requires an ongoing relationship of an evaluative nature with the consultee. In an educational relationship, there is a defined curriculum, which is developed outside a consultative relationship and must be imparted during the instructional process. In contrast, consultation excludes positional authority and a priori educational objectives. It is contracted for on a time-limited basis. The consultant and the consultee have a co-equal relationship. Both are responsible for professional activities and knowledge development. The consultant does not bring an agenda; consultation develops through an exploration of the consultee's needs and the consultant's expertise.

According to Caplan (1970), consultation is a specialized method of intervention. It employs information and concepts that are often unfamiliar to professionals schooled in treatment relationships. It has a specific knowledge base with distinct principles and concepts to guide its methods. Training and certification in one's own profession does not translate into competence in consultation knowledge and skills. Further, helping others with their work problems is a much more complex process than working directly with one's own work-related problems. Specialized preparation is needed so that one understands the consultation process, consultation phases, different models of consultation practice, and the unique functions of the consultant's role.

The Role of Federal Government and Contributions of Allied Professions

School social workers and mental health workers have traditionally utilized consultation as an expected part of their roles. In 1963, the federal government became a major catalyst in the development of consultation theory, practice, and research with the signing of the Mental Retardation Facilities and Community Mental Health Centers Construction Act, PL 88-164. This statute mandated the provision of mental health consultation and education by publicly funded community mental health centers. The National Institute of Mental Health furthered the intellectual base of this method of intervention when it established the Mental Health Study Center. The center developed a series of monographs and supported publications on mental health consultation. The purpose of these monographs was: to assist community mental health centers in the planning, development, and evaluation of consultation; to provide technical resources to universities in developing consultation training programs; and to stimulate research on the impact of consultation (Grady, Gibson, & Trickett, 1981; Mannino, 1981; Mannino, 1969; Mannino & MacLennan, 1978; Mannino, MacLennan, & Shore, 1975; Mannino & Shore, 1971, 1979; Mannino, Trickett, Shore, Kidder, & Levin, 1986; McClung & Stunden, 1970). This body of work remains one of the richest original sources of professional consultation knowledge.

Current consultation literature now has a very eclectic knowledge base. Each of the allied helping professions, such as social work (Kadushin, 1977; Reiman, 1992; Rapoport, 1963), psychiatry (Caplan, 1970; Caplan & Caplan, 1993), psychology (Brown, Pryzwansky, & Schulte, 2001; Erchul & Martens, 2002), school psychology (Conoley & Conoley, 1992; Gutkin & Carlson, 2001; Parsons, 1996), school counseling (Dinkmeyer & Carlson, 2001), and early childhood education (Carlson, Splete, & Kern, 1975; Donahue, Falk, & Provet, 2000) have published texts on the theory and practice of consultation. Further, there is growing literature that documents the need for professional associations to provide continuing education, training, and professional development programs (Allen, & Blackston, 2003; Berkovitz & Sinclair, 2001; Bramlett, Murphy, Johnson, Wallingsford, & Hall, 2002; Fowler & Harrison, 2001; Luellen, 2000; Martens & Ardoin, 2002; Sterling-Turner, Watson, & Moore, 2002; Wesley, 2002; Wesley, Buysee, & Keyes, 2000; Wilczynski, Mandal, & Fusilier, 2000). Seminal works and current research on consultation are found in the professional literature for the various school disciplines (Dinkmeyer & Carlson, 2001; Dougherty, 2000; Erchul & Martens, 2002; Hughes, 2000). Special issues of professional journals are devoted to consultation (see, for example, *Child and Adolescent Psychiatric Clinics of North America*, January 2001, or *School Psychology Quarterly*, Summer 1998). Retrospective reviews analyze consultation literature by the decades (Berlin, 2001).

Indeed, consultation literature in the allied helping professions is now classified according to specific *types* of consultation (Alpert & Meyers, 1983). These are behavioral consultation (Sheridan, Eagle, Cowan, & Mickelson, 2001; Wilkinson, 1999), mental health consultation (Berlin, 2001; Bostic & Bagnell 2001; Bostic & Rauch, 1999), program consultation (Kerr, 2001; Lusky & Hayes, 2001), and organization consultation (Blake & Mouton, 1983; McDowell, 1999; Packard, 2001; Schein, 1999; Sperry, Kahn, & Heidel, 1994; Wilson & Lubin, 1997). The issues of culture and ethnicity are two important recent additions to the literature (Annotated Bibliography, 2000; Fischer et al., 2002; Goldstein & Harris, 2000; Henning-Stout & Meyers, 2000; Ingraham, 2000; Rogers, 2000; Sheridan, 2000).

MODELS: GOALS, OBJECTIVES, SKILLS, AND TECHNIQUES

The Profession and Practice of Consultation by Gallessich (1982) remains a seminal text in its area. The book compares and contrasts six different types of consultation models providing a comprehensive presentation and analyzing each model using specific dimensions. The dimensions identified by Gallessich are the following: 1) the conceptualization or formulation of the problem, 2) the overall or broad goal of consultation, 3) the major methods used by the consultant, 4) the consultant's assumption about change, 5) the consultant's role or source of power, and 6) the underlying value of the model. Information applicable to one dimension of a model naturally leads to the other dimensions of the model to build an internally consistent and specific consultation approach. Clarifying one's thinking on one or two of these dimensions helps to lead the practitioner toward or away from other types of consultation.

We present a brief synopsis of each consultation model in order to assist school social work consultants to select the most appropriate model for the problem.

1. *Education and Training Consultation*. In the education and training consultation model, the assessed problem is the consultee's lack of technological knowledge, information, or skill. The consultant's goal is to provide the needed knowledge, information, or skill. Methods used may include lectures, multimedia presentations, distance learning, Internet activities, instructional materials, structured laboratory experiences, small-group discussion, modeling, and feedback measures. It is assumed that the consultee changes through cognitive learning processes. The consultant is viewed as an expert who values the growing fields of information and technology services to sustain the future of a group, organization, agency, or program. This model assumes that, in a school, the administrators have conferred with the faculty and reached mutual agreement that there is a benefit from the proposed education and training.

The phenomena of student growth, development, and differentiation in the educational context provide limitless subject matter for education and training programs. The breadth of issues that may confound educational progress is endless. Education and training programs are an important and familiar way to impart new knowledge that supports the teaching-learning process. These programs let school personnel see the vast amount of information available to assist them in their roles and tasks. Dupper (2002) offers a framework for consideration when conducting a needs assessment for staff development training and education. Programs might revolve around students' externalizing behaviors such as classroom behavior problems, bullying, peer harassment, suspension, and expulsion. Internalizing behaviors that might puzzle a teacher include anxiety, loneliness, trauma, grief, and depression. Social problems, economic problems, groups of vulnerable students, cultural diversity issues, and parent involvement are other topics that lend themselves to education and training.

After the tragedies of Columbine, Red Lake, and Virginia Tech, school leaders spoke about the importance of information and support provided by consultants. Professional development and training programs are vital to successful classroom climates, the school organization, and administrative structures (Gottlieb & Polirstok, 2005). The literature now documents the value and effectiveness of pre-service and in-service training (Agresta, 2004; Bartels & Mortenson, 2002; Boyle-Del Rio et al., 2000; Curtis, Hunley, & Grier, 2002; Davis, 2003; Rosenberg, 2001; Sawka, McCurdy, & Mannella, 2002; Watkins, Crosby, Pearson, & Jeremy, 2002).

2. *Clinical Consultation.* The clinical consultation model reflects assumptions consistent with a medical model. The need is for an expert diagnosis and authoritative recommendation regarding a client's disease or dysfunction due to the consultee's lack of technical expertise in the identified problem area. The consultant's goal is limited to the diagnosis and amelioration of a particular set of problems in order to restore normal psychosocial functioning or to remediate symptoms. The methods include diagnosis, prescription, and treatment. It is assumed that the diagnosis is outside the consultee's range of competencies; therefore, the consultant's expertise is essential for providing knowledge to bring about change. The consultant may be collegial or directive in relating to the consultee, but in either case, the consultant values the healthy functioning of the client. This model assumes that, in a school situation, the student's problem is so complex it requires a specialist for evaluation, management, and disposition.

School social workers always use clinical consultation as one of their professional roles in the school system, when they conduct the psychosocial evaluation for special education evaluations and for prereferral interventions. Here, school social workers are viewed as the team members with expertise in psycho-social-spiritual factors that must be ruled in or ruled out for a specific learning problem. Given resource problems and the need for workable solutions, where a more restrictive environment is less necessary, prereferral interventions are becoming more and more important. There are also many issues other than those related to special education in which the school social worker might offer expertise (Buck, Polloway, Smith-Thomas, & Cox, 2003; Jackson & White, 2000). Some of these include the ramification of poverty, teacher-student ethical dilemmas, and the impact of trauma on psychosocial and academic development.

3. *Mental Health Consultation.* In mental health consultation the consultant's goal is to increase competencies and strengthen the consultee's professional functioning, with improvement in the client as a side effect. The problem is differentiated by the consultee's need for knowledge, skill, self-confidence, or objectivity (Lambert, Hylander, & Sandoval, 2004). Although methods differ for each of these four problem categories, all use education, facilitation, and support. The model assumes that the consultee has the capacity to solve the work problem with cognitive and emotional support. The consultant brings many sources of power to the role and becomes a model teacher, resource, collaborator, and encourager. The consultant's primary underlying value is the infusion of mental health concepts and principles as a form of mental health intervention. This model assumes that there is administrative sanction and support, which provides the consultant and the consultee with the necessary time to analyze the identified problem and to plan and implement interventions.

The President's New Freedom Commission on Mental Health Executive Report (2003) identifies six goals for transforming mental health in America. Goal 4 specifically addresses the promotion of mental health in young children and calls for improvement and expansion in school mental health programs. Two national centers to conduct research, training, technical assistance, and networking have been federally funded. The Center for School Mental Health Assistance at the University of Maryland, School of Medicine (2005) and the University of California, Los Angeles, School Mental Health Project, Center for Mental Health in Schools (2005) are advancing effective school-based mental health programs. Each center offers an extensive reference list related to mental health practice and research in the schools. The challenge for social workers is to publish findings related to school mental health theory, practice, and research because most of the literature referenced by the centers are by other professions (See *Children & Schools*, Special Issue: Mental Health in Schools, January 2001; Lynn, McKay, & Atkins, 2003).

4. *Behavioral Consultation.* In the behavioral consultation model, the problem is formulated in terms of dysfunctional behavior. The goal is to reduce or eliminate undesirable behaviors and to increase the frequency of desired behaviors. The method used is the systematic application of cognitive-behavioral learning principles. It is similar to methods of clinical consultation with its case-centered focus on the methods of diagnosis, prescription, and treatment. The method involves the following elements: the problem is defined in behavioral terms; behaviors are observed and recorded; antecedents and consequences are analyzed; and, reinforcement contingencies are designed and implemented. When these activities are completed, the consultant withdraws and the consultee assumes responsibility for the client's behavioral management program. The model assumes

that change is possible with the consultant's empirical and rational expertise, which is the consultant's source of power. The behavioral consultation model places great value on technology and the scientific method. It assumes that the teacher is willing to collaborate with the consultant in recording observed behaviors, implementation of behavior modification strategies, evaluation of behavior changes, and integration of a new behavioral management program.

Today behavioral consultation is a common strategy used in the schools to provide treatment and support to an increasing number of students with behavioral challenges that interfere with their learning (Wilkinson, 2003). It has taken on far greater importance since Congress mandated the development of functional behavioral assessments (Raines, 2002), underscoring the worth of behavioral interventions. In fact, recent literature is replete with materials that document its use for individual students, classroom-wide interventions, home-school partnerships and whole school programs (Cowan & Sheridan, 2003; Lewis & Newcomer, 2002; Luiselli, 2002; Metzler, Biglan, Rusby, & Sprague, 2001; Noell, Duhon, Gatti, & Connell, 2002; Sheridan & Kratochwill, 2007; Sheridan, Clarke, Knoche, & Edwards, 2006). The Department of Education, Office of Special Education Programs, Technical Assistance Center on Positive Interventions & Supports (2005) offers technical assistance guides, literature searches, online articles and school-wide positive behavior support literature. Again, the challenge is for social workers to publish their practice and research perspective in this area of consultation.

5. *Program Consultation* formulates the consultation issue in terms of a lack of expertise needed to successfully carry out specialized services designed to benefit a target population. Methods used vary considerably because of the diversity of programs. Generally, they include some or all of the following elements: needs are assessed, specific goals are delineated, and methods to achieve identified goals are selected. Then resources are identified, benefits assessed, and constituencies identified. Administrative procedures are established. Staffing needs and funding guidelines are determined. Later, outcomes are evaluated and new programs are integrated with existing services and programs. The consultant assumes that theory and research is the foundation for changes made to alter or develop a program. The consultant is viewed as an expert who values the scientific approach to program planning or supports the values reflected in the program.

Although program development is traditionally the role of school administrators, recent surveys of school social work roles validate that program development is a vital component of practice (Agresta, 2004; Boyle-Del Rio, Carlson, & Laibeck, 2000; Constable, Kuzmickaite, Harrison, & Volkmann, 1999). Research has found that some federally mandated programs are not in compliance when school social workers are not present (Sabatino, 2001). School social workers must expand their thinking and view themselves as program planners who intend to influence education, based on policies that drive program development.

6. *Organizational Consultation*. Organizational consultation concerns may fall into several domains. These are technological, structural, managerial, and human relations. The goal is to increase organizational productivity and morale. The methods used by organizational consultants vary widely depending on the domain of concern. In some instances, teams composed of consultants with certain specialties are used. Consultants assume that change is brought about by empirical knowledge and re-education. The consultant's authority comes from expert knowledge. In addition, the consultee usually identifies with the consultant's area of expertise and the consultant's role performance. Organizational consultants base their models on the values inherent in technological information and human development services. As with education and training consultation, this model assumes that members of the organization agree that the services of a consultant are of value.

Organizational consultation is a new role for school social workers (Packard, 2001). However, there are reviews of the literature and outcome studies that document that organizational consultation yields robust effects (Matheny & Zimmerman, 2001; Reddy, Barboza-Whitehead, Files, & Rubel, 2000). School social workers are well situated to provide this type of consultation given their ecological approach, with the assumption that students and their families are embedded in social and environmental contexts. With this analytical framework, they are capable of introducing strategic change for the entire school organization (Mishna & Muskat, 2004).

Curtis and Zins (1981) offer another framework for sifting consultation theory and practice to select an appropriate consultation practice model. They ask the following questions: *What should be changed?* (value orientation); *For whom is change intended*? (target); *Through whom is change brought about?* (operational level); *How will change take place?* (consultative methods); and *What is the style of interpersonal interaction between the consultant and the consultee?* (consultant role). Gallessich (1982) would vary these questions by focusing on the *problem definition,* the *goal* of consultation, the *target* of change, the requisite *skills* and *techniques*, and the *role* of the consultant. Both of these models, however, emphasize a common *process* of consultation, matching the *type* of consultation to the *needs* of the situation.

PHASES OF CONSULTATION

Regardless of the theoretical framework or type of consultation, all models of consultation have a common set of phases. Gallessich (1982) identifies the following phases of the consultation process. Each needs to be explored in relation to both the school social work consultant's and the consultee's roles and responsibilities. Each may have several subphases, and there is fluidity among the phases (Tindel, Parker, & Hasbrouck, 1992). The value of identifying these phases is that it provides a common framework for reference and discussion if the consultation process becomes unproductive, thereby helping the consultation to remain focused. The phases are presented along with a series of questions adapted from Gallessich to reflect issues relevant to the development of school-based consultation service.

1. **Preliminary exploration**
   - What are the school's needs?
   - What are the consultant's qualifications regarding these needs?
   - Is there a satisfactory fit between the consultant and the consultee?
   - Are there any value conflicts among the parties?
2. **Negotiation of a contract**
   - What are the terms for working together?
   - Is this a formal or legal contract?
   - Is this an informal or oral contract?
   - Does the contract include consultation goals, length of contract, consultant responsibilities, school responsibilities, consultant's role, and evaluation or termination procedures?
3. **Entry**
   - Where will consultation take place?
   - What physical, social, or psychological barriers to entry are encountered?
   - What school dynamics might be a barrier to being trusted and accepted in this school system?
   - What tensions arise in the course of building a relationship with the consultee?
4. **Diagnosis of problems or needs assessment**
   - Do the consultant and consultee collaborate in data collection?
   - Is assessment seen as an ongoing activity?
   - Has the entire context for consultation been examined or is the assessment narrowly focused on the presenting problem?
   - Have hard data and soft data been used for the assessment?
   - Has more than one theoretical perspective been used to sort and analyze the problem? Is further data gathering required?
5. **Goal setting**
   - Who has proposed the goal(s)?
   - Have the merits of a number of goals been evaluated?
   - Are there realistic solutions to the problem?
   - If not, is the consultant prepared to terminate the consultation?
   - Can the goals be reached by the school staff without consultation?
   - How urgent is it to achieve a goal?
   - How successful might this goal be?
   - How feasible is a goal?
   - What is the cost of this goal in time and money?

6. **Exploration and selection of alternative consultation approaches**
   - What is the best method for achieving the goal?
   - Have alternative methods been generated and examined?
   - Is there a clear definition of the objective?
   - Is there a clear plan of action to reach the objective?
   - What problems are anticipated?
   - Which school personnel are responsible for which actions?
   - Have the consultant's role, function, and responsibility been delineated from those of the consultee's?
7. **Implementation of intervention**
   - Does implementation involve the consultant?
8. **Evaluation of outcomes**
   - To what degree have the goal(s) been achieved?
   - Is evaluation one of the consultant's functions?
   - What factors contributed to the positive and the negative outcomes?
   - Is the evaluation informal and anecdotal?
   - Is the evaluation formal and quantifiable?
   - Has the consultant's performance been evaluated?
9. **Institutionalization of changes**
   - Have new procedures or behaviors been incorporated to become standard practice?
   - Does this change require additional training and monitoring?
   - Does this change require that incentives be institutionalized?
10. **Termination of consultation**
    - What are the criteria for termination?
    - What are the emotional reactions surrounding the termination?
    - Will termination occur through a series of steps?
    - Are there follow-up plans to termination?

CHALLENGES FOR SCHOOL SOCIAL WORK CONSULTANTS

The interpersonal relationships established during these phases are crucial to the success of the consultation services. It is important for the consultee to feel comfortable, accepted, and respected. The consultant establishes this atmosphere by being trustworthy, accepting, respectful, nonjudgmental, and collegial. Throughout the consultation phases, it is important to remember that it takes time for a consultee to build a relationship, to understand what consultation is, and to learn how to use it. The consultee needs to learn how to present relevant information, what kind of help to expect from the consultant, and what the consultant has to offer. Sometimes the consultee will have a hidden agenda in consultation. For example, the consultant might be invited into a conflict as an "expert" to support one viewpoint. In other instances, the consultant might be expected to share the emotional burden of making a difficult decision, or to enable someone to abdicate responsibility for a difficult problem. Sometimes there is a wish to substitute consultation services for clinical, programmatic, or organizational efforts. In any case, there may need to be several preliminary meetings for the consultee to understand the processes and use them effectively.

It is important that the consultee understand what consultation is and how it is to be used. Caplan and Caplan (1993) note that what is labeled as "resistance" may only be a lack of professional preparation for consultation. Or it may signal the belief that asking for consultation is an admission of professional incompetence. To overcome these barriers, the consultee may be reminded that problems often are complicated and confusing and that the request for consultation services is a sign of professional competence. No significant problem can be resolved quickly.

Further, it is important to distinguish consultation from therapy. In consultation, material is discussed that is often delicate in nature, personal to the consultee, and risky to share with others. In order to meet the agreed-upon goal of solving work-related problems, it is not appropriate for the consultant to interpret or reflect unconscious or personal material or to foster the development of a therapeutic relationship. In fact, these traditional elements of psychodynamic intervention distract the consultant and the consultee from their central task of focusing on the presenting problem.

Thus, in a school setting the consultation relationship is a *coordinate* relationship, wherein two differently prepared professionals concentrate on helping students reap the full benefit of their education. The faculty and school system are entirely competent and retain full authority and responsibility. They are free to accept or reject the consultant's ideas and recommendations. In fact, it is best to avoid advice-giving and jargon. These imply some level of ignorance on the part of the consultee. They may be seen as a devaluation of the consultee's abilities. To reinforce this coordinate relationship, it is important to develop a joint language for communicating with each other about work-related difficulties by exploring the semantic meanings of the consultee's narrative (Saleeby, 2006) and by using language that is understandable and acceptable to him or her. The nature of the concepts communicated must fit the culture of the school and teacher. The goal is to enable the teacher or school system to deepen the understanding of those aspects of the presenting problem that are puzzling.

A MENTAL HEALTH CONSULTATION MODEL FOR SCHOOL SOCIAL WORKERS

A practice model contains rules for practitioners in defining and assessing target problems and delineating sequences of interventions to be used in attempts to alleviate problems (Reid, 1979). A model organizes discrete principles, methods, and procedures into coherent strategies. Models are bridges between theory and practice, the translation of theory into how-to-do-it descriptions of activities.

The following *mental health consultation* model has been adapted for school social workers from Caplan (1993). It is a research-based and practice-based model that has been significantly effective for providing remedial and preventive services within private and public school systems (Sabatino, 1986). Specifically, this model builds on one of Caplan's four specific categories of mental health consultation, *consultee-centered case consultation*. The author has found that the theory and practice of consultee-centered mental health consultation may be easily applied to school social work consultation. Further, the paradigm is easy to teach in staff development workshops to groups of school social workers.

According to Caplan's theory, there are four reasons why a teacher might have a problem with a student: need for ***knowledge***, need for ***skill***, need for ***self-confidence***, and need for ***objectivity*** (Caplan, 1970). These four reasons provide the core concepts of the model.

1. *Need for Knowledge*. The school social work consultant is able to assess the need for knowledge when, owing to lack of specific psychosocial knowledge, the teacher misunderstands or draws erroneous conclusions about a student's puzzling behavior. In some instances, the teacher possesses the professional knowledge necessary to understand the situation but does not see its relevance or application to this particular child and problem. Interventions consist of imparting missing general information or sharing specialized expertise.

Caplan takes the position that the need for knowledge should be the least frequent reason for consultation because the consultee is a trained professional. In a regular classroom setting, however, the teacher's primary training is in elementary or secondary education. Sometimes teachers are lacking in complex theoretical knowledge about the cognitive, emotional, social, or interactional processes that accompany a child's problem in the teaching-learning process. Other times a specific problem arises that would rarely be part of a teacher's training or expertise. It is inevitable that teachers will be confronted with experiences for which they received no professional education. Trauma and child abuse are examples. In such instances, the task of the consultant is to impart the missing information in the most economical manner. This may call for continued individual consultation but also lends itself to in-service workshops that disseminate information more broadly and may benefit the entire faculty and administration.

2. *Need for Skill*. Sometimes the consultant will become aware that the teacher possesses the requisite professional knowledge to understand the presenting problem but does not possess the ability to apply appropriate

skill to solve it. It is one thing to discern cognitively the difficulty, but quite another matter to call forth and exercise the appropriate problem-solving skill. The main task for the consultant is to explore with the teacher how he or she might develop skill. The teacher might invoke the assistance of colleagues, the principal, or a specialist. By offering to model skill development, there is a risk that the consultant may threaten the collegial relationship and be perceived to be violating the norms of the role. Sometimes the skill necessary is fairly obvious, and it is a matter of support for the teacher's efforts to acquire it. At other times, the consultant may want to suggest to the teacher that he or she review the case with the principal or another teacher, who can assist in developing techniques of intervention. In some instances, however, the social worker is the ideal staff person for skill development. For example, the Individual Family Service Plan calls for assessment of family priorities, resources, and concerns. In many school districts, teachers, who often lack basic family interviewing skills, are expected to assist in the development of this document. Tasks such as interviewing families and helping them to identify their views of their child's developmental delay are very challenging. The social worker, as a team member, might assist the teacher to do this.

3. *Need for Self-Confidence*. There are instances when the teacher demonstrates adequate psychosocial knowledge and skill performance but does not use it because of personal insecurities or lack of self-confidence. This problem may be detected in the teacher's tentativeness and uncertainty, or worse, in feelings of incompetence and worthlessness. In this case, the consultant listens to the teacher describe how the situation was handled and provides support for these work efforts. Another intervention centers on assisting the teacher to seek out experienced faculty members who have had similar experiences and, thereby, engender the very powerful support of the "all in the same boat" phenomenon.

A heartrending illustration of this concept occurs when a student suddenly dies. One often hears teachers recount catastrophic losses they have suffered, where they were when it occurred, how they reacted, what they thought, how they felt, what was helpful, and what was not helpful. Their students may experience the same range of reactions. Supporting teachers in recognizing the linkages between their experiences and students' struggles offers them a way to gain confidence in using themselves effectively to help students express their feelings and perceptions and to mourn.

4. *Need for Objectivity*. Lack of objectivity is defined as the teacher's loss of professional focus by becoming too close or too distant from the child or the family. When this occurs, conscious or unconscious factors invade the teacher's role functioning, distort perception, and cloud judgment. Five causes for loss of objectivity are 1) direct personal involvement, 2) simple identification, 3) transference, 4) characterological distortions, and 5) theme interference (Caplan, 1970; Caplan & Caplan, 1993, 1999). *Direct personal*

involvement takes place when the teacher's professional relationship evolves into a personal relationship. The teacher receives personal satisfaction rather than professional satisfaction in relation to the child. The task of the consultant is to help the teacher control the expression of personal needs in the workplace and develop professional goals and a professional identity. Modeling empathy, while maintaining appropriate distance, is one technique of intervention to be used. Another is to recount a similar experience the consultant has had in mastering personal feelings. When it is not feasible to discuss directly the teacher's over-involvement and the difficulties that come from that, the problem can be reversed and reframed. What would the teacher do if the child or family might wish to have a personal relationship with him or her to the exclusion of classmates? It may be easier to discuss the ramifications of a direct personal relationship in this way.

When the teacher describes a problem in such a way that one person is perceived in glowing terms and the other person is perceived in derogatory, stereotypic terms, a tendency toward *over-identification* with a pupil might be evident. One might expect the teacher to possess some similar characteristics or experiences to the person seen in sympathetic terms. The same process can also result in excessively *negative or hopeless characterizations* of the subject. The task of the consultant is to weaken the identification by having the teacher re-analyze the data about the entire situation. As this process unfolds, the consultant helps the teacher to see individuals as separate and unique people rather than extensions of the teacher. *Transference* problem*s* occur when the teacher imposes a preordained set of attitudes, perceptions, or expectations derived from the teacher's own life experiences that block an objective assessment and work with the child and family. The danger is that the teacher will use the child to act out or resolve the teacher's own unconscious conflicts or fantasy. One way to detect this problem is the teacher's paucity of data to support assertions made about the child. The consultant identifies the conflict that has stimulated the teacher's transference reaction, and then asks the teacher to observe the child more closely in this area. Sometimes the newly collected observational data will help the teacher identify the conflict. In other cases, the best the consultant can do is to offer emotional support, allow the teacher to vent feelings, and steer the teacher toward more appropriate outlets for the conflict.

The concept of *theme interference* refers to a teacher's temporary ineffectualness in a limited segment of the work field when suddenly confronted by a situation that is confusing and upsetting. Caplan and Caplan (1993, p. 122) postulate that an unresolved life experience or a fantasy persists in the consultee's "preconscious or unconscious as an emotionally toned cognitive constellation . . . a theme." A major component of the theme is its repetitive quality that links an initial category to an inevitable outcome. The teacher is reminded of an unresolved conflict and associates it with the current situation. This condition is perceived to lead to one particular outcome, usually involving pain and suffering. For example, a teacher may say, "Immigrant children whose parents do not learn English [initial category] will not succeed in school [inevitable outcome]." One intervention technique to use with theme interference is to influence the teacher to change his or her perceptions about the child so as to remove the initial category. This "unlinking" frees the child from the inevitable outcome. An unintended consequence of the technique, however, may be the consultee's displacement of the conflict onto another child. To avoid this problem the consultant can use a technique called *theme interference reduction*. The consultant accepts the placement of the child in the initial category but, through examination of the specifics of the child's case, influences the teacher to see that the inevitable outcome is only one of several possible outcomes for the child. In fact, the data often suggest a different outcome.

In all professions, some members have serious psychiatric problems that Caplan and Caplan (1993, p. 119) label "characterological distortions of perception and behavior." The work-related difficulty may largely be due to the teacher's own mental health problems. The task of the consultant is to support the teacher's defense structure and lower anxiety so that the teacher maintains an optimal level of professional functioning. The goal is to help the teacher maintain control over impulses, fantasies, and regression and develop appropriate role boundaries.

A CASE EXAMPLE FOR MULTIPLE CONSULTATION MODELS

You are the school social worker at Washington-Lee High School (W&L), which has an enrollment of 1,500 students. W&L is located in a large metropolitan community in the Mid-Atlantic region, where employment revolves around federal and state government, the military, tourism, national corporations, and private businesses. The high school offers a rigorous academic curriculum that includes many advanced placement courses and the International Baccalaureate Program; however, parents of "students in the middle" have expressed concern about the lack of attention and resources for their children. The school is academically ranked 15th of 150 high schools in the region. At the same time, 37 percent of the student body is eligible for reduced or free lunch. Many of these students are first generation immigrants from Central America, although the school population is evenly divided among African Americans, Asians, Caucasians, and Hispanics, with no one group in the majority.

You are a member of the multidisciplinary special education evaluation team. The principal often asks you to help with issues that arise in the high school that are not related to your clinical assessment role. The faculty perceives you as a valuable member of the professional school community and seeks your input on a range of issues. This year you have been asked to serve on the school's cultural diversity committee.

Cas is a 14-year-old freshman. He has been referred to you by his English teacher for academic and behavioral problems. He has great difficulty with term paper assignments and struggles with any form of written expression. In

> class, Cas has taken the role of class clown and often avoids using class time to draft his papers and, in fact, disrupts the others during this time. In meeting with Cas and his family, you learn the following: Mr. and Mrs. Choudry emigrated from India to the United States ten years ago with their two children. Cas has a younger sister, Sala, who is 12-years old and in the seventh grade. The father is a successful professional, and the mother has remained at home to care for the children. The family has an economically stable, middle-class lifestyle. They have lived in the same neighborhood for the last six years, where they have been well accepted and integrated into a predominately white community. The children have attended private elementary and middle schools in the community. Cas enrolled in the local public high school, where he hoped to become a member of the cross-country team and to compete in regional meets because he is a gifted long-distance runner. In the eighth grade, Cas's academic work began to slip. He failed one of the sections of the standards of learning test mandated by the state department of education and required special classes to pass the exam. At the end of the first quarter in high school, he received failing grades in English and History, two Cs and one B. Though Cas entered high school with some of the same classmates from the private middle school he attended, he found himself now being excluded by them. Cas injured his knee at the beginning of the school year and was unable to try out for any fall sports teams. According to his parents, Cas has begun to hang around with the wrong crowd, and they are worried that, in addition to poor academic performance, Cas may get into drugs or into trouble with the law. He refuses to attend religious services with his family. This is very painful for Mr. and Mrs. Choudry, who strongly believe that religion is a central feature of one's daily life activities. Sala is performing well academically, but her mother has noticed that she is no longer invited over to friends' homes as much as she used to be, nor is she inviting classmates to their house. Mr. and Mrs. Choudry do not understand what is happening or how to make things better for their children (Plionis & Sabatino, 1998).

This brief vignette provides the school social worker with a variety of consultation opportunities. Clinical consultation is required, if Cas is referred for a special education evaluation. Behavior consultation might be useful in changing Cas's classroom actions, and mental health consultation might be helpful in expanding the teacher's understanding of Cas's bicultural experiences during adolescent development. Honoring ethnic, racial, and cultural differences among the student population might call for program consultation through the school's cultural diversity committee, while responding to the "students in the middle" might call for organizational consultation at the school system level. Further, there might be the need for interagency collaboration to bring various resources from the community, such as the recreation department, the career center, and private businesses, into the school for enrichment programs and after-school activities. What other consultation models do you think might be applied to this case vignette? Which would be more important, and which less important as you approached this situation?

CONCLUSION

In this age of evidence-based practice, we must document school social work effectiveness (Berkovitz, 2001; Graham, 1998; Mattison, 2000; Medway & Updike, 1985; Rones & Hoagwood, 2000). Collaboration and consultation are well-established methods of delivering professional services to students, families, schools, and the community. The materials presented in this chapter offer a rich theoretical, conceptual, and empirical foundation to guide practice and research in collaboration and consultation.

References

Abramson, J. S., & Rosenthal, B. B. (1995). Interdisciplinary and interorganizational collaboration. In R. L. Edwards and J.G. Hopps (Eds.), *Encyclopedia of social work* (19th ed., Vol.2; pp. 1479–1489). Washington, DC: National Association of Social Workers Press.

Agresta, J. (2004). Professional role perceptions of school social workers, psychologists, and counselors. *Children & Schools, 26*(3), 151–163.

Agresta, J. (2006). Job satisfaction among school social workers: The role of inter professional relationships and professional role discrepancy. *Journal of Social Service Research, 33*(1), 47–52.

Allen, S., & Blackston, A. (2003). Training preservice teachers in collaborative problem solving: An investigation of the impact on teacher and student behavior change in real-world settings. *School Psychology Quarterly, 18*(1), 22–51.

Allen-Meares, P. (1994). Social work services in schools: A national study of entry-level tasks. *Social Work, 39*, 560–565.

Allen-Meares, P., Washington, R. O., & Welsh, B. (2000). *Social work services in schools* (3rd ed.). Boston: Allyn and Bacon.

Alpert, J. L., & Meyers, J. (1983). *Training in consultation: Perspectives from mental health, behavioral, and organizational consultation*. Springfield, IL: C.C. Thomas.

Altshuler, S. (2003). From barriers to successful collaboration: Public schools and child welfare working together. *Social Work, 48*(1), 52–63.

Anderson-Butcher, D., & Ashton, D. (2004). Innovative models of collaboration to serve children, youths, families, and communities. *Children & Schools, 26*(1), 39–54.

Annotated bibliography for the mini-series on multicultural and cross-cultural consultation in schools. (2000). *School Psychology Review, 29*(3), 426–28.

Barker, R. (2003). *The social work dictionary* (5th ed.). Washington, DC: National Association of Social Workers Press.

Bartels, S., & Mortenson, B. (2002). Instructional consultation in middle schools: Description of an approach to training teachers to facilitate middle school teams. *Special Services in the Schools, 18*(1), 1–21.

Berkovitz, I. H. (2001). Evaluations of outcome in mental health consultation in schools. *Child & Adolescent Psychiatric Clinics of North America, 10*(1), 93–103.

Berkovitz, I. H., & Sinclair, E. (2001). Training program in school consultation. *Child & Adolescent Psychiatric Clinics of North America, 10*(1), 83–92.

Berlin, I. N. (2001). A retrospective view of school mental health consultation. *Child & Adolescent Psychiatric Clinics of North America, 10*(1), 25–31.

Blake, R., & Mouton, J. S. (1983). *Consultation: A handbook for individual and organization development* (2nd ed.). Reading, MA: Addison-Wesley.

Bostic, J. Q., & Bagnell, A. (2001). Psychiatric school consultation: An organizing framework and empowering techniques. *Child & Adolescent Psychiatric Clinics of North America, 10*(1), 1–12.

Bostic J. Q., & Rauch, P. K. (1999). The 3 R's of school consultation. *Journal of American Academy of Child & Adolescent Psychiatry, 38*(3), 339–341.

Boyle-Del Rio, S., Carlson, R., & Hailbeck, L. (2000). School personnel's perception of the school social worker's role. *School Social Work Journal, 25*(1), 59–76.

Bramlett, R., Murphy, J., Johnson, J., Wallingsford, L., & Hall, J. (2002). Contemporary practices in school psychology: A national survey of roles and referral problems. *Psychology in the Schools, 39*(3), 327–335.

Bronstein, L. (2003). A model for interdisciplinary collaboration. *Social Work, 48*(3), 297–306.

Brown, D., Pryzwansky, W. B., & Schulte, A. C. (2001). *Psychological consultation: Introduction to theory and practice* (5th ed.). Boston: Allyn and Bacon.

Buck, G., Polloway, E., Smith-Thomas, A., & Cox, K. W. (2003). Prereferral intervention processes: A survey of state practices. *Exceptional Children, 69*(3), 349–360.

Bye, L., & Alvarez, M. (2007). *School social work: Theory to practice*. Belmont, CA: Thomson Brooks/Cole.

Caplan, G. (1970). *The theory and practice of mental health consultation*. New York: Basic Books.

Caplan, G., & Caplan, R. (1993). *Mental health consultation and collaboration.* New York: Jossey-Bass.

Caplan, G., & Caplan, R. (1999). *Mental health consultation and collaboration.* Prospect Heights, IL: Waveland Press, Inc.

Carlson, J., Splete, H., & Kern, R. (Eds.). (1975). *The consulting process*. Washington, DC: American Personnel and Guidance Association.

Carr, L. D. (1976). *Report on survey of social work services in schools*. Washington, DC: National Association of Social Workers. Mimeograph.

Children & Schools (2001). Special Issue: Mental health in schools *23*(1).

Conoley, J. C., & Conoley, C. (1992). *School consultation: Practice and training* (2nd ed.). Boston: Allyn and Bacon.

Constable, R., Kuzmickaite, D., Harrison, W. D., & Volkmann, L. (1999). The emergent role of the school social worker in Indiana. *School Social Work Journal, 24*(1), 1–14.

Costin, L. B. (1969). A historical review of school social work. *Social Casework, 50*(8), 439–453.

Cowan, R., & Sheridan, S. (2003). Investigating the acceptability of behavioral interventions in applied conjoint behavioral consultation: Moving from analog conditions to naturalistic settings. *School Psychology Quarterly, 18*(1), 1–21.

Curtis, M. J., & Zins, J. E. (Eds.). (1981). *The theory and practice of school consultation.* Springfield, IL: Thomas.

Curtis, M., Hunley, S., & Grier, J. E. (2002). Relationships among the professional practices and demographic characteristics of school psychologists. *School Psychology Review, 31*(1), 30–42.

Davis, K. (2003). Teaching a course in school-based consultation. *Counselor Education and Supervision, 42*(4), 275–82.

Dinkmeyer, D. C., & Carlson, J. (2001). *Consultation: Creating school-based interventions* (2nd ed.). Philadelphia: Brunner-Routledge.

Donahue, P. J., Falk, B., & Provet, A. G. (2000). *Mental health consultation in early childhood*. Baltimore: Paul H. Brookes Publications.

Dougherty, A. M. (2000). *Psychological consultation and collaboration in school and community settings* (3rd ed.). Australia: Belmont, CA: Wadsworth.

Dryfoos, J., & Maguire, S. (2002). *Inside full-services community schools*. Thousand Oaks, CA: Corwin Press.

Dupper, D. (2002). *School social work: Skills and interventions for effective practice*. Hoboken, NJ: John Wiley & Sons.

Erchul, W. P., & Martens, B. K. (2002). *School consultation: Conceptual and empirical bases of practice* (2nd ed.). New York: Kluwer Academic/Plenum.

Fischer, D., Hoagwood, K., Boyce, C., Duster, T., Frank, D., Grisso, T., et al. (2002). Research ethics for mental health science involving ethnic minority children and youths. *American Psychologist, 54*(12), 1024–1040.

Fowler, E., & Harrison, P. (2001). Continuing professional development needs and activities of school psychologists. *Psychology in the Schools, 38*(1), 75–88.

Franklin, C., Harris, M. B., & Allen-Meares, P. (2006). *The school services sourcebook: A guide for school-based professionals*. New York: Oxford University Press.

Gallessich, J. (1982). *The profession and practice of consultation*. San Francisco: Jossey-Bass.

Goldstein, G., & Harris, K. (2000). Consultant practices in two heterogeneous Latino schools. *School Psychology Review, 29*(3), 369–377.

Gottlieb, J., & Polirstok, S. (2005). Program to reduce behavior infractions and referrals to special education. *Children & Schools, 27*(1), 53–57.

Grady, M. A., Gibson, J. J., & Trickett, E. J. (1981). *Mental health consultation, theory, practice, and research 1973–78. An annotated reference guide*. (DHHS Publication No. ADM 81-948). Rockville, MD: National Institute of Mental Health.

Graham, D. S. (1998). The need for empirical studies in school consultation. *School Psychology Quarterly 13*(2):92–93.

Graham, J. R., & Barter, K. (1999). Collaboration: A social work practice method. *Families in Society, 80*, 6–13.

Gutkin, T., & Carlson, J. (2001). *Consultation: Creating school-based interventions* (2nd ed.). Florence, KY: Brunner-Routledge.

Henning-Stout, M., & Meyers, J. (2000). Consultation and human diversity: First things first. *School Psychology Review, 29*(3), 419–425.

Hoagwood, K., & Erwin, H. D. (1976). Effectiveness of school-based mental health services for children: A 10-year research review. *Journal of Child and Family Studies, 6*, 435–451.

Hughes, N. (2000). The essential role of theory in the science of treating children: Beyond empirically supported treatments. *Journal of School Psychology, 38*(4), 301–330.

Ingraham, C. (2000). Consultation through a multicultural lens: Multicultural and cross-cultural consultation in schools. *School Psychology Review, 29*(3), 320–343.

Jackson, S., & White, J. (2000). Referrals to the school counselor: A qualitative study. *Professional School Counseling, 3*(4), 277–286.

Jonson-Reid, M., & Kim, J. (2007). Maltreated children in schools: The interface of school social work and child welfare. *Children & Schools, 29*(3), 182–191.

Jozefowicz-Simbeni, D., & Allen-Meares, P. (2002). Poverty and schools: Intervention and resource building through school-linked services. *Children & Schools, 24*(2), 123–136.

Kadushin, A. (1977). *Consultation in social work*. New York: Columbia University Press.

Kapp, S. (2000). Defining, promoting, and improving a model of school social work: The development of a tool for collaboration. *School Social Work Journal, 24*(2), 21–41.

Kerr, M. M. (2001). High school consultation. *Child & Adolescent Psychiatric Clinics of North America, 10*(1), 105–115.

Lambert, N., Hylander, I., & Sandoval, J. H. (2004). Consultee-centered consultation: Improving the quality of professional services in schools and community organizations. Mahwah, NJ: Lawrence Erlbaum.

Lewis, T., & Newcomer, L. (2002). Examining the efficacy of school-based consultation: Recommendations for improving outcomes. *Child & Family Behavior Therapy, 24*(1–2), 165–181.

Lopez, S. A., Torres, A., & Norwood, P. (1998). Building partnerships: A successful collaborative experience between social work and education. *Social Work in Education, 20*(3), 165–176.

Luellen, W. (2000). An examination of consultation training in National Association of School Psychology approved programs and its relationship to professional practice. *Dissertation Abstracts, 61*(4–A), 1308.

Luiselli, J. (2002). Focus, scope, and practice of behavioral consultation to public schools. *Child & Family Behavior Therapy, 24*(1–2), 5–21.

Lusky, M. B., & Hayes, R. L. (2001). Collaborative consultation and program evaluation. *Journal of Counseling & Development, 79*(1), 26–38.

Lynn, C., & McKay, M. (2001). Promoting parent-school involvement through collaborative practice models. *School Social Work Journal, 26*(1), 1–14.

Lynn, C., McKay, M., & Atkins, M. (2003). School social work: Meeting the mental health needs of students through collaboration with teachers. *Children & Schools, 25*(4), 197–209.

Mannino, F. V. (1969). *Consultation in mental health and related fields: A reference guide*. (PHS Publication No. 1920). Rockville, MD: NIMH.

Mannino, F. V. (1981). Empirical perspectives in mental health consultation. *Journal of Prevention, 1*(3), 147–155.

Mannino, F. V., & MacLennan, B. W. (1978). *Monitoring and evaluating mental health consultation and education services*. (DHEW Publication No. ADM 77-550). Rockville, MD: NIMH.

Mannino, F. V., MacLennan, B. W., & Shore, M. F. (1975). *The practice of mental health consultation*. (DHEW Publication No. ADM 74-112). Rockville, MD: NIMH.

Mannino, F. V., & Shore, M. F. (1971). *Consultation research in mental health and related fields: A critical review of the literature*. (PHS Publication No. 2122). Rockville, MD: NIMH.

Mannino, V. F., & Shore, M. F. (1979). Evaluation of consultation: Problems and prospects. *New Directions for Mental Health Services, 3*, 99–114.

Mannino, F. V., Trickett, E., Shore, M., Kidder, M. G., & Levin, G. (1986). *Handbook of mental health consultation*. (DHHS Publication No. ADM 86-1446). Rockville, MD: NIMH.

Martens, B., & Adroin, S. (2002). Training school psychologists in behavior support consultation. *Child & Family Behavior Therapy, 24*(1–2), 147–163.

Matheny, A., & Zimmerman, T. (2001). The application of family systems theory to organizational consultation: A content analysis. *American Journal of Family Therapy, 29*(5), 421–433.

Mattison, R. E. (2000). School consultation: A review of research on issues unique to the school environment. *Journal of the American Academy of Child & Adolescent Psychiatry, 39*(4), 402–413.

McClung, F., & Stunden, A. (1970). *Mental health consultation to programs for children.* (PHS Publication No. 2066). Rockville, MD: NIMH.

McDowell, T. (1999). Systems consultation and Head Start: An alternative to traditional family therapy. *Journal of Marital & Family Therapy, 25*(2), 155–168.

Meares, P. A. (1977). Analysis of tasks in school social work. *Social Work, 22*(3), 196–201.

Meares, P. A. (1982). A content analysis of school social work literature, 1968–1978. In R. T. Constable and J. P. Flynn (Eds.), *School social work: Practice and research perspectives* (pp. 38–41). Homewood, IL: Dorsey.

Medway, F. J., & Updyke, J. F. (1985). Meta-analysis of consultation outcome studies. *American Journal of Community Psychology, 13*(5), 489–505.

Metzler, C., Miglan, A., Rusby, J., & Sprague J. (2001). Evaluation of a comprehensive behavior management program to improve school-wide positive behavior support. *Education and Treatment of Children, 24*(4), 448–479.

Meyers, J., Parsons, R. D., & Martin, R. (1979). *Mental health consultation in the schools*. San Francisco: Jossey-Bass.

Mishna, F., & Muskat, B. (2004). School-based group treatment for students with learning disabilities: A collaborative approach. *Children & Schools, 26*(3), 135–150.

Mizrahi, T., & Rosenthal, B. (2001). Complexities of coalition building: Leaders' successes, strategies, struggles, and solutions. *Social Work, 4*(1), 63–78.

New Freedom Commission on Mental Health. (2003). *Executive report*. Washington, DC: Author.

Noell, G., Duhon, G., Gatti, S., & Connell, J. (2002). Consultation, follow-up, and implementation of behavior management interventions in general education. *School Psychology Review, 31*(2), 217–234.

Openshaw, L. (2008). *Social work in schools: Principles and practice*. New York: The Guilford Press.

Oppenheimer, J. J. (1925). *The visiting teacher movement with special reference to administrative relationships* (2nd ed.). New York: Joint Committee on Methods of Preventing Delinquency.

Packard, T. (2001). Enhancing site-based governance through organization development: A new role for school social workers. *Children & Schools, 23*(2), 101–113.

Parsons, R. P. (1996). *The skilled consultant: A systemic approach to the theory and practice of consultation*. Boston: Allyn and Bacon.

Plionis, E., & Sabatino, C. (1998). Personal communication. Washington, DC: The Catholic University of America.

President's New Freedom Commission on Mental Health (2003). Achieving the promise: Transforming mental health care in America. Final report. DHHS Pub. No. SMA-03-3832 Rockville, MD: Department of Health and Human Services.

Raines, J. (2002). Brainstorming hypotheses for functional behavior assessment: The link to effective behavioral intervention plans. *School Social Work Journal, 26*(2), 30–45.

Rapoport, L. (Ed.), (1963). *Consultation in social work practice*. New York: National Association of Social Workers Press.

Reddy, L. A., Barboza-Whitehead, S., Files, T., & Rubel, E. (2000). Clinical focus of consultation outcome research with children and adolescents. *Special Services in the Schools, 16*(1–2), 1–22.

Reid, W. J. (1979). The model development dissertation. *Social Service Research, 3*(2), 215–225.

Reiman, D. W. (1992). *Strategies in social work consultation: From theory to practice in the mental health field*. New York: Longman.

Roberts, R., & Greene, G. (2002). *Social workers' desk reference*. New York: Oxford University Press.

Rogers, M. R. (2000). Examining the cultural context of consultation. *School Psychology Review, 29*(3), 414–418.

Rones, M., & Hoagwood, K. (2000). School-based mental health services: A research review. *Clinical Child and Family Psychology Review, 3*(4), 223–241.

Rosenberg, M. (2001). Introduction to program descriptions. *Teacher Education and Special Education, 24*(3), 262.

Sabatino, C. A. (1986). The effects of school social work consultation on teacher perception and role conflict–role ambiguity in relationship to students with social adjustment problems. *Dissertation Abstracts International, 46*(1), 2443.

Sabatino, C. A. (2001). Family-centered sections of the IFSP and school social work participation. *Children & Schools, 23*(4), 241–251.

Saleeby, D. (2006). *The strengths perspective in social work practice* (4th ed.). Boston, MA: Pearson/Allyn& Bacon.

Sawka, K., McCurdy, B., & Mannella, M. (2002). Strengthening emotional support services: An empirically based model for training teachers of students with behavior disorders. *Journal of Emotional and Behavioral Disorders, 10*(4), 223–232.

Schein, E. H. (1999). *Process consultation revisited: Building the helping relationship*. Reading, MA: Addison-Wesley Publishing.

Sessions, P., & Fanolis, V (2006). Partners for success: A collaborative project in school-based mental health practice and training. In L. Combrinck-Graham (Ed.). *Children in family contexts: Perspectives on treatment* (pp. 356–381). New York: Guilford Press.

Sheridan, S. M. (2000). Considerations of multiculturalism and diversity in behavioral consultation with parents and teachers. *School Psychology Review, 29*(3), 344–353.

Sheridan, S. M., Clarke, B. L., Knoche, L. L., & Edwards, C. P (2006). The effects of conjoint behavioral consultation in early childhood settings. *Early Education and Development, 17*(4) 593–617.

Sheridan, S. M., Eagle, J. W., Cowan, R. J., & Mickelson, W. (2001). The effects of conjoint behavior consultation: Results of a 4-year investigation. *Journal of School Psychology, 39*(5), 361–385.

Sheridan, S. M., & Kratochwill, T. R. (2007). *Conjoint behavioral consultation: Promoting family-centered connections and interventions* (2nd ed.). New York: Springer

Sperry, L., Kahn, J. P., & Heidel, S. H. (1994). Workplace mental health consultation. A primer of organizational and occupational psychiatry. *General Hospital Psychiatry, 16*(2), 103–111.

Sterling-Turner, H., Watson, T. S., & Moore, J. W. (2002). The effects of direct training and treatment integrity on treatment outcomes in school consultation. *School Psychology Quarterly, 17*(1), 47–77.

Strand, V. C., & Badger, L. (2007). A clinical consultation model for child welfare supervisors. *Child Welfare, 86*(1), 79–96.

Thousand, J. S., & Villa, R. A. (1992). Collaborative teams: A powerful tool in school restructuring. In R. A. Villa, J. S. Thousand, W. Stainbeck, & S. Stainbeck (Eds.), *Restructuring for caring and effective education* (pp. 73–107). Baltimore: Paul H. Brookes.

Timberlake, E. M., Sabatino, C. A., & Hooper, S. N. (1982). School social work practice and P.L. 94-142. In R. T. Constable and J. P. Flynn (Eds.), *School social work: Practice and research perspectives* (pp. 49–71). Homewood, IL: Dorsey.

Tindel, G., Parker, R., & Hasbrouck, J. (1992). The construct validity of stages and activities in the consultation process. *Journal of Educational & Psychological Consultation, 3*(2), 99–118.

Tourse, R. W. C., & Mooney, J. F. (Eds.). (1999). *Collaborative practice: School and human service partnerships*. Westport, CT: Praeger.

Tourse, R. W. C., Mooney, J., Kline, P., & Davoren, J. (2005). A collaborative model of clinical preparation: A move toward interprofessional field experiences. *Journal of Social Work Education, 41*(3), 457–477.

University of California, Los Angeles, School Mental Health Project, Center for Mental Health in Schools (2005). Retrieved November 10, 2007, from http://www.smhp.psych.ucla.edu

University of Maryland, School of Medicine, Center for School Mental Health Assistance. (2005). Retrieved November 10, 2007, from http://www.csmha.umaryland.edu

U.S. Department of Education, Office of Special Education Programs, Technical Assistance Center on Positive Behavioral Interventions and Supports (2005). Available from http://www.pbis.org

Watkins, M., Crosby, E., & Pearson, J. (2001). Role of the school psychologist: Perceptions of school staff. *School Psychology International, 22*(1),64–73.

Weist, M., Ambrose, M. G., & Lewis, C. (2006). Expanded school mental health: A collaborative community-school example. *Children & Schools, 28*(1), 45–50.

Wesley, P. (2002). Early intervention consultants in the classroom: Simple steps for building strong collaboration. *Young Children, 57*(4), 30–34.

Wesley, P. W., Buysse, V., & Keyes, L. (2000). Comfort zone revisited: Child characteristics and professional comfort with consultation. *Journal of Early Intervention, 23*(2), 106–115.

Wilczynski, S. M., Mandal, R. L., & Usuilier, I. (2000). Bridges and barriers in behavioral consultation. *Psychology in the Schools, 37*(6), 495–504.

Wilkinson, L. A. (1999). School-based behavioral consultation: Delivering treatment for children with externalizing behavior problems. *Dissertation Abstracts International, 59*(7–A), 2350.

Wilkinson, L. A. (2003). Using behavioral consultation to reduce challenging behavior in the classroom. *Preventing School Failure, 47*(3), 100–105.

Wilson, C. D., & Lubin, B. (1997). *Research on professional consultation and consultation for organizational change*. Westport, CT: Greenwood Press.

Zischka, P. C., & Fox, R. (1985). Consultation as a function of school social work. *Social Work in Education, 7*(2), 69–79.

21

A Case Example of School and Mental Health Agency Collaboration

Mary Constable Milne
Kari Centre
Auckland, New Zealand

- Collaboration in a Crisis Situation
- Establishing the Collaborative Relationship
- Working with the Child, the Family and the School

In every educational system, collaborative and innovative service delivery approaches to meeting the needs of children, family, schools, and communities are essential. This chapter describes three case examples based on collaborative relationships developed between a mental health service provider and schools in New Zealand.

New Zealand (NZ) has a population of about four million (almost half of whom reside in the Auckland region). It has well-developed government child and adolescent community mental health services (CAMHS). Unique to New Zealand, mental health teams have Maori and Pacific Island (PI) Cultural Advisors for Maori and P.I. clients. CAMHS are offered free to children and adolescents who are considered to have a moderate to severe mental health issue. Young people are seen within the context of their families. A range of interventions is provided (e.g., parenting programs, group therapy, individual and family therapy). A concern is that, while perhaps 2 percent of youth directly access CAMHS (Vague, 2005), up to 20 percent of young people may have a mental health problem (U.S. Department of Health and Human Services, 1999). Intervention often occurs late in the process, when patterns of behavior are more difficult to change. A significant number of families will only tentatively engage with the mental health service when they are in crisis, and these are often the disorganized families that are in the greatest need of support. The mental health setting often carries stigma and may seem artificial and removed from the normal worlds (particularly the school world) of the adolescent. Clinicians often do not have the relationship with school staff that makes collaboration possible.

Central Auckland, NZ is diverse economically and socially. It hosts 181 different ethnic groups, many of which comprise recent immigrants. Primary ethnic groups include Maori (the indigenous people of New Zealand), Pakeha (Caucasians), Asians and Pacific Islanders. The thirty high schools reflect the diversity of the area. Common issues for students include learning disabilities, family issues, poverty, self-harm, teen pregnancy, abuse, eating disorders, depression, drug use, truancy, and anxiety. Suicide and intentional self-inflicted injury make up the greatest proportion of all injury-related fatalities for adolescents. Most high schools do not have school social workers, school nurses, psychologists, or other health professionals located in the school. Almost all high schools have at least one school guidance counselor (SGC). The role of the SGC has become pivotal in reaching young people in need of social/emotional support. They are the people who are on the front line of intervention with students and key links for CAMHS.

The Liaison Education Adolescent Project (LEAP) programme of the Kari Centre for Mental Health, a CAMHS in central Auckland, offers one example of a program response to developing a partnership between high schools and mental health services so that both are better able to carry out their missions. Schools are better equipped to educate students if they can address the mental health issues that interfere with students' ability to achieve. In turn, CAMHS are more able to bridge barriers in order to reach a wider group of young people at primary and secondary prevention levels. The goal of LEAP has been to develop a partnership between the Kari Centre and high schools to assist in addressing their common concerns for vulnerable students. Mary Constable Milne is an MSW with specialized preparation in school social work. She co-ordinates LEAP half time and works clinically with adolescents and families the other half.

LEAP links people with mental health resources through in-service education, other information, and an active website (headspace.org.nz). It also provides consultation/liaison to high school educators. Ongoing consultation/liaison and collaboration is the best way to develop a partnership relationship. Of the thirty high schools in the Kari Centre area, two-thirds of these schools are actively involved with LEAP. A top priority of the clinic, schools are assigned two mental health clinicians and a cultural advisor if appropriate. The clinicians negotiate with the school in terms of the frequency of visits. They are also available for phone consultation in between visits. LEAP stresses that the school retains accountability and has the choice to carry out its suggestions or not.

COLLABORATION IN A CRISIS SITUATION

The link between LEAP and a school can be particularly crucial in times of school crisis. This case example demonstrates how developing a partnership with schools can aid CAMHS to intervene at the primary, secondary, and tertiary levels:

> A large public school in Auckland was hosting a rock concert, mostly attended by their own students. "Sione," a Samoan student at the school joined a crowd of young people at the front entrance of the school. During an altercation with another boy from South Auckland, Sione was fatally stabbed. Before the ambulance arrived, Sione died on the front entrance of the school, surrounded by students. As soon as we heard of the crisis, we contacted the SGC team to offer support and arranged a school visit. Through regular consult/liaison visits, we had already established good relationships with the SGC team. At the visit, the SGC team had been struggling to identify and support the many students suffering from trauma reactions and were emotionally exhausted. They first of all needed collegial support from us. Students who witnessed the stabbing were mainly of Pacific Island background from socially disadvantaged families. Together, we discussed the most useful ways of supporting students. They were wondering whether Kari Centre would immediately take the many students who seemed to need mental health intervention. We stressed the need to normalize trauma reactions rather then refer the students to mental health services. We provided the SGC team with up-to-date information on psychological trauma. It relieved them to know that the majority of young people who witnessed the stabbing would not necessarily develop post-traumatic stress disorder (PTSD). They wondered if we could run groups in the school for the students most impacted. While we wanted to help them in any way we could, we also understood that they were a capable team. We did not want to undermine their authority. Instead, we provided suggestions and guidelines for them to facilitate the groups. We suggested that groups should only run for a few sessions with the purpose of psycho-education and normalizing trauma reactions. Intense and longer-term groups might do more harm than good. We supported their idea of hosting a parent night and offered to attend along with our Pacific Island cultural advisor. They responded that they now felt capable of handling the night on their own. After the initial meeting, we had a few subsequent meetings to support them with the fallout from the crisis. We helped them to triage and refer students who would benefit from Kari Centre.

ESTABLISHING THE COLLABORATIVE RELATIONSHIP

Schools differ in their receptiveness to collaboration with outside agencies. The school in the previous case study was familiar with working with outside agencies, and so the process of consultation did not take long to develop. For many schools, mainly small private schools, the model of consult/liaison with mental health is a new way of working. They are not always clear on what we are offering. Sufficient trust and mutual respect between an outside agency and school need to be established in order to collaborate and consult effectively. Clinicians unfamiliar with schools sometimes expect to enter a school and immediately consult on cases. The example below illustrates the good working relationship and mutual trust needed before effective consultation can take place:

> St. James' School has a pastoral care team headed by the deputy principal (D.P.). The team consists of a part-time SGC (who is also a teacher), a school health worker, and a few student counselors on placement. They have little understanding of mental health or the Kari Centre. They do have a system in which each student has a staff mentor. The mentor directs any concerns about students to the pastoral care team. We have been meeting with the pastoral care team for over a year to help them learn about the Centre. After describing several times what the Kari Centre does, we were initially unsuccessful in directing the conversation toward actual consultation. We were feeling frustrated and wondered if these meeting were actually useful. Finally, at the last meeting, the DP and the school counselor produced a list of students needing extra support. We were able to suggest useful community resources. In some cases we were able suggest a Kari Centre referral and walk them through the referral process. We were also able to suggest useful strategies for dealing with difficult students. At the end of the meeting, the team was able to agree that the process was useful. We agreed to keep to this format in subsequent meetings. Most recently, the DP requested a training session for school staff on identifying and supporting students who might be depressed.

WORKING WITH THE CHILD, THE FAMILY AND THE SCHOOL

In our clinical role, there are some cases where we work with the child, the family, and the school at the same time and in relation to each other:

> Kate is a 15-year-old girl currently experiencing low mood, triggered by a recent parental divorce and subsequent move to the city with her mother. Kate feels disconnected from her mother and her new school. Her grades have dropped significantly and she becomes so distressed that she calls her mother several times a week to get her out of school. We have been working with mother and daughter to change the patterns of interaction in order to strengthen their relationship and the mother's ability to nurture her daughter. Individual work has been focused on helping Kate build skills to cope with her emotions (i.e., relaxation techniques) and deal with some aspects of her relationship with her mother. With Kate's permission, we have been in close contact with her SGC about our shared concern for the amount of school she has been missing. We organized a joint school meeting. The purpose of the meeting was to collaborate on a plan for when Kate becomes distressed at school. At the school meeting (attended by Kate and her mother), it became apparent

> that Kate is struggling in the school and is being bullied. This was the trigger for calling her mom to pick her up. Together, we worked out a plan. The SGC agreed to ask her teachers to be vigilant for students bullying Kate. Instead of going home when distressed, we agreed that Kate could have a pass to leave class twice a week for up to twenty minutes. During that time, she would go to a quiet place in the library and practice calming herself with relaxation techniques from a tape. We also encouraged Kate to join a girl's group in the community to have a safe place to practice social skills and develop friendships. We are planning to work with the school to discuss issues of bullying and the process of creating a safe environment.

Evaluations of the LEAP programme have been quite positive. One SGC commented, "I've found the consultation/liaison service very helpful . . . in working with clients and it means that there's a working relationship in place . . . for when it's needed. There is ongoing communication about our different roles . . . and how best to mesh these for the benefit of the client."

Throughout the world, social workers, community agencies, and schools are working together to address the needs of children, families, schools, and communities. Effective collaborations, such as those described in this chapter, can exponentially increase a community's capacity to cope with crisis, and to work with children and families.

References

Vague, R. (2005). Mental health information national collection: Analysis for the Stocktake Project. Auckland, NZ: The Werry Centre.

U.S. Department of Health and Human Services. (1999). *Mental health: A report of the Surgeon General.* Rockville, MD: U.S. Department of Health and Human Services.

22

Assessment of the Learning Environment, Case Study Assessment, and Functional Behavior Analyses

Galen Thomas
Southern Illinois University

Marguerite Tiefenthal

Robert Constable
Loyola University Chicago

Erin Gleason Leyba
University of Illinois at Chicago

- Ongoing Assessment and Decision Making
- The Strengths Perspective
- Dynamics of the Learning Environment
- Prereferral Interventions
- The Case Study Assessment (CSA) and the Social Developmental Study (SDS)
- Special Education Assessment
- Adaptive Behavior Assessment
- Functional Behavior Assessment

ONGOING ASSESSMENT AND DECISION MAKING

Assessment is a systematic way of understanding what is happening in the pupil's relations within the classroom, within the family, with peers, and between family and school. It provides a basis for deciding which interventions will be most effective. Thus, it is an individualized effort to identify and evaluate the interrelations of problems, people, and situations (Siporin, 1975). The objective of assessment is effective intervention with a system that is itself in process. Assessment is more than a one-time, required procedure, or a formal evaluation. It is a continuous, ongoing process in which school social workers engage as they work with students, their families, school personnel, and community agencies. Its power is its focus on the identification of strengths in individuals and systems rather than on deficits alone. It is geared toward collective decision-making processes potentially involving the social worker, the parent, the pupil, and the team. The social worker's decision about which intervention to use comes from integrating data and drawing conclusions about the interrelated factors contributing to the problem(s) and the potential effectiveness of various interventions. Because assessments are individualized to the purpose and context of the assessment, the worker needs to develop a systematic way to gather and evaluate information, sifting out significant details from the potentially vast universe of information available.

THE STRENGTHS PERSPECTIVE

Because assessment procedures are often used to determine whether a student has a disability and is eligible for special education, they often concentrate on documenting limitations in student performance. Although some information about deficit or risk areas is needed, attending to a student's strengths and talents can ensure that the assessment provides a holistic, balanced perspective of overall functioning (Gleason, 2007). A strengths-based assessment focuses on a student's resiliencies, talents, connections, skills, and gifts (Cowger, Anderson, & Snively, 2006). It attempts to understand the supportive elements in the environment that help a student grow or respond effectively to stress. It explores how a student has been resilient or has adapted successfully when faced with challenges (Wang, Haertel, & Walberg, 1999). In a strengths-based assessment, questioning strategies attempt to identify "what works" and "how it works." During assessment interviews, the social worker might use:

- Exception questions ("When things were going well, what was different?")
- Survival questions ("How have you managed to survive this far?")
- Support questions ("What people have given you special understanding, support, and guidance?")

- Esteem questions ("What accomplishments in your life have given you pride?") (Parton & O'Byrne, 2000; Saleebey, 2006).

The relationship-oriented process of eliciting examples of a student's strengths and talents builds trust between the social worker, the student, and the family (Gleason, 2007). When the social worker communicates a student's strengths in reports and at meetings, the interdisciplinary team is able to acknowledge the student's progress, existing skills, humanity, heroism, and courage. The team can use detailed information about previously successful supports and interventions to advocate that these effective strategies be replicated and further developed (Gleason, 2007). The team can also use information about a student's strengths and talents to address problems and risk areas through creative methods.

DYNAMICS OF THE LEARNING ENVIRONMENT

Assessment of the complex dynamics of learning environments, especially the classroom environment, is essential to any understanding of a pupil in school. Information is gathered through observations and conversations that occur throughout the school day. Through sensitivity to signs of potential problems with individual students as well as indications of more general systemwide problems, the social worker is able to take a proactive approach to identify issues that need to be addressed either individually or through a broader base of team effort. This information is shared with others who function as part of the decision-making process. Prior to their work in a school setting, social workers should have a good general understanding of human development, family interaction, relationships of children in a community context, and group dynamics.

On this foundation, school social workers need to develop an understanding of classroom group dynamics. Teaching styles and classroom group composition have an impact on pupil behavior and the learning process. Classroom management often takes a great deal of the teacher's time, yet some teachers have little or no training in group dynamics. The understanding of the classroom is an interactive understanding, coming from direct observation and from the teacher's account. Social workers may look for negative patterns so they can be extinguished. Consider a situation where children may feel fearful, unsafe, or challenged by their peers. If the teacher feels uncertain or unequipped to deal with the problem, the behavior of one child may increase and become "contagious" to others. Perhaps an overwhelmed teacher is unwittingly fanning the flames of general out-of-control behavior with a fearful or excessively rigid response. Perhaps the legitimate need to clamp down on an out-of-control situation overlooks the needs of other children in the class. While understanding problematic issues is important, social workers can also notice and examine the contextual conditions present when things are going particularly well in the classroom so they can be further developed (Gleason, 2007). For example, when students are listening, behaving, and learning, what conditions are in place? What is the teacher doing? How is the classroom arranged? What directions were given? How were students supported, reinforced, or engaged? By providing an objective, strengths-based perspective through classroom observation and consultation with the teacher, the social worker may help the teacher identify more effective solutions for managing the classroom.

The first prerequisite to any person's effective functioning in any group is safety. Nothing else can be done without the belief that one is safe, that one's personhood and dignity will be respected. Both teachers and students need safety. This is so important that a person's energies will be deflected by safety concerns before investing in anything else. A classroom or school environment that does not value each person's contribution and that permits bullying, scapegoating, or other abusive behavior will hardly be able to do much other than cope with its own toxic surroundings. In addition to outlawing bullying, the school community must work at developing a climate of acceptance and positive value for each person. Effective schools present learning and social processes to which all students can connect. The atmosphere of productive work, respect, and comfortable order is noticeable immediately when one enters the building or classroom. Leadership is clear and uncontested. The climate is safe and orderly. There is an emphasis on basic skills and continuous assessment of pupil progress. There are high expectations for achievement (Finn, 1984; Purkey & Smith, 1983). In the effective school or classroom, these are taken for granted by the students and faculty, but they are not accidental. They are the result of a good deal of work over a number of years by the school leadership, and by teachers, students, and community. When something upsets this equilibrium, the school community (or classroom) may go into a crisis mode, but it can be a productive crisis if members work constructively together to restore the lost (and remembered) equilibrium.

Assessments of the learning environment start with observation and concrete description. To learn the process of assessment of the learning environment it is best to begin with a student the teacher has some concern about and a classroom where you are welcome to observe unobtrusively. Forms for observation, such as the ones in chapter 24, are useful ways to begin to find the patterns and sequences of the student's interaction with learning tasks, the teacher, and other students. To look further for patterns and sequences, a good model to follow is the Antecedent-Behavior-Consequences (ABC) model. Here you, as an observer, record in anecdotal form in each instance of (A) significant antecedent events, (B) the behavior of concern, and (C) the immediate and longer-term consequences of the behavior. From repeated observations and interviews with the teacher and parents, you can begin to map out the *times* and *conditions* where the student *did* or *did not* exhibit the particular behavior of concern (Raines, 2002; Repp & Horner, 1999). You can then begin to develop some hypotheses about the possible *functions* or purposes of the behavior. Hypotheses are plausible explanations of the function of the behavior that predict the general conditions under which the behavior is most likely to occur, as well as the possible consequences that serve to maintain the behavior (Raines, 2002). The key is to develop a conceptual language for nonacademic, developmental learning, such as those illustrated in the sampler of developmental (functional) learning objectives in table 26.1 in chapter 26. With this approach, you can begin to explain classroom behavior and develop a positive behavior intervention plan, changing the antecedents and/or consequences of the behavior and/or assisting students to develop skills to deal with certain situations.

Functions of Behavior

Normally students are expected to behave in class in ways that address the tasks of their own learning and do not interfere with the learning of others. When students are off-task or interfere with others, it is assumed that their behaviors may serve functions of *seeking attention* from the teacher or others in the class, *communicating* their needs to teacher or peers, or *avoiding* academic tasks (Zuna & McDougall, 2004). These functions cover motivations for a wide range of behavior and are a good beginning. Raines (2002) goes further to suggest needs from the perspective of normal development: for autonomy, individuation, and control, for self-esteem, to regulate stimulation, and to set some structure in what may be perceived as an unstructured environment. Other functions of behavior, maladaptive and less amenable to immediate change, may be a need to repeat a learned scapegoat role, to create safety from imagined threats, to display grandiose invulnerability, to be punished, to have revenge, or to derive pleasure from the discomfort of others (Raines, 2002).

Antecedents in the Classroom

Each classroom is different, reflecting the teacher's preferred style and the composition of the classroom group. To begin to understand these differences we need to consider:

1. The number of students in the classroom;
2. The resources available;
3. The amount of freedom a teacher has to individualize and modify curriculum or select alternative behavior management techniques;
4. The amount of time to individualize for one student's needs;

5. The degree of pressure placed on teachers for accountability through state and district "high-stakes" testing and the effect of that on the learning process;
6. The group composition and atmosphere of the class: How many "prosocial" students? How many students with difficulties? How much time is available "on task"? How much distraction is there? and
7. The teacher's preferred style and repertoire of teaching approaches to respond to a situation or to the needs of particular students.

Details about the classroom environment that can be significant to the student can include seating arrangement, lighting, window location, noise from outside the room, total number of students in the room, number of interesting items hanging around the room, and so on. Distractions (being close to a window, etc) can make a big difference for students with learning difficulties or ADHD. Class size, class structure, number of discipline problems, student-to-teacher ratios, classroom management rules, direction and frequency of teacher attention, and the number of opportunities for students to respond academically all affect student learning (Roberts, 1995). Teachers teach in different ways. Where do teachers position themselves in proximity to the student? Are modifications made to individualize material to students who are having difficulties? Does the teacher appear confident dealing with issues of discipline?

Understanding the learning environment demands that we first understand the realities a particular teacher is facing. We cannot really advocate for an individual student without advocacy for the teacher's needs, and without empathy for the teacher's reality. Without some understanding of the pressures on teachers, social workers will have difficulty developing a working relationship with them or even gaining their acceptance of the assessment information. Teachers have different styles that can be effective with certain types of students. Some teachers are very comfortable with their firmness and can work compassionately with students needing limits. Others do better with youngsters by using patience, warmth, and nonpossessive concern. Each of us responds to every situation within the framework and limits of ourselves as persons. Experienced teachers often can call on a variety of approaches to a situation, especially if they can analyze it objectively. It is important for school social workers to practice with teachers the same attitudes they typically are trained to use with students and parents. They should exhibit a nonjudgmental attitude, start where the teacher is, exercise positive regard, and assume teachers are doing their best given the amount of support they have, available resources, and the extent of their experience.

An understanding of the pupil's perspective often comes with experience, from the teacher's account, and from observation, but there is hardly a substitute for the learning contained in a direct interview with the pupil.

In the interview, the social worker can explore whether personal or family factors are supporting, assisting, discouraging, or distracting the student. The social worker might ask the student about his or her interests and supports through questions such as: "If you had to join one sport, hobby, or club, what would it be?" "What is one way you're a good friend?" "What is your favorite part of the day?" "Of what are you most proud?" "How has your family helped you out?" (Gleason, 2007). Answers can offer rich clues as to how to potentially rekindle the student's motivation, build on talents, and capitalize on existing supports. The student might communicate other important information during the interview. Perhaps a student could be motivated by a different tangible or social reward than the ones currently available in the classroom. Sometimes a child needs glasses, warm clothes and shoes, a medical exam, a hearing test, or a welcoming friend in a new and frightening environment. Teachers are often more receptive to trying alternatives when they understand that they can make some impact on what they see as an initially impossible situation or that problems are more complex than initially perceived. The small steps of progress that they see are in reality very important. The social worker often needs to reframe the student in positive terms to the teacher. The child is not simply being oppositional or lazy. Both the teacher and the social worker need to give up the idea of a quick, mechanically smooth solution to the problem. Solutions eventually do emerge with trial and error, persistent support, time, patience, and appropriate engagement with the problem and the people involved in it.

PREREFERRAL INTERVENTIONS

The Individuals with Disabilities Education Act (IDEA) encourages prereferral intervention. It specifically mandates that eligibility as a student with emotional disabilities requires that the student have the characteristics of disability over an extended period of time and that the problem behavior has persisted even after attempts at intervention have been made. It emphasizes school-wide approaches and early intervention services to reduce the need to label children as disabled. Documentation of efforts to work with the student through the identification of appropriate functional areas of learning and Goal Attainment Scaling (see chapter 26) are critically important from a compliance standpoint as well as for practical reasons.

When students are experiencing nonacademic difficulties and are not showing clearly identifiable disabling conditions, it is appropriate for teachers to seek consultation with the team of colleagues designated to assist in reviewing possible interventions to support positive changes in student performance and/or the school social worker. The support team will often review interventions already attempted, conduct a functional assessment of the student's behavior, and monitor student response to interventions over a designated period. It is essential that interventions focus not only on ameliorating problems directly, but also on building on student strengths with the expectation that these interventions will activate the motivation, self-esteem, confidence, or social support that is also needed to improve the student's problem area. As a general rule of thumb, at least three interventions should be attempted to achieve objectives over the course of six weeks. If the student shows progress on the objectives, even though not "cured," the team has to make a decision. On the one hand there is progress and more time and further interventions could be tried rather than proceeding with the referral for special education assessment. On the other hand there could be pressure to "get on with the referral," because the minimum time has been expended. If there is progress, the need to maintain the student in the least restrictive environment would support going with the progress. However, this will not be successful without discussion and the commitment of everyone: the student, the parents, and the teacher(s).

THE CASE STUDY ASSESSMENT (CSA) AND THE SOCIAL DEVELOPMENTAL STUDY (SDS)

Purpose and Definition

Assessment brings everything together by creating a picture of how pupils function in a learning situation, with their families, and with their peers in their school and in the larger community. *Case Study Assessment* (CSA) is a more formal assessment process in which school social workers participate. The CSA is a compilation and analysis of information concerning those life experiences of the child, both past and present, that pertain to his or her problems in school. It provides a comprehensive baseline of the pupil's personal and social functioning as well as identifying significant environmental realities and assisting with planning interventions. One major purpose of the CSA is to assist the team, the parents, and the pupil in understanding the pupil's life circumstances as they relate to school performance or behavior. A second major purpose is to assist parents and school personnel to develop the most suitable educational environment and to intervene in a way that would be most helpful for the optimum learning and development of the child. The CSA includes information from many sources, including the student, parents/foster parents, teachers, other school personnel, involved agency personnel, and other significant people outside the school, such as extended family or other caretakers. Each is significant in developing a profile of the student's current social and developmental functioning. When the CSA is used as part of the evaluation for services for a child with a disability, it should include an assessment of the pupil's adaptive behaviors, discussed later in this chapter. Although the CSA is sometimes referred to as the *social history*, a tool often used by social workers to understand client dynamics, the CSA has additional components that make it more comprehensive than a social history. The CSA includes a basic description of the following:

1. The pupil,
2. The pupil's current social functioning and the presenting problem,
3. Observations in classroom(s) as well as other less structured school environments,
4. An individual interview with the pupil,
5. The pupil's sociocultural background,
6. Any events or stressors possibly contributing to the problem,
7. Other significant life experiences, and
8. Current abilities of the pupil.

The CSA is an assessment of the whole child in his or her environment. It focuses on identified strengths as well as areas in need of support. It brings into focus the developmental systems and ecological factors that affect the child's learning and behavioral patterns. By involving the family in this information gathering, the school social worker can begin a cooperative working relationship between parents or guardian and the school that may not have been present earlier. A relationship can be established through which emotional support, counseling, information about community resources, and legal rights can be discussed, and the mediation of significant differences between home and school can begin. The relationship with the family formed by the social worker when compiling a CSA can continue through the development and implementation of an educational plan. Even if it is a brief contact, this relationship frequently can have a positive impact on the parents or guardians, helping them to address feelings of anxiety or alienation from their child's educational experience. During this process the social worker needs to help parents gain an understanding of the implications of the assessment for their child's long-range educational needs. Giving parents or guardians the chance to vent frustration, anger, or fear of the future for their child is time well spent. In a few cases this may lead to more than one meeting, but it will pay off later when active parent or guardian cooperation will be necessary for the success of the child. Parents may also be eager to share positive information about their children. Social workers can ask, "What is your son or daughter good at?" "What does your son or daughter do that makes you proud?" "What time do you enjoy most with your son or daughter?" By eliciting positive stories and examples of the child's resiliency from parents, the social worker can build trust and help the team further understand the child's gifts and needs (Gleason, 2007).

Components of a Case Study Assessment

The CSA assembles the evaluations done by the school social worker into a single written statement. With the addition of professional judgment, the foundations for the social worker's recommendations emerge. We outline ten components that contribute to the gathering of information for a CSA:

1. Pupil interview(s),
2. Parent interview(s),
3. Social history and current functioning,
4. Significant health history and current health needs,
5. Socioeconomic and cultural background,
6. Assessment of the pupil's learning environment,
7. Observation of the pupil in the school (in classrooms, in individualized tasks, in a structured group, in the playground, and ideally in the home environment),
8. Consultation with the pupil's current and (preferably) previous teachers,
9. Review of student files (grades, discipline, achievement testing),
10. Consultation with other staff and agencies when necessary.

Although the potential wealth of descriptive information gathered through this process may go beyond the scope of one's assessment focus, only information directly pertinent to the child's educational progress that does not breach the right to confidentiality of the parent or child may be included in the written report. As a useful concrete framework, we can outline nine components of the CSA:

I. Identifying Information

A. The child's name, birth date, school, grade, and teacher
B. Each family member's name, age, relationship to the child, educational background, occupation, employment, address, and marital status
C. Names of other persons living in the home and their relationship to the child
D. Race/ethnicity of the family
E. Brief impression of the child at your initial meeting

II. Reasons for Referral

A. The stated reasons for the referral and any specific questions that should be addressed
B. The problem (the child's learning or behavior) as described by the teacher, parent, or others
C. What has been done to try to correct the situation (should include at least three significant interventions)?
D. What were the immediate precipitating events that prompted the referral?
E. A checklist of specific behaviors that interfere with the learning process

III. Sources of Information. A list of dates and sources of data obtained should include, but not be limited to, the following:

A. Home visit(s) or alternative modes of interviewing parents, guardians, or other relatives
B. Social worker's or other's interview(s) with the child
C. Review of school records
D. Outside evaluations
E. Observations of the student ideally in various settings, but at least in the classroom and one unstructured situation (e.g., recess)
F. Review of health history
G. Teacher interviews

IV. Developmental History

Developmental milestones may be significant and can include problems that occurred during pregnancy, delivery, or any unusual conditions at birth. This information conveys an understanding of the child over time to determine whether development is progressing appropriately. Developmental history from infancy forward should include tolerance of frustration, sources of frustration, and what parental coping strategies have been employed. Emotional development includes the ability to successfully get needs met and to develop satisfying age-appropriate relationships. Lucco's (1991) tables of developmental evaluation provide an excellent developmentally informed guide for this phase of assessment. In addition, for a child between ages 3 and 5, the social-developmental profile may include an assessment of the following:

Infancy to 5 years of age

A. Degree of independence
B. Quality of and types of interpersonal relationships experienced
C. Self-image
D. Adaptability
E. Play behavior

Children 5 years and older

A. Level of independence
B. Interpersonal relationships, including quality of
    1. Peer interactions
    2. Adult interactions
    3. Range and intensity of play activity
C. Self-image
D. Self-awareness
E. Self-esteem
F. Self-confidence

G. Coping and effectiveness in social situations
H. Sensitivity to others
I. Adaptability and appropriate persistence
J. Problem-solving abilities

The CSA can include any traumas, hospitalizations, accidents, health problems or chronic conditions, disabilities, unusual problems, or chronic need for medication, if relevant to the child's educational functioning. The reasons for absences from school need to be considered. The child's stamina, energy level, and length of attention span in specific situations or times of day can be significant. The child's physical appearance and conduct while in the company of the social worker should be noted. This information can form the basis for an evaluation of the child's strengths and areas of need. It will be useful for the team, particularly if the information provides a different perspective on the youngster. Significant health issues can provide important clues to why children have developed learning or behavioral problems. Previous interventions to address medical or health issues may not have been reported. More detailed family and student risk factors should be covered as part of the assessment process. This would include vision or hearing problems during early development, as well as recent screenings.

V. School History

The school history for young children begins with day care, nursery school, preschool, and early childhood classes and experiences. Increasingly, children experience group learning and day-care facilities from infancy forward. This section should include a chronological account of informal and formal learning experiences, including their changes and interruptions and the progress or lack of progress the child has made to date. School records are quite useful. For an experienced school social worker often a cumulative record gives a clear indication of the issues and directions in the pupil's life, learning patterns, and what appears to work and not work. The record would reveal attendance patterns, progress rates, special instructional assistance, testing results, and remarks of teachers. Teacher's remarks should be interpreted cautiously, but they often reveal what the pupil's behavior may have brought out in others, as well as insights into the pupil's progress at different periods. School records can also be reviewed to identify academic or social strengths such as "child does not give up, even when tasks are difficult," "child excels in group projects," or "child has perfect attendance." Parents frequently recall the pupil's difficulties making transitions, and their own difficulties, and significant changes, problems, and traumatic experiences that have affected their child's learning progress over the years. The parents' attitudes toward early learning situations, their involvement with their child's learning, and their expectations of the school are all important data. The school history includes a current classroom observation.

VI. Cultural Background, Family History, and Current Issues

The assessment of cultural background is done to determine how the child's culture or background affects his or her ability to function in school as well as whether the school and community are responding appropriately. All children have a cultural background. It includes the family's ethnicity and primary language spoken in the home, the degree of English-speaking proficiency, the usual mode of communication (spoken, sign, etc.) utilized by the student and the family, and the family's socioeconomic status relative to the community. In a dynamic sense, how do the family and the student process the meanings from their culture and from the broader culture? Children's understanding of their cultural background may include ethnic customs, special observances, and unique dress or food not shared by others their age, but also how they come to experience the larger society. An appropriate assessment might read in part:

> Ranjit's family is of East Indian origin, and they observe Sikh traditions. They currently reside in a community with about 25 percent minority population; however, only one other family is of East Indian background, also of Sikh tradition. Fluent in English and in their own language, both of Ranjit's parents come from professional families in India. Economically, Ranjit's family seems to be about average in this solidly middle-class community. Though the family is close knit, they feel well respected and comfortable with their neighbors. Ranjit only speaks English and in many ways appears more adapted to the culture of his peers than to the culture of his parents.

In addition, this section may include information specific to this family's history or dynamics—for example, length of marriage, separations, divorces, deaths, remarriages, moves, transfers, changes in child care, presence or absence of various family members, and other significant events. Observations of the child's role in the family, family expectations, opportunities for friends outside of school, and sense of humor can all contribute to understanding the child as a person in the environment. The atmosphere within the family (which may be temporarily in crisis) should be noted, along with the family's methods and abilities, individually and as a unit, to cope with stressful situations. Because, as previously mentioned, some of this information may be highly sensitive and confidential, an agreed-to substitute statement may be needed, such as, "Some current difficulties in the home make consistent parental support difficult at this time." Because the focus is on the pupil's functioning, the impact of the situation on the pupil's functioning is more important than what actually happened in the family.

VII. Current Functioning

Sensitivity of family members to the child's problem and the family's ability, time, temperament, and willingness to be helpful are important. The parents' view of the child's personality, the interrelationships between family members, the family's interests, activities, hobbies, and leisure activities all give clues to possible recommendations to help the child. Special attention is given to a child's interests at home, how he or she seems to learn best, areas of giftedness, hobbies, and special opportunities the child has for learning. Any maladaptive tendencies toward temper tantrums, fears, impulsivity, enuresis, sleep disturbances, stealing, or other difficulties should be noted.

VIII. Evaluation, Summary, Conclusions, and Recommendations

The final part of the CSA is a concise summary of the meaningful information, including how these experiences affect the child's educational progress. This forms the basis for the social worker's recommendations regarding the educational needs of the child, the best learning environment, parent counseling, available school-based services, and further diagnostic evaluations. Specific recommendations about how parents can be helpful and supportive are appropriate. Because the CSA is a diagnostic tool and is often essential in assessing the severity of emotional problems and mental retardation, the data must be carefully collected and evaluated to ensure its accurate contribution to a differential assessment.

IX. Signature

The CSA ends with the name and professional qualification of the writer (Susan Smith, MSW and/or LCSW) and the date of completion of the document.

Confidentiality is a frequent concern in writing a CSA. The social worker may be given sensitive information that has a direct bearing on the pupil's problem, but it may be inappropriate to share the information with other school personnel. "Sometimes social data is very personal and its potential prejudicial effect may outweigh its diagnostic values" (Byrne, Hare, Hooper, Morse, & Sabatino, 1977, p. 52). If the assessment focuses more on a student's strengths and coping mechanisms rather than the details of his or her "problems," then confidentiality quandaries can dissipate (Gleason, 2007). Another important approach to managing confidentiality in the CSA is to ensure the parents early in the initial interview that this confidential information will not be shared with the school unless the parents give their permission or unless withholding it would endanger the health or welfare of the child. One procedure in keeping with this approach is to prepare the study in the form in which it will be presented and give the parent(s) the opportunity to read it and correct factual inaccuracies. This procedure gives the parents concrete emotional assurance that confidentiality will be honored and adds trust to the social worker–parent relationship. Often the social worker and parent can collaborate on wording that will convey concern without revealing sensitive details. In rare cases, information to which the parents object may need to be included. Such information is included only if it is accurate and critical to decisions to be made about the child's educational needs.

SPECIAL EDUCATION ASSESSMENT

The CSA is sometimes called a *Social Developmental Study* (SDS) when it evaluates a student's possible eligibility for special education services. The SDS is the social worker's contribution to the complete, multifaceted nondiscriminatory evaluation of the student's needs as required by law. This complete evaluation becomes the basis for the team's planning for and with pupils with special needs through development of individualized education programs (IEPs). The SDS is an analysis and synthesis of the information gathered from various sources into a concise presentation of those life experiences of the child, both past and present, that pertain to the child's educational experiences. It needs to address cultural, environmental and familial influences on the student's behavior and learning processes. It should contain an adaptive behavior assessment of the youngster's behavior patterns and functional abilities both in and outside of the learning environment. In the case of youngsters with discipline problems, it may need to contain a *functional behavior assessment*, the basis for a *behavioral intervention plan.* The SDS provides information to the team that can guard against inappropriate labeling or placement of a child. Such inappropriate placement is more likely to occur when test scores and school performance evaluations are the only data used. The inclusion of developmental and ecological information provides a more complete view of the child and expands the range of possibilities appropriate to address the needs of the child (see Bronfenbrenner, 1979; Hobbs, 1976). The SDS is written in educational language (behavioral descriptions, not psychological diagnoses) and should not include the social worker's recommendations for interventions that address the stated concerns. These will be developed later at the team meeting and by the entire team. Thus, specific identification of a special education category or recommendation for placement is not appropriate. A special education category designation, such as behavior disordered, learning disabled, and so forth, is the result of the compilation of the findings of the full multidisciplinary team, including the parents, as an outcome of the multidisciplinary conference. Only when the child's learning needs have been identified from a variety of different perspectives in the meeting can the multidisciplinary team determine the most appropriate and least restrictive environment (or placement) in which these needs can be met.

ADAPTIVE BEHAVIOR ASSESSMENT

There is disagreement in the professional community on the definition of adaptive behavior (MacMillan, Gresham, & Siperstein, 1992; 1995). A simplified definition of adaptive behavior is the effectiveness with which the individual functions independently and meets culturally imposed standards of personal and social responsibility. The American Association on Mental Retardation (AAMR) specified in 1992 that mental retardation refers to substantial limitations in present functioning. It is characterized by significantly subaverage intellectual functioning, existing concurrently with related limitations in two or more of the following applicable adaptive skills areas: communication, self-care, home living, social skills, community use, self-direction, health and safety, functional academics, leisure, and work. Mental retardation manifests itself before age 18. The concept of adaptation historically has been used to differentiate a person's general functioning from his or her measured intellectual functioning (IQ) and was used before the term adaptive behavior was adopted. Assessment of children's levels of adaptive behavior is intended to be a significant step toward two important objectives: 1) that children from minority and culturally diverse groups are not overrepresented in special education designations as a result of cultural influences rather than true disabilities, and 2) that children of all ages and cultural backgrounds are appropriately diagnosed and placed. A child may display behavior that the school environment considers to be maladaptive or emotionally disturbed, but it may be simply *emotionally disturbing* to the adults at school. The overrepresentation of minority children in special education suggests that the intention of this policy has not yet been realized.

Adaptive behavior is understood to be dependent on three primary factors: age, cultural expectations, and environmental expectations. As children get older, they are normally expected to function more independently. The age when this increased independence is to be demonstrated varies dramatically across different cultures. On the other hand, children may have to learn to work with others in coordinating relationships, to trust others, or to appropriately depend on them. It is the immediate environment of a child that ultimately determines what is adaptive or maladaptive. Since children spend the majority of their lives outside of school, it is important to understand how they function in the community and home environments—how a child's behavior is viewed as adaptive in the child's regular environment outside of school. For example, a student who appears significantly delayed in school may function quite independently in the community.

Viola

Viola, a kindergartener, was verbally and physically attacking other students. She attacked a third-grade boy after he pulled the kindergartener's hair braids in the hallway. After she was returned to the classroom, she threatened the rest of the class if any of them "mess with her too." The school social worker contacted the kindergartener's mother to make a home visit and discuss the incident. The mother was very concerned for Viola and supported the need for her to change her behavior. The family was poor, but the household composition was most important. She had two older brothers, who were already in special education classes for emotional/behavioral problems, and both were very rough around home. The mother acknowledged that Viola had learned to deal with any provocation with an immediate counterattack, to avoid getting hurt even more. When the social worker returned to school she discussed the home dynamics with school personnel. It was decided that, rather than beginning the process of seeking an evaluation for special education referral, school personnel would work with Viola to help her recognize that the school is different from home. There were many adults at school to intervene on her behalf. Over the course of the next two months, Viola steadily improved in her willingness to let teachers and others provide protection when other students provoked her.

Informal Adaptive Behavior Assessments

The social worker, a generalist and an expert in family patterns and cultural differences, is often identified as the professional responsible for administering this assessment, reporting results to the team and contributing to its interpretation. Adaptive behavior information is typically gathered either through paper-and pencil instruments or qualitatively and informally through observations and interviews. It is useful to understand the applications of informal, qualitative assessment, as well as the use of formal, quantitative assessment instruments. Informal, qualitative assessments, using interviews and systematic observations (see chapter 24), compare the child's functioning in the classroom with his or her functioning out of the classroom: at home, in the community, and during external school activities. The areas of functioning, outlined in table 22.1, include *independent functioning*, *personal responsibility*, and *social responsibility*. When addressing independent functioning, the informal, qualitative assessment will answer the question "Does he or she have (or can he or she acquire) the necessary skills in each area?" When addressing the child's personal responsibility, the assessment will answer the question "Does he or she use the skills in each behavior setting?" When addressing social responsibility, the question to be answered is "Does he or she use the skill appropriately, that is, in the appropriate place, at the appropriate time?" Table 22.1 presents a conceptual model that may be used in acquiring this information systematically. The child's age and sociocultural background are, of course, essential ingredients in such an informal, qualitative assessment, as they are in formal assessments, using quantitative instruments.

Formal Adaptive Behavior Assessments

Formal, normed assessment of adaptive behavior is most appropriate in the determination of two special education eligibility categories: mental retardation and emotional disturbance. As previously discussed, the assess-

TABLE 22.1 Informal Adaptive Behavior Assessment: A Conceptual Model

	Areas of Functioning		
Environmental Settings	*Independent Functioning*	*Personal Responsibility*	*Social Responsibility*
Academic school: subject areas *Nonacademic school:* playground, halls, gym, to and from school and classes *Out-of-school:* home, neighborhood, peers, parents, other adults	Does he/she have/can he/she acquire the necessary skills?	Does he/she use the skills?	Does he/she use the skills appropriately (time and place)?

All criteria must be appropriate to the age of the child and to the sociocultural setting.

SOURCE: Suggested design by George Batsche, director, School Psychology Program, Eastern Illinois University, NASW Workshop on Adaptive Behavior, March 1981.

ment of mental retardation requires more than an identification of academic and intellectual deficits. The use of appropriately normed instruments is intended to avoid the disproportionate placement of children in special education classes simply because they are culturally different from the majority of the school population. Yet it is quite common that instruments may be considered culturally biased. There are literally hundreds of instruments with varying degrees of precision available. The choice of an instrument is probably best done by the team, where there is often expertise on tests and measurements and a good deal of combined experience. There are ten criteria that should be applied to every scale. There are no scales that will meet all of these, but a number will meet most:

1. Scales should be relevant to the referral question. Use the correct measure for each individual and never expect the child to conform to the scale.
2. Scales should contribute to collaborative decisions about how to help a child. They should help to determine the restrictiveness of the milieu, the frequency of treatment, which interventions (medical and psychological) receive priority, the urgency for intervention, and the prognosis for improvement.
3. Scales should have clear instructions for both administration and scoring. For example, they should clearly indicate the reading level required for the respondent.
4. The normative sample used by the scale should be diverse and stratified by age, gender, race, or disability status. The best scales update their norms every ten years.

5. Scales should be reliable, consistent with a correlation coefficient of .80 or above.
6. Scales should be valid, measuring what they purport to measure and reporting how this was determined, using content, criterion, or construct validity measures.
7. Scales should triangulate their sources. Ideally, rating scales will have separate versions for the parent(s), teacher(s), and student.
8. Scales should avoid a response set. This is most commonly done by having some questions reverse scored, so that a "5" on one item measures adaptive behavior, while a "5" on another item measures maladaptive behavior.
9. Scales should take into account diversity characteristics during administration. Persons with visual impairments may need an audiotaped version of the test and some will need a version in their own language.
10. Scales should enable the evaluator to present the results in a clear manner. This is often accomplished by plotting results onto a graph, sometimes with separate colors for each source. (Illinois State Board of Education, 2007, Appendix F).

A useful resource for reviewing the strengths and weaknesses of any specific instrument is the *Mental Measurements Yearbook* (Geisinger, Spies, Carlson, & Blake, 2007), which is available in most university libraries and online. Raines (2003) and Van Acker (2006) and chapter 23 also provide guidelines on how to identify which instrument may be best suited to the evaluator's needs. It is particularly important to consider issues such as whether the instrument has data to demonstrate that the scales are reliable and valid for the characteristics being assessed, and whether it is possible to triangulate information from more than one informant. It is also essential to consider whether the social worker has the educational background and training to use the instrument being considered. Some instruments specify that the user is expected to have the background and training of a psychologist. Others qualify the instruction with the admonition that it is ultimately the responsibility of the evaluator to determine whether he or she has the training to adequately administer, report, and interpret the results of the assessment instrument.

The necessary training to administer and report the results of an instrument is often available from others in the district or through workshops. The person administering will usually make a report to the team. Here there must be some selection of relevant findings from a mass of quantitative scores, but the qualitative information gathered as part of the SDS will make a considerable difference. Interpretation is best done by the team as a whole, particularly persons with graduate training in tests and measurements and day-to-day familiarity with the instrument.

In any case, the key element in the SDS is the social worker's analysis and synthesis of significant information from a variety of sources using multiple methodologies. This requires going well beyond the computer-generated reports produced by some assessment instruments. If the computer-generated report is used as a part of the SDS, the social worker needs to be prepared to explain and defend it. To do this, it is important to see the fit of the adaptive behavior assessment into the total social work assessment scheme. While formal instruments are very popular with school districts, the computerized report that is automatically generated by some of the instruments—even if it may look professional in its presentation of data—is not a substitute for a comprehensive social work assessment. Sometimes formal instruments are not available or appropriate. Sometimes their rigid format is not adapted to the situation or misses what the social worker has learned about the pupil's functioning, cultural background, or environmental conditions in other parts of the assessment. Thus, even if a formal instrument is used, the social worker may need to add to the findings or discuss them further with qualifications.

FUNCTIONAL BEHAVIOR ASSESSMENT

When IDEA was reauthorized in 1997 and 2004, it specified that when disciplinary action is being considered, students who receive special education services are to be provided with some additional procedural safeguards. A multidisciplinary team in the school is directed to conduct a functional behavior assessment. This in turn assists in developing a behavioral intervention plan for (and with) the student. The assessment is based on:

- An objective, detailed, and behaviorally specific definition or description of the behaviors of concern
- A description of the frequency, duration, intensity, and severity of the behaviors of concern and the settings in which they occur
- A description of other environmental variables that may affect the behavior (e.g., medication, medical conditions, sleep, diet, schedule, social factors, etc.)
- An examination and review of the known communicative behavior and the functional and practical intent of the behavior
- A description of environmental modifications made to change the target behavior
- An identification of appropriate behaviors that could serve as functional alternatives to the target behavior (see Clark, 2001)

The key questions in functional behavior assessments are the following: How is the student currently performing? and How does the student respond to interventions suggested by the problem-solving team? The focus is on gathering systematic information not only on the student but also on the factors in the school, home, and community settings that may be contributing to the difficulties. Analysis of the functional behavior assessment focuses on understanding:

- The purpose and function of the behaviors of concern
- The factors/conditions that may precipitate these behaviors
- The person's social, emotional, and behavioral functioning in relation to expectations
- The development of interventions
- The identification of needed supports
- The identification of desired behavior(s) that could serve as functional alternatives (see Clark, 2001)

There is a beginning guide to the development of a functional behavior assessment in the earlier discussion of assessment of the dynamics of the learning environment in this chapter. There is also a good sampler of developmental learning objectives in chapter 26 (table 26.2). Using these principles and this language, the school social worker can contribute to the team's mapping of the *functions* of a targeted behavior, and the *antecedents* and *consequences* of the behavior *as the student perceives them*. The key is to think of the student's perceptions of the functions, antecedents, and consequences of behavior. How does Viola understand certain boys' aggression in school and what she has to do to deal with it? Using the student's perspective, antecedents (triggers) can be lessened. The student can be assisted to manage them. And the student can be assisted to get what he or she legitimately wants and needs (e.g., safety) in a less disruptive and dysfunctional way.

In many ways the functional behavior assessment is not very different from the way social workers ordinarily think, except that it is quite behaviorally specific. It does not explicitly compare or classify the pupil in relation to an abstract norm of the behavior of other pupils (often the problem with normed, paper-and-pencil evaluative instruments). Rather it begins where the pupil is and looks at what may trigger a behavior and what might be workable next steps and goals for social participation. What antecedent conditions might possibly trigger the behavior? What functional payoff might there have been for the student? What did he get or avoid? Multiple methods such as interviews, observations, checklists, and so on should be used to gather the information. This process would then result in the development of a behavioral intervention plan (BIP) (see chapter 26) with interventions linked to the functional assessment.

Social workers have traditionally used observation and interviews as their basic tools for gathering information for assessing the dynamics of persons in their environments, preparing social histories, and conducting needs assessments. This chapter has addressed the application of these skills in the school environment. This chapter has also presented an introduction to some of the additional tools that are necessary for the school social worker to be of service to school personnel, students, and families. Conducting assessments of the learning environment is essential if we are to move beyond a focus on the student alone. Being prepared to assist in conducting functional assessments of behavior will be essential for not only meeting the needs of students, but also for demonstrating the social worker's ability to help schools meet the mandates that are being placed on them. Fortunately, functional assessments are very close to the analysis of person-environment relations social workers have always done, now applied to the educational setting. Gaining some experience with adaptive behavior assessment and being able to do either informal, qualitative assessments or to use formal instruments will require going beyond the traditional generalist skills provided in graduate schools of social work. However, the results can give additional credibility to the clinical impressions gained through the interviews and observations. This is especially important when we are being called on to assist in special education decisions about a student's possible eligibility for additional services. Our role is essential for ensuring that environmental and familial factors are taken into consideration as well as for helping parents be aware of their rights.

References

American Association on Mental Retardation (AAMR) (1992). *Mental retardation: Definition, classification, and systems of supports* (9th ed.). Washington D.C.: Author.

Bronfenbrenner, U. (1979). *The ecology of human development*. Cambridge, MA: Harvard University Press.

Byrne, J. L., Hare, I., Hooper, S. N., Morse, B. J., & Sabatino, C. A. (1977). The role of a social history in special education evaluation. In R. J. Anderson, M. Freeman, & R. L. Edwards (Eds.), *School social work and PL 94-142: The Education for All Handicapped Act* (pp. 47–55). Washington, DC: National Association of Social Workers.

Clark, J. (2001). *Functional behavioral assessment and behavioral intervention plans: Implementing the student discipline provisions of IDEA '97.* NASW school social work hot topics. Washington, DC: National Association of Social Workers. Available at http://www.naswdc.org/sections/SSW/hottopics/schalark.htm

Cowger, C. D., Anderson, K. M., & Snively, C. A. (2006). Assessing strengths: The political context of individual, family, and community empowerment. In D. Saleebey (Ed.), *The strengths perspective in social work practice* (4th ed., pp. 93–115). Boston: Allyn & Bacon.

Finn, C. E. Jr. (1984). Toward strategic independence: Nine commandments for enhancing school effectiveness. *Phi Delta Kappan, 65*(8), 513–524.

Geisinger, K. E., Spies, R. A., Carlson, J. F., & Blake, B. S. (Eds.) (2007). *Mental measurements yearbook*, 17th ed. Lincoln, NE: Buros Institute.

Gleason, E. T. (2007). A strengths-based approach to the social developmental study. *Children & Schools, 29*(1), 51–59.

Hobbs, N. (Ed.). (1976). *Issues in the classification of children*. San Francisco: Jossey-Bass.

Illinois State Board of Education (2007) *Student service providers recommended practices and procedures manual: School social work.* author, www.isbe.net, Appendix F

Individuals with Disabilities Education Act, PL 105-17. U.S.C. 11401 et seq.

Individuals with Disabilities Education Improvement Act (IDEA 2004). Public Law 108-446.

Lucco, A. A. (1991). Assessment of the school-age child. *Families in Society: The Journal of Contemporary Human Services, 81*(5), 394–407.

MacMillan, D. L., Gresham, F. M., & Siperstein, G. N. (1992) Conceptual and psychometric concerns about the 1992 AAMR definition of mental retardation. *American Journal on Mental Retardation, 98*, 325–335.

MacMillan, D. L., Gresham, F. M., & Siperstein, G. N. (1995) Heightened concerns over the 1992 AAMR definition: Advocacy vs. precision. *American Journal on Mental Retardation, 100*, 87–97.

Parton, N., & O'Byrne, P. (2000). *Constructive social work: Towards a new practice.* New York: St. Martin's Press.

Purkey, S. C., & Smith, M. S. (1983). Effective schools: A review. *The Elementary School Journal, 83*(4), 427–452.

Raines, J. C. (2002). Brainstorming hypotheses for functional behavior assessment: The link to effective behavioral intervention plans. *School Social Work Journal, 26*(2), 30–45.

Raines, J. C. (2003). Rating the rating scales: Ten criteria. *School Social Work Journal, 27*(2), 1–17.

Repp, A. C., & Horner, R. H. (1999*). Functional analysis of problem behavior: From effective assessment to effective support*. Belmont, CA: Wadsworth.

Roberts, M. (1995). Best practices in assessing environmental factors that impact student performance. In A. Thomas & J. Grimes (Eds.), *Best practices in school psychology* (pp. 679–688). Washington, DC: National Association of School Psychologists.

Saleebey, D. (2006). The strengths approach to practice. In D. Saleebey (Ed.), *The strengths perspective in social work practice* (4th ed., pp. 77–92). Boston: Allyn & Bacon.

Siporin, M. (1975). *Introduction to social work practice*. New York: Macmillan.

Van Acker, R. (2006). The assessment of adaptive behavior. In R. Constable, C. R. Massat, S. McDonald, & J. P. Flynn (Eds.). *School social work: practice, policy, and research* (6th ed., pp. 379–391). Chicago: Lyceum.

Wang, M. C., Haertel, G. D., & Walberg, H. J. (1999). Psychological and educational resilience. In A. J. Reynolds, H. J. Walberg, & R. P. Weissberg (Eds.), *Promoting positive outcomes: Issues in children's and families' lives* (pp. 329–366*).* Washington, DC: CWLA Press.

Zuna, N., & McDougall, D. (2004). Using positive behavioral support to manage avoidance of academic tasks. *Teaching Exceptional Children, 37*(1), 18–24.

23

The Screening & Assessment of Adaptive Behavior

James C. Raines
Illinois State University

Richard Van Acker
University of Illinois at Chicago

- Reasons for Screenings of Adaptive Behavior
- Reasons for Assessing Adaptive Behavior
- Why Social Workers Are Qualified to Assess Adaptive Behavior
- Defining Terms
- The Assessment of Adaptive Behavior
- Common Instruments Used to Measure Adaptive Behavior
- Using Clinical Judgment in the Assessment of Adaptive Behavior

For decades, social workers, psychologists, educators, and others have attempted to identify and measure accurately those behaviors related to competence that distinguish individuals as they interact with their physical and social environments (see Kelly, 1927), that is, assess their adaptive behavior (Schmidt & Salvia, 1984). Adaptive behavior assessments fall into two major types: formal and informal. This chapter will discuss primarily the formal measures that use semistructured interviews or standardized scales. Informal adaptive behavior assessment is discussed in chapter 22. Understanding how individuals adapt themselves to the requirements of their physical and social environment is the goal of many of our social sciences. The ability to function effectively across a range of adaptive skill areas is essential for personal success and adjustment in life. Maximizing adaptive behavior skills for individuals with physical, mental, or emotional challenges is often a goal for social work intervention. Thus, the construct of adaptive behavior is becoming increasingly important in the identification and treatment of individuals with various disabilities, such as cognitive impairments, emotional disturbance, and mental impairments. The American Association on Intellectual & Developmental Disabilities (AAIDD), formerly the American Association on Mental Retardation (AAMR), is the international and multidisciplinary leader in the conceptualization, definition, and classification of mental retardation (see www.aaidd.org). Founded in 1876, this organization has included adaptive behavior as a critical factor in defining mental retardation since the late 1950s (Heber, 1959).

REASONS FOR SCREENINGS OF ADAPTIVE BEHAVIOR

There are three major reasons to do screenings for adaptive behavior. First, the Individuals with Disabilities Education Improvement Act (IDEA) of 2004 (IDEA 2004) requires that all states have policies and procedures in place to find children who are in need of special education regardless of whether they are homeless, attend private schools (including religious schools), or are wards of the state. Therefore schools require quick and accurate ways to determine which children require further evaluation and which ones do not. Second, as more school districts adopt a Response-to-Intervention model of services (see Figure 23.1) providers of related services need to be able to identify which children require more intensive services than general education, but less intensive services than special education. Response-to-Intervention can be defined as the practice of providing scientifically based interventions that fit student needs along with frequent monitoring of the student's level of performance and learning rate over time in order to make important educational decisions (National Association of State Directors of Special Education, 2006). For these children, screening instruments can be an efficient way of monitoring which children are responding to intervention and which ones are not (Torgesen, 2004). Finally, early screening can lead to early intervention and ultimately save the government from having to fund costly remediation programs (Barnett, 2000). Early intervention programs are cost efficient when one realizes that for every dollar spent, society saves $17 in remedial costs (Glascoe, 2006).

REASONS FOR ASSESSING ADAPTIVE BEHAVIOR

There are a number of reasons for assessing adaptive behavior. Federal regulations and state school codes began to require that adaptive behavior be assessed before a pupil could be considered eligible for special education services under the category of mental retardation, developmental disability,

FIGURE 23.1 A Response-to-Intervention Model

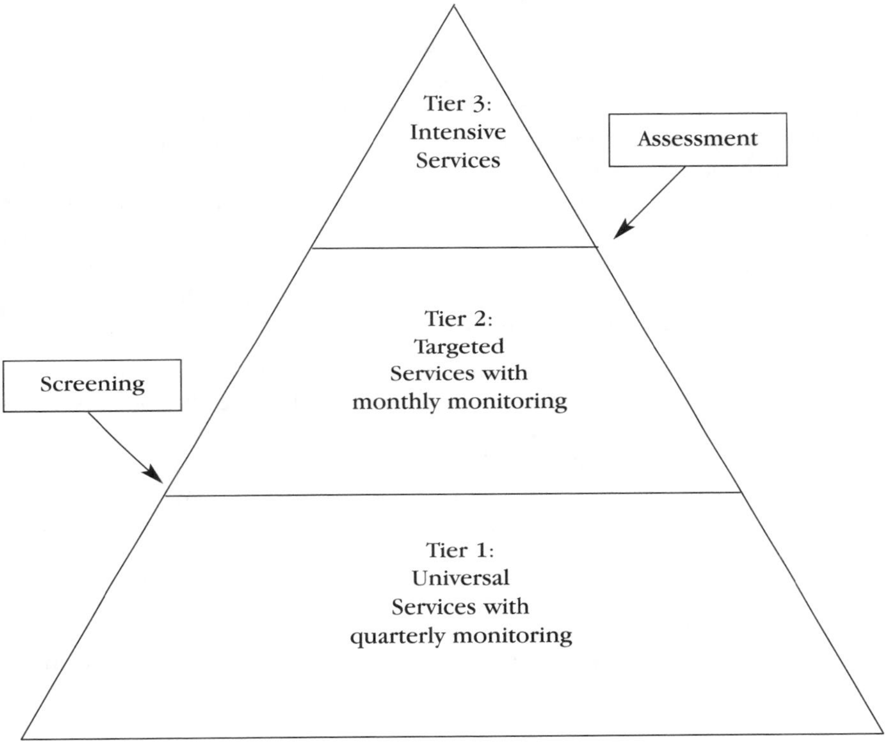

or autism. Adaptive behavior may also be assessed when students are evaluated for other disabilities. For example, when the possibility of an emotional disturbance or learning disability is explored, an assessment of adaptive and maladaptive behavior is often recommended. The latest reauthorization of the Individuals with Disabilities Education Act in 2004 clarified that any evaluation of a child's school performance was meant to be inclusive of both academic achievement and functional performance (Raines, 2006).

Another reason for assessing adaptive behavior relates to program planning. The reauthorization of IDEA in 1997 specified the need to develop educational objectives and behavior management plans for students with disabilities whose behavior interferes with their own learning or that of others. Thus, the assessment of both adaptive and maladaptive behavior has an increased level of importance in the identification of target behaviors. This legislation also specified increased responsibility for the development of educational objectives to promote the transition of students with disabilities into the workplace. Again, the assessment of adaptive behavior can play an important role in the identification of appropriate goals and objectives.

WHY SOCIAL WORKERS ARE QUALIFIED TO ASSESS ADAPTIVE BEHAVIOR

Social workers have assessed people's functioning in their various environments throughout the history of the profession. Assessments are made in comparison to others in the same cohort, controlling for age, gender, ethnicity, community, environment, socioeconomic status, and any perceived or suspected disabilities, as well as other defining characteristics. For most people, functional abilities are relatively stable across various settings, however, for some there is significant variation. Describing this variability is an essential component of a social developmental study and is identified as the adaptive behavior assessment. It is important that in school settings the social worker take responsibility for adaptive behavior assessments, for three reasons:

1. Social workers are well trained in the interviewing process.
2. The professional focus of social work is the functioning of persons in their environment. The central theme of social work practice is improving the fit between the person and the environment.
3. Finally, one of the requirements of the Individuals with Disabilities Education Act (IDEA, PL 108-446) is the multidisciplinary approach to assessment and decision making in determining the academic, developmental, or functional needs of each referred student.

Thus, both through training and theoretical framework, adaptive behavior assessment falls well within the professional responsibilities of the social worker.

DEFINING TERMS

There are three terms that require definition before moving further. The first is related to the now obsolete term "mental retardation" (Glidden, 2006; Greenspan, 2006; Schalock & Luckasson, 2005). While that term is still widely used, the more accurate and current term is intellectual disability. The (2007) AAIDD definition for intellectual disability is:

> A disability characterized by significant limitations both in intellectual functioning and in adaptive behavior as expressed in conceptual, social, and practical adaptive skills. This disability originates before the age of 18. A complete and accurate understanding of mental retardation involves realizing that mental retardation refers to a particular state of functioning that begins in early childhood, has many dimensions, and is affected positively by individualized supports. As a model of functioning, it includes the contexts and environment within which the person functions and interacts and requires a multidimensional and ecological approach that reflects the interaction of the individual with the environment, and the outcomes of that interaction with regards to independence, relationships, societal contributions, participation in school and community, and personal well-being. (AAIDD, July, 2007; Schalock et al., 2007)

This new definition of intellectual disability allows it to be more aligned with the federal definition for developmental disabilities:

> A severe, chronic disability of an individual that is attributable to a mental or physical impairment or combination of mental and physical impairment; is manifested before the individual attains age 22; is likely to continue indefinitely; results in substantial functional limitations in 3 or more of the following areas of major life activity: self-care; receptive and expressive language; learning; mobility; self-direction; capacity for independent living; and economic self-sufficiency; and reflects the individual's need for a combination and sequence of special, interdisciplinary, or generic services, individualized supports, or other forms of assistance that are of lifelong or extended duration and are individually planned and coordinated. An individual from birth to age 9, inclusive, who has substantial developmental delay or specific congenital or acquired conditions may be considered to have a developmental disability without meeting 3 or more of the criteria described above in (A) through (E) if the individual, without services and supports, has a high probability of meeting those criteria later in life. (Developmental Disabilities Act & Bill of Rights Act of 2000, PL 106-402, see http://dhs.sd.gov/ddc/faq.aspx)

Both the definition of intellectual disability and developmental disabilities, therefore, require an evaluation of a child's functional limitations. According to the AAIDD, limitations in adaptive behavior can be determined by:

> [. . .] using standardized tests that are normed on the general population including people with disabilities and people without disabilities. On these standardized measures, significant limitations in adaptive behavior are operationally defined as performance that is at least 2 standard deviations below the mean of either (a) one of the following three types of adaptive behavior: conceptual, social, or practical, or (b) an overall score on a standardized measure of conceptual, social, and practical skills. (AAIDD, July, 2007)

Thus, the AAIDD identifies three major categories of adaptive skills, including conceptual, social, and practical. Conceptual skills include: 1) receptive and expressive language, 2) reading and writing, 3) money concepts, and 4) self-directions. Social skills include: 1) interpersonal, 2) responsibility, 3) self-esteem, 4) gullibility, 5) naïveté, 6) follows rules, 7) obeys laws, and 8) avoids victimization. Practical skills include: 1) personal activities of daily living (such as eating, dressing, mobility, and toileting), 2) instrumental activities of daily living (such as preparing meals, taking medication, using the telephone, managing money, using transportation, and doing housekeeping), 3) occupational skills, and 4) maintaining a safe environment (AAIDD, 2007). Altogether, there are over 25 specific skills that must be assessed for a comprehensive view of an individual's adaptive functioning. Most standardized tests will assess many more items than this number since most of these areas will vary based on the age and culture of the identified person.

Adaptive Behavior as a Function of Age

The age of the target individual must be considered when assessing adaptive behavior. When assessing adaptive behavior, the person completing the measure must take care to be sensitive to the realities of child development. As most assessment measures call for the respondent to rate the frequency with which the target individual displays a given behavior (e.g., usually, sometimes, seldom, or never), knowledge of what is developmentally appropriate is assumed. Only a subset of the adaptive skill areas identified by the AAMR may be relevant at a given age. For example, when one is assessing early elementary–age students, the skills related to work will be significantly less important than issues related to functional academics, communication, and self-care (Gresham, MacMillan, & Siperstein, 1995; Reschly, 1987). The nature of the expectations placed on the individual for the display of adaptive behavior changes dramatically over the life span. As children grow, assessment of adaptive behavior targets learned behavior. We expect young children to communicate socially with others and to demonstrate social skills as they play together. We anticipate that children will demonstrate increased independence in self-care (e.g., dressing, feeding), community use (e.g., mobility in their neighborhood), self-direction, and engagement in leisure time activities as they mature. With adolescence come expectations for eventual transition into the adult world of work.

Adaptive Behavior as a Function of Cultural Expectations

Cultural awareness and sensitivity play a critical role in the assessment of adaptive behavior. Culture, by definition, affects the display of language, behavior, and beliefs. For example, some cultures support personal independence and individual achievement more so than others. The age at which children are expected to display specific behaviors related to self-care, self-direction, and independent community use differ dramatically across cultures. The respondent must be aware of the cultural expectations of the individual being assessed. Moreover, the validity of the score obtained will depend on the similarity or difference of the person being assessed to those individuals included within the normative sample of the measure being employed (Eikeseth, 2006; Zhang & Yao, 2003). That is, if the target individual differs significantly in level of acculturation from those individuals used to norm a particular measure, the score should be interpreted with great care.

Adaptive Behavior and the Environment

Successful adaptation requires a good "person-in-environment fit." The individual's capabilities must match the environmental demands. The concept of environment in the assessment of adaptive behavior includes those specific settings in which the individual functions, in particular the home, school, work, and community environments. What is considered adaptive in one environment may prove maladaptive in another. A behavior that proves adaptive in a rural setting may have quite a different outcome in an urban setting (Bornstein, Ginsti, Leach, & Venuti, 2005). For example, as children mature, greater independence and greater self-directed mobility within and between neighborhoods in the community are expected. For many children growing up in the inner cities of our large urban centers, such mobility might significantly increase the personal danger to which these children are exposed. Movement through rival gang territories can lead to confrontation, assault, and death (Salcido, Ornelas, & Garcia, 2002). Therefore, increased mobility and independence could be viewed as maladaptive in some contexts.

Not only can the environment affect the individual's pattern of adaptive behavior, but the opposite is true as well. Children's adaptive abilities can change the environmental climate in which they develop. For example, Weiss and colleagues (2003) found that children with lower adaptive functioning increased parental stress. Given the relationship between parental stress and child abuse, it should come as no surprise that children with disabilities experience a higher rate of abuse than those without disabilities (Sullivan & Knutson, 2000). In short, adaptive behavior and the environment have a complex and reciprocal relationship.

The Assessment of Maladaptive Behaviors

The inclusion of maladaptive behavior in measures of adaptive behavior often increases the confusion and difficulty in the interpretation of findings. For obvious reasons, the identification of maladaptive behavior is important in its own right. The relation of adaptive to maladaptive behavior, however, is not that of behaviors at opposite ends of a continuum. Most children with disabilities have both strengths (adaptive behaviors) and weaknesses (maladaptive behaviors) that need to be assessed (Geschwind & Dykens, 2004). In fact, these behaviors can appear to exist quite independently of one another and both can increase as a function of age (Cohen, Schmidt-Lackner, Romanczyk, & Sudhalter, 2003). An individual can display both adaptive and maladaptive behavior in the same area. For example, many individuals who practice many acts of great care in the area of health and safety (e.g., good diet and exercise) also will engage in significant levels of substance abuse (e.g., smoking and alcohol consumption). Moreover, the absence of maladaptive behavior does not imply the presence of adaptive behavior.

THE ASSESSMENT OF ADAPTIVE BEHAVIOR

Adaptive behavior is measured across multiple environmental settings using typical, everyday functioning rather than optimal performance. Adaptive behaviors are those that are performed regularly (habitually and customarily), spontaneously, and without prompting or assistance from others.

When assessing adaptive behavior, we are not interested in what the target individual can do (ability), but rather what the individual typically does (performance). This is an important and often misunderstood distinction. Individuals who have the knowledge and skills necessary to perform a given response often fail to do so routinely in their everyday interactions with their environment. For example, a student might know how to solve a given social problem (e.g., peer conflict) in an acceptable fashion (e.g., verbally expressing his feelings in a calm manner). When confronted with a peer conflict, however, the student might routinely respond with aggression. The assessment of his adaptive behavior is not aimed at the discovery of his potential response (verbal problem solving), but rather at a measure of his typical response (aggression). Behaviors are rated as performed regularly (habitually and customarily). Moreover, behaviors must be displayed spontaneously without prompting or assistance from others.

Adaptive behavior information may be gathered either through a standardized measure or through observations and interviews as a more qualitative assessment. IDEA 2004 does not specify that standardized measures are required to make an adaptive behavior assessment. Informal adaptive behavior assessments can bring an understanding of the effect of environmental conditions on behavior. Informal or qualitative assessments can be used to assess a child's functioning in the classroom and compare this to his or her functioning in other settings. The child's age and sociocultural background are, of course, essential ingredients in such an informal assessment, as they are in formal assessments. Areas of functioning include independent functioning, personal responsibility, and social responsibility. For each of these areas, the school social worker needs to determine whether the child has necessary skills to function at his/her grade level.

Adaptive behavior is most often assessed using a formal, standardized instrument. The report usually comes from a third person (respondent), and this in turn generates a standardized rating of a target individual. Rather than employing systematic observation of the behavior of the target individual, the examiner relies on the cumulative observations of a respondent who is familiar with the target individual. This method of assessment is susceptible to various types of limitations, errors, and biases. The respondents are limited to those behaviors they have had the opportunity to observe. Often different respondents will observe individuals in only a limited number of contexts (e.g., the school classroom, the lunchroom, the home setting). Some of these environments place different demands on students, so children will often display different behavior in these various contexts. This is why Achenbach, McConaughy, and Howell (1987) concluded that the best way to get a three-dimensional view of the child within his or her environment is to use multiple informants and multiple methods.

There also is a concern that respondents can differ significantly in their awareness and/or tolerance for some behaviors. Most assessments of adaptive behavior ask respondents to rate on a scale the frequency or seriousness of various behaviors with an underlying assumption that respondents will employ a similar standard. Thus, there is an assumption that one respondent's "sometimes" is assumed to differ from another respondents "usually." This may not be a safe assumption. A related problem results from the fact that these ordinal level measurements are often treated as interval level measurements to calculate the target individual's scores. These scores are obtained by assigning numbers (e.g., 0, 1, or 2) to the various ratings and manipulating these numbers mathematically. Remember, what are really being added are subjective ratings (e.g., a "sometimes" + a "usually" + a "seldom" = ______). This is why clinical judgment is required whenever one interprets the results of either formal or informal assessments (AAIDD, 2007).

Another concern with the traditional approach to assessing adaptive behavior is that the individual being assessed may conceal important behaviors from the respondent, perhaps owing to cultural demands, fear of consequences, or other personal agendas. Thus, the respondent may not report the presence of a potentially important adaptive or maladaptive behavior; or a respondent might be less than truthful when completing an assessment. This is especially true if the respondent has a stake in the outcome. For example, parents might be more willing to give their child the benefit of the doubt or provide responses based on ability rather than typical performance if they are concerned that their child might be stigmatized as having an intellectual disability or emotional disturbance. On the other hand, a teacher might be inclined to magnify the frequency or magnitude of a maladaptive behavior if it will increase the likelihood of removing a particularly challenging child from her classroom.

Given these potential limitations, errors, and biases, the examiner is advised to seek information and assessments of adaptive behavior from multiple people across a variety of settings within which the target individual interacts. The goal of multiple measurements of adaptive behavior is the identification of patterns in responding, and the development of a reliable understanding of the target individual's adaptive and maladaptive behavior. Best practice involves multiple data collection strategies that can be recalled using the acronym, RIOT, for Reviewing records, Interviewing primary caregivers (parents and teachers), Observing the child within multiple contexts, and Testing for mastery. One has to keep in mind that disparate ratings do not necessarily indicate error but could signal the differences in behavior of an individual in distinct settings and/or with different people.

COMMON INSTRUMENTS USED TO MEASURE ADAPTIVE BEHAVIOR

It has been estimated that there are over 200 instruments designed to measure adaptive behavior (Spreat, 1999). In the next section of this chapter, both screening instruments (see table 23.1) and assessment instruments

TABLE 23.1 Common Screening Measures of Adaptive Behavior

Instrument (Authors)	*Age range*	*Informant*	*Type of Measure*
Ages & Stages Questionnaire (Bricker & Squires, 1999)	4 mos.–5 yrs.	Parent	Rating Scale
Battelle Developmental Inventory Screener (Newborg, 2005)	Birth–7 yrs.	Parent	Rating Scale
Parents' Evaluation of Developmental Status (Glascoe, 2002)	Birth–8 yrs.	Parent	Rating Scale
Prescreening Developmental Questionnaire (Frankenburg et al., 1992)	1 mo.–6 yrs.	Parent	Rating Scale

(see table 23.2) used to measure adaptive behavior are reviewed. The 2002 AAMR manual clearly states that a valid determination of adaptive skills requires that "adaptive behavior should be measured with a standardized instrument that provides normative data on people without mental retardation" (p. 83). The purpose of this section, therefore, is to familiarize the reader with some of the most commonly used measures and to point out some of the important features related to scoring the measure, the normative samples available for interpretation, and critical psychometric properties of the measure. This information should help the reader select the appropriate measure for a specific need and aid in the interpretation of results.

TABLE 23.2 Common Assessment Measures of Adaptive Behavior

Measure (Authors)	*Age Range*	*Informant*	*Type of Measure*
AAMD Adaptive Behavior Scale: School (Lambert, Nihira, & Leland, 1993)	3–21 years	Teacher	Interview Questionnaire
AAMD Adaptive Behavior Scale: Residential & Community	18–79 years	Professional	Interview Questionnaire
Adaptive Behavior Inventory (Brown & Leigh, 1986)	6–18 years	Teacher	Interview Questionnaire
Adaptive Behavior Assessment System (Harrison & Oakland, 2000)	0–21 years	Parent & Teacher	Rating Scale
Adaptive Behavior Evaluation Scale (McCarney & Arthaud, 2006)	4–18 years	Parent & Teacher	Rating Scale
Bayley Scales of Infant Development (Bayley, 2005)	1–42 months	Professional	Observation
Scales of Independent Behavior-Revised (Bruininks et al., 1996)	3 mos.–90 yrs.	Parent or Teacher	Interview Questionnaire
Vineland Adaptive Behavior Scales (Sparrow, Cicchetti, & Balla, 2005, 2007)	Birth–90 yrs.	Parent & Teacher	Interview or Rating Scale

Screening Measures

Screening measures are broad measures that attempt to uncover multiple risk factors with a minimum of effort. All the measures below cover five standard domains for developmental disabilities, including personal-social, adaptive, motor, communication, and cognitive functioning. Hamilton (2006) identified a number of screening measures that were brief, reliable, and easy to administer. The ideal amount of time for screening is ten to fifteen minutes per child. Good screening measures strike a balance between sensitivity and specificity (Jenkins, 2003). Sensitivity is the degree to which the instrument correctly identifies those children who are at risk for future problems. Specificity is the degree to which the instrument also correctly identifies those children who are not at risk (Raines, 2008). Too much sensitivity can lead to false positives—those children who score poorly but are really doing well. Too much specificity can lead to false negatives—those children who score well, but really need help. The Child Seek program in Hawaii has summarized these measures in both a table and narrative description (Shapiro & Derrington, 2007). The following four scales are widely employed and have good sensitivity and specificity.

Ages & Stages Questionnaire. The *Ages & Stages Questionnaire* (ASQ) was developed in 1999 (Bricker & Squires, 1999). The ASQ was normed on 388 nondisabled children and 1,620 children with clinical problems. About 65 percent of the sample was White and 35 percent was minority (including Asians and Pacific Islanders). Test-retest reliability and interobserver reliability were both high at .94. It covers five standard domains with six questions for each domain. It is appropriate for ages 4 months—5 years and is available from Brookes Publishing (www.brookespublishing.com).

Battelle Developmental Inventory Screener. *The Battelle Developmental Inventory*—Second edition—Screener (BDI-2S) was developed in 1984 and revised in 2005 (Newborg, 2005). The BDI-2 was normed on more than 2,500 children closely matching the U.S. 2000 census. Test-retest reliability ranges from .92 to .99 over the five domains and interrater reliability ranges from .94 to .98. The BDI also covers the same five domains with one hundred questions that can be used as a screener prior to employing the full BDI. It is appropriate for ages birth—seven years and is available from Riverside Publishing (www.riverpub.com).

Parents' Evaluation of Developmental Status. The *Parents' Evaluation of Developmental Status* (PEDS) was developed in 1997 (Glascoe, 2002). The PEDS was normed on 771 children from various socioeconomic statuses and racial-ethnic backgrounds. Test-retest reliability and interrater reliability are both high at .88. The PEDS relies solely on parent report and covers the same five domains with ten questions per age level, making it the shortest of the screening measures. The PEDS is appropriate for ages birth–8 years and is available from www.pedstest.com.

Prescreening Developmental Questionnaire. The *Prescreening Developmental Questionnaire*—Second edition (PDQ-II) is based on the longer Denver Developmental Screening Test—Second edition (DDST-II) (Frankenburg, Dodds, Archer, Shapiro, & Bresnick, 1992). Both the DDST-II and the PDQ-II were normed on more than 2,000 children living in Colorado. Test-retest reliability is high at .94 and interrater reliability ranges from .80 to .95. While the DDST-II uses direct observation and has 125 questions, the PDQ relies on parent report and has 105 items. The DDST-II and the PDQ-II are appropriate for ages 1 month to 6 years and is available from www.denverii.com.

Assessment Measures

Assessment measures perform a more in-depth function of pinpointing specific problems and even aiding in the diagnosis of specific disorders. All of the scales below focus specifically on adaptive functioning. Most of these scales are longer, more expensive, and better studied than the screening instruments above. Because of the time and expense of administering these scales, they probably should be used only when previous measures have alerted the school social worker to the need for greater clarity about the problem or the child has failed to respond to targeted interventions.

***AAMD Adaptive Behavior Scales* (ABS).** As an organization, the AAMR has developed its own rating scale, titled Adaptive Behavior Scales (ABS), which correlates with the ten behaviors they identify as crucial. The revised ABS are composed of a school version—The AAMR Adaptive Behavior Scale-School 2 (ABS-S2) (Lambert, Nihira, & Leland, 1993); and a Residential and Community version—the AAMR Adaptive Behavior Scale: Residential and Community Scale 2nd edition. Both are individually administered measures. The school edition is designed for children and youth ages 3–21 years and was normed on 3,328 students (2,074 with an intellectual disability and 1,254 without an intellectual disability). The residential and community version is designed for individuals aged 18 to 79 and was normed on 4,103 individuals with developmental disabilities stratified by living arrangements (living at home, small-group home, community-based residence, and large institution). Sample members represented individuals from forty-six states and the District of Columbia and were predominantly between the ages of 18 and 39. The norm sample was generally representative of the nation as a whole with regard to race, ethnicity, and geographical region. Two independent critiques of the Adaptive Behavior Scale suggest it measures two major components of adaptive behavior (personal independence and social behavior) rather than the five components suggested by the original authors (Stinnett, Fuqua, & Coombs, 1999; Watkins, Ravert, & Crosby, 2002). Therefore, test users should be cautious about specifying discrete domains of adaptability. It is available from www.proedinc.com.

Adaptive Behavior Inventory. The *Adaptive Behavior Inventory* (ABI) (Brown & Leigh, 1986) is an individually administered, norm-referenced measure to assess the behavior of students who range in age from 6 to 18 years. The test was normed on 1,296 nondisabled students and 1,076 students with mental retardation in 21 states. The typical respondent when using the ABI is the target student's classroom teacher or other professional with whom the child frequently interacts. The ABI is specifically developed to explore the adaptive behavior skills of a given target individual. Both a full-scale and a short form (sometimes referred to as a "screening" instrument) of the ABI are available. While this instrument is still available from the publisher, the ABI has not been revised in over twenty years and is no longer recommended for today's youth.

Adaptive Behavior Assessment System. The *Adaptive Behavior Assessment System* was created by Harrison and Oakland (2003) and quickly revised to meet the new standards set by the AAMR in 2002. The Adaptive Behavior Assessment System–Second edition (ABAS-II) has five forms depending on the age of the child and who does the rating. There are two parent forms for ages 0–5 and 5–21 and two teacher forms for ages 2–5 and 5–21. There is also a self-report form for ages 16 to 89. The ABAS-II measures functioning in the 11 skills areas of communication, community use, health and safety, leisure, self-care, self-direction, functional pre-academics, home (or school) living, social skills, work, and motor skills. These skills are then translated into four domain scores: conceptual, social, practical, and general adaptive composite (GAC) to conform to the AAMR's (2002) definition of adaptive behavior. The average GAC score is 100 with a standard deviation of 15 points. The instrument was measured using at least one hundred participants in each age group as well as clinical samples (e.g., children with ADHD, autism, learning disabilities, and hearing/visual impairment). Rust and Wallace's (2004) review concluded that the ABAS-II is both theoretically and technically sound with excellent reliability and validity. The ABAS-II is available from: http://harcourtassessment.com.

Adaptive Behavior Evaluation Scale. The *Adaptive Behavior Evaluation Scale*–Revised (ABES-R2) comes in two versions, one for children 4–12 years of age and one for adolescents 13–18 years old (McCarney & Arthaud, 2006). Both revisions were completed in 2006. The former was standardized on 3,288 children and the latter was standardized on 1,998 students. Both drew samples from 30 states and tried to replicate the demographic diversity of the 2000 census. Both have home and school versions of the scale. The home version is also available in Spanish. The school version is linked to another Hawthorne product called the Adaptive Behavior Intervention Manual that helps users to formulate IEP goals linked to each of the 55 items on the scale. Norms are based on age, grade, and gender of the child. Like the ABAS-II, it is designed to meet the AAMR's (2002) tripartite definition for adaptive behavior: conceptual, social, and practical.

Since the ABES-R2 has only been available since 2006, there have been no published reviews. Correlation coefficients for the children's version are in the moderate range (.61–.78) and the interrater reliability is also in the moderate range (.60–.80). Correlation coefficients for the adolescent version are somewhat better (.60–.85), but interrater reliability is lower (.61–.73). Developers used the Adaptive Behavior Scale (1993) and the Vineland Adaptive Behavior Scales (1985) to establish concurrent validity for the child version and added the Scales for Independent Behavior–Revised (1996) to establish concurrent validity for the adolescent version. The Vineland now has a newer version available (see below). The ABES-R2 is available from: http://www.hes-inc.com.

Bayley Scales of Infant Development. With the 1986 amendments to IDEA, there was an increased emphasis on early intervention, especially for children of pre-school age. The Bayley Scales of Infant Development-Second edition has been one of the most widely used instruments for early identification of infants and toddlers with special needs. In 2005, Bayley issued a completely revised set of scales called the Bayley Scales of Infant and Toddler Development (Bayley-III). The Bayley-III is appropriate for children between 1 month and 42 months and was normed on 1,700 children (Bayley, 2005). There are five scales used to measure cognitive, language, motor, social-emotional, and adaptive behavioral development. The latter scale adopts the Infant and Preschool forms of the Adaptive Behavior Assessment System–Second Edition (ABAS-II) (Harrison & Oakland, 2003). Albers & Grieve (2007) concluded that the Bayley-III is accurate for children down to 6 months of age, does a good job of separating cognitive skills from expressive language skills, and possesses excellent psychometric properties. Its utility for treatment planning, however, is yet to be determined. The Bayley-III is available from: http://harcourtassessment.com

Scales of Independent Behavior–Revised. The *Scales of Independent Behavior–Revised* (SIB-R) (Bruininks, Woodcock, Weatherman, & Hill, 1996) is an individually administered measure to be used with individuals aged 3 months through 90 years. There are three forms of the SIB available: the full-scale form, the short form, and the early-development form. The short form of the SIB-R is intended to serve as a screening device and consists of 40 items selected from the 259 items of the full-scale version. The early-development form has been developed to assess "the development of preschoolers and the adaptive skills of youths or adults with serious disabilities" (Bruininks et al., 1996, p. 16). The SIB-R is specifically intended to be used to assess independent functioning within various settings such as the home, school, community, or workplace. The SIB-R lends itself well to purposes such as the establishment of appropriate instructional goals, making placement decisions, and evaluating program outcomes. This measure is frequently employed for both clinical and research purposes.

The SIB-R is normed on a sample of 2,182 individuals ranging in age from 3 months to 90 years of age. Norms are a composite of those established for the first edition of this measure (N = 1,764) and a separate standardization conducted for the revised edition (N = 418). The sample approximates the population as specified in the 1990 U.S. census in terms of gender, race, and community size. The SIB-R is available from: http://www.riverpub.com

***Vineland Adaptive Behavior Scales* (VABS).** The Vineland Adaptive Behavior Scales (VABS) have been around since 1984 and the second edition (VABS-II) was recently completed in 2007. The VABS-II is administered individually and is completed by a respondent familiar with the target individual. There are now four separate forms, each with its own technical manual. Two of the forms are termed interview versions: the survey form and the expanded survey form. The survey form includes fewer items than the expanded interview form and consequently requires less administration time. Interviews are conducted in a semistructured format with the interviewer asking questions in her own words to probe the respondent about the target individual's functioning (rather than simply reading the interview items). When the interviewer has gathered enough information about a given skill area, she rates the individual on the scale's items. Thus, the VABS requires that the interviewer gain familiarity with the instrument before administering it and provides a manual with a good deal of data about scoring the items. Two of the forms are rating scale versions: the parent/caregiver form and the teacher rating form. The interview forms and parent form are designed for assessment of individuals from birth to 90 years. The teacher form can be completed by a teacher or day-care provider in approximately twenty minutes. This version is suitable for children ages 3 to 21 years.

When the items for the VABS-II were being developed, the authors used a general population sample of 1,843 individuals from birth to 77 years old. To avoid racially biased items, one third was African American, one third was Hispanic, and one third was White. Gender, socioeconomic status, community type, and geographic region were also controlled. The authors also used a clinical sample of 392 individuals diagnosed with autism, Asperger's syndrome, mental retardation, and pervasive developmental disorder not otherwise specified. After the items were selected for clinical importance, comprehensiveness, reliability, freedom from bias, and validity, standardization was established using a nationally representative sample of 3,695 individuals—from birth to 90 years old, from 44 states. Norms were developed for twenty age groups with each one evenly split for gender and matching U.S. demographic diversity for race/ethnicity, socioeconomic status, and geographic region (Northeast, North central, South, and West). Norms were also established for ten clinical groups having: ADHD, autism-nonverbal, autism-verbal, emotional/behavioral disturbance, hearing impairment, learning disability, three levels of mental retardation (mild, moderate, and profound), or visual impairment (Sparrow, Cicchetti, & Balla, 2005).

Like the ABES-R2, the VABS-II is too new to have been externally reviewed. Correlation coefficients for internal reliability are high with more than half over .90 and only six below .80. Three of the lowest coefficients are for the 22-90 year old age group, a cohort that is unlikely to be evaluated by school social workers. Correlations between the two parent forms were moderate to high, ranging from .71 to .98 for the 3-21 age group. The authors used the ABAS-II, the Behavior Assessment System for Children, 2nd edition (BASC-II), and the original VABS to establish criterion validity. The VABS-II is available from: http://ags.pearsonassessments.com

USING CLINICAL JUDGMENT IN THE ASSESSMENT OF ADAPTIVE BEHAVIOR

Test results do not interpret themselves, they require a clinically skilled and perceptive examiner to make sense and derive educationally relevant implications. The AAMR (2002) guide to diagnosis defines clinical judgment as "A special type of judgment rooted in a high level of clinical expertise and experience; it emerges directly from extensive data. It is based on the clinician's explicit training, direct experience with people who have mental retardation, and familiarity with the person and the person's environments. (p. 95). The AAMR then discusses ten guidelines for clinical judgment. First, social workers must ensure a match between the evaluation's purpose and the assessment measure chosen. Practitioners who want to screen which children are at risk for autism, for example, are better off using the Modified Checklist for Autism in Toddlers (M-CHAT) (Robins, Fein, Barton, & Green, 2001). Second, social workers must review the appropriateness and psychometric properties of the measures in terms of the client's age, gender, ethnic-racial group, primary language, and sensory-motor limitations. For example, if adult respondents do not follow directions on a rating scale, it may be appropriate to question their literacy. Third, social workers must be sensitive to the instrument's examiner qualifications and ensure that they have been properly trained in its use. Most of the publishers' web sites provide training materials for their instruments. Fourth, social workers must administer the instrument with fidelity to its directions and avoid taking liberties in its application. Remember that an instrument's reliability and validity depend on consistent application. Fifth, social workers must stay abreast of the scientific literature and ethical concerns regarding available instruments. As new editions become available, clinicians should dispose of their old forms and utilize the latest versions (Raines, 2003). Sixth, social workers should choose informants carefully by determining how well they know the client and can provide reliable and valid information. For example, parents with mental illness may not be the best informants about their own children. Seventh, when interpreting test results, social workers should consider the client's experiences as they relate to participation, interactions, and roles. For example, children born with very low birth weights (less than three pounds) should be measured against their "due date" rather than their "birth date" (Pritchard, Coldwitz, & Beller, 2005). Eighth, when interpreting test results, social workers should be sensitive to physical or mental health issues that influence their responses. Depression, for example, often lowers an individual's estimates of his or her abilities. Ninth, social workers should utilize other members of the multidisciplinary team as resources. Psychologists may be especially useful in understanding an instrument's psychometric qualities. Finally, social workers should follow published guidelines for the interpretation of the specific test used. Clinical judgment should never be a justification for setting aside test results in favor of subjective hunches or impressionistic generalizations.

The assessment of adaptive behavior is an increasingly important activity for teachers, social workers, and psychologists. When assessing adaptive behavior, the examiner is generally interested in how well a target individual meets the needs of his or her physical and social environment. Does the individual function well enough not to represent a significant risk to self or others? Unfortunately, there is a lack of agreement as to exactly which behaviors need to be assessed. Adaptive behavior is greatly influenced by societal expectations. The developmental level and cultural heritage of the individual must be taken into consideration when assessing adaptive behavior.

Adaptive behavior is usually not measured directly, but rather through information provided by a third-party respondent familiar with the target individual. When assessing adaptive behavior, one is interested in what the target individual does on a regular basis (not on what the individual can demonstrate under optimal conditions). The assessment of adaptive behavior suffers from a lack of adequate measures. There is a lack of reliability across many of the subscales in the various measures that results in serious error measurement. Moreover, the norms available are often inadequate.

Care must be taken when selecting measures for assessing adaptive behavior. Examiners may wish to select scales, or subscales, from any number of measures to maximize the validity and reliability of the results. When conducting an assessment of adaptive behavior, seek multiple respondents who are very familiar with the target individual. Look for patterns of behavior displayed in the target individual as reported across respondents. When behavior varies across respondents the evaluator attempts to identify elements in the contexts assessed that might affect behavior. The ultimate goal of an assessment of adaptive behavior is to identify both the strengths and weaknesses displayed by individuals as they interact with the world. With care and understanding of the potentials as well as the limitations of current measures of adaptive behavior, one can proceed to identify possible areas of both adaptive and maladaptive behavior.

References

Achenbach, T. M., McConaughy, S. H., & Howell, C. T. (1987). Child/adolescent behavioral and emotional problems: Implications of cross-informant correlations for situational specificity. *Psychological Bulletin, 101*(2), 213–232.

Albers, C. A., & Grieve, A. J. (2007). Test review of the Bayley Scales of Infant and Toddler Development–Third edition. *Journal of Psychoeducational Assessment, 25*(2), 180–198.

American Association on Intellectual and Developmental Disabilities (2007). *User's guide: Mental retardation, definition, classification, and systems of support* (10th ed.). Washington, DC: Author.

American Association on Intellectual and Developmental Disabilities (April, 2007). *The American Association on Intellectual and Developmental Disabilities (AAIDD, formerly AAMR) announces the definition of the term intellectual disability, and renames "mental retardation" in its upcoming classification and terminology manual.* AAIDD F.Y.I. 7(4), 1–3. Retrieved August 7, 2007 from http://www.aamr.org/FYI/fyi_vol_7_no_4.shtml

American Association on Intellectual and Developmental Disabilities (July 5, 2007). *Definition of mental retardation*. Retrieved August 29, 2007 from http://www.aaidd.org/Policies/faq_mental_retardation.shtml

American Association on Mental Retardation (AAMR). (2002). *Mental retardation: Definition, classification, and systems of supports* (10th ed.). Washington, DC: Author.

Barnett, W. S. (2000). Economics of early childhood intervention. In J. P. Shonkoff & S. J. Meisels (Eds.), *Handbook of early childhood intervention* (2nd ed., pp. 589–610). New York: Cambridge University Press.

Bayley, N. (2005). *Bayley Scales of Infant and Toddler Development*—Third edition. San Antonio, TX: Harcourt Assessment.

Bornstein, M. H., Giusti, Z., Leach, D. B., & Venuti, P. (2005). Maternal reports of adaptive behaviours in young children: Urban-rural and gender comparisons in Italy and United States. *Infant and Child Development, 14*(4), 403–424.

Bricker, D, & Squires, J. (1999). *Ages and stages questionnaire: A parent-completed, child-monitoring system*. Baltimore: Brookes.

Brown, L., & Leigh, J. (1986). *Adaptive behavior inventory manual*. Austin, TX: Pro-Ed.

Bruininks, R., Woodcock, R., Weatherman, R., & Hill, B. (1996). *Scales of independent behavior, revised, comprehensive manual*. Chicago, IL: Riverside Publishing Company.

Cohen, I. L., Schmidt-Lackner, S., Romanczyk, R., & Sudhalter, V. (2003). The PDD Behavior Inventory: A rating scale for assessing response to intervention in children with pervasive developmental disorder. *Journal of Autism and Developmental Disorders, 33*(1), 31–45.

Developmental Disabilities Act & Bill of Rights Act of 2000, PL 106-402. 114 Stat. 1677 (2000).

Eikeseth, S. (2006). The Vineland Adaptive Behavior Scale in a sample of Norwegian second-grade children: A preliminary study. *Tidsskrift for Norsk Psykologforening, 43*(10), 1036–1039.

Frankenburg, W. K., Dodds, J., Archer, P., Shapiro, H., & Bresnick, B. (1992). The Denver II: A major revision and restandardization of the Denver Developmental Screening Test. *Pediatrics, 89*, 91–97.

Geschwind, D. H., & Dykens, E. (2004). Neurobehavioral and psychosocial issues in Klinefelter syndrome. *Learning Disabilities Research & Practice, 19*(3), 166–173.

Glascoe F. P. (2002). *Collaborating with parents: Using Parents' Evaluation of Developmental Status (PEDS) to detect and address developmental and behavioral problems*. Nashville, TN: Ellsworth & Vandermeer Press.

Glascoe, F. P. (2006). *Talking points on developmental-behavioral screening*. Retrieved September 24, 2007 from http://www.pedstest.com/content.php?content=download_resources.html

Glidden, L. M. (2006). An update on label and definitional asynchrony: The missing mental and retardation in mental retardation. In H. N. Switzky & S. Greenspan (Eds.), *What is MR: Ideas for an evolving disability* (pp. 39–49). Washington, DC: American Association on Mental Retardation.

Greenspan, S. (2006). Mental retardation in the real world: Why the AAMR definition is not there yet. In H. N. Switzky & S. Greenspan (Eds.), *What is MR: Ideas for an evolving disability* (pp. 165–183). Washington, DC: American Association on Mental Retardation.

Gresham, F. M., MacMillan, D., & Siperstein, G. N. (1995). Critical analysis of the 1992 AAMR definition: Implications for school psychology. *School Psychology Quarterly, 10*, 1–19.

Hamilton, S. (2006). Screening for developmental delay: Reliable, easy-to-use tools. *Journal of Family Practice, 55*(5), 415–422.

Harrison, P. L., & Oakland, T. (2003). *Adaptive behavior assessment system*-Second edition. San Antonio, TX: Harcourt Assessment.

Heber, R. (1959) A manual on terminology and classification in mental retardation. *American Journal of Mental Deficiency, Monograph Supplement* (Rev.). 56

Holman, J., & Bruininks, R. (1985). Assessing and training adaptive behaviors. In K. Lakin & R. Bruininks (Eds.), *Strategies for achieving community integration of developmentally disabled citizens* (pp. 73–104). Baltimore, MD: Paul H. Brookes.

Individuals with Disabilities Education Improvement Act of 2004, PL 108-446, 118 Stat. 2647 (2004).

Jenkins, J. R. (December 4–5, 2003). *Candidate measures for screening at-risk students. Responsiveness-to-Intervention Symposium*. Kansas City, MO. Retrieved May 19, 2005 from http://www.nrcld.org/symposium2003/jenkins/index.html

Kamphaus, R. W. (1987). Conceptual and psychometric issues in the assessment of adaptive behavior. *Journal of Special Education, 21*(1), 27–35.

Kelly, T. (1927). *Interpretation of educational measurements*. Yonkers, NY: World Book.

Lambert, N., Nihira, K., & Leland, H. (1993). *AAMR adaptive behavior scale–school* (2nd ed.). Austin, TX: Pro-Ed.

MacMillan, D. L., Gresham, F. M., & Siperstein, G. N. (1992). Conceptual and psychometric concerns about the 1992 AAMR definition of mental retardation. *American Journal on Mental Retardation, 98*, 325–335.

MacMillan, D. L., Gresham, F. M., & Siperstein, G. N. (1995). Heightened concerns over the 1992 AAMR definition: Advocacy versus precision. *American Journal on Mental Retardation, 100*, 87–97.

McCarney, S. B., & Arthaud, T. J. (2006). *Adaptive Behavior Evaluation Scale—Revised* (2nd ed.). Columbia, MO: Hawthorne Educational Services.

McGrew, K., & Bruininks, R. (1989). Factor structure of adaptive behavior. *School Psychology Review, 18,* 64–81.

McGrew, K., & Bruininks, R. (1990). Defining adaptive and maladaptive behavior within a model of personal competence. *School Psychology Review, 19*, 53–73.

National Association of State Directors of Special Education (2006). *Response-to-Intervention*. Retrieved May 19, 2006 from http://www.nasdse.org/documents/RtIAn AdministratorsPerspective1-06.pdf

Newborg, J. (2005). *Battelle Developmental Inventory–Second edition* (BDI-2). Rolling Meadows, IL: Riverside Publishing.

Pritchard, M. A., Coldwitz, P. B., & Beller, E. M. (2005). Parent's evaluation of developmental status in children born with a birthweight of 1250 grams or less. *Journal of Paediatrics and Child Health, 41*(4), 191–196.

Raines, J. C. (2003). Rating the rating scales: Ten criteria to use. *School Social Work Journal, 27*(2), 1–17.

Raines, J. C. (2006). The new IDEA: Reflections on the reauthorization. *School Social Work Journal, 31*(1), 1–18.

Raines, J. C. (2008). *Evidence-based practice in school-based mental health: A primer for school social workers, psychologists, and counselors*. New York: Oxford University Press.

Reschly, D. J. (1987). Adaptive behavior in classification and programming with students who are handicapped. St. Paul, MN: Minnesota Department of Education.

Robins, D., Fein, D., Barton, M., & Green, J. (2001). The Modified Checklist for Autism in Toddlers: An initial study investigating the early detection of autism and pervasive developmental disorders. *Journal of Autism and Developmental Disorders, 31*(2), 131–144. Test available from: http://www.firstsigns.org/

Rust, J. O., & Wallace, M. A. (2004). Test review of the Adaptive Behavior Assessment System–Second edition. *Journal of Psychoeducational Assessment, 22*, 367–373.

Rust, J. O., & Wallace, M. A. (2004). Book review. Adaptive behavior assessment system–second edition. *Journal of Psychoeducational Assessment, 22,* 367–373.

Salcido, R. M., Ornelas, V., & Garcia, J. A. (2002). A neighborhood watch program for inner-city school children. *Children & Schools, 24*(3), 175–87.

Schalock, R. L., & Luckasson, R. A. (2005). AAMR's definition, classification, and systems of support and its relation to international trends and issues in the field of intellectual disabilities. *Journal of Policy and Practice in Intellectual Disabilities, 1*, 136–46.

Schalock, R. L., Luckasson, R. A., & Shogren, K. A. (2007). [Perspectives] The renaming of mental retardation: Understanding the change to the term intellectual disability. *Intellectual and Developmental Disabilities, 45*(2), 116–24.

Schmidt, M., & Salvia, J. (1984). Adaptive behavior: A conceptual analysis. *Diagnostique, 9*, 117–25.

Shapiro, B., & Derrington, T. (2007). *Screening tool options and psychometrics*. Retrieved on September 24, 2007 from http://www.seek.hawaii.edu/Products/4-Info-Binder/ScreeningToolTBL.pdf

Sparrow, S., Cicchetti, D. V., & Balla, D. A. (2005). *Vineland Adaptive Behavior Scales–Second edition, Survey forms manual.* Circle Pines, MN: American Guidance Service.

Spreat, S. (1999). Psychometric standards for adaptive behavior assessment. In R. A. Schalock (Ed.), *Adaptive behavior and its measurement: Implications for the field of mental retardation* (pp. 103–117). Washington, DC: American Association on Mental Retardation.

Stinnett, T. A., Fuqua, D. R., & Coombs, W. T. (1999). Construct validity of the AAMR Adaptive Behavior Scale–School: 2. *School Psychology Review, 28*(1), 31–43.

Sullivan, P. M., & Knutson, J. F. (2000). Maltreatment and disabilities: A population-based epidemiological study. *Child Abuse & Neglect, 24*(10), 1257–1273.

Torgesen, J. K. (2004). Avoiding the devastating downward spiral: The evidence that early intervention prevents reading failure. *American Educator, 28*, 6–19.

Watkins, M. W., Ravert, C. M., & Crosby, E. G. (2002). Normative factor structure of the AAMR Adaptive Behavior Scale-School, Second edition. *Journal of Psychoeducational Assessment 20*(4), 337–345.

Weiss, J. A., Sullivan, A., & Diamond, T. (2003). Parent stress and adaptive functioning of individuals with developmental disabilities. *Journal on Developmental Disabilities, 10*(1), 129–135.

Zhang, Q., & Yao, S. (2003). Development of adaptive skill rating scale for school age children. *Chinese Mental Health Journal, 17*(3), 161–163.

24

Classroom Observation

Carol Rippey Massat
University of Illinois at Chicago

David Sanders

- The Sanders Classroom Observation Form
- Recording Event Sampling
- Observing Multiple Students
- Observing Teacher-Pupil Interactions

Classroom observation is a key assessment tool of the school social worker. The current literature supports the use of classroom observation for evaluating teacher effectiveness (VanTassel-Baska, Quek, & Feng, 2007), assessment of student learning (Baker, Gersten, Haager, & Dingle, 2006), and assessment of children's behavior (Vile Junod, DuPaul, Jitendra, Volpe, & Cleary, 2006).

School social workers use classroom observations as an objective way of understanding the interactions in a classroom and their impact on students. The instruments described in this chapter provide ways to examine student and teacher classroom behaviors. They provide a useful foundation for a report to the multidisciplinary team but also can be excellent vehicles for consultation with teachers, helping them to match their repertoire of teaching skills to the needs of the classroom situation and individual students.

Classroom observations are also used by school social workers to evaluate children for eligibility to receive special services, to assist physicians in diagnosing attention deficit disorders, to measure the effectiveness of a treatment plan, and to document results of classroom intervention strategies. It is important to know how the target student compares to particular criteria: for example, he was "aggressive" three times more often than the average student in the room, or his "on-task" performance went from 58 percent to 82 percent after he began a medication regime, or his "off-task" behavior dropped from 32 percent to 18 percent after a new classroom management plan was implemented. This kind of precise information gives practitioners confidence in their decisions and helps them make good decisions.

But classroom observations rarely produce this kind of precision or uniformity. Typically, an observer arranges to visit a classroom, sits in as unobtrusive a position as possible, observes as long as his or her schedule permits, and then departs with notes to assess what has happened. The ensuing staffing report goes something like this: "He appeared to be off task much of the time. He fidgeted around a lot in his seat and fiddled with objects in his desk. He got up and moved around the room quite a bit and bothered his neighbor many times. He was certainly more active than the rest of the students." This format has served well enough, usually because of the integrity of the participants and the needs of the process, but mostly because there are few alternatives. Where this anecdotal and essentially casual approach fails is in its objectivity, reliability, and precision. This approach is not objective. It allows the observer too much latitude: What, precisely, is "off-task" behavior? How are "fidgeting" and "bothering others" interpreted? Is the observer too much influenced by peripheral issues that may distort conclusions? Is he or she under pressure from administrators to "do something" with a troublesome student? Is the observer's relationship with the classroom teacher too close, or strained? No matter how mature and professional we think we are, we often respond to subtle and disquieting pressures that, in the absence of objective and standardized observation procedures, are often difficult to resist.

And reliability? Can the observation process be duplicated by new personnel or by the same professional at another time and place, with enough consistency and uniformity to produce meaningful results? Criteria for such classroom behaviors as "fidgeting," "bothering others," and being "off task" can have various meanings. This lack of a common reference base can result in misleading conclusions and poor understanding of critical classroom behaviors. Can we expect decision makers to have any faith in our conclusions when our methods are varied and haphazard?

And precision is totally lacking. How much more "off task" was Jane than Astrid? Was it enough to be significant? And how much more "on task" is Tommy after starting his medication? A lot? Quite a bit? These terms are not helpful and do not build confidence. To give classroom observation uniformity, consistency, and definition, this chapter suggests observational procedures.

To acquire skill in classroom observation, school social workers need to spend many hours unobtrusively observing classes. The teacher's permission to do this must be received. Teachers will grant permission willingly only if they see the observation as supportive and helpful to them, as a part of team problem solving, or as a part of a consultative relationship in which teacher and social worker put their heads together to help a student and to assist the teacher to be helpful. Some teachers will resist having school social workers in their classes. Social workers often find themselves beginning with the more personally secure members of the teaching faculty until their confidence and positive reputation increase.

THE SANDERS CLASSROOM OBSERVATION FORM

The procedure for using the Sanders classroom observation form is nothing more than the well-established, timed-interval technique. But to provide a framework for collecting, organizing, standardizing, and presenting data, a classroom observation form is introduced (figure 24.1).

The first line of the Sanders form has spaces for all pertinent identifying information. Next, the legend gives brief explanations of the four critical student behaviors to be observed (on task; off task, passive; off task, active; off task, severe), as well as two important observations about the classroom (group on task; transitions). Starting time, finishing time, notation interval, and observer's identification are noted on the next line.

Conduct the process as follows: First, complete all preliminary consultations with the teacher, administrator, parent, or physician to legitimize the observation. Then, confer again with the classroom teacher to set a date and time, and during these conferences emphasize that you will be measuring time on task and that lessons should be presented as usual and the classroom management plan followed—no special changes should be made just for the observation.

Tell the teacher that you will be observing two students: the target student and a sample student. The sample student should be of the same sex and selected at random from the seating chart. Allow the teacher to veto your selection if he feels the student you have chosen has similar symptoms. After selecting the sample student, decide on a place from which to observe. You should be comfortable and as unobtrusive as possible, and in a position to see their facial expressions.

You will need two classroom observation forms: one for the target student and one for the sample student. Fold the target student's at the top arrows (with the identifying information folded under) and place it over the sample student's at the bottom arrows so that you can easily make entries under "class" and "student" for both. You need to keep the target student's form on top because you will be making frequent notes in the spaces below.

You need to decide on a time interval to record your observations. The more data you collect, the more reliable your conclusion will be, provided of course the data are good. The most comfortable time interval is thirty seconds. This requires a notation every fifteen seconds: one for the target student, then one for the sample student, alternately. At fifteen-second intervals the pace is lively but still manageable, unless you fall behind with your note taking. This interval also allows you to complete the form's one hundred

FIGURE 24.1 Classroom Observation Form

CLASSROOM OBSERVATION FORM

NAME:__________ GRADE:__________ TEACHER:__________ SCHOOL:__________ DATE:______

LEGEND: **For "Student":**
O-On Task (attentive, productive)
P-Off Task, Passive (distracted, daydreaming)
A-Off Task, Active (aggressive, interfering)
S-Off Task, Severe (interventions needed, time-out)

For "Class":
O-Group on Task (clear direction and purpose)
X-Transitions (changing subjects, unmanageable interruptions)

STARTING TIME:__________ FINISH:__________ NOTATION INTERVAL:__________ OBSERVER:__________

CLASS:	O	oooooooooo oooooooooo oooooooooo oooooooooo oooooooooo oooooooooo oooooooooo oooooooooo oooooooooo oooooooooo
	X	oooooooooo oooooooooo oooooooooo oooooooooo oooooooooo oooooooooo oooooooooo oooooooooo oooooooooo oooooooooo
STUDENT:	O	oooooooooo oooooooooo oooooooooo oooooooooo oooooooooo oooooooooo oooooooooo oooooooooo oooooooooo oooooooooo
	P	oooooooooo oooooooooo oooooooooo oooooooooo oooooooooo oooooooooo oooooooooo oooooooooo oooooooooo oooooooooo
	A	oooooooooo oooooooooo oooooooooo oooooooooo oooooooooo oooooooooo oooooooooo oooooooooo oooooooooo oooooooooo
	S	oooooooooo oooooooooo oooooooooo oooooooooo oooooooooo oooooooooo oooooooooo oooooooooo oooooooooo oooooooooo
NOTE REF:		
ACTIVITY:		
NOTES:		
COMMENTS:		

TEACHER'S INTERACTIONS WITH STUDENT, VERBAL AND/OR PHYSICAL:

Positive:__________ (encouragements, acknowledgements) Neutral:__________ (clarifications, cues) Negative:__________ (reprimands, scoldings)

TEACHER'S OPINION OF OBSERVER'S PRESENCE ON STUDENT'S BEHAVIOR:

____NEGLIGIBLE (typical behavior) ____POSITIVE (improved behavior) ____NEGATIVE (worse behavior)

TOTAL:__________

O:__________ = % O:__________
P:__________ = % P:__________
A:__________ = % A:__________
S:__________ = % S:__________
X:__________ = % X:__________

SOURCE: © 1990 David Sanders, LCSW.

spaces in fifty minutes; this is a good time period for most classrooms, and you can always return for more information later, if needed—and it makes the math calculations easy.

Position your timepiece where you can watch the seconds go by. At the minute, observe the target student, make a decision about his or her behavior, then mark the form. At the quarter-minute, do the same for the sample student, and mark his or her form. Then, at the half-minute, go back to the target student. Every fifteen seconds observe either the target or sample student, alternating between them, analyzing and categorizing their behaviors into one of the four categories mentioned earlier:

1. On task (attentive, productive). This is the "O" line under "student." All clues tell you that the student is attending to the given task. Obvious clues, such as thoughtful engagement in completing the assignments or responding to a discussion question, are easy to assess, but others, such as apparent daydreaming or looking about the room, can be misinterpreted. Contextual information will help you make a good decision here. None of your decisions will be isolated from the ones you made thirty seconds earlier; if the student has established a pattern of listening and participating in a discussion, then his sudden, daydreamlike appearance is probably due to his trying to recall the correct response to the question.

2. Off task, passive (distracted, daydreaming). This is the "P" line. Observed behaviors tell you that the student is detached from the given task and has little interest in completing it. Obvious clues are looking about absentmindedly, playing with things in or on the desk, or having an unusual preoccupation with his or her thumb.

3. Off task, active (aggressive, interfering). This is the "A" line. This behavior is usually easy to identify because it is likely to be obvious, at least to you. It often escapes the teacher's attention because the student may be quite clever concealing it until the teacher's back is turned or the student is busy helping other students. Common behaviors that fall under this category are whispering or talking with neighbors; aggravating, teasing, or otherwise disrupting a classmate's attention; being out of seat or moving about the room without permission; talking out, silliness, or throwing things.

4. Off task, severe (interventions needed, time-out). This is the "S" line. This category is for those times when the student's behavior is severe enough that the teacher has to confront the student, invoke a time-out, or give a negative consequence to preserve enough control and authority to continue the lesson. As mentioned earlier, it is important to reassure the teacher that you want to observe the student under normal classroom conditions and under the management plan in place. Some teachers feel you need to see the student at his or her worst, so they will allow unruly behavior to go unchecked, but it is more important to see how the student responds to the teacher's classroom methods.

The line for "class" (above the "student" line) is there to record any disruptions in the classroom routine, because only students with exceptional self-discipline and control can remain "on task" when the teacher is distracted. If the task is well defined and the directions are clear, note the *O* line, but when there is an interruption of the lesson and the teacher is preoccupied (such as when the principal interrupts to confer with the teacher, or during transitions to new subjects), note the "X" line. (You will save time by noting the "O" line once and then noting the "X"s only as they occur because there are usually few of them.)

This division of classroom behaviors into four basic categories will suffice for nearly all behaviors you will witness. When you have made your observation and categorized the behavior, darken the circle on the line corresponding to its code letter at the interval. If necessary, you can also make other supplemental notations on the form using the following guidelines:

The line for "note ref" is used to refer to an explanation in the "notes." You may want to describe in detail a particular student behavior so you can refer to it later during your report. These spaces are provided to organize those observations. For example, during one interval you see the student poking his neighbor with a pencil. At that moment you would darken the circle on the "A" line, and in the "note ref" space below it you would jot down a reference number (e.g., 1). Then in the space for "notes," you would write, "1. jabbed neighbor with pencil." Usually these details are only important to note for the target student.

The "activity" line is important because it provides a reminder of what the classroom activity was during the observation. But more important, it sometimes gives clues about how students react differently to various teaching methods and learning activities. For instance, it may reveal that the student maintained good attention during a cut-and-paste activity but lost all interest during a classroom discussion, or that the student was on task when doing desk work but became very active during a small-group activity. This kind of information is helpful when planning intervention strategies.

The "comments" space is used for general comments on the observation period and physical classroom features, as well as any unusual events that occurred to minimize or alter the legitimacy of the conclusion.

There is space at the bottom of the form to tally the teacher's interactions with the target student. Positive interactions are clearly encouraging and rewarding. "Good job, Billy." "That's exactly right, Sally." Neutral interactions are informative, inquisitive: "Did you bring your note back, John?" "It's time to put your book away, Doris." Negative interactions are usually reprimands or warnings: "I told you to sit down!" "Put that back in your desk!" Be aware that "interactions" are not just verbal; also count physical interactions (looks, smiles, frowns) when you observe them. Try to note all interactions you witness, not just the ones that occur during an observation interval.

This information is important for two reasons: first, it reveals the frequency, or lack of, such interactions; second, it reveals the nature (positive, neutral, or negative) of such interactions. This will be helpful when discussing strategies for amelioration, because if positive interactions are infrequent, then a legitimate recommendation can be made to increase them, but if they are frequent, then the teacher can be commended and valuable time can be spent brainstorming other strategies.

The final notation to record is whether the student's behavior during the observation period was typical. Some students love to "perform" for guests while others seem unaware of visitors in the room. When naturally curious students ask, "What are you doing here?" probably the best response is simply to say, "I'm here to visit for a while and I promised Ms. Jones I wouldn't talk to anyone." Check with the teacher on this final question and mark the teacher's response; if the behavior appeared to be much different than typical, you will have to make a decision about how valid the results are.

The table in the lower right-hand corner is to summarize the data you observed and to record the final percentages. As mentioned earlier, this will be easy when all one hundred spaces are used because the calculations can be done quickly; otherwise, a pocket calculator will be useful to speed things up. Because it would be unfair to penalize a student for general class transitions and interruptions, observations made when the class "X" line is noted are overridden and calculated as an "X" percentage.

Another difficult time to assess is when students finish their work and are not sure what to do next. For instance, should the sample student be marked "off task" when he or she completes the work and has nothing to do while the target student is still working? Typically, this is when students begin to talk with their neighbors and "active" behaviors begin, even for otherwise compliant students. Most teachers anticipate this with clear directions about what to do when work is finished, but not all. It might be wise to bring this to the teacher's attention before the observation begins. Your previous experiences will be your best guide. Figure 24.2 is an example of a completed classroom observation form.

RECORDING EVENT SAMPLING

Another type of observation is event sampling (Boehm & Weinberg, 1987). Event sampling records observations of behaviors each time they occur. Event sampling often involves behaviors that occur infrequently. Time sampling, or observing within a limited time frame, may not capture these behaviors. The school social worker may ask teachers or parents to do event sampling in a given day. Event sampling may be used to record completion of homework, completion of in-class assignments, or whether a child completes an activity without assistance. A format for an individual child's event sample may be a simple grid, such as tables 24.1 and 24.2.

FIGURE 24.2 Classroom Observation Form

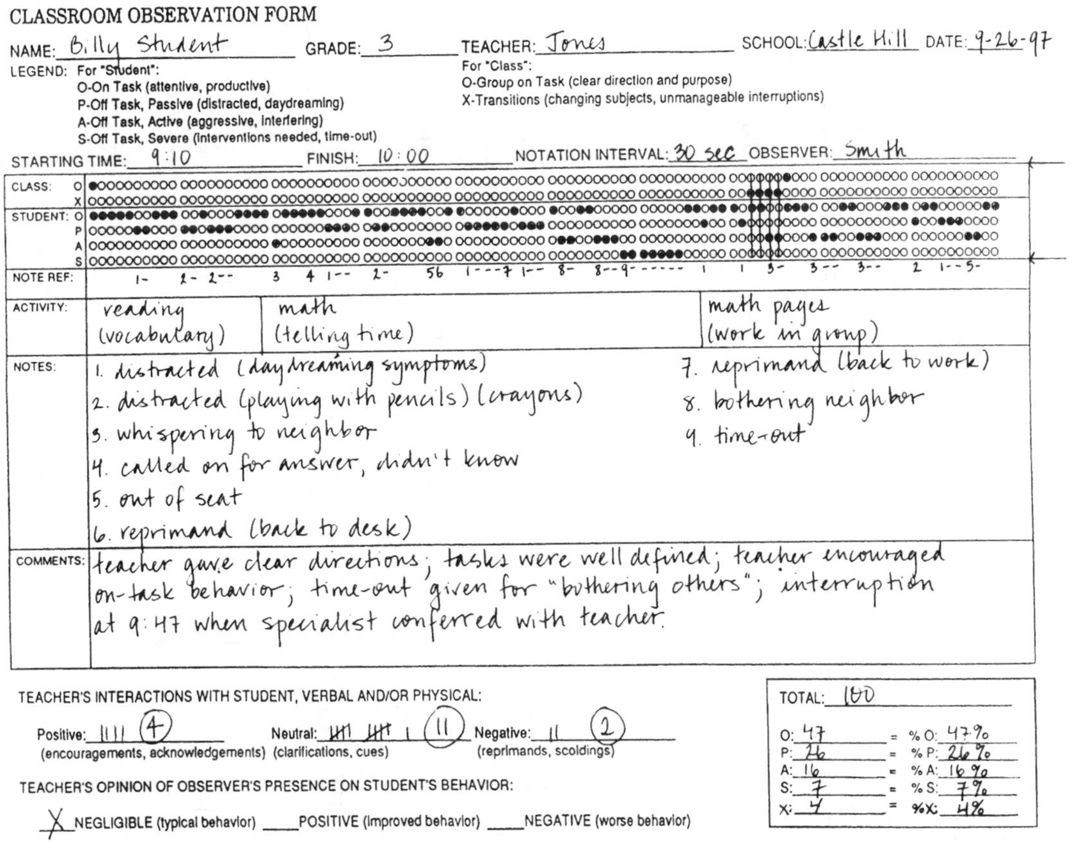

CLASSROOM OBSERVATION FORM

NAME: Billy Student GRADE: 3 TEACHER: Jones SCHOOL: Castle Hill DATE: 9-26-97

LEGEND: For "Student":
O-On Task (attentive, productive)
P-Off Task, Passive (distracted, daydreaming)
A-Off Task, Active (aggressive, interfering)
S-Off Task, Severe (interventions needed, time-out)

For "Class":
O-Group on Task (clear direction and purpose)
X-Transitions (changing subjects, unmanageable interruptions)

STARTING TIME: 9:10 FINISH: 10:00 NOTATION INTERVAL: 30 sec OBSERVER: Smith

CLASS: O, X

STUDENT: O, P, A, S

NOTE REF: 1- 2- 2-- 3 4 1-- 2- 56 1---7 1-- 8- 8--9----- 1 1 3- 3-- 3-- 2 1--5-

ACTIVITY: reading (vocabulary) | math (telling time) | math pages (work in group)

NOTES:
1. distracted (daydreaming symptoms)
2. distracted (playing with pencils) (crayons)
3. whispering to neighbor
4. called on for answer, didn't know
5. out of seat
6. reprimand (back to desk)
7. reprimand (back to work)
8. bothering neighbor
9. time-out

COMMENTS: teacher gave clear directions; tasks were well defined; teacher encouraged on-task behavior; time-out given for "bothering others"; interruption at 9:47 when specialist conferred with teacher.

TEACHER'S INTERACTIONS WITH STUDENT, VERBAL AND/OR PHYSICAL:

Positive: |||| (4) (encouragements, acknowledgements) Neutral: ~~||||~~ ~~||||~~ | (11) (clarifications, cues) Negative: || (2) (reprimands, scoldings)

TEACHER'S OPINION OF OBSERVER'S PRESENCE ON STUDENT'S BEHAVIOR:

X NEGLIGIBLE (typical behavior) ____ POSITIVE (improved behavior) ____ NEGATIVE (worse behavior)

TOTAL: 100

O: 47	=	% O: 47%
P: 26	=	% P: 26%
A: 16	=	% A: 16%
S: 7	=	% S: 7%
X: 4	=	% X: 4%

TABLE 24.1 Event Sample for Individual Child: School Behaviors

Date	Time	Completed spelling	Completed math	Completed language arts

TABLE 24.2 Event Sample for Individual Child: Home Behaviors

Date	Got dressed independently	Got to bus on time independently	Completed homework	Packed all homework in backpack

Event sampling can also be used by a school social worker to record the acquisition of skills for a group of children or a classroom. For example, the school social worker might record when each child in a social skills group demonstrates a new skill for the first time. Table 24.3 demonstrates an example of a recording format for such an application.

TABLE 24.3 Social Skills Group Skill Acquisition

Child	Greets others	Starts conversation	Requests a behavior change appropriately	Independently makes "I" statements	Takes turn in the group

OBSERVING MULTIPLE STUDENTS

To observe the behavior of multiple students in a classroom it is important to have in mind no more than 10 codes for behavior, since trying to recall more than ten codes is difficult to impossible (Medley & Mitzel, 1963). Each code must reflect an exhaustive and mutually exclusive category of behavior (categories cannot overlap and each category must include all possibilities). Observing thirty students at a time is unrealistic, so it may be useful to observe students in sequence, during a five-minute observation period, and then repeat this process to count the number of behaviors observed in a classroom during a thirty-minute period. Table 24.4 is an example of a recording format for this type of observation. For this example, each child in each cluster would be observed in turn for ten seconds. Observations for that child would be recorded, and then this process would be repeated for each time sequence.

TABLE 24.4 Observing Classroom Patterns of Social Behavior

Setting: Social Studies Class, Mr. Smith's fourth grade

Time Period: 9:00 am–9:40 am

Environmental Notes: Classroom is set up with desks in clusters of four. There is a total of six clusters. The class is studying the topic of Jane Addams and the settlement house movement, and each cluster is working on a group project to construct a diorama of Hull House.

Codes: 1 = talking to peer, 2 = listening to peer, 3 = direct aggressive behavior toward peer, 4 = indirect aggressive behavior toward peer, 5 = working, hands on, mutually with peer, 6 = ignoring peer

Child	*Time Period*								*Total*
	9:00	9:05	9:10	9:15	9:20	9:25	9:30	9:35	

OBSERVING TEACHER-PUPIL INTERACTIONS

Teacher-pupil interactions are also critical in understanding what is occurring in the classroom. The interactions are affected by differences in teaching style that can profoundly affect students' development and learning. Each teacher develops a personal teaching style, compatible with his or her personality, that generally works for certain students. Some teachers, for example, have a no-nonsense, limit-setting style that lets students know exactly where they stand. Other teachers are less directive, more accepting of differences, but less clear about their expectations. These styles will have different effects on students. At best, the students who do well with one style may do less well with another. Good, experienced teachers may have more than one style, indeed a repertoire of teaching styles to match the needs of different students. They may vary their styles with certain students without undermining their effectiveness with the rest of the class. They may keep students on task in different ways, use other members of the class group to help a student, or manipulate rewards in different ways.

An experienced school social worker needs to understand classroom dynamics. Having some formal preparation in group dynamics, the social worker applies this knowledge to the classroom. Just as teachers are different, so is each class different in the dynamics of interaction between its members and the effect of these dynamics on individual students. Group contagion among students with certain behavior problems is particularly challenging to the teacher and dangerous for the educational process. Frequently teachers have no formal training in dealing with the dynamics of the class as a group, and so the problem is particularly disabling.

Understanding how teaching styles and classroom dynamics interact, the social worker needs to examine both in relation to individual students, who may be less responsive to a particular teaching style, or who may become negative targets of classroom dynamics. This examination is a prelude to a more developed understanding of alternative ways of working with classroom dynamics or the needs of individual students.

According to Boehm and Weinberg (1987), the Flanders system for observing teacher-pupil interactions is the foundation for most current systems of teacher-pupil observations. Flanders categorizes teacher behaviors into seven categories: 1) accepts students' feelings, 2) praises or encourages pupils, 3) accepts pupils' ideas, 4) asks questions, 5) lectures, 6) gives directions, or 7) criticizes or justifies authority. Student behaviors fall into three categories: 1) student talk, narrow response, 2) student talk, broad response, or 3) silence or noise.

In using the Flanders system, "the observer makes a notation for every change in category and also records one category number at least every three seconds, whether there is a category change or not" (Boehm & Weinberg, p. 81). The recording format could simply record the setting, activity, date, and time and then sequentially list the category codes of the interactions that were observed during that time period. The Flanders system is helpful for observing classroom patterns of teacher-student communication and may be helpful in completing a functional behavioral analysis. By observing patterns of teacher-student behaviors, school social workers can identify antecedents and consequences of student behavior.

By using standard procedures for classroom observations, social workers can give objective, reliable, precise information about students' classroom behavior and teacher-pupil interactions. They can present this information in easily understood and readily accessible formats. Observers will be able to repeat the process in standardized format, and they will be able to share these results with other practitioners with the confidence only consistency provides.

References

Baker, S. K., Gersten, R., Haager, D., & Dingle, M. (2006). *Elementary School Journal, 107*(2), 199–219.

Boehm, A. E., & Weinberg, R. A. (1987). *The classroom observer: Developing observation skills in early childhood settings*. New York: Teachers College Press.

Medley, D. M., & Mitzel, H. E. (1963). Measuring classroom behavior by systematic observation. In N. L. Gage (Ed.), *Handbook of research in teaching* (pp. 247–328). Chicago: Rand McNally.

VanTassel-Baska, J., Quek, C., & Feng, A. X. (2007). The development and use of a structured teacher observation scale to assess differentiated best practice. *Roeper Review, 29*(2), 84–92.

Vile Junod, R. E., DuPaul, G. J., Jitendra, J. K., Volpe, R. J., & Cleary, K. S. (2006). Classroom observations of students with and without ADHD: Differences across types of engagement. *Journal of School Psychology, 44*(2), 87–104.

25

Mental Health and School Social Work

Michael S. Kelly
Loyola University Chicago

Helene Moses

Eric D. Ornstein

Carol Rippey Massat
University of Illinois at Chicago

- Mental Health Policies and School Social Work
- Children's Mental Health and Academic Achievement
- The Role of the School Social Worker in Mental Health Services
- Assessment
- Use of the *DSM-IV-TR*
- School Social Workers' Use of the Evidence-Based Practice (EBP) Process
- Disorders Commonly Encountered in Schools

Children often receive core mental health services in schools, and many students are affected by mental health concerns. Therefore, every school social worker needs to be familiar with the field of mental health, including relevant federal and state policies, the impact of mental health on academic achievement, the role of the school social worker in mental health service provision, mental health assessment, and use of evidence-based practice in mental health. This chapter is an overview of mental health issues and services delivered in the schools. It reviews mental health policy, as well as assessment and interventions with selected disorders that may present themselves in the school setting. Special attention is given to an evidence-based practice (EBP) process that can empower school social workers and clients to use the best available evidence to address common children's mental health problems.

School social workers encounter many children with mental disorders. According to the first-ever Surgeon General's Report on children's mental health (1999), one in five American children has a mental disorder, with 5 to 9 percent of all children aged 9 to 17 having a serious emotional disturbance. Other federal estimates say that 1 in 10 children may have a mental disorder severe enough to cause significant impairment in their school, home, and social functioning, and 80 percent of children with such disorders do not receive treatment (NIMH, 2004). The President's New Freedom Commission on Mental Health (2003) identified a disjointed, fragmented system of provision of mental health care with significant disparities in the availability of treatment. Services vary from state to state and from community to community. The commission's subcommittee on children and families called for better and earlier screening of children for mental disorders and argued that schools are one of the most important areas to focus on in improving the nation's mental health infrastructure for children (President's New Freedom Commission, 2003). The commission recommended that the mental health field and schools be partners in the provision of early mental health screening, assessment, and referral to services:

> The mission of public schools is to educate all students. However, children with serious emotional disturbances have the highest rates of school failure. Fifty percent of these students drop out of high school, compared to 30% of all students with disabilities. Schools are where children spend most of each day. While schools are primarily concerned with education, mental health is essential to learning as well as to social and emotional development. Because of this important interplay between emotional health and school success, schools must be partners in the mental health care of our children. Schools are in a key position to identify mental health problems early and to provide a link to appropriate services. (p. 58)

Though public schools are charged with educating all students, those who are members of vulnerable populations and who are also affected by mental illness face obstacles beyond those of the general population. Racial and ethnic minority students are at greater risk for poverty. Both poverty and its related stressors can exacerbate mental health issues and create obstacles to the receipt of needed services. African American and Latino families are less likely to use mental health services (Miranda, Azocar, Organista, Munoz, & Lieberman, 1996; Pumariega, Glover, Holzer, & Nguyen, 1998; Snowden, 2001). Kataoka, Zhang, and Wells (2002) found that nearly 80 percent of children needing mental health services did not receive them, and that Latinos and the uninsured were at particularly high risk for unmet mental health needs. It is critical to reduce these barriers to mental health services, because children who live in persistent poverty are at the greatest risk of negative mental health outcomes (Brooks-Gunn & Duncan, 1997). Gay and lesbian students also have special mental health needs and risks. They are frequent victims of violence and harassment in school and at home (Morrow, 1993), which may lead to symptoms of post-traumatic stress disorder (Thompson & Massat, 2006).

MENTAL HEALTH POLICIES AND SCHOOL SOCIAL WORK

There is a long history of state involvement in mental health services. Federal involvement, contemplated from the days of Dorothea Dix, was limited mainly to veterans' services until the passage of the National Mental Health Act of 1946. This act established the National Institute of Mental Health (NIMH) to promote research about mental disease, to encourage training of personnel, and to establish state mental health authorities to develop mental health programs. The first federally administered program that focused specifically on the mental health needs of children was the Comprehensive Children's Mental Health Services Program, administered by the Substance Abuse and Mental Health Services Administration (SAMHSA) through the U.S. Department of Health and Human Services. The program, first authorized in 1992, offers grants to states, territories, Indian tribes, and communities to develop systems of care for children with mental health needs. Services must involve families, be need driven, collaborative, community based, and culturally responsive.

Federal initiatives to promote safe schools are also related to school mental health issues. The Safe and Drug-Free Schools and Communities Program (SDFSC) is intended to reduce drug, alcohol, and tobacco use and violence through prevention, early intervention, referral, and education in elementary and secondary schools. This program began in 1986 with the Drug-Free Schools and Community Act (SDFSCA), (20 U.S.C. 4601), which was reauthorized in 1994 as the Safe and Drug-Free Schools Act (20 U.S.C. 7101). The Principles of Effectiveness were established in 1998, and are still used by federal and state agencies to evaluate grant applications by school districts for school-based mental health and prevention services. These principles are the standard for Safe and Drug-Free Schools. As of July 1998, a grantee must:

1. Base its programs on a thorough assessment of objective data about the drug and violence problems in the schools and communities served.
2. With the assistance of a local or regional advisory council where required by the SDFSCA, establish a set of measurable goals and objectives and design its programs to meet those goals and objectives.
3. Design and implement its programs for youth based on research or evaluation that provides evidence that the programs used prevent or reduce drug use, violence, or disruptive behavior among youth.

4. Evaluate its programs periodically to assess its progress toward achieving its goals and objectives, and use its evaluation results to refine, improve, and strengthen its program, and to refine its goals and objectives as appropriate (Safe and Drug Free Schools Newsletter, 2007).

The legislation was most recently reauthorized as part of the No Child Left Behind Act (NCLB), which imposed new accountability requirements.

CHILDREN'S MENTAL HEALTH AND ACADEMIC ACHIEVEMENT

Children's mental health has a demonstrable impact on their academic achievement. According to the U.S. Department of Education (2001), many students with serious emotional disturbances drop out of school. It is estimated that 12 to 30 percent of children have serious emotional disorders that will ultimately cause severe academic difficulty (Institute of Medicine, 1994; Kazdin, 1993; U.S. Department of Education, 1994). Children who have experienced child abuse and foster care are also at risk for school failure and poor mental health outcomes (Stone, 2007). Other research has found that children with positive early psychosocial development have higher achievement test scores later on in school (Teo, Carlson, & Mathieu, 1996), and that mental health has a direct impact on children's grade point averages (Gutman, Sameroff, & Cole, 2003). Ialong, Edelsohn, and Kellam (2001) found that first-graders' reports of depressed mood and feelings were associated with poor academic functioning later on and the subsequent need for mental health services due to suicidal ideation, and major depressive disorder.

THE ROLE OF THE SCHOOL SOCIAL WORKER IN MENTAL HEALTH SERVICES

Nationwide, problems in the provision of mental health services to children place a greater burden on school social workers, who may be the first—and perhaps the only—social service providers to children and youth. Often the school social worker has far greater natural access to parents and children than any other community service provider. The role of the school social worker varies widely, even within school districts. In most cases, school social workers are responsible for providing services to children who have behavioral or emotional disorders that impede their academic functioning. In some settings, school social workers are responsible for providing extensive therapy in schools. However, in most situations, ongoing family work and medication management are delivered outside of the school setting. According to recent survey data, the most critical role of the school social worker is consultation, teamwork, and short-term support as well as referral and linkage to community services (Jonson-Reid, Kontak, Citerman, Essma, & Fezzi, 2004). School social workers are the bridge between outside professionals, school administration, and teaching staff. They attend staffings in hospitals when a student has a psychiatric hospitalization. They help to develop transition plans to ease the student's return to school from the hospital, and it is their job to translate medical jargon into functional information for the students, teachers, and allied staff. School social workers help multidisciplinary teams to gain a holistic picture of the student. If community services are unresponsive, however, school social workers find themselves doing much more. A few schools offer psychiatric services and medication management (Costello-Wells, McFarland, Reed, & Walton, 2003). When children are receiving services outside of the school, the school social worker must identify issues of concern, understand effective work with children experiencing mental health disorders, support children's work in school, and assist students who are making a transition from hospitalization.

School social workers may also partner with community agencies and schools to bring into the school additional social workers, psychiatrists, and other mental health professionals to provide longer-term or more intensive therapeutic services. In this model, the school district contracts with one or more agencies to come into the school to provide services. Grant funding may be used to support services (Anderson-Butcher, Iachini, & Wade-Mdivanian, 2007; Anderson-Butcher & Ashton, 2004). The full-service school offers mental health services to students and community members in the school setting as one of an array of on-site services. Full-service schools may include vaccination and health clinics, family planning services, drug and alcohol treatment, as well as mental health services (Ghuman, Weist, & Sarles, 2002). School social workers are in a great position to draw upon the resources around them to establish such community-school partnerships, family-school interventions, and school-wide interventions, as well as individual and group interventions, in caring for mental health needs of children.

Both intervention in the school and collaboration with service providers outside of the school are critical in preventing costly outcomes for children with serious emotional disturbances. Therapeutic schools and out-of-state care are costly for the school district and often costly for children. Children placed in residential treatment or therapeutic schools may need such an environment, but there is an emotional cost to the children when they lack normative school socialization. The student may feel isolated from the community and may lose out on critical social support and family contact. If effective services can be provided in the community, these more restrictive alternatives may be avoided.

ASSESSMENT

State and federal mental health agencies increasingly focus on schools as a primary site for early screening for possible mental disorders (President's

New Freedom Commission, 2003). A critical role of a school social worker is assessment, which is often part of a larger process done with the multidisciplinary team and outside professionals. A mental health concern is one aspect of the pupil-in-school assessment. The school social worker emphasizes student strengths and aspirations, sensitizes the team to the student's cultural, familial, and spiritual needs and shows how these factors interface with the student's mental health issues and learning requirements.

The school social worker needs to be skilled in making differential decisions as a member of a team. Some students can be well served in the school environment through social skills groups, individual counseling, and crisis intervention. Other students require referral to outside providers for psychiatric evaluation, long-term mental health care, and family counseling. In schools and communities with few resources, school social workers are sometimes the only mental health professional that the student will ever see. School social workers must prioritize and determine which students have the most pressing needs and which interventions will be most efficient and effective. Those students at risk for suicide, child maltreatment, or criminal justice involvement require partnership with outside resources. These partnerships often involve outside professionals with a limited understanding of school social work and with whom it is necessary to develop a common language and a mutual process of learning and sharing.

USE OF THE *DSM-IV-TR*

One common language of mental health professionals is the *Diagnostic and Statistical Manual* IV Text Revision (DSM-IV-TR; APA, 2000), which is the major classification and assessment tool used by the mental health system. *DSM-IV-TR* is a multiaxial system consisting of five axes. Axis I lists clinical syndromes, such as schizophrenia, mood disorders, anxiety disorders, and substance abuse. V Codes and behavioral and situational problems are also coded on Axis I. Axis II lists developmental disorders such as mental retardation and personality disorders. Axis III lists physical health conditions or disorders. Axis IV lists psychosocial and environmental problems such as poverty, housing problems, and issues of loss. Axis V is a global assessment of a person's functioning and adjustment currently and within the past year. The student is rated from 0 to 100, based on social, psychological, and school functioning. Many manuals can assist school social workers to understand and to utilize the *DSM-IV-TR* (House, 2002; Morrison, 2001; Pomeroy & Wambach, 2003).

There are advantages and limitations in using the *DSM-IV-TR* diagnostic system (Shea, 1998). On the one hand, *DSM-IV-TR* provides a common language across disciplines to discuss students' mental health issues, and this can assist in effective treatment planning and service delivery. An accurate diagnosis can lead to determining the most evidence-based intervention and the appropriate medication regimen. The multiaxial system encourages social workers to understand students' mental health problems within the context of multiple interacting systems. It allows social workers to consider a wide array of possible interventions (Shea, 1998). On the other hand, diagnoses are labels and can be abused. People may be more prone to use diagnoses as stereotypical explanations of human behavior rather than seeing each person as an individual. Critics of the *DSM* (and even its proponents) acknowledge that the construct validity and reliability of the diagnostic categories need further research, particularly when used with minority populations and children (Chodoff, 2005; Pincus, 1998). There is a realistic danger that clients can become stuck with an inappropriate diagnosis. A *DSM* diagnosis needs to be viewed as an evolving process that is always subject to reexamination and revision. Diagnoses can have ramifications in terms of the student's culture, family, and social situations. For instance, a peer group may scapegoat the student because of a lack of understanding of the meaning of a diagnosis. Finally, the *DSM-IV-TR* does not address the etiology of the mental disorders that it describes; nor does it directly address issues of management of the disorder (Shea, 1997).

SCHOOL SOCIAL WORKERS' USE OF THE EVIDENCE-BASED PRACTICE (EBP) PROCESS

Evidence-based practice (EBP) is defined for this chapter as a process of transparent, culturally sensitive, and evidence-informed practice with clients that draws on the best available empirical evidence to help clients solve their problems. In a school context, this EBP approach is particularly useful in helping parents, teachers, and students understand the myriad problems that present in schools (Franklin, 2007; Raines, 2007). EBP is often caricatured as being rigid or dependent solely on manualized treatments; the EBP approach described in this chapter, based on the work of social work scholars like Gambrill (2001) and Gibbs (2003), is characterized by the use of evidence to inform practice choices that ultimately are implemented by a collaboration between the social work practitioner and his or her client, based on cultural, developmental, and ethical factors. This section describes the basic tenets of this EBP approach and describes the advantages of using it in school social work practice. Additionally, in the following section EBP resources and research findings will be shared to help readers quickly access the best available research evidence to enhance their service to children in schools.

Evidence-based practice is a movement that began in medicine (Corcoran, 2007; Gambrill, 2001; Sackett, Rosenberg, Gray, Haynes, & Richardson, 1996) and quickly spread into mental health disciplines including social work (Gibbs, 2003). The EBP movement in medicine and mental health has sought to equip health care providers and mental health practitioners with the best and most current empirical evidence to help them assist their patients/clients (Gambrill, 2001; Gibbs, 2003). In addition to using practitioners' experience and "practice wisdom," EBP challenges school social workers to collaborate with clients on solving client problems using interventions that emphasize both client preferences and empirical evidence, rather than interventions that solely emanate from the "expert" status of the practitioner.

The EBP process being advanced in this chapter acknowledges the importance of the practitioner-client relationship in making EBP work. This chapter's approach to EBP preserves the all-important clinical relationship school social workers create with their clients while still incorporating the best available empirical evidence to inform the choice of how best to intervene in the presenting problem of the school client. This crucial client-practitioner piece is at times absent from some of the discussions in educational settings of EBP. Indeed, the field has seen calls for empirically-validated treatments (often referred to as "EVTs") in numerous social work, psychological, education, and special education regulations and policy statements. These policy statements and laws have called for practitioners to use "research-based," "scientifically-based," or "empirically-validated" interventions in their work with children (Hoagwood & Johnson, 2003). The EBP process discussed in this chapter allows for the use of EVTs, but not at the expense of failing to establish the school social worker–client rapport that is central to successful work in schools.

Applications of an EBP process to practice can differ in small but significant ways for each client and problem context. An overall process tends to follow similar steps based on Gibbs's (2003) conceptual framework and includes the following: 1) identification of a problem that the client (and often in the case of children, the client system) wants to resolve; 2) creation of an answerable question related to the problem. This answerable question should engage the interest of the client, speak to the client's particular context (culturally, developmentally, and socioeconomically) and assist either in understanding the problem more clearly or in selection of an appropriate and effective intervention; 3) consultation of the evidence base by the school social worker (usually through online research databases) to identify the best available evidence to address the problem; 4) presentation of that evidence in the next session to the client in concise and developmentally appropriate language to help the school social worker and client make decisions about next steps to take, including interventions to implement to address the problem; 5) evaluation of the intervention plan undertaken with consideration either of termination or a repeat of this five-step process to address another problem that has arisen in treatment (Gibbs, 2003). This process can be seen in Figure 25.1.

FIGURE 25.1 Evidence-based Practice (EBP) Process for School Social Workers

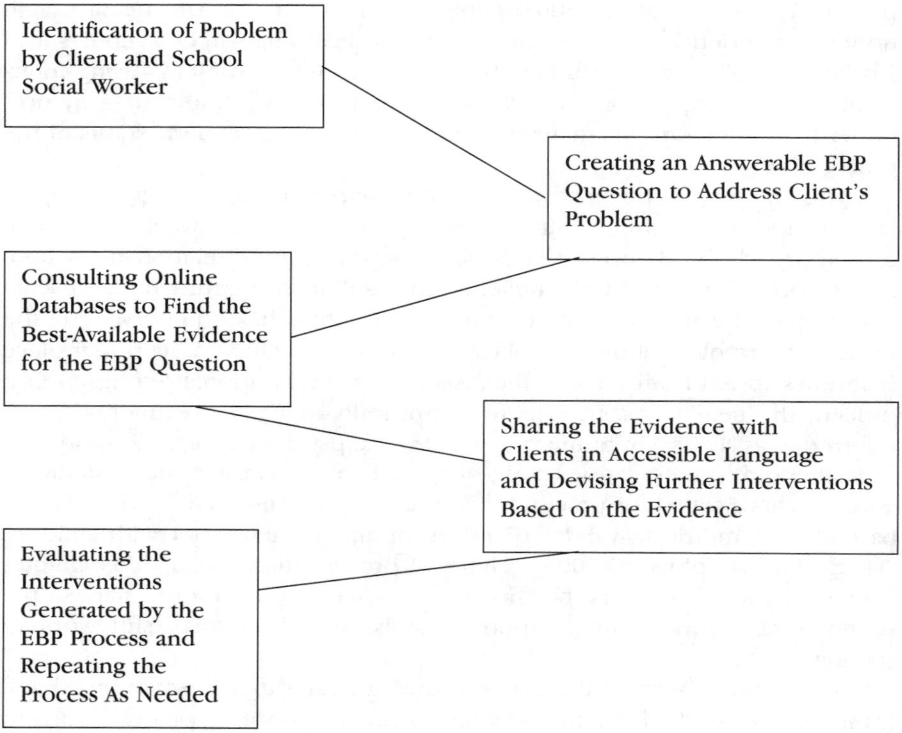

In applying this model to school social work practice, situations often involve complex, multifaceted situations. Consider the case of Marty

> Marty, a 16-year-old high schooler with Asperger's Disorder has great difficulty understanding the complexity of social relationships around him. He feels anxiety and severe depression as he struggles with the contrast of his expectations of himself and the actuality of his situation. Some classmates, noticing his awkwardness, tease him unmercifully; others are sympathetic, but reserved. His unusual behavior and growing stance of victimhood reinforces the teasing. With almost a phobia about numbers, structure, and time, he has a math learning disability. His intelligence is fairly high and his verbal skills are excellent. With his energy taken up with his situation, he does poorly academically. His teachers either come down hard on him or sympathize with him and modify expectations below his actual ability. At home his verbal abuse of his high-achieving younger sister is extreme. His mother feels caught in a protective relationship with him. She constantly modifies expectations in his favor. Father,

a busy and successful engineer, withdraws from Marty into work. Marty mainly sees himself as a victim, has very little awareness of his difficulty in social skills, and has little motivation to change. Although he is generally related to his situation, Hadley, his school social worker, wonders whether some of his discussion and perceptions might have a psychotic quality or whether he could ever act on his depression. He is able to talk about his suicidal thoughts, but denies any desire or plan to go further.

Marty's situation involves multiple transactions—with schoolmates, teachers, parents, and his sister. The school social worker must work with this constellation of issues and attempt to find appropriate interventions at multiple levels. For example, there is a sizeable evidence base related to bullying issues in schools, and Hadley may begin with Marty's concern about being a bullied victim, using the social work maxim, "Start where the client is." Hadley is likely to work with the school environment around the bullying problem.

Hadley is also likely to use their long-term relationship to help Marty stabilize his coping and his perceptions and to plan together around social skill development. Once again, there is a literature upon which to draw to find a range of social skills interventions, including participation in social skills groups, such as those described by Lecroy in chapter 33.

Hadley will also try to help Marty to refine his concerns and his "question" to include himself as well as the others in school. He will help Marty to discover that *he* can impact his situation. He will work with teachers around Marty's identified academic concerns. He will work with the family around their concerns as part of his plan with Marty. He will use his collaborative relationship with the mental health clinic to get consultation, an appointment for Marty, and some possible planning in case his adjustment deteriorates.

There is available research evidence, mainly reflecting individual and family clinical interventions, for each of the identified problems. Another source of knowledge is Hadley's three years of experience in a high school, where he has seen a number of boys like Marty, and is generally familiar with the changing and developing evidence base for the different problems involved.

This case illustrates the ways in which each relational situation is different, and the ways in which complex and multisystemic interventions are often needed to address mental health issues. The school social worker is not the only person working with Marty and his family. The school social worker brings together work done by the assistant principal (school bullying policy), Marty's teachers, his parents, and a psychiatrist and psychologist from the mental health center. The school social worker works towards—not a cure—but a better adjustment. His overall purpose is to help Marty to become more productively engaged in school, in the community, with his family, and with some friends.

Gibbs's basic five-step process differentiates itself in a number of ways as one deals with the complexity of any problem, the developing evidence base, the actuality of a school and family situation, and the uniqueness of every relationship. Right now, Marty may not be ready for much of step four. He only knows his victimhood, his hurt, and some of his own resulting distortions. It may take quite a bit of work to assist him to come to a point where he feels *he* could do anything constructive about his problems. Hadley may need to do a lot of environmental modification to create safety before Marty can begin to form a stable and productive relationship with any part of it. Moreover, each practitioner has a personal style, as unique as a great painting of the same theme by Pablo Picasso or Georges Braque. Hadley knows what can be effective. He has to fit the possibilities in the school at large and the possibilities that emerge from their unique relationship into his own personal style. EBP provides general principles of effective practice, now in balance with personal style and uniqueness, which arises from any real relationship of two persons. EBP can inform a general helping process, but the process is ultimately unique to the persons involved and to their relationship.

The approach to EBP described here should not be conflated with an EBP approach that emphasizes specific interventions over others because those interventions are considered "empirically validated" treatments that have been rigorously evaluated by intervention researchers using large sample sizes, control groups, and random assignment to treatment conditions (Stone & Gambrill, 2007). While evidence from such studies (usually referred to as randomized controlled trials, or RCTs) are useful and do often show strong evidence of intervention effectiveness, such evidence is ultimately unlikely to have a significant impact if the critical components of client preference and school social worker "practice wisdom" are removed from the process and made subservient to the intervention itself. The EBP process advocated in this chapter provides for numerous advantages for school social workers wishing to become more evidence-based and to increase their engagement with their clients. Advantages of using this EBP process approach include: 1) ability for school social workers to feel confident that they are using the best available evidence to help clients with their problems; 2) increase in engagement between client and school social workers as they work together collaboratively on client problems (many clients have come to their next EBP session eager to hear "what the evidence says"; and 3) enhancement of cultural competency skills for school social workers, as the EBP process discussed here challenges practitioners to adapt empirical evidence to client's cultural contexts.

Additionally, a robust finding in the psychotherapy literature indicates that the therapist-client alliance and client strengths are more important for psychotherapy treatment effectiveness than specific techniques (Wampold, 2001). Practitioners will need to cultivate a degree of skepticism and critical thinking skills when presented with interventions that are called "best practices" for treating childhood mental health disorders, pending further evidence that specific ingredients of therapeutic interventions with children make the most difference for most students. While it is certainly possible that programs and interventions may someday become "universal best practices" for students with specific mental health disorders (and tables 25.1 and 25.2 list several programs and interventions that have met rigorous evaluation standards and can be considered to be "effective"), the evidence base is still too thin to state categorically that specific school-based interventions for childhood mental health disorders are effective for most children most of the time, without also considering client preferences, client co-morbidity factors (for example, children who are diagnosed with both ADHD and anxiety), the skills of the practitioners delivering the intervention, and other socioeconomic/cultural/developmental variables that are often screened out of the intervention research process (Gibbs, 2003; Mullen, Bellamy, Bledsoe, & Francois, 2007).

DISORDERS COMMONLY ENCOUNTERED IN SCHOOLS

According to the National Mental Health Information Center (2005) schools ranked the following mental health issues as the most common: 1) social, interpersonal, or family problems; 2) aggression/disruptive behavior/bullying; 3) behavior problems associated with neurological disorders [such as ADHD]; 4) adjustment issues; 5) anxiety/stress/school phobia; and 6) depression/grief reactions. These issues affected boys and girls differently, with boys having more problems with aggression and disruptive behavior problems than girls and girls exhibiting more difficulty with social, interpersonal or family problems, adjustment issues, anxiety and depression.

Attention Deficit Hyperactivity Disorder (ADHD)

Attention deficit hyperactivity disorder (ADHD) can be related to most of these issues, and is the most commonly identified problem for students in a school setting (Costello-Wells, McFarland, Reed, & Walton, 2003). It is most apparent in the school setting and is problematic not only for the student but also for peers, teachers, and parents. It is marked by a student's lack of attention, often combined with hyperactive behavior and impulsivity. To be diagnosed, symptoms must be present before the age of 7, although the actual diagnosis might not come until an older age. The disorder is more often noted in boys and can remain an impairment throughout adolescence and adulthood (American Psychiatric Association, 2000). Some of its behavioral manifestations include: poor time management, incomplete or superficially written assignments, poor problem-solving strategies for learning, and poor recall (Sattler, 1998). Diagnosis of this disorder is difficult. In families

TABLE 25.1 School-based Attention Deficit Disorder Interventions: Results from an EBP Search Process

Intervention	Population Studied	Experimental or Quasi-Experimental Design?	Study Conducted in a School Setting?	Results of Study	Six-Month Follow-up Results	Material and Training Costs How to find out more
Promising						
Behavioral Management Interventions (DuPaul & Eckert, 1997)	Meta-analysis of 63 ADD school-based intervention studies from 1971–1995 (for another smaller meta-analysis, see Reid et al., 2005)	Qualified Yes; some of the studies were single-subject designs, but most were quasi-experimental	Yes (one of the criterion for including in the meta-analysis)	Studies with a control group had a moderate (.45) effect size for helping students manage their behavior through a variety of behavior-based intervention strategies	n/a	All the studies used for the meta-analysis are clearly listed in the article's references. Lead author's e-mail: gjd3@lehigh.edu
Challenging Horizons Program (CHP) (Evans et al., 2005)	Middle school students (*N*=7)	No	Yes (on school grounds after school)	Based on multiple measures of single-subject designs, most students demonstrated moderate gains in both academic and social functioning	No (authors are still analyzing initial data and plan further follow-up)	No information on cost of materials and training possibilities; program has a Web site that describes its program in more detail: http://chp.cisat.jmu.edu/chp.html
Modifying Classroom Environment and Instructional Strategies (Zentall, 2005)	Students in K–12 settings; this is a review of ADD school intervention strategies	No	Yes	No method is specified for how studies were selected or evaluated; still, the studies cited do indicate that making the classroom environment more stimulating and sensory-rich can help students with ADD maintain their attention more successfully	No	No training or materials are listed in the article; Author's e-mail address: zentall@purdue.edu

NOTE: For this table, we used a search of EBP article databases to evaluate intervention studies that met the following criteria: Promising: a school-based study that had at least one of the following: an experimental or quasi-experimental design, random assignment of subjects, with intervention results maintained at a six-month follow-up.

TABLE 25.2 School-Based Anxiety Interventions: Results from an EBP Search Process

Intervention and Intervention Rating (Effective or Promising)	Population Studied	Experimental or Quasi-experimental Design?	Random Assignment of Subjects?	Study Conducted in a School Setting?	Results of Study	Six-Month Follow-up Results?	Material and Training Costs How to find out more
Effective							
Coping Cat (Kendall et al., 1994; Kendall et al., 1997)	Children ages 8–13	Yes, Random assignment of students to treatment or wait-list control group; first study N=47, second study N=94	Yes	Yes, though initial studies were done in a clinic setting	Based on pre- and post-tests and self and parent reports, students showed improvement on their coping skills and decreased anxiety level	Yes, both initial studies showed gains were maintained at one year	*Coping Cat Workbook* by Kendall & Hedtke (2006) $27 at amazon.com; a DVD of the *Coping Cat* for use with students is available for $56 at www.workbookpublishing.com; No cost information on training for the Coping Cat Program: contact Dr. Philip Kendall at pkendall@temple.edu for more information
FRIENDS (Lowry-Webster, Barrett, & Lock, 2003)	Children ages 6–16	Schools randomly assigned to FRIENDS or no-treatment control N=594	Yes	Yes	Students in the FRIENDS group reported fewer anxiety symptoms at post-test	Yes, gains maintained at one-year follow-up	Program is based out of Australia at http://www.friendsinfo.net/ Cost of initial packet containing manual and materials $150; Website is unclear about whether trainings are available outside of Australia
Promising							
Cool Kids Program (Mifsud & Rapee, 2005)	Children ages 9–10, from low-income schools in Australia	Yes, schools randomly assigned to treatment or control	Yes	Yes	Symptoms of anxiety decreased in treatment group compared to control	No, researchers only did follow-up at 4 months (though they claim the students had main-tained their gains)	Cool Kids manuals available for $75 for child/adolescent levels at the researcher's website: http://www.psy.mq.edu.au/MUARU/books/prof.htm Training is encouraged, though training appears to only be offered in Australia at present.

NOTE: For this table, we used a search of EBP article databases to evaluate intervention studies that met the following criteria: Effective: a school-based study that had an experimental or quasi-experimental design, random assignment of subjects, with intervention results maintained at a six-month follow-up. Promising: Any study that met at least one of the "effective" criteria but didn't meet all of them.

and classrooms with a high threshold or tolerance for ADHD, symptoms in these children can often be overlooked. On the other hand, sometimes normally active children are inappropriately diagnosed and treated for a disorder where none exists (Sattler, 1998). ADHD has many co-occurring conditions such as learning disabilities, oppositional defiant disorder, and mood disorders. These co-occurring conditions further complicate a student's ability to learn and pose significant challenges to social workers and teachers as they attempt to accommodate the student's learning needs. These co-occurring conditions (often referred to in research literature as "co-morbidities") also can complicate efforts by school social workers to design effective, school-based interventions for children with ADHD (Teasley, 2006).

In addition to working with the family and coordinating medication, school social workers can also work with teachers to develop effective behavior strategies and classroom management techniques that will allow for optimal student learning. In some cases, students will need specific classroom accommodations. These accommodations might include; shortened assignments, breaking tasks into smaller parts, peer tutoring, untimed tests, and taking breaks. Students might need to have their desks placed in the quietest part of the room to avoid overstimulation and distractions (Silver, 1999). School social workers will need to educate students with ADHD about this disorder and how it is affecting their learning, social relationships, and school adjustment (Silver, 1999). Students may also require social skills interventions. Some students will be best served in a group and others will require individual counseling. Research suggests that multimodal treatment strategies for ADHD present the most promising likelihood of success for most children, combining family therapy, classroom behavior modification, stimulant medication, and individual behavioral therapy (Jensen et al., 2001). Though all of these approaches individually have shown some promise for children with ADHD, the significant problems with medication compliance and family and school disruptions that are caused by students with ADHD have created more interest in the multimodal approach. Examples of screening measures for ADHD and anxiety can be found in Table 25.3. Examples of effective, school-based intervention programs can be found in table 25.1.

Mood Disorders

Depression. The study of depression in children and adolescents is a relatively recent phenomenon. Children and teenagers can and do experience depression, although it may manifest itself differently in young people than in adults. Diagnosis of depression in children requires a significant change in mood and functioning that persists over time (Sattler, 1998). The causes of depression are not fully understood, although it is thought to have both biological and psychosocial origins. Depression is diagnosed in

TABLE 25.3 Screening Measures for ADHD and Anxiety in Children and Adolescents

Measure	Age (approximate years)	Reading level (grade)	Spanish version	Cost	Time to complete (minutes)	Contact Information for Ordering Scale
Child Behavior Checklist (pre-school)	1 1/2–5 (completed by parents)	6	Yes	$150	10–15	http://www.aseba.org/products/cbcl6-18.html
Child Behavior Checklist (school age)	6–18 (completed by parents)	6	Yes	$395	10–15	http://www.fmhi.usf.edu/amh/homicide-suicide/assess_dep.html
Conner's Teacher Rating Scale	3–17 (completed by parents) 12–17 (adolescent self-report)	6–9	Yes	$268	10–15	http://www.pearsonassessments.com/tests/crs-r.htm

NOTE: All of the above three scales have subscales that address anxiety and attention problems.

females almost five times more often than in males (Sattler, 1999). Some paper- and-pencil assessment tools for depression in childhood can be found on table 25.4.

Depressed children and adolescents may experience loss of interest in activities, feelings of helplessness and hopelessness, and disturbances in sleep and appetite (Johnson, Rasbury, & Siegel, 1997). Although adults might become withdrawn and lethargic when experiencing depression, children

TABLE 25.4 Screening Measures for Depression in Children and Adolescents

Measure	Age (approximate years)	Reading level (grade)	Spanish version	Cost	Time to complete (minutes)	Contact Information for Ordering Scale
Children's Depression Inventory	6–17	1	Yes	$73	10–15	http://www.pearsonassessments.com/tests/cdi.htm
Center for Epidemiological Studies-Depression Scale for Children	12–18	6	Yes	Free (public domain)	5–10 10–15	http://www.fmhi.usf.edu/amh/homicide-suicide/assess_dep.html
Reynolds Child Depression Scale	8–12	2	Yes	$138		http://www3.parinc.com/products/product.aspx?Productid=RCDS
Beck Depression Inventory	14 and older	6	Yes	$83	5–10	http://harcourtassessment.com/hai/SearchResults.aspx?Search=Beck%20Depression

SOURCE: This table was synthesized from information at the following sources: Sharp, L. & Lipsky, M. (2002, September 15). American Family Physician, 1001-1008 and the above websites for each scale.

and adolescents tend to exhibit high degrees of irritability and agitation. The symptoms of adolescent depression tend to be similar to those of adults and include: an inability to experience pleasure, low self-esteem, fatigue, boredom, aggressive behavior, somatic complaints, and irritability. Sometimes depressed teenagers express their symptoms behaviorally. They may run away from home, engage in low-level criminal behavior such as stealing or shoplifting, or engage in conflict with peers and authority figures. They may experience an increase in suicidal ideation or behavior. Diagnosis of depression in children can be difficult because they are in a constant state of developmental flux, and typically children and adolescents experience fluctuations in mood and affect. Students are rarely referred to the school social worker for obvious symptoms of depression, but rather for abrupt behavioral changes or acting out at home or in the classroom. Students with moderate or severe depression often experience disruptions in their ability to learn. Teachers may mistakenly assume that a student's low energy, impaired concentration, or defiance is a result of a behavior disorder when the student may be suffering from an underlying depressive disorder.

Some psychosocial or environmental factors that contribute to a student's depression can include family neglect or abuse, or victimization by peers. There is also some evidence that some students may be predisposed to depression because of a family history of depression (Kendler et al., 1995). Students who are vulnerable to depression may come to school with inadequate problem-solving and self-regulatory skills and are often overwhelmed by stressors that other children might be able to manage. Major life stressors such as the loss of a parent, pregnancy, moves, divorce, or remarriage can also trigger depressive reactions in children and adolescents (Sattler, 1998).

Bipolar Disorder. Sometimes the first episode of depression for children and adolescents can turn out to be what will later be diagnosed as bipolar disorder. Some estimates suggest that nearly half of the children who develop major depression before puberty subsequently experience mania by age 20. The Child & Adolescent Bipolar Foundation (2001) identifies bipolar disorder as a treatable neurobiological brain disorder characterized by severe fluctuations of mood and activity level. The manic phase of bipolar disorder in children can include periods of crankiness, insomnia, hyperactivity, expansive mood, and racing thoughts. The depressed phase in children with bipolar disorder is not distinguishable from the symptoms of childhood depression discussed above. Some children experience rapid cycling; in the morning they appear depressed, but by afternoon they are displaying a full-blown manic episode with unmanageable behavior. Scientists believe that a predisposition to the disorder is inherited and can be triggered by trauma, or it may occur with no identifiable cause (The Child & Adolescent Bipolar Foundation, 2001).

Diagnosis of this disorder is controversial and difficult to make. It can often be confused with unipolar depression, substance abuse, attention deficit disorder, or oppositional defiant disorder. This would have significant consequences with regard to appropriate medication and treatment planning. For instance, if there has been a misdiagnosis and the child is prescribed medication such as Ritalin for ADHD, instead of correcting the problem the medication can exacerbate the child's condition and may trigger a manic episode (Parmelee, 1996).

At school, students with bipolar disorder might be viewed as creative and verbally skilled but would have difficulty with organization, and problem solving. They might appear very distracted and inattentive. School expectations in the early years—learning to follow rules, taking turns, and completing tasks—place stress on these students by demanding that they perform in areas where they have deficits. In later school years, the hormonal changes of puberty can further exacerbate the symptoms of bipolar disorder. Most adolescents experience moodiness and powerful emotions; for those students with bipolar disorder these fluctuations are more extreme and may lead to risky or dangerous behavior. Teenagers with bipolar disorder are at an increased risk for suicidal behavior and substance abuse (Kluger et al., 2002).

Practices based on current research for treating students with mood disorders involve a multimodal approach involving counseling, medication, and other psychosocial interventions (McLellan & Werry, 2003). The primary aim of treatment is to shorten the period of the mood disorder and decrease negative consequences of episodes of illness. Students need to be encouraged to continue to be active in school and with their studies even when they are still feeling badly. Adding structure to the day will help stabilize the student's mood. Positive reinforcement needs to be implemented to assist students in completing tasks of daily living such as getting ready for and going to school, completing assignments and staying at school for the whole day (Parmelee, 1996). Recent studies suggest that a focus on cognitive and behavioral skills is effective in treating students with mood disorders (Johnson, Rasbury, & Siegel 1997). Group treatment can have an especially important role in work with these students. Students can learn social skills from their peers. In the group they can hear about successful recovery, and this might increase their own compliance with medication and/or counseling (Reinecke, Ryan, & DuBois, 1998).

Pervasive Developmental Disorders (PDD)

With the trend toward inclusion in the last decade, more and more students with a pervasive developmental disorder (PDD) are attending local public schools. This has posed many opportunities and challenges for students, school social workers, and staff. PDD is an umbrella term that includes a heterogeneous group of conditions. PDDs are characterized by impaired social interactions, communication deficits, and stereotypical behaviors such as rocking, head banging, and echolalia (Johnson, Rasbury, & Siegel, 1997).

Impairments in these areas can be so severe that they require multiple interventions and services to allow these students to participate in school. It is important to state that the term pervasive does not imply that there are no areas of normal functioning. These students can have significant strengths and talents in some areas that can include musical or artistic ability.

Autism. Students with autism can range from being mentally retarded and having no communication or social skills to having some speech and the ability to be trained to improve social interaction. These students are often not aware of the existence of other people and rarely give eye contact or demonstrate a need for closeness. This disorder is often diagnosed during infancy or the preschool years and can be lifelong in duration. The most common presenting concern that brings these children to a professional's attention is the failure to acquire language at the expected age (Parmelee, 1996).

Asperger's Disorder. Students with Asperger's disorder are different from students with autism because they do possess some communication skills and have average or above average intellect. The main deficit for students with Asperger's is in the area of social skill development. These students have trouble with nonverbal behaviors such as maintaining eye contact or maintaining appropriate physical boundaries with others (Johnson et al., 1997). Children with this disorder frequently have slowed motor skill development and can be clumsy and awkward. Students with Asperger's can become consumed with highly personalized interests that don't require other peer involvement. Examples of this might be collecting many facts about baseball or trains to the exclusion of other interests or relationships. Many students with Asperger's do want to connect with others but they lack knowledge and skills about how to make these connections.

The role of the school social worker with children having PDD begins in early intervention programs before the child starts kindergarten. These students will require early intervention by an interdisciplinary team of school professionals. School social workers can be a bridge between the school, the teacher, and the family, and be part of a team that would assess eligibility for special education services and identify areas for growth and development. When a diagnosis such as PDD is made, many families experience shock, grief, and denial. For many years, parents were "blamed" for their child's autistic symptoms. As a result, an adversarial relationship could develop between families and the medical or education system on which they depended. It is now well understood that pervasive developmental disorders are neurological conditions, and that parents have not caused the problem but rather are an integral part of the team that will attempt to remediate the student's deficits. In order for parents to function in collaboration with the school, the social worker needs to establish a strong and supportive alliance that acknowledges parents' feelings and aspirations for their child. The school social worker can provide social skills groups and other behavioral interventions as part of the treatment team. They will be responsible for a thorough case-study evaluation and for developing individualized educational program (IEP) goals for social work service.

Suggested interventions based on current intervention research would focus on fostering normal development and helping students to compensate for their developmental deficits. Since the social worker's role is in the domain of social and emotional development (Bryson, Rogers, & Fombonne, 2003), the goal of the work will be to increase the pleasure that a child can experience when engaging in social connections with peers and adults. These students will need repetitive training in areas such as greeting skills, personal hygiene, and appropriate classroom behaviors. They may need to be taught how to play with others and to become more aware of social nuance. If students are engaging in self-injurious or aggressive behaviors they will need behavior modification to reduce the frequency of these behaviors.

Conduct Disorders

Behavior problems are the reason why most children are referred for mental health services (Costello-Wells et al., 2003; Parmelee, 1996). Most children who have a behavior problem do not go on to develop a diagnosable disturbance of conduct. Some will go on to develop disturbances that get worse over time and cause multiple problems with relationships, undermining their adult functioning. Johnson, Rasbury, and Siegel (1997) describe children with conduct disorders who exhibit behaviors that bring them into conflict with their environment. These behaviors can include: tantrums, stubbornness, defiance, disobedience, and spitefulness. Children with more severe behavior problems can become aggressive with people or animals, destroy property, set fires, steal, lie, run away, and ultimately become involved with the juvenile justice system. According to *DSM-IV-TR*, disruptive behavior disorders can be divided into two categories: conduct disorder and oppositional defiant disorder. Features of a conduct disorder involve a repetitive pattern of behavior where the rights of others are violated and/or societal norms are broken. Oppositional defiant disorder (ODD) is defined as a pattern of defiant, disobedient, and hostile behavior directed toward authority figures (APA, 2000). Disruptive behavior disorders are often associated with a number of co-occurring conditions including ADHD, substance abuse, and mood disorders (House, 2002).

Students with conduct or behavior disorders take up significant amounts of time from school social workers, teachers, and administrators. Not only is learning impeded for those children, but their behavior may also have a negative impact on the learning of other children in the classroom. Students with conduct disorders are often the school bullies, can be involved in gang activity, and are openly defiant to school authority. Teachers bring these students to the social worker's attention, hoping that behavior plans can be put in place or that the student can be identified as needing special education services. Animosity often develops between school staff and parents because of frequent phone calls home with concerns about noncompliant behavior. Some parents withdraw from school meetings and activities because of feelings of shame or helplessness. These disconnections between home and school leave more room for student misbehavior and manipulation. When communication has broken down, these students are vulnerable and may fall through the cracks. School shootings and random violence are worst-case scenarios. In recent years, many schools have taken on the challenge of teaching moral values and character development as a school-wide strategy to address the issues that contribute to disruptive school behavior.

It is important to learn the meaning or function of a student's disruptive behavior. A functional assessment (see chapter 22) includes a detailed description of behavioral antecedents and consequences, frequency, duration, intensity, location, and the function of the behavior. Additional information needs to be collected regarding the child's history, including age of onset of the problematic behaviors, symptoms that might suggest a difficult temperament, and whether the child's problematic behavior has occurred alone or in the presence of others, within the family, or in the community. Children should receive a medical assessment to find out whether there has been a head injury or central nervous system or auditory processing difficulties. Any past involvement with the legal system should be documented. Awareness of any family history of mental illness, substance abuse, or abuse or neglect will assist in the treatment planning process (Sattler, 1998).

An outcome of a careful assessment will include appropriate interventions designed to target disruptive behaviors. The most effective approach needs to be multisystemic and focused on cognitive and behavioral skills. Specific techniques may include brainstorming and problem-solving strategies, role-playing, behavioral rehearsal, as well as teaching various self-soothing techniques such as progressive muscle relaxation and positive imagery (Parmelee, 1996). Increasing structure throughout the school day is critical for these children. Parent and teacher education is important, with the focus on assisting them to respond to provocative behavior appropriately. They need to provide consistent, positive reinforcement for prosocial behaviors and predictable and natural consequences for negative or antisocial behaviors (Fonagy & Kurtz, 2002).

Anxiety Disorders

DSM-IV-TR describes ten different types of anxiety disorders in childhood. The most common disorders include: separation anxiety, panic disorder, social phobia, obsessive-compulsive disorder, and post-traumatic stress disorder. Anxiety disorders are considered internalizing disorders, which means that they are directed toward self and the symptoms primarily involve excessive inhibition of behavior (Sattler, 1998). Symptoms of anxiety involve avoidant or escape behaviors. The subjective experience often involves a sense of dread, despair, and impending doom. Physical symptoms can include: rapid heartbeat, sweating, difficulty breathing, and impaired speech and coordination. Intense anxiety is an aversive experience, and phobic behaviors often result from avoiding the anxiety-producing stimuli. Anxiety problems can be conceptualized as exaggerated fear responses in situations where the fear is no longer functional. For example a child who encounters a strange dog in his neighborhood and feels frightened is normal. A child with an anxiety disorder would no longer be able to feel at ease in the same area of the neighborhood even though the dog was no longer present (House, 2002). Separation anxiety and post-traumatic stress disorder will be described in more detail because of their prevalence among school-aged children and the impact they have on learning.

Separation Anxiety. Children with separation anxiety disorder show obvious distress when separating from their parents (Johnson et al., 1997). These children often refuse to go to school and may be mislabeled as school phobic. The fear for these students is not of going to school per se but instead is a fear of leaving their parents. These children may have physical symptoms such as nausea, headaches, and stomachaches. They may describe fears of getting lost or kidnapped, and nightmares are a common experience. Separation anxiety is frequently the reason why families initially seek help for their children. More girls are diagnosed with this disorder than boys, and onset is usually between the age of 9 and 11. One-third of these children have co-occurring depression and later may go on to have other features of anxiety (Parmelee, 1996; see Chapter 34).

Post-traumatic stress disorder is also classified as an anxiety disorder in *DSM-IV-TR*. The central feature for children with post-traumatic stress disorder (PTSD) is the experience of a severe trauma such as witnessing a murder, being kidnapped, or living through a natural disaster, followed by the recurrent intrusive recollection of the trauma, avoidance of trauma-related stimuli, and hyperarousal (Parmelee, 1996). This is more fully discussed in chapter 34.

Students with anxiety disorders present many challenges in the school setting. In the early years, getting to school can be difficult and taking risks in the learning process can be slowed. In later years, separation anxiety that is stopping students from attending school can lead to chronic truancy or dropping out of high school entirely. Even when these students attend school on a regular basis they are often so anxious and preoccupied with managing their fears that they are unavailable for learning. They may be slow to make friends, unable to establish trusting relationships with teachers or social workers, and unwilling to try new activities. When severely anxious students perceive the outside world as dangerous and anticipate impending doom, they may respond with rigidity, and inflexibility in dealing with the everyday demands of school. Their reactions may include temper tantrums, aggressive outbursts, and petulant withdrawal. These behaviors are attempts to maintain sameness and predictability in the school. See table 25.2 for a list of some evidence-based interventions for school social workers to consider when treating students with anxiety.

Suicidality

Almost 5,000 young people between the ages of 15 and 24 commit suicide every year. Suicide is the third leading cause of death among adolescents and the second leading cause of death for college age youth (Brown University, 2004; NIMH, 2006).

School social workers are frequently the first adults who become aware that a student is experiencing suicidal ideation. This can be one of the most anxiety provoking and troubling issues in school social work practice. Sometimes students reveal these thoughts to the social worker; sometimes a student's friend comes to the social worker; and there are times when a student or teacher passes on a suicide note to the social worker. Many times parents are unaware of their children's suicidal feelings. When they are aware, they can be at a loss about what to do and will frequently turn to the school social worker for support and direction.

Students with a diagnosed mental illness are at greater risk for suicide than other students (Parmelee, 1996). The pain of depression, anxiety, or bipolar disorder can be accompanied by hopelessness, isolation, and despair. These negative feelings can trigger both suicidal ideation and behavior. Students who feel alone and are not part of a social support structure at home or at school are particularly vulnerable to suicidal feelings. Because adolescents are impulsive and may not have a developed a vision for their future, they can idealize suicide and see it as a solution to their problems without any thought to the consequences of their self-destructive behavior (Cooper & Lesser, 2005).

Some students who voice suicidal feelings are actually crying out for help and may wish for an adult to rescue them from their agony. It is a common myth that discussing suicidal ideation will promote suicidal behavior. Rather the opposite is true. When a student can verbalize these thoughts he or she may be less likely to act them out (American Association of Suicidology, 2007).

Other students may present to the school social worker as having chronic suicidal feelings and may make significant demands on school personnel for their time and attention. Although these students may not always require hospitalization, they are at risk and need ongoing services to manage the emotional disregulation that they experience. When a student poses a threat of self-harming it is necessary to breach confidentially and inform parents, outside service providers, and school administration.

A major goal of work with this student population is to teach them cognitive and behavioral skills to help them to manage their painful emotions (Linehan, 1993). School social workers need to develop clinical judgment and skills that enable them to evaluate the level of a student's lethality and the possible need for hospitalization and/or other services. An interview protocol can include: determining the frequency and duration of suicidal ideation, the specificity of the suicidal plan, and the extent of action already taken in carrying out the plan (Shea, 1998). Shea recommends a chronological assessment of suicide events (the CASE approach). The school social worker needs to explore the presenting suicidal ideation or events, the degree of the student's suicidal ideation within the last two to six weeks, any past suicidal ideation or events, and current ideation or intent. By breaking up the interview into four discrete time frames, the worker can be more confident that she has captured a complete picture of the student's suicide risk (Shea, 2002).

Obtaining information from collateral sources, such as parents, family members, and friends, is a critical step in assessing lethality. It is wise to get another opinion about the student's risk through a referral for a psychiatric assessment. However, hospitalization is not a magical solution to a student's acute suicidal crisis. In this age of managed care, students who are hospitalized often return to school in a few days. Sometimes the hospitalization is so brief that the suicidal ideation is not fully resolved. Often the underlying issues or problems that led to the crisis continue to need attention.

Safety contracts have been a popular and often used tool during risk assessment. However research has not shown that safety contracts in themselves are effective deterrents (Shea, 2002). They can be appropriately used as part of an assessment to further explore the student's ambivalence about living or dying. For a more complete list of evidence-based suicide treatment and prevention resources, consult the American Foundation for Suicide Prevention's Best Practices Registry at http://www.sprc.org/featured_resources/bpr//index.asp.

Suicide Risk with Gay and Lesbian Youth. Gay and lesbian youth may be two to three times more likely to kill themselves than heterosexual youths and constitute 30 percent of all adolescent suicides (McBee & Rogers, 1997). The negative reactions of family and society and internalized homophobia appear to sometimes lead to a pervasive sense of hopelessness and despair in this population. Hetrick and Martin (as cited in Morrow, 1993) reported that one-third of their adolescent gay and lesbian clients had suffered violence because of their sexual orientation. Of those who reported suffering violence, nearly half of the violence (49 percent) was inflicted by family members. Uribe and Harbeck (1992) in their description of a program to assist gay and lesbian youth write:

> Although most in this early group were very intelligent, few were performing at the level of their native capacity. Many were involved in self-destructive behavior, including substance abuse and attempting suicide, and were on the

> verge of dropping out of school. They felt they existed in a box, with no adults to talk to, no traditional support structures to lean on for help in sorting out problems, and no young people like themselves. In effect, they felt stranded in an environment that shunned their very existence. (pp. 51–52)

Alcohol and substance use compounds risks for gay and lesbian youth. Substance abuse is greater among gay and lesbian youth than other youth (Gibson, 1989; Whitbeck, Chen, Hoyt, Tyler, & Johnson, 2004), and recent research has shown that substance abuse is a significant risk factor along with depression and previous suicide attempts for gay youth (Russell & Joyner, 2001).

This chapter discussed mental health issues commonly encountered by school social workers and has focused on related policies, research, assessment, and intervention. School social workers have long been involved with mental health issues in schools. These issues continue to be crucial, given the large number of students affected and the negative impact of such issues on academic achievement. School social workers provide direct mental health services as well as working collaboratively with families, schools, and community partners. Throughout this work, school social workers must understand mental health assessment, including use of the *DSM-IV-TR*. The contemporary models of evidence-based practice (EBP) are now part of the language of mental health service provision across settings. A considerable literature is available to draw upon related to mental health issues of children and youth and effective interventions, although most of this research does not involve school social workers. Thus, there are complexities in translating EBP into ecologically based, multisystemic, complex, school social work practice. This chapter develops a foundation for school social work mental health practice that draws upon the available resources to address issues commonly found in schools. Such issues include ADHD, mood disorders, PDD, conduct disorders, and anxiety disorders. The following Web sites offer opportunities to expand upon this foundation and to build knowledge and skill in addressing mental health issues in schools.

Internet resources for ADHD

Children and adults with learning disabilities (including ADHD) http://www.ldonline.org/

National Attention Deficit Disorder Association www.add.org

Internet resources for mood disorders

Depression and Bipolar Support Alliance www.dbsalliance.org

Child and Adolescent Bipolar Foundation www.bpkids.org

All About Depression www.allaboutdepression.com

Internet resources for PDD

Center for the Study of Autism www.autism.org

Online Asperger Syndrome Information and Support www.udel.edu/bkirby/asperger

Internet resources for conduct disorders

Conduct Disorders http://www.conductdisorders.com/

Explosive Child resources (based on *The Explosive Child* by Ross Greene) http://www.explosivechild.com/

Internet resources for anxiety disorders

Anxiety Disorders Association of America www.adaa.org

Internet resources for suicide

American Association of Suicidology www.suicidology.org

American Foundation for Suicide Prevention www.sprc.org/featured_resources/bpr//index.asp

Evidence-based practice resources for designing school-based interventions (this is only a partial list of free EBP resources to use)

Campbell Collaboration Systematic Reviews of Social Work and Education Interventions http://www.campbellcollaboration.org/index.asp

Cochrane Collaboration (for mental health interventions based on *DSM-IV* diagnoses) http://www.cochrane.org/index.htm

Colorado Blueprints for Violence Prevention http://www.colorado.edu/cspv/blueprints/

National Registry of Evidence-based Programs and Practices (SAMHSA) http://www.nrepp.samhsa.gov/

What Works Clearinghouse (U.S. Department of Education) http://ies.ed.gov/ncee/wwc/

References

American Association of Suicidology. (2007). *The youth suicide prevention school-based guide.* Retrieved on September 10, 2007 from http://www.suicidology.org

American Psychiatric Association. (2000). *Diagnostic and statistical manual of mental disorders: Text revision* (4th ed.). Washington, DC: Author.

Anderson-Butcher, D., Iachini, A., & Wade-Mdivanian, R. (2007). *School linkage protocol technical assistance guide: Expanded school improvement through the enhancement of the learning support continuum.* Columbus, OH: College of Social Work, Ohio State University.

Anderson-Butcher, D., & Ashton, D. (2004). Innovative models of collaboration to serve children, youths, families, and communities. *Children & Schools, 26*(1), 39–53.

Brooks-Gunn, J., & Duncan, G. J. (1997). The effects of poverty on children. *Future of Children,* 7(2), 55–71.

Brown University. (2004). Teen suicide. *Brown University Child & Adolescent Behavior Letter, 20*(8), 2.

Bryson, S., Rogers, S., & Fombonne, E. (2003). Autism spectrum disorders: Early detection, intervention, education, and psychopharmacological management. *Canadian Journal of Psychiatry, 48,* 506–516.

Child & Adolescent Bipolar Foundation. (2001). *Early-onset bipolar disorder fact sheet.* Retrieved February 27, 2005, from http://www.bpkids.org

Chodoff, P. (2005). Psychiatric diagnosis: A 60 year perspective. *Psychiatric News, 40*(11), 17.

Cooper, M. G., & Lesser, J. G. (2005). *Clinical social work practice: An integrated approach*. Boston: Allyn & Bacon.

Corcoran, K. (2007). From the scientific revolution to evidence-based practice: Teaching the short history with a long past. *Research on Social Work Practice, 17*, 548–552.

Costello-Wells, B., McFarland, Reed, J., & Walton, K. (2003). School-based mental health clinics. *Journal of Child and Adolescent Psychiatric Nursing, 16*, 60–71.

Drug-Free Schools and Community Act (20 U.S.C 4601).

Fonagy P., & Kurtz A. (2002), Disturbance of conduct. In P. Fonagy (Ed.), *What works for whom? A critical review of treatments for children and adolescents.* New York: Guilford.

Franklin, C. (2007). Teaching evidence-based practices: Strategies for implementation: A response to Mullen et al. and Proctor. *Research on Social Work Practice, 17,* 592–602.

Gambrill, E. (2001). Social work: An authority-based profession. *Research on social work practice, 11*(2), 166–175.

Ghuman, H. S., Weist, M. D., & Sarles, R. M. (Eds.) (2002). *Providing mental health services to youth where they are: School and community based approaches*. New York: Taylor & Francis.

Gibbs, L. (2003). *Evidence-based practice for the helping professions*. New York: Brooks/Cole.

Gibson, P. (1989). Gay male and lesbian youth suicide. In U.S. Department of Health and Human Services (Ed.), *Report of Secretary's Task Force on Youth Suicide* (pp. 11–142). Washington, DC: U.S. Department of Health and Human Services.

Gutman, L. M., Sameroff, A. J., & Cole, R. (2003) Academic growth curve trajectories from 1st grade to 12th grade: Effects of multiple social risk factors and preschool child factors. *Developmental Psychology, 39*(4), 777–790.

Hoagwood, K., & Johnson, J. (2003). School psychology: A public health framework. *Journal of School Psychology,* 3–21.

House, A. E. (2002). *DSM-IV diagnosis in the schools*. New York: Guilford.

Ialong, N. S., Edelsohn, G., & Kellam, S. G. (2001). A further look at the prognostic power of young children's reports of depressed mood and feelings. *Child Development, 72*(3), 736–747.

Institute of Medicine. (1994). *Reducing risks for mental disorders: Frontiers for preventive intervention research*. Washington, DC: National Academy Press.

Jensen, P. S., Hinshaw, S. P., Swanson, J. M., Greenhill, L. L., Connors, C. K., Arnold, L. E., Abikoff, H. B., Elliott, G., Hechtman, L., Hoza, B., March, J., Newcorn, J. H., Severe, J. B., Vitiello, B., Wells, K., & Wigal, T. (2001). Findings from the NIMH Multimodal Treatment Study of ADHD (MTA): Implications and Applications for Primary Care Providers. *Journal of Developmental & Behavioral Pediatrics, 22*(1), 60–73.

Johnson, J. H., Rasbury, W. C., & Siegel, L. J. (1997). *Approaches to child treatment* (2nd ed.). Needham Heights, MA: Allyn & Bacon.

Jonson-Reid, M., Kontak, D., Citerman, B., Essma, A., & Fezzi, N. (2004). School social work case characteristics, services and dispositions: Year one results. *Children & Schools, 26*(1), 5–22.

Kataoka, S. H., Zhang, L., & Wells, K. B. (2002). Unmet need for mental health care among U.S. children: Variation by ethnicity and insurance status. *American Journal of Psychiatry, 159*(9), 1548–1555.

Kazdin, A. E. (1993). Adolescent mental health: Prevention and treatment programs. *American Psychologist, 48*, 127–141.

Kendler, K. S., Kessler, R. C., Walters, E. E., MacLean, C., Neale, M. C., Heath, A. C., & Eaves, L. J. (1995). Stressful life events, genetic liability, and onset of an episode of major depression in women. *American Journal of Psychiatry, 152*, 833–842.

Kluger, J., Song, S., Cray, D., Ressner, J., Dequine, J., Sattley, M., et al. (2002). Young and bipolar. *Time, 160*(8), 38–48.

Linehan, M. M. (1993). *Skills training manual for treating borderline personality disorder*. New York: Guilford.

McBee, S. M., & Rogers, J. R. (1997). Identifying risk factors for gay and lesbian suicidal behavior: Implications for mental health counselors. *Journal of Mental Health Counseling, 19*(2), 1–8.

McLellan, J. P., & Werry, J. S. (2003). Evidence-based treatments in child and adolescent psychiatry, *Journal of the American Academy of Child and Adolescent Psychiatry, 42*, 1388–1400.

Miranda, J., Azocar, F., Organista, K. C., Munoz, R. F., & Lieberman, A. (1996). Recruiting and retaining low-income Latinos in psychotherapy research. *Journal of Consulting & Clinical Psychology, 64*(5), 868–874.

Morrison, J. (2001). *DSM-IV made easy*. New York: Guilford.

Morrow, D. (1993). Social work with gay and lesbian adolescents. *Social Work, 38*(6), 655–660.

Mullen, E., Bellamy, J., Bledsoe, S., & Francois, J. J. (2007). Teaching evidence-based practice. *Research on Social Work Practice, 17(5)*, 574–582.

National Institute of Mental Health. (2004). *Treatment of children with mental disorders*. Retrieved January 6, 2008 from http://www.nimh.nih.gov/health/publications/treatment-of-children-with-mental-disorders/summary.shtml

National Mental Health Information Center. (2005). *School mental health services in the United States, 2002–2003*. Retrieved Sept. 8, 2007 from http://mentalhealth.samhsa.gov/publications/allpubs/sma05-4068/

No Child Left Behind Act of 2001, PL 107-110.

Parmelee, D. X. (1996). *Child and adolescent psychiatry*. St. Louis, MO: Mosby-Yearbook.

Pincus, H. A. (1998) Clinical significance and DSM-IV. *Archives of General Psychiatry, 55*, 1145.

Pomeroy, E., & Wambach, K. (2003). *The clinical assessment workbook*. Pacific Grove, CA: Brooks/Cole.

President's New Freedom Commission on Mental Health. (2003). *Achieving the promise: Transforming mental health care in America. Final report*. (DHHS Publication No. SMA 03-3832). Rockville, MD: Department of Health and Human Services.

Pumariega, A., Glover, S., Holzer, C. E., & Nguyen, N. (1998). Utilization of mental health services in a tri-ethnic sample. *Community Mental Health Journal, 34*(2), 145–156.

Raines, J. (2007). *Evidence-based practice in schools*. Presentation at School Social Work Association of America, April 2007.

Reinecke, M. A., Ryan, N. E., & DuBois, D. L. (1998). Cognitive-behavioral therapy of depression and depressive symptoms during adolescence: A review and meta-analysis. *Journal of the American Academy of Child and Adolescent Psychiatry, 37*(1), 26–34.

Russell, S. T., & Joyner, K. (2001). Adolescent sexual orientation and suicide risk: Evidence from a national study. *American Journal of Public Health, 91*, 1276–1281.

Sackett, D. L., Rosenberg, W. M. C., Gray, J. A. M., Haynes, R. B., & Richardson, W. D. (1996). Evidence based medicine: What it is and what it isn't. *British Medical Journal, 312*, 71–72.

Safe and Drug-Free Schools and Communities Act, 20 U.S.C. 7101.

Safe and Drug Free Schools Newsletter. (2007). *The principles of effectiveness*. Retrieved Sept. 8, 2007 from http://www.acde.org/educate/challenge/v9n4prin.htm

Sattler, J. M. (1998). *Clinical and forensic interviewing of children and families*. San Diego, CA: Sattler.

Shea, S. C. (1997). The practical use of DSM-III-R. In M. Hersen & S. M. Turner (Eds.), *Adult psychopathology and diagnosis* (pp. 23–43). New York: Wiley & Sons.

Shea, S. C. (1998). *Psychiatric interviewing: The art of understanding*. Philadelphia: W. B. Saunders.

Shea, S. C. (2002). *The practical art of suicide assessment*. Hoboken, NJ: John Wiley & Sons.

Silver, L. B. (1999). *Attention-deficit/hyperactivity disorder* (2nd ed.). Washington, DC: American Psychiatric Press.

Snowden, L. (2001). Social embeddedness and psychological well being among African Americans and whites. *American Journal of Community Psychology, 29*(4), 519–537.

Stone, S., & Gambrill, E. (2007). Do school social work textbooks provide a sound guide for education and practice? *Children & Schools, 29*(2), 109–118.

Stone, S. (2007). Child maltreatment, out-of-home placement and academic vulnerability: A decade review of evidence and future directions. *Children & Youth Services Review, 29*(2), 139–161.

Surgeon General's Report. (1999). *Mental health: A report of the surgeon general*. Retrieved February 27, 2005, from http://www.surgeongeneral.gov/library/mental health/home.html

Teasley, M. (2006). Effective interventions for students with ADHD. In C. Franklin, M. B. Harris, & P. Allen-Meares (Eds.). *The school services sourcebook: A guide for social workers, counselors, and mental health professionals* (pp. 45–56). New York: Oxford University Press.

Teo, A., Carlson, E., & Mathieu, P. J. (1996). A prospective longitudinal study of psychosocial predictors of achievement. *Journal of School Psychology, 34*, 285–306.

Thompson, T., & Massat, C. R. (2006). Experiences of violence, post-traumatic stress, academic achievement and behavior problems of urban African Americans. *Child and Adolescent Social Work Journal, 22*(5–6), 367–393.

United States Department of Education. (1994). *To assure a free appropriate public education of all children with disabilities: Sixteenth annual report to Congress on the implementation of the Individuals with Disabilities Education Act.* Washington, DC: Author.

United States Department of Education Office of Special Programs. (2001). *Twenty-third annual report to Congress on the implementation of the Individuals with Disabilities Education Act: Results.* Washington, DC: Author.

Uribe, V., & Harbeck, K. M. (1992). Project 10 addresses needs of gay and lesbian youth. *Education Digest, 58*(2), 50–55.

U.S. Department of Health and Human Services. (1999). *Mental Health: A Report of the Surgeon General.* Rockville, MD: U.S. Department of Health and Human Services.

Wampold, B. E. (2001). *The great psychotherapy debate: Models, methods and findings.* Mahwah, NJ: Erlbaum.

Whitbeck, L. B., Chen, X., Hoyt, D. R., Tyler, K. A., & Johnson, K. D. (2004). Mental disorder, subsistence strategies, and victimization among gay, lesbian and bisexual homeless and runaway adolescents. *Journal of Sex Research, 41*(4), 329–342.

26

Planning and Setting Goals: Behaviorial Intervention Plans, the Individualized Educational Program, and the Individualized Family Service Plan

Robert Constable
Loyola University Chicago

Galen Thomas
Southern Illinois University

Erin Gleason Leyba
University of Illinois at Chicago

- The Behaviorial Intervention Plan (BIP)
- The Individualized Educational Program (IEP)
- The Process of Setting Goals and Objectives
- What is the IEP Team?
- Developing Agreements and Integrating Resources

- Involving Children in the IEP
- The Individualized Family Service Plan (IFSP)

The planning process, formalized in Behaviorial Intervention Plans (BIP), the Individualized Educational Program (IEP), and the Individualized Family Service Plan (IFSP), builds on strengths-based assessment, discussed in chapter 22. In the United States, the IEP and the IFSP are the chief documents for the child's right to a free, appropriate, public education. They are formal planning instruments under the Individuals with Disabilities Education Act (IDEA) and central to the school social worker's work with any child or infant with a disability. The IEP deals with children aged 3 through 21; the IFSP generally deals with infants and toddlers, from birth to three years of age, and their families, although IDEA 2004 permits the use of the IFSP for children until they enter kindergarten under certain circumstances. Although the family is important in both, in the IFSP the family is a principal agent to manage and implement a plan using a variety of resources to meet the young child's educational needs. The greater the need and complexity of family involvement, the more important the social worker's role becomes.

Strengths are the starting point for assessment and planning. The strengths-based perspective assists students to discover and develop capabilities where they often lack authentic confidence and belief in themselves (Kam-shing, 2003). Social work or educational interventions that make use of strengths minimize resistance to change by capitalizing on things the student enjoys and by creating positive (constructional) behaviors rather than simply eliminating negative behaviors. (See Table 26.1 for examples of this process). As social workers reframe stories in a strengths-based manner, such stories eventually become accepted as the dominant understanding (Dietz, 2000). Positive reframing can occur while brainstorming individualized educational program goals and objectives, services, accommodations, scheduling, strategies for professionals, or placement options. Although formal accommodations are usually made on the basis of deficits, social workers can advocate that they also be based on strengths. Aversive activities may be paired with reinforcing activities to encourage growth. Parents may be guided by family strengths. When family strengths open the possibility of social support, they can form the basis for referrals for special programs, resources, or extracurricular activities.

THE BEHAVIORAL INTERVENTION PLAN (BIP)

When disciplinary action is being considered, it is important to develop a functional behavior assessment (discussed in chapter 22), the basis for a

TABLE 26.1 Examples: Using Strengths to Solve Problems Creatively

Protective Factor/Strength	*Key Risk Factor/Need*	*Creative Problem Solving*
Parent indicates that child is a real leader around younger children. Child loves to help younger kids around the neighborhood.	Child is highly disruptive during art class.	Arrange for child to be a helper/model/co-teacher for younger children's art classes one to two times per week.
Child loves to watch music videos and sing along at home.	Child has low self-esteem.	Arrange for child to sing a holiday song over the PA system.
Child loves to make things, to put things together.	Child cannot follow classroom routine.	Post daily or weekly classroom routine on puzzle. Have child put it together (in order) for the class.
Child is on-task and alert during the morning.	Child has difficulty with social studies and tends to "tune out" during lessons.	Arrange a schedule change so child has social studies in the morning.
Child knows a significant amount of historical facts.	Child makes bullying comments to others during morning announcements.	Arrange for child to formulate a history question/riddle during morning announcements to be presented daily to the history class.
Child is close to uncle and loves animals.	Child does not practice reading at home.	Arrange for child to read with uncle about animals.
Child scored high on adaptive behavior scale for community orientation, or "knowing where things are."	Child's adaptive behavior scale weaknesses are in socialization, peer interaction, and expressive language.	Arrange for child to be a school tour guide with another peer for children who are new to the school.

behavioral intervention plan (BIP). The BIP is the responsibility of the entire team, and, in particular, the teacher, who may have the most contact with the student. It is an integral part of teamwork and consultation. Social workers may assist in the construction of the plan and in its implementation. They may have responsibilities in skill development and in modifying antecedent conditions and consequences.

The BIP should be designed to fulfill the original function of the student's negative behavior (i.e., power and control, task avoidance, attention, belonging, fun) through positive interventions so the negative behavior can be diminished. For example, if a student constantly talks out in class to achieve a sense of belonging, the interventions listed in the BIP should include positive alternatives to help the student belong, such as giving the student a special role in the class, linking the student with a peer buddy, or helping the student feel more included in small-group work. One of the most important aspects of the BIP is that its interventions should provide the same payoff (serve the same function) as the negative behavior, but through appropriate means (Van Acker, Boreson, Gable, & Potterton, 2005).

The BIP should focus on the behaviors of concern. Building on the ABC functional behavior analysis, described in Chapter 22, a plan would specify:

- Needs for development: motivation, behavior, social skills, self-esteem (see figure 26.1.);
- Antecedent conditions (these might be modified);
- Consequences (these might be modified).

Antecedent conditions that could be modified might include: task or instructional modifications, incorporation of student interests, "chunking" or reducing assignments, use of advance organizers, peer tutors or models, student choices, instruction in alternative forms of communication, or limitation of homework to tasks that the student has mastered, shared power, alternating tasks, increased supervision, decreased sensory input, or decreased classroom overcrowding (Raines, 2002; Zuna & McDougall, 2004). It may involve a short, daily check-in with the social worker. It may involve a group program at the YMCA that indirectly teaches social skills. Consequences that could be modified might include: ignoring or redirecting mildly inappropriate behavior, providing incentives, or noticing and reinforcing appropriate behavior (Raines, 2002). Auxiliary supports may include parent training, family therapy, couples counseling, psychiatric referral for medication, outpatient child therapy, case coordination with other agencies, or youth programs at local YMCAs (Raines, 2002). Under different circumstances they may either be antecedents or consequences.

The BIP should have measurable goals and objectives and a clear description of how to increase positive behaviors rather than simply trying to reduce the undesirable ones. These measurable goals and objectives should clearly describe the desired improvement or remedy for the problem. Here the charts of functional behavior objectives in this chapter may be a useful beginning in assessment and treatment planning. The plan should include strategies for generalizing and maintaining positive behavior outside of the educational situation and planned disciplinary procedures, if necessary. The BIP would have a list of responsible participants and resources to access. Evaluation can take place by comparing a measure of the initial target behavior with a later period. When the plan is developed, it should be monitored regularly, and modified when necessary. It should be documented in a way that conveys to parents and others whether or not the student is making progress (Clark, 2001).

THE INDIVIDUALIZED EDUCATIONAL PROGRAM (IEP)

The school social worker's role is only one part of a broader assessment and planning process done by the multidisciplinary team. In the case of the IEP or the IFSP, an individualized assessment (including the social worker's case study assessment [CSA]) done by the team results in goals and a statement of special education and/or related services necessary for the student to attain these goals. The planned interventions, the "program" needed (special education and related services) become a civil right when they are defined in the IEP/IFSP. Social workers need to fit their assessment and planning processes into this broader team process, which then defines the civil right. The specific description and the justification for the school social work services needed as a part of this overall plan must come from this relationship.

The IEP is the central management tool used to ensure the child with disabilities the right to a free, appropriate, public education. The IEP assembles recent evaluation, present decision making, and future expectations in one document. It is a synopsis of the service efforts of the IEP team. It reflects the assessment effort that has previously taken place and the areas of need identified by a team of qualified professionals and the parents of the child. It involves the people who have interest in the child's education and who attend the IEP staffing: the parents, various members of the IEP team (e.g., the teacher, administrator, psychologist, and other specialized personnel) when appropriate, and the child.

The IEP goes beyond a simple report or a plan. It is the living record of a complex evaluation and goal-setting process, which has taken place among parents, school, and child. The IEP is also a *program* that outlines the educational resources necessary to accomplish the goals. And these become the basis for the civil right of the child with disabilities to free, appropriate public education (FAPE). If signed and not contested, it is concrete evidence that consensus has been reached. The decision-making process aims for an agreement in seven crucial areas:

1. *The child's present level of academic achievement and functional performance.* The social work social developmental study (SDS) has studied the relation between appropriate social and developmental tasks, present functional performance, and academic achievement. These establish baselines in different areas upon which measurable goals and objectives can be constructed. The school social worker will mainly contribute to the child's IEP in the areas of functional performance (see Table 26.1).

2. *How the child's disability affects the child's involvement and progress in the general education curriculum.* This begins to align the assessment with the general education curriculum and its district-wide assessment processes. When a child cannot participate in the regular assessment, there must be an appropriate alternate assessment, aligned to alternate achievement standards, selected by the team.

3. *Measurable annual goals.* Goals are measurable academic and behavioral (functional) outcomes achievable over a period of one year or less. Goals are made up of short-term objectives, the measurable steps or bench-

marks that may lead to the achievement of goals. Annual academic and functional goals, reflecting the baseline assessment, are geared both toward progress in the general education curriculum and toward meeting other needs coming from the disability. There needs to be a description of how the progress toward meeting the annual goals will be measured and when the reports will be provided. Objective criteria are components of the child's behavior that may be observed and measured. Such criteria may be used to compare the child's current performance with previous levels of performance, or they may be compared with a classroom norm that is typical of children his or her age. The results of these comparisons indicate whether or not objectives are being achieved or whether new and different objectives may be in order (20 U.S.C. 1414[1]). Only when there is an alternate assessment with alternate standards (i.e., not geared to existing grade level standards) there is a need for measurable short-term objectives or benchmarks leading to the annual goals. Otherwise periodic progress reports are needed, using academic measures or possibly variations of goal attainment scaling described later in this chapter. On the other hand, it may be difficult to think about measurable annual goals without intermediate objectives or benchmarks, and so these are included in our discussion. Good practice would dictate thinking of longer-term goals, signifying the achievement of a sequence of short-term objectives.

4. *The "program,"* that is, the special education and related services to be provided for or on behalf of the child. This includes *program modifications* to enable the child to make progress in general education and/or *supports* for school personnel. For school social workers, direct individual or group work with the pupil can be a *related service*. Consultation on behalf of the pupil can be a *support* or involve a *program modification*.

5. *A statement of the extent to which the child will not participate with nondisabled children in the regular class, with or without support services.* This underlines the importance of the least restrictive environment for the child with disabilities. The negative wording (not participate) is meant to bring the team to justify nonparticipation in a general education environment, rather than assume an environment that is directly matched to the child's learning needs but is more restrictive. School social workers have important responsibilities assisting the team to develop this optimal match (see chapter 19).

6. *The projected dates for initiation of services, planned modifications, and the anticipated frequency, location, and duration of those services and modifications.*

7. *Beginning at age 16, goals of postsecondary transition to training, education, employment and, where appropriate, independent living skills, as well as the needed transition services to reach these goals* 34 C.F.R. 300.320; 20 U.S.C. 1414 et seq).

Transition Services are a coordinated set of activities for a student, designed within an outcome-oriented process that promotes movement from school to post-school activities. The coordinated set of activities is based on the individual student's needs, taking into account the student's preferences and interests. It includes instruction, community experiences, the development of employment and post-school adult-living objectives, and, when appropriate, acquisition of daily living skills and a functional vocational evaluation. If a participating agency other than the educational agency fails to provide agreed-on services, the educational agency would reconvene the IEP team to identify alternative strategies to meet the transition objectives.

Although the law specifies an Individualized Transition Plan (ITP) for pupils 16 or older with certain variations as the student grows older, the term *transition* has also been applied to all movement from one level to another. For example, as a 5-year-old child with severe disabilities moves from early childhood special education to kindergarten, an appropriate transition plan should be developed. Whenever there is a delicate transition from one environment to another, there needs to be planning, and the social worker probably should be involved. Preparations for inclusion of a new student and transition planning are discussed in greater detail in Chapter 19. To do good transition planning, the school social worker needs a broad, ecological perspective on the relations of the student to the home, the school, and community resources. She needs to understand the possible process of transition, and the supports needed to make the transition successful.

All of the IEP assessment and planning has to result in a *statement of needed special education and related services*, building on the annual goals. The social work services are justified as related services that assist the pupil to attain these academic and functional goals and benefit from education. These services need to be specific and related to the annual goals. Global descriptors, such as "a unit of casework," are not adequate. Rather, much more precise descriptors such as "the social worker will spend an hour a week working with the student on attendance and motivation for achievement," or "in a group to help him develop social and friendship skills. This will take place for a half semester with continuance based on evaluation" should be used.

The IEP encapsulates the entire provision of special education and related services as well as the evaluation of effectiveness. It is ultimately a list of services to be provided to reach agreed upon goals. Although the IEP cannot guarantee the child will actually reach these particular goals, it is an agreement on the school's part to provide or purchase (if it cannot directly provide) the special education and related services listed in the document. If necessary resources are unavailable within the school district, the school must contract with outside agencies, individuals, or other school districts to ensure their provision—thus the importance of listing the "program" and setting measurable goals for each program component.

The full potential of what school social work can offer to children cannot be achieved without a significant level of participation by the social worker in the IEP process. Social workers cannot expect to offer services to children with disabilities in the school without IEP involvement. Their unique contribution to the IEP process takes place in at least three major areas. The social worker (1) participates in the process of setting annual goals (and intermediate objectives), (2) helps the multidisciplinary team to develop sufficient consensus among itself and with parents to proceed, and (3) is involved with case management and integration of school and outside agency resources.

THE PROCESS OF SETTING GOALS AND OBJECTIVES

Goals and achieved objectives provide a way for educators and parents to track the child's progress in special education. They should not be confused with the goals and objectives that are normally found in daily, weekly, or monthly instructional plans. Otherwise, there could be hundreds of educational goals for one IEP. They should *signify*; they should be milestones in the pupil's expected progress. They should be measurable, even if "measurable" means the presence or absence of an observed behavior, such as making a friend. Such objectives for children with disabilities reflect the confluence of academic and functional (social) goals. The concept of education is broad and includes social skills, life skills, problem-solving skills, and developmental steps. For children with disabilities these are often the most important parts of their education. The education of the child with disabilities is in large part a preparation for his or her best level of social functioning outside of the school situation. Particularly for children with severe disabilities, a large part of this preparation has to do with the learning of life skills: those skills that promote appropriate independence, appropriate and satisfying interpersonal relationships, problem-solving skills, an appropriate self-image, and tolerance for unavoidable stress (see chapter 33). These are areas where social workers have particular expertise and can make a crucial contribution to the educational process.

Functional Performance and Developmental Needs: Functional Behavior Objectives

As long as school social workers have been participating in the IEP, they have sought to develop frames of reference for the developmental goals and objectives that underlie the academic content and fall within their areas of expertise. Some social workers may tend to think in terms of psychological disorders. While these deficit frameworks open up a useful literature, they do not translate well into the normalizing, strengths-based, learning and functional orientations that characterize education. The problem of translating developmental objectives into measurable learning objectives has challenged school social workers since the inception of IDEA. From David Sanders' (2002) perspective, there are four basic categories of developmental needs that impede a student's functioning in school. These are:

1. *Motivation*—referring to the desire to achieve and develop within school expectations;
2. *Behavior*—referring to actions dysfunctional to one's own learning and development or the learning and development of others;
3. *Social skills*—referring to skills in relation to others, difficulties making friends, or problems fitting into groups positively;
4. *Self-image*—referring to difficulties in self-esteem or self-confidence.

Each need category implies underlying needs as well as presenting behavior. It is only after careful evaluation of the pertinent data that a confident decision can be made. In an example of aggressive and defiant behaviors, fighting might at first indicate that *behavior* would be the appropriate basic category. But aggressive behavior is often symptomatic of weak or nonexistent social skills, or of a profound and pervasive feeling of inferiority. In these cases either *social skills* or *self-image* would be the more appropriate category (Sanders, 2002). Table 26.2 provides a sampler of strengths-based, developmental learning objectives, together with the way each item could be measured. The list is not exhaustive and in any case should be individualized to develop goals and objectives for each student's situation. To assist the student to achieve a goal or objective, the social worker's "program" could range from direct, individual work, crisis work, group work, social skills groups, consultation, direct classroom intervention or modifications, parent consultation or coaching, or other interventions appropriate to the situation. These also translate readily into an assessment framework, such as the functional behavior assessment and a resulting intervention system, such as positive behavior interventions and support (PBIS), discussed in chapter 17.

Goal attainment scaling (GAS) is a popular way to provide an individualized, criterion-referenced approach to describing, measuring, and documenting changes in student performance (Roach & Elliott, 2005). Members of the team first identify target behaviors—behaviors of concern where desirable change is possible and that can be used as benchmarks of progress. These behaviors are defined in objective terms so that they can be understood and accurately paraphrased. Interventions are planned and a scale for measuring change is constructed. The scale could be developed from three to five descriptions of the possible outcomes, ranging from "least favorable" to "most favorable." Table 26.3 (Roach & Elliott, 2005) illustrates this process and shows at least ten different possible dimensions of change, ranging from "frequency" of an activity through "engagement" with a process. After the scale is developed with the team and the student, the intervention can be implemented and the resulting behaviors evaluated.

TABLE 26.2 Developmental Learning Objectives Sampler

Area of Learning	*Measurement*
I. **Motivation**	
A. Profile: Poor homework completion, weak organization skills, poor study skills	
1. Student will learn the importance of completing homework assignments and being prepared for class.	Tests (content based)
2. With an incentive plan, student will complete homework as assigned and be prepared for class.	Charting (contracting, incentive plans) Daily log (teacher's records, assignment notebooks)
3. Independently, student will complete homework as assigned and will be prepared for class (receive passing grades in (*x*) class, maintain credits to graduate with class).	Charting (contracting incentive plans) Daily log (teacher's gradebook) Other (midterm reports, report cards)
B. Profile: Off-task behavior	
1. Student will learn the importance of listening and being on task at school.	Tests (content based)
2. With an incentive plan, student will begin in-class assignments and (with appropriate cues from the teacher) will be on task for (*x*) minutes (until work is completed).	Charting (contracting, incentive plans) Observations (documented) Other (formal classroom observations)
3. Independently, student will be consistently and appropriately on task.	Charting (contracting, incentive plans) Observations (documented) Other (consultations, formal classroom observations)
C. Profile: Poor school attendance, truancy	
1. Student will learn the importance of daily school attendance.	Tests (content based)
2. With an incentive plan, with a behavior modification schedule, student will decrease school absences to less than one (two) per month.	Charting (contracting, incentive plans) Other (attendance records)
3. Independently, student will be at school each attendance day unless ill (excused, etc.).	Other (attendance records)
II. **Behavior**	
A. Profile: Disruptive Behavior	
1. With an incentive strategy, student will follow the behavior	Charting (contracting, incentive plans) Daily log (teacher's records)

plan specifically written as part of his IEP.	
2. Independently, student will follow the behavior plan specifically written as part of his IEP.	Charting (contracting, incentive plans) Daily log (teacher's records, office records)
B. Profile: Poor listening skills, not following directions	
1. Student will learn why paying attention and following directions are important in the classroom (on the playground, in the cafeteria, etc.).	Tests (content based)
2. With an incentive plan, student will listen for and follow directions in the classroom with appropriate cues from the teacher).	Charting (contracting, incentive plans) Observations (documented) Other (consultations, formal classroom observations)
3. Independently, student will listen for and follow directions.	Observations (documented) Other (consultations, formal classroom observations)
C. Profile: Chronic classroom misbehavior	
1. Student will understand the importance of rule systems in school and will know the classroom (school, playground, cafeteria) rules and consequences of noncompliance.	Tests (content based)
2. Student will learn the purpose of time-out and will learn and practice correct time-out behavior.	Tests (content based) Daily log (record of practice sessions)
3. With an incentive plan, student will take time-out correctly in the classroom in compliance to the classroom behavior plan.	Charting (schedules, contracting) Daily log (teacher's behavior records) Observations (documented)
4. Independently, with an incentive plan, student will accept and follow the classroom behavior plan (increase acceptable classroom behaviors, decrease classroom disruptions to (*x*) or less per (*x*)).	Charting (schedules, contracting) Daily log (teacher's behavior records) Observations (reports from teachers, staff) Other (office discipline records)
D. Profile: Bothering others, aggressive behaviors	
1. Student will learn why every student should feel safe and be safe at school.	Tests (content based)
2. Student will learn to identify motivations and causes of aggressive behavior (teasing, baiting).	Tests (content based)
3. With a conflict resolution program, student will learn and practice a conflict resolution strategy	Tests (content based) Daily log (record of practice sessions)

(assertive, nonaggressive problem-solving techniques).	
4. Independently, with an incentive plan, student will decrease incidents of physical aggression at school (in the classroom, in the cafeteria, to less than (*x*) per (*x*)).	Charting (contracting, incentive plans) Daily logs (teacher's behavior logs) Other (office discipline records)
E. Profile: Accepting consequences, respecting authority	
1. Student will understand cause and effect relationships as they relate to behavior and prescribed negative consequences.	Tests (content related)
2. Student will be able to explain how his or her behavior precipitates a prescribed negative consequence.	Tests (content related) Observations (reports from staff)
3. Independently, student will cooperatively accept prescribed negative consequences of his or her behavior.	Charting (contracting, incentive plans) Observations (reports from staff)
4. Independently, student will accept legitimate direction, criticism, and/or negative consequences.	Observations (reports from staff) Daily log (daily record of incidents)

III. **Social Skills**	
A. Profile: Uncooperative, dysfunctional social behavior	
1. Student will learn the importance of cooperative social behavior.	Tests (content based)
2. Using a conflict resolution strategy, student will learn and practice a conflict resolution (problem-solving) strategy.	Tests (content based) Daily log (record of practice sessions)
3. Independently (with an incentive plan), student will decrease incidents of social conflict in the classroom (school environment, on the playground) to one (two) or less per day (week).	Charting (contracting) Daily log (teacher's behavior records) Other (office discipline records)
B. Profile: Poor social skills, difficulties making friends	
1. With group work intervention, student will learn and practice basic social skills (taking turns, waiting politely, saying nice things, sharing, respecting differences, accepting others, good manners, controlling teasing and name calling).	Tests (content based) Daily log (content based)

2. Independently, student will use (increase) positive, cooperative interpersonal social skills in the classroom (on the playground, at school, that can be observed by (*x*)).	Observations (documented)
C. Profile: Anger control	
1. Student will be able to identify telltale feelings and body signals when becoming angry.	Tests Charting
2. Student will develop a understanding of reactions to and perceptions of anger.	Tests Charting
3. Student will learn a self-talk (cool-down) technique to reduce angry feelings.	Tests (content based) Charting
4. Independently, student will use a self-talk (cool-down) technique to reduce and control his or her anger.	Observations (documented)

IV. Self-Esteem

A. Profile: Poor self-esteem, elementary, intermediate	
1. Student will successfully complete a copyrighted esteem-building curriculum.	Tests (content related)
2. Student will keep a personal journal and will enter one positive statement about self each (*x*).	Charting (entries) Daily log (record of entries)
3. Independently, student will increase and maintain positive feelings of self-esteem.	Charting (self-evaluation) Other (Piers–Harris base and intervals)
B. Profile: Poor self-esteem, intermediate, secondary	
1. Student will recognize unique positive personal attributes.	Tests
2. Student will learn and practice personal goal-setting strategies.	Charting (contracting)
3. Student will experience success by setting and achieving realistic personal (educational, social) goals.	Charting (contracting, incentive plan)
4. Independently, student will increase and maintain positive feelings of self-esteem.	Charting (self-evaluation) Other (Piers–Harris base and intervals)
C. Profile: Poor self-confidence	
1. Student will recognize unique positive personal qualities and attributes.	Tests

2. With an incentive plan, student will volunteer positive statements about self to (ask clarifying questions of) teacher (familiar staff) when asked (with prompts).	Charting (contracting, incentive plans) Observations (documented) Daily log (record of occurrences)
3. With an incentive plan, student will ask clarifying questions and/ or make appropriate declarative statements spontaneously in the classroom.	Charting (contracting, incentive plans) Observations (documented) Daily log (record of occurrences)
4. Independently, student will gain self-confidence, increasing participation in playground activities (joining a school club, starting a conversation with a familiar staff person, eating lunch with classmates (*x*) days of the week, applying for a job).	Charting (self-evaluation) Observations (documented) Others (Piers–Harris base and intervals, consultations)

D. Profile: Poor hygiene and weak self-care skills

1. Student will learn the importance of good grooming, appearance, and personal hygiene.	Tests (content based)
2. Independently, student will show increased healthful personal hygiene habits in the classroom (school, cafeteria) (that will be noticed by (*x*)).	Observations (documented)

E. Profile: Drug use

1. Student will learn the consequences of drug abuse.	Tests
2. Student will learn strategies for assertively refusing offers from others to participate in drug use.	Tests
3. Student will set healthful personal goals about drug and substance use.	Charting (contracting) Other (consultations with student)
4. Independently, student will abstain from harmful drug use.	Other (consultations, medical, parental)

F. Profile: Gang involvement

1. Student will identify social and emotional needs and how those needs are met through gang affiliations.	Tests
2. Student will identify potential dangers and hazards of gang affiliations.	Tests
3. Student will identify satisfying and healthy alternatives to gang affiliations.	Observations (documented)

4. Independently, student will choose satisfying and healthy alternatives instead of gang affiliations.	Charting (contracting) Observations (documented) Daily log (record of specific behaviors) Other (consultations with significant others)

TABLE 26.3 Goal Attainment Scaling Model to Rank Objectives

Predicted Levels Of Attainment	*Goal 1: Devin will interact appropriately with peers.*	*Goal 2: Devin will dress for gym without special accommodations.*	*Goal 3: Devin will maintain successful effort and grades in all classes.*
Much less than expected –2	Significant conflicts with peers in regular and special classes involving more than six rule violations per day.	Refuses to dress even with accommodations.	Failing one or more classes.
Somewhat less than expected –1	At least four class rule violations per day.	At least three "no dress" gym days per week, even with accommodations.	Grades drop in one or more subjects.
Expected level 0	Devin will attend social skills class and participate appropriately, with no more than three rule violations per day.	Devin will dress for gym with accommodations and no more than two "no dress" days per week.	Devin will maintain grades in all classes.
Somewhat more than expected +1	Devin will transfer behavior learned in group and practice it with peers in special calluses.	With accommodations, Devin will dress every day for gym.	Devin will improve grades in two classes.
Much more than expected +2	Devin will interact comfortably with peers in regular and special classes.	Devin will dress for gym without accommodations.	Devin will improve grades in four classes.

WHAT IS THE IEP TEAM?

The IEP team means a group of individuals composed of: 1) the parents of a child with a disability, 2) a regular education teacher of the child (if the child is, or may be, participating in the regular education environment), 3) at least one special education teacher of the child, 4) a representative of the local educational agency who provides or supervises special education and who is knowledgeable about the general education curriculum, and 5) an individual who can interpret the instructional implications of evaluation results.

Parents, as part of the multidisciplinary team, must be included in the decision-making process that determines these resources. "Parents" may include: a biological or adoptive parent, an individual who may have special knowledge of the child, such as a foster parent, a guardian (but not the state), a person who is acting in the place of the parent (such as a grandparent, stepparent, or other relative) with whom the child lives, or a legally appointed surrogate parent (34 CFR 300.30[a])

Also, whenever appropriate, the pupil should be included, especially when post-secondary transition is part of the IEP considerations. The emphasis on self-determination would require participation whenever the student is going to be able to manage appropriately in the meeting. Recent reviews of best practices suggest preparation of the student for the meeting when necessary. This preparation may involve some form of verbal rehearsal, role-playing, or the use of verbal, visual, and/or physical prompts as part of this. In addition, student involvement in the meeting can be facilitated by avoiding jargon, using understandable language and vocabulary, and directing questions to the student (Test, Mason, Hughes, Konrad, Neale, & Wood, 2004).

DEVELOPING AGREEMENTS AND INTEGRATING RESOURCES

The attainment of IEP and transition plan goals, particularly with children having more serious disabilities, often demands coordination and integration of a variety of services outside as well as inside the school. Most social workers have developed problem-solving and consensus-building skills through their professional education. These skills are often crucial to the successful completion of the IEP process. Social workers are often most likely to have a holistic perspective on the child. The social worker is usually the only member of the multidisciplinary team who is in everyday contact with outside resources and whose educational preparation includes concepts of coordination among these services. Consequently, many school districts routinely use the social worker as a coordinator of the initial multidisciplinary team and in the later IEP staffing with the parents. The high level of professional specialization within the school and the different interests often represented by parent and school create the potential for conflict. Agreements, if reached, are frequently perceived as accommodations between weaker and stronger sets of interests. Children with disabilities receive services from a variety of agencies: medical services, respite care, child welfare, mental health, financial assistance, transportation, vocational education, and so on. In addition to formal agency services, they can receive a variety of help from neighbors, relatives, and informal community groups. These can work against each other if they are not coordinated. The U.S. Department of Education lists the social worker as one of three professionals (the others are counselor and psychologist) who might serve as coordinator or case manager of the IEP process for an individual child or all children with disabilities served by an agency. Case managers might: 1) coordinate the multidisciplinary evaluation, 2) collect and synthesize evaluation reports and other relevant information about a child that might be needed at the IEP meeting, 3) communicate with the parent, and 4) participate in or conduct the IEP meeting itself (U.S. Department of Education, 1981). Chapter 30 discusses case management and coordination in greater detail.

A Hypothetical Case Study

Let us begin by following a simple referral for a case study evaluation of Devin, with the IEP process, and service sequence through each of the stages of the process. For purposes of our first illustration let us assume that Devin cannot participate in the district-wide general education assessment. Thus he will require annual goals and short-term objectives, as every child has required through the implementation of IDEA 2004.

We will break down the steps that should be followed to arrive at those goals and objectives in the school social worker's contribution to the IEP. The steps represent a way of clarifying our own goals and involvement in developing the IEP. The reader should keep in mind that this is a hypothetical case study and that the type and extent of the school social worker's involvement in a particular case will depend on the individual child's needs as determined by the IEP team. We will begin with the presenting problem:

The Presenting Problem. In order to be eligible for funding, the problem must relate to the categories of disabilities written into the regulations. However, the fact that the child fits into one of the categories, for example, hearing impaired, does not automatically make him a candidate for social work intervention. Inability to deal with stress, potential breakdown of social functioning, or needed improvement of social functioning are general reasons for referral to a social worker. The additional stress of a disability and the need for individualized environmental support systems are reasons that many exceptional children need social work help. The child with a particular disability may have difficulty coping with the educational and social skill demands of the school. He may need help in acquiring such skills and/or in dealing with experiences that are new.

> Devin is a 12-year-old with multiple physical disabilities who is borderline educable mentally disabled. He was referred because of his teacher's concern that his excessive demands for attention were impeding his learning process in several general education classes, particularly in gym.

The Problem as a Whole. The school social worker's conference with teacher and parents resulted in a picture of a boy whose performance in school has been uneven and whose ability to function in school has been hampered by parental overprotectiveness and disagreement on the degree of independence he should be allowed. He is currently enrolled in both special and regular education classes with poor adjustment to some of these classes, overwhelming needs for attention from adults, and withdrawal from relations with other children. In the family, the parents have had difficulty agreeing on the tasks he should be involved in and on his expected level of self-care. Consequently, Devin's participation in the family and in care of himself is considerably less than his potential. The parents are in conflict about this, and his two brothers and a sister reflect this ambivalence in their relationships with him. The social worker's assessment draws some connections between Devin's role in the family, the parents' feelings, and the way Devin has played out some of these family-role interactions in school behaviors, particularly with parentlike school figures and teachers. The statement also includes alternative plans for working with the family, Devin, and his teachers. The results of the social worker's assessment, combined with the information gathered by the other team members, will be used by the team in the evaluative conference and later to formulate the statement of present levels of educational functioning in the IEP.

The Problem as It Is Experienced in the Context of Education. The next step is to define the problem as it is being experienced in the classroom and in relation to the goals of education. At the risk of oversimplifying, we may provide several social parameters of the educational problem. One parameter is that of engagement or withdrawal from educational tasks appropriate to the child's capabilities. The child may either engage in the learning process with distracting, attention-getting, inappropriately aggressive behavior or may withdraw from the process, attempting to compensate in other ways for the withdrawal. A second parameter is that of engagement or withdrawal from relationships with other children. Pupils need to learn social skills appropriate to their own maturational level. The learning of these social skills influences the performance of educational tasks. Thus, there is a direct relation between the learning environment and the child's social maturation.

To follow our example, the school wishes to place Devin in a general education gym class. We can predict with some certainty that Devin will place high demands on the gym teacher and the other pupils. The parents, although accepting of the idea, might endanger the arrangement because of their own anxiety and worries about Devin. Failure in the gym class could generalize to several other classes where he has recently made some adjustment. There is particular concern with the gym class because of dressing, showers, and inherent physical competition. Any one of these factors might place Devin's use of what the school could offer him at risk. What we know about the problem allows us to predict with some degree of accuracy the chances of goal achievement within a behavior setting and some ability to generalize to the overall ecology of the school. This understanding allows us to move to the next stage, definition of the problem in behavioral terms.

The Problem as Behavior. The purpose of this stage is to state the school social worker's formulation of the problem in behavioral terms and to relate it to the educational goals established earlier. Behavioral terms are statements of a person's present functioning, or what Devin is presently doing. These terms establish a baseline for goals and objectives and must be specific.

Behavioral objectives risk fragmentation and meaninglessness if they do not flow from the process of problem definition discussed earlier. The school social worker may find himself in the position of choosing from a seemingly infinite range of behaviors for any child. Actually, a few well-chosen examples are much better, particularly if they may serve as indicators or "milestones" of the pupil's progress.

To go back to our example, Devin has difficulty dealing with a situation that seems competitive and draws attention to his poor functioning. Under stress he has tended to retreat into social relations with adults, from whom he demands high levels of attention. He is particularly uneasy with the dressing and showering aspects of gym. His parents' anxiety adds to the situation and reveals another set of needs. Teachers also can tend to overreact to the situation, increasing the chances of failure. To enumerate specific aspects of the problem:

1. Devin withdraws from situations involving physical competition. Without intervention, the pattern is expected to continue or increase in gym class.
2. Devin tends not to interact with peers in his general education classes.
3. Social interaction is limited with peers in special education.
4. Devin has no close friends.
5. Devin makes excessive demands on adults, especially teachers, but doesn't function in the classroom up to his own capacities without constant support from the teacher.
6. Devin is particularly self-conscious concerning dressing and showering aspects of gym.
7. His parents have tended to protect Devin from situations that demand independence or involve any risking of self. Devin's home patterns are related to his school patterns.
8. Teachers have tended toward either excessive protection or excessive expectations of independence with Devin.

Annual Goals, Objectives, and Resources

Finally, we may define goals and objectives. Annual goals are specific statements of the skills the student should be progressing toward within the framework of the school year. Annual goals evolve out of the assessment of the child's needs and abilities and should be an index of student progress. Although there are different formats that may serve as examples for a particular child's IEP, most would probably contain:

1. The direction of change desired—to increase, to decrease, to maintain.
2. Deficit or excess—the general area that is identified as needing special attention.
3. Present level of performance—what the child now does in deficit or in excess, expressed in measurable terms whenever possible.
4. Expected level—where the child realistically could be or what he could gain, with proper resources.
5. Resources needed—to accomplish the needed level of performance. Resources could be specialists, materials, situations, or methods required to bring about the desired change.

Measurable terms can be derived in some cases from counting performances, such as attendance, suspensions, grades, homework returned, test scores, extracurricular activities, referrals to the principal, time-outs, etc. They can be derived from performance (or nonperformance) of a particular targeted activity. Or experienced teachers (natural experts for the normal range for the age group who know the student best) may rate the student on a 1–10 scale on some quality in comparison with a normal range for the age group (How does the student get along with his peers, or come prepared to school, or exhibit healthy hygiene?) (Raines, 2002). Or, data can be gathered by observation of the pupil's on- and off-task behavior as in chapter 24. The measurement should obviously fit the purpose and the meaning of the objective as much as possible.

In Devin's case, there are three major annual goals. The components are listed in brackets.

> **Annual Goal 1:** For Devin to increase [direction] positive social relations with peers in general education [deficit] from limited [from] to more informal [to] through interaction experiences in a group with the social worker and regular social work contacts with the parents and teacher [resources].
>
> **Annual Goal 2:** For Devin to increase [direction] his independence in dressing for gym [deficit] from never dressing for gym to dressing at least two days per week.
>
> **Annual Goal 3:** For Devin to maintain [direction] his current academic adjustment.

Note that the direction set in the third goal is maintenance of current functioning. Maintenance equates present and expected levels of functioning.

Short-Term Objectives (Benchmarks)

Pupils who cannot participate in the district-wide general education assessment would need to follow alternate assessments and would need short-term objectives as well as annual goals. For purposes of illustration let us assume that Devin will not participate in the district-wide assessment. Short-term objectives can be thought of as measurable intermediate steps toward achievement of each annual goal. These steps are benchmarks or major milestones through which progress toward the annual goals can be assessed (see Lignugaris-Kraft, Marchand-Martella, & Martella, 2001). They should specify the conditions under which the behavior is to be exhibited by the student in his class—in unstructured group tasks, the lunchroom, gymnasium, and so on. For the social worker, these can be indicators or changes in behavior and do not have to reflect every single objective that might be defined for that goal. For Devin, our hypothetical case example, some short-term objectives, with which the social worker would be involved, might be:

1. Devin's level of class participation and quality of assignment completion in his regular education classes will be maintained at his current level through January 15.
2. Devin will interact compatibly with general education peers in an unstructured group task by March 15.
3. Devin will interact comfortably and spontaneously with general education peers in an unstructured lunchroom situation by May 15.
4. Devin will form casual friendships with peers in general and special education by June 15.
5. Devin's distractibility and talking out in class will reduce by 50 percent by June 15.
6. Devin will be able to dress for gym without special arrangement by January 15.

For our second illustration, let us assume that Devin *can* participate in the regular assessment and requires annual goals and periodic progress reports, based on goal attainment scaling. In Devin's case periodic progress reports, based on a series of objectives, could be established on a quarterly basis, since this is the typical frequency of report cards being sent to students in general education classes. Table 26.3 outlines reasonable objectives using a goal attainment scaling model.

Monitoring these goals will be a joint responsibility of the classroom teacher and the school social worker. Devin will share in the monitoring by carrying a card with him so the goals can be marked each period and reviewed with his teacher and the social worker to reinforce his progress.

The social worker often assists the team by developing the appropriate goals and objectives in their own area of the student's social functioning. These are worked out individually for every student. For general reference, David Sanders' sampler of developmental learning objectives has been included in this chapter (see table 26.2). School social workers have developed lists of areas of learning using various developmental and social skill formulas (see Micek et al., 1982; Huxtable, 2004; Sanders, 2002).

Resources

The list of services and persons responsible is essentially a resource statement. There may be external barriers to Devin's accomplishing these goals and objectives.[1] For example, teachers and parents may need help to avoid overprotecting Devin or some modifications in the gym program may be necessary. A list of the specific educational services required must be written into the IEP so that the goals and objectives can be implemented. Parents have a right to request that educational services that are included in the IEP but are not available in the school be purchased by the school district for the child or otherwise be provided at no cost to the parents.[2] Examples of such services might include:

1. The social worker will see Devin once a week for a 45-minute period with a group of other children with disabilities who are also dealing with the stress and social skills demands of a general education class. The appropriateness of whether Devin should continue in the group will be reevaluated on or about January 15.
2. The social worker will monitor Devin's group progress and act as liaison between the IEP team and the family service agency working with Devin's family and will inform Devin's parents of progress.
3. The teacher will monitor Devin's achievement of these objectives, reinforcing independent and peer-affiliative behavior.

INVOLVING CHILDREN IN THE IEP

It is a good practice to involve the schoolchild in IEP plans. Sometimes the plan's goals may seem abstract to the child, and so a mechanism, such as the car-in-the-garage technique developed by Fairbanks (1985), is useful. This technique involves the following steps:

---

1. See *Federal Register*, Education of Handicapped Children, Tuesday, August 23, 1977, 121a.552(d). "In selecting the least restrictive environment, consideration is given to any potentially harmful effect on the child or on the quality of services which he or she needs." While the concept of external barriers is not highlighted in the law, it is a traditional concept in dealing with persons with handicapping conditions. Lack of focus on such tangible or nontangible barriers would be in effect "blaming the victim" for a condition that he or she did not create.

2. A free appropriate public education is defined in the law as: special education and related services that a) have been provided at public expense, under public supervision and direction and without charge; b) meet the standards of the state educational agency; c) include an appropriate preschool, elementary, or secondary school education in the state involved; and d) are provided in conformity with the individualized education program (20 U.S.C. 1401[8]).

1. The school social worker draws a rough sketch of a garage on a piece of paper, connects it to a road, indicates that the garage is to be the child's destination, and asks the child to identify what should be placed in the garage as goals.
2. The child tells the school social worker what changes are desired, and the social worker or the child writes these goals inside the garage.
3. The child places one or more cars at various points along the road to the garage, symbolizing how far away from the goals and objectives he or she is. Sometimes the child leaves one or more cars off the road completely, indicating extreme lack of progress toward the goals represented by those cars.
4. The social worker asks the child for additional information about the cars and records the responses. The child's stated goals and objectives then become part of the IEP that is formally drafted at the planning team meeting.
5. The child draws new cars on the road as treatment progresses, relocating the cars on the road either closer or farther away from the garage.
6. The child places one or more cars inside the garage when particular objectives are attained and either establishes a new set of objectives or terminates treatment.

Figure 26.1 illustrates use of the technique in clarifying initial objectives for Mike, age 12, and Jerry, age 8, in a public school day treatment program. Following the clarification of objectives, the technique can be used to measure progress and change objectives. In some cases, it can be used with a group because the technique becomes a visual and verbal metaphor for their accomplishments.

Where do parents fit into this picture? Chapter 29 outlines how social workers relate their family focus to the goals of education (Welsh, 1985). Following the example of Devin, the problem in school was related to a long-established pattern of inconsistent expectations at home that caused Devin's self-care and participation in the family to be far below his capabilities. The social worker worked with the child and the parents and indirectly with siblings to develop an agreement on specific aspects of participation and contribution in family, through chores, helping with younger siblings, learning more responsibility in maintaining his room, choosing his clothes, and dressing himself. In the process of planning with the parents and with Devin, it became clear that parental differences over how to respond to Devin were reinforcing immaturity, and that these differences were not easily dispelled. The social worker identified some of these issues in the context of a focus on Devin. The parents could continue to work on these in the context of Devin, or begin marital counseling at a family agency in the community. The result was that the parents went into marital counseling in their efforts to deal with the problem.

FIGURE 26.1 Using the Car-in-the-Garage Technique to Clarify Objectives

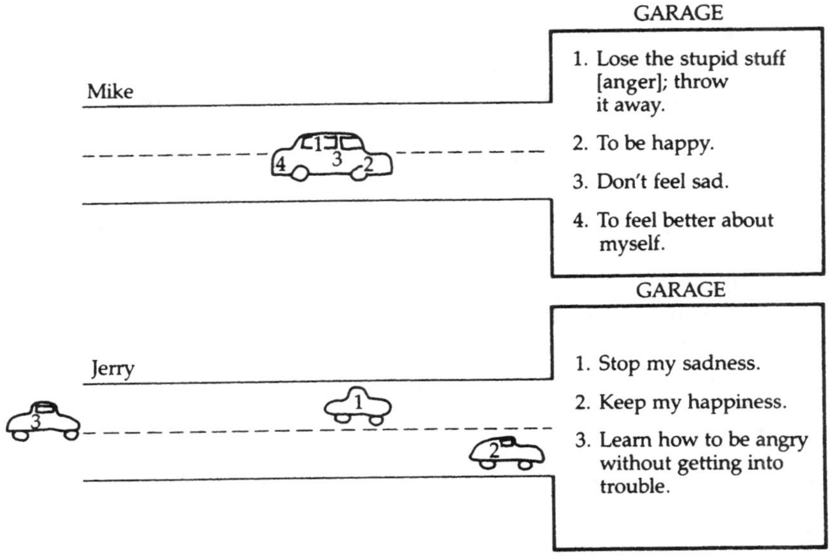

From Involving children in the IEP: The car-in-the-garage technique, by N. McDowell Fairbanks, 1987, *Social Work in Education, 9*(3).

THE INDIVIDUALIZED FAMILY SERVICE PLAN (IFSP)

The individualized family services plan (IFSP) grows out of early intervention programs for infants and toddlers and the obvious necessity of family involvement with children from birth through two years of age, especially children with multiple disabilities. Many of the principles underlying the IEP are also applicable to the IFSP and need not be repeated. There are several differences, because the IFSP is more comprehensive than the IEP and takes in a wider universe. The focus of the IFSP is first of all on development, rather than a more static focus, appropriate to the older child. This is evaluated through a variety of means and instruments. In addition, a statement of the family's strengths and needs relating to enhancing the child's development is needed. A statement of the family's strengths and needs requires a family assessment and is best carried out by the school social worker. An agreement on goals, objectives, and tasks needs to emerge from this mutual assessment between social worker and family. In addition, the coping and adaptation of parents, siblings, and support systems in an extended family and friendship network need to be assessed.

The IFSP must contain:

1. A statement of the child's present levels of development (cognitive, speech/language, psychosocial, motor, and self-help);
2. A statement of the family's strengths and needs relating to enhancing the child's development;
3. The measurable outcome criteria, procedures, and timelines for determining progress;
4. The specific early intervention services necessary to meet the unique needs of the child and family, including the method, frequency, and intensity of service;
5. The projected dates for the initiation of service and the expected duration;
6. The name of the case manager;
7. Procedures for transition from early intervention into the preschool program.

The IFSP must be evaluated at least once a year and must be reviewed every six months or more, where appropriate.

The family is of crucial importance at the earliest stages of dealing with the possibility that a child has a disability. There is often a heavy involvement with the health-care system, and this is confusing at a time when parents are just beginning to bond with a child—Whose child is this, ours or the health-care system's (or the school's)? The health-care system and the school actually have similar concerns with families. If either system seeks to displace the family, the result can be chaotic. When there are multiple specialists, parents often have a great deal of case management to do at a time when they are most uncertain of their role. They are often mourning the loss of the perfect child they had dreamed of, and thus the loss of their fondest hopes and expectations (Lachney, 1982). The heavy caretaking demands can split even well-established marital relations into extremes: overadequate and enmeshed roles or underadequate and disengaged roles. These roles may follow conventional gender expectations. The resulting marital and family patterns are disruptive of other aspects of family living and may account for the higher rates of divorce, suicide, and child abuse among families of children with disabilities (Gallagher, Beckman, & Cross, 1983). Working with the parents, while they are actively mourning their losses and when care patterns have not been completely solidified, may prevent the most crippling effects of these disrupting patterns on the family and especially on the child with a disability. A certain amount of inactivity associated with being overwhelmed and with mourning, and the potential distortion of relationships inherent in heavy caregiving demands, often can be expected in these situations, and thus the risks should be assessed. The teaching role of parents can be distorted by the loss of hope implicit in a mourning process, and by the same relational distortions involved in the discussion of caregiving roles. Parents may be reluctant to accept help and may isolate themselves from other potential support systems in the process. Success in this process presupposes a good contact between the social worker and parents when the pressures and risks are discussed in a normalizing context.

Expected Outcomes

The IFSP, a statement of expected outcomes and an agreement on a type of partnership, can be used as the basis for the social worker's intervention with the child and the family. Based on the assessment and the particular contacts developed with the family, major expected outcomes now can be stated in a way that reinforces the primary roles of parents as educators as well as caregivers and the appropriate assistance of the school in carrying out its related mission. A key outcome will be the family's participation in the teaching and caregiving roles and ability to use the case management process. The expected outcomes are largely based on (1) the assessments previously made of the child's present levels of development and (2) the new coping and adaptation patterns becoming established in the family. Although educational and medical specialists have an important role in setting achievable developmental outcomes, social workers should also be involved in setting such family outcomes and showing their relation to the pupil's developmental outcomes.

Service Coordination

The IFSP must contain the name of the service coordinator from the profession most immediately relevant to the infant's, toddler's, or family's needs who will be responsible for the implementation of the plan in coordination with other agencies or persons. She coordinates services to the family of an infant or toddler with a disability to assist in gaining access to early intervention services identified in the IFSP. Service coordination includes:

1. Coordinating assessments and participating in the development of the IFSP;
2. Assisting families in identifying available service providers;
3. Coordinating and monitoring the delivery of services, including coordinating the provision of early intervention services with other services that the child or family may need or is receiving, but that are not required under this part;
4. Facilitating the development of a transition plan to preschool services where appropriate. (*Federal Register* 52(222): 303.6)

The coordinator then assists parents in gaining access to these services. However, parents themselves should take responsibility as much as possible for the coordination roles (Garland, Woodruff, & Buck, 1988) or at least have a major role in the selection of a service coordinator. The social worker's role places him or her closest to the parents in carrying out service coordination responsibilities.

The final part of the IFSP is that of the child's transition from an early intervention program to the preschool program. Although this is frequently the domain of the educational specialists, the process and the timing of the entry of the child from a family context into a new program with new demands may be an area in which the school social worker needs to participate.

The family involvement projected in the IFSP need not be confined to infants and toddlers. When children present complex vulnerabilities and long-established patterns that inevitably affect the educational process, it is simply good practice to involve the parents in the work of the school. The IEP and the IFSP can be no better than the process of thinking, communicating, and decision making they represent. They certainly are accountability documents, but they also are vehicles for collaboration with parents and for coordination of resources and development of the working agreements necessary for complex goals to be achieved. The IFSP and the IEP are challenges for social workers in developing clarity about what they will be offering students, parents, and the school, while providing an opportunity to work systematically with all of the influences on the full educational process. It is an opportunity that we cannot afford to let pass.

References

Clark, J. (2001). *Functional behavior assessment and behavior intervention plans: Implementing the student discipline provisions of IDEA '97*. NASW school social work hot topics. Washington, DC: NASW Home Page: Retrieved from http://www.naswdc.org/sections/ssw/hottopics/schalark.htm

Dietz, C. A. (2000). Reshaping clinical practice for the new millennium. *Journal of Social Work Education, 36*, 503–520.

Fairbanks, N. M. (1985). Involving children in the IEP: The car-in-the-garage technique. *Social Work in Education, 7*(3), 171–182.

Gallagher, J. J., Beckman, P., & Cross, A. H. (1983). Families of handicapped children: Sources of stress and its alleviation. *Exceptional Children, 50*(1), 10–18.

Garland, C., Woodruff, G., & Buck, D. (1988). *Case management. Division for early childhood white paper.* Reston, VA: Council for Exceptional Children.

Huxtable, M. (2004). *Defining measurable behavioral goals and objectives. SSWAA Bell*. January, Northlake, IL: SSWAA. (see also SSWAA@aol.com or www.sswaa.org). For a 26-page list of behavioral goals and objectives in a PDF format from the Tucson Unified School District's Web site, see http://edweb.tusd.k12az.us/exced/forms03/Forms_pdf/behavioralgoals_Obj_021027.pdf

Individuals with Disabilities Education Act, PL 105-17. U.S.C. 11401 et seq.

Individuals with Disabilities Education Improvement Act. (IDEA 2004). Public Law 108-446.

Kam-shing, Y. (2003). A strengths perspective in working with an adolescent with dual diagnosis. *Clinical Social Work Journal, 31*, 189–204.

Lachney, M. E. (1982). Understanding families of the handicapped: A critical factor in the parent-school relationship. In R. T. Constable & J. P. Flynn (Eds.), *School social work: Practice and research perspectives*) (pp. 234–241). Homewood, IL: Dorsey Press.

Lignugaris-Kraft, B., Marchand-Martella, N., & Martella, R. C. (2001). Strategies for writing better goals and short-term objectives or benchmarks. *Teaching Exceptional Children, 34*(1), 52–8.

Micek, D., Barnes, J., Newman, C., Roelofs, M., Rosenbaum, M., & Sices, M. (1982). School social work objectives. In R. Constable & J. Flynn (Eds.), *School social work: Practice and research perspectives* (pp. 251–255). Homewood, IL: Dorsey Press.

Raines, J. C. (2002). Present levels of performance, goals and objectives: A best practice guide. *School Social Work Journal, 27*(1), 58–72.

Roach, A. T., & Elliott, S. N. (2005). Goal attainment scaling: An efficient and effective approach to monitoring student progress. *Teaching exceptional children, 37*(4), 8–16.

Sanders, D. (2002). Annual goals and short-term objectives for school social workers. In R. Constable, S. McDonald, & J. Flynn (Eds.), *School social work: Practice, policy, and research perspectives* (pp. 279–288). Chicago: Lyceum.

Test, D. W., Mason, C., Hughes, C., Konrad, M., Neale, M., & Wood, W. (2004). Student involvement in individualized education program meetings. *Exceptional Children, 70*(4), 391–412.

U.S. Department of Education. (1981). *The case study evaluation*. Washington, DC: Author.

Van Acker, R., Boreson, L., Gable, R. A., & Potterton, T. (2005). Are we on the right course? Lessons learned about current FBA/BIP practices in schools. *Journal of Behavioral Education, 14*(1), 35–56.

Welsh, B. L. (1985, March). *The individualized family plan (IFP): A social work component to the IEP*. Paper presented at the NASW School Social Work Conference, Philadelphia, PA.

Zuna, N., & McDougall, D. (2004). Using positive behavioral support to manage avoidance of academic tasks. *Teaching Exceptional Children, 37*(1), 18–24.

27

Response to Intervention (RTI) and the School Social Worker

Carol Rippey Massat
Jane Addams College of Social Work
University of Illinois at Chicago

Robert Constable
Loyola University Chicago

Galen Thomas
Southern Illinois University

- Public Policy and RTI
- The Process of RTI
- The Evidence Base for RTI

Response to Intervention (RTI) is a classroom- and team-based approach in general education for identification, assessment, planning, and intervention with students who are at risk for academic failure. This chapter addresses the policies that relate to RTI, the process of implementing RTI, the evidence base for RTI, and the school social worker's involvement in this process. Written into the Individuals with Disabilities Education Act (IDEA) 2004, and supported by public policy, RTI refines and individualizes classroom intervention for students in a manner similar to positive behavior intervention and support (PBIS). Students at risk for failure may have severe learning disorders, but also may have problems in specific areas such as social behavior, taking initiative, or math anxiety. They may have motivational problems.

They may be distractible, and certain classroom dynamics may contribute to their distractibility. Teaching methods, effective with other students, may not be as effective with them. (Indeed the general teaching approach may be ineffective or inadequate.) A class's energy may be absorbed by internal conflicts, conflicts with the teacher, or conflicts within the school or outside. Working within an RTI framework, school social workers, as team members, provide consultation to teachers and work in focused ways with parents and other resource persons and systems.

The central focus of RTI is on the student's performance in the general education curriculum, and thus on the teaching relationship. The focus is extended whenever needed to other interveners, other resource persons, and to the parents. Assessments are performance-based, and evidence-based interventions depend on the assessment. More individualized interventions depend on the student's response to a less targeted, group-oriented intervention.

RTI models organize educational approaches to students at risk of failure. There are three levels of intervention, *Tier 1, Tier2,* and *Tier 3.* At each step of this progressive intervention process there is a role for the school social worker and the parents. These models typically contain: 1) a continuum of evidence-based services available to all students, from universal interventions and procedures to very intensive and individualized interventions; 2) decision points to determine whether students are performing significantly below the level of their peers in academic and social behavior domains; 3) ongoing monitoring of student progress; 4) employment of more intensive or different interventions when students do not improve in response to current interventions; and 5) systematic decision points to screen students for an evaluation for special education services if warranted (Fairbanks, Sugai, Guardino, & Lathrop, 2007; Fuchs, Mock, Morgan, & Young, 2003; Zirkel & Krohn, 2008). Assessment is rooted in performance. Targeted intervention for pupils at risk of academic failure comes earlier and mainly takes place in general education. Special resources become progressively available when the student is unresponsive to more general interventions.

Some approaches to RTI emphasize it as a screening tool for special education (Torgeson et al., 2001 as cited in McMaster, Kung, Han, & Cao, 2008). Other approaches are rooted in general education, so that high-quality general classroom instruction would be provided to at-risk students *before* any decision is made to implement more intensive intervention (Fuchs, 2003; McMaster, Kung, Han, & Cao, 2008). School social workers will encounter both emphases, and from an emergent perspective, they are not mutually exclusive. While the context for intervention for most students is be general education, the process should also result in the provision of specialized services for those who need it. At the same time, education in the least restrictive environment could become more effective for the many students who can benefit from a strengthened and more individualized general-education process. But the strengthening and individualizing of general education is a long-term project.

Thus RTI could become a catalyst for changes already taking place in education and in school social work. Teaching is becoming more individualized, and more open to using different outside resources. It is not simply geared to a middle range of students within a class. Many effective and focused intervention methods for at-risk individuals simultaneously broaden the educational process to the larger classroom. Also many educators are rediscovering powerful and effective partnerships with parents. For social workers this demands a heightened collaborative process, now with a focus on the classroom and the learning process. In many ways the role is not different from the essential school social work role and focus developed in this book.

PUBLIC POLICY AND RTI

The specific learning disability (SLD) category has long grown beyond its predicted incidence in a school population. Traditionally SLD has been established by demonstrating through testing a severe IQ-achievement discrepancy for a specific child (the severe discrepancy [SD] approach). Services were then relegated to special education, requiring some removal from the general education classroom. A problem with this approach to assessment is that there are a number of students in the SLD category who test as "false positives." They may have been given a disability label, but, rather than having an inherent disability, they are low achievers, perhaps because of poor instruction (Fuchs & Fuchs, 2005) or other reasons. An alternative to this approach to assessment and intervention would be RTI. RTI comprises an identification and intervention process "based on the child's response to scientific, research-based intervention." (34 CFR 300.309(a)(2)). IDEA 2004 permits educators to use an RTI identification process for SLD as a substitute for, or supplement to, the traditional SD approach: Schools will "not be required to take into consideration whether a child has a severe discrepancy between achievement and intellectual ability." (Section 1414(b)). Instead it permits children to be systematically observed in their learning environments, considering the child's response to ordinarily effective teaching interventions, as part of a possible determination process for an SLD (34 CFR 300.307, 300.309, 300. 310 & 300.311).

The 2006 IDEA regulations spelled out three possibilities for states to do this: 1) A state can require its school districts either to prohibit or to permit the severe discrepancy (SD) approach to determining specific learning disabilities, 2) states must permit use of RTI to determine whether or not a child has a specific learning disability, or 3) states may permit other research-based alternatives. According to Zirkel and Krohn's (2008) review, in 2007 six states had proposed or finalized plans to mandate RTI procedures and prohibit SD: Colorado, Delaware, Florida, Georgia, Indiana, and West Virginia. Four states had proposed or adopted transitional policies. Iowa adopted a transitional policy of permitting RTI and other research-based approaches but prohibiting SD. Illinois and Maine adopted transitional plans to permit RTI and to permit SD until the year 2010. Louisiana proposed a policy of permitting all three options, with the intention of implementing RTI. Twenty-one states had proposed or adopted permissive policies that would allow both RTI and SD.[1] Fourteen states had proposed or adopted policies to permit SD and other research-based alternatives.[2] Two states, Mississippi and Utah, adopted permissive policies that permitted SD or a combination of SD and RTI. These can be found in each state department of education's rules and regulations for special education. In addition, different local educational agencies (LEA's) are adopting within state guidelines different approaches to RTI, some focusing more on general education, some gravitating more toward changing the screening process for special education.

THE PROCESS OF RTI

The first step in the RTI process is an initial screening to find students at risk of academic failure. Screening should take place the first month of the school year. Students below the 25th percentile in reading or math on recent achievement tests would be considered to be at academic risk (Fuchs & Fuchs, 2005).

Tier 1 (universal) interventions would apply to everyone in a class. Curricula and teaching methods should be effective—that is, evidence based. Classroom outcomes should be closely and continuously monitored. Experienced teachers and new recruits would need strong professional development. Effective teaching methods would include classroom management skills, such as consistently implementing an acknowledgment system to recognize appropriate behavior in class, minimizing transition time between activities and/or providing multiple and varied opportunities for students to respond during instruction. Regular monitoring of the learning of all students is critical to providing high-quality instruction to all students at each tier. Fuchs and Fuchs (2005) recommend weekly monitoring of at-risk students in general education classes for eight weeks, using either local or national estimates of weekly improvement or the use of specific criteria for

1. These states are Arizona, Idaho, Maine, Maryland, Missouri, Montana, New Mexico, North Carolina, North Dakota, Nebraska, Nevada, Oklahoma, Oregon, Pennsylvania, Rhode Island, South Dakota, Texas, Vermont, Wisconsin, Washington, and Wyoming.

2. These states are: Alabama, Arkansas, California, Connecticut, Hawaii, Kansas, Kentucky, Massachusetts, Michigan, New York, Ohio, South Carolina, Tennessee, and Virginia.

expected weekly improvement. A most important contribution of the school social worker is to provide such things as consultation to the teacher on conditions within the classroom and its group dynamics; support teacher strengths, cultural awareness, and responsiveness to the ongoing classroom situation; and help with limit setting. Case examples of school social work consultation can be found in this chapter and throughout the book.

Pro-social Behaviors

Students can't learn without a safe and orderly learning environment. Teachers generally take a great deal (sometimes even a majority) of instructional time simply attempting to establish this safety and order. When such problems become endemic to particular schools or classes, safety and order need restoration. School social workers are involved with these efforts in anti-bullying work, social skills groups, peer mediation and other strategies described elsewhere in this book. As part of this larger process, a school social worker might also do units of instruction with classes on feelings, self-awareness, social responsiveness to others, acceptance of differences within the class, anti-bullying curricula or character education:

> An elementary school has a school-wide program to encourage pro-social behaviors. The school social worker has been an active participant in developing various activities, such as an honor day program for students who have achieved goals in such areas as academics, athletics, and attendance. There are quarterly "good behavior" activities for students who have not had detentions, etc. The school social worker also is responsible for leading character education presentations in each classroom on a monthly basis. She provides materials, ideas, and consultation for the teachers to use as applications of the concept throughout the day, and provides the means to reinforce students who demonstrate that they are practicing the pro-social behaviors. For example, in some situations tickets are given to students who are "caught being good." The students can turn in the tickets for the monthly drawing of various rewards donated by local merchants. Data collected can demonstrate that the number of referrals to the office for disciplinary issues has declined since the combination of reinforcements was started. The majority of students seem to have responded well to the program.

Some *Tier 1* interventions bridge to *Tier 2* as well. While they involve everyone, they involve different groups in slightly different ways. There can be advantages for everyone when *Tier 2* interventions are encapsulated and normalized in whole-class and whole-school programs.

> A school developed a general parent-involvement program to strengthen academics and use of homework, etc. The school social worker worked on the planning team, in outreach, and at parents' night. There was a special focus on strengthening the 25 percent highest risk students, so that plans between teacher, pupil and parents could be developed at an early point without appearing to have singled out these students.

A school developed an after-school tutoring program for everyone, but with special focus on at-risk students. The social worker worked with parents, pupils, and teachers around access and use of this program.

Peer-Assisted learning-strategies (PALS) programs involved students helping each other with math (Kroeger & Kouche, 2006) or learning English for non-native students (McMaster, Kung, Han, & Cao, 2008). Learning to help another student offers as much for the peer assistant as for the student assisted. The social worker helped the teacher develop this general strategy and helped with problem solving when difficulties were inevitably encountered.

Tier 2 (targeted) interventions would supplement instruction for students who do not respond as expected to universal interventions. Some of these have been illustrated above in a mix of *Tier 1* and *Tier 2*. Another possibility is that different instruction be developed for subsets of the class with different needs. A best-practice recommendation is that a certified teacher conduct this instruction, three times a week, with a 30-minute duration, with no more than three students involved in a small-group instructional format for approximately eight weeks (Fuchs & Fuchs, 2005). Student progress would be assessed weekly, using brief assessment instruments with strong evidence of reliability and validity. Or the teacher might develop a "check-in and check-out" system to provide additional structure, prompts, instruction, feedback, and acknowledgment for students who are having difficulty with certain classroom tasks (Fairbanks, Sugai, Guardino, & Lathrop, 2007) or develop Peer Assisted Learning Strategies (PALS) (Kroeger & Kouche, 2006) for particular groups of students. Teachers may need help to accommodate these individualized educational subgroups within the total class learning process. School social workers might develop in-class or out-of-class groups with different foci, perhaps on social skills, experienced losses, shyness, gender themes, etc. Teachers might get consultation on dealing with subgroups in the class, etc. Many of the reasons for school failure go far beyond education.

Teachers identified a need for more effective ways to address students who had conflicts with peers on the playground. The school social worker secured some funding to purchase a set of videos dealing with conflict situations and pro-social ways to deal with frustrating situations. Students, required to miss recess because of peer conflicts, watched the videos in the school social worker's office and discussed more appropriate ways of dealing with similar situations. Particular concerns about ganging up and bullying emerged here. Students role-played better ways of dealing with such conflicts. They were let back into recess with access to the social worker, when needed. There was improvement. Near the end of each semester parents of the students were invited to an evening program to praise the students on how well they had learned to deal with conflicts. The parents received the program very well. One parent commented that it was the only time she had attended a school to have her children praised.

Tier 3 (individualized) interventions apply to individuals who do not respond to targeted group interventions. These students may need more than tier 2 interventions. There are specific and time-intensive assessments to determine individual gaps in skills (Fairbanks, Sugai, Guardino, & Lathrop, 2007). Students may receive a comprehensive, individualized evaluation that would include all of the elements included in IDEA, including parental consent. Mental retardation, emotional disturbance, and other possible causes of the failure to respond to tier 1 and 2 would be included as part of this more comprehensive evaluation. There may be further linkage to special education resources. Consultation is also important in these team-based interventions. A great deal of social work consultation consists of helping a teacher to find an effective way in his/her repertoire of teaching experience and skill to work with the complex needs of a pupil, and to connect parents and the pupil with the process as well as to connect the process with their needs. The class and the school experience, however, remains a major focus. The total process can be seen in the cases of Angela and Ronnie.

> Angela, a fourth grader, had average cognitive abilities, but significant attention/anxiety problems, poor attendance, and poor peer relationships. Marcia, her parent, had bipolar disorder, a history of substance abuse, and lacked energy or interest to participate in any classroom-based, management/reinforcement system. Previous attempts at counseling, disciplinary referrals, and contacts with Marcia had met with limited or no changes in the pupil's behaviors. The teacher requested the social worker conduct a functional behavior assessment of Angela in the classroom situation to provide some ideas. The social worker noticed that whenever Angela perceived work to be too difficult or success was not assured, she mostly avoided the work. Otherwise, she might blurt out to get immediate help, or create conflict with the teacher or classmates, so that she would not have to do the work. Consulting with Marcia, they worked out a number of interventions. Angela would be seated closer to the teacher so more immediate help was available, while also providing some separation from her classmates. The social worker completed a "preferred reinforcement" questionnaire with her to identify what rewards might work with her. They implemented a "Check and Connect (Sinclair & Kaibel, 2002)" plan for her to report to an adult in school each morning, and at the end to report how the day had gone. They worked with Marcia to reinforce these maturational goals at home, to help increase regular attendance, and to find support for her coping with family needs using a community wrap-around approach.
>
> A new teacher in an early-childhood pre-kindergarten class sought consultation regarding 4-year-old Ronnie. Ronnie is the only child of a busy, but fairly well-functioning professional couple. He had poorly developed social skills to the extent that special education referral was considered for when he would enter kindergarten. He was noncompliant with classroom routines and would push other children whenever an adult was not in the immediate vicinity. The functional behavior assessment pointed out that he did not seem to understand that pushing was not an appropriate way to interact with his classmates.

> Nor could he directly verbally communicate either with children or adults. At Ronnie's age there could be a variety of possible explanations, whether it was a form of autism, a pragmatic language disorder, or simply a child with few social expectations at home and some level of ADHD. Time and systematically trying different things would tell. The preschool teacher gathered baseline data on the frequency of the pushing behavior by carrying at least a dozen items in one pocket, transferring one to the other pocket each time she observed pushing. After two days (owing to the potential harm to other children) the team stopped the testing and met and consulted with the parents. As a result of this meeting, the teacher was directed that when Ronnie pushed another child, she was to put him in her lap and wrap her arms around him, while explaining that pushing was not the way to play with others. This enforced timeout was to continue for three or four minutes. Then he was to be released with the stated belief that he had made a mistake and now could learn to play with other children appropriately. The parents agreed to spend more time with Ronnie, working on specific maturational and social skills learning objectives. They would jointly assess how this was working in a month. The pushing behavior rapidly decreased over the course of two weeks. Ronnie did not, however, develop verbal interactions or more appropriate interactions with adults or peers. With time, the progressive use of RTI, and further testing prior to kindergarten, it is expected that Ronnie's needs will be more clearly understood.

Ronnie's case points out the use of both RTI and testing to gradually clarify the situation and possibly move to yet another level, where the child might be involved with special education as the appropriate level of intervention. It also illustrates this collaboration in RTI assessment and intervention extending to the parents. At the same time, unless Ronnie is eventually moved into a totally self-contained setting, he would remain involved with school-wide and whole-class, (*Tier 1, 2,* and *3*) intervention programs. Thus, tiers should not be considered categories, but maps of a graduated intervention system rooted in general education, a mix, which would operate toward Ronnie's ultimate advantage as he is helped to find his best level of coping with schooling.

THE EVIDENCE BASE FOR RTI

While RTI is new and experimental and there are many versions, its intervention methods are not particularly new. It draws upon many effective interventions from other areas, now with a focus on educational processes. While the social-behavior domain in school needs more study and research development (Fairbanks, Sugai, Guardino & Lathrop, 2007), there is a substantial body of research on positive behavioral interventions, functional behavior assessment, and early intervention. Wraparound planning and behavior support is well established (see chapter 30). Social skills approaches and classroom management are likewise well established. There have been a number of studies of RTI approaches in schools (Glover & DiPerna, 2007; Marston,

Meuystens, Lau, & Canter, 2003; Reschly & Starkweather, 1997; Tilly, 2003). These generally support the different levels of response implicit in the tier approach. In addition, there is an extensive body of research on curriculum-based measurement (Deno, 1985) and universal academic and behavioral screening (Glover and DiPerna, 2007). Such research has focused on the measurement of student skills via brief direct methods, or via behavior ratings or observations, to (a) discriminate among categories of students (e.g.,; Marston & Magnusson, 1988), (b) assess risk status and predict future student behavior or performance (Albers, Glover, & Kratochwill, 2007; Glover & Albers, 2007), and/or (c) evaluate intervention effectiveness (Deno, 1985; Glover & DiPerna, 2007). There is also a growing body of evidence-based research on teaching effectiveness (Glover & DiPerna, 2007), but all of this will develop further on an established framework.

School social workers are particularly important in joint assessment and intervention with emotional and behaviorial disorders related to low academic achievement and in the connections of RTI intervention with the parents. While RTI approaches specifically address academic concerns of potentially failing students, they eventually have to include social and emotional concerns as well. Approaches such as positive behavioral intervention and supports (PBIS) also involve a tiered approach, evidence-based interventions, and measurement of student progress. They all demand teamwork and consultation.

RTI is based on pragmatic, evidence-based ways of responding to students with learning disabilities, testing their responses to teaching rather than attempting to categorize them on the basis of a severe discrepancy between intellectual ability and achievement (Fuchs & Fuchs, 2005). As such, it becomes an alternative to a deficit approach. Although its language is new, it is quite compatible with traditional social work thinking and methodology. School social workers, traditionally connected to the process of education, need to learn more about RTI to develop better and more effective collaboration with the aims of education, the lives of pupils, and their families.

References

Albers, A., Glover, T. A., & Kratochwill, T. R. (2007). Where are we and where do we go now? Universal screening for enhanced educational and mental health outcomes. *Journal of School Psychology, 45*(2), 257–263.

Deno, S. L. (1985). Curriculum based measurement: The emerging alternative. *Exceptional Children, 52*, 219–232.

Fairbanks, S., Sugai, G., Guardino, D., & Lathrop, M. (2007). Response to intervention: Examining classroom behavior support in second grade. *Exceptional Children, 73*(3), 288–310.

Fuchs, L. S. (2003). Assessing intervention responsiveness: Conceptual and technical issues. *Learning disabilities research and practice, 18*, 172–186.

Fuchs, D., & Fuchs, L. D. (2005). Responsiveness to intervention: A blueprint for practitioners, policymakers, and parents. *Teaching Exceptional Children, 38*(1), 57–61.

Fuchs, D., Mock, D., Morgan, P. L., & Young, C. L. (2003). Responsiveness-to-intervention: Definitions, evidence and implications for the learning disabilities construct. *Learning Disabilities Research and Practice, 18*, 157–71.

Glover, T. A., & Albers. C. A. (2007). Considerations for evaluating universal screening assessments. *Journal of School Psychology, 45*(2), 117–135.

Glover, T. A., & DiPerna, J. C. (2007). Service delivery for response to intervention: Core components and directions for future research. *School Psychology Review, 36*(4), 526–540.

Individuals with Disabilities Education Improvement Act of 2004. (IDEA 2004). Public Law 108-446. 20 U.S. C. 1401 et seq.

Kroeger, S. D., & Kouche B. (2006) Using peer-assisted learning strategies to increase response to intervention in inclusive middle math settings. *Teaching Exceptional Children, 38*(5), 6–13.

Martson, D., & Magnisson D. (1988). Curriculum based measurement: District level implementation. In J. Garcia, J. Zims & M Curtis (Eds.). *Alternative educational delivery systems: Enhancing instructional options for all students* (pp. 137–172). Washington, DC: National Association of School Psychologist.

Marston, D., Meuystens, P., Lau, M., & Canter, A. (2003) Problem solving model for decision-making with high incidence disabilities: The Minneapolis experience. *Learning Disabilities Research & Practice, 18*(3), 187–200.

McMaster, K. L., Kung, S., Han, I., & Cao. M. (2008) Peer-assisted learning strategies: A "Tier 1" approach to promoting English learner's response to intervention. *Exceptional Children, 74*(2), 194–214.

Reschly, D. J., & Starkweather, A. R. (1997). Evaluation of an alternative special education assessment and classification program in the Minneapolis Public Schools. Minneapolis: Minneapolis Public Schools.

Sinclair, M., & Kaibel, C. (2002). *Dakota county check and connect program evaluation*. Final summary report. Minneapolis: University of Minnesota Institute on Community Integration.

Tilly, D. (2003, December). *How many tiers are needed for successful prevention and early intervention? Heartland Area Agency's evolution from four to three tiers.* Paper presented at the National Research Center on Learning Disabilities Responsiveness-to-Intervention Symposium, Kansas, City, MO.

Torgeson, J. K., Alexander, A. W., Wagner, R. K., Rashotte, C. A., Voeller, K. K. S., & Conway, T. (2001). Intensive remedial instruction for children with severe reading disabilities: Immediate and long term outcomes from two instructional approaches. *Journal of Learning Disabilities, 34*, 33–58, 78.

Zirkel, P. A., & Krohn, N. (2008). RTI after IDEA: A survey of state laws. *Teaching Exceptional Children, 40*(3), 71–73.

Section Four

Practice Approaches in Schools

28

Developing and Defining the School Social Worker's Role

Robert Constable
Loyola University, Chicago

Helen Wolkow
(retired) School District 159
Matteson, Illinois

- Role Development
- Clinical Social Work in a School
- Units of Attention and School Social Work Role(s)
- Evidence-Based Practice

ROLE DEVELOPMENT

The role of a school social worker develops according to an assessment of the situation and the decisions reached within the team, with parents, and with students. The foundation skills of school social workers are focused on deciding (with others) what to do, who should do it, and with whom. These skills were discussed in Section III on assessment, multidisciplinary teaming, and consultation. The next set of skills concentrates on role development, that is, doing what has been decided. The school social worker helps pupils, parents, and the school to work with each other in ways that would best assist students in their tasks of learning and developing.

CLINICAL SOCIAL WORK IN A SCHOOL

The following is an example of a case quite common to the caseload of the school social worker. It involves a child with whom the social worker worked over a period of six years (second through eighth grade), his parents, his teachers, the school administration, and outside agencies.

Alan was referred for evaluation by his 2nd-grade classroom teacher about five weeks after the start of school. He was a transfer student from another school district and was experiencing great difficulty with reading and spelling. He also had difficulty following directions and concentrating on his work; he was easily distracted, and he had poor fine-motor coordination and poor visual perception. Alan often would try to copy from his neighbors or just sit and not attempt to do his work. At times he would sit and suck his fingers. Teachers described him as shy and withdrawn. The teacher presented the situation to the pupil personnel service team, and they agreed testing should be done. The parents were contacted and agreed to the evaluation. As part of this evaluation I completed a Social Developmental Study. This provided us with some insight into possible causes for his academic, developmental, and social difficulties.

Case Study Findings. Alan, a nice-looking, blond, blue-eyed white male, was age 7 at the time of our initial interview. When interviewed, he had a very quiet and shy manner, almost withdrawn. He spoke very softly, and at times it was difficult to understand what he said. A lot of his emotional energy seemed to be tied up with his parents' divorce process, which had started a year-and-a-half earlier. He felt school was rather difficult, especially reading, but math was okay. He believed his older brother had learned to read as a baby. Later I found out his older brother had been retained, had reading difficulties, and still seemed to be having some academic problems. He felt that his parents yelled a lot, both at him and his brother. He talked quite a bit about this, and many of his answers to my questions referred to this. He was able to say that he felt angry when he could not get his way.

Alan's Family History. Alan, at the time of the evaluation, lived with his mother, his 10-year-old brother, and his 3-year-old sister. His mother and father had separated at the end of Alan's kindergarten year. Initially, the mother stayed home with the children during the day but went to her parents' home for the night when the father returned from work. The mother was attending school at a local community college at the time. The father works as an accountant and recently had become a born-again Christian; the mother is Catholic and attends church on a weekly basis. The divorce became final the summer after Alan completed first grade. That summer, mother and children moved to the same mobile home park where her parents resided. This move placed them within our district boundaries. The park had many children in residence and was comprised mostly of working-class people. The family fit within the norms of that community. During this time, the father usually would take the children on weekends. He was most consistent in doing so, and both children and father seemed to enjoy the time very much. Both sets of grandparents were involved with Alan and supportive of the family situation. Alan often would visit a country cottage with the maternal grandparents, and he was quite fond of those times.

Alan's Educational Background and Evaluation. Alan attended preschool a few days a week at age four and then kindergarten and first grade in a standard educational placement. He came to his present district at the beginning of second grade, and he was evaluated shortly after entry. The assessment pointed out that his support systems were eroding and that his self-concept was rapidly deteriorating, along with his academic performance. To shore up Alan's self-esteem and to assist in rebuilding him to former levels of functioning, resources needed to be utilized within the educational system, within the family, and within the community. Coordination of resources would be essential, or there was the potential for some systems to impact negatively on the efforts of the others, even when each support system worked within its individual sphere toward the best interests of the child. Such a case normally requires an extended period of time, both because of the amount of work indicated and the nature of the goals of the service delivery plan. As a result of the evaluation, Alan was placed on a learning disabilities watch status, which meant that the learning disabilities specialist consulted with his classroom teacher weekly about possible interventions in the classroom for the perceived problems. In addition, Alan was placed with the reading specialist in a small group to see if this would strengthen his reading skills. The social worker was identified as the interim case manager because it was clear that case management was going to be crucial to Alan's case. As a case manager, I met jointly with the classroom teacher, learning disabilities specialist, and reading specialist to arrange mutual consultation. With regard to direct social work service, Alan needed help with divorce issues, self-esteem, socialization skills, and learning appropriate ways to express his needs. I explored with his parents the possibility of outside counseling. They did not agree to this, so I monitored him on a consultative basis until further direct work could be arranged.

Alan had been wrestling with events in his life with which his cognitive abilities were not yet capable of dealing. Emotionally, he had been challenged by events that went right to the core of his worst fears, both in terms of potential abandonment and of his sense of self-competence. Efforts to soothe himself or put events in perspective generally had met with failure. Thus, he was becoming increasingly overwhelmed and anxious, and as a result some regressive behavior was noted (finger sucking, passivity, and disengagement).

Services Offered Alan, Progress, and Results. Alan's second-grade teacher was highly structured and somewhat inflexible. She was not, initially, very encouraging with him, nor did she recognize his artistic and creative strengths and his good problem-solving skills. She found his slow pace of working, which was part of his perfectionistic need, difficult to relate to. This teacher was not particularly receptive to direct suggestions from me, so I had to develop some alternative strategies to implement through our already established consultation with the reading specialist. In these meetings, we discussed what my goals were in my work with Alan's situation. We discussed some parallel goals that might be implemented by the reading specialist, and the classroom teacher was able to discuss her approach. She was able to draw on an approach that she had used with a similar student a few years back. In fact, the earlier situation was close enough to be useful, and she felt she could use the same approach with Alan. By seeing the similarities between students, she was able to accept other suggestions. At the end of February of second grade,

Alan's classroom teacher went on maternity leave. Alan's new teacher was very warm, caring, and creative. She liked Alan and wanted suggestions on how to help him. The consultation meetings continued. He seemed to be having great difficulty, and we suspected that Alan needed more intensive support. We requested a new Individualized Educational Program conference to amend the findings of the original case conference. In order to arrange this meeting in a timely manner, the school administration had to be consulted about Alan's high-priority status. Given this information, the special education director in particular put in extra effort to reschedule the team and the parents so we could meet within the following week. As a result of the conference, Alan was changed from the learning disabilities watch list to direct learning disabilities services with the learning disabilities [LD] teacher in a resource room. I would work with him thirty to sixty minutes a week in a small group of 7-year-old boys struggling with learning problems. A week after this meeting and Alan's being placed in the learning disabilities program, his regular education teacher brought to my attention a picture Alan had drawn of himself with a noose around his neck. When I questioned him about it, he said he had just been kidding around, but then did admit he had some very sad feelings. I told him that I wanted to check in with him every day for a while because his being this sad concerned me. I also told him I needed to talk to his mother and father because it was important that they also know about it. When I approached his mother regarding my concerns, she said that she felt it really was not serious, and that in fact Alan seemed to be doing much better. His father felt it was serious and wanted Alan in outside counseling. I sensed the mother's resistance and that I had ventured into an old area of marital disagreement. I was certain that she would not accept a referral at the time. I suggested to both that I continue to work with him until school was out in June and that then they should think about an outside therapist, if not sooner. Both agreed. I felt that I needed to have another conference with his mother to support her awareness that in many ways Alan was doing much better, but that this new development was still something I hoped she would take seriously. She listened attentively, asked some very perceptive questions, and although she did not seem as convinced about the seriousness of Alan's situation as I had hoped, her attitude did seem to be much more open and cooperative. Alan started to do much better after he started seeing the learning disabilities teacher. She continued to consult with me and the classroom teacher until the end of the year, and the classroom teacher began implementing similar strategies in the classroom to support his progress. Alan became more outgoing and started displaying improved social skills, first in our group and then in the classroom setting. When it was determined that he was starting to generalize the skills he was learning in our small group, I met with each of his teachers to request that they encourage his fledgling efforts to become more assertive and outgoing. Most of them were cooperative and actively helped him with this. They regularly reported to me informally. Retention still was considered at the end of the year because his academic progress was not as great as we had hoped, but the parents agreed that they wanted to wait to see how things would progress for him in third grade. I then went to the principal to encourage her to consider placing Alan with the more flexible and caregiving third-grade teachers. She said she would take my request into consideration when making class assignments.

When the school year was nearly ended, I contacted the mother and father about making arrangements for Alan to see an outside therapist and gave them some names I could recommend. I asked that when they had made arrangements, they give the therapist permission to call me regarding Alan's case, and that they give me permission to discuss the case with the new therapist. The mother was very uncomfortable about the whole arrangement, stating that Alan would not be comfortable talking with a stranger, just as she would not be. Because I felt that my relationship with the mother was fairly strong by this time, I encouraged her to at least meet with the people I had recommended; then, if she wished, she could call me to talk further about her concerns. She thanked me but did not act on this offer. In two weeks, just at the end of the school year, I received a call from the therapist whose name topped the list, who mentioned that the father had made the arrangements for the meeting, and only the father came. However, the therapist had called the mother, and she had agreed to cooperate in getting Alan to his appointments. At the beginning of third grade, I met with Alan and his parents separately after discussing his progress with his outside therapist. We all agreed that, following a few visits to assist in his adjustment to the new school year, direct social work service would not be indicated at this time.

Third grade generally went well for Alan. He made good academic progress. He was seen by the reading specialist and the learning disabilities specialist two times a week, with one other student. I had regular contact with his classroom teacher to make sure he was progressing both academically and socially. Initially, I discussed with her his previous struggles and alerted her to watch for signs of depression. I also helped her to institute a behavior modification plan for the whole class, focused on positive social interaction, as a way of keeping a handle on Alan's real social progress, aside from his teacher's impressions. Alan finished third grade on a positive note and was promoted to fourth grade.

Alan continued doing well in fourth grade. He had a male teacher whom he seemed to enjoy. The teacher noted that after entering fourth grade, Alan improved greatly in his academic, organizational, and social skills—and going up several grade levels in reading, health, and social studies. Grades in other subject areas stayed the same or went up slightly. He became more organized and began writing his assignments down each day; his daily homework assignments were consistently completed. My work with his teacher that year was less intense than previously. I consulted with him weekly for the first few weeks of school, giving him essentially the same background information as I had done for the third-grade teacher, though in less detail. This was followed by monthly check-ins, except when specific concerns arose.

Alan became more involved in class discussions, although he still was shy about sharing experiences. One thing he did share, slowly, with each of us involved with him, was his mother's remarriage at the end of the summer. He was beginning to enjoy his stepfather, although he felt the stepfather sometimes was not confident when problems arose, but, as Alan suggested, perhaps this was because he had never had children before. I learned of this by asking Alan if he would like to come to talk with me a few times once I learned from his teacher of this new development. I also asked him for permission to contact his mother and stepfather to ask them if they would like to come in to talk to me about any issues surrounding their relationship with the children, especially with Alan. Surprisingly, they agreed and came in the following week. We decided to keep in contact throughout the rest of the year. I also agreed to start seeing Alan again in a small group of boys. He interacted with the other students, but he still needed work on social skills. At times he reacted negatively and physically to others when annoyed; however, he eventually learned to walk away from those situations. I reinforced the importance of therapy for Alan for the summer months, given those latest developments, more to prevent backsliding than because of the former concerns regarding serious depression.

Alan became more comfortable with his academics and the school setting. He would have liked more friends. He enjoyed being with his stepfather and no longer thought so much about the divorce. He visited with his father every weekend and also became involved with outside activities, such as Boy Scouts. His mother then started to work part-time in the office of one of the district schools.

Alan completed his middle and junior high school years successfully. He was placed on a consult basis for learning disability/resource (LD/R) services the last two years of junior high and continued in the Chapter I reading program through sixth grade. Socially, he interacted well with others and was involved in the chess club. He was very involved with the youth group at his father's church.

Alan's Current Progress. Alan is now a freshman in high school and doing well academically. He does not seem to have many friends in the mobile home park but does have friends in his father's neighborhood, which he visits regularly. He is still somewhat shy and a "loner." His mother states that he may move in with his father, after his junior year, as did his oldest brother. The move would be prompted by the fact that he would be attending a much smaller and more personal high school in a small-town setting. Alan continues to maintain the progress he made, academically, socially, and emotionally—the progress began when he first came to the attention of the multidisciplinary team many years ago.

UNITS OF ATTENTION AND SCHOOL SOCIAL WORK ROLES

The focus of concern for the social worker rested at different times and in different ways on Alan, the regular and special education teachers, the principal, mother, father and stepfather, and the outside therapist. One way to organize these complex choices for assessment and for intervention is to think of them as units of attention. A unit of attention is a chosen point of most effective change, a point or set of points in the system where, if change takes place, other positive changes will also become possible. For example, the social worker started by assessing the situation, interviewing Alan, the teacher, and the parents. Initially, the social worker did an assessment and case management. She suggested an outside therapist to the parents and brought in resources from the school to support Alan's coping with school and dealing with a possible learning disability. The mother would not accept outside counseling. The social worker continued to monitor the situation in the meantime and provided consultation to the classroom teacher and the learning disability and reading specialists. Shifts in the situation brought out different units of attention. Alan's new second-grade teacher was able to make better use of consultation, but then Alan's drawing changed the nature of the problem and brought out a different focus on everyone's part. The worker got directly involved with Alan and worked through others. She was eventually successful with the parents getting outside help and getting somewhat more involved themselves. The principal became a unit of attention in planning Alan's third-grade placement. At different points during the following years there were different responses to the changing situation. Their focus depended on the school social worker's assessment of the needs in the situation, the worker's competence in different areas, the time available, and the extent of development of the social work program in the school. In other words, the social worker was responding to the realistic limitations and opportunities of a changing process.

The School Program as a Unit of Attention

The first unit of attention of the school social worker is the school program offered to pupils. Here the school social worker may work with others in the school to develop programs for particular groups, such as pregnant adolescents or children being mainstreamed from special education programs, or for individual students. In one instance, the high school may be in crisis with the suicide of a well-known third-year student. The social worker is part of the crisis team, having helped prepare a general crisis plan, and will take part in working with different parts of the school community as it copes with the crisis. In another instance, the social worker assists in the development of regular education classroom environments that appropriately accommodate certain children with special needs. He or she may be involved in transition planning for these children and consultation on placements. The social worker may design special group experiences to meet the needs of diverse populations, such as young parents, children of divorce, pregnant adolescents, eighth graders with developmental disabilities learning social skills, or teachers finding an appropriate role for themselves in dealing with children who tell them about abuse. The social worker may develop a mediation program to help the school find better and fairer ways for adolescents to deal with disputes and fights.

The social worker provides a good deal of consultation to teachers, consistently a most important part of the role (Constable, Kuzmickaite, Harrison, & Volkmann, 1999). Many times, developing a program or consulting with teachers is enough to accomplish desired change. The change in the classroom affords the pupil an opportunity to accomplish learning and social developmental tasks. Sometimes nothing more is needed than consultation.

Extending intervention to the parents or pupil would be unnecessary and therefore intrusive. In Alan's case, at different times it was necessary to work with him, with the parents, and with an outside therapist. This was built on continuing consultation with the teachers and other resources in the school.

The Family as a Unit of Attention

The second unit of attention is the family of the pupil, discussed further in the next chapter. In harmony with the work begun by the teacher, the potential alliance of the school with family members may need to be developed through routine communication and consistent mutual understanding of what they should expect and what support the pupil needs to take the next steps toward appropriate, developmental maturity. With many students, contact with the family and some ongoing work with teachers is enough.

In Alan's case the parents had just divorced and Alan was reacting to it. For the parents, Alan's issues brought out the old, unresolved issues around parenting. The social worker could help each one focus appropriately on Alan's needs and encourage positive involvement in a realistic, strengths-based approach. This opened the possibility of Alan getting outside help, for the social worker to collaborate with the therapist and for both to relate to Alan's needs in different ways. She did the same with the stepfather when he appeared. By that time, Alan was able to accommodate relationships both with father and stepfather, a major indicator of some resolution of his concerns.

The Pupil as a Unit of Attention

The third unit of attention is the pupil. Whatever changes take place in the classroom environment and in what the school is able to offer, the pupil needs to use them and to deal with personal change. Building on the sound base of a connection with home and school, the combination of small changes in home, school, and pupil is often much more powerful than an intensive focus on a single factor.

Alan's developmental needs, his learning process, and the family and school worlds that surround that process have centrality in the case. The family and school worlds were dysfunctional in relation to his attempts at active coping and learning. A whole environmental world—from parent through school secretary, janitor, school psychologist, social worker, teachers, and principal—waits to see whether and how Alan will cope. The social worker moved among all the parts of this world to help it work for Alan. She adapted methodology to the particular needs in the situation—to help Alan make sense of his world and discover what *he* could do. With Alan she used individual and group modalities. She used relational qualities of empathy and good communication to help him cope with himself and his relational world. She would be "there" for him, even though they might not get together always. Alan did the work. From Alan's perspective, the learning process in school has to be a central developmental event. But his eroding relationships, his learning disabilities, and his social skills problems make it difficult to carry out these tasks. Educational tasks are so salient to the maturation of many children that there may be no more powerful way to help Alan grow, particularly if the family can participate in and support the process.

The social worker worked with Alan's surroundings, with Alan when necessary, and then indirectly through others. The daily check-ins were crucial in second grade. In third grade, with Alan's progress and another therapist involved, there were only a few contacts in the beginning of the school year and availability when needed. In fourth grade, there was some contact with Alan around accommodating his stepfather. Alan also attended a social skills group led by the social worker.

The Community as a Unit of Attention

A fourth unit of attention is the agencies and resources in the community. The community provides a variety of resources, such as child care, health care, employment, and so on, that may make it possible to achieve certain goals. In most cases, the social worker would have difficulty making the connection without first establishing a firm base with school, family, and pupil. In Alan's case, the school social worker helped the parents and Alan to use an outside therapist. As long as the parents refused to use the therapist, the social worker did what she could with Alan's situation. When they did make contact, she maintained a liaison with the therapist, but her role was different and in some ways more complex than the therapist's.

In addition to helping people to use existing resources, frequently the school social worker is in a position to develop resources in the community. This is particularly possible when the school is used as the center in the community for developing family services. A child with a severe disability is usually more vulnerable and depends on complex relations with systems external to the family, as well as the family itself, to meet his or her emergent needs. These external systems provide special education, physical and mental health services of different sorts, job training, transportation, and a variety of temporary or permanent care arrangements when family care is no longer adequate. The family of the child with disabilities is under considerable pressure and cannot really function without some assistance from the outside. The school social worker needs to negotiate networks of service agreements with the family and the appropriate providers. The school social worker may also use informal resources. For example, a school social worker made use of a student volunteer in a public park system to help an extremely isolated 13-year-old move into group game activities and eventually translate these gains into his relationships with others in school. Considerable professional skill is necessary to keep such a network going, but these networks could make the difference between a child's remaining in the community or going to an institution.

Using firsthand accounts, let us consider a few examples of the process of working with different units of attention.

Tommy—Working Between Parents, Teachers, and Pupil

Here the school social worker had to work between Tommy, his teachers, and his parents to redevelop a relationship around his learning.

> Tommy is a third grader who was initially referred for his out-of-control behavior. He is not on grade level, tends to disrupt the class, seldom finishes assignments, and steals and lies both in and out of class. He seldom tells the same story about an incident and has alienated himself from his classmates. He is a late reader and appears to have marginal learning disabilities in verbal and math skills. Tommy lives with his mother, stepfather, and his half-brother, aged 2. The parents, who work as orderlies in an extended-care facility, were married a year ago. Last year after his parents had punished him for something, Tommy reported to the school that his parents were abusing him, and that his father had a drinking problem. The resulting referral to the child welfare agency (with no contact with the parents) was unfounded. Tommy admitted later that there had been no physical punishment. Tommy's parents responded to these accusations by refusing to meet, or have Tommy meet, with anyone from the school. Communications broke down, and Tommy's behavior worsened. At this point, Tommy's behavior was referred to Julia Alvarez, the social worker. The teacher was determined to get Tommy into a class for the behaviorally disordered. The mother was very angry and reluctant to meet with anyone from the school. She saw the teacher (and the school) as an enemy, disrupting her marriage and undermining her authority with her son. She said that Tommy had the same problems at home, but that there had been no physical abuse and that her husband had stopped drinking. It took a great deal of work to regain the trust of the parents and help them to find alternate ways to deal with Tommy. Both parents agreed to form a united front in relation to Tommy. They made a plan where the stepfather agreed to walk Tommy back to school if he didn't bring homework home. Neither had a high school diploma, and they felt hampered in helping him with his homework, but they did find a neighbor girl who would help him. Tommy agreed to go along with this plan.
>
> In spite of these changes, the teacher was still determined to remove him from her class. The principal initially supported her in this. It was only with the involvement of the district-wide prereferral committee that the principal and teacher agreed to make an effort to work with the parents on this at all. Working between the teacher, Tommy's parents, and Tommy, it took Ms. Alvarez about a semester of constant work, together with Tommy's gradual, but evident improvement, for the teacher to change her attitude. For every

step Tommy took, he sabotaged his progress the next moment. On the other hand, for the first time in his life Tommy was being exposed to consistent expectations and clear, appropriate consequences from everyone. Ms. Alvarez had to help the teacher overcome a tendency either to overreact to Tommy or to ignore him. She had to help the parents back up the teacher. She had to help Tommy adjust to the changes in class, and to accept his stepfather's, as well as his mother's, involvement with him. Later testing confirmed Tommy's borderline learning disabilities and now marginal behavior problems. Over the next three years, Tommy did improve gradually, and Ms. Alvarez continued to work with the parents, his teachers, and Tommy. When he went to junior high school, he didn't do badly. He came back to tell Ms. Alvarez how he was managing himself. His favorite subjects were shop and gym, and he was on the stage crew.

Cathy

With Cathy the focus was always on helping her manage her anxieties, but in the process John Atwood, the social worker, also worked over a period of four years at different times with her teachers, her parents, and a psychiatrist in the community.

On the first day of freshmen orientation at West Oakwood Senior High School, students were having a cookout, prepared by the administration and joined by faculty and staff. A senior girl came up to Mr. Atwood and asked for assistance with a girl in her group who was crying uncontrollably. At first, Cathy was almost unable to communicate, and he worried that she might hyperventilate from her sobbing. He was able to help her to calm herself. Later she stated that she was scared to death of being in this big school and away from her mother. Mr. Atwood helped her to stabilize, contacted the parents, and with their permission then met with Cathy to help her deal with her anxiety about the transition to West Oakwood. As part of this plan, he also wrote to Cathy's teachers that she was having difficulty with her transition, asking them for any input they might have and also letting them know he would be available. In the beginning, he would see Cathy before school started three days a week and then touched base with her before her study hall period to help get her through the second half of the day. He coordinated with the parents, with some of her teachers, and with the psychiatrist, who evaluated her and prescribed medication. As she began to adjust, Mr. Atwood would see her once a week to help her maintain her gains, with monitoring by one of her teachers and occasional contact with her parents.

Cathy lives with her parents and younger brother and sister. Both of Cathy's parents work in the small family business they own. They are having marital problems, and the mother has been in therapy a year and a half. Her two younger siblings are state and national champion gymnasts, something her father is deeply involved with. Cathy is slightly overweight, feels awkward, neglected by her father and siblings, and closer to her mother. Since sixth grade, she has had panic attacks whenever she begins something new, such as going to summer camp. She had received help in a middle-school group addressing anxiety issues and was working with a counselor in the community. In Mr. Atwood's contacts with her, Cathy became increasingly worried about her attacks. She was afraid that something would happen to her father and mother when she was not with them. She recalled her father injuring his back at work, and getting the call just when she came home from school. As a freshman, she became more and more distraught and began to make comments about harming herself so that she would not have to come to school. When Mr. Atwood shared this with her parents, the family was initially reluctant to place Cathy on medication. But when Cathy started talking about harming herself, she was evaluated and prescribed an antidepressant. Gradually, Cathy showed signs of improvement and stabilized. He encouraged Cathy, who has always loved creative writing, to get involved with the school paper, and encouraged her parents to support her in this. Cathy gradually developed greater self-confidence and a few friends. The following year she did much better, and he reduced their contacts to check-ins every month. She had a difficult junior year, when she had a very disappointing experience with a boy who was on the school paper with her. Mr. Atwood saw Cathy weekly for a while and stayed in occasional contact with her up to graduation. She came back to visit him once, looking for encouragement when she started at a local junior college.

Dealing with Sexual Harassment at Northwood Junior High School

The social worker first became aware of a big problem of peer sexual harassment in eighth-grade gym class when several girls told her about it with great embarrassment. It was going on mostly in the locker room and the showers, which were unmonitored. The gym teacher wasn't sure what constituted harassment and wasn't sure how to deal with it, if it was. He agreed to check into it. We developed an anonymous survey, which asked students whether they had experienced particular harassing behaviors (which were defined in the questionnaire) in school over the past year. When we received the returns, 75 percent of the boys and 85 percent of the girls had experienced sexual harassment in school. When they thought about these behaviors as harassment, they didn't like them. They had been uncertain whether this was just something to be expected in school. When the principal and the teachers saw the data, they were surprised. They also found themselves changing their thinking about harassment, and so did community members and parents when the issue was discussed. A policy was eventually developed that sexual harassment would not be tolerated. Later the social worker worked with the principal and faculty on ways to implement this policy. Students had to learn that the penalty for harassment was removal from school until it was clear that the harassment would stop. When this actually occurred, the social worker found herself working professionally with groups and individual victims on the meaning of what had happened to them. Students mediated some of the problems. She worked with perpetrators on the meaning of what they had done and on ways to rejoin the school community. This eventually created a profound change in the school.

In actual practice, the social worker will work with a variety of units of attention at the same time. The focus on these units will also change over time. In Alan's situation there were various permutations of units of attention over the years as the family situation, the teachers, and Alan himself changed. A paradox is that although the worker actively shifted her role to fit the developing situation, most of the "work" was done by Alan, his family, and the school, as all of them shifted over time and in relation to each other. The worker did not need to be centralized at any time or to give an exhaustive amount of energy to the situation. She could use the energy from their tasks in relation to each other as the main tool for change. With the situation and its dynamics accurately assessed, the principal actors did the work. The task of the social worker was to work with the principal actors, using a variety of intervention modalities, and to develop situations in which this work could be done most productively. Effectiveness did not come from the use of a single modality, but from matching modalities with the situation and the energies and capabilities of its participants. This approach to assessment and intervention is more complex, but undoubtedly more effective. As any team member will recognize, effective interventions are accomplished not by one member alone, possibly the school social worker, but by all the participants in the arena. Ineffective interventions are likewise a product of the participants in interaction.

Evidence-based Practice

The school social worker translates evidence from a variety of sources for this diverse and complex practice. Except for reviews of multimethod and multisystemic practice done with problems of youth violence (National Institutes of Health, 2005; Sexton & Alexander, 2003; Sheidow, Henggeler & Schoenwald, 2003) it is difficult to find studies to match the complexity and diversity of school social work, even dealing with fairly ordinary situations such as Alan's. Indeed, the economics of research mostly permit studies of single-method interventions. Thus there is a need for translation of a gradually developing literature of findings from other areas, particularly mental health (Franklin, Harris, & Allen-Meares, 2006), and from single-method studies in school social work (see Chapter 12). Every situation is unique, resisting conformity to a stereotyped "problem." Using Alan's case as an example, the problem(s) could be seen as family relational, as adjustment to a new school, as learning disability, as depression with suicidal ideation in a young child, and as a poor match between learner's needs and teaching style. Depression occurs in about two percent of elementary age children (Corcoran & Hanvey-Phillips, 2006), and most discussion of working with suicidality comes from literature on adolescents (Roberts, 2006). There is a burgeoning literature on learning disabilities, usually in middle to upper-grade levels, and the effect of school failure on self-esteem and social skills (Raines, 2006). In any case, there will rarely be a perfect fit between the evidence and the situation one is encountering. Evidence about probabilities of success comes into play at crucial points when one makes a decision, and so there has to be room for judgment. In Alan's case, the worker applied the evidence from other areas pragmatically to the situation she was encountering, given the emergent and hoped-for outcomes. On the other hand, the worker knew that the situation demanded an assessment, work with the parents, referral and ongoing teamwork with the school, and possible work with Alan. The advent of the suicidal drawing demanded another urgent assessment, contact with the parents, and a shift in plans. When the parent's refused her recommendation for outside therapy, she shifted again and started the check-ins, assessing Alan's state and providing direct support within her limited resources of time. Alan joined the worker's group of 7-year-olds with learning problems. However, it was the thrust of Alan's need to adapt to school and the support developed for this that carried the situation, and the worker facilitated this. In different circumstances, she would have proceeded differently.

School social workers will shape and hone their practice to meet the needs and possibilities of the actual situation, the school, and its community environment. As a result, the practice of one social worker will emphasize resource development and teamwork facilitation, while another will emphasize the traditional treatment model, and so on. Each becomes an adaptation to an environment of expectations and a professional decision on the worker's part about what is the most efficient, effective, and timely investment of self in service to a common social work commitment and perspective.

References

Constable, R., Kuzmickaite, D., Harrison, D., & Volkmann, L. (1999). The emergent role of the school social worker in Indiana. *School Social Work Journal, 24*(1), 1–15.

Corcoran, J., & Hanvey-Phillips, J. (2006). Effective interventions for adolescents with depression. In C. Franklin., M. B. Harris., & P. Allen-Meares, P. (Eds) (2006). *The school services sourcebook: A guide for school-based professionals* (pp. 111–118). New York: Oxford University Press.

Franklin, C., Harris, M. B., & Allen-Meares, P. (Eds.) (2006). *The school services sourcebook: A guide for school-based professionals.* New York: Oxford University Press.

National Institutes of Health. (2005). *State of the science conference statement: Preventing violence and related health-risking behaviors in adolescents* October 13–15, 2004. Final statement January 18, 2005. Retrieved February 24, 2005, from http://concensus.nih.gov/ta/023/YouthViolenceFinalStatement011805.htm

Raines, J. (2006). Improving educational and behavioral performance of students with learning disabilities. In C. Franklin, M. B. Harris, & P. Allen-Meares. (Eds) (2006). *The school services sourcebook: A guide for school-based professionals* (pp. 201–212). New York: Oxford University Press.

Roberts, A. R. (2006). School-based adolescent suicidality: Lethality assessments and crisis intervention protocols. In C. Franklin, M. B. Harris., & P. Allen-Meares. (Eds) (2006). *The school services sourcebook: A guide for school-based professionals* (pp. 3–14). New York: Oxford University Press.

Sexton, T., & Alexander, J. (2003). Functional family therapy: A mature clinical model for working with at-risk adolescents and their families. In T. Sexton, G. Weeks & M. Robbins (Eds.). *Handbook of family therapy* (pp. 323–350). New York: Brunner-Routledge.

Sheidow, A., Henggeler, S., & Schoenwald, S. (2003). Multisystemic therapy. In T. Sexton, G. Weeks & M. Robbins. (Eds.). *Handbook of family therapy* (303–322). New York: Brunner-Routledge.

29

School Social Work Practice with Families

Robert Constable
Loyola University Chicago

Herbert J. Walberg
Stanford University

- The School as a Community of Families
- The Necessary Arrangement of Relations between Family and School
- Family Conditions, Family Risks, and Resilience
- The School Social Worker's Role with Families

Families are essential to schools, and schools cannot accomplish their missions without connections with families. Since family is essential to the functioning and socialization of children, schools cannot forget that their clientele are members of families. Otherwise they risk failure. Families, including extended families, are the most important of the mediating systems that connect and stand between public and private life. These mediating systems allow each person to cope with the complexity of modern society with its necessary institutions—schools, workplaces, and health-care organizations. Families, in turn, need assistance from their surrounding relational and institutional communities. The modern family often experiences social isolation. Sometimes conflict, loss, family dissolution, even a physical move can cut off generational linkages and place families at risk. Losses can create social pathologies and progressive vulnerabilities in succeeding generations. And all of these have important effects on the child's success or failure in school.

Some of the key functions of social workers in schools are to repair the mismatches between school and family and in situations of potential difficulty, to develop real partnership. More than simply working with schools and families as separate units, their relationship is the natural focus. When children have difficulty or special needs in school, the relationship of family to school often needs special attention. The school, as a complex community, so salient to development, can either aggravate a youngster's vulnerabilities or compensate somewhat for personal and/or family vulnerability. It can provide alternate socializing relationships and maturational experiences. But it also can damage delicate relationships and create conflicts in loyalty.

THE SCHOOL AS A COMMUNITY OF FAMILIES

The school is a community of families, of teachers, parents, and others working in partnership with one another as socializers of children. The development of this supportive community is even more important when children, families, communities, and schools have special needs, where the connection between home and school is not easily developed, or where there is cultural or linguistic diversity. The social worker can help develop this community (Nebo, 1963). The cultural diversity of the contemporary U.S. school is now enormous. Pupil diversity is family diversity. In areas such as Chicago, it would not be unusual to find as many as thirty-five linguistic groups in an elementary school with a population of perhaps 200 pupils. Where there is cultural difference between family and school, families may have ambitions for their children, but they are often fearful of involvement and participation. Schools may not be well connected with some of these diverse communities. Parents need help to participate in education and to build an effective school community (Paik & Walberg, 2007).

There is a strong evidence base that resilience in children is promoted when the resources in the school, family, and community are united and dedicated to their healthy development and educational success (Christenson & Sheridan, 2001; Kelleghan, Sloane, Alvarez, & Bloom, 1993; Redding, 2000; Subotnik & Walberg, 2006; Wang, Haertl, & Walberg, 1998). Students whose parents are involved with their education show improved social competence (Elias, 2003; Lybolt & Gottfred, 2003; Whitbread, Bruder, Fleming, & Park, 2007; Webster-Stratten, Reid, & Hammond, 2001) and lower rates of adolescent high-risk behavior (Resnick et al., 1997). They show better academic achievement across family background, whether racial, income level, or educational levels (Jeynes, 2005). The family is the crucial arena for young children to develop self-determination (Lee, Palmer, Turnbull & Wehmeyer, 2006). Jeanne Brooks-Gunn (2004–2005), summarizing developmental research, suggests parents interact with their children along at least six dimensions: they nurture them; they manage the home and provide a climate of language and communication; they set standards, expectations, and discipline; they provide materials that children can use for learning and development; they monitor the child's behavior; and finally, they directly teach skills to survive and flourish in their environment. The climate of language, materials in the home, and direct teaching of skills are aspects of parenting most linked with the child's school success. Reflecting these six dimensions, she estimates that one-third to one-half of the variation in school outcomes between poor and not-poor children can be accounted for by differences in parenting.

Parents and teachers may have different perspectives on the same child. A survey of parents showed that they were better at understanding their children's "internalizing" emotions, such as being anxious, sad, lonely, or physical complaints, real or imagined. Teachers, on the other hand, were better at recognizing "externalizing" behaviors, arguing, teasing, threatening, cheating, and lying (Konold, 2006).

What Do Parents Expect?

Whether schools are ready or not, parents are clearly asking for partnership. This relationship, particularly necessary when the pupil has special needs, can easily break down when schools need to include parents in their processes. In these cases, mediation could change the situation. Focus group research done with adult family members of children with and without disabilities resulted in six broad indicators of what parents would expect from collaborative partnership with professionals in schools:

- Communication—positive, understandable, and respectful;
- Commitment—shared loyalty to the child and family, accessible, sensitive, child is "more than a case";
- Equality—in decision making and service implementation; equal power to influence outcomes;
- Skills—demonstrated competence to fulfill their roles; being willing to learn;
- Trust—assurance about the dependability of the character, ability, strength, and truth of the others;
- Respect—mutual regard and esteem in actions and communications (Blue-Banning, Summers, Frankland, Nelson, & Beegle, 2004).

This climate of parental expectations crosses national and cultural boundaries. Japanese mothers of children with disabilities came up with a similar list, with particular concerns about schools' negative-segregative views of disability. They wanted understanding, empowerment, coordination, and advocacy from school professionals (Kasahara & Turnbull, 2005).

Partnerships Between Home and School

Schools are beginning to recognize that families are essential to their mission. Family partnership has become a major school policy objective. There is an explicit and expected link of families to schools in national education goals pertaining to school readiness and parent participation (PL 103-227). Special education has expected some use of partnership with parents for at least thirty years since the inception of the Individuals with Disabilities Education Act (IDEA) in 1975. General education is moving in the direction of enhanced parental involvement and partnership as a matter of public policy in PL 107-110, the *No Child Left Behind Act* (NCLB). Many commentators (Paik & Walberg, 2007; Carter & CADRE, 2002; Lee et al., 2006; Whitbread et al., 2007; Bristol & Gallagher, 1982; & Walberg, 1984) have suggested different ways schools can develop effective partnerships with parents. Programs can be made more flexible, with individualized planning, the establishment of meaningful parent roles, and the involvement of the father as well as the mother. Programs would focus on goals important to the family and would also expect something of the parents. Parents often need help to see the importance of the often-small gains made. Meetings can be scheduled at times when parents are available. School personnel can be available who speak the native language of the parent, or translators can be present. School personnel can get involved with the community. Social workers can make home visits. The school social worker might help the parents develop their own support network of friends and relatives, or assist in expanding their network. Associations of families of children with disabilities are especially important. Parental involvement can be developed in a meaningful way through sharing power with families. This is not just a matter of asking parents to carry out an existing school agenda, raise money, or do volunteer work in the school (although each of these tasks has value). Often schools overtly state a commitment to parental involvement, but want it only on their own terms. A true partnership exists when there is time to listen and respond to all voices. This takes time but is well worth the effort.

Parent Participation

In the late 1960s, Project Head Start, reflecting a general philosophy governing community action programs, was the first to initiate planned parent participation as an essential dimension of schooling. James Comer (1995), a psychiatrist, developed a model of education in disadvantaged communities, where parents were often initially perceived as "unmotivated" or "hard to reach." The model is built on parent participation as essential to the creation of an effective school community, and thus effective education. Social workers would take the lead in activities that, over time, developed a community of parents involved in the schools. Here Schraft and Comer (1979) envisioned three progressive levels of parent participation: 1) general activity geared to involving the majority of families, such as potluck dinners and fun fairs; 2) parents involved specifically in the daily life of the school, such as in the role of classroom assistants, as participants in workshops, or making materials for teachers; and 3) parents able to participate meaningfully in the decision-making process in the school. Parents might move from level to level, but they cautioned against expecting involvement in the third level without much development of the first two levels over a relatively long period of time, that is, without a chance to develop a relationship with the school and its functions.

Adolfi-Morse (1982) applied these concepts to her work in a school for children with emotional disturbances in Fairfax County, Virginia. The school, which served a wide geographic area with many ethnic differences, is conceived of as a community of families. Events such as back-to-school night, potluck dinners, and parent-teacher organization meetings were used to reinforce this concept. Parents of children with disabilities, who may have been less involved than others, were often able to find important roles for themselves with their children as they were making the school community work. Their involvement resulted in a change in their children's estimate of their own roles.

On a broader scale states, such as Florida, Kentucky, and Tennessee, have developed Family Resource Centers as part of state school reform. Schools in Kentucky sponsor family centers if at least 20 percent of pupils qualify for the federal free and reduced-price meals program (nine out of every ten schools in that state). These centers provide a range of programs, including family crisis counseling, referrals for health and other social services, and preschool and after-school child care. Evaluation results have been very positive (Southern Regional Education Board, 2001). These centers are now being developed in many other areas. They are a new and potentially very effective service delivery system for children, and school social workers have very important and natural roles in them.

THE NECESSARY ARRANGEMENT OF RELATIONS BETWEEN FAMILY AND SCHOOL

Summaries of research on educational effectiveness (Henderson & Mapp, 2002; Boethel, 2004) suggest a necessary order in the relationship between families of all cultural backgrounds and schools. Families would have difficulty educating their children in a complex modern society without the assistance of schools; nor can schools readily educate without the cooperation of families (Paik & Walberg, 2007; Subotnik & Walberg, 2006; Walberg, 1984, Walberg & Lai, 1999). Each can prevent the other from accomplishing its proper function. This is particularly true for vulnerable children and families.

Families are the first educators of their children through their developing years. School functions exist to help the family carry out its prior functions in accordance with the needs and standards of society and the rights of members of the family. The community, often represented by the school, is obligated to ensure that families have all the assistance—economic, social, educational, political, and cultural—that they need to face all their responsibilities in a human way.

The relationship of the family unit to the school and the community can be encapsulated by three principles:

1. The family has primary functions in the care and socialization of its children. It has rights and responsibilities derived from this function that include the economic, social, educational, and cultural provision for the needs of its members. As such, the family is the basic social unit of society.

2. The school's primary functions are helping the family to meet its responsibilities and supplying certain cognitive instruction that the family cannot. The work of the family is always personal. Transactions *en famille* are expected to be based on affection and respect for the other person. Particular types of learning would be distorted if they excluded this dimension of affection and respect for the person *as a person*, as worthwhile in his or her own right. In families, this personal dimension is experienced and learned in work, worship, gender roles, respect for others in social relations, and respect for one's developing sexuality. When affection and respect break down, the partnership of home and school can be developed through social work services that assist the family in developing or redeveloping the complex interactive relationships necessary for their children's survival and personal development.

3. A secondary function of the school (and in a broader sense, the community) is to monitor potential abridgment of rights of children as pupils and citizens when external conditions of society or internal conditions within the family make it impossible for the family to accomplish its primary function. This must be done, without inappropriately abridging the family's exercise of those functions it is able to accomplish.

There is a balance between family and school, an order, and a defined relation between their respective functions. The increased awareness of the importance of effective families, the increasing numbers of vulnerable families, and the increasing school responsibility for the education of vulnerable children inevitably leads to the need for more integrated relationships between school and family. Even if many parents spend less time with their children (Elias & Schwab, 2004), schools could not necessarily fill the vacuum. Indeed the development of school services closing the gap between family and school could also pose a threat to family autonomy and effectiveness.

A balance needs to be mediated between the need for collaboration and the need to protect the rights of children to appropriate family nurture and socialization—to support the family in carrying out its responsibility. In the face of the weakness of the family and the complexity of the child's problems, schools may attempt to substitute for family functions. This never works well. This situation is legendary among school social workers: providing consultation to an intensely involved and otherwise effective special education teacher who feels the need to rescue a student from the parents. When services take over, rather than empower families to carry out their tasks, the parent's response may be to become either less adequate or more angry. Defining a relationship of collaboration, so that vulnerable children in vulnerable families are helped to make the most of what school has to offer, demands skill and commitment.

FAMILY CONDITIONS, FAMILY RISKS, AND RESILIENCE

Collaborative relationships are often difficult to manage, particularly with vulnerable families. The stress experienced by families with children with disabilities has a well-established evidence base. Children with disabilities have high needs for caregiving. Their families are often isolated from community support systems. Severe family stresses and losses are ordinary experiences for many children. There may be few actual and continuing supports to buffer risk. Parents' energies may be "indentured" by demanding work roles or the need to survive. Parents of children under age 6 have difficulty balancing the demands of participating in the workforce with child-care responsibilities (Children's Defense Fund, 1994; Hanson & Carta, 1995). Children of younger parents are at risk for cognitive, emotional, and physical difficulties (Smith, 1994).

Research and practice experience with children with special needs points out a heightened need for parental involvement and participation in education. Paradoxically, the greater the child's difficulties, the greater the magnitude of disagreement between schools and parents (Victor, Halvorson, & Wampler, 1988). Thus, the greater the difficulties, the greater the need for specialized attention of the school to the relationship with families. Partnership between family and school is particularly important when pupils show problems such as conduct disorders (Webster-Stratton, 1993), attention deficit hyperactivity disorder (ADHD) (August, Anderson, & Bloomquist, 1992), and difficulties in social interaction with others (Sheridan, Kratochwill, & Elliott, 1990). Nevertheless, families of children with disabilities, even after long mandated participation in school decision making, still come up as predominantly passive in response to this process (Fine, 1993; Harry, Allen, & McLaughlin, 1995). Often the school itself creates estrangement from families.

It is helpful to keep the strengths perspective in mind when working with schools and families of children with disabilities. So much of testing, grading, and assessment focuses on the deficits of the child that this process is likely to create defensiveness, despair, or overprotectiveness in parents. A good deal of work is necessary on both sides. Both research and practice experience suggest that parents of children with disabilities, low-income parents, and people with cultural and other differences can become quite actively involved when their school has an inclusion policy that helps them to feel encouraged, supported, and valued (Lewis & Henderson, 1997; Schraft & Comer, 1979).

Poverty is associated with great risks for children. These risks are greater for single-parent families and persons with lower job skills. In addition, the gap between relatively well-off and poor people is increasing, with children the largest age group caught in poverty. Children born in poverty have their risks, including illness, family stress, lack of social support, and health and environmental risks, compounded (Hanson & Carta, 1995; Schorr, 1988). Further risks are experienced by children in families where there is substance abuse or violence (Hanson & Carta, 1995). On the other hand, resilient children seem to maintain cognitive skills, curiosity, enthusiasm, goal-setting behavior, and high self-esteem. They appear less vulnerable to some of these adverse environmental factors (Hanson & Carta, 1995). In some instances, family characteristics, such as rule setting, respect for individuality, and parental responsiveness, can "inoculate" children against adverse environmental factors (Bradley, Whiteside, Mundfrom, Casey, & Pope, 1994). Social support from the larger community or kinship group can also act as a buffer (Keltner, 1990). Usually, resilient children will identify some significant adult in their environment who encouraged their positive growth. Such family or extended-family arrangements, which can occur naturally and in spite of very difficult circumstances, can also be constructed and encouraged with the assistance of professionals, such as school social workers.

Family Processes and Family Resilience

There is an extensive literature on family process, family structure, and family intervention (Constable & Lee, 2004; Fine & Carlson, 1992). Every family must create for itself an environment of safety, belonging, and appropriate communication and socialization. These family relational tasks involve the mutual construction of:

- A *safe* environment for each of their members, protecting dignity and often fragile and developing identities;
- A place where members can *belong*, that is, can be treated as unique persons of worth;
- Sufficient opportunities and models for effective *communication*, so that members can learn to communicate, respond to each other, and adapt to changes within the family and in its outside environment;
- Building on these prerequisites, each family needs to develop an environment where there is appropriate freedom, concern, respect, and care capable of enabling members to make appropriate developmental choices, to be concerned about each other, to respect each other, and to be able to care for others appropriately. (Constable & Lee, 2004)

These are not simply needs and requirements; they are interactive family tasks, which uniquely organize family process. In their absence, the effect on the younger members can be devastating. Since these complex, interactive tasks are related to the socializing mission of education, the school social worker may become involved when this breakdown inevitably affects the child's development and an educational process.

The concept of *family resilience*, developed by Froma Walsh (2003, 1999), extends the concept of family responsiveness to stressful situations. The resilient family forges transformation and growth from adverse circumstances (Walsh, 2003). In the midst of difficulty, the family is somehow able to develop its meanings, interact with its surroundings, adapt creatively to them, and preserve its own values. It manages to carry on as a family. Resilience is not a matter of a particular family structure, but of family process. When families are resilient, their members are able to communicate their needs and solve problems. Paradoxically, the effects of oppressive conditions may act on families in different ways, depending on external conditions and the family's own subjective processing of the situation. These conditions may act either to suppress the qualities that could lead to survival or stimulate them. According to Walsh, the resilient family is able to:

- Approach adversity as a challenge shared by the whole family
- Normalize and contextualize distress
- Use adversity to gain a sense of its own coherence
- Make sense of how things have happened through causal or explanatory attributions
- Have a hopeful and optimistic bias
- Master the art of the possible
- Draw upon spiritual resources
- Develop flexibility and adaptability
- Develop its internal connections
- Use social and economic resources appropriately
- Communicate clearly and openly with each other
- Solve problems collaboratively

The recognition of individual and family resilience connects with a large body of literature on family intervention and therapy and provides a conceptual map for a strengths-based approach. An ultimate test of the functional power of families is the way they continue their work even under stress. In spite of extreme stresses—slavery and subsequent discrimination, the Holocaust, deportation to refugee camps—some families have attempted to preserve as many of their human processes and functions as possible, often living a more human existence than conditions warranted. They have learned to be responsive, to support each other in difficult conditions as islands of humaneness in a hostile sea.

THE SCHOOL SOCIAL WORKER'S ROLE WITH FAMILIES

Working with Pupil, Family, and School

The school is a powerful stage where each student plays out the great developmental issues: separation-individuation, self-esteem, social relationships, language, imagination, emotions, assertiveness, achievement, competition, productive work, justice, and the discovery and use of one's self. The quality of a child's interaction with learning tasks and with others in school is usually a very accurate barometer of his or her broader developmental issues and of the family situation. The normal tasks of adapting to school can absorb the student's developmental energy. The possibility that this energy can be harnessed makes school a logical intervention point. The school social work role demands a systems perspective applied to families and schools and the skills to work with each in a mutually reinforcing relationship. The key to family-school intervention comes from the fact that family tasks and school tasks are intertwined and interdependent. Partnership in these tasks, mediated by family culture and history, is possible. Shared tasks place social workers uniquely on the inside of both, facilitating their complex relationship, without taking over the family's natural exercise of its own, appropriate functioning. This is particularly important where pupil or family vulnerability or school conditions might interfere with the effectiveness of their work.

The Family Systems Perspective Applied to Schooling

The current body of couple and family therapy literature establishes both the general efficacy of the field and the effectiveness of certain approaches (Sexton, Weeks, & Robbins, 2003, p. 460). This evidence base gives legitimacy to family intervention and allows its methodology to be adopted across a wide variety of areas. School outcomes—that is, whether family interventions are sufficiently effective to specifically produce a change in school behavior—are infrequently measured in studies of the efficacy of general family intervention (Carlson, 2006). The four recent social work studies of the relation of family intervention in schools to other student outcomes did show positive outcomes (see table 3.1 in chapter 3). This is a promising result, but more research is needed. Social workers have worked with families for over a century. Their intervention integrates a systems perspective with family development theory (Constable & Lee, 2004). They have long transferred research and practice from other parts of their field to the situations of school pupils and their families. In this context two therapeutic programs dealing with youth violence and criminal behavior have shown comparatively high effectiveness (National Institutes of Health, 2005) with problems of alcohol and drug abuse, and serious emotional disturbance as well. These focus on the family and its surrounding systems as well as on the youth. *Multisytemic Therapy* (Sheidow, Hengeller, & Shoenwald, 2003) and *Functional Family Therapy* (Sexton & Alexander, 2003), have each in their own way succeeded in systematizing the broad approach social workers have always taken to families and their surrounding institutions with intensity of contact. Full-time, social work masters-level multisystemic therapists carry four to six families at any one time (Sheidow, Hengeller, & Shoenwald, 2003). Functional family therapists work with perhaps twenty-six families over the period of a year (Sexton & Alexander, 2003). Both programs have shown their effectiveness with problems of youth violence through high-quality, randomized controlled trials (RCT) with effects sustained for at least one year postintervention and with at least one external RCT replicating the results (National Institutes of Health, 2005). The similarity of both practice models to what many school social workers have been doing, albeit on short rations and without elaborate research protocols, points out possible applications of this research to school intervention with families. Other models focusing on the family system, such as strategic family therapy (Carlson, 2006; Cody, 2006) and solution-focused family interventions (Franklin, Kim, & Tripoldi, 2006) have a good evidence base and have been applied in schools.

Family-systems concepts can enrich the interventive repertoire of the school social worker when they are applied to the processes of education. They are useful for complex, systemic problems. The route toward health goes through the family, the student in question, and the living, surrounding institutions, which assist both in their related life tasks. The family-systems perspective applied to schooling means that, to help children cope better with developmental needs and life circumstances, it probably would be ineffective to work with the child without working with the teacher, who can influence the school environment, and without some focused connection with parents, who can influence the home environment. The nature of this involvement depends on the assessment of the total situation. It is important to begin with environmental changes, for from a systems perspective these may have the most rapid results. When changes in the child's real environments take place, the social worker can assist the child to change correspondingly. Or the child will respond without direct, personal intervention. Even small changes taking place in the classroom environment, with the teacher, or in the home environment, with the parents, may be enough to give the child an opportunity to cope more effectively. Children who experience a small shift in the classroom or at home may see themselves differently.

We know from developmental research that children are for the most part responsive and flexible, that the child will inevitably be a part of these changes, and that they often do use well what opportunities they perceive (Fine & Carlson, 1992). On the other hand, to focus on the child alone, in the absence of a focus on school or family, would be to expect heroic changes in the child's patterns of behavior and in the multiple worlds the child inhabits. This focus alone is likely to be ineffective and an exercise in frustration. Small changes in the worlds that children inhabit, and corresponding changes in their relations to each other, create larger changes in the total environment supporting the child's learning to cope differently. When there are changes in classroom and family relations, working with the child individually, when necessary, becomes much less complicated. In addition, the social worker would be less prone to take on a role that teachers and/or parents should play, when both are already part of the team.

There are five foundational principles for school social work with families:

1. *Understand Family Structure and Process.* This principle presupposes an understanding of family assessment and social work with families. Families have unique structures, which evolve out of their particular stories and cultures, but common processes, illustrated above. School social workers need to be able to identify these structures and processes to understand the context of meanings that family members and individual pupils bring with them, to work with them and to develop partnership (Constable & Lee, 2004).

2. *Use a Strengths-Based Approach.* The diversity of family structures encountered in school social work and the individualistic approach often taken by school personnel could lead to misunderstandings and pathological labeling of families. The point where school social workers can work with families is at the point of their strengths, helping families to respond and compensate for parts that are breaking down and schools to support this process while it is taking place (Constable & Lee, 2004; Kral, 1992).

3. *Develop Partnership.* Because parents are the first educators of their children, a workable home-school partnership needs to develop, characterized by communication, respect, general agreement on important issues, and reflexivity (appropriate responsiveness) in relation to the changing needs of the pupil. This is especially necessary when the pupil or the family is having difficulty or is under stress (Lee et al., 2006; Whitbread et al., 2007; Christenson & Sheridan, 2001; Fine & Carlson, 1992).

4. *Use the School as a Holding System for Development While Changes Take Place.* Schools often provide some elements of relational stability, a natural "holding system," that pupils experiencing chaos and relational confusion at home are able to use. The school social worker can work between the pupil, the school, and the home to make this arrangement work.

5. *Never Work with a Pupil without Some Connection with the Family.* No matter how limited the connection or how difficult the involvement, parents need to become your allies. Just one contact may be sufficient to establish some collaboration. More may be necessary to reinforce and support a working relationship. Working with a student without the parents brings parents to work against you. Rarely will they lose this unnecessary competition.

Assessment and Intervention

To construct effective relationships between school and vulnerable families, the school social worker needs to have all the assessment and intervention abilities of a good family therapist. Assessment involves understanding relationships, tasks, and expectations in the classroom and in the home, as well as the child's developmental progression and patterns of coping in the context of the small changes that lead to systemic shifts. Much of school social work intervention is working to assist parents and teachers to find different ways of responding to and working with the child's active coping strategies. Working between the worlds of home and school, the school social worker assists teachers and parents to discover their own personal repertoire of ways to assist the child's coping, often modifying their expectations of themselves in relation to the real needs of the child. When intervention with the child is necessary, the social worker can assist the child in relation to those changes and assist parents and teachers to respond to the child's present efforts at coping, and correspondingly the child's efforts to respond to the changing environment in new ways.

The skill of making a good assessment of the whole system in interaction, leads to the skill of assisting parents, teachers, and children to manage that interaction. Social workers have not always understood that such a broad, balanced assessment clarifies the possible intervention between school, home, and pupil. The paradox is that it takes less effort to focus on the whole, and then respectfully intervene where needed, than to exclude someone from the assessment and the joint effort and then attempt to compensate for what the excluded person might have offered. In the assessment process, it is critical to maintain a focus on strengths—what we have to build upon in order to reach our mutual goals. Every assessment interview with parents should include questions such as "What is something that your child does very well?" or "What do you do that really works when you are helping your child?" or "What are some of your favorite things about your child?"

Choosing Units of Attention

School social work can take two directions: 1) helping family, school, and community work with one another and with the pupil, and 2) helping the pupil find his or her own resources and make use of what the family, school, and community have to offer. The school social worker must choose units of attention, that is, discover where to focus and what to do to enable the best match to take place between pupil-family needs and school-community resources. A unit of attention should be a point of most effective change, a point or set of points in the systems where, if change takes place, other positive changes will also become possible. Working with each unit of attention demands its own skills. Choosing the most efficient and effective focus, in the context of the time and resources available, is a complex professional task, and by no means a random process. There is a logical progression to it, reflecting the systems framework, and commitment to family partnership.

Some Case Examples of School Social Work Practice with Families

School social work services may continue throughout the school experience of a student at different levels of intensity as the education process continues. The case of *Tommy* in the previous chapter outlines work with a conflicted relationship between school, parents, and Tommy, which was directly related to Tommy's failure in school tasks. The case of *Alan* in the same chapter is another example of similar work done over a number of years. Instead of centralizing the therapist and the method, the focus is on the ongoing educational process—school tasks in every pupil's life and their individual meanings for the child and the family. This focus on tasks brings in a different type of process with the total network of school relationships, which becomes a natural holding system for this process and these tasks. There is also a different way of approaching time. In an elementary school it would be possible for a school social worker to know and work with a child for up to nine years.

The case of *Alan* is a good example of the school social worker working over a number of years through every part of the student's relational system, through the home and through the school. While the home went through great changes, the school became a natural holding system, allowing Alan's development to stabilize as the home stabilized. The school social worker carried out a wide range of functions with different units of attention supporting the holding system, supporting the parents' better functioning, as well as supporting Alan's functioning and his developmental maturation. In the beginning Alan had great difficulty. His world, as he knew it, was falling apart. He could not deal with major changes in his family, his move from his old neighborhood, his learning disabilities, and the demands of schooling. When the school situation showed responsiveness and support, he began to let out his depression and suicidal ideation. Over seven years, Alan showed considerable growth while working steadily on the same problems. He was able to use the constancy and support of this system to avert possible deterioration.

His family went through profound changes over four years—severe marital upset, separation, divorce, single parenthood with joint custody, and remarriage. While the school social worker's focus remained on Alan, she was also a resource for the changing family system. The social worker brought both parents and school into communication and support of Alan's best functioning. She helped the parents access outside helping resources for Alan. She worked with the complex family system and Alan in the context of the remarriage. Working between the worlds of family and school, the social worker helped the teacher, the parents, and Alan in different ways to develop this holding system, to support Alan's strengths, and—as Alan grew and matured—to help him to put things together. Alan's breakdown of school functioning—the massive breakdown of his ability to cope with educational and social tasks, his thoughts of dying, and his chronic sadness—were essentially concerns about himself and his family. And here Alan's developmental thrust to adapt to school became the key to the helping process. The parents expected to have some relationship with the school. They were open to the school social worker and the school at a time when they would not be open to any other resource, and certainly not to each other.

The social worker, from her position in the school, worked at different levels of intensity throughout Alan's elementary school experience, attempting to bring all the elements of the situation together. The focus on different units of attention varied according to the particular situation. At different times she provided consultation to everyone. She met with Alan according to Alan's current need, whether individually or in groups. She set the conditions for Alan and his family to find some resolution of this complicated situation. As a skilled clinician, she used a variety of modalities in the context of Alan's developmental tasks and the school to orchestrate a larger healing process.

The two following cases briefly illustrate practice of clinical social work in the school with families and students. As in Alan's case, the school is used as a holding system for simultaneous work with the student and with the family. Given this basic temporal and organizing framework of school, which both adds a further ingredient and provides limits, a variety of different effective models of family therapy, such as the two cited earlier, can be drawn from to assist the social worker's understanding of the intervention process. Both cases below involved fragmented and fragile family systems and students whose reactions to these systems were evidence of their developmental risks. Both cases involved outreach to parents and home visits, an outreach that was geared to what the parent(s) could tolerate and what seemed appropriate in the situation. In both cases there was a remarkable healing process. For parent(s) and student the relationship with school, facilitated through the worker, provided the protection and the time (a holding system) necessary for a natural healing and maturing process to take place. For these early adolescents there is a close connection between the educational goals and developmental goals. The descriptions below contain brief outlines of the process.

> Lynda began seventh grade as a very anxious, educationally and socially limited 13-year-old with placement recommended to remedy the abuse she was experiencing. She had a mutually explosive, provocative, and destructive relationship with her mother, who was struggling with mental illness. In a rage the mother

had once thrown a hot iron at Lynda, and these explosions were becoming the pattern in their relationship. Her father was concerned about the situation but felt helpless and passive in the face of his wife. The family is Jewish, but isolated from any extended family system. When Lynda was in a self-contained class in her elementary school, the Alliance for Jewish Children (AJC) had made an extensive evaluation of Lynda and her home. They strongly recommended that Lynda be placed in a foster home. However, there was no home available. Lynda was put on a waiting list and went on to junior high school. For any early adolescent it would be a great challenge to move from the relative safety and predictability of self-contained classes in a smaller elementary school to the multidepartmental, subject-oriented junior high school. Lynda would not cope with it as long as safety at home was the prerequisite need. The school social worker worked intensively over a period of two years with Lynda, with her teachers, and with her parents and collaborated with the AJC. Since the parents were unable to get to school, there were weekly home visits on the father's lunch hour. The structure provided by these weekly visits with both parents provided some safety. The parents gradually became responsive. The father became more appropriately involved with Lynda. The mother backed off from the intensity of some of their relationship, checking in with the worker when she felt prone to violence. Lynda became less anxious and provocative. Building on the safer relationships the family was constructing, the worker assisted both parents to move to a better connection with Lynda. At the same time, she assisted Lynda to use her school experience and what her parents could offer her. Gradually feeling less stressed at home, Lynda responded to weekly meetings with the social worker, and over the period of two years translated them into improved school and peer relations. She showed a good deal of creativity, particularly in art. Her grades, once failing, improved. She was eventually able to develop normal friendships with other pupils. At this point, the social worker provided consultation to a volunteer group leader at the local YWCA. Lynda's membership in this group was an important developmental experience for her. With her graduation from junior high school, Lynda was able to recognize and celebrate with her family the major steps she and they had taken.

Ed, a 12-year-old in a Swedish American family, lived in a world of his own. Although he was not psychotic, his relationships, patterns, and perceptions were decidedly schizoid and often his fantasies simply took over. He had superior intelligence but never engaged with his sixth-grade teacher or the class. Instead, he spent most of his time in fantasy, drawing spaceships and imagining himself on them. He had no social relationships at all and actively rejected any attempts on the part of classmates to make relationships. At one point he would spend free time mapping and exploring the town sewers. He lived with his grandparents and his mother in an emotionally impoverished environment. His mother had never married and was mainly invested in her work. His father was in prison. The mother related to Ed casually, as an older sister, but otherwise avoided him. The grandparents actively rejected Ed as an unwanted child. The social worker learned quickly in their first home visit that he could not ask much of the mother in relation to Ed. She would not come to the school ("too busy"), and it was clear that she would reject implicit pressure to get more involved in a parental role with Ed. She did agree to work together in twice-yearly home visits with some phone follow-up. In their contacts, the social worker deliberately moved slowly with her, providing a nondemanding, affirmative, strengths-building experience, always with its focus on her relationship with Ed. The social worker saw Ed twice weekly, then weekly, and later biweekly over a three year period. Ed made major gains in involvement with school and friends. He became better connected with his surroundings through his wonderful sense of humor and his art. The mother eventually felt free enough to make office contacts, and gradually became more effectively involved with her son. Between Ed's seventh and eighth grade this went so far as the two of them taking an enjoyable auto trip through the West together. When Ed's father got out of prison, the worker had some good sessions with him and with Ed as they got to know each other for the first time. The connection with school held everything together as they developed a better relationship. Ed's gains assisted the mother to find a connection with him. Her better connection helped Ed to take major developmental and social steps. Together they celebrated his readiness for high school.

Respecting Relational Structure

In working with parents and children in the present family structure, the necessary power of the parent(s) in relation to their children, their concerns, their educational functions, and their responsibilities need to be respected. In Tommy's case, the family felt a lack of respect from the school. In Alan's case, multiple changes had made the parental hierarchy confused and dysfunctional. In Lynda's case, the mother-daughter relationship was explosive and unsafe. In Ed's case, the mother would have preferred not to take charge or invest much in their relationship, and the power was unclear in the family unit. How does the social worker avoid taking over the process and thus displacing the parents? The temptation will be very strong for the social worker to enter a dysfunctional family as an "expert" and undercut the already tottering parental power. When the "expert" takes charge, both parents and child(ren) either move into further dysfunction and invest energy elsewhere or fight the agency and social worker in order to remain in control. It may be better for parents to fight with the agency and the worker, since moving into dysfunction is usually self-confirming and relationally circular. It eliminates the possibility of improvement. But even conflict may be unnecessary.

Home Visits. All of these cases involved at least initial home visits with parents. Normally an office interview at the school is preferable. The office interview relates the parents to the school, to their child's experience, and to his or her emerging developmental world. It is also an effective use of the school social worker's time. On the other hand, sometimes parents will not or cannot come to school for an interview, even to a school open house. A home visit becomes the only way to develop a connection and the basic mutual understandings and agreements to work together in the interests of the student (Allen & Tracy, 2004; Wasik & Shaffer, 2006). In Lynda's case, her safety demanded a more intensive outreach and the social worker simply decided to use her lunchtime once a week for this. It appeared at the time to be the only effective way to help the parents to work on Lynda's safety and their relationship with her. Not every school system would give the social worker the amount of time needed to do fine work with the family. In Ed's case, the combination of a home visit and phone contacts maintained a relationship that supported the mother's functioning while she supported Ed's development and began to discover a relationship with him. On the other hand, sometimes the neighborhood or the immediate circumstances preclude home visits. Sometimes a neutral spot, such as a community center, can be chosen. Social workers should avoid any situation where they are afraid or they sense danger. Parents for the most part do understand this and will usually go out of their way to facilitate an outreach of the social worker and make sure that everyone is safe. In Appendix B of this book we have included some practice-tested guidelines on personal safety, developed by the School Social Work Association of America. They are well worth reading.

It is also very important to involve the school principal with your making these contacts in the community (without sharing particular details of the contacts). Such contacts are often new to schools. Schools are generally not accustomed to collaboration with parents other than on open house night or in the parents' organization. However, a more extensive involvement is often precisely what is needed in the situations social workers encounter, particularly in special education. Generally, principals will support this if it is discussed with them. You are not practicing extramural family therapy. Rather you are taking the process of education and the school into the community, developing a partnership with parents over your shared concerns, and helping parents carry out their roles. Time spent with parents often pays enormous dividends, particularly with the overstressed, often single-parent, families of today. As in Ed's case, from a systems perspective a small change, even an attitude turned cooperative, makes other things possible.

School social workers will find an enormous range and variety of family structures in their school communities, for which the task-oriented, family-strengths, whole-system approach discussed here, will be equally effective. Alan's family went through a variety of structures—two parents, single parent, both spouses remarried. Ed's family was more complex—mother and grandparents in a confused power hierarchy, father in prison. The social worker found a different role with each part of the family system as the situation developed. There are over half a million children living in out-of-home placements. The majority of children in foster care attend public schools (Altshuler, 2006). Foster children can have many problems with school, reflecting some of their losses, their uncertainty and ambivalence about their foster parents, while they still have contact with birth parents. With these uncertainties, the school remains an important holding system; and the foster parents and child must still carry out relational tasks. All of this can be difficult and complex. The social worker can work with foster parents, develop a collaborative relationship with the child welfare agency (discussed in Chapter 36), and work with the pupil as well. The difference will be the need to understand the meanings of relational losses and new, but insecure, relationships being formed. In addition, there is always a need to coordinate with the child welfare agency.

Many children in school are raised by kinship caregivers—a network of relatives: uncles, aunts, and grandparents who have taken responsibility for the child in the absence of a birth parent. The case of Danny in Chapter 30, raised by a grandmother struggling with some incapacities, his parents out of the picture, and supported by a complex agency wraparound structure, is a good example of the situation of the kinship caregiver. Here the agencies provided support to help the grandmother to manage. In other cases there is a large family network. While each member of the network may be more or less available, it is the family network itself that with the school becomes the holding system. Here there is some similarity with working with tribal or clan arrangements, such as that found in traditional Hmong society, where the clan system itself provides security and stability, and the leaders of the system and appointed index parent(s) (perhaps an aunt or grandparent) become the key people for the school to work with. It is important for the social worker to assess the system and its cultural understandings to work out what type of a partnership may be possible.

Social workers often work with parents in groups. Discussed in chapters 31, 32 and 33, the strength of any group of peers is its ability to normalize a situation everyone in the group is experiencing, to support its members' confrontation of a problem they would have great difficulty facing alone. There are groups of parents around child-rearing issues using a variety of programs available. Parents with something in common, whether kindergartners, children with certain disabilities, or early adolescents; newly arrived parents in a school community; and parents undergoing divorce or grieving losses are among the many parents who can use a group as a vehicle for learning, support, and problem solving.

In addition, groups are very useful in crises as well as in longer-term healing processes when a tragedy has taken place. There is a great deal to learn from the coping of others, particularly if this is the first time one has faced a particular situation. For mobile families, the group often becomes a substitute family network where they can discuss concerns. For school social workers, it is an effective and productive use of their time in a type of family education cum group therapy. Their needs assessment for the particular school will dictate their approach to the school community and their use of the limited amount of time available.

The Child with Disabilities and the Family

All families experience some stress; however, families of children with disabilities face special levels of stress, frequently related to increased child care demands. The special needs of a child with a disability levy a heavy physical, financial, and emotional tax on the family. Most obvious are the financial burdens (Moore & McLaughlin, 1988). There are also needs for information, particularly medical and diagnostic information (Bailey, Blasco, & Simeonson, 1992; D'Amato & Yoshida, 1991). Moreover, parents must develop the skill to manage the specialized services needed. Otherwise, these services might seriously intrude on other aspects of the child's development, sense of mastery, self-esteem, and the family's ability to function independently. These families can experience increased divorce and suicide rates, a higher incidence of child abuse, increased financial difficulties, and a variety of emotional manifestations, such as depression, anger, guilt, and anxiety. Different types of disabling conditions may create secondary problems. Families of children with difficulty in communication (Frey, Greenberg, & Fewell, 1989), delay in developmental tasks, difficult temperament, need for constant supervision, or repetitive behavior patterns experience increased family stress. As the child develops physically and emotionally, increased age and caregiving demands can exacerbate the situation (Gallagher, Beckman, & Cross, 1983; Hanson & Hanline, 1990; Harris & McHale, 1989; McLindon, 1990). The perceived need for more complex support and protection may make real self-determination an elusive, although crucial, goal. Special educators are finding that specific collaborative partnerships with parents can assist reaching this goal (Lee, et al., 2006). Parents of children with serious, permanent disabilities go through a mourning process that includes all the usual stages of anger, guilt, depression, and grief over loss of the "perfect child who never came." A realistic acceptance of the child may eventually be reached. Yet chronic sorrow for what some parents see as a "loss" is often experienced in the day-to-day struggle to meet the needs of the child while maintaining personal self-esteem, integrity as a family, and a meaningful place in the community (Bernier, 1990; Bristol & Gallagher, 1982; Lachney, 1982; Olshansky, 1962; Turnbull & Turnbull, 1978). The initial grieving may return, continue, or intensify when the child is unable to accomplish developmental milestones adequately or at the prescribed times (Davis, 1987).

Coping with a Child with Special Needs. Intense and unrelieved involvement in caregiving for a child with special needs can put severe pressure on parents and siblings. If family members cannot adaptively share the caring role, the result is often rejection of the child or a split in the family into caregivers and noncaregivers, with the child empowered by the disability itself, and thus able to exploit the split. The effect of such increased and unresolved caregiving demands on spousal relations can be dramatic. Increased caregiving demands and perhaps excessive feelings of personal responsibility for a disability may cause parental roles to split into caregiving and noncaregiving specialties. One parent (often the mother) assumes the caregiving role to the (often voluntary) exclusion of the other parent. Without constructing shared responsibility together, the stress becomes overwhelming for the caregiver or can lead to other pathological relationship outcomes. The effect for parents of such overadequate-underadequate role patterns is to seriously split and distort the spousal relationship. The distortion is often carried to the siblings, generating caregiving and noncaregiving specialists. Such families often need professional help to balance caregiving over the entire family and to use the support of other informal or formal caregiving systems in the community. For various reasons connected with feelings of personal responsibility, families of children with disabilities may have real difficulty accepting help from the outside and often suffer profound isolation at the time they most need workable social relations with friends, kin, and neighbors, as well as extended community resources. Such informal support can be a source of respite care, advice, information, and material assistance, as well as empathy and emotional support. This support can be a buffer against the stresses of child care (Beckman, 1991; Beckman & Pokorni, 1988), but it still may not be sufficient to prevent parental dysfunction (Seybold, Flitz, & MacPhee, 1991).

Tavormina and associates noted four major parental styles of adapting to the realities of raising a child with disabilities:

1. One parent emotionally distances himself or herself from the child, leaving the care of the child entirely up to the other parent, and concentrates entirely on outside activities unrelated to the child, such as job and organizations.
2. The parents draw together in rejecting the child. The child in this type of family is most apt to be institutionalized, regardless of the severity of his or her disability.
3. The parents make the child the center of their universe, subordinating all of their own desires and pleasures to the service of the child.
4. The parents join in mutual support of the child, and of each other, but maintain a sense of their own identities and create a life as close to "normal" as possible. (As cited in Bristol & Gallagher, 1982)

The relations of such parents with institutions and organizations, such as schools, may become complicated. Despite an assumed community expectation that families be assisted in their functions, formal social support (from formal organizations: schools, social agencies, etc.) does not seem to have a significant effect in reducing stress in parents of young children with developmental delays (Beckman, 1991; Beckman & Pokorni, 1988). Indeed, parent-professional relations can be a source of additional stress (Gallagher et al., 1983). These paradoxical findings point out the problems of organizations or professionals attempting to supplant the parents. They challenge school social workers to assist families to construct appropriate relationships with formal resources. Families desperately need to benefit from these relationships, without distorting their own internal relationships.

Parenting a child with disabilities is a 24-hours-a-day, 7-days-a-week involvement, drawing considerable energy from other children and other responsibilities. When parents attempted to describe their experiences, they described great pressure from the child:

> Christine stated, "He'll do a lot of things purposely to get my attention, like break something or turn on the TV, turn off the TV, or start yelling." Luz stated emphatically that Juan's behavior was about attention, "Twenty-four hours he wants my attention. And that's the problem. That's why he breaks things, writes on the walls, and everything. He just wants my attention."
>
> Carmen shared with us, "Everything is difficult. And then when you've got other kids and they've got homework and they've got to be at school in time and everything. It's just hard to put everything together. . . . At that point I was working full time, but I couldn't do it because I had so many appointments with Arturo, so then I cut my hours to part-time. . . . We didn't know about it. It was a world we were thrust into when Arturo was born." (Fox, Vaughn, Wyatte, & Dunlap, 2002, p. 445)

Research points out that the disability systemically affects every internal and external relationship, whether family relationships, physical circumstances, social networks, or daily routines and activities. There is a need for community and network resources, policy development, and an ecological approach to assessment, going well beyond the simple focus on child-in-school, and certainly involving the home (Fox et al., 2002).

A Family with Severe Caregiving Demands

Many families of children with disabilities are at the point of breakdown, when the extreme caregiving demands of the child do not mesh with what family members see themselves as able to do. The school social worker works with both family and the pupil to help them to develop a workable environment. A child with severe disabilities, Betty did better at school than at home. The mother wanted Betty placed. Placement was unavailable and the family's difficulties left the school in an unwanted position of offering the major consistent, developmentally appropriate relationships that Betty was experiencing.

> Betty is a 6-year-old with cerebral palsy who currently ambulates by rolling and crawling. She has a 7-year-old brother doing well in school. She shows "autistic-like" behavior but seems to have higher ability than her current diagnosis of

profound developmental disability. Although her use of language at home is minimal, she follows directions in school and is able to indicate her need to use the toilet. She is expected to get a walker and orthopedic shoes from United Cerebral Palsy by the end of the year. At home her dominant activities are described by the parents as screaming, crying, grabbing, hitting, head banging, pulling her own hair out, and self-stimulating. Her mother works in a factory, and her father is a janitorial worker. The mother is gone in the mornings and the father in the afternoon and the evening. The grandmother sometimes watches the children during the day, and the family receives twenty-five hours a month of respite care. The mother is overwhelmed. She feels her only way to handle Betty is to give in to her demands to keep her from screaming and insists that the brother do the same. The father feels that Betty's main problem is that she cannot walk, and this limits her contact with other children. Neither parent seems to have a clear idea of what can be expected from Betty in the future or how far she could advance in her ability to function normally.

Betty shares a classroom with five other students, a teacher, and an aide. She showed no behavior problems this year. Last year when the teacher used restraining techniques to manage her, she would scream, grab, and hit. This year the teacher is more nurturing. Betty appears happy and follows directions. When observed in class, she quietly worked behind a screen, putting paint brushes together. She kept trying, even when it was difficult for her, and managed to have some success. The school would like the parents to use medication and behavior modification techniques at home, but they refused. The mother didn't feel that she could "change her own behavior." The parents did put Betty briefly on medications but discontinued them after a short trial. The school felt they should have waited longer for them to take effect. The parents are requesting a residential placement for Betty. The school administrator feels that Betty is currently placed in the least restrictive environment and is adequately served in their program. She feels the district should not pay for residential treatment because of home problems. In any case, she believes Betty would get more services from their school than from a residential placement. Both parents were surprised at how well Betty is doing in school this year. Her father would like to know specifically how they are handling Betty in school, so they could do the same things with her at home. Her mother is fearful that if Betty were doing well, it might endanger the possibility of placement.

Because she is doing well in school, there is no likelihood of the school (or the state) funding residential placement; everything now depends on the social worker working between family, school, and Betty. There needs to be a channel of ongoing communication with the school. As the father indicates, it may be possible to help Betty generalize her gains made in school, thus relieving some of the pressure on the parents and brother. The mother feels desperate and hopeless and will need additional help. The parents need to be worked with at home together to explore rebalancing their roles and the support they might receive and provide each other in this stressful situation. They need to be able to mourn their situation and then to begin to see Betty as a real person, with real strengths. Some additional respite help might be possible. There is also the possibility of helping these very isolated parents connect with a group of parents of children with severe disabilities. As the social worker follows the situation over a period of time, the capabilities of the home to care for Betty could become more evident. In the meantime, concrete supports for the parents, the possibility of a walker, orthopedic shoes for Betty, and most of all help and encouragement for the parents in management of Betty are important.

The case illustrations of Tommy, Alan, Lynda, Ed, Betty, and their complex families are emblematic of clinical social work with pupils and families. A wide range of help was offered in a minimally intrusive way, using the child's and the family's own adaptive efforts to cope with the life tasks and family transitions. The ordinary "work" of a social institution, the school, the child, and the family was used to enhance the positive coping skills eventually developed in a remarkable healing process.

References

Adolfi-Morse, B. (1982). Implementing parent involvement and participation in the educational process and the school community. In R. T. Constable & J. P. Flynn (Eds.), *School social work: Practice and research perspectives* (pp. 231–234). Homewood, IL: Dorsey.

Allen, S. F., & Tracy, E. F. (2004) Revitalizing the role of home visiting by school social workers. *Children & Schools, 26*(4), 197–208.

Altshuler, S. J. (2006). School social work collaboration with the child welfare system. In R. Constable, C. R. Massat., S. McDonald. & J. P. Flynn (Eds.), *School Social Work: Practice, Policy and Research*, sixth edition (pp. 544–558). Chicago: Lyceum.

August, G. J., Anderson, D., & Bloomquist, M. L. (1992). Competence enhancement training for children: An integrated child, parent and school approach. In S. L. Christenson & J. C. Conoley (Eds.), *Home-school collaboration: Enhancing children's academic and social competence* (pp. 175–192). Silver Spring, MD: National Association of School Psychologists.

Bailey, D., Blasco, P., & Simeonson, R. (1992). Needs expressed by mothers and fathers of young children with disabilities. *American Journal on Mental Retardation, 97*, 1–10.

Beckman, P. (1991). Comparison of mother's and father's perceptions of the effect of young children, with and without disabilities. *American Journal of Mental Retardation, 95*, 585–595.

Beckman, P., & Pokorni, J. (1988). A longitudinal study of families of preterm infants: Changes in stress and support over the first two years. *Journal of Special Education, 22,* 55–65.

Bernier, J. (1990). Parental adjustment to a disabled child: A family system perspective. *Families in Society, 71*, 589–596.

Blue-Banning, M., Summers, J. A., Frankland, H. C., Nelson, L. L., & Beegle, G. (2004). Dimensions of family and professional partnerships: Constructive guidelines for collaboration. *Exceptional Children, 70*(2), 167–184.

Boethel, M. (2004). *Readiness: School, family and community connections*. Austin, TX: National Center for Family and Community Connections with Schools. Southwest Educational Development Laboratory (available as a full-text PDF at www.sedl.org/connections/resources or in print from Southeast Educational Development).

Bradley, R. H., Whiteside, L., Mundfrom, D. J., Casey, P. H., & Pope, S. K. (1994). Early indicators of resilience and their relations to experiences in the home environments of low birthweight, premature children living in poverty. *Child Development, 65*, 346–360.

Bristol, M. M., & Gallagher, J. J. (1982). A family focus for intervention. In C. T. Ramey & P. L. Trohanis (Eds.), *Finding and educating high risk and handicapped infants* (pp. 137–161). Baltimore: University Park Press.

Brooks-Gunn, J. (2004–2005, Winter). A conversation with Jeanne Brooks-Gunn. In *Evaluating family involvement programs. The evaluation exchange, 10*(4), Harvard Family Research Project. Retrieved February 1, 2005, from http://www.gse.harvard.edu/hfrp/eval/issue28/qanda.html

Carlson, C. (2006). Best models of family therapy. In C. Franklin, M. B. Harris, M. B. & P. Allen-Meares (Eds.), *The school services sourcebook: A guide for school-based professionals* (pp. 663–670). New York: Oxford University Press.

Carter, S., & CADRE. (2004). *Educating our children together: A sourcebook for effective family-school-community partnerships*. Retrieved October 8, 2006, from http://www.directionservice.org/CADRE/EducatingOurChildren_01.cfm

Children's Defense Fund. (1994). *The state of America's children*. Washington, DC: Children's' Defense Fund.

Christenson, S. L., & Sheridan, S. M. (2001). *Schools and families: Creating essential connections for learning*. New York: Guilford.

Cody, P. A. (2006). Working with oppositional youths using brief strategic family therapy. In C. Franklin, M. B. Harris, & P. Allen-Meares (Eds.), *The school services sourcebook; A guide for school-based professionals* (pp. 671–680). New York: Oxford University Press,

Comer, J. P. (1995). *School power: Implications of an intervention project*. New York: Free Press.

Constable, R., & Lee, D. (2004). *Social work with families: Content and process*. Chicago: Lyceum Books.

D'Amato, E., & Yoshida, R. (1991). Parental needs: An educational life cycle perspective. *Journal of Early Intervention, 15*, 246–254.

Davis, B. (1987). Disability and grief. *Social Casework, 68*, 352–357.

Elias, M. J. (2003). *Academic and Socio-emotional learning*. Educational Practices Series 11. Geneva: International Academy of Education, United Nations Educational, Scientific and Cultural Organization. (available free at http://www.ibe.unesco.org/publications/practices.htm)

Elias, M., & Schwab, Y. (2004, October 20). What about parental involvement in parenting? *Education Week, 24*(8), 39, 41.

Fine, M. J. (1993). (Ap) parent involvement: Reflections on parents, power, and urban public schools. *Teachers' College Record, 94*, 682–711.

Fine, M. J., & Carlson, C. (1992). *The handbook of family-school intervention: A systems perspective*. Boston: Allyn & Bacon.

Fox, L., Vaughn, B. J., Wyatte, M. L., & Dunlap, P. G. (2002). "We can't expect other people to understand": Family perspectives on problem behavior. *Exceptional Children, 68*(4), 437–450.

Franklin, C., Kim, J. S., & Tripoldi, S. J. (2006). Solution-focused, brief therapy interventions for students at risk to drop out. In C. Franklin, M. B. Harris & P. Allen-Meares (Eds.), *The school services sourcebook: A guide for school-based professionals* (pp. 691–704). New York: Oxford University Press.

Frey, K., Greenberg, M., & Fewell, R. (1989). Stress and coping among parents of handicapped children: A multidimensional approach. *American Journal on Mental Retardation, 95*, 240–249.

Gallagher, J. J., Beckman, P., & Cross, A. H. (1983). Families of handicapped children: Sources of stress and its alleviation. *Exceptional Children, 50*(1), 10–18.

Hanson, M. J., & Carta, J. J. (1995). Addressing the challenges of families with multiple risks. *Exceptional Children, 62*(3), 201–212.

Hanson, M. J., & Hanline, M. (1990). Parenting a child with a disability: A longitudinal study of parental stress and adaptation. *Journal of Early Intervention, 14*, 234–248.

Harris, V., & McHale, S. (1989). Family life problems, daily caregiving activities, and the psychological well-being of mothers of mentally retarded children. *American Journal on Mental Retardation, 94*, 231–239.

Harry, B., Allen, N., & McLaughlin, M. (1995). Communication vs. compliance: African-American parents' involvement in special education. *Exceptional Children, 61*(4), 364–377.

Henderson, A. T., & Mapp, K. L. (2002) *A new wave of evidence: the impact of school-family and community connections on student achievement*. Austin, TX: National Center for Family and Community Connections with Schools. Southwest Educational Development Laboratory (available as a full-text PDF at www.sedl.org/connections/resources or in print from Southeast Educational Development Laboratory, 211 E. 7th St, Austin, TX 78701).

Jeynes, W. H. (2005). A metaanalysis of the relation of parent involvement to urban elementary school student academic achievement. *Urban Education, 40*, 237–269.

Kasahara, M., & Turnbull, A. P. (2005). Meaning of family-professional partnerships: Japanese mothers' perspectives. *Exceptional Children, 71*(3), 249–265.

Kelleghan, T., Sloane, K., Alvarez, B., & Bloom, B. S. (1993). *The home environment and school learning*. San Francisco: Jossey-Bass.

Keltner, B. (1990). Family characteristics of preschool social competence among black children in a Head Start program. *Child Psychiatry and Human Development, 21*(2), 95–108.

Konold, T. (2006). *Who knows their children best, teachers or parents?* The University of Virginia, Accessed 4-24-06 at newswise.com/p/articles/view/519445/

Kral, R. (1992). Solution-focused brief therapy: Applications in the schools. In M. J. Fine & C. Carlson (Eds.), *The handbook of family-school intervention: A systems perspective* (pp. 330–346). Boston: Allyn & Bacon.

Lachney, M. E. (1982). Understanding families of the handicapped: A critical factor in the parent-school relationship. In R. T. Constable & J. P. Flynn (Eds.), *School social work: Practice and research perspectives* (pp. 234–241). Homewood, IL: Dorsey.

Lee, S., Palmer, S. B., Turnbull, A. P., & Wehmeyer, M. L. (2006). A model for parent-teacher collaboration to promote self-determination in young children with disabilities. *Teaching exceptional children, 38*(3) 36–41.

Lewis, A. C., & Henderson, A. T. (1997). *Urgent message: Families crucial to school reform*. Washington, DC: Center for Law and Education.

Lybolt, J., & Gottfred, C. (2003). *Promoting pre-school language.* Educational Practices Series 13. Geneva: International Academy of Education, United Nations Educational, Scientific and Cultural Organization. (available free at http://www.ibe.unesco.org/publications/practices.htm)

McLindon, S. (1990). Mother's and father's reports of the effects of a young child with special needs on the family. *Journal of Early Intervention, 14*, 249–259.

Moore, J., & McLaughlin, J. (1988). Medical costs associated with children with disabilities or chronic illness. *Topics in Early Childhood Special Education, 8*, 98–105.

National Institutes of Health. (2005). *Preventing violence and related health-risking social behaviors in adolescents* October 13–15, 2004. State-of-the-Science Conference Statement. Final Statement, January 18, 2005. Washington, D.C.: National Institutes of Health. Retrieved February 24, 2005, from http://concensus.nih.gov/ta/023/YouthViolenceFinalStatement011805.htm

Nebo, J. (1963). The school social worker as community organizer. *Social Work, 8*, 99–105.

No Child Left Behind Act of 2001. P. L. 107-110.

Olshansky, S. (1962). Chronic sorrow: A response to having mentally defective children. *Social Casework, 43*, 190–192.

Paik, S. J., & Walberg, H. J. (Eds.) (2007). *Narrowing the achievement gap: Strategies for educating Latino, Black, and Asian students.* New York, NY: Springer.

Redding, S. (2000). *Parents and Learning*. Educational Practices Series 2. Geneva: International Academy of Education, United Nations Educational, Scientific and Cultural Organization. (available free at http://www.ibe.unesco.org/publications/practices.htm)

Resnick, M. D., Bearman, P. S., Blum, R. W., Bauman, K. E., Harris, K. M., Jones, J. et. al. (1997). Protecting adolescents from harm: Findings from the National Longitudinal Study on Adolescent Health. *Journal of the American Medical Association, 278*, 823–832.

Schorr, L. B. (1988). *Within our reach*. New York: Doubleday.

Schraft, C. M., & Comer, J. P. (1979). Parent participation and urban schools. *School Social Work Quarterly*, *1*(4), 309–326.

Sexton, T. L., & Alexander J. F. (2003). Functional family therapy: A mature clinical model for working with at-risk adolescents and their families. In T. L. Sexton, G. R. Weeks, & M. S. Robbins (Eds.), *Handbook of family therapy* (pp. 323–350). New York: Brunner-Routledge.

Sexton, T. L., Weeks, G. R., & Robbins, M. S. (Eds.) (2003). Handbook *of family therapy*. New York: Brunner-Routledge.

Seybold, J., Flitz, J., & MacPhee, D. (1991). Relation of social support to the self-perceptions of mothers with delayed children. *Journal of Community Psychology, 19*, 29–36.

Sheidow, A. J., Hengeller, S. W., & Schoenwald, S. K. (2003). In T. L. Sexton, G. R. Weeks, & M. S. Robbins (Eds.), *Handbook of family therapy* (pp. 303–322). New York: Brunner-Routledge.

Sheridan, S. M., Kratochwill, T. R., & Elliott, S. N. (1990). Behavioral consultation with parents and teachers: Delivering treatment for socially withdrawn children at home and at school. *School Psychology Review, 19*, 33–52.

Smith, T. M. (1994). Adolescent pregnancy. In R. J. Simeonson (Ed.), *Risk, resilience, and prevention: Promoting the wellbeing of all children* (n.p.). Baltimore: Paul H. Brookes.

Southern Regional Education Board (SREB). (2001). *Helping families to help students*: Kentucky's family resource and youth services centers. Atlanta: Author.

Subotnik, R. F., & Walberg, H. J., (Eds) (2006). *The scientific basis of educational productivity*. Greenwich, CT.: Information Age Publishing.

Tavormina, J. B., Boll, T. J., Dunn, N. J. Luscomb, R. L., & Taylor, J. R. (1981). Psychosocial effects on parents of raising a physically handicapped child. *Journal of Abnormal Child Psychology, 9*, 121–131.

Turnbull, A. P., & Turnbull, H. R. (1978). *Parents speak out: Views from the other side of the two-way mirror.* Columbus, OH: Merrill.

Victor, J. B., Halvorson, C. F., Jr., & Wampler, K. S. (1988). Family-school context: Parent and teacher agreement on temperament. *Journal of Consulting and Clinical Psychology, 56*, 573–577.

Walberg, H. J. (1984). Improving the productivity of America's schools. *Educational Leadership, 41*(8), 19–27.

Walberg, H. J., & Lai, J. (1999). Meta-analytic effects for policy. In G. J. Cizek (Ed.), *Handbook of educational policy* (pp. 418–454). San Diego, CA: Academic.

Walsh, F. (1999). *Strengthening family resilience*. New York: Guilford.

Walsh, F. (2003). Family resilience: A framework for clinical practice. *Family Process, 42*(1), 1–18.

Wang, M. C., Haertl, G. D., & Walberg, H. J. (1998). *Building educational resilience*. Bloomington, IN: Phi Delta Kappan Educational Foundation.

Wasik, B. H., & Shaffer, G. L. (2006). *Home visiting: Essential guidelines for home visits and engaging with families.* In C. Franklin, M. B. Harris, M.B. & P. Allen-Meares (Eds.), *The school services sourcebook: A guide for school services professionals* (pp. 745–752). New York: Oxford University Press.

Webster-Stratton, C. (1993). Strategies for helping children with oppositional defiant and conduct disorders: The importance of home-school partnerships. *School Psychology Review, 22*, 437–457.

Webster-Stratton, C., Reid, M. J., & Hammond, M. (2001) Preventing conduct problems, promoting social competence: A parent and teacher training partnership in Head start. *Journal of Clinical Child Psychology, 30*, 283–302.

Whitbread, K. M., Bruder, M. B., Fleming, G., & Park, H. J. (2007) Collaboration in special education: Parent-professional training. *Teaching Exceptional Children, 39*(4), 6–7.

30

Case Management, Coordination of Services, and Resource Development

Robert Constable
Loyola University Chicago

Richard S. Kordesh
Bluehouse Institute, Inc.
Oak Park, IL

- The Continuing Challenges of Resource Development
- Case Management
- The Transagency Team in the Schools
- Wraparound Planning
- Social Workers as Resource Developers

From the very beginnings of practice, school social workers had to find resources, connect clients with them, make sure they were providing appropriate services, work out difficulties between different service providers, and develop new services or fight for their accessibility. As early as 1906 Louise Montgomery developed and coordinated resources at Hamline School and did case management. Resource development and coordination roles remain essential and continuing aspects of school social work practice. These roles have become even more critical with the growing desire to work with vulnerable children in the community, with the broadening scope of schools, and with school reform.

THE CONTINUING CHALLENGES OF RESOURCE DEVELOPMENT

Research points out multiple benefits of developing collaborative frameworks between schools and community agencies. Among these benefits are academic achievement, higher test scores, better attendance rates, and reduction of suspensions (Anderson-Butcher & Ashton, 2004). As schools develop services for vulnerable children, they are beginning to address the implications of their centrality in the community and the potential effectiveness of collaborative frameworks for services. The movement to include youngsters with more severe disabilities in public education, especially infants and toddlers (see chapters 13 and 14), has created a greater need for professionals who can do case management and develop complex support systems. The more severe the problem or the gap between home and school, the greater the need for complex and individually constructed supportive resource systems. Other community agencies, such as mental health (Weist, Ambrose & Lewis, 2006; chapter 25), child welfare (chapter 36), and juvenile justice, are also motivated to develop collaborative networks to serve their clientele in the community, if at all possible. Collaboration between schools and community agencies means working together and sharing responsibility for results (Anderson-Butcher & Ashton, 2004). It means the school social worker would often do resource development and coordinate services for children who might not otherwise be able to remain in the community. To recap the implications of this:

- Schools and families often cannot accomplish their own functions without specialized help from other agencies. These agencies might provide health services, counseling services, concrete assistance, respite care, summer camp, or other necessary services. Students being served in the community may be involved with other systems that have legal claims on them, such as the juvenile justice system or the child welfare system.
- The service delivery system tends to be segmented and divided by special functions within mental health, health care, child welfare, vocational rehabilitation, educational systems, and so on. There could be an unlimited array of services, each with particular functions, missions, and rationales for helping. Even if these were integrated at the organizational level (discussed in chapter 30), it is still more important that service be integrated at the level of the case.
- Integration builds on the centrality of school and family to the child. Family and school, with a focus on the whole child and the environment, have concerns that would transcend segmentation. Both have natural roles in addressing the difficulty in accessing services for vulnerable children. The school social worker, working with both worlds, is the person most likely to coordinate services and provide case management.
- The more vulnerable the child, the greater the need to coordinate services from different service providers and the greater the potential damage,

including family breakdown, if something goes wrong. The more services needed, the greater the likelihood that something will go wrong, and thus the greater the need for a problem-solving professional to address the configuration and delivery of services.

◆ Schools have particular concerns for young children with severe disabilities and older youngsters with disabilities nearing transition into the world of work. With both populations, some case management is mandated, but effective service cannot be provided to either of these populations without the larger structure of interagency agreements and the smaller structure of case management that appropriately involves the family and other resource persons in individual case plans.

Often parents of children with disabilities are not aware of what resource systems exist. Access to resources is usually difficult and accompanied by multiple and conflicting behavioral demands. The family's attempts to support the youngster and to compensate for gaps in socialization and capability place it under pressure. Family units, such as single-parent households or households where both parents work, are already under strain. Whatever takes place in the family inevitably will affect what the pupil is able to do in school, and so it is artificial to draw a sharp boundary between what is educational and what is noneducational. A commitment to vulnerable children places the school in the difficult position of having to interact with families and community agencies in complex planning efforts, to bring children and educational resources together in an appropriate environment and to maintain a support system. Some research suggests that educators may not have generally developed such relationships, even with out-of-school programs (Anderson-Butcher, Stetler, & Midle, 2006) and would be quite unprepared for this task. School social workers are frequently the only members of the school team whose orientation and general skill development includes interaction with community agencies. Their investment of time in informing parents, removing barriers to obtaining services, and helping parents use services could have a high payoff in the child's adjustment to a learning situation and remaining in the community. Particularly where resources are scarce and there is much to do, it can be a very effective use of time.

Resources in the community can be divided into two groups. First, there are services available from formally constituted organizations, often purchased by either family or school, and, if not purchased, subject to complex eligibility determinations for entitlement. Second, there are informal, helping networks of neighbors, community people, relatives, members of church and civic groups, local merchants, and other schoolchildren who may be willing and able to help in a variety of ways. Possible uses of such networks are almost limitless. Social workers often maintain an ongoing consultative relationship with some network members so that they do not become disappointed or confused at the initial response of the child with disabilities or his or her family. The authors have used volunteers, police officers, and a wide variety of other persons in many ways to provide structure, an element of caring, and vitally needed help for the child with disabilities and his or her family.

Interagency Agreements

As schools have become more central to service provision to children with severe disabilities, particularly the very young and those transitioning into the world of work, they are only gradually seeing themselves as members of a larger community of services. The demand for case management is accompanied by the need for interagency collaboration. Efficiency of service provision and indeed the effectiveness of any case management attempts would demand agreements reached beforehand among various agencies serving particular populations. For these networks to be viable, interagency agreements have to include some commitment on the local or regional level, a means of communication between all levels, as well as practitioners equipped to implement and coordinate service agreements on the direct-practice level. A good interagency agreement needs to be written in simple and clear language. It should contain sections that 1) describe the reason for writing the agreement; 2) identify the responsibilities of each agency and the method for performing those responsibilities; 3) identify the standards each agency must meet when performing an activity; 4) describe the process of exchanging information on clients in common; and 5) describe the method for modifying the agreement. The agreement should be flexible, focusing on the desired outcome rather than on the process of getting there. It should not jeopardize an agency's funding or turf. Instead, the agreement should seek to clarify these issues. Finally, and obviously, a mutual benefit should be evident. The mutual benefit should enhance the opportunity for future agreement as well as the full implementation of the current agreement (Anderson-Butcher & Ashton, 2004; LaCour, 1982).

CASE MANAGEMENT

A movement to a wider range of services based on legal entitlement is taking place, not only in the schools, but also in most other agencies serving children with disabilities. To cope with the implications of this entitlement, laws have prescribed or agencies have developed case management approaches. Case management has become an instrument of compliance and a tool for keeping clients in charge of their services, ensuring that they get what they are entitled to and have the opportunity to be active, rather than passive, consumers of services. Case management involves an individualized plan founded on a data-based assessment of needs. It is driven by specific objectives to be attained, placed in a time frame with a date for specific initiation and duration of services, and given expectations for evaluation and review and participation in setting objectives and deciding on appropriate resources. Table 30.1 illustrates seven major case management approaches coming out of different enabling legislation or frameworks. There are obvious similarities. With agencies having parallel approaches to case management, the next step would be to coordinate them into a species of joint planning.

In social work, case management is also a commonly accepted approach to the delivery of service to populations having ongoing or fairly complex needs, which necessitate that different services work together. It is not simply a routinized meshing of agency policies and practices to fit the case. Rather, it is an approach to practice that requires considerable skill. The social worker is working simultaneously with pupil, parent, teacher, school, and a network of agencies. Indeed, from a systems perspective the combination of small changes in each sector often creates broader change that no one sector—pupil, parent, teacher, school, or network—could ever accomplish on its own. Case management tasks described in the literature (Compher, 1984; Frankel & Gelman, 1998; Garland, Woodruff, & Buck, 1988) include assessing client needs, developing service plans, coordinating service delivery, monitoring service delivery, evaluating services, and advocating on behalf of the needs and rights of the client.

To coordinate the diverse segments of a service delivery system, the case manager needs to move beyond the confines of his or her agency or discipline and include other services with full respect for the differences they offer the totality. Two models of teamwork have emerged at different levels to meet the demands of case management: the transdisciplinary team and the transagency team.

TABLE 30.1 Seven Case Management Approaches

Case Management Approach	*Entitling Legislation or Framework*
The Individualized Habilitation Plan	PL 94–103, for developmentally disabled
The Individualized Education Program	PL 105–17, for all children with disabilities
Individualized Written Rehabilitation Program	Rehabilitation Act of 1973
Individualized Service Plan	Title XVI, for children with disabilities eligible for social security income
Individualized Care Plan	For Title XIX Medicaid
Individualized Program Plan	Mandated by Joint Committee on Accreditation of Hospitals
Individualized Program Plan	Title XX, purchase of service

Typically, the transdisciplinary team, composed of the family and professionals from a variety of disciplines, collaborates in assessment and program planning. One individual, chosen from among the team members, works in consultation with colleague specialists to carry out the individualized plan. Together with the family, the case manager integrates the information and skills of the entire team to work with the child and family on goals established, to ensure coordination and communication among providers, and to monitor services to make sure that services planned are provided. In the transdisciplinary model the case manager typically is both primary provider and service coordinator.

The transagency team provides a broader, horizontally nested structure for case management. It brings together not only the many disciplines working with a single agency but also a variety of agency representatives to assess needs and plan services. In many models the transagency team is created specifically for the purpose of a particular population, and the agencies represented on the team are determined by the nature of the program (Garland et al., 1988).

THE TRANSAGENCY TEAM IN THE SCHOOLS

We developed a transagency team in the Chicago south suburban area for students with disabilities, transitioning from special education. The area is heterogeneous, with patches of severe poverty mixed with blue-collar and middle-class suburbia. There are large populations of black and Hispanic minorities and white ethnic populations of eastern or southern European background. The area has experienced considerable development over the past twenty years, development that has outstripped the capacities of the traditional service resources and provided the opportunity for a fairly innovative type of planning effort. A transagency committee was established, composed of the major public and private agencies that are resources to children with disabilities and their families.

The transagency committee reached agreements on individualized service plans and provided a means of communication around resource issues affecting children with disabilities. A major focus of the committee was to develop agreements on individualized service plans for particular situations of need. With participation of the client, family, or informal resource network, one particular agency was designated as the focal agency. A particular worker from that agency would develop an agreement with the family about their overall goals and what resources they would need to reach them. This agreement would involve the client system, any appropriate informal support systems, and the committee. The social worker from the focal agency, who would work with the client, family, or informal support system, needed to be sufficiently skilled to:

- Help the client and family define the problem, some resultant goals, and what resources, services, and supports are needed;
- Define with the family the supportive network available to the client;
- Involve the client, family, or informal resource network in decision making by working with them individually, coordinating with other sectors, and bringing them together when they are ready to come to an agreement;
- Identify formal resources needed, maintain a steady communication with the formal resource systems in the network, and carry out problem solving with these systems as questions arise;
- Help the client or family and members of the informal resource network relate to the formal agency resources as collaborators, without a feeling of loss of dignity or control and with the assumption that agency actions must be related to client need;
- Help clients to use the situation of receiving service to identify their own aspirations for change, to embark on a change process, to adapt to realities in the environment, and to change attitudes or accustomed ways of relating to others.

In providing means of communication around issues of service development and planning among agencies working with a particular clientele, the transagency team focused on gaps in services, situations where the client would be at high risk, has needs involving a number of agencies, and requires coordination of services. It cannot represent any one agency if it is to carry out its function.

The social worker is the crucial link between planning processes. On the one hand, the social worker has a close relationship with an individual client and his or her family or informal support system. On the other hand, there is a working relationship with formal agency resources through the committee. Except for the social worker, members of this particular committee generally did not have direct service responsibilities. They would be far enough up the agency hierarchy to deal with potential resource commitments but close enough to practice and service delivery to communicate with the direct service level of the agency.

WRAPAROUND PLANNING

Wraparound planning, now part of the lexicon of human service reform, is a method of resource development geared to particular cases of children presenting severe or complex need, particularly where there is the possibility of institutionalization if fragile and overloaded community resource systems and/or family fail. In general, the term refers to the involvement of multiple formal and informal resources in all phases of service delivery to particular clients. Often these clients, if not served by a more complex network of family, community, and social services, would be facing institutionalization or would be returning into the community from institutional settings.

Wraparound planning is a process that takes the interagency professional team another step toward comprehensiveness. In addition to agencies, it would involve, when necessary, family members, friends, neighbors, pastors, or other significant persons in a client's life in problem definition, goal setting, implementation, and evaluation of services. It relates these informal resources to the formal social agency and school systems. It also stresses the importance of involving the client as part of the team. The emphases on comprehensiveness, integration of formal and informal resources, and client empowerment all reflect the policy reforms discussed in chapter 8.

Wraparound planning creates a new avenue for the school social worker to engage in mobilization activities on behalf of children in school. The very commitment by a school to wraparound planning will usually trigger a more intensive outreach effort to families, friends, kin, and neighbors. Resource development activities for the school social worker, who participates in, or leads, a wraparound effort, will begin with the formation of the team (including child and parents). It continues through the assessment, planning, and implementation phases as the team identifies additional resources needed to "wrap around" the child, forming new supports for that child and bolstering the child's chances for school success.

To some school social workers, the components that define wraparound planning might not sound so new. Indeed, Louise Montgomery seems to have done a form of it a century ago. Wraparound is simply a good use of the natural position of the school in the life of the child and family and the perspective of the social worker. It is a response to the growing awareness of the need for community alternatives to institutionalization as well as a recognition of the continuing work toward developing comprehensive, family-centered, ecologically based practice for vulnerable people in the community. Obstacles include policy fragmentation, overspecialization in treatment, services that neglect the family context, and a growing disassociation of clinical practice from community practice.

Eber, Nelson, and Miles (1997) described the uniqueness of the wraparound approach as it is utilized in a school-based setting for students with emotional and behavioral challenges:

> An important characteristic separating wraparound plans from other types of student plans is that they are driven by needs rather than by the parameters of programs currently available. In contrast to the traditional practice of evaluating student needs on the basis of available educational placements, existing

> program components and services are analyzed and employed according to their usefulness in meeting student needs. Services are not based on a categorical model (i.e., services are embedded in a program in which "eligible" students are placed), but are embedded or created on the basis of specific needs of the student, family, and teacher. The child and family team consists of persons who know the student best, and who can provide active support to the student, his or her teacher, and family. Extended family members, neighbors, family, friends, and mentors also are frequently participants in child and family teams. (pp. 547–549)

Eber illustrates wraparound planning as a process in table 30.2.

The diverse perspectives recruited into the child and family team ensure that diverse domains of a student's life will be viewed as a whole. Specialists are challenged to open the boundaries of their own vision as well, working collaboratively to formulate strategies to resolve the difficulties students face academically as well as socially.

School-Based Family Empowerment as Resource Development

Although wraparound planning brings the school social worker into resource development, another trend that broadens the school social worker's resource-development activities is multifaceted family-empowerment projects in schools. As related in chapter 8, one type of project that increases the potential for school-based family empowerment is the family resource center in the school. Through school-based family resource centers, school social workers are able to mobilize a variety of assets for families. These assets help support families and bolster the productive roles families might play in the community. School-based or school-linked family resource centers have also become critical components of community revitalization strategies in impoverished neighborhoods. Although such centers represent innovations in school-based institutions, reshaping the service delivery system in impoverished communities, they are also grounded in classical social work principles (Dupper & Poertner, 1997).

Family Support America (formerly the Family Resource Coalition of America) issued guidelines for practice that illustrate how intrinsically important resource development is to empowering families.[1] Although phrased to pertain to community-based family support programs in schools and outside of schools, the principles reveal the practical opportunities for working with community assets that will emerge for school social workers. The Family Support America's (2004) principles for practice in schools are as follows.

---

1. The Family Support America Web site (familysupportamerica.org) contains resources and links useful for social workers. Also see: Alliance for Children and Families (alliance1.org) Jewish Communal Service Association (jcsana.org).

TABLE 30.2 Community-Based Wraparound Planning Steps

Step	*Definition*	*Purpose*
Issue identification	Prior to the team meeting, facilitator contacts key stakeholders, which include, at minimum, the parents, child, and significant others (e.g., agency providers, relatives, community mentors).	• Identifies issues that might affect outcomes of the plan, as well as concrete steps that must be taken immediately. • Identifies strengths of the child, parents, and others to use as a foundation for future planning. • Builds a sense of being listened to and heard by the persons most involved in the child's care. • Prepares facilitator to understand system and personal issues affecting the child's performance. • Develops knowledge of the situation as seen by the persons most involved in the child's care. • Allows the facilitator to understand points of agreement and disagreement between the parents and providers. • Allows the facilitator to develop immediate crisis response, if needed, prior to the first meeting.
Introductions and agenda setting	Facilitator allows participants to identify their roles and relationship to the student and sets expectations for the product to be developed in the meeting.	• Allows meeting participants to understand their relationship to the family. • Sets expectations against which the process can be measured (i.e., building practical support plan that will produce better outcomes for the child). • Begins to build a sense of team as well as communicating to the parents that they do have access to support in their care for the child. • Builds a sense of hope about the capacity for improved outcomes if all team members can agree on areas for improvement.

TABLE 30.2 Community-Based Wraparound Planning Steps—*(Continued)*

Step	*Definition*	*Purpose*
Strengths presentation	Facilitator presents a summary of family, student, and other participants' strengths as developed from conversations in the issue identification step.	• Begins to build appreciation across meeting participants relative to the family strengths as well as provider capacities. • Identifies strengths as the foundation for strategy and plan development. • Allows persons in attendance to move from the role of meeting participants to team members. • Builds an alliance between the parents and providers in appreciating each other's strengths. • Allows team members to commit to the possibilities of improved outcomes and creates a sense of commitment to the child. • Allows team members to see providers as both assets and as persons in need of support.
Goal setting and needs identification	Facilitator leads team through goal-setting exercise, focusing on present performance levels of a typical child. Information is presented and commented on by team members. When goals have been set, parents and significant others are asked where strategies need to be developed to bring the child's functioning level to the defined "typical" functional level.	• Allows team members to set realistic outcomes that are easily understandable to all team members. • Builds a framework in which team members can pinpoint areas of need as measured against the description of a typical child. • Builds an alliance between parents and providers as they begin to view their similarities in terms of needs statements. • Allows participants to voice expectations and feel "heard" by other team members.

Needs prioritization	Facilitator asks parents and providers to identify needs that must be addressed first. Prioritized needs are limited to no more than five per meeting. Other team members are asked if other areas are seen as needing to be addressed first.	• Allows the team to break the need for interventions into manageable parts. • Creates the expectation that other team members will provide support to the persons most closely involved with the child's daily life. • Solidifies the team's commitment to working together, creating interventions, and building a commitment to improved outcomes. • Strengthens alliance between parents and providers. • Expectations for future planning around other need areas often are set, in order to foster the expectation that when first priority needs are met, others will be added.
Strategy development	Facilitator leads the team through a brainstorming process in which strategies to meet identified needs are developed. Members are asked to be as specific as possible. Suggestions do not focus solely on linking traditional services or settings. The facilitator continually verifies with the parent whether the strategies suggested might be helpful for the child.	• Allows team members to create a plan that is tailored to the needs of the child as well as building team ownership of the action plan. • Sense of ownership is likely to pay off in terms of task completion and follow-through. • Allows team members to identify creative strategies that are tailored to the needs of the child rather than the programs or services currently in place. • Allows the team to specify target behaviors, potential reinforcement strategies, as well as support activities implemented by certain adults involved in the planning.
Securing team member commitments	After needs have been brainstormed and listed on a flip chart, team members are asked to commit to certain strategies.	• Builds a sense of public commitment to specific action steps by team members. • Allows the team to move toward self-management by requiring the facilitator to wait for their commitment. • Gives the team a sense of direction and response in building a student support plan.

TABLE 30.2 Community-Based Wraparound Planning Steps—*(Continued)*

Step	*Definition*	*Purpose*
Follow-up communication	As the plan is formalized, the facilitator identifies a communication plan by which team members can have contact with each other. Team members are encouraged to commit to contact other participants. The facilitator commits to contact stakeholders regarding the child's progress.	• Builds a sense of team functioning that is likely to occur between meetings. • Allows team members to build alliances and communication protocols apart from formal team meetings. • Creates an environment of volunteerism among team members when participants commit based on their ability to follow through rather than on their job descriptions. • Allows parents and other providers to feel supported and that help is nearby.
Process evaluation and closure	Facilitator checks with stakeholders regarding whether the plan developed will be helpful, whether the meeting was productive, and whether participants felt their ideas were heard. A follow-up meeting is scheduled within the next five weeks. Procedures for calling an emergency meeting are identified.	• Allows the team to gain ownership by evaluating the process. • Parents feel supported and heard in the teaming process. • Communicates a sense that help is available regarding day-to-day needs. • Allows the facilitator to set expectations regarding communication and crisis as well as establishing action steps to determining their efficacy.

- Create a community of equal partners with parents, staff, and the community.
- Identify families' needs and use community resources to meet them.
- Build relationships with parents and create leadership opportunities within the school.
- Celebrate diversity and foster respect among people with cultural, religious, and other differences.
- Create "community schools" that offer a range of supports before, during, and after school.
- Involve parents in school governance and decision making.
- Make vital services accessible at school (for example, dental cleanings, skill building and child care, parent-to-parent support groups).
- Empower parents to address community issues of concern and provide needed supports to affect change.
- Provide strengths-based child and family development training to staff, administrators, and parents.

Through family resource centers, school social workers find more support in reaching the families, neighbors, and agencies that can be helpful in working with their own students. New opportunities for empowering families to wield more influence in the school and the community will continue to emerge.

The family is central to all of these processes, bringing together family and child with school and community resources. The case of Betty in chapter 29 involves a family at an early stage of dealing with the complex needs of their 6-year-old child with profound developmental disabilities. Much of the focus of the social worker is on helping the parents to deal with the complex needs of their child, to divide tasks, to reframe their pictures of Betty and of themselves, and to support each other in the process. At the same time, the social worker is working with United Cerebral Palsy, a physician, a respite care provider, and eventually a group of parents of such children. The worker is working between the parents, as they begin to see and care for Betty in a different way, and the agencies as together they assist the parents to do this.

The following cases illustrate work with the family and agency systems of a 10-year-old boy in school and two young adults in transition out of school.

> Danny is a 10-year-old African American boy with pervasive developmental disorder. In class he is disruptive, shows poor attention to tasks, even with assistance, has very poor academic performance, is aggressive with other children, and tends to isolate himself from them. They are afraid of him. Having come recently from living in Germany, his father in military service, he speaks a mixture of English and German, which isn't easily understood by others. According to his paternal grandmother, with whom he lives, he had been developing

reasonably well in early childhood and walked and talked normally. Both parents have a history of severe drug and alcohol abuse. When he went to Germany, he experienced severe physical abuse by his mother, neglect by his father, and was heavily involved in the military social service program for children. His mother is in a residential substance abuse program. His father is still in the army. Danny is being raised by his grandmother. She has given up her twenty-year business to take care of him. The following agencies are involved with the case: the state child protection agency, the state Department of Mental Health, Adair School, a Big Brother program, and a homemaker services agency. In addition, Danny received karate lessons from a community volunteer, has in-home therapy from a contract therapist trained in pervasive developmental disorders, and is tutored twice a week.

The state child protection agency sponsors the wrap team through the school and pays for the services provided through its local area network services program. Danny's grandmother is overwhelmed with all the services involved. The placement needs to be stabilized, particularly if the mother returns. There are differences of opinion within the team about whether Danny should remain in this placement or be hospitalized. The main goal at the moment is that Danny maintains himself at school and that the home continues to provide appropriate parenting, belonging, and security for him. This is beginning to happen although the situation both at home and at school is very delicate. The team meets monthly, including the grandmother, to discuss and work out issues.

The following two cases involve the transition out of school of young adults with severe disabilities:

Doris is an 18-year-old adolescent with severe psychological disturbance. Her reactivity to a symbiotic conflict with her mother and resultant self-destructive behavior has led to several hospitalizations. Whenever there is a possible separation from her mother, she shows increased disturbance. The school had found itself reacting to the behavior, and programming for Doris alone, rather than getting the mother and daughter into contact with help. Mother and daughter have now begun with a social worker in private practice. The school will now bring Doris into a daily one-hour class in ceramics with only the instructor present. If this can be established without incident, Doris will be involved with a petting zoo run by another agency. Because the situation between mother and daughter is potentially explosive, a shelter arrangement with a relative to be used in a crisis will be worked out. This would keep Doris in the community as long as possible. If the social worker is able to make further gains with the mother and Doris's school adjustment stabilizes, the next step is to develop a program with the Illinois Department of Vocational Rehabilitation. The state agency is involved in the plan and will give special consideration to Doris's needs.

Michael is a 21-year-old severe and barely stabilized diabetic, legally blind, who lives in a nursing home because his single, working parent was unable to care for him. He is about to graduate from his special education program because of his age. A plan is developed in the wrap team to make it possible for him to

> return home through utilization of public assistance, Medicaid, and homemaker and home health care services. Some further medical assessment is planned, and based on this assessment, some vocational assessment would be done. The social worker from the school will work with Michael and his mother, coordinating with other agencies, with the goal of passing on case management responsibilities to another agency when the two have solidified their own direction and connections with other services.

Although such cases present complex, chronic needs and will take work over a span of years, they are not particularly unusual. A combination of resources could prevent institutionalization or make movement from an institutionalized setting possible. Furthermore, none of the "hard" service provision, no matter how flexible, could have been effective or even possible without the "soft" services to parent and child that helped them deal with the situation and link their processes and needs with programs and resources. To make complex plans for families without their choice, involvement, and participation, indeed not to make the individual-in-family-unit the center of the decision process, is to court disaster and set up an unproductive struggle around power and control. And so, in addition to highly skilled family-oriented work, the social worker inevitably becomes an active member of the transagency team, a colleague, and a consultant.

SOCIAL WORKERS AS RESOURCE DEVELOPERS

Whatever the future holds for new school-based services, it certainly will continue to call for the many traditional resource development activities that social workers have conducted. School social workers will continue to serve as facilitators of school-community relations. Such activities will remain as varied as organizing services around particular children, building collaborations with agencies in the school, and monitoring the quality of service. Remedial, crisis-oriented, and preventive methods will endure as well. Moreover, negotiating, facilitating, drafting, and brokering interagency agreements will remain a resource-development task of the school social worker. Fashioning such agreements will at times take place through the function of case management, at other times through participation as a member of an interagency team.

The expanded family-support and empowerment programs that are growing in schools also create different possible scenarios for the resource-development activities of school social workers. At a minimum, one might imagine school social workers conducting case management with some of the families present in the school in the family resource center. More broadly, one might envisage school social workers helping families form their own empowering associations, which could be either school-based or school-linked. Family empowerment associations will enable families to deliver more support to one another, exercise stronger roles as co-teachers through tutoring and mentoring, and exercise more influence over school governance. In short, many experiments with family-based institutions in schools will take place. Some school social workers will likely lead in their design and formation.

From Louise Montgomery on, school social workers have had a long history of involvement with the community, developing community resources and doing a type of community organization work with education at the forefront of community activity and the school as a type of community center. Newer models of responsive, family centered, school community services reinforce this. They carry forward traditional social work practices in schools into newer institutional and community-building initiatives.

References

Anderson-Butcher, D., & Ashton, D. (2004). Innovative models of collaboration to serve children, youths, families and communities. *Children & Schools, 26*(1), 39–53.

Anderson-Butcher, D., Stetler, E. G., & Midle, T. (2006). A case for extended partnerships in support of positive youth development. *Children & Schools, 28*(3), 155–163.

Compher, J. V. (1984). The case conference revisited: A systems view. *Child Welfare, 63*(5), 411–418.

Dupper, D., & Poertner, J. (1997). Public schools and the revitalization of impoverished communities: School-linked, family resource centers. *Social Work, 42,* 415–422.

Eber, L., Nelson, M. C., & Miles, P. (1997). School-based wraparound for students with emotional and behavioral challenges. *Exceptional Children, 63*(4), 539–555.

Family Support America. (2004). *Are schools ready for families: Case studies in school-family relationships*. Chicago, IL: Author.

Frankel, A., & Gelman, S. R. (1998). *Case management*. Chicago: Lyceum.

Garland, C., Woodruff, G., & Buck, D. (1988). *Case management. Division for Early Childhood white paper*. Reston, VA: Council for Exceptional Children.

LaCour, J. A. (1982). Interagency agreement: A rational response to an irrational system. *Exceptional Children, 49*(3), 265–267.

Weist, M. D., Ambrose, M. G., & Lewis, C. P. (2006). Expanded school mental health: A collaborative community-school example. *Children & Schools, 28*(1), 45–50.

31

Working with Groups in Schools: Planning for and Working with Group Process

Joan Letendre
University of Connecticut

- Evidence Based Practice and Group Work
- Planning the Group: A Group for Shy Children
- Stages of Group Process: Seventh-Grade Girls Group
- Group Facilitation: From Beginning Stage to Work Stage to Ending

This chapter focuses on principles of social work groups in schools, with special emphasis on the stages of that work starting with the planning stage, continuing through the initial engagement stage, the work stage, and then the ending stage. Examples of groups illustrating processes of planning and facilitation are provided. In one example, the social worker plans to develop a group for socially shy third and fourth graders. In another example, the school social worker facilitates the group work, through the initial engagement, work stage, and ending stage, of a group of seventh grade girls, who have had disciplinary referrals for fighting.

Group work historically has been and continues to be a method used by school social workers. An early study conducted in a school district in the Midwest (1949–1951) found that boys who had problems getting along with peers gradually gained skills in social relationships through small club groups, where a skilled group worker facilitated interactions through the use of age-appropriate activities, games, and discussions. In 1959, the practice committee of the School Social Work Section of the National Association of Social Workers (NASW) surveyed its members to determine the use of group-work practice in schools. Caseworkers reported: 1) a lack of education and training in leading groups, 2) requests from school staff for group services for children, and 3) an interest in a role combining group-work and case-work services that might provide help for children experiencing problems in the school environment (Johnson, 1962).

Besides the obvious benefit to busy school social workers of serving numerous children simultaneously, the group offers a real-life experience, where children are guided and reinforced for offering mutual aid and support to their peers. It provides opportunities to experience positive peer reinforcement and camaraderie as well as to engage in mutual sharing and problem solving that modifies beliefs and behaviors toward children of different statuses (Bierman, 1986; Bierman & Furman, 1984; Rose & Edleson, 1987). A lonely child, unskilled in friendship, can practice social skills through the use of fun activities with same-age children in a safe and structured environment. A pre-adolescent child experiencing a difficult family situation such as divorce, incarceration, illness, or death of a family member can hear the experiences of peers and realize that he/she is not alone. An adolescent girl struggling with anger can be a member of an all-girl group where she can practice effective skills to calm angry thoughts, and where she can develop more adaptive ways of coping with situations that generate strong emotional reactions.

EVIDENCE-BASED PRACTICE AND GROUP WORK

The populations served and the problems addressed by school social workers in groups are many and varied, each with its own emerging best-practices literature. Pawlak, Wozniak & McGowan (2006) report school social workers facilitating groups to address a wide variety of issues including substance abuse, ADHD, race and culture, socialization and peer interaction skills, adolescent parenting, trauma, drop out prevention and grief and loss. Parents were also served in support and educational groups. A study by Garrett (2004) reporting on the findings of a survey of the members of the School Social Work Association of America (SSWAA) found that groups were used to serve multiple needs of children and adolescents. The majority of groups (87 percent) taught social skills. Fifty-nine percent focused on peer difficulties, including bullying or aggression. Groups focused on a variety of social-emotional and behavioral issues affecting self-esteem, emotional regulation, and self-management of behaviors. Other groups addressed grief and loss. Some groups involved pupils with specific diagnoses such as ADHD, anxiety disorder, substance abuse, and eating disorders. Family changes, such as divorce or remarriage, were addressed somewhat more often in elementary schools.

In an evidence-based world, the school social worker needs knowledge of best practices. There is knowledge, specific to the issues, that guides the content of sessions with various populations (age, ethnicity, gender, sexual orientation) and problems, such as shyness, anger control, or grief and loss. The field of social work has a broad foundation of knowledge regarding group process and group work methodology that guides a group through the stages of its development. An intersection of knowledge of problems, populations, process, and methodology comprises the knowledge base available to practitioners (Kurland & Salmon, 1998; Northen & Kurland, 2001; Toseland & Rivas 2005). The effective group practitioner must integrate this evidence base related to specific problem areas with a general understanding of group processes and interventions.

Group methodologies that focus on specific skill-set development and use empirically tested curricular models to help children model and practice new ways of thinking and behaving have become popular (LeCroy, 2006). Behavioral changes learned in the group can be readily observed, measured, and documented. However, when such groups are led by social workers who know little about the dynamics of groups, the focus can simply rest on didactic learning with no attention given to the process elements that connect the members. When the social worker integrates the process of the group with the behavioral changes being taught, the children simultaneously learn how to interact positively with the other children and become a part of the process of helping each other (Letendre & Davis, 2004). Such informed facilitation insures that school social workers understand the current knowledge base for working with specific social-emotional problems as well as understanding the group factors that contribute to helping members feel comfortable sharing concerns, offering mutual aid, and practicing different ways of thinking and behaving.

PLANNING THE GROUP: A GROUP FOR SHY CHILDREN

Planning is necessary to anticipate what may follow as the group gets underway. Careful attention to the planning stage is an often-overlooked aspect of group work in schools. All too often groups are haphazardly developed with no attention to the elements affecting group functioning. Lack of prior planning, sometimes fostered by the pressure that school social workers feel to provide services to troubled children quickly, can create barriers to the ongoing work of a group (Letendre, 2007a). A systematic planning process (Northen & Kurland, 2001) prepares the worker and members for the group. This planning process should include: 1) recognition of the need for the group, 2) development of a clear purpose, 3) attention to structure, 4) careful consideration of group composition, 5) development of content that is focused specifically on the best practices for the needs of the group members, and 6) inviting each member for a pre-group contact. Throughout this section of the chapter, the example of a group for shy children of elementary school age will be used to illustrate the planning process.

Need

The first element to which school social workers must attend is *need*. A need for a group can be identified by the various stakeholders (students, teachers, support staff, parents, and administrators) who raise concerns about a specific problem that is surfacing or populations of children who need a service. In our example, several teachers at an elementary school asked the school social worker to facilitate a group for children who are shy and apparently friendless. Some of the children are known to the school social worker as she has had individual sessions with two of them who had been refusing to go to the cafeteria for lunch with the other children. The parents of the students are in support of the group because they recognize their children's anxiety about social relationships.

Agency Contact: The Group Within the School

The structure of the group is often determined by the specifics of its setting. With the growing emphasis on academic proficiency and accountability, teachers are increasingly less willing to release their students for support services such as social work groups. It becomes an essential part of the planning process to include teachers as stakeholders and to help them to understand how such a group can aid its members with social-emotional problems that interfere with their success in school. Effective work with shy children includes components of: 1) modeling, 2) coaching in conversational skills, 3) peer-mediated interventions, and 4) group contingencies (Gresham & Evans, 1987). Some of these interventions are classroom based, such as peer tutoring, peer pairing, highlighting accomplishments, and giving low-risk tasks that promote conversation. For these, teacher involvement is key (Brophy, 1996). If teachers can see the relationship between a group-work intervention for shy children and the child's ability to attend school and interact more easily with peers, they may be more likely to support attendance at the group sessions (Pawlak et al., 2006). When teachers and school social workers support the same purposes for the group, the recruitment and ongoing implementation of the group is facilitated (Letendre, 2007a; Malekoff, 2004; Toseland & Rivas, 2005).

Purpose

Once the need for the group has been established, defining a clear purpose helps to inform members about its focus, and directs the work of the sessions. Developing a clear and convincing rationale guides the purpose of the group (Corey & Corey, 2006). The social worker can ask the questions: Why is the group being established? What does the social worker hope to accomplish? The purpose of the group is a clear and concise statement that informs the members and referral sources of the reason that the group is being formed, for example, "The *purpose of the group for shy children is to provide a place to learn how to talk to and play with other children.*" When the group purpose is defined, the worker is better able to develop clear objectives that are specific, measurable, and attainable within a specified period of time (Corey & Corey, 2006). The objectives for the group in our example are to teach children the specific conversational skills of initiating conversation, asking questions of peers, and developing the ability to take the lead in conversations. Additionally, the school social worker plans to assess how the child interacts in the larger social context (i.e., classroom, playground, home, community activities) to promote group content that may teach the child skills to be generalized to these settings. Skill development is assessed weekly in and out of the group, so that objectives can be modified to include more complicated development of skills.

Composition: Group Membership

The composition of the group refers to number and characteristics of the worker and the group members (Northen & Kurland, 2001). The social worker in our example decides to include a teacher in some of the groups to support generalization of the new behaviors to the classroom setting. Cofacilitation of groups offers additional input on group dynamics and support in working with the group members (Corey & Corey, 2006). This can be especially helpful if the group of children is lively and if numerous interactions are occurring throughout the group. Recognizing that the number and characteristics of group members affect how much time each member will have to take part in the group learning, the worker decides that the group will be composed of five shy children and two peer mentors.

In our example of a group for shy children, combining children from grades three and four enhances the heterogeneity of skills and age level and responds to the referrals by the third- and fourth-grade teachers. Differences in membership characteristics of group members provide opportunities to learn different perspectives and ways of interacting (Toseland & Rivas, 2005). In our example, the school social worker also would include two peer mentors of the same age. These would be chosen by teacher ratings that reported strong social skills and helpful relationships with classmates. Such peer mentors could model peer socialization skills and promote acceptance in social situations outside of the group (Bierman, 1986; Bierman & Furman, 1984; Brophy, 1996).

Structure of the Group

The structure of the group refers to the concrete arrangements that will define the group (Kurland & Salmon, 1998), including when, where, the number of sessions, duration of each session, and whether the group will be closed or open to new members. Coordination of the structure of the group is complicated, particularly when group members are being recruited from different classrooms. Teacher schedules, purpose of the group, and characteristics of members influence the structure of the group. Consultation with teachers can facilitate developing structure for groups since, with the pressure to focus on academic subjects based on No Child Left Behind (Executive Summary, N.D.), teachers may be reluctant to allow students to leave the classroom during certain academic subjects. The number of sessions, as well the amount of time in each session are influenced by teacher and school schedules necessitating flexibility from the school social worker.

In our example, the plan is to close the group to new members for the ten-session curriculum, allowing the children to become comfortable with one another and adept in progressive social skill development (otherwise the social worker can be blindsided by late requests to join an already composed group). Depending on teacher schedule (with children coming from two classrooms), it may be preferable to conduct two, thirty-minute sessions per week for five weeks rather than one sixty-minute session per week. Such exposure increases the comfort of group members and the learning of new skills and may be easier for teachers to accommodate. In our example, the worker alternates group sessions between an early-morning group, that accommodates the needs of two of the children who have frequent absences triggered by fear of coming to school, and a lunchtime group, that allows the group members opportunities to practice social interactions on the playground with the help of their peer mentors.

Content of the Sessions: What Will Be Done to Achieve Goals?

Birnbaum & Cicchetti (2000) suggest that each session have a defined structure with flexibility to change as the sessions demand. The worker examines several skill-building curricula, because development of specific skill sets is essential in improving the interactional skills of shy, somewhat fearful children. The curricular models provide the worker with current evidence based practices for socio-emotional and behavioral change, specifying the content to be delivered over a set number of sessions and ensuring that the designated skills are being delivered across settings and practitioners (Galinsky, Terzian, & Fraser, 2006). Bierman and Furman (1984) recommend focusing on three conversational skills with shy and withdrawn children: 1) sharing information about self; 2) asking others about themselves; and 3) giving help, suggestions, invitations and advice. Keeping in mind that generalization of social skills to settings outside of the group is essential if the children are to master the skills and have opportunities to interact with peers (Frey & George-Nichols, 2003), the social worker chooses as a "program" a school-wide poster project related to kindness. This would be a theme for conversational practice in the group. The theme was also chosen because the teachers have noted that two of the shy children are quite "talented artistically."

Skills would be learned through pairing with a socially skilled peer, who would attempt to model each skill and role-play situations in which the skill could be used. Each exercise is directed by the group facilitator with ample opportunities for both child and mentor to be rewarded with praise or concrete rewards, as positive reinforcements are important for behavioral change (Frey & George-Nichols, 2003; Mattaini, 2001). In our example, the mentor might initially demonstrate beginning a conversation about a poster contest with one of the shy children. The shy child then would be coached in initiating a similar conversation with the mentor. Finally, the child would be coached to have conversations about the poster project (with the support of the peer mentor) with other children in the classroom and on the playground.

Evaluation

Assessment and evaluation of both individuals and group interactions are an ongoing part of the group experience. The social worker assesses each individual's conversational skills of sharing information about self; asking questions of others and giving help, suggestions, and advice to others before the group begins. Specific development of each skill may be evaluated after each training session with a simple check list: (See below).

Weekly Evaluation of Conversational Skill Development

Has the child:

Initiated conversation about the art project with the peer buddy?
Asked the peer buddy questions about his/her art project?
Asked another group member questions about his/her art project?
Offered ideas or help to the peer buddy about his/her art project?
Offered ideas or help to another group member about his/her art project?

By evaluating the skill development after each session, the social worker determines the acquisition of skills, and also defines the specific behaviors that must continue to be practiced and reinforced. In the following chapter, there are a number of such examples of evaluation of groups in schools. The social worker also evaluates whether the children are interacting more easily and comfortably in the group as they learn the various conversational skills. Teacher evaluation of the child's acquisition of skills is also measured with a similar simple checklist that monitors how children interact in the classroom and on the playground. It is important for the social worker to keep the teacher apprised of the various practiced skills to support reinforcement in the classroom. For instance, the social worker could report that the children are discussing a poster contest with the theme of kindness and suggest that the teacher could arrange for the shy child to talk about it in a small group of supportive peers (with the help of the peer mentor).

Pre-Group Contact: Mutual Conversation—Getting to Know Each Other

An important step in recruiting members to the group is the pre-group interview that allows prospective group members to more fully understand the purpose of the group, to ask clarifying questions, and to form an initial bond with the leaders. This may ease transition to the group (Corey & Corey, 2006). Children who have difficulty making friends because of their shyness and lack of social skills may experience considerable trepidation at the idea of joining a group of peers. As the school social worker presents the group as a way for them to have fun, learn how to make friends, and work with other students on a project that they enjoy, anxiety may be decreased. Concrete examples can be used to suggest specific issues that the children may have concerns about. For instance, some children may feel scared that other children will laugh at them in a group. Children can be invited to participate and, if reluctant, encouraged to "try the group" for several sessions. If they find that they do not like the group, children have the option of dropping out. The pre-group interview also allows the worker to assess the strengths and challenges of each member. It allows prospective members to decide whether they are ready for a group experience at this time as well. An initial screening interview may lead to exclusion of potential members who are not appropriate at this time for the group intervention, such as children who are vehement that they do not want to take part in the group, children with parents opposed to the group, or children who are highly anxious about interacting with more than one peer.

STAGES OF GROUP PROCESS: SEVENTH-GRADE GIRLS GROUP

After careful planning and recruitment of members for the group, the worker's next task is to understand the needs of individual members and the group process as the group progresses through beginning, work stage, and ending stages. The role of the school social worker is to lead the group in such a way that positive group experiences for members are maximized. The social worker facilitating the group must have a clear understanding of the purpose of the group and be ready to help members become comfortable sharing concerns and changing behaviors that interfere with optimal social interactions. In order to do this, school social workers must be knowledgeable about group-work principles and must develop awareness of the skills used to further positive group movement at various stages of group development.

The school social worker must be a keen observer of interactions between group members and must actively intervene in encouraging members to focus on both the session theme and their relationships with each other within the group. Each group, whether it be a structured, time-limited, curricular-based group with the same core group of members meeting for several weeks, or an open-ended support group that invites members for support for a common issue, goes through predictable stages that mirror the members' comfort levels in working on specific themes. When the worker is aware of the meaning of various behaviors at each stage of group development, he or she will be more able to support group members in positive interactions with peers, encouragement of mutual aid, and learning new behaviors that will lead to more satisfying interactions in the world.

The following is an example of how the worker intervenes in processes and helps the members to engage productively in different stages of the group's development. The group involves seventh-grade girls referred to the assistant principal for fighting.

Principal's Request

The principal of an urban middle school has asked the social worker to convene a group for seventh-grade girls who have had disciplinary actions for fighting with classmates. Some girls have had only verbal battles where staff has intervened to de-escalate the conflict, while others have had physical altercations that resulted in suspension from a school that has a zero-tolerance rule for fighting. The principal believes that this group of girls needs additional intensive intervention to learn new ways of managing conflict and has requested that the school social worker develop a group for six to eight girls identified as having fighting behaviors.

Evidence-Based Practice for Group Work with Girls Who Are Aggressive

The increase in violent behavior among children and adolescents has promoted development of a knowledge base that informs mental health practitioners about the multiple contexts for learning of aggressive behaviors and the best practices for intervening in each context. Peer group, school, and family have been identified as contexts where children and adolescents learn and are reinforced for aggressive behaviors. Gender-specific methods for working with girls have fine-tuned the interventions that respond to the unique needs that girls have for methods that take into account female socialization and its influence on the ways that girls have learned to express anger, solve conflict, and protect themselves from physical and sexual victimization (Baer, 1999; Crick & Grotpeter, 1995; Letendre, 2007b). Group interventions are an ideal method of working with young adolescent girls because of the importance of relationships and connectedness to others in the lives of females (Walsh-Burke & Scanlon, 2000). Garrett (2004) reported that the majority of school social workers who completed the SSWAA survey used cognitive-behavioral curricula as resources in their groups (with modifications for their population of children). The challenge of using the cognitive-behavioral curricular model chosen by the school social worker is that of also allowing time to attend to the interactions between members. In this case, an all-female skill-building group can teach the girls ways to calm hurt and angry feelings by using self-talk that promotes problem-solving methods, cognitive changes, and nonaggressive actions. Helping the girls to practice the skills in the group as situations arise will further enhance the skills. Including teachers and parents in the learning of the skills can ensure generalization and reinforcement in the classroom and family.

The Plan

In pre-group interviews and beginning sessions it is important to carefully assess the specific strengths and challenges that each girl brings to the group (Toseland & Rivas, 2005). An individual assessment will enable the school social worker to understand how the girl's strengths and challenges will impact the group process. The release from specific classes for an eight-week group needs to be supported by teachers who see the behavior of the girls as detrimental to individual and class learning. The groups would last 60 minutes during lunch and the next academic class period. Skill building with an empirically tested curriculum will be combined with ample opportunities to modify the generic curriculum to the needs of this group of urban girls, with integration of cultural components throughout the session (Letendre, 2007a; Peeks, 1999; Scott, 2002;). The social worker recruits two eighth grade girls, recommended by teachers and peers for their ability to interact positively with peers and model pro-social ways of behaving, to be mentors. Bi-weekly contact with families is maintained to ensure that parents are also participants in the change process.

GROUP FACILITATION: FROM BEGINNING STAGE TO WORK STAGE TO ENDING

Engaging Group Members in the Beginning

When members first come together in a group, they experience typical fears and exhibit predictable behaviors associated with entering new situations (Corey & Corey, 2006; Kurland & Salmon, 1998). Young adolescent girls, who see each other daily in school, may fear appearing foolish, being rejected by peers, having their participation in the group known by other students, being talked about outside of group, and not being competent to perform the tasks of the group. Such fears may be masked by behaviors that interfere with the work of the group, such as monopolizing group time when a topic is raised, giving advice without waiting for discussion of the problem, putting other members down, clowning, refusing to participate, acting superior, socializing with one or two other members, and allying with other group members against the leader (Corey & Corey, 2006). Members who have not voluntarily sought the group but are "sent" to sessions by the principal or urged to attend by a teacher/parent may remain silent, hostile, and withdrawn. The worker's ability to refrain from taking such behaviors personally and to actively provide structure allows the girls to discuss their feelings and to calm their fears.

In the beginning stage of the group the emphasis is on: 1) helping members to get to know one another, 2) connecting the purpose of the group with individual needs, and 3) developing group norms that assure members of a safe experience where positive interactions are reinforced and every voice will be heard. Use of a positive, nonpunitive behavioral system may be helpful to facilitate the work of the group for students with challenging behaviors (Mattaini, 2001; Wodarski, Feldman & Flax, 1973).

The following example illustrates how group members can be engaged in the group process and taught skills of active listening, empathy, and problem solving while setting norms for confidentiality:

> In the first meeting of the group, the social worker introduced the discussion of confidentiality. This is particularly important to encourage open sharing of the many concerns that might lead to destructive behaviors. The worker stated that she has responsibility to protect the girls in the group from harm and therefore would need to intervene if a girl were to say that she or someone else could be hurt. She also said that there are ways other than physical harm by which the members can be hurt in the group. Rather than authoritatively dictating "What is said in the group, stays in the group," the worker modeled active listening when she asked each member how she might feel if her personal story about a friend, boyfriend, or family member was shared with peers outside the group. She repeated each girl's statements as a way of underscoring the hurt, betrayal, and ensuing anger that might result from this breach of confidentiality. Next, the social worker led a discussion on ways to problem-solve and prevent girls from sharing stories outside of the group. What should be the consequences if this should occur?

By bringing the problem into the group and sharing it, the worker provided an opportunity for the girls to listen to each other, to develop empathy for their peers, and to engage in a problem-solving method that encourages brainstorming nonaggressive solutions to a problem. By encouraging active involvement of this group of girls, who are frequently disempowered in the school setting, the worker has demonstrated that their input is a valued part of this group intervention.

Since schools often fail to provide the support and encouragement that aggressive students need to change their behaviors, it is important to avoid allying with the administration as disciplinarians when discussing participation in the group. It is critical to be honest with the girls about why they were chosen and to clarify both the purpose of the group and the specifics of the sessions. Members must be involved in the discussion of how specific skills may apply to situations in their lives. This provides them an opportunity to discuss how the group can be of help to them. This opportunity for the young adolescent girls to be heard and understood by a caring, nonjudgmental adult furthers the work of trust building and connection to the group as a helpful place to meet.

Work Stage: Encouraging Interaction

In the working stage, the school social worker is looking for opportunities to help each girl to try out different roles and ways of thinking and behaving. For many of the girls in the group, who habitually react rather than communicate their needs calmly and assertively, changing roles is difficult. The group offers opportunities for this kind of practice. As the school social worker models new skills (methods of calming down when angry and generating "cool" thoughts) for practice and role-play situation, she is scanning the group to observe how members are reacting to the material and to each other and using group facilitation skills to encourage open communication. Members can be challenged in a caring and respectful way to talk about issues that may be painful and/or difficult. It may be hard for one girl to apologize to another after a put-down, and she may need much support from the group for gradually being able to do this. Gently encouraging exploration of feelings and actions related to sharing hurtful situations offers opportunities for empathy building and mutual support among the girls. Making observations as "hunches" empowers the girls to either accept or reject interpretations of their actions and behaviors. Demonstrating sensitivity to racial, cultural, and oppressive attitudes can set the tone for girls to express to the group ways that they have felt "put down" because of their skin color or ethnicity (being followed by a clerk in a store, being laughed at for her accent). Encouraging listening and step-by-step problem solving trains members to think before acting. Inviting members to share positive and negative feedback in caring, nonoppressive ways increases their repertoire of skills for showing appreciation and asking for what they need, skills that have been poorly developed and reinforced in this group of girls.

Conflict around Difference

As the girls become more comfortable within the group and begin to share differences, renewed conflict may emerge. When an issue arises in the group related to stereotyping or lack of comfort with differences, the worker invites exploration of the issue. When one member, a new immigrant, is scapegoated by the other members for her "funkiness" (hygiene) and the "dumb" statements that she makes to the members and leaders, the group worker provides guidance in helping the girls talk openly with each other about the specific reasons that the girls are shunning this group member and the normally taboo subject of "hygiene." Throughout the discussion, the worker encourages the girl to express how being shunned makes her feel. This is an opportunity for the worker to reframe existing concerns around female socialization and stereotypical behaviors and roles, an important topic in the curriculum. The worker asked the girls whether any of them had ever experienced not knowing what to do in a situation and having others make fun of them. This discussion helps the girls to be empathic with the plight of the formerly shunned group member. The worker also asks other group members to share with the shunned member some ways she might behave differently that might bring greater approval from her peers. Finally, the worker asks the members if they would like to do anything to help the girl to fit in more easily in this new social setting. Such a discussion, although difficult, teaches the girls to listen to another's point of view, put themselves in her place, and even offer support to someone who is different from themselves. Helping members to talk to each other models ways of interacting that are more adaptive and less destructive than the girls have previously learned. This is quite a different scenario than one that might have occurred before the girls entered the group, and the leader commends them for the way they have handled the situation.

Ending the Group with Good-byes, Gains, and Next Steps

The ending of the group involves sharing feelings about leaving the group, saying good-byes, celebrating gains, and planning for using the newly learned skills and behaviors outside the group. The most important part of ending is that the *group members* need to be helped to wrap up the group. For this group of girls, many of whom have not had satisfying relationships with other girls, the ending of a group experience that was fun and where they felt accepted and valued can be difficult, and the worker must help members to discuss their feelings of loss as well as the gains that they have made while in the group. Revisiting the initial purpose of the group as well as the goals that each girl set for herself can help to consolidate the gains. Knowing from the principal, teachers, and parents about changes that they have observed outside of the group can also reinforce the successes that the girls have achieved. The group also discusses plans for continuing to use their newly acquired skills, challenges that might interfere with their successes, and plans for possibilities for periodic booster groups. A celebration with food chosen by the girls and certificates of achievement that are individualized for each member end the group.

School social workers have long known that group work is a powerful method for helping children to solve problems and learn to interact with peers in ways that promote positive social and emotional growth. In recent years, the importance of including evidence based practice in work with groups has fostered the inclusion of best-practice methods in group sessions. Many group methods have specific skill sets that have shown efficacy with certain populations and problems. School social workers must attend to the specific content of the sessions as well as to planning and facilitation if the group interventions are to be effective. As school social workers continue to become trained and educated in group work models of practice as well as best practices for different populations, problems, and stages of group development, they can continue to provide the group-work services that children and adolescents need for skill development, belonging, mutual support and problem solving. The next chapter builds further on this model to focus on monitoring of group processes and outcomes.

References

Baer, J. (1999). Adolescent development and the junior high environment. *Social Work in Education, 4*(21), 238–248.

Bierman, K. L. (1986). Process of change during social skills training with preadolescents and its relation to treatment outcome. *Child Development, 57*, 230–240.

Bierman, K. L., & Furman, W. (1984). The effects of social skills training and peer involvement on the social adjustment of preadolescents. *Child Development, 55*, 151–162.

Bierman, K. L., Miller, C. L., & Stabb, S. D. (1987). Imposing the social behavior and peer acceptance of rejected boys: Effects of social skills, training with instructions and prohibitions. *Journal of Consulting and Clinical Psychology, 55*(2), 194–200.

Birnbaum, M., & Cicchetti, A. (2000). The power of purposeful endings in each group encounter. *Social Work with Groups, 23*(3), 37–52.

Brophy, J. (1996). *Working with shy or withdrawn students* (Report No.EDO-PS-96-14). Washington DC: Office of Educational Research and Improvement (ED). (ERIC Document Reproduction Service No. ED402070 1996-11-00.

Corey, M. S., & Corey, G. (2006). *Groups: process and practice* (7th edition). Belmont, CA: Thomson/Brooks Cole.

Crick, N. R., & Grotpeter, J. K. (1995). Relational aggression, gender, and social-psychological adjustment. *Child Development, 66*, 710–722.

Frey, A., & George-Nichols, N. (2003). Intervention practices for students with emotional and behavioral disorders: Using research to inform social work practice. *Children & Schools, 25*(2), 97–103.

Galinsky, M., Terzian, M. A., & Fraser, M. W. (2006). The art of group work practice with manualized groups. *Social Work with Groups, 29*(1), 11–26.

Garrett, K. J. (2004). Use of groups in school social work and group processes. *Social Work with Groups, 27*(2–3), 75–92.

Gresham, F. M., & Evans, S. E. (1987). Conceptualization and treatment of social withdrawal in the schools. *Special Services in Schools, 3*(3–4), 37–51.

Johnson, A. (1962). *School social work: Its contribution to professional education.* New York: National Association of Social Workers.

Kurland, R., & Salmon, R. (1998). *Teaching a methods course in social work with groups.* Alexandria, VA: Council on Social Work Education.

LeCroy, C. W. (2006). Social skills training in school settings: Some practical considerations. In R. Constable, C. R. Massat, S. McDonald, & J. P. Flynn (Eds.), *School social work: Practice, policy and research* (pp. 598–617). Chicago: Lyceum Press.

Letendre, J. (2007a). "Take Your Time and Give It More": Supports and Constraints to Success in Curricular School Based Groups. *Social Work with Groups, 30*(3), 65–84).

Letendre, J. (2007b). Sugar and spice but not always nice: Gender socialization and its impact on development of aggression in adolescent girls. *Child and Adolescent Social Work Journal.* (on-line version)

Letendre, J. A., & Davis, K. (2004). What really happens in violence prevention groups? A content analysis of facilitator behaviors and child responses in a school-based violence prevention project. *Small Group Research, 35*(4), 367–387.

Malekoff, A. (2004). *Group work with adolescents: Principles and practice* (2nd edition). New York: Guilford Press.

Mattaini, M. (2001). *PEACEPOWER for adolescents: Strategies for a culture of non-violence.* Washington, DC: NASW Press.

Moote, G. T., Smythe, N. J., & Wodarski, J. S. (1999). Social skills training with youth in school settings: A review. *Research on Social Work Practice, 9*(4), 427–465.

Northen, H., & Kurland, R. (2001). *Social Work with Groups,* 3rd edition. NY: Columbia University Press.

Pawlak, E., Wozniak, D., & McGowan, M. (2006). Perspectives on groups for school social workers. In R. Constable, C. R. Massat, S. McDonald and J. P. Flynn (Eds.), *School social work: Practice, policy and research* (pp. 598–617). Chicago: Lyceum Press.

Peeks, A. L. (1999). Conducting a social skills group with Latina adolescents. *Journal of Child and Adolescent Group Therapy, 9*(3), 139–153.

Rose, S. D., & Edleson, J. L. (1987). *Working with children and adolescents in groups.* San Francisco: Jossey-Bass Publishers.

Scott, C. C. (2002). The sisterhood group: A culturally focused empowerment group model for inner city African-American youth. *Journal of Child and Adolescent Group Therapy, 11*(2–3), 77–85.

Toseland, R. W., & Rivas, R. F. (2005). *An introduction to group work practice* (5th edition). Boston, MA: Allyn & Bacon.

Walsh-Burke, K., & Scanlon, P. (2000). Beyond reviving Ophelia: Groups for girls 12–14 and women who care about them. *Social Work with Groups, 23*(1), 71–81.

Wodarski, J. S., Feldman, R. A., & Flax, N. (1973). Social learning theory and group work practice with antisocial children. *Clinical Social Work Journal, 1*, 78–93.

32

Working with Groups in Schools: Monitoring of Process and Evaluation of Outcomes

Kendra J. Garrett

The College of St. Catherine and the University of St. Thomas

- Evidence-Based Practice with Groups
- Monitoring Individual and Group Goals
- Monitoring Group Process
- Methods for Monitoring Groups

This chapter describes principles of evidence-based practice (EBP) with groups and monitoring of individual and group goals. Evidence-based practice mandates that social workers use methods shown empirically to be effective, to think critically in making practice decisions, and to monitor interventions to be certain that they are being implemented as intended and are effective (Howard, McMillen, & Pollio, 2003; Roberts & Yeager, 2004). School social workers are increasingly asked to show that their practice is effective. While the No Child Left Behind Act (NCLB) (2002) created a mandate that practice methods be scientifically based and have positive and demonstrable results (Raines, 2004), the push for monitoring outcomes is nothing new to social workers. The National Association of Social Workers (NASW) *Code of Ethics* (1999) and *Standards for School Social Workers* (2002) call for school social workers to use proven interventions and to monitor practice outcomes.

EVIDENCE-BASED PRACTICE WITH GROUPS

School social workers using group methods need to be aware of intervention methods backed by convincing evidence and must know how to find answers to new questions. This challenges school social workers to stay abreast of a rapidly changing knowledge base. Fortunately, there are excellent resources available for this search, many of which are listed in chapters 3 and 25.

The second tenet of evidence-based practice with groups is that social workers must use critical thinking regarding existing research. The school social worker must critically evaluate the research to determine if it is of high quality, and if it is applicable to clients and their specific needs (Raines, 2004). Evidence-based practice involves adapting programs as needed to meet the unique needs of clients (Raines, 2004).

We know that school social workers do adapt programs with some regularity. Garrett (2004) found that school social workers freely change manual-based group-work curricula to meet needs of students in their groups and to fit with stages of group development. When an evidence-based program is altered, however, even for such a desirable reason as to fit with client needs, it must be noted that the program no longer is, strictly speaking, research based. Therefore such changes must be made with caution and be strictly monitored.

This leads to the third tenet of evidence-based practice. In addition to using methods known to be effective and applying them judiciously, school social workers must monitor their own practice outcomes to determine if the work they are doing is helpful in meeting client needs. Such evaluation is more challenging to school social workers who conduct small counseling groups than it is for monitoring individual interventions. Toseland and Rivas (2005) suggest that both outcomes and dynamics should be monitored, and that monitoring and evaluation should be an ongoing process that occurs over the lifespan of a group. Such monitoring with groups is further complicated by the need to monitor the experiences of each individual member as well as the group as a whole.

MONITORING INDIVIDUAL AND GROUP GOALS

The purpose and goals of a group need to be congruent with what members hope to accomplish, and group members need to understand them (Toseland & Rivas, 2005). Sometimes younger students may need to discuss goals in concrete terms before they can set goals for themselves in the group (Rose & Edleson, 1987). Goals for students in social work counseling groups need to be congruent with the educational purposes of the school (Dane & Simon, 1991), and group members need to be able to articulate, to the extent they are able, the purposes of the group in which they are participating as well as what they will accomplish as part of that group.

Goal setting in groups may be complicated by the fact that goals may be either group goals, common to everyone in the group, or individualized goals (Toseland & Rivas, 2005). When the entire group is working on a project, understanding the goals should be very clear to the members. For example, students who are working on a leadership project in a character-education group by gathering books for Africa need to understand that they are learning to be good citizens. Group goals are often quite easy to evaluate, as the project, when accomplished, defines the successful outcome of the group. When all members of a group are working on similar goals (e.g., increasing their self-esteem, managing their anger, coping with a death in the family, learning parenting skills, or leaving abusive relationships), goals can be discussed together, and measurements can be the same for all students in the group. Goal monitoring is most complicated when each member has a different goal. For example, a group might be working on increasing social skills, but each member might have different skills he or she is hoping to gain. One student might be working to be more assertive, another may be working to become more tolerant, and others may be working on impulse control, verbalizing anger, and so on. In a situation such as this, each student's goals would need unique measurement strategies, and the group would also need frequent reminders of the various member goals so that they can give each other support and help. In this complicated example, the group might want to be particularly tolerant of an angry statement from the student wanting to become more assertive, while giving another student, whose goal is anger management, gentle feedback to be more patient. Setting the stage in a group with a number of individual goals requires social workers to have good organization and communication skills. They need to see the relationship between group goals, group processes, and individual goals.

Good goals are measurable, attainable, and specific (Raines, 2002; Toseland & Rivas, 2005). Making goals measurable requires the school social worker and group members to articulate what they are hoping to accomplish together in the group, so they will recognize when they have been successful. In making goals specific, members must be able to understand how their goals will be measured and how they will work to accomplish the goals. Goals need to be attainable, so that members can reasonably hope to accomplish them.

Setting goals with members can have considerable clinical or therapeutic merit, especially for students who have not previously been involved in setting their own goals. Students often gain clearer understanding of why they are participating in the group as they talk about teachers' and parents' concerns (although they usually have some inkling about this already). But they are often surprised to learn that they might have a say in what they are to work on. The process of negotiating a student-stated goal of, say, "getting the teacher off my back" might lead to productive work on the student's behavior. This contracting around goals is extremely important because interventions are more likely to be successful when there is a shared understanding between group members and the social worker about what they were working to accomplish (Toseland & Rivas, 2005). In other words, the group is more likely to be effective when the group leader and the group members are on the same page.

School social workers working with students with individualized educational programs (IEPs) may have an advantage in measuring goals, to the extent goals and objectives are clarified in the IEP. Group goals, however, and the purpose of the group probably will not fit exactly with the IEP. In this situation, and for all other students who do not have IEP goals, the school social worker should help members specify these goals as part of the beginning stage of the group.

Monitoring Outcomes

It is wise to use a variety of strategies to monitor goals (Monette, Sullivan, & DeJong, 2008; Toseland & Rivas, 2005). Quantitative measures require workers to find ways to count or assign numbers to measure goals. Qualitative methods use words, pictures, or descriptions to explain changes in goals. Both can be useful in monitoring the success of group work in schools.

One important caveat in monitoring goals, whether through numbers or with narratives, is that measurements and markers used must be reliable and valid. Reliable measurements are those that are stable (Monette et al., 2008). This means that there is shared understanding among all parties about what the goals are; that they are well defined enough that everyone understands what they mean, and they are consistent from one measurement to the next and from one "observer" to another. Measurements must also be valid, meaning that they must adequately measure what they are intended to measure (Monette et al., 2008). For example, the number of times a student volunteers to help other students in the classroom is not a valid measurement of self-esteem, even though there may be a presumption that students with high self-esteem volunteer more often to help others.

Another consideration in choosing measurements for goals is that the unit of analysis must match the measurement strategy (Monette et al., 2008). For example, if members have individual goals, it would make little sense to measure success by changes made by the group (e.g., group cohesion) or school-wide changes (such as total discipline incidents).

Quantitative Measurement

There are a number of quantitative ways to measure goals for group members. Perhaps the easiest one is to count behaviors that are to be targets for change. Students who have angry outbursts, are sent out of class for discipline purposes, receive detentions, get into fights, disrespect others, or fail to do homework have countable behaviors that can be used as a baseline. These behavioral goals are, perhaps, the easiest kind of goal to identify and monitor. But it is important for the school social worker, group members, teachers, and parents to be clear on what those behaviors mean; part of the goal-setting discussion is to clarify with everyone involved what constitutes the behavior to be counted and who will observe the behavior. If parents define a behavior in one way, the teacher defines it differently, and the students define it in yet another way, the measurement is not clear or specific enough to be an effective marker of a student's behavior change. If, for example, the target behavior is doing homework, the worker and group members (and maybe also the teacher) need to discuss what constitutes homework, what quality of work is acceptable, and whether it is sufficient to do the homework and leave it in the backpack or if the homework must also be turned in on time.

A second way to quantify individual change is through standardized measurements. These measurements are those that have been administered to large numbers of students to determine the range and average scores for students at various ages. Many of these standardized measurements exist and are readily available to school social workers for use with students, although some have restrictions that require coursework in psychometrics for those who administer or score them (Raines, 2003). A complete discussion of these scales is beyond the scope of this chapter, but some commonly known standardized measures are the Multidimensional Self-Concept Scale (Pro Ed, 2007), the Children's Behavior Checklist (Achenbach, 2007), the Beck Youth Inventories (anger, anxiety, depression, behavior, self-concept) (Harcourt Assessment, 2005), and Connors' Rating Scales-Revised (attention deficit disorder) (Multi-Health Systems, Inc., 2006). One advantage of standardized scales is that their reliability and validity are known and clearly discussed in the manuals that accompany the tests. Some have subscales so that school social workers can limit the time needed to administer and score the tests to the specific areas that relate to group goals.

A third quantitative way of measuring goals is through the use of available data. Student records are rich sources of information on group members (Dibble, 1999). Cumulative files contain standardized test scores, attendance information, discipline reports, and grades. Teacher records may be additional sources of such information. For example, a teacher's grade book may have information on homework completion rates and ongoing grades.

The fourth measurement strategy is to find or develop measurement scales. Fischer and Corcoran (2006) have compiled a sourcebook of measurements for children and families that may fit the goals of group members. The Hudson Scales (e.g., parental attitudes, children's attitudes toward parents, peer relations) (Walmyr, 2007) are considered rapid-assessment instruments (RAIs), so named for their ease in administration and scoring (Monette et al., 2008).

If specific measurements are not readily available, it may be necessary to develop questions to assess progress. Group members may be involved in this process, and some wonderful therapeutic work can be done in the process by identifying the work the group will be doing and how the worker and members will know if it is successful. A goal-attainment scale (GAS) (Toseland & Rivas, 2005) is a good example of such an instrument. The school social worker and group members consider what they are trying to accomplish and what markers will tell them when they have reached an acceptable solution. They also consider what markers would be less than acceptable and what would be beyond expectations. A simple GAS would have three levels of markers (although many have five levels, two below and two above the acceptable level). So if a member is working on anger management, the less-than-acceptable level might be to lose his temper daily; the acceptable level might be to lose his temper less than twice each week; and the more-than-acceptable level might be to lose his temper less than once a month.

The school social worker might want to make up a survey to measure a goal and use it as a pretest and then to monitor progress at regular intervals. Such an instrument is probably not as reliable as a standardized instrument, but it might be more personal, and therefore, more accurate for the members in a particular group (so it might be valid in measuring the student's goals). Another strategy is to measure the goal on a scale of 1 (low) to 10 (high). For example, a member whose goal is to manage his anger more effectively could rate his anger management for the past week. When group members have common goals, one instrument could be used consistently by all members of the group.

Another measurement strategy is to use satisfaction reports. Questions about whether or not members are happy with the group can be very helpful. Member satisfaction, while not necessarily linked to goal attainment, can tell the school social worker if groups are meeting member needs and can provide ideas for making changes in the way group services are provided. Satisfaction can be measured by using a survey when the group terminates or by asking students to rate their satisfaction with various aspects of group sessions on a scale of 1 (low) to 10 (high) (Rose, 1998).

Qualitative Methods

While there are a number of quantitative ways to monitor practice, Garrett (2004) found that school social workers in her study tended to focus on qualitative methods of monitoring their group work. In her study, group leaders tracked statements from group members, teachers, and parents regarding improvement in school problems; comments on group process; statements about improved peer relationships; notations about member enjoyment of the group; and improvement in ability to cope with difficult situations. Their narrative group reports included charming anecdotes of the group and quotes from students, parents, and teachers regarding member progress. The direct quotes in these reports added a human dimension to the group results that would not have been as apparent through reporting only numerical results.

MONITORING GROUP PROCESS

While we know that many group interventions are successful, that is to say, they have successful outcomes, we know less about what specifically contributes to this (Corey & Corey, 1997). So in order to monitor groups effectively, school social workers need to assess what is happening within the group as it progresses (Northen & Kurland, 2001; Wayne & Cohen, 2001). We know that groups that function effectively together are better able to accomplish tasks and meet goals. For example, group-centered communication leads to increased commitment to goals and improved morale; and cohesiveness, effective group norms, and positive climate lead to more positive outcomes (Toseland & Rivas, 2005). Macgowen (2000) found that the ability to work with and relate to others was the best predictor of positive outcomes in his stress-reduction groups.

"Knowing what normative behavior is at each stage [of group development] can help a group worker assess whether the group is making progress toward achieving its goals" (Toseland & Rivas, 2005, p. 89). Monitoring the development of group process is important in determining if the group is headed in a positive direction. When a worker gathers data on group dynamics on an ongoing basis, he or she should let members know that the purpose is to share the information gathered with the members and use it to improve functioning of the group (Rose & Tolman, 1989). For example, McCullagh and Koontz (1993) monitored trust, listening, and self-disclosure in groups with special education students. They found that these three dynamics improved as the group progressed.

Any process monitoring needs to be minimally intrusive and time efficient. Rose (1998) suggests using a post-session questionnaire in groups for children and adolescents. Such a questionnaire may be a rating scale that asks members to comment on member perception of the usefulness of the group, their own involvement, the degree of mutual help and self-disclosure, cohesion, on-task behavior, and anxiety. These can be quickly summarized to track member satisfaction as the group progresses. The worker can identify concerns and bring them to the group, which can then problem solve to address them.

METHODS FOR MONITORING GROUPS

School social workers lack time and funding to become researchers, but it is essential for them to find efficient ways to monitor their practice outcomes. Three such methods seem particularly appropriate for monitoring groups in school settings. The first method is the single-system design (SSD) (Monette et al., 2008; Toseland & Rivas, 2005). Following the identification of goals and quantitative measurements for the goals, the worker tracks students' progress on the goals for several measurements, usually over a period of two to three weeks, to determine if the goals are stable before the group begins. Should the goals be improving of their own accord or because of some external interventions (for example, the parents have changed the way they interact with the student at home or a new teacher is praising good behavior), the worker would not be able to identify the group as the source of positive outcomes. If the goals are stable or, sadly, getting worse before the group begins, the worker has greater assurance that gains toward goal improvement are a result of the group rather than some other factor unrelated to the group. This baseline time is a good time for the school social worker to conduct the search for evidence regarding effective interventions for the problems and the goals of the group members (see chapter 25). When the group begins, the worker continues to monitor goals on a regular basis, perhaps by weekly checks on the goals with the member, teachers, or parents. In SSDs, these monitoring efforts are carefully tracked, usually with graphs, so progress (or the lack thereof) can be easily identified and discussed with group members. If members are improving in their goals after the group begins, the worker might assume that the group intervention is the "cause" of the improvement and continue until the goals are reached (or until the predetermined time for the group to end). Should some or all members not be making progress, the worker would need to consider the course of action, perhaps by adjusting the group method and assessing changes that need to be made to help members succeed in reaching their goals. SSDs are particularly useful in school-based groups because of their flexibility. They can be used when members have different goals or when everyone has the same goal. They can also simultaneously monitor group goals (like developing cohesion or accomplishing a group task). SSDs can be simple or complicated, depending on the needs of the group members. Members can have several goals simultaneously (if they are able to conceptualize several goals), can change the criteria for their goals, and can add new goals as they progress. Graphs give school social workers records of progress that can be added to IEP records or used for summary reports.

The second way of monitoring goals is the pre-experimental design (PED) (Monette et al., 2008). Instead of continuous measurement with several baseline measurements, the worker gathers data on goals only once before beginning the group. Then the same measurements are repeated at the end of the group to see if members have made progress on goals. PEDs have the advantage of less record keeping and, therefore, less work. The disadvantage is that the worker cannot be as certain that the group was the cause of positive change (students naturally grow and change over time, and they may have improved of their own accord). And if the students are not improving, the information may not be available until after the group ends.

Like the SSD, PEDs are flexible and can be used for multiple goals and for group goals.

Another way of monitoring process is through records on the progress students are making in the group. The worker can record attendance, make qualitative observations of member behavior, teacher and parent feedback, interactions among members, and narratives of group sessions. Ongoing reflection of group and member progress provide a supplement to any quantitative methods the worker is using and can be used for supervision and consultation regarding the progress of the school social workers' group interventions. MacKenzie (1990) suggests that group records might illustrate major issues for each member, a sociogram of member interaction, major themes, critical incidents, therapist issues, supervision comments, and notes for the next session. Another recording approach is to record groups in a consistent format that includes session number, a seating chart, notes on communication flow, and a brief summary of group content, processes, developmental stage, plans for the future, and a worker reflection on the group (Cohen & Garrett, 1995). These ongoing records should be summarized regularly, perhaps at report-card time and the end of the school year (Raines, 2002).

Monitoring process and outcomes is a professional imperative for school social workers leading small groups. School social workers should define emergent goals with students in those groups, search carefully for research on the most effective ways to meet those goals, evaluate the quality of that research, and make decisions about the use of those interventions. Because each student is unique, both individuals and the group must be monitored to determine the effectiveness of a group. Monitoring *process* requires careful monitoring of implementation to document what was done, and how the intervention was similar to and different from evidence-based interventions that research indicates "should" work. Monitoring *outcomes* of group work requires assessment of achievement of member and group goals. Finally, school social workers must keep adequate records to identify group and member goals, how those goals were monitored, and what the outcomes were. School social workers need this information as they determine what methods to use in future groups and to evaluate where best to devote their all-too-limited time in schools. School administrators need this information as part of their evaluation of social work services. Parents want to know how their children are progressing towards their goals in school-based counseling groups. And student members need feedback as they grow and change.

References

Achenbach, T. (2007). *Achenbach system of empirically based assessment* (ASEBA) retrieved August 9, 2007, from http://www.aseba.org/products/forms.html

Cohen, M. B., & Garrett, K. J. (1995). Helping field instructors become more effective group work educators. *Social Work with Groups, 18*(2–3), 135–146.

Corey, M. S., & Corey, G. (1997). *Groups: Process and practice.* (5th ed.) Pacific Grove: Brooks Cole.

Dane, B., & Simon, B. (1991). Resident guests: Social workers in host settings. *Social Work, 36*(3), 208–213.

Dibble, N. (1999). Outcome evaluation of school social work services. Retrieved August 23, 2004 from www.dpi.state.wi.us/dpi/dlsea/sspw/pdf/outcmeval999.pdf

Fischer, J., & Corcoran, K. (2006). *Measures for clinical practice: A sourcebook.* (4th ed.). New York: Oxford University Press.

Garrett, K. J. (2004). Practice evaluation and social group work in elementary schools. *Journal of Evidence-Based Social Work, 1*(4), 15–32.

Harcourt Assessment. (2005). Beck youth inventories-second edition. Retrieved August 9, 2007 from http://harcourtassessment.com/HAIWEB/Cultures/en-us/Productdetail.htm?Pid=015-8014-197&Mode=summary

Howard, M. O., McMillen, C. J., & Pollio, D. E. (2003). Teaching evidence-based practice: Toward a new paradigm for social work education. *Research on Social Work Practice, 13*(2), 234–259.

Macgowen, M. G. (2000). Evaluation of a measure of group engagement for group work. *Research on Social Work Practice, 10*(3), 348–361.

MacKenzie, K. R. (1990). Introduction to time-limited group psychotherapy, Washington DC: American Psychiatric Press, Inc.

McCullagh, C. E., & Koontz, B. A. (1993). A self-report questionnaire for group work: Monitoring the outcome of group work intervention with special education students. *Iowa Journal of School Social Work, 6*(3), 5–19.

Monette, D. R., Sullivan, T. J., & DeJong, C. R. (2008). *Applied social research: A tool for the human services* (7th ed.) Belmont CA: Thomson Wadsworth.

Multi-Health Systems, Inc. (2006). Connors' Rating Scales-Revised (CRS-R). Retrieved August 9, 2007 from https://www.mhs.com/ecom/(j0ndna453xehkc55sfwscbri)/product.aspx?RptGrpID=CRS

National Association of Social Workers. (1999). *Code of Ethics.* Washington DC: NASW Press.

National Association of Social Workers. (2002). *NASW Standards for School Social Work Services*. Washington D.C.: NASW Press.

No Child Left Behind Act of 2001, Pub. L. No 107-110 § 101, 115 Stat. 1425 (2002).

Northen, H., & Kurland, R. (2001). *Social work with groups* (3rd ed.). New York: Columbia University Press.

Pro Ed (2007). The multidimensional self-concept scale (NSCS). Retrieved August 9, 2007 from http://www.proedinc.com/customer/productView.aspx?ID=685

Raines, J. C. (2002). Present levels of performance, goals, and objectives: A best-practice guide. *School Social Work Journal, 27*(1), 58–72.

Raines. J. C. (2003). Rating the rating scales: Ten criteria to use. *School Social Work Journal, 27*(2), 1–17.

Raines, J. C. (2004). Evidence-based practice in school social work: A process in perspective. *Children & Schools, 26*(2), 71–86.

Roberts, A. R., & Yeager, K. (2004). Systematic reviews of evidence-based studies and practice-based research: How to search for, develop, and use them. In A. R. Roberts & K. R. Yeager (Eds.). *Evidence-based practice manual: Research and outcome measures in health and human service* (pp. 3–14). New York: Oxford University Press.

Rose, S. D. (1998). *Group therapy with troubled youth: A cognitive behavioral interactive approach.* Thousand Oaks CA: Sage.

Rose, S. D., & Edleson, J. L. (1987). *Working with children and adolescents in groups.* San Francisco: Jossey Bass.

Rose, S. D., & Tolman, R. (1989). Measuring and evaluating individual achievements and group process. In S.D. Rose (Ed.) *Working with adults in groups* (pp. 109–136). San Francisco: Jossey Bass.

Toseland R. W., & Rivas, R. F. (2005). *An introduction to group work practice.* (5th ed.) Boston: Allyn and Bacon.

Walmyr Publishing Company. (2007). Welcome to the WALMYR Publishing home page. Retrieved August 9, 2007 from http://www.walmyr.com/index.html

Wayne, J., & Cohen, C. S. (2001). *Group work education in the field.* Alexandria, VA: Council on Social Work Education.

33

Social Skills Training through Groups in Schools

Craig Winston LeCroy
Arizona State University

- Defining and Conceptualizing Social Skills
- The Evidence Base for Social Skills Groups
- Practical Considerations in Conducting Social Skills Groups
- Guidelines for Practitioners
- Social Skills Training Illustrated
- Classroom Social Skills Approaches

School is the major socializing institution for children. In school, children develop social behavior as well as learn academic skills. Although schools focus on children's educational and cognitive skills and capabilities, they recognize an important but neglected area of concern—the healthy social development of children. The National Mental Health Association Commission on the Prevention of Mental-Emotional Disabilities recommended, "programs should be developed in schools (preschool through high school) that incorporate validated mental health strategies and competence building as an integral part of the curriculum" (as cited in Long, 1986, p. 828). In general, the public supports a broader educational agenda that includes enhancing children's social and emotional competence (Rose & Gallup, 2000).

Without proper social skills, children face numerous negative consequences later in life. For example, poor social skills are linked to later psychiatric disorders, externalizing problems, and internalizing problems. Self-regulation skills (e.g., being able to communicate thoughts and needs, being sensitive to others, and following instructions) are critical to school readiness (Blair, 2002). Teachers most often cite the self-regulation of pupils as more important than academic skills, because it is easier to help a child catch up academically when he or she has the expected and needed self-regulation capabilities.

Lela Costin (1969) argued some forty years ago that social workers should apply group-work methods more broadly in school settings. Social skills groups can equip children with prosocial skills to replace aggressive or withdrawn behaviors with appropriate coping strategies. For example, interpersonal skills can be taught to enhance communication with peers, parents, and authority figures. Self-regulation skills can be taught to enhance classroom processes such as taking turns and following instructions. Numerous opportunities exist for the implementation of various skills-based programs that can help facilitate the successful socialization of children and adolescents in our schools. School social workers can play an important role in the design and implementation of social skills programs that: (1) enhance children's ability to learn and interact successfully with others and (2) enable teachers to focus on and better accomplish educational goals.

DEFINING AND CONCEPTUALIZING SOCIAL SKILLS

Social skills can be defined as a complex set of skills that facilitate successful interactions between peers, parents, teachers, and other adults. *Social* refers to interactions between people; *skills* refers to making appropriate discriminations deciding what would be the most effective response and using the verbal and nonverbal behaviors that facilitate interaction. The conceptualization of social skills as training suggests that problem behaviors can be viewed as remediable deficits in a child's response repertoire (King & Kirschenbaum, 1992; LeCroy, 2002). This perspective focuses on building prosocial responses as opposed to eliminating excessive antisocial responses. Children learn new options in coping with problem situations. Learning how to respond effectively to new situations produces more positive consequences than using behaviors, which may have been used in similar situations in the past. This model focuses on the teaching of skills and competencies for day-to-day living rather than on understanding and eliminating defects. This model is an optimistic view of children and is implemented in an educative-remedial framework.

Research supports the relationship between various problem behaviors and the lack of social skills. For example, depressed adolescents have less satisfying peer relationships than nondepressed adolescents and this problem exacerbates their isolation and feelings of loneliness (Weisz, 2004). Social skill deficits also play a role in the difficulties faced by children with conduct disorder and oppositional defiance disorder. It is estimated that up to 40% of children who are rejected because of poor social skills have problems with aggression (Fonagy & Kurtz, 2002), and children who are both rejected and have aggression are at the highest risk of developing antisocial behavior in adolescence (Coie, Underwood, & Lochman, 1991). Children with attention deficit hyperactivity discorder (ADHD) are well known for their social deficits, and they struggle to modulate their behavior in demanding social interactions (Fonagy, Target, Cottrell, Phillips, & Kurtz, 2002).

THE EVIDENCE BASE FOR SOCIAL SKILLS GROUPS

There is a growing body of research supporting the use of social skills training as an evidence-based treatment strategy (LeCroy, in press). In a comprehensive review, Tobler, Roona, Ochshorn, Marshall, Streke, & Stackpole (2000) examined outcome studies with children and adolescents over a 20 year time period. The greatest benefits were found with programs that included life skills models, refusal skills, goal setting, assertiveness, communication, and coping strategies—all aspects of different social skills programs. Other studies (Hinshaw, Buhrmester, & Heller, 1989; LeCroy & Rose, 1986; Lochman & Wells, 2002; Kazdin, Siegel, & Bass, 1992; Wilson, Gottfredson, & Najaka, 2001) have documented the effectiveness of social skills training. However, it is important to note that often social skills training is one component of a multifaceted program.

PRACTICAL CONSIDERATIONS IN CONDUCTING SOCIAL SKILLS GROUPS

Social skills training is usually conducted in a group format. The group format provides support and a reinforcing context for learning new responses and appropriate behaviors in a variety of social situations. The group is a natural context for social skills training because of the peer interactions that take place as the group members work together. In addition, the group allows for extensive use of modeling and feedback, and these are critical components of successful skills training. However, it is important to note that not all children do well in group settings, and on some occasions certain children experience negative effects from working in groups. In these situations, social skills are best taught on a one-to-one basis.

Group Composition

Conducting group prevention and intervention services is an efficient use of a school social worker's time, because several students can be seen at one time. However, groups must be recruited and constructed with certain key factors in mind. First, recruitment for social skills training groups will depend on the goals of the particular program. It may be necessary to limit the number of participants involved, in which case procedures must be used to help identify students most likely to benefit from the program. This screening process can be accomplished by administering assessment devices, identifying students who meet specified risk criteria, conducting pre-group interviews, or designing a referral system for teachers and other professionals to use to refer children directly to the group. On the other hand, limiting groups only to children who meet certain risk criteria may not be best in some groups. Often including participants who do not have social skills difficulties but are highly socially competent can have positive implications. Because some groups will contain children who act out antisocially, a higher degree of poor social skill modeling could initially take place. By including high-functioning children in an antisocial group, the opportunity for prosocial modeling increases. Moreover, it may be less difficult to maintain order (Merrell & Gimpel, 1998).

Finally, group composition will be influenced by factors such as how well the group participants know one another, how heterogeneous the group is, how large the group is, the age and developmental level of the participants, and their gender. It is important that all members of a group have the time and attention they need to practice skills and receive important feedback; social skills groups should have between six and ten members, and there should be a low leader-to-participant ratio. Two group leaders are recommended, especially if the group has as many as ten participants. Merrell and Gimpel (1998) proposed that the members in the group should not vary in age by more than two or three years, and, depending on the developmental level of the group, the level of structure and language used may need to be altered. Presenting social skills that require a high level of cognitive ability will not be effective for group members who are either too young or who are functioning at a lower developmental level than the skill requires. For certain purposes, mixed-gender groups may provide a realistic context for interaction and increase the possibilities of generalization of particular skills.

Developing Program Goals

The first step in developing a successful social skills training program is to identify the goals of the program based on the needs and strengths of the target population. A program goal, for example, might be for withdrawn children to be able to initiate positive social interactions. Once the goals of the program are clearly defined, the next step is to select the specific skills that are to be taught. Then you may help the group get ready for the skills by discussing with them the details of the skills as well as when, where, and why this skill could or should be used.

Selecting Skills

Depending on the type of problem to be addressed, a number of different skills may be appropriate. Skills for withdrawn and isolated children include greeting others, joining in ongoing activities, managing a conversation, and sharing/cooperation around things (e.g., toys) and ideas (King & Kirschenbaum, 1992; Weiss & Harris, 2001). Barth (1996) elaborated assertiveness skills needed for preventing teen pregnancy, including problem solving and refusing unacceptable demands. The basic principles are 1) to break the preferred behavior down into a number of skills and 2) to assist the group in practicing the skills. It is important to remember each member's developmental level of communication, motor skills, and cognition. This is especially important when working with children who have disabilities (Nevil, Beatty, & Moxley, 1997; Weiss & Harris, 2001).

Refining Selected Skills

The process of social skills training requires continual attention to refining each skill that is to be taught. After identifying the broad social skills desired, it is important to divide each broad skill into component parts so that they can be more easily learned. For example, LeCroy (in press) breaks down the skill "beginning a conversation" into six component parts (see also Cartledge & Milburn, 1995; Elias & Tobias, 1996):

1. Look the person in the eye and demonstrate appropriate body language.
2. Greet the person, saying one's own name.
3. Ask an open-ended question about the person. Listen attentively for the response.
4. Make a statement to follow up on the person's response.
5. Ask another open-ended question about the person. Listen attentively to the response.
6. Make another statement about the conversation.

Depending on the program, the same basic skill, such as starting a conversation, may be broken down differently. The important thing to remember is that social skills are more complex than they appear on the surface.

Major Skill Areas for Healthy Development

Five major social skill areas have been identified as critical for healthy child and adolescent development. The following is a list of major skill areas and the most important skills within those areas. Each specific skill can be further broken down into subskills:

Peer Relationship Skills

1. Compliments, praises, or applauds peers;
2. Offers help or assistance to peers when needed;

3. Invites peers to play or interact;
4. Participates in discussions; talks with peers for extended periods;
5. Stands up for rights of peers; defends a peer in trouble;
6. Is sought out by peers to join activities; everyone likes to be with him or her;
7. Has skills or abilities admired by peers; participates skillfully with peers;
8. Skillfully initiates or joins conversations with peers;
9. Is sensitive to feelings of peers;
10. Has good leadership skills; assumes leadership role in peer activities;
11. Makes friends easily; has many friends;
12. Has sense of humor; shares laughter with peers.

Self-Management Skills

1. Remains calm when problems arise; controls temper when angry;
2. Follows rules; accepts imposed limits;
3. Compromises with others when appropriate; compromises in conflicts;
4. Receives criticism well; accepts criticism from others;
5. Responds to teasing by ignoring peers; responds appropriately to teasing;
6. Cooperates with others in a variety of situations.

Academic Skills

1. Accomplishes tasks or assignments independently; displays independent study skills;
2. Completes individual seatwork and assigned tasks;
3. Listens to and carries out teacher directions;
4. Produces work of acceptable quality for ability level; works up to potential;
5. Uses free time appropriately;
6. Is personally well organized;
7. Appropriately asks for assistance as needed; asks questions;
8. Ignores peer distractions while working; functions well despite distractions.

Compliance Skills

1. Follows instructions and directions;
2. Follows rules;
3. Appropriately uses free time;
4. Shares toys, materials, and belongings;
5. Responds appropriately to constructive criticism or when corrected;
6. Finishes assignments; completes tasks;
7. Puts toys, work, or property away.

Assertion Skills

1. Initiates conversations with others;
2. Acknowledges compliments;
3. Invites peers to play; invites others;
4. Says and does nice things for self; is self-confident;
5. Makes friends;
6. Questions unfair rules;
7. Introduces self to new people;
8. Appears confident with opposite sex;
9. Expresses feelings when wronged;
10. Appropriately joins ongoing activity/group

Constructing Realistic Social Situations

It is important to construct realistic social situations that demand the use of social skills being taught, and that the social situations and skills are determined empirically. Okamoto, LeCroy, Dustman, Hohmann-Marriott, & Kulis (2004) constructed problematic or difficult situations that American Indian youth encounter involving drugs and alcohol. The process involved conducting a series of focus groups and recording the kinds of situations that American Indian youth typically face when confronted with situations that involve substance use. These "difficult" situations were then put into a survey and American Indian youth were asked to rate each situation in terms of frequency and difficulty. At the end of this process there is a list of common and difficult situations with "social" validity (in this case cultural validity) that can be used for skills training. For example, in this study we found that many of the difficult situations for American Indian youth revolved around family interactions and social gatherings. When conducting substance abuse prevention groups with this population, we include these exact situations and help young people to learn appropriate skills for handling relevant situations in their social contexts.

Owing to the uniqueness of each interpersonal interaction, most practitioners must develop their own problematic situations or elicit them from the group during social skills training. For example, a substance abuse prevention program could address the following problem situation:

> You ride to a party with someone you've been dating for about six months. The party is at someone's house; their parents are gone for the weekend. There is a lot of beer and dope, and your date has had too much to drink. Your date says, "Hey, where's my keys—let's get going."

This situation ends with a stimulus for applying the skills of resisting peer pressure. An effective response to this situation would include the steps involved in resisting peer pressure: name the trouble, say no quickly, suggest alternatives, and leave the situation.

Social skills programs must be sensitive to racial and ethnic considerations. Cultural differences are often also differences in communication. Thus, the goals that are targeted in social skills groups must be culturally sensitive and depend on the major cultural values of the participants in the program (Meyer, Park, Grenot-Scheyer, Schwartz, & Harry, 1998). Selection of social skills must be tailored to be an effective social interaction in a variety of cultures.

GUIDELINES FOR PRACTITIONERS

After program goals are defined and skills are selected, there is a sequential process for teaching social skills. The following seven basic steps delineate the process that leaders can follow (based on LeCroy, in press). These guidelines were developed for social skills groups with middle school and high school students. Social skills groups with younger children would use modified guidelines (see King & Kirschenbaum, 1992). In each of the seven steps of the process for teaching social skills outlined below there is a request for group member involvement because it is critical that group leaders involve the participants actively in the skill training. In addition, such requests keep the group interesting and fun for the group members.

1. *Present the social skill being taught.* The first step for the group leader is to present the skill. The leader solicits an explanation of the skill, for example, "Can anyone tell me what it means to resist peer pressure?" After group members have answered this question, the leader emphasizes the rationale for using the skill. For example, "You would use this skill when you're in a situation where you don't want to do something that your friends want you to do; you should be able to say no in a way that helps your friends to be able to accept your refusal." The leader then requests that group members voice additional reasons for learning the skill.
2. *Discuss the social skill.* The leader presents the specific skill steps that constitute the social skill. For example, the skill steps for resisting peer pressure are good nonverbal communication (including eye contact, posture, and voice volume), saying no early in the interaction, suggesting an alternative activity, and leaving the situation if there is continued pressure. Leaders then ask group members to state examples of times they used the skill, or examples of times they could have used the skill but chose not to.
3. *Present a problem situation and model the skill.* The leader presents a problem situation. For example, the following is a problem situation for resisting peer pressure.

> After seeing a movie, your friends suggest that you go with them to the mall. It's 10:45 and you are supposed to be home by 11:00. It's important that you get home by 11:00 or you won't be able to go out next weekend.

The group leader chooses members to role-play this situation and then models the skills. Group members evaluate the model's performance. Did the model follow all the skill steps? Was his or her performance successful? The group leader may choose another group member to model if the leader believes he or she already has the requisite skills. Another alternative is to present videotaped models to the group. This has the advantage of following the recommendation by researchers that the models be similar to trainees in age, sex, and social characteristics.

4. *Set the stage for role-playing the skill.* For this step the group leader needs to construct the social circumstances for the role play. Leaders select group members for the role play and give them their parts. The leader reviews with the role players how to act out their roles. Group members not participating in the role play observe the process. It is sometimes helpful if these observers are given specific instructions for their observations. For example, one member may observe the use of nonverbal skills; another member may be instructed to observe when "no" is said in the interaction.

5. *Have group members rehearse the skill.* Rehearsal or guided practice of the skill is an important part of effective social skills training. Group leaders and group members provide instructions or coaching before and during the role play and provide praise and feedback for improvement. Following a role-play rehearsal, the leader will usually give instructions for improvement, model the suggested improvements, or coach the person to incorporate the feedback in the subsequent role play. Often the group member doing the role play will practice the skills in the situation several times to refine the skills and incorporate feedback offered by the group. The role plays continue until the trainee's behavior becomes more and more similar to that of the model. It is important that "overlearning" takes place, so the group leader should encourage many examples of effective skill demonstration, followed by praise. Group members should be taught how to give effective feedback before the rehearsals. Throughout the teaching process the group leader can model desired responses. For example, after a role play the leader can respond first and model feedback that starts with a positive statement.

6. *Practice using complex skill situations.* The next-to-last phase deals with more difficult and complex skill situations. Complex situations can be developed by extending the interactions and roles in the problem situations. Another possible and relevant way to construct complex social situations is to ask group members to describe a situation in their own lives or in the lives of their friends that relates to the skill the group is working on. Most social skills groups also incorporate the teaching of problem-solving abilities. Problem solving is a general approach to helping young people gather information about a problematic situation, generate a large number of potential solutions, evaluate the consequences of various solutions, and

outline plans for the implementation of a particular solution. Group leaders can identify appropriate problem situations and lead members through the seven steps. Problem-solving training is important because it prepares young people to make adjustments as needed in particular situations. It is a general skill with large-scale application (for a more complete discussion on the use of problem-solving approaches, see Elias & Clabby, 1992; Rose, 1998).

7. *Train for generalization and maintenance*. The success of a social skills program depends on the extent to which the skills young people learn transfer to their day-to-day lives. Practitioners must always be planning for ways to maximize the generalization of skills learned and promote their continued use after training. There are several principles that help facilitate the generalization and maintenance of skills. The first is the use of overlearning. The more overlearning that takes place in the group the greater likelihood of later transfer of skills. Therefore, it is important that group leaders insist on mastery of the skills. Another important principle of generalization is to vary the stimuli as skills are learned. To accomplish this, practitioners can use a variety of models, problem situations, role-play actors, and trainers. The different styles and behaviors of the people used produces a broader context in which to apply the skills learned. Perhaps most important is to require that young people use the skills in their real-life settings. Group leaders should assign and monitor homework to encourage transfer of learning. This may include the use of written contracts to do certain tasks outside of the group. Group members should be asked to bring to the group examples of problem situations where the social skills can be applied. Last, practitioners should attempt to develop external support for the skills learned. One approach to this is to set up a buddy system whereby group members work together outside the group to perform the skills learned.

SOCIAL SKILLS TRAINING ILLUSTRATED

This methodology may be applied to a whole range of problem areas. Table 33.1 illustrates some common focus areas for social skills training in the schools, along with general skills to be developed and resources for more specific information about these focus areas.

Although the examples in table 33.1 examine particular aspects of social skills training interventions, many practitioners use multiproblem social skills training in groups with children experiencing a variety of problems. For example, groups could include children with such problems as acting-out behavior, withdrawn behavior, fear, and so forth.

TABLE 33.1 Problem Behaviors and Related Social Skills Training

Type of Program and Resources	*Social Skills Focus*
Aggressive behavior Bierman & Greenberg, 1996 Feindler & Meghann, in press Olweus, 1996 Lochman & Wells, 2002 Waterman & Walker, 2001	*Skills to work on* 1. Recognizing interactions likely to lead to problems; 2. Learning responses to negative communications; 3. Learning to request a behavior change.
Depression Clarke, Lewinsohn, & Hops, 2001 Stark, Schnoebelen, Simpson, Hargrave, Glenn, & Molnar, 2004	*Skills to work on* 1. Conversation skills; 2. Planning social activities; 3. Making friends; 4. Increasing pleasant activities; 5. Reducing negative cognitions.
Anxiety or withdrawn, isolated behavior Gottman, 1983 Hops, Walker, & Greenwood, 1979 Kearney, in press Kendall, Choudhury, Hudson, & Webb, 2002 Chorpita, 2007 Weiss & Harris, 2001	*Skills to work on* 1. Greeting others; 2. Joining in ongoing activities; 3. Starting a conversation; 4. Sharing things and ideas.
Substance abuse prevention Botvin, 2000 Hohman & Buchik, 1994 Henggeler, Clingempeel, Brondino, & Pickrel, 2002	*Skills to work on* 1. Identifying problem situations; 2. Learning effective refusal skills; 3. Making friends with non-using peers; 4. Learning general problem-solving techniques.
Teen pregnancy and HIV prevention Barth, 1996 Jermmott & Jermmott, 1992 Wang et al., 2000 Wingood & DiClemente, in press	*Skills to work on* 1. Identifying risky situations; 2. Refusing unreasonable demands; 3. Learning new interpersonal responses; 4. Learning problem-solving techniques.
Peer mediation for interpersonal conflict Begun, 1995 Schrumpf, Crawford, & Usadel, 1991	*Skills to work on* 1. Learning communication skills; 2. Focusing on common interests; 3. Creating options; 4. Writing an agreement.
Children with cognitive and other disabilities Sargent, 1991 Walker, Todis, Holmes, & Horton, 1988 Weiss & Harris, 2001	*Skills to work on* 1. Gaining teacher attention; 2. Following classroom rules; 3. Being organized; 4. Drinking from the water fountain appropriately (and other skills appropriate for this population).

In groups designed for prevention purposes, the goal is to promote positive prosocial alternative behaviors (LeCroy, 2001; LeCroy & Rose, 1986). Such programs may be tailored to meet the needs of specific populations. Although social skills training will likely be the major component of the treatment, other treatment procedures also can be used; for example, a social skills training program may be enhanced by the addition of a psychoeducational component. A specific example of the development of one such prevention program follows.

A Prevention Program for Early Adolescent Girls

A social skills training psychoeducational prevention program called Go Grrrls (LeCroy & Daley, 2001) was developed specifically for early adolescent girls. Program goals were identified through empirical investigation of problems common to this population and through direct interaction with middle-school girls. In response to these identified problems, a group of "core" social skills—for example, assertiveness skills and basic conversational skills—are presented and taught during the first half of a twelve-session program. Participants are then asked to build on core skills by applying them to more specific situations, such as substance abuse refusal, during the latter half of the program.

Two examples of program goals for the Go Grrrls program are to equip girls with assertiveness skills, and with the skills necessary to build healthy peer relationships.

Building a Solid Foundation of Skills. For the focus area of "assertiveness," the Go Grrrls program provides three sessions that help girls to learn this skill. In one of the early group meetings, girls are introduced to the general concept of assertiveness and are given practice using this skill. In two later sessions, girls are given additional practice using assertiveness skills in the context of refusing substances and unwanted sexual advances. As the program progresses, girls are able to combine several of the core social skills they learned in early sessions to help them deal with more specific problem areas in the later curriculum. For example, by the time participants reach the curriculum section dealing with substance abuse, they have already completed sessions on the core social skills of assertiveness and starting conversations. They can draw from both of these areas in learning to effectively deal with peer pressure to use drugs. Table 33.2 illustrates how social skills may be combined in a complementary fashion to help participants build strengths. Research studies (LeCroy, 2004) have found that this program produced significant outcomes in comparison to a control group of participants who did not receive the program.

TABLE 33.2 *Go Grrrls* Skill Building

Go Grrrls Program Goal	*Related Social Skills Training*
Core skill: Assertiveness Goal: To teach girls to act assertively rather than passively or aggressively. Rationale: Teaching basic assertiveness skills to girls will help them speak up in classrooms and withstand peer pressure and will serve as a foundation for learning more specific refusal skills.	1. Discuss the skill of assertiveness. 2. Group leaders demonstrate assertive, passive, and aggressive responses to sample situations. 3. Group members practice identifying assertive behavior. 4. Group members practice assertiveness skills. 5. Group leaders and other members provide feedback. Sample scenario: You are in science class, and the boy you are partners with tells you that he wants to mix the chemicals and you can be the secretary. What do you do?
Core skill: Making and keeping friends Goal: To equip girls with the tools they need to establish and maintain healthy peer relationships. Rationale: Disturbances in peer relationships are among the best predictors of psychiatric, social, and school problems. Teaching friendship skills can reduce these problems.	1. Discuss the components of a successful conversation, including the beginning, middle, and end. 2. Group leaders demonstrate both ineffective and effective conversational skills. 3. Group members practice identifying effective conversational skills such as making eye contact and asking questions of the other person. 4. Group members practice conversation skills in role-play situations. 5. Group leaders and other members provide feedback. Sample scenario: It is your first day of junior high and you don't know anyone in your homeroom. Start a conversation with the girl who sits next to you.
Specific skill: Avoiding substance abuse Goal: To teach girls coping strategies and skills they may use to avoid using alcohol, tobacco, and other drugs. Rationale: More girls are using drugs, and at earlier ages, than ever before. Early drug use may place girls at risk for serious health and psychological problems.	1. Discuss the reasons why some girls use drugs. (Reasons may include: They don't know how to say no, they don't have friends and get lonely, etc.) 2. Discuss reasons why some girls don't use drugs. 3. Group members practice refusing drugs in role-play situations. They build on the core skill of assertiveness learned earlier. 4. Group members list coping strategies they can use instead of turning to drugs. They build on the core skill of starting conversations, by recognizing that they can build healthy friendships with non-using friends to help them stay drug free.

CLASSROOM SOCIAL SKILLS APPROACHES

Although few evidence-based interventions have been developed specifically for teaching social skills in the classroom, such efforts are gaining greater appeal in order to target a large number of students that could benefit from such interventions (see Webster-Stratton & Taylor, 2001 for an exception). Practitioners can take many of the same methods as used in teaching child-management skills to parents and apply them in classroom settings with teachers. Studies have found that modifying teacher-child interactions can have an impact on child engagement and behavior (Howes, 2000). Such classroom-based interventions are more typically established with younger children. Teachers are taught skills in promoting positive social behavior using attention, praise, and encouragement (Webster-Stratton & Taylor, 2001).

Additionally, teachers can be taught the specific skills of helping improve students' self-regulation. Research is documenting that self-regulation and its component parts (working memory, executive attention, and emotional regulation) can be harnessed to improve children's mental health and social functioning (Buckner, Mezzacappa, & Beardslee, 2003). This may be accomplished by guiding students in tasks that require higher-order cognitive skills to successfully negotiate, or using situations that heighten negative emotional arousal that require higher-order reasoning and executive-function skills to successfully resolve.

As school social workers work toward the goal of enhancing the socialization process of children, methods for promoting social competence, such as social skills training, have much to offer. Social workers can make an important contribution to children, families, and schools through preventive and remedial approaches like those described in this chapter. As we have seen, children's social behavior is a critical aspect of successful adaptation in society. The school represents an ideal place for children to learn and practice social behavior. It provides the needed multipeer context and offers multiple opportunities for newly learned behaviors to be generalized to other situations and circumstances.

Social skills training provides a clear methodology for providing remedial and preventive services to children. This direct approach to working with children has been applied in numerous problem areas and with many child-behavior problems. It is straightforward in application and has been adapted so that social workers, teachers, and peer helpers can successfully apply the methodology. Although we have emphasized the group application, social skills training also can be applied in individual or classroom settings.

References

Barth, R. P. (1996). *Reducing the risk. Building skills to prevent pregnancy STD and HIV* (3rd ed.). Santa Cruz, CA: ETR Associates.

Begun, R. W. (1995). *Ready-to-use social skills lessons & activities for grades 4–6*. West Nyack, NY: Center for Applied Research in Education.

Bierman, K. L., & Greenberg, M. T. (1996). Social skills training in the fast track. In R. D. Peters & R. J. McMahon (Eds.), *Preventing childhood disorders, substance abuse, and delinquency* (pp. 65–89). Thousand Oaks, CA: Sage.

Blair, C. (2002). School readiness: Integrating cognition and emotion in a neurobiological conceptualization of children's functioning at school entry. *American Psychologist, 57*, 111–127.

Botvin, G. J. (2000). *Life skills training: Promoting health and personal development*. New York: Princeton Health.

Buckner, J. C., Mezzacappa, E., & Beardslee, W. R. (2003). Characteristics of resilient youths living in poverty: The role of self-regulatory processes. *Development and Psychopathology, 15*, 139–162.

Cartledge, C., & Milburn, J. F. (1995). *Teaching social skills to children and youth: Innovative approaches* (3rd ed.). Boston: Allyn & Bacon.

Chorpita, B. F. (2007). *Modular Cognitive-Behavior Therapy for childhood anxiety disorders.* New York: Guilford Press.

Clarke, G. N., Lewinsohn, P. M., & Hops, H. (2001). *Instructor's manual for the Adolescent Coping with Depression course*. Retrieved January 20, 2005 from: http://www.kpchr.org/public/acwd/acwdl.html.

Coie, J. D., Underwood, M., & Lochman, E. (1991). Programmatic intervention with aggressive children in the school setting. In D. J. Pepler & K. H. Rubin (Eds.), *The development and treatment of childhood aggression* (pp. 389–410). Hillsdale, NJ: Lawrence Erlbaum Associates.

Costin, L. B. (1969). An analysis of the tasks of school social work. *Social Service Review, 43*, 247–285.

Elias, M. J., & Clabby, J. F. (1992). *Building social problem-solving skills*. San Francisco: Jossey-Bass.

Elias, M. J., & Tobias, S. E. (1996). *Social problem solving: Interventions in the schools*. New York: Guilford.

Feindler, E. L., & Gerber, M. (in press). TAME: Treatment Anger Management Education. In C. LeCroy (Ed.). *Handbook of evidence-based child and adolescent treatment manuals*. New York: Oxford University Press.

Fonagy, P., & Kurtz, A. (2002). Disturbance of conduct. In P. Fonagy, M. Target, D. Cottrell, J. Phillips, & Z. Kurtz. *What works for whom? A critical review of treatments for children and adolescents* (pp. 106–192). New York: Guilford Press.

Fonagy, P., Target, M., Cottrell, D., Phillips, J., & Kurtz, Z. (2002). *What works for whom? A critical review of treatments for children and adolescents.* New York: Guilford Press.

Gottman, J. M. (1983). How children become friends. *Monographs of the Society for Research in Child Development, 48*, 410–423.

Henggeler, S. W., Clingempeel, W. G., Brondino, M. J., & Pickrel, S. G. (2002). Four-year follow-up of multisystemic therapy with substance-abusing and substance-dependent juvenile offenders. *Journal of the American Academy of Child and Adolescent Psychiatry, 41*(7), 868–874.

Hinshaw, S. P., Buhrmester, D., & Heller, T. (1989). Anger control in response to verbal provocation: Effects of stimulant medication for boys with ADHD. *Journal of Abnormal Child Psychology, 17*, 393–407.

Hohman, M., & Buchik, G. (1994). Adolescent relapse prevention. In C. LeCroy (Ed.), *Handbook of child and adolescent treatment manuals* (pp. 200–239). NY: Lexington.

Hops, H., Walker, H. M., & Greenwood, C. R. (1979). PEERS: A program for remediating social withdrawal in school. In L. A. Hamerlynch (Ed.), *Behavior systems for the developmentally disabled: I. School and family environments* (pp. 224–241). NY: Brunner/Mazel.

Howes, C. (2000). Social-emotional classroom climate in child care, child-teacher relationships, and children's second-grade peer relations. *Social Development, 9*, 191–204.

Jermmott, L. S., & Jermmott, J. B., III (1992). Increasing condom-use intentions among sexually active inner-city adolescent women: Effects of an AIDS prevention program. *Nursing Research, 41*, 273–278.

Kazdin, A. E., Siegel, T. C., & Bass, D. (1992). Cognitive problem-solving skills training and parent management training in the treatment of antisocial behavior in children. *Journal of Consulting and Clinical Psychology, 60*, 733–747.

Kearney, C. A., (in press). Manualized treatment for anxiety-based school refusal behavior in youth. In C. LeCroy (Ed.), *Handbook of evidence-based child and adolescent treatment manuals*. New York; Oxford University Press.

Kendall, P. C., Choudhury, M., Hudson, J., & Webb, A. (2002). *The C. A. T. project workbook for the cognitive-behavioral treatment of anxious adolescents*. Ardmore, PA: Workbook Publishing.

King, C. A., & Kirschenbaum, D. S. (1992). *Helping young children develop social skills*. Pacific Grove, CA: Brooks/Cole.

LeCroy, C. W. (2001). Promoting social competence in youth. In H. E. Briggs & K. Corcoran (Eds.), *Social work practice: Treating common problems* (pp. 199–212). Chicago, IL: Lyceum Books.

LeCroy, C. W. (in press). Social skills training. In C. LeCroy (Ed.). *Handbook of evidence-based child and adolescent treatment manuals* (pp. 99–138). New York: Oxford University Press.

LeCroy, C. W. (2004). Experimental evaluation of the 'Go Grrrls' preventive intervention for early adolescent girls. *Journal of Primary Prevention, 25*, 457–473.

LeCroy, C. W., & Daley, J. (2001). *Empowering adolescent girls: Examining the present and building skills for the future with the Go Grrrls program*. New York: W.W. Norton.

LeCroy, C. W. (2002). Child therapy and social skills. In A. R. Roberts & G. J. Greene (Eds.), *Social Work Desk Reference* (pp. 406–412). New York: Oxford University Press.

LeCroy, C. W., & Rose, S. D. (1986). Evaluation of preventive interventions for promoting social competence in adolescents. *Social Work Research and Abstracts, 22*, 8–17.

Lochman, J. E., & Wells, K. C. (2002). *The coping program for preadolescent aggressive boys and their parents.* Unpublished manuscript.

Long, B. B. (1986). The prevention of mental-emotional disabilities: A report from a National Mental Health Association Commission. *American Psychologist, 41*, 825–829.

Merrell, K. W., & Gimpel, G. A. (1998). *Social skills of children and adolescents: Conceptualization, assessment, treatment*. Mahwah, NJ: Lawrence Erlbaum Associates.

Meyer, L. H., Park, H., Grenot-Scheyer, M., Schwartz, I. S., & Harry, B. (1998). *Making friends: The influences of culture and development*. Baltimore: Paul H. Brookes.

Nevil, N. F., Beatty, M. L., & Moxley, D. P. (1997). *Socialization games for persons with disabilities: Structured group activities for social and interpersonal development*. Springfield, IL: Charles C Thomas Pub.

Okamoto, S. K., LeCroy, C. W., Dustman, P., Hohmann-Marriott, B., & Kulis, S. (2004). An ecological assessment of drug-related problem situations for American Indian adolescents in the southwest. *Journal of Social Work Practice in the Addictions, 4*, 47–64.

Olweus, D. (1996). Bullying at school: Knowledge base and an effective intervention program. *Annals of the New York Academy of Sciences, 794*, 265–276.

Rose, S. D. (1998). *Group therapy with troubled youth*. Thousand Oaks, CA: Sage.

Rose, L. C., & Gallup, A. M. (2000). *The 32nd Annual Phi Delta Kappa/Gallup poll of the public's attitudes towards the public schools*. Retrieved July 10, 2002 from http://www.pdkintl.org/kappan/kpol0009.htm.

Sargent, L. R. (1991). *Social skills for school and community: Systematic instruction for children and youth with cognitive delays*. Preston, VA: Division on Mental Retardation, Council for Exceptional Children.

Schrumpf, F., Crawford, D., & Usadel, H. C. (1991). *Peer mediation: Conflict resolution in the schools*. Champaign, IL: Research Press.

Stark, K. D., Schnoebelen, S., Simpson, J., Hargrave, J., Glen, R., & Molnar, J. (2004). *Treating depressed children: Therapist manual for ACTION*. Ardmore, PA: Workbook Publishing.

Tobler, N. S., Roona, M. R., Ochshorn, P., Marshall, D. G., Streke, A. V., & Stackpole, K. M. (2000). School-based adolescent drug prevention programs: 1998 meta-analysis. *Journal of Primary Prevention, 20*, 275–337.

Walker, H. M., Todis, B., Holmes, D., & Horton, G. (1988). *The ACCESS program*. Austin, TX: Pro-Ed.

Wang, L. I., Davis, M., Robin, L., Collins, J., Coyle, K., & Baumler, E. (2000). Economic evaluation of safer choices: A school-based human immunodefiency virus, other sexually transmitted diseases, and pregnancy prevention program. *Archives of Pediatric Adolescent Medicine, 154*, 1017–1024.

Waterman, J., & Walker, E. (2001). *Helping at-risk students*. New York: Guilford.

Webster-Stratton, C., & Taylor, T. (2001). Nipping early risk factors in the bud: Preventing substance abuse, delinquency, and violence in adolescence through interventions targeted at young children (0–8 years). *Prevention Science, 2*, 165–192.

Weiss, M. J., & Harris, S. L. (2001). *Reaching out, joining in: Teaching social skills to young children with autism*. New York: Woodbine House.

Weisz, J. R. (2004). *Psychotherapy for children and adolescents: Evidence-based treatments and case examples.* New York: Cambridge University Press.

Wilson, D. B., Gottfredson, D. C., & Najaka, S. S. (2001). School-based prevention of problem behaviors: A meta-analysis. *Journal of Quantitative Criminology, 17*, 247–272.

Wingood, G. M., & DiClemente, R. J. (2008). HIV prevention with African American females. In C. W. LeCroy (Ed.), *Handbook of evidence-based child and adolescent treatment manuals* (pp. 85–98). New York: Oxford University Press.

34

School-Based Crisis Intervention for Traumatic Events

Jay Callahan

- Social Work Involvement
- Definitions
- Type I versus Type II Trauma
- Common Post-Traumatic Reactions
- Predictors of Distress
- Trauma versus Grief
- Definitions of Crisis and Crisis Intervention
- Crisis Team and Levels of Crisis
- Crisis Plan
- On-Scene Interventions
- Team Activation
- Teachers' Meeting
- Notification of Students
- Support Services
- Scope of School Response
- Screening of Victims
- Critical Incident Stress Debriefing
- Ongoing Support Groups
- Consultation and Assistance to Faculty
- Ongoing Tracking and Review
- Media
- Community Meeting
- Rumor Control Mechanisms
- Reducing Suicide Contagion
- Community Healing

In the aftermath of the terrorist attacks of September 11, 2001, the psychological impact of traumatic events has become all too clear to many people throughout the world. The emotional consequences of these events spread far beyond New York and Washington, and people across the country experienced intrusive images, anxiety, and fear that the attacks would happen again.

The 21st century brought another dramatic example of the emotional consequences of trauma in the tsunami that struck south Asia at Christmas, 2004. The World Health Organization issued a statement expressing concern for the "millions of children" who were expected to have "psychological scars" from the disaster, which killed over 157,000 people (Huuhtanen, 2005). These devastating incidents, one human-caused and the other an act of nature, are overwhelming in their scope and impact. Other incidents emotionally devastating to victims and survivors took place in schools:

◆ On April 20, 1999, the deadliest public-school shooting in U.S. history took place in Littleton, CO, at Columbine High School. Two students, reportedly angry at being bullied and humiliated, brought bombs and guns to school. They killed 12 students and a teacher, and wounded 23 others, before committing suicide (Verhovek, 1999). This incident has so affected U.S. culture that the term "Columbine" has now come to mean a mass shooting in a generic sense.

◆ In a small Arkansas town in March 1998, two schoolboys dressed in fatigues hid in the woods near their middle school, armed with several semiautomatic rifles. The boys, ages 11 and 13, set off a false fire alarm and then fired twenty-seven shots at students and teachers who came out on the playground. They killed four young girls and a teacher and wounded ten others (Bragg, 1998).

◆ Early one morning in the mid-1990s, in a small town west of Chicago, a substitute school bus driver drove across a pair of railroad tracks and stopped for a red light. Distracted by the noise of the engine and the students in the bus, she was unaware that the rear of the bus was hanging over the railroad tracks. A commuter train plowed into the bus, killing five high school students and injuring thirty others. Virtually everyone in their high school was traumatized (Washburn & Gibson, 1995).

◆ In the late 1980s in a small town in southeastern Michigan, during the summer a 10-year-old boy committed suicide by hanging. Just after school began in the fall, a 12-year-old girl from the same neighborhood also committed suicide, also by hanging. The middle school in that neighborhood was thrown into crisis. Friends and acquaintances of the second suicide victim attempted to cope with her death, while faculty, parents, and administrators feared that additional suicides would occur (Callahan, 1996).

Thus it has become quite clear that schools are not immune to the traumatic events that occur in all facets of our society, and, indeed, the entire world. Traumatic events take place in schools, on the way to and from schools, and in the communities to which schools belong. Many of these situations precipitate crises for schools and their surrounding communities. In this chapter we will discuss traumatic events and the crises they often cause, as well as crisis intervention techniques to respond to these tragic situations.

SOCIAL WORK INVOLVEMENT

In all of these cases, and in many others, school social workers have been central to the interventions that have followed these traumatic events. As individual professionals, and as members of school crisis teams, social workers are frequently leaders in providing crisis intervention to traumatized schools, faculty, and students. By virtue of training and education, social workers are often better prepared to respond appropriately than other school professionals. However, this is not to imply that all school social workers have an adequate background in crisis intervention and responding to traumatic stress; indeed, the purpose of this chapter is to outline this advanced level of training. Nonetheless, social workers are ideally suited to provide crisis intervention activities in the aftermath of a traumatic event.

DEFINITIONS

Traumatic events are extraordinary situations that are likely to evoke significant distress in many people. Such events involve the threat of death or serious physical injury. They include homicide, suicide, or accidental death; specific examples include gang-related violence, the abrupt heart attack and death of a teacher, and an auto accident in which students are seriously injured. A traumatic stressor is defined by the American Psychiatric Association as an event in which

> the person experienced, witnessed, or was confronted with an event or events that involved actual or threatened death or serious injury, or a threat to the physical integrity of self or others [and] the person's response involved intense fear, helplessness, or horror. (American Psychiatric Association [APA], 1994, p. 431)

Traumatic stressors include both individual events as well as certain ongoing or chronic circumstances. Other terms that are synonymous with traumatic stressor are psychic trauma, psychological trauma, and emotional trauma.

It has only been in the past twenty years that empirical studies of children's and adolescents' responses to traumatic stressors have been carried out. Prior to the early 1980s, a few psychoanalytic case studies existed, but little research was done. In 1980, the American Psychiatric Association's *Diagnostic and Statistical Manual of Mental Discorders* (*DSM-III*), was published (APA, 1980), which included the new category of post-traumatic stress disorder (PTSD). Although the impetus for this inclusion was the experience of Vietnam veterans, it soon became evident that other traumatic events and stressors also could lead to PTSD. Moreover, it was also evident that children and adolescents frequently experienced a variety of traumatic events and exhibited reactions that could be understood, not as manifestations of previous psychopathology, but as responses to the trauma (Pynoos & Nader, 1988; Terr, 1991). PTSD was conceptualized as a syndrome of persistent reactions following a traumatic stressor that was fairly similar among children, adolescents, and adults. A new disorder, acute stress disorder (ASD), was included in the *DSM-IV* in 1994. ASD is essentially PTSD in the short term—that is, less than one month; PTSD can only be diagnosed when the symptoms have persisted for one month or more. In this chapter we will not focus on diagnosable disorders, but rather on the spectrum of post-traumatic reactions and phenomena in general, which will be labeled traumatic stress. Even though traumatic events are defined as extraordinary situations that are likely to evoke significant distress in a large proportion of the population, victims can exhibit a wide range of reactions. Even in highly stressful events, reactions range from mild to severe. As traumatic stress reactions become better understood, it is evident that many individuals experience only mild, transient responses (Bonanno, 2004).

TYPE I VERSUS TYPE II TRAUMA

Traumatic stressors can take many forms. One helpful distinction is between acute, "single-blow" traumatic events and multiple or long-standing traumas (Terr, 1991). Type II traumas are multiple or continuous and occur in a context of physical or psychological captivity. Multiple or long-standing traumas for adults include experiencing combat, concentration camps, or being a prisoner-of-war, or the victim of political torture. Among children and adolescents, prolonged childhood physical and sexual abuse are the primary examples. Crisis intervention, such as the activities that are described in this chapter, is not appropriate for Type II traumas. In these situations, the full nature of the trauma is frequently not evident to authorities and individuals in a position to intervene until months or years of abuse have passed. After such continued trauma, much more extensive treatment is required than the relatively brief interventions described here for Type I individual traumas.

Type I traumas that affect a school community include suicides, homicides, and sudden accidental deaths of faculty members; transportation accidents; significant violence occurring in the school; and disasters in the surrounding community, such as tornadoes, hurricanes, earthquakes, and wildfires. Rare but overwhelming events include hostage situations and sniper attacks on school grounds. Occasional national disasters, such as assassinations and the explosions of the *Challenger* and *Columbia* space shuttles can also have a powerful impact on a school community.

COMMON POST-TRAUMATIC REACTIONS

Although many social workers may think of the word *post-traumatic* as shorthand for post-traumatic stress disorder, the word means "after a trauma." Therefore, in discussing common post-traumatic reactions, no implication is intended that these are symptoms of PTSD. Post-traumatic reactions occur on a continuum, as noted earlier, and span many different aspects of human functioning; only in the most severe cases is it appropriate to assign a diagnostic label. Recent research has also focused on the positive side of this equation—that many people experience highly stressful events and do not develop post-traumatic symptoms. In fact, the evidence suggests that, at least in some instances, the majority of people exposed to a traumatic stressor will experience only mild and transient symptoms (Kessler, Sonnega, Bromet, Hughes, & Nelson, 1995). It appears that in our tendency to focus on helping people who are harmed, we have overlooked the fact that many individuals are resilient in the face of traumatic events (Bonanno, 2004; Bonanno et al., 2002). In fact, at least in some cases, stress can lead to adaptive and constructive psychological growth. Receiving appropriate support and intervention is frequently crucial in producing these positive outcomes. However, it is also true that many people are able to handle traumatic stress in their own way and with their own natural support systems.

Among those who are harmed, post-traumatic stress disorder is not the only consequence. The negative sequelae of trauma include depression, maladaptive alcohol and drug use, somatic symptoms, such as headaches and muscle aches, and various manifestations of anxiety. The most common post-traumatic symptoms can be conceptualized as occurring in four major categories. These four clusters of reactions are: a) intrusive thoughts and images that are frequently re-experienced; b) purposeful avoidance of places, people, and situations that remind the individual of the traumatic stressor; c) dissociative phenomena; and d) increased anxiety and autonomic arousal. These are described next, along with some consideration of the different reactions of children and adolescents. Adolescents' reactions tend to resemble adult reactions in most ways.

Re-experiencing

Re-experiencing phenomena include intrusive thoughts about the event that occur unbidden, and usually unwanted, and are relatively resistant to conscious control. Adults and adolescents may experience "flashbacks," in which they visualize the trauma and feel as if it is happening again. Children do not seem to experience flashbacks in the same way, although they may visualize images or hear sounds briefly (Pynoos & Nader, 1988). Flashbulb memories are so traumatic and dramatic that the individual retains the image like a flash photograph. Powerful and painful images of this kind that accompanied the explosion of the *Challenger* have been described among children of Concord, New Hampshire, who attended the school in which Christa McAuliffe taught (Terr et al., 1996). Dreams and nightmares are common, and children often incorporate trauma themes into their play (Terr, 1991).

Purposeful Avoidance

The second cluster of symptoms consists of conscious and purposeful avoidance of situations, places, and people that remind a victim of the traumatic event. Adolescents as well as children are reluctant to return to places where traumas occur, including school or home. In the aftermath of a sniper shooting at a school in Los Angeles, daily absenteeism increased to a peak of 268 per day from its normal level of 64 and remained elevated for a month (Pynoos et al., 1987). In addition, some individuals consciously avoid talking about the event, so as not to stir up strong feelings that may be overwhelming; such avoidance has been termed affect avoidance. Because children often have even more difficulty tolerating strong feelings than adults do, affect avoidance may be particularly persistent in children.

Dissociation

The third cluster of symptoms refers to mild to moderate kinds of dissociation. Usually these experiences are described as "emotional shock" or "numbing of responsiveness." In this instance individuals report a variety of experiences such as "It didn't seem real" or "I couldn't believe it was actually happening." Dissociation is the structured separation of normally integrated functions of memory, emotion, consciousness, and identity (Spiegel & Cardena, 1991). Dissociation of memory is the common experience of being unable to remember all the details of a traumatic event afterwards, or of having "patchy amnesia." Dissociation of emotion is the frequent experience of feeling numb or of feeling nothing immediately after a trauma. Dissociation of consciousness is the feeling of unreality or disbelief that many individuals have during and after a traumatic event. Finally, dissociation of identity is the extreme separation of an individual's personality into several partial personalities. This extreme form sometimes occurs in the aftermath of chronic and severe sexual and physical abuse and has previously been labeled multiple personality disorder.

Dissociation has received renewed attention in recent years, and it has become increasingly clear that not only is dissociation a frequent consequence of a trauma, it is a marker or indicator of distress. The common conception of emotional numbing, or feeling of unreality, for example, is that it is a protective mechanism in the aftermath of a traumatic event that shields the individual from the full realization of the horror that has taken place. However, recent research has overwhelmingly demonstrated that individuals who make frequent use of dissociation fare poorest in the long run (Griffin, Resick, & Mechanic, 1997; Marmar et al., 1994; Marmar, Weiss, Metzler, Ronfeldt, & Foreman, 1996). During the occurrence of an emotional trauma, victims frequently experience dissociation of consciousness, in which the passage of time seems altered (usually slowed down), the world seems unreal, the event seems to not really be happening, and similar phenomena. Dissociation at the time of the trauma is termed peritraumatic dissociation, and a variety of studies have shown that victims who experience peritraumatic dissociation have the highest probability of developing PTSD (Griffin et al., 1997; Marmar et al., 1994, 1996).

Hyperarousal and Anxiety

The fourth symptom cluster is that of hyperarousal or heightened anxiety. In the aftermath of a traumatic stressor, people very frequently report difficulty sleeping, an increased startle reflex, jumpiness or a sense of being "keyed up," and anxiety in general. One particular aspect of this anxiety is fear of recurrence of the trauma; it is as if one occurrence, no matter how rare, suggests that the event could happen again. Similarly, the experience of being exposed to one trauma opens up the possibility of other traumas happening as well. For example, individuals of all ages who lose a family member or friend to sudden illness worry that others may die in car accidents.

Guilt is another common reaction and can have many referents. Frequently individuals who have been present when others were killed or injured feel guilty that they were not able to prevent or lessen the loss, or that there is no discernible reason that they survived while others died.

PREDICTORS OF DISTRESS

Because there are many different types of post-traumatic reactions, the general term distress is used here to indicate the severity of possible symptoms. Although a traumatic event is distressing to almost everyone, some people react more intensely than others, as noted above. Recent research has sought to clarify the factors that are associated with the severity of response. Across virtually all studies, for adults, adolescents, and children, the amount of exposure to the trauma is the single most powerful predictor of the intensity of the post-traumatic reaction. A helpful example, empirically validated, was presented by Pynoos et al. (1987). Near the end of a school day, a sniper opened fire on a school playground in Los Angeles from a nearby apartment building window, killing one child and one adult and wounding thirteen others. He was found to have committed suicide when the police broke into his apartment. A group of 159 children were studied, and exposure to the gunfire was found to be the strongest predictor of distress. Children who were actually on the playground, who saw others being shot and heard the gunfire, were most severely affected. Children who were still in school at the time, and who were kept in their classrooms by their teachers, who feared an assault on the school, were next most affected. Children who had already gone home for the day were less affected. Finally, children who were "off track" in their twelve-month school schedule, who were not attending school that month, were least affected. The degree of exposure to the violence and the threat of death were the most powerful variables.

Other variables, however, have been shown to make significant differences in the severity of distress; the meaning of the event to the individual is perhaps one of the most important (Webb, 1994). In the Los Angeles situation, a twelve-month follow-up found that the children who were in the school building during the sniper attack, who feared that armed men would storm the school and kill students and teachers, had reappraised their risk. That is, in the days following the event it became evident that the gunman acted alone, that he shot from an apartment window across the street, and that the fear of an armed assault on the school was groundless. Consequently, many of the children revised their appraisal of risk and altered the meaning of the event to them, now concluding that they were never in any danger. As a result, their level of distress decreased markedly, whereas the children who were on the playground continued to have high levels of anxiety and other post-traumatic reactions a year later (Nader, Pynoos, Fairbanks, & Frederick, 1990).

Traditionally, theories of stress have included the concept of appraisal (Lazarus & Folkman, 1984). That is, the meaning that the individual attaches to the event is paramount in predicting and understanding his or her response. Controlling for the amount of loss of life and property damage, natural disasters are usually less distressing than human-caused accidents, and accidents are less distressing than incidents caused by human malevolence. These distinctions are thought to be due to most people's attributions that conscious human intent to harm others, such as the 9/11 terrorist attacks, are considered more preventable and less understandable than a human-caused accident, such as many airplane crashes, which are frequently due to pilot error. Human error is thought to be preventable in theory, but most people realize that it is impossible to prevent 100 percent of accidents. Finally, natural weather disasters are considered inevitable/not preventable; they simply happen.

Another aspect of meaning is the possible violation of basic assumptions about life and the world. According to Janoff-Bulman (1985) and other theorists, adolescents and adults from all Western cultures share a small number of common, unstated, but deeply held assumptions. One primary assumption is that the world is predictable, which gives rise to long-standing searches to find an understandable meaning. Survivors of trauma struggle to understand why it happened to them. Many people believe "everything happens for a reason" and that a victim "must have done something to have this happen to him," or they ask "what did I do to deserve this?" Of course, children may draw a variety of personal and malignant meanings from an event, partly due to cognitive immaturity.

Malignant meanings that individuals attach to events lead to higher levels of distress. Individuals who are able to find benevolent or positive meanings in events fare better. Furthermore, there appears to be a natural inclination to try to find some positive meaning in the aftermath of a trauma, and eventually many people find satisfaction in having survived, in having done the best they could under the circumstances, and similar conclusions.

Other factors that affect the outcome include prior trauma. As noted earlier, in the past theorists suggested that repeated trauma may provide a kind of "inoculation" against the destructive effects of additional trauma. However, recent research has indicated that multiple or continued trauma is harmful. For example, Vietnam veterans who were physically abused as children were more likely, given a certain amount of exposure to combat, to develop PTSD than those who were not (Pynoos & Nader, 1988; Schlenger et al., 1992). Clearly, this suggests that children and adolescents who have been victims of prior trauma are more likely to be severely affected by current trauma than those who have not. Family discord or a personal history of depression or other emotional problems are also associated with more negative outcomes. Conversely, individuals with stable backgrounds and psychologically healthy families frequently possess the personal qualities of "resilience" or "hardiness" that enables them to withstand very stressful events.

Finally, social support plays an important role in shielding an individual from the most severe impact of traumatic stress. Numerous studies of stress, both normative and traumatic, have demonstrated that people with supportive family and friends cope with trauma better than those without. Especially important may be the initial response of significant others—the "homecoming" of Vietnam veterans and the initial response of the spouse of a woman who has been sexually assaulted (Johnson et al., 1997). In a trauma that affects a school, supportive and positive responses of teachers and staff to traumatized children are crucial.

TRAUMA VERSUS GRIEF

Death or the threat of death has a central role in many, perhaps most, of these traumatic situations. School social workers and other mental health professionals tend to conceptualize students' and teachers' reactions to death as grief or bereavement. However, such a conception is incomplete. Grief is the reaction to the death of a significant other, but post-traumatic reactions are a separate aspect and involve a variety of other symptoms and cognitive phenomena, which will be described next. Recent research suggests, in fact, that when both are present, post-traumatic reactions must be attended to first, before the grieving process can proceed (Nader, 1997). Almost all deaths of young people, as well as unexpected deaths of adults, involve trauma as well as grief. Many of these deaths are by suicide, homicide, or sudden accidents, and many involve violence; these events evoke trauma responses as well as grief reactions.

DEFINITIONS OF CRISIS AND CRISIS INTERVENTION

A crisis is a period of psychological disequilibrium, during which a person's normal coping mechanisms are insufficient to solve a problem or master a situation (Callahan, 1994). A state of crisis necessarily persists for at least a few days, up to perhaps six weeks, during which the individual usually feels tense, anxious, depressed, and frequently overwhelmed. However, the disequilibrium and tension of the crisis state cannot last indefinitely; individuals naturally reach a new equilibrium. However, depending on a variety of factors, including the type and appropriateness of help received, this new equilibrium may be at a lower level of functioning than the person's previous level. Individuals may enter a state of crisis in reaction to a variety of precipitating events, including many that may be thought of as normative or common. For example, parental divorce may precipitate a crisis for many children and adolescents. Although "traumatic" in the ordinary sense of the word, a divorce is not a traumatic stressor in the sense that we have been describing here (i.e., involving the threat of death or serious physical injury).

Many crises are precipitated by traumatic stressors. In fact, in particularly severe events, many people experience a state of crisis. This does not mean that they necessarily qualify for a diagnosis of ASD, but it does mean they are significantly distressed, do not function at their normal levels, and are in danger of ongoing dysfunction—which may eventually justify a diagnosis of ASD or PTSD if appropriate help is not received in a timely fashion.

In a similar way, a system may be thought of as being in a state of crisis when many of its members experience tension, anxiety, and depression and when the system as a whole does not function at its normal level and in its normal fashion. A school as a whole may experience a crisis after a traumatic event, and its continued health and ability to function effectively may depend on receiving appropriate help in a timely fashion.

CRISIS TEAM AND LEVELS OF CRISIS

The school social worker is often one of the primary professionals who can offer this help. In fact, a team of professionals is necessary to offer intervention to a school in crisis, and usually this team is designated the "crisis team" or the "traumatic event response team." The remainder of this chapter consists of guidelines on responding to traumatic events, along with suggestions on how to decrease the possibility of cluster or contagious suicide when the original event is a student suicide.

It is helpful to conceptualize a variety of levels of severity, usually corresponding to the nature and breadth of impact of the event itself. A common typology defines three levels of crisis:

- *Level I*—a personal tragedy for one individual or a threatening incident primarily affecting a student, teacher, or administrator at one site. Examples are the death of a parent or family member, the serious illness of a student or faculty member, a suicide threat in school, or a student bringing a weapon to school.
- *Level II*—a major personal crisis or a major threatening incident at a single school, or a major disaster elsewhere that affects students and teachers. Examples include the death of a student or teacher while not in school, an accident with severe injuries, a student abduction, or gang violence.
- *Level III*—a disaster or threatened disaster that directly affects one or more schools. Examples include a tornado or flood; the taking of hostages or sniper fire at a school; an air crash, explosion, or fire at or near the school; cluster suicides; or a death at a school.

A graded series of interventions should be planned, corresponding to the level of crisis. A Level I crisis can often be responded to by one or two school social workers or other school mental health or health professionals and may not require the active intervention of a larger team. In contrast, a Level II or Level III crisis clearly requires a crisis team, made up of at least six to eight individuals, and may require additional help from other schools or the community (Dallas Public Schools, 1997; Smith, 1997).

CRISIS PLAN

Each school, and each school district, should have a carefully designed and periodically updated crisis plan. Such a plan would indicate a variety of activities, described next. Annual in-services for all faculty and staff should be provided, so that the plan is not simply filed and forgotten. In many schools, a school social worker is the director or leader of the crisis team; in any case the school social worker usually has an important role in the development of the crisis plan. Members of the crisis team usually include the school nurse, the school psychologist, and several volunteer teachers who are interested. A Level I crisis can usually be managed by just a few members of the team. Six to eight members on the crisis team is enough to provide most of the leadership and actual coverage in a Level II crisis. With a Level III crisis, outside help will always be necessary. It is always advisable to include at least one school social worker or other school mental health professional from another school in the same district, or an outside mental health consultant. In certain crises, in which the members of the crisis team are personally affected, or in which teachers need particular attention, the use of a consultant or professional from outside eliminates the undesirable situation in which the school social worker needs to provide personal support and intervention to faculty members who are his or her peers during regular school days. Such dual relationships should be avoided if at all possible.

ON-SCENE INTERVENTIONS

The vast majority of social work interventions for school crises take place in the aftermath of the traumatic event, that is, after the event itself is over. Postvention is another term for these responses, which indicates the timing of the activities, relative to prevention and intervention activities (American Association of Suicidology, 1997). Rarely does the event last long enough or occur in a place close enough for school personnel, including the school social worker, to become actively involved while the event is still unfolding. In the case of the sniper who fired at children on a school playground described earlier, teachers and other school personnel were involved in the traumatic situation itself. In fact, several hours passed after the gunfire stopped before it became clear that the sniper had killed himself and that it was safe to leave the school building. In other cases, such as fires or suspected fires, parents may arrive at the school and congregate on the playground or in the parking lot, and it may appear that some kind of intervention by the social worker is indicated.

During the event, no psychological interventions should be attempted. The only activities that are appropriate in this kind of situation are keeping order, providing information, and responding to rumors. Occasionally, social workers have attempted to engage parents or students in discussions of their feelings and thoughts at the time of an incident, before it is resolved. Such attempts are ill advised. Until the safety of everyone concerned is assured, parents and students are in a psychologically vulnerable state and are primarily experiencing fear, anxiety, and a sense of vulnerability. It is not appropriate to engage them in a discussion of these fears and anxieties when the outcome is unknown. In such situations parents and students have not explicitly or even implicitly agreed to such a discussion. Providing information about support activities that will be scheduled for the near future is appropriate, as are periodic informational updates and rumor control. The only possible exception would be to provide informal support on a one-to-one basis with an individual who is already obviously upset.

TEAM ACTIVATION

Many traumatic events, fortunately, take place away from school. As soon as knowledge of such an event becomes known to anyone on a school staff, the crisis team and the principal should be notified. If the school social worker is the leader of or a member of the crisis team, it may be her responsibility to coordinate a meeting of the crisis team either late on that same day, if staff are still at school, or early the next morning. Most school crisis teams meet early in the morning prior to school, and before a special teachers' meeting that itself is scheduled for thirty or forty-five minutes prior to the opening of school. In the crisis team meeting, the current situation and the crisis plan are reviewed, and a general approach to the current crisis is outlined. If no representative of administration is on the team, close communication with administration must be established and maintained.

As part of team activation, the principal of the school or superintendent of the school district should confirm the details of the event. Most often this entails talking to the police, or a hospital, or the medical examiner, or the family of the individuals affected by the traumatic event. Although most of the details of these situations may be confidential, authorities usually understand that the event will have a powerful impact on the school and that accurate information is essential in order to plan an effective response. Confirming the names of the deceased, for example, is often the central issue in a traumatic death.

With Level II and Level III crises, crisis team members need to spend most if not all of their time for at least several days responding to the traumatic event. Teachers who are team members will need to be replaced by substitute teachers, and school social workers will rarely be able to carry out many of their regular responsibilities.

TEACHERS' MEETING

Using a "phone-fan-out" system or other emergency notification system, teachers are notified as soon as possible about the crisis situation and ask them to attend a special meeting. This special meeting is usually held thirty to forty-five minutes before school begins the next morning. At this meeting, the principal usually briefs the faculty on the nature of the event and then turns the meeting over to the crisis team leader. The team leader describes the range of reactions expected from students, notes interventions and activities to be held over the next few days, and provides an opportunity for faculty to ask questions. If possible, an expert in the specifics of the traumatic event can be brought in to provide more detailed information. However, the range of reactions to almost all traumatic events is similar enough that general knowledge of the nature of traumatic stress is usually sufficient. In addition, a later voluntary meeting or other opportunity for faculty to talk with the crisis team and each other is essential. Faculty and staff cannot effectively help students if they are themselves distracted and preoccupied by their own reactions to the tragedy.

It is strongly recommended that information about the event be communicated to students through a prepared statement written by the crisis team and read to first-period classes by each teacher. Therefore, the written statement is prepared and duplicated by the crisis team in advance and distributed to the faculty at the early morning meeting. The written statement should include only information that has been confirmed definitely. Distributing a vague and generic announcement is not useful; by the time school has begun, many students will know more details about what happened than most of the faculty, and if the school does not appear knowledgeable, the crisis team and the faculty in general will lose credibility. If the death is a suicide and the family has indicated that they do not want this fact to be announced, the school should gently suggest to the family that little is gained by trying to conceal the manner of death and that the school must abide by the ruling of the medical examiner or coroner. If the medical examiner or coroner does not provide a definitive decision (in some cases, a decision with regard to mode of death is not available for some weeks), the statement should simply indicate that no ruling has yet been reached.

NOTIFICATION OF STUDENTS

As noted previously, notification of students should take place in a personal manner, with teachers reading the statement previously prepared by the crisis team and administration. Announcements over the public address system are impersonal and inevitably poorly received, whereas classroom-by-classroom notification by teachers is usually appreciated by students. Inevitably, time for discussion must be provided immediately, and little normal work will be accomplished. In a Level II crisis, there are usually some students and some classes that are not intensely affected by the event, and discussion can be brief. In cases where students knew the victims well, much more time will be needed. If a student or students have died, a member of the crisis team should attend each of the deceased student's classes throughout the day and assist the teacher in structuring the discussion.

SUPPORT SERVICES

Throughout the first few days of a Level II or Level III crisis, a school "drop-in" center or centers should be established. These centers are easily accessible offices or rooms where students are encouraged to go if they feel the need to talk about the traumatic event or other related concerns. Drop-in centers should be staffed by members of the crisis team, with extra assistance if needed. Group or individual discussions should be conducted.

Some experts in the field of traumatic stress have recommended that individual sessions be emphasized (Leenaars & Wenckstern, 1999), but the consensus of the field is that group sessions are preferable and more practical, given the limitations of time and staff.

In a Level II crisis, students are typically permitted to leave their regular classes without an excuse to go to these drop-in centers for the first two or three days. After two to three days, school should begin to move back toward "business as usual." Many students will not be intensely affected and deserve to have their education continue with as few interruptions as possible. In a Level III crisis, return to normalcy may take considerably longer. Limiting the availability of the drop-in centers is also appropriate given some students' tendency to become emotionally involved in the trauma in a melodramatic fashion. Such students seem to be "seduced" by intense feelings and seem to unconsciously desire to continue the crisis state's emotional intensity as long as possible (Callahan, 1996). In addition, it is possible that some students will simply take advantage of the opportunity to miss class and to do something else that appears to be more interesting, whether they really need to or not.

SCOPE OF SCHOOL RESPONSE

For some time, the consensus of experts has been that opportunities for discussion, processing of trauma, and grief work be made available to as many students as possible. The reasoning was that it is impossible to really know, after a given traumatic incident, who is affected and who is not. Therefore, it was considered important to "cast a wide net," so that students who might find it awkward to come forward on their own, or those who are confused about their own responses, would still receive help.

Recently, however, many experts in the field of traumatic stress have adopted a different philosophy. This new consensus is that we should not try to provide interventions to everyone, but rather devise a screening system to identify those most strongly affected. Our limited resources can then be utilized to assist these individuals. This new philosophy is highlighted in the 2002 report of a National Institute of Mental Health (NIMH) consensus conference on severe traumatic events ("mass violence"), which states:

- A sensible working principle in the immediate post-incident phase is to expect normal recovery;
- Effective early intervention following mass violence can be facilitated by careful screening and needs assessment for individuals, groups, and populations;
- Follow-up should be offered to individuals and groups at high risk of developing adjustment difficulties following exposure to mass violence, including those: a) who have acute stress disorder or other clinically signifi-

cant symptoms stemming from the trauma; b) who are bereaved; c) who have a preexisting psychiatric condition; d) who require medical or surgical attention; and e) whose exposure to the incident is particularly intense and of long duration.

This means in schools that widespread support or grief groups should not be made available to everyone, but only to those who manifest some indications of difficulties.

SCREENING OF VICTIMS

The new NIMH approach described above recommends "screening" of victims and survivors. In a school setting when a death has occurred, the friends and close classmates of the deceased would obviously be included. In addition, "screening" for other affected individuals can be done fairly unobtrusively by requesting that teachers observe students for signs of distress, and communicate the names of those students to the crisis team. In addition, any student who is frequently absent after the event, or who evidences other indirect indicators of distress, should be followed up. Certainly help should be provided to any student who requests it.

CRITICAL INCIDENT STRESS DEBRIEFING

In previous editions of this chapter, the author recommended a crisis intervention technique called critical incident stress debriefing (CISD), a structured one-session group discussion (Bell, 1995; Mitchell & Bray, 1990; Mitchell & Everly, 1995). In recent years a controversy has developed about the usefulness of CISD, centered on its originators' claim that it forestalls the later development of post-traumatic stress disorder. The bulk of the empirical evidence now suggests that CISD does not prevent the development of PTSD, and some studies seem to suggest that participation in CISD, especially mandated or involuntary participation, interferes with some individuals' natural recovery processes.

In addition, for most individuals who do need assistance, a "one-shot" group meeting is frequently insufficient. Ongoing individual or group support and treatment is usually necessary.

ONGOING SUPPORT GROUPS

Multiple-session group discussions or support groups should be arranged with all naturally occurring groups who were strongly affected by the traumatic incident. Homogenous groups are preferable. For example, one group might be made up of the close friends of any students who died, with a separate group of peers from classes. A third group might be composed of an athletic or extracurricular group of which those students were members. In all cases, participation should be voluntary. (Students who request help but who are uncomfortable in groups should be seen individually.)

Support groups are ideal for helping students cope with a traumatic event. A typical group might meet a half-dozen times on a weekly basis, with a stable and fixed membership. The group leader should be a social worker or other school mental health professional who is experienced in group process. Support groups are not therapy groups: the material discussed is at a conscious level; the leader does not interpret hidden feelings or unconscious motivations. Support groups should be held at a time and place where there will be no interruptions, and the content of the group must be kept confidential (although the usual exceptions apply). Because support groups usually continue for six weeks or so, there is often a rich opportunity to more fully process the traumatic material. In addition, because support groups normally include the students most affected by the trauma, the social worker can observe how well or poorly individuals are processing and coping with the incident. The social worker is in a unique position to recommend additional individual help if necessary.

CONSULTATION AND ASSISTANCE TO FACULTY

As noted previously, in many situations faculty members are deeply affected and distressed themselves. A meeting, debriefing, or other structured discussion with faculty is an important aspect of crisis team functioning, although it is frequently overlooked. This session should be conducted by a school social worker or other mental health professional from outside the school in question, or an outside community professional, so that the teachers are not put into a position of talking about their personal emotional reactions with the school social worker, a peer with whom they work on a daily basis.

The school social worker and crisis team can also assist teachers in small ways. For example, some teachers are so distressed that they have difficulty reading the prepared statement to their first-period classes in the immediate aftermath of the traumatic event. A crisis team member could accompany them to class, read the announcement, and cofacilitate the ensuing discussion.

ONGOING TRACKING AND REVIEW

As the first few days of the crisis unfold, periodic feedback needs to be established, so that the crisis team and the social worker can make corrections as needed. A combined teachers' and crisis team meeting after school on the second or third day is quite helpful; the experience up to that point can be reviewed, and changes can be made if necessary. It may be time to suspend the drop-in centers, for example, or it may be decided to continue them for another day. Specific students who are particularly distressed can be discussed, and in some cases, plans can be made for the social worker to speak to those students individually, or call their parents. If faculty are still distressed themselves, their difficulties can be addressed individually.

MEDIA

Especially in a Level III crisis, print and electronic media may be present at the school and demand information, access to witnesses, or statements from children. One member of the crisis team, or one member of the administration, should be designated the media representative, and everyone else should refuse to comment. Students should be informed that they are not obligated to speak to media personnel and that in fact the school suggests that they do not. Media representatives can be quite persistent and will often cite the illusory "public's right to know," which has no legal standing at the time of a crisis. For example, during a Level II crisis in a midwestern middle school in which five members of one family were killed in a fire, TV reporters (with cameras and microphones) walked uninvited into the school that the remaining child attended and attempted to interview his classmates. They refused to leave the building until directed to by the police and then set up their cameras on the sidewalk, just off school property (P. Reese, school psychologist, personal communication, 1990).

The media representative should provide information and answer questions concerning the school's response to the traumatic event. No information about the actual event—what happened, who was injured, who was killed—should be provided; this information should properly be obtained from the family, or from legal authorities. The media representative should be straightforward and nondefensive, even in response to what might be perceived as provocative questions. The most effective way to respond to media inquiries is to provide the information that the school wants to provide, regardless of the question asked.

COMMUNITY MEETING

Within a few days of the traumatic incident, a community meeting for parents and others should be held. This meeting should normally take place in the school auditorium on a weekday evening, and the principal should lead it. Representatives of the crisis team should also attend. They will frequently be called on to explain the details of the school's response to the traumatic event. Community members and parents can be confrontative and demanding at community meetings, and staff speaking to them must be prepared for this. If the community turnout is large, as it may be for a Level III crisis, it is helpful to present some information in a large group, but then to break down into small discussion groups. These would be each led by a crisis team member or teacher who is knowledgeable about traumatic stress and the school's response. If the community includes groups whose native languages are not English, it is helpful to have one or more group facilitators who are fluent in those languages.

RUMOR CONTROL MECHANISMS

Throughout the period of crisis, numerous rumors will be circulated among students, parents, and the community in general. Frequently these rumors represent peoples' fears about additional trauma, or their attempts to find a "cause." For example, in the aftermath of an adolescent suicide, and especially following two suicides, rumors of additional "suicide pacts" are extremely common, even though actual suicide pacts are quite rare (Gibbons, Clark, & Fawcett, 1990). Similarly, after an accidental death, whatever the circumstances, rumors may circulate that the driver was drunk, or that this student was walking on that road because she had been thrown out of her parents' house, or that the student was secretly a gang member.

Various procedures to attempt to defuse and debunk these rumors can be useful. Foremost among these is frankly answering questions from students and parents as they arise, and explaining that there is no basis in fact to a particular rumor. Making announcements to large groups or to the media that a particular rumor is untrue is often not effective; in this era, a denial of a rumor that some people have not yet heard is, unfortunately, a very effective way of promoting that rumor. On the other hand, debunking rumors when meeting with small groups of students or parents is usually effective.

REDUCING SUICIDE CONTAGION

When the traumatic event is a student suicide, which is usually a Level II crisis, school officials and community members are frequently concerned about the possibility of suicide "clusters." This is the phenomenon of one suicide's leading to other "copycat" suicides, and it has been observed in groups such as schools and hospitals. After one suicide, especially of a well-known or popular student, additional suicides are a possibility, although the number of actual suicide clusters in the United States has been fairly small (Davidson, Rosenberg, Mercy, Franklin, & Simmons, 1989; Gibbons et al., 1990).

The only research that has demonstrated the contagious nature of suicide has been carried out using the United States as a whole, following heavily publicized suicides of famous people. Only on such a large scale can a statistically significant increase be convincingly demonstrated. In these situations, some celebrity suicides have been shown to result in an increase in suicide over a three- to four-week period, primarily among adolescents and young adults (Phillips, Lesyna, & Paight, 1992).

Other studies have focused on specific cases with small numbers of subjects. One well-conducted study of specific individuals followed fifty-eight friends and acquaintances of ten different suicides for a six-month period. These friends and acquaintances had no more thoughts of suicide or suicidal behavior than a control group but did have significantly higher rates of depression, which may have represented complicated grief (Brent et al., 1992). These same researchers also studied twenty-eight high school students who witnessed another student committing suicide on a school bus, after accidentally shooting another student while taking out his gun. In this report, the witnesses did not develop suicidal behavior themselves but did develop post-traumatic symptoms (Brent et al., 1992). These studies suggest that after an adolescent suicide, grief, depression, and trauma are much more likely to occur than additional suicides.

Nonetheless, the prospect of cluster suicides is anxiety-provoking (Centers for Disease Control, 1988). In fact, when a traumatic event is a completed suicide, the goal of a school's crisis intervention program is frequently not only to assist students to process the trauma but also to forestall additional suicides. Many of the crisis intervention activities already described are also useful in reducing suicide risk, in that they provide arenas for students to voice their concerns and feelings and give and receive support. These activities also provide opportunities for the crisis team members and the faculty to observe students for signs of unusual distress, and therefore for the need for intervention. However, above and beyond these standard activities, there are a number of other steps that can be taken to lessen the possibility of contagion.

Perhaps most important is undermining the tendency of students to identify with the deceased suicide victim. Although cluster suicides are not well understood, it appears that the primary mechanism of the contagion is identification and imitation in someone already experiencing suicidal impulses. Adolescents are prone to perceive the world in rather judgmental and rigid categories and frequently see themselves and their friends as heroes and heroines attempting to combat an evil and corrupt adult society. Thus a teen suicide is often viewed as a defiant gesture by a heroic individual who was beaten down by powerful but destructive adult forces. The story of Romeo and Juliet exemplifies this concept, and adolescents' tendency to view a suicide as a "romantic tragedy" (Smith, 1988) could set the stage for a possible cluster suicide.

The key to prevention, therefore, is to undermine the atmosphere of romantic tragedy. One clear way to do this is to portray the deceased student, in all announcements and especially in small-group and individual discussions, as a troubled or depressed or substance-dependent isolated young person who made a bad decision. This portrayal must of course be done with sensitivity and tact and must remain sympathetic, but it will counter students' tendency to idolize and make heroic what is almost always a result, in part, of psychopathology.

Other activities can also help prevent additional suicides. Any student with a history of serious depression, previous suicide attempts, or suicide in the family must be sought out and interviewed individually by a member of the crisis team. Many of these students may benefit from a debriefing or support group, even if they do not belong to any of the naturally occurring groups for whom sessions will have already been planned. Alternatively, many of these students may need to be referred to a community mental health professional for traditional outpatient treatment.

A confidential list of students thought to be at risk for suicidal behavior should be prepared and maintained by the crisis team or school social worker. In addition to students with histories of suicidal behavior, the close friends of the victim should be considered at risk, along with any other students who appear to be strongly affected. Every student on this list should be interviewed privately by a mental health professional experienced at suicide risk assessment, and in any instances in which more than trivial risk exists, parents should be contacted and asked to come to the school and arrange suitable community treatment, outpatient or inpatient, with the assistance of school staff.

Although it may seem counterintuitive, the resumption of business as usual in a school is also an antidote to possible suicide contagion. The structure of the school routine is comforting and helpful to most students (and faculty). A long-lasting crisis atmosphere, in which usual classes or programming are canceled or altered, can easily contribute to an atmosphere of romantic tragedy and artificially elevated melodrama. A more detailed discussion of reducing suicide contagion may be obtained in the author's case study of a "postvention" program that appeared to inadvertently worsen the situation (Callahan, 1996).

COMMUNITY HEALING

In recent years, memorials, rituals, and anniversary ceremonies have arisen, as a way to help groups and communities continue to heal in the aftermath of a traumatic event. Especially in the case of major events, these rituals help victims and survivors integrate the event into the context of their lives. Perhaps counterintuitively, occasions to look back and remember seem to help victims and survivors move on with their lives. One recent example was the 10th anniversary of the bombing of the Oklahoma City federal building. In April 2004, a week-long series of activities were held, including tree plantings, public lectures, a national symposium on terrorism, an evening candlelight service, and a day of remembrance.

Traumatic events lead to crises in many schools and for many students, but it must be remembered that a crisis manifests both "danger" and "opportunity" (Slaikeu, 1990). The danger in a crisis, of course, is that an individual will be unable to cope effectively with the traumatic stress involved and that the lack of resolution will result in long-term distress and a reduced ability to function. This long-term psychopathology typically takes the form of PTSD, major depression, alcohol or drug dependence, or some other disorder. On the other hand, the opportunity is due to the uncharacteristic openness that individuals exhibit while experiencing a crisis. During a crisis, people are much more open to considering and trying out alternative coping techniques than they are at any other time, since (by definition) their customary coping mechanisms have not worked to resolve the current situation (Golan, 1978). Thus, with appropriate assistance, such as that provided by an effective school crisis team, an individual may work through a crisis and adopt new coping techniques. These could be self-reflection, realizing the value of talking with friends and family about important and personal matters, the ability to tolerate strong feelings, adoption of a more adaptive worldview, and the like. When a crisis leads an individual to adopt these or other new coping techniques, that individual becomes stronger, more capable, and more resilient than before the crisis. Many survivors of traumatic events feel "if I survived that, I can survive anything." This sense of confidence and mastery is especially important for children and adolescents, who may otherwise begin to perceive themselves as generally helpless and prone to victimization. The growth that students can build out of tragedy is one of the most gratifying processes that a school social worker can experience.

References

American Association of Suicidology. (1997). *Suicide postvention guidelines* (2nd ed.). Washington, DC: Author.

American Psychiatric Association. (1980). *Diagnostic and statistical manual of mental disorders* (3rd ed.). Washington, DC: Author.

American Psychiatric Association. (1994). *Diagnostic and statistical manual of mental disorders* (4th ed.). Washington, DC: Author.

Bell, J. L. (1995). Traumatic event debriefing: Service delivery designs and the role of social work. *Social Work, 40*, 36–43.

Bonanno, G. A. (2004). Loss, trauma, and human resilience. Have we underestimated the human capacity to thrive after extremely aversive events? *American Psychologist, 59*(1), 20–28.

Bonanno, G. A., Wortman, C. B., Lehman, D. R., Tweed, R. G., Haring, M., Sonnega, J., Carr, D., & Nesse, R. M. (2002). Resilience to loss and chronic grief: A prospective study from preloss to 18-months postloss. *Journal of Personality and Social Psychology, 83*(5), 1150–1164.

Bragg, R. (1998, March 26). Arkansas boys held as prosecutors weigh options. *New York Times*, pp. A1, A20.

Brent, D. A., Perper, J., Moritz, G., Allman, C., Friend, A., Schweers, J., Roth, C., Balach, L., & Harrington, K. (1992). Psychiatric effects of exposure to suicide among friends and acquaintances of adolescent suicide victims. *Journal of the American Academy of Child and Adolescent Psychiatry, 31*, 629–640.

Callahan, J. (1994). Defining crisis and emergency. *Crisis, 15*, 164–171.

Callahan, J. (1996). Negative effects of a school suicide postvention program: A case example. *Crisis, 17*, 108–115.

Centers for Disease Control. (1988). CDC recommendations for a community plan for the prevention and containment of suicide clusters. *Morbidity and Mortality Weekly Report, 37*(Suppl. S–6), 1–12.

Dallas Public Schools. (1997). *Crisis management plan: Resource manual*. Dallas, TX: Author.

Davidson, L. E., Rosenberg, M. L., Mercy, J. A., Franklin, J., & Simmons, J. T. (1989). An epidemiologic study of risk factors in two teenage suicide clusters. *Journal of the American Medical Association, 262*, 2687–2692.

Golan, N. (1978). *Treatment in crisis situations*. NY: The Free Press.

Gibbons, R. D., Clark, D. C., & Fawcett, J. (1990). A statistical method for evaluating suicide clusters and implementing cluster surveillance. *American Journal of Epidemiology 132*(Supp. 1), S183–S191.

Griffin, M. G., Resick, P. A., & Mechanic, M. B. (1997). Objective assessment of peritraumatic dissociation: Psychophysiological indicators. *American Journal of Psychiatry, 154*, 1081–1088.

Huuhtanen, M. (2005, January 14). *WHO fears psychological tsunami damage*. Retrieved from www.comcast.net/News/healthwellness//xml/1500_Health_medical/b20e.

Janoff-Bulman, R. (1985). The aftermath of victimization. Rebuilding shattered assumptions. In C. R. Figley (Ed.). *Trauma and its wake* (Vol. 1, pp. 15–35). NY: Brunner/Mazel.

Johnson, D. R., Lubin, H., Rosenheck, R., Fontana, A., Southwick, S., & Charney, D. (1997). The impact of the homecoming reception on the development of posttraumatic stress disorder: The West Haven Homecoming Stress Scale (WHHSS). *Journal of Traumatic Stress, 10*, 259–277.

Kessler, R. C., Sonnega, A., Bromet, E., Hughes, M., & Nelson, C. B. (1995). Posttraumatic stress disorder in the National Comorbidity Survey. *Archives of General Psychiatry, 52*, 1048–1060.

Lazarus, R., & Folkman, S. (1984). *Stress, appraisal, and coping*. NY: Springer.

Leenaars, A. A., & Wenckstern, S. (1999). Principals of postvention: Applications to suicide and trauma in schools. *Death Studies, 22*(4), 357–391.

Marmar, C. R., Weiss, D. S., Metzler, T. J., Ronfeldt, H. M., & Foreman, C. (1996). Stress responses of emergency services personnel to the Loma Prieta earthquake, Interstate 880 freeway collapse and control traumatic incidents. *Journal of Traumatic Stress, 9*, 63–85.

Marmar, C. R., Weiss, D. S., Schlenger, W. E., Fairbank, J. A., Jordan, B. K., Kulka, R. A., & Hugh, R. L. (1994). Peritraumatic dissociation and posttraumatic stress disorder in male Vietnam theater veterans. *American Journal of Psychiatry, 151*, 902–907.

Mitchell, J. T., & Bray, G. P. (1990). *Emergency services stress*. Englewood Cliffs, NJ: Prentice-Hall.

Mitchell, J. T., & Everly, G. S. (1995). *Critical incident stress debriefing: An operations manual for the prevention of traumatic stress among emergency services and disaster workers* (2nd ed.) Ellicott City, MD: Chevron.

Nader, K. O. (1997). Childhood traumatic loss: The interaction of trauma and grief. In C. R. Figley, B. E. Bride, & N. Mazza (Eds.), *Death and trauma* (pp. 17–41). Washington, DC: Taylor & Francis.

Nader, K., Pynoos, R., Fairbanks, L., & Frederick, C. (1990). Children's PTSD reactions one year after a sniper attack at their school. *American Journal of Psychiatry, 147,* 1526–1530.

National Institute of Mental Health. (2002). *Mental health and mass violence: Evidence-based early psychological intervention for victims/survivors of mass violence. A workshop to reach consensus on best practices*. NIH Publication No. 02-5138, Washington, D.C.: U.S. Government Printing Office.

Phillips, D. P., Lesyna, K., & Paight, D. J. (1992). Suicide and the media. In R. W. Maris, A. L. Berman, J. T. Maltsberger, & R. I. Yufit (Eds.). *Assessment and prediction of suicide* (pp. 499–519). New York: Guilford.

Pynoos, R. S., & Nader, K. (1988). Psychological first aid and treatment approach to children exposed to community violence: Research implications. *Journal of Traumatic Stress, 1,* 445–473.

Pynoos, R. S., Frederick, C., Nader, K., Arroyo, W., Steinberg, A., Eth, S., Nunez, F., & Fairbanks, L. (1987). Life threat and posttraumatic stress in school-age children. *Archives of General Psychiatry, 44,* 1057–1063.

Schlenger, W. E., Kulka, R. A., Fairbank, J. A., Hough, R. L., Jordan, B. K., Marmar, C. R., & Weiss, D. S. (1992). The prevalence of posttraumatic stress disorder in the Vietnam generation: A multimethod, multisource assessment of psychiatric disorder. *Journal of Traumatic Stress, 5,* 333–363.

Slaikeu, K. A. (1990). *Crisis intervention: A handbook for practice and research* (2nd ed.) Boston: Allyn & Bacon.

Smith, J. (1997). *School crisis management manual: Guidelines for administrators*. Holmes Beach, FL: Learning Publications.

Smith, K. (1988). October. *One town's experience with teen suicide*. Presentation at the annual meeting of the Michigan Association of Suicidology, Lansing, MI.

Spiegel, D., & Cardena, E. (1991). Disintegrated experience: The dissociative disorders revisited. *Journal of Abnormal Psychology, 100,* 366–378.

Terr, L. C. (1991). Childhood traumas: An outline and overview. *American Journal of Psychiatry, 148,* 10–20.

Terr, L. C., Block, D. A., Michel, B. A., Shi, H., Reinhardt, J. A., & Metayer, S. (1996). Children's memories in the wake of the Challenger. *American Journal of Psychiatry, 153,* 618–625.

Verhovek, S. H. (1999, April 22). Terror in Littleton: The overview; 15 bodies are removed from school in Colorado. *New York Times*, p. A1.

Washburn, G., & Gibson, R. (1995, October 26). Ride to school ends in tragedy. *Chicago Tribune*, 1.

Webb, N. B. (1994). School-based assessment and crisis intervention with kindergarten children following the New York World Trade Center bombing. *Crisis Interventions, 1,* 47–59.

Section Five

School Social Work Practice Applications

35

Tier 2 Behavioral Interventions for At-Risk Students

Brenda Lindsey
University of Illinois at Urbana Champaign

Margaret White
Illinois Positive Behavior Intervention and Supports Network

- Cueing and Group Social Skills Instruction
- *The Journey*: A Group Counseling Intervention
- *Challenging Horizons Program*
- *Kids Together*
- Peer-Pairing
- Behavior Education Program
- Anger Management Group: Using Animals
- Solution-Focused Intervention for LD Students At-Risk of Behavior Problems

Positive behavior interventions and supports (PBIS) is an evidence-based, school-wide approach for promoting socially appropriate behavior among students and creating safe, effective learning environments. Schools implementing PBIS create uniform behavior expectations for all classrooms and building locations, develop systematic procedures for teaching and reinforcing expectations for students and staff, and utilize school teams that employ data-based decision-making to guide implementation (Sugai & Horner, 2002). Schools implementing PBIS with fidelity have reported reductions in discipline referrals, decreased amounts of administrative time devoted to addressing problem behavior, and improved positive school climates (Carr et al., 2002; Horner et al., 2004; Irvin et al., 2006; Irvin, Tobin, Sprague, Sugai, & Vincent, 2004; Lewis & Sugai, 1999; Luiselli, Putnam, & Sunderland, 2002; Scott, 2001; Scott & Barrett, 2004; Sugai et al., 1999; Sugai, Sprague, Horner, & Walker, 2000; Sugai et al., 2000; Sugai & Horner, 2002). These findings suggest that PBIS is an effective behavior intervention.

PBIS uses a three-tier model to illustrate an integrated school-wide approach for providing academic and behavioral interventions (Sugai, 2006). Tier one interventions are universal, provided to all students to prevent academic and behavior problems. Examples of tier one academic interventions include scientifically validated reading and math curricula taught in general education classrooms. Tier one behavior interventions establish and provide methods to teach all students how to display expected behaviors, proactively pre-correct students, and acknowledge students for exhibiting the expected behaviors. PBIS expects that 80–90 percent of students will respond to tier one interventions (Sugai, 2006).

Tier two interventions are specially designed group interventions that target students at-risk of displaying challenging academic and behavior problems. These interventions are designed to be quickly accessed, highly efficient, flexible, and to bring about rapid improvement (Hawken & Horner, 2003). PBIS estimates that 10–15 percent of students will need tier two level interventions to be successful in school. An example of a tier two academic intervention is an additional 30 minutes of small-group reading instruction that is provided to students over and above the amount of reading instruction they receive in general education classrooms. Tier two behavior interventions include specially designed small-group counseling interventions provided by school social workers, school psychologists, school counselors, and other behavioral specialists (Crone, Horner, Hawken, 2004).

Tier three interventions are provided to students with intensive academic and/or behavior needs. Interventions at this level are individualized and tailored to meet the unique academic and/or behavior needs of students. An example of a tier three academic intervention is an extra 60 minutes of concentrated small-group reading instruction that is provided in addition to the time devoted to reading instruction in general education classrooms. Tier three behavior interventions include wraparound planning. Wraparound is a planning process based on student strengths and needs across home, school, and community. Individualized intervention plans are developed and tailored to meet the unique needs of students who exhibit chronic problem behaviors (Scott & Eber, 2003). PBIS estimates that 1–5 percent of students will require tier three level interventions. All three tiers work together to provide a continuum of school-wide instructional and behavioral support (Scott & Eber, 2003).

The purpose of this chapter is to describe various tier two behavior interventions for students at risk of developing problem behaviors due to poor social skills, low academic achievement, and/or challenging family situations

FIGURE 35.1 Continuum of Academic and Behavior Support. From: OSEP Technical Assistance Center on Positive Behavior Interventions and Supports

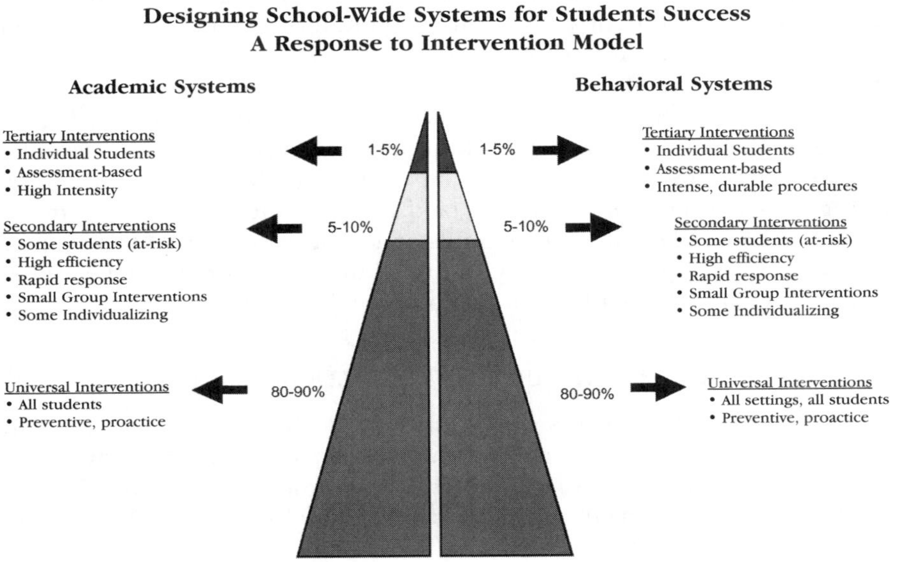

(Lewis & Sugai, 1999). These students require added support over and above the tier one interventions that are provided to all students but they do not require the type of help associated with tier three interventions. Tier two interventions offer at-risk students additional opportunities to learn expected behaviors that lead to educational success (Lee, Sugai & Horner, 1999). Key components of tier two interventions include 1) continuous availability; 2) minimal effort required from staff; 3) voluntary student participation; and 4) ongoing data collection and evaluation that guides implementation.

School social workers frequently provide or coordinate tier two interventions. Students may be identified as in need of tier two behavior interventions by analyzing trends in the number of office discipline referrals, suspensions, detentions, attendance, and tardies. Those students with a greater number of incidents may be targeted to receive additional support. Tier two interventions must reflect the frequency and complexity of students' problem behaviors (Sugai, et al., 2000). Student progress is monitored over time to determine if the identified problem behaviors have decreased or if tier three interventions should be considered. A common method of evaluating progress is through rating scales that require teachers or another adult to record their opinion of a specific problem behavior during a class period (Sandomierski, Kincaid, & Algozzine, 2007). The rater should provide verbal feedback to students that explain why they received a given score. Additional data used to evaluate progress include reductions in the number of office discipline referrals, suspensions, detentions, and tardies. Other progress indicators are increased attendance days as well as pre/post group intervention testing, and student grades. By integrating ongoing data evaluation methods into tier two interventions, progress is monitored continuously to ensure that implementation efforts meet student needs.

Tier two interventions integrate practices that are developed based upon the best available research. Interventions must be implemented consistently and correctly before a decision can be made regarding student progress. This means that attention must be paid to what interventions are implemented as well as how they are administered. The remainder of this chapter will describe examples of effective tier two interventions that can be implemented for students at-risk of various problem behaviors.

CUEING AND GROUP SOCIAL SKILLS INSTRUCTION

Children and adolescents with poor impulse control frequently talk out of turn, fail to listen to directions, blurt out answers before being called upon, and have difficulty waiting their turn. Posavac, Sheridan and Posavac (1999) described an effective behavior intervention for students that demonstrate disruptive classroom behaviors. These students received social skills instruction as part of a small-group counseling intervention that focused on enhancing listening and anger management skills. In addition, students were assigned a target goal behavior to focus on for the duration of the intervention. The goals were stated in positive terms such as "keep hands to myself." A critical component of the intervention involved a cueing procedure that required students to evaluate themselves as well as their fellow group members at five minute timed intervals during social skills instruction periods as to whether they had met their goal. The cueing procedure culminated with the group leader making the final determination regarding goal attainment. Students were recognized and positively reinforced for performing the identified behavior. The cueing procedure provided in conjunction with small-group social skills instruction for children that displayed disruptive classroom behaviors resulted in a decrease in impulsive behaviors.

THE JOURNEY: A GROUP COUNSELING INTERVENTION

The Journey is a six-week, small-group, school-based counseling intervention for students with attention deficit hyperactivity disorder (ADHD) (Webb & Myrick, 2003.) The group sessions include structured learning activities that teach students cognitive behavioral strategies designed to increase their ability to pay attention, listen closely to instructions, and to identify personal cues to manage difficult situations. Using the metaphor of

ADHD as a journey, students learn that even though their ADHD symptoms can make their school experience different from that of other students, it is possible to be successful. Each of the six sessions presents a different social skill and includes opportunities for guided practice:

1. *Our journey.* This session introduces the notion that students with ADHD must learn to be a different kind of traveler and must learn new ways to demonstrate socially appropriate behavior at school.
2. *Pack it up.* The need to learn effective organizational skills is emphasized and students are exposed to assorted organizational strategies that facilitate classroom learning.
3. *Stop lights and traffic cops.* Students learn various strategies designed to help them pay close attention when faced with distractions.
4. *Using road signs as a guide.* This session helps students identify personal cues that lead to socially appropriate classroom behavior.
5. *Road holes and detours.* Students are instructed on selected cognitive behavioral techniques intended to help identify and maneuver around obstacles that interfere with classroom learning.
6. *Roadside help and being your own mechanic.* This session emphasizes social skills with the expectation that students use the skills to self-manage their behavior.

The Journey is most effective when combined with teacher reinforcement in the classroom of social skills acquired during the group intervention.

CHALLENGING HORIZONS PROGRAM

The *Challenging Horizons Program* is an after-school program for middle school students who demonstrate disruptive classroom behaviors (Evans, Axelrod, & Langberg, 2004.) The program provides interpersonal skills training, recreational activities, educational skill instruction, and family support in two-hour sessions three days a week over a three-month period. The interpersonal skills training component of the program is a small-group intervention designed to teach, practice, and reinforce socially appropriate communication skills. The recreational segment of the program provides an opportunity for students to practice the social skills learned during the interpersonal skills training.

Small-group instruction on educational skills accompanies the *Challenging Horizons Program*. This segment of the program focuses on developing the skills necessary to succeed in the classroom. These skills include: note-taking, study skills, recording assignments in assignment notebooks, gathering required materials for completing homework assignments, organizing lockers, book bags, and notebooks. The family assistance part of the program includes regular parent meetings that provide information on topics such as homework management and supporting positive peer relationships. Evans, et al. (2004) found that students that participated in the *Challenging Horizons Program* reported decreased problem behaviors and improved academic performance.

KIDS TOGETHER

Kids Together is an effective group play-therapy intervention for students who exhibit impulsive, disruptive behaviors, and poor communication skills (Hansen, Meissler, & Owens, 2000). The fifteen-week program targets students age 5–17 and aims to increase socially appropriate peer and adult interactions. The group curriculum includes skill topics such as listening, organization, self-monitoring, impulse control, and problem solving. Students receive step-by-step instructions on how to seek and maintain positive social relationships. Once students demonstrate skill competencies, they identify cues and prompts to help them generalize the new behaviors to classrooms, hallways, and lunchrooms. Using a combination of play, art, and recreational therapeutic activities, *Kids Together* has been shown to reduce problem behaviors while increasing socially appropriate ones.

PEER-PAIRING

Mervis (1998) reported that peer-pairing is an effective model for children with poor impulse control, hyperactivity, or high levels of aggression. Peer-pairing is a good option to consider when traditional small-group, individual, or classroom interventions have been ineffective. The model is well suited for students who become overstimulated in a group setting. Peer-pairing provides ongoing social skills instruction and coaching to two students who are matched based on similar levels and types of problem behaviors. Students who have acquired an emerging level of social skills acquisition can invite a guest student to the peer-pairing sessions. The guest student is someone whom both students agree to invite. A guest student does not have to have social skills deficits. Peer-pairings with guest students are another way to provide the student pairs an opportunity to rehearse what they have learned. By providing targeted training and coaching in peer-paired arrangements, students with poor impulse control or highly aggressive behaviors can develop the skills necessary to be successful in school.

BEHAVIOR EDUCATION PROGRAM

The Behavior Education Program (BEP) is a daily check-in, check-out intervention for students at-risk of exhibiting severe behavior problems (Hawken & Horner, 2003). Students attend daily meetings with an adult before and after school to monitor their progress in meeting identified behavior goals. In addition, students check in with teachers after each class to receive immediate feedback about their behavior during that class period. Progress is monitored through daily behavior performance reports that are sent home for parents to sign. Data is summarized weekly and the results are communicated to the students, their teachers, and parents. The Behavior Education Program has been found to reduce problem behaviors while helping students become more consistent in exhibiting socially appropriate classroom behaviors. More importantly, the program has shown a decreased need for more intensive tier three behavior interventions (Hawken, MacLeod, & Rawlings, 2007).

ANGER MANAGEMENT GROUP: USING ANIMALS

A unique tier two behavior intervention that targets adolescents who display aggressive behavior combines cognitive behavior therapy and pet therapy in a 12-week group intervention (Hanselman, 2002). Two dogs are present at each group session and are available for petting as members discuss emotionally charged issues. Group members learn to identify anger and aggression triggers, consider consequences of aggressive behaviors, and implement alternative behavior responses during the group intervention. The pets provide a means for assessing empathy skills and capacity for attachments. By identifying irrational beliefs about anger and the consequences for displaying aggressive behaviors, students increase their ability to consistently express anger in appropriate ways.

SOLUTION-FOCUSED INTERVENTION FOR LD STUDENTS AT-RISK OF BEHAVIOR PROBLEMS

Solution-focused therapeutic interventions utilize cognitive behavioral therapy techniques aimed at increasing socially appropriate behaviors (Franklin, Bievier, Moore, Clemons, & Scamardo, 2001). Applied to students with learning disabilities who exhibit school-related behavior problems, solution-focused interventions aim to rapidly increase displays of socially appropriate behaviors while reducing maladaptive ones. Each session follows a similar format. Students are asked the "miracle question" followed by scaling questions to help them identify small, measurable steps for change. The miracle question asks students to speculate what would happen if they woke up to learn that a miracle had taken place to solve their problem. This technique is followed by a series of questions that require students to rate their problem and potential progress on a scale of 1 to 10. In as few as 5-10 sessions, students can show improved functioning in appropriate school-related behaviors.

Tier two behavior interventions, implemented as part of a systematic approach to promote socially appropriate behavior on a school-wide basis, provide additional support to at-risk students. The interventions highlighted in this chapter are evidence-based practices that can be implemented by school social workers. Tier two interventions should match the frequency and intensity of student needs and incorporate ongoing data collection to monitor student progress. By providing tier two behavior interventions to at-risk students, school social workers can effectively meet the needs of children experiencing social difficulties at school.

References

Carr, E., Dunlap, G., Horner, R., Koegel, R., Turnbull, A. P., Sailor, W., Anderson, J., Albin, R., Koegel, L., & Fox, L. (2002). Positive behavior support: Evolution of an applied science. *Journal of Positive Behavioral Interventions, 4*(1), 4–16.

Crone, D., Horner, R., & Hawken, L. (2004). *Responding to problem behavior in schools: The behavior education program*. New York: Guilford.

Evans, S., Axelrod, J., & Langberg, J. (2004). Efficacy of a school-based treatment program for middle school youth with ADHD. *Behavior Modification, 28*(4), 28–547.

Franklin, C., Bievier, J., Moore, K., Clemons, D., & Scamardo, M. (2001). The effectiveness of solution-focused therapy with children in a school setting. *Research on Social Work Practice, 11*(4), 411–434.

Hansen, S., Meissler, K., & Owens, R. (2000). Kids Together: A group play therapy model for children with ADHD symptomatology. *Journal of Child and Adolescent Therapy, 10*(4), 191–211.

Hanselman, J. (2002). Coping interventions with adolescents in anger management using animals in therapy. *Journal of Child and Adolescent Group Therapy, 11*(4), 159–195.

Hawken, L., & Horner, R. (2003). Evaluation of a targeted intervention within a school wide system of behavior support. *Journal of Behavioral Education, 12*(3), 225–240.

Hawken, L., MacLeod, K., & Rawlings, L. (2007). Effect of the behavior education program (BEP) on office discipline referrals of elementary school students. *Journal of Positive Behavior Interventions, 9*(2), 94–101.

Horner, R., Todd, A., Lewis-Palmer, T., Irvin, L., Sugai, G., & Boland, J. (2004). The School-wide Evaluation Tool (SET): A research instrument for assessing school-wide positive behavior support. *Journal of Positive Behavior Interventions, 6*(1), 3–12.

Irvin, L., Horner, R., Ingram, K., Todd, A., Sugai, G., Sampson, N., & Boland, J. (2006). Using office discipline referral data for decision making about student behavior in elementary and middle schools: An empirical evaluation of validity. *Journal of Positive Behavior Interventions, 8*(1), 23.

Irvin, L., Tobin, T., Sprague, J., Sugai, G., & Vincent, C. (2004). Validity of office discipline referral measures as indices of school-wide behavioral status and effects of school-wide behavioral interventions. *Journal of Positive Behavior Interventions, 6*(3), 131–147.

Lee, Y., Sugai, G., & Horner, R. (1999). Effect of component skill instruction on math performance and on-task, problem, and off-task behavior of students with emotional and behavioral disorders. *Journal of Positive Behavior Interventions, 1*, 195–204.

Lewis, T. J., & Sugai, G. (1999). Effective behavior support: A systems approach to proactive school-wide management. *Effective School Practices, 17*(4), 47–53.

Luiselli, J., Putnam, R., & Sunderland, M. (2002). Longitudinal evaluation of behavior support intervention in a public middle school. *Journal of Positive Behavior Interventions, 4*(3), 182–188.

Mervis, B. (1998). The use of peer-pairing in schools to improve socialization. *Child and Adolescent Social Work Journal, 15*(6), 467–477.

Posavac, H., Sheridan, S., & Posavac, S. (1999). A cueing procedure to control impulsivity in children with Attention Deficit Hyperactivity Disorder. *Behavior Modification, 23*(2), 234–253.

Sandomierski, T., Kincaid, D., & Algozzine, B. (2007). Response to intervention and Positive Behavior Support: Brothers from different mothers or sisters with different misters? *Positive Behavior Interventions and Supports Newsletter, 4*(2). Retrieved October 10, 2007 from http://pbis.org/news/New/Newsletters/Newsletter4-2.aspx

Scott, T. (2001). A school wide example of positive behavior support. *Journal of Positive Behavior Interventions, 3*(2), 88–94.

Scott, T., & Barrett, S. (2004). Using staff and student time engaged in disciplinary procedures to evaluate the impact of school-wide PBS. *Journal of Positive Behavior Interventions, 6*(1), 21–27.

Scott, T., & Eber, L. (2003). Functional assessment and wraparound as systemic school processes: Primary, secondary and tertiary systems examples. *Journal of Positive Behavior Interventions, 5*(3), 131–143.

Sugai, G. (2006, February 13). *School-wide positive behavior support: Getting started.* Retrieved October 2, 2007 from http://www.pbis.org/files/George/co0206a.ppt

Sugai, G., Horner, R., Dunlap, G., Hieneman, M., Lewis, T., Nelson, C., Scott, T., Liaupsin, C., Sailor, W., Turnbull, A., Turnbull, H., Wickham, D., Reuff, M., & Wilcox, B. (2000). Applying positive behavioral support and functional behavioral assessment in schools. *Journal of Positive Behavioral Interventions and Support, 2*, 131–143.

Sugai, G., Horner, R., Dunlap, G., Hieneman, M., Lewis, T., Nelson, C., Scott, T., & Liaupsin, C. (1999). *Applying positive behavioral support and functional behavioral assessment in schools: Technical Assistance Guide.* U.S. Department of Education, Office of Special Education Programs, Center on Positive Behavioral Interventions and Support.

Sugai, G., & Horner, R. (2002). The evolution of discipline practices: School-wide positive behavior supports. *Child & Family Behavior Therapy, 24*(1/2), 23–50.

Sugai, G., Sprague, J., Horner, R., & Walker, H. (2000). Preventing school violence: The use of office discipline referrals to assess and monitor school-wide discipline interventions. *Journal of Emotional and Behavioral Disorders, 8*(2), 94–101.

Webb, L., & Myrick, R. (2003). A group counseling intervention for children with Attention Deficient Hyperactivity Disorder. *Professional School Counseling, 7*(2), 108–115.

36

School Social Work Collaboration with the Child Welfare System

Sandra J. Altshuler
University of South Carolina

- Social and Emotional Needs of Children Involved with Child Welfare
- Educational Needs of Children Involved with Child Welfare
- Collaboration Between Schools and Child Welfare
- Mandated Reporting
- Promising Practices: Tiers One, Two, and Three

Schools have a wide range of connections with the child welfare system, having in common the care and well-being of children involved with both systems. Some of these children are still living with their own parents or family; others are at risk of child abuse or neglect; others live in foster care homes or group homes or are returning from substitute care. This chapter focuses on the current research on the social, emotional, and academic needs of such children and applies that knowledge in exploring promising practices for school social work collaborations with the child welfare system to address the needs of these highly vulnerable children.

The number of students living in foster care has been growing exponentially for twenty years, with over one-half million children living in out-of-home placements (U.S. Department of Health and Human Services, 2003b). The majority come from poor minority families, with African-American children the largest overrepresented ethnic group in the foster care population (Mech, 1983; Tate, 2001; Zetlin & Weinberg, 2004). Many of these children are at risk for school failure based upon their low socioeconomic status (SES), minority status, and special education needs. Because the majority of children involved with the child welfare system attend public schools, school social workers are in a unique position to assist these students, but they must first become aware of their extensive needs. Children in foster care are often the most vulnerable children in schools, because they are struggling with personal, familial, and educational challenges that other students may not need to confront.

SOCIAL AND EMOTIONAL NEEDS OF CHILDEN INVOLVED WITH CHILD WELFARE

Children involved with the child welfare system have experienced physical or sexual abuse, neglect, and, in most cases, some type of separation from parents. A great deal of literature has convincingly documented that these experiences significantly increase the risk of serious emotional, behavioral, or developmental problems, and attachment disorders (DHHS, ACF, 2003b; Clausen, Landsverk, Ganger, Chadwick, & Litrownik, 1998; Halfon, Berkowitz, & Klee, 1992; Hughes, 1999; Manly, Kim, Rogosch, & Cicchetti, 2001; McIntyre & Keesler, 1986; Orme & Buehler, 2001; Pilowsky, 1995; Stein, Evans, Mazumdar, & Rae-Grant, 1996).

One of the first national longitudinal studies examining characteristics and needs of children and families involved in the child welfare system found that these children scored below general population norms on virtually every developmental measure, thus demonstrating a profile similar to children living in poverty. These children are particularly lacking social skills and daily living skills. They have lower cognitive abilities and language development and higher levels of behavioral problems, yet only about 25 percent received at least one specialty service to address those problems (DHHS, ACF, 2003a).

Using standardized measures of child behavior or diagnostic criteria for psychological disturbances, other studies have assessed the emotional difficulties of children living in foster care, who consistently demonstrate clinically high levels of externalizing and internalizing behavioral problems, as evidenced on the CBCL, and/or the American Psychiatric Association's *Diagnostic and Statistical Manual of Mental Disorders (DSM)* (Clausen et al., 1998; Heflinger, Simpkins, & Combs-Orme, 2000). The prevalence of psychiatric disorders is comparable to that for children who receive services in mental health settings (Stein, et al., 1996).

EDUCATIONAL NEEDS OF CHILDREN INVOLVED WITH CHILD WELFARE

Concerns about the educational needs of students involved with the child welfare system have arisen over the past 25 years. Many or most of such children are placed in substitute care. They change schools often, usually in mid-year, and have consistently demonstrated lowered achievement and academic performance in school. In the following section, the research on the educational needs of children living in substitute care will be reviewed.

There is a body of research on the academic performance of children in nonrelated foster care (placed with a family to whom the child is not related), kinship foster care (placed with a blood relative), and group home care.[1] These studies all found that, compared to normed expectations, students in foster care demonstrate significantly lower academic achievement and performance. The conclusions were based primarily upon standardized achievement tests, school cumulative records, teacher assessments, or parent ratings. Compared with other students in similar classes, students living in foster care consistently perform and are placed below age-appropriate grade levels, demonstrate inappropriate school-related behaviors more frequently, have poorer attendance records, change schools more frequently, and have higher retention rates.

Students living in foster care demonstrate a variety of academic difficulties, including weaker cognitive abilities (Fanshel & Shinn, 1978; Fox & Arcuri, 1980) and poorer academic performance and classroom achievement (Evans, 2004; Heath, Colton, & Aldgate, 1994; Runyan & Gould, 1985; Sawyer & Dubowitz, 1994). These difficulties lead many of these students to experience grade retentions and placement below age-appropriate grade levels (Benedict, et al., 1996; Sawyer & Dubowitz, 1994; Smucker, Kauffman, & Ball, 1996).

Students living in foster care demonstrate behavioral problems in school settings that range from aggressive, demanding, immature, and attention-seeking behaviors to withdrawn, anxious, and overcompliant behaviors (Smucker, et al., 1996; Wolkind & Rutter, 1973; Zima, et al., 2000). They have higher rates of absenteeism and tardiness than their classroom peers (Benedict, et al., 1996; Canning, 1974; Runyan & Gould, 1985) and lower levels of school engagement or participation in extracurricular activities (Kortenkamp & Ehrle, 2002). They change schools more frequently, drop out in significantly higher numbers than students not living in foster care, or do not continue on to higher educational opportunities (Burley & Halpern, 2001; Cook, 1994; Eckenrode, Rowe, Laird, & Brathwaite, 1995; Vinnerljung, Oman, & Gunnarson, 2005). These attendance difficulties also contribute to poor academic performance and behavioral problems.

Students living in foster care receive special education services at higher rates than children in the general population (Geenen & Powers, 2006; U.S. Department of Health and Human Services, 2003a; Zetlin, 2006; Zetlin & Weinberg, 2004). The primary disabling condition identified for a majority of children placed in foster care and special education is either a learning disability or a serious emotional disturbance (Berrick, Barth, & Needall, 1994;

1. More restrictive placements, such as institutional care, are not discussed in this chapter because these children do not usually attend public schools.

Goerge, VanVoorhis, Grant, Casey, & Robinson, 1992). Interestingly, Goerge and his colleagues speculate that children in foster care are actually under-identified for emotional disturbances, given that research has demonstrated the extensive mental health needs of these children (DHHS, ACF, 2003b; Clausen, et al., 1998; Stein, et al., 1996).

Poor educational functioning while in care has led to poorer functioning as adults. Retrospective reports from adults placed in foster care as children indicate that they experienced significant school difficulties while growing up in foster care and regret not receiving extra help to succeed academically (Blome, 1997; Courtney & Dworsky, 2006; Courtney, Piliavin, Grogan-Kaylor, & Nesmith, 2001; Martin & Jackson, 2002; Pecora, et al., 2006). Benedict and her colleagues (1996) highlighted school failure and retention, behavioral, and attendance problems as some of the most significant difficulties experienced by former foster children. High school graduation is particularly important. Former foster children who had not graduated from high school were less likely than those who did graduate to be employed, maintain stable housing, have strong leisure interests, feel satisfied with their lives (Pilling, 1987, as cited in Jackson, 1988), or have higher levels of self-sufficiency, including the ability to maintain stable housing and full-time employment (Cheung & Heath, 1994; Stein, 1994). Studies of adult functioning after foster care have demonstrated the importance of academic success for employment, self-sufficiency, and self-esteem (Aldgate, Heath, Colton, & Simm, 1993; Benedict & Zuravin, 1996; Courtney, et al., 2001; Kerman, Wildfire, & Barth, 2002).

COLLABORATION BETWEEN SCHOOLS AND CHILD WELFARE

Despite the obvious need for collaboration, public child welfare systems and public educational systems have often had difficulty working collaboratively (Altshuler, 2003). Child welfare systems tend to focus on achieving safety and permanency, whereas the educational mission is academic achievement. The No Child Left Behind Act (NCLB) has placed even greater pressure upon schools to meet standardized testing goals, while over the past twenty five years child welfare legislation has created similar imperatives to move children out of substitute care and into more permanent placements.

Because of these external pressures, schools may be unprepared to deal with the vast array of needs of children involved with the child welfare system, while public policy has failed to make academic achievement a central goal of that system. Perhaps because of the obstacles posed by these differing policy mandates, few mechanisms exist to support successful collaboration between schools and the child welfare system. Thus children served by both systems may receive inadequate services from either, while neither system works collaboratively with the other (Altshuler, 2003; Johnson-Reid, et al., 2007; Zetlin, Weinberg, & Kimm, 2003; Zetlin, Weinberg, & Luderer, 2004).

Nonetheless, school social workers can work to collaborate with agencies from the child welfare system on behalf of these vulnerable students. They need to ensure that these students experience schools as safe and appropriate havens, and they need to provide them appropriate, individualized services.

MANDATED REPORTING

Sometimes, the first point of contact between the school social worker and the child welfare system is due to the mandated reporter role of school social workers. School social workers, and all professionals working in a public school system, are legally defined as "mandated reporters" of suspected child abuse and neglect. This means that all legitimate suspicions of abuse and neglect must be reported to the child abuse hotline, or professionals risk losing their licenses. A "legitimate suspicion" is one in which school social workers have some reason to suspect abuse or neglect has occurred. School social workers or teachers, however, do not need to assess the validity of their suspicions; indeed, they should not even attempt to do so. Rather, after documenting the details that explain their suspicions, they should immediately report their concerns by calling the local, state, or federally available child abuse hotline. As mandated reporters, school social workers or teachers will be required to identify themselves and their professional positions, but can request that the family not be informed of the identity of the reporter. They cannot, however, remain anonymous in their reporting.

Once they have filed a report, they will receive a report number and the name of the person with whom they spoke, and include that information in their ongoing documentation. Depending on the circumstances, the investigating child protection worker may then contact the reporting professional to arrange for an immediate interview with the child at the school. Usually the school social worker will eventually be notified of the outcome of the investigation, but, unfortunately, this does not necessarily occur, it may take more time than expected, or the outcome may not match the hopes of the reporter. The implications of school personnel being mandated reporters will demand a good deal of assistance by the school social worker in the form of consultation and workshops for teachers and others who may be less familiar or less equipped to deal with these requirements. Such workshops are one component of planful school social work practice that addresses the needs of children involved with child welfare.

PROMISING PRACTICES: TIERS ONE, TWO AND THREE

Interventions to address the social, emotional, and academic needs of children involved with the child welfare system span an array of promising practices beyond the mandated reporter role. First of all, school social workers need to be mindful of the potential consequences that result from the trauma of abuse, neglect, and/or separation from primary caregiving parents. School social workers should anticipate a wide and somewhat unpredictable range of problems. What is predictable is knowing that these students are struggling with emotional challenges on a daily basis: a profound change in their living situation; the knowledge that they have been removed from their primary caregiver; the uncertainties they feel about their parents and their future living arrangements; and the difficulty in overcoming the actual experiences of abuse or neglect at the hands of their loved ones. Additionally, children in foster care often struggle with the challenges of low SES, minority status, and the tendency to change schools frequently owing to changes in placements. It is easy to understand why the challenges at school may not be the top priority for these children, as they struggle to give meaning to the upheavals in their lives. Nonetheless, school social workers can support these students by ensuring that the schools they attend are a "safe haven" from these concerns, offering a stable, consistent, accepting, and predictable environment in which they can thrive.

Evidence-based practice (EBP) has become a priority for many social workers (see, e.g., Bilson, 2004; Gambrill, 1999, 2003, 2006; Proctor & Rosen, 2003). In effect, the push for EBPs may be best understood as an attempt to support our ethical obligation to ensure that clients are receiving the most effective, efficient, and efficacious practices that exist. Establishing an evidence base for practice calls for experimental designs with methodologically rigorous group designs and random assignment. The difficulty for school social work practice is that implementing such rigor to test the efficaciousness of practice approaches is seldom practical or feasible. Furthermore, there are still very few published research projects on evidence-based approaches for improving academic success of students in foster care. Thus, this section will discuss "promising practices," that is, approaches that may not yet have rigorous design support but have a degree of evidence demonstrating their potential to be effective.

School social workers are in a strong and unique position to help support the educational functioning of students living in foster care by implementing promising practices at all three tiers of intervention in schools. Tier 1 interventions are designed to be preventive in nature, and attempt to target the whole school and its relationships with those outside the school. Tier 2 interventions address more specifically the needs of children who may be at risk for academic, social, or emotional problems. Tier 3 interventions are intended to focus on the needs of students who clearly demonstrate immediate and pressing concerns.

Tier 1 Intervention: Increase collaboration with public child welfare

Tier 1 interventions attempt to prevent school problems from developing, by addressing the wider environment that encompasses the school and its community relationships. For students living in foster care, strengthening collaborations between schools and child welfare systems has the potential to be a powerful force in preventing problems and concerns when they enter public schools.

Increase trust. The first step in strengthening school/child welfare collaborations is to increase trust. There is a tendency for educators and child welfare workers not to understand or trust each other to carry out their professional duties toward students in foster care (Altshuler, 2003; Jonson-Reid, et al., 2007; Stone, D'Andrade & Austin, 2007). Child welfare workers may be concerned that school systems would not follow through on educating students living in foster care. They may believe that schools simply do not want students in foster care—especially those with behavioral problems—in their schools, and are therefore uncommitted to working with them. They may believe that schools do not maintain high academic expectations for students in foster care, or do not act promptly on academic concerns. On the other hand, these beliefs may be symptomatic of the child welfare worker not having the time, the energy, or even the knowledge to engage with the education system. Despite the importance of the school, child welfare workers are sometimes unmotivated to prioritize school collaboration over other issues such as achieving safety and permanence for children. Unfortunately, this allows educators and school social workers to believe that child welfare workers are unreliable, uncaring, and uninvolved. Educators often complain about the child welfare workers' "obvious lack of caring" toward students (Altshuler, 2003). As a result, successful collaboration remains difficult to achieve, and the child who needs the joint services of the school social worker and the child welfare worker may become lost in a "sea of professional adversity" (Altshuler, 1997).

School social workers and child welfare workers must begin to alleviate that sea of adversity by mutually developing trust. School social workers could initiate contact with the local child protective agency to discuss how the two systems can best support and complement each other's work. In addition, they should contact the specific child welfare workers responsible for children currently placed in foster care in their school to discuss each child's unique educational needs. They may be pleasantly surprised at child welfare workers' responsiveness to these efforts, ultimately supporting the vulnerable children for whom they are all responsible.

Improve communication to increase information-sharing. A second step in strengthening collaboration is to improve communication between the systems.[2] Schools and public child welfare systems may perceive each other as uncommunicative or unhelpful. Professionals in one system might place the responsibility for communication upon the professionals in

---

2. The American Bar Association has developed a guide entitled *Mythbusting: Breaking Down Barriers to Meet the Education Needs of Children in Foster Care,* for addressing such barriers. It would be useful for all school social workers (McNaught, 2005).

the other system, creating a lack of information sharing. Currently, while educators generally understand the legal and policy constraints faced by child welfare workers, they nonetheless often feel that child welfare workers either deliberately withhold vital information from them or are simply unresponsive and therefore do not warrant contact (Jonson-Reid, et al., 2007). Conversely, while child welfare workers generally understand the justification for school systems to know about the educational needs of the students, they often feel that educators expect them to divulge confidential, nonessential information (Altshuler, 2003). In actuality, however, schools often know a great deal about the child's current functioning and capabilities because of their testing of and proximity to students.

Clear and consistent guidelines for sharing confidential information (see chapters 4 and 5) need to be developed within and across both systems to increase the timely flow of needed information. With these guidelines, school social workers can exchange vital, timely information with child welfare workers more freely and understand more clearly, based upon written policy, when they cannot. Since the concerns they share have to do with the child's current functioning, it is less important to share history, except in relation to what the child has told them already. More complex issues arise when the child is suddenly removed from the home and from the school as well.

Improve professional relationships. A third step to strengthen collaboration is to build stronger, long-term relationships with each other. Once school social workers are aware of a student's foster care status, it is their responsibility to initiate and maintain ongoing contact with the student's child welfare worker. This would include inviting the child welfare worker to meetings, informing child welfare workers about available in-school programs (e.g., tutoring, mentoring), and asking about specific problems or issues of which the school should be aware.

School social workers can provide workshops and training opportunities for local child welfare workers about educational policies and laws, especially those related to special education and accommodations for disabilities. Child welfare workers often do not attend school meetings because they do not understand the complexity of schools today and feel unable to provide professional input (Altshuler, 2003; Rittner & Sacks, 1995). Teaching child welfare workers about the processes and practices of multidisciplinary conferences, the educational language and acronyms, and the importance of alerting the school promptly about a child's special educational or disability needs can help improve collaborative relationships. Secondarily, it may also increase the frequency with which child welfare workers attend meetings and initiate contacts with school social workers.

Some governing bodies have successfully legislated the necessity for interagency collaboration between child welfare and public education. The Foster Youth Services Program was enacted in 1981 in California (Ayasse, 1995) and the Manchester Teaching Service was implemented in Great

Britain in 1989 (Walker, 1994). Both programs are designed to increase the collaboration between child welfare and education and both employ independent social workers to accomplish their goals. In Los Angeles County, an Education Initiative provided for Education Specialists, co-located liaisons from local education agencies placed in child welfare offices (Zetlin & Weinberg, 2004; Zetlin, et al., 2004). All three programs demonstrate promising outcomes that suggest replication and further study is warranted.

In summary, collaboration requires a balancing of the diverse roles of school social worker and child welfare worker. Clarifying the distinct roles of school social workers and child welfare workers is the first step in developing collaboration. The school social worker has the advantage of weekly or even daily contact with the child. This degree of contact may be difficult or impossible for the child welfare worker. The school social worker may also have easier access to family caregivers for the child, without the constraints of the power relationship that exists between the child welfare system and families. On the other hand, the child welfare worker has access to the courts and decision-making power that is inaccessible to the school social worker. Each role has different strengths and opportunities. By working together, a synergy can be created that will benefit children and families.

The need for systemic collaboration between schools and child welfare goes far beyond individual collaboration between a school social worker and a child welfare worker. It is important for schools to develop systemic collaborative partnerships with agencies serving children and families, and, specifically, with child welfare. Such partnerships are described in greater detail in chapter 30 of this book, which focuses on coordination of services and resource development, particularly on the development of wraparound systems, to develop a holding environment and prevent institutionalization.

Tier 2 intervention: Improve the school environment

Tier 2 interventions are designed primarily to focus on preventing further deterioration in functioning for students who are at risk for academic, social, or emotional problems. All children involved with the child welfare system should be considered to be at risk owing to their troubled life experiences, and, therefore, could benefit from a variety of Tier 2 interventions.

Create a safe and welcoming environment. Foster care status can significantly affect both how the students perform in school and how teachers react to them (Altshuler, 2003). As noted earlier, school success understandably can become less of a priority for children who have experienced abuse, neglect, and/or separation from their primary caregivers. It is crucial to ensure that students in foster care are treated with sensitivity to their unique circumstances, and to their potentially more urgent needs. This would include maintaining consistent structure and expectations for both behavioral and academic performance. In addition, school social workers should be at the forefront in implementing multicultural and diversity education for the entire school system to improve the educational climate for diverse students (Dupper & Evans, 1996).

Foster parents also need a warm and welcoming educational environment that values them. Despite the knowledge that parent participation in school has a beneficial effect on student achievement, the public education system has not always reached out to foster parents to participate in schools (Kurtz, 1988; Kurtz & Barth, 1989). They may be ignored or only superficially included in multidisciplinary and special education planning meetings, school functions, and the PTA. Foster parents often do not have the history of working with the school that other parents have and may be uncertain of their role there. Because of their overall uncertainty, they may remain on the sidelines unless the school and/or the child welfare agency encourages them to get involved with the school. This situation can be exacerbated if the foster parents are ethnically, culturally, or socioeconomically different from the majority of the school (Outland-Mitchell & Anderson, 1992; Pine & Hilliard, 1990) and no professional addresses these issues.

School social workers and child welfare workers together must take a leadership role to change this, knowing the inherent vulnerability of foster children. They can solicit the foster parents' opinions regarding how the school can best meet the children's educational needs through home visits, phone calls, or face-to-face meetings. They can also carry out their role as advocates by joining the parents and caregivers at meetings with teachers and administrators, and ensuring that their solicited opinions are heard and valued.

School social workers and/or other team members may offer sessions for all parents, including foster parents, about educational policies and laws, especially those related to special education and accommodations for disabilities. Teaching foster parents about the processes and practices of multidisciplinary conferences, the educational language, and the importance of alerting the school promptly about a child's special educational or disability needs can help empower the parents to advocate more effectively for the children in their care. The National Court Appointed Special Advocates (CASA) organization has created an e-learning curriculum to train CASA volunteers and Guardian ad Litem professionals about the educational rights and needs of youth in foster care (see www.nationalcasa.org). School social workers could use this already-designed curriculum in their collaborative work with foster parents. Additionally, the Child Welfare League of America has recently developed a 6 hour in-service training for foster parents, entitled the PRIDE Education Module (see, www.cwla.org), designed to provide them with the knowledge and skills they would need to be effective educational advocates for the youth in their care.

The 100 Black Men of America program (see, www.100blackmen.org) has a mission to enhance educational opportunities for all African Americans. While this program does not directly address the discomforts of African American parents, it does provide promising model programs, using mentors and tutors for improving the academic success of youth.

Teach the educators. Teachers and school administrators should be an integral part of the school social worker's efforts. Teachers need information on the stresses faced by students living in foster care, and how they may be manifested academically, behaviorally, emotionally, and developmentally. Teachers also need to understand when to allow for different responses in different environments, since the previous environment was undoubtedly stressful. Through workshops and consultation, school social workers can provide educators with an overview of some of the challenges faced by child welfare workers and foster parents, to strengthen the collaboration between the parties. Workshops can be offered either at the beginning of the school year, or periodically throughout the year, as specific issues and challenges arise. Additionally, individual contacts and consultations about particular issues are of paramount importance. It is important for teachers to know that students in foster care not only want to be treated equally to other students, but also want their teachers to be sensitive to their unique needs.

Despite extensive searches and reviews of the major publications regarding best or promising practices for supporting the educational needs of foster youth, nothing that is designed specifically for educators in understanding the unique needs of foster youth has yet emerged from the literature. While it is highly likely that there are many iterations of such trainings in existence, there was no one specific training to highlight for school social workers to use. One training, however, that is easily accessible for school social workers was developed by the College of Education at California State University–San Marcos in collaboration with the Foster Youth Services division of the San Diego County Office of Education. Their supplemental curriculum for training future teachers about the needs of youth in foster care is available online. Evaluations of the curriculum have shown significant increases in levels of knowledge and understanding about child welfare and foster care issues after course completion, which, it is hoped, will in turn support better outcomes for such youth.

Ensure Support within the School. Across the country, there is wide variation in the extent of support and social services provided within any school. Programs such as tutoring, mentoring, social skills training, and peer counseling in schools have all demonstrated their effectiveness in helping at-risk students (Bein, 1999; Durlak, 1995). Like other at-risk students, those living in foster care may also benefit from such services. For example, there has been some promising research showing that mentoring programs specific for meeting the needs of children in foster care can enhance their educational success, if implemented well (Altshuler, 2001; Rhodes, Haight, &

Briggs, 1999). In-school mentors could be particularly beneficial for students who change schools mid-year, by offering an ability to provide specific direction for students in negotiating the demands of a new school.

Minimize school disruptions. Frequent disruptions in placements negatively affect students' ability to establish a connection with a home school and have serious detrimental effects on the students' ability to succeed educationally. Keeping students in their home school, regardless of their movement within the foster care system, is one approach for reducing the disruption. Recently, however, advocates for youth have suggested that moving to a new school may be more beneficial for youth, especially if the newer school has an increase in resources, services, and supports (see, e.g., Berrick, 2006); but this should be balanced with the network of relationships already established, the student's current success, the student's preferences, and any inconvenience attached to staying put. In any case, it is crucial for school social workers to minimize the impact of such disruptions, by ensuring continuity in teaching, educational planning, and parental involvement.

Tier Three: Provide appropriate interventions

Tier 3 interventions are designed to meet the needs of children who clearly demonstrate immediate and pressing concerns. The following section describes promising practices for addressing the needs of children involved with the child welfare system who have already demonstrated their need for specific intervention.

Address concrete needs. A first step is to address the often overlooked, concrete needs of children and family systems in foster care. Both school social workers and child welfare workers often overlook the importance of ensuring that family systems have the requisite concrete needs for optimal functioning that are often outside the purview of their own systems. Concrete assistance, important for children living in low SES families, is also especially important for children living in kinship care. Kinship foster parents are more likely to have lower incomes, be single female heads of households, and live in publicly subsidized housing than other parents, including nonrelated foster parents (Berrick, et al., 1994; Dubowitz, Feigelman, & Zuravin, 1993; Le Prohn, 1994). Without adequate finances, food, shelter, or clothing, it is very difficult for foster families to support their children's educational needs. School social workers and child welfare workers can enhance the possibilities of success of these children by acting as advocates in securing needed economic supports and other concrete services for their families.

Be More Pro-Active in Anticipating Student Needs. Research suggests that virtually every student in foster care has some type of special need that should be addressed if they are to succeed academically. School social workers should be pro-active in anticipating these needs. As effective as tier two interventions may be, a focus on the needs of each individual student is crucial as well. School social workers need to urge the local child welfare agency to develop a policy of immediate notification whenever a student in foster care begins to attend a new school. Upon notification, the school social worker or the child welfare worker should organize a joint meeting involving, at a minimum, the classroom teacher, the school administrator, and the foster parents to develop collaboration. The student should be involved as well, unless age or developmental functioning prohibits appropriate participation. The purpose of the meeting would be to create a clearly delineated plan for individualizing each student's needs, and specifying who is responsible for what activities (e.g., What is the child welfare worker going to do, what is the teacher going to do, and what are the foster parents and pupil going to do?). If these meetings were held routinely, it is likely that collaborative efforts between the professionals in both systems would be enhanced, and students in foster care would be less likely to slip through any educational cracks.

In addition to the above advocacy actions, school social workers should seek out and utilize already existing educational support programs designed for students in foster care. One of the most well-known organizations designed specifically to support education for foster youth is the Treehouse Program, located in Seattle Washington. For the past 20 years, this program has been providing a wide range of enrichment and educational support programs for youth in foster care, specifically targeting educational achievement through such efforts as tutoring, advocacy, and college preparatory coaching (see www.treehouseforkids.org). Another program option, the Strategic Tutoring Program manual, has been developed at the University of Kansas. The program is designed to provide a customizable education support program for at-risk youth (see www.ku-crl.org). The curriculum's instructional methods are based upon over 25 years of research that has focused specifically on the needs of at-risk, underprepared students.

Counseling and Consultation. Group counseling can be helpful for students in foster care, particularly for those who have not yet established friendships among classmates. A group approach can normalize the fostering experience for students and allow them to rely on peer support in a meaningful way (Altshuler, 1999). It can also help students learn the norms and expectations of a new school system.

Individual consultation with teachers regarding specific student needs can also support the educational functioning of children living in foster care. For example, school social workers can arrange a behavioral management plan for attendance, tardiness, or behavioral problems. By providing consultation to teachers, school social workers can target specific behavioral or emotional problems of students in their classes, to ensure that their unique needs are being met.

Children in foster care are often the most vulnerable children in the school system. They struggle with personal, familial, and educational challenges that other students may not need to confront. School social workers must play a critical role in creating a safe and supportive haven for children in foster care, and are in a unique position to support the academic success of these students by increasing collaboration with the child welfare system, by ensuring a welcoming school environment for diverse students and foster parents, and by providing direct, individualized services. Although school social workers are not always in a position to prevent children from experiencing the consequences of abuse or neglect, they are certainly in a pivotal position to advocate for them in the school system, so that children in foster care do not suffer further harm by lacking the educational skills they may need to successfully meet life's challenges.

While education may not be the top priority for these students, their foster parents, or child welfare workers, school social workers must support their school functioning. Not only has academic success consistently predicted successful adult functioning, but school itself is a potential anchor for a child whose life has been uprooted. The stability and security of a familiar school system can help children weather the storm of foster care placement, but only if the key participants make active commitments to truly work in the best interests of these children.

References

Aldgate, J., Heath, A., Colton, M., & Simm, M. (1993). Social work and the education of children in foster care. *Adoption and Fostering, 17*(3), 25–34.

Altshuler, S. J. (1997). A reveille for school social workers: Children in foster care need our help! *Social Work in Education, 19*, 121–127.

Altshuler, S. J. (1999). The educational needs of children in foster care: The perceptions of teachers and students. *School Social Work Journal, 23*(2), 1–12.

Altshuler, S. J. (2001). When is mentoring not helpful for students living in foster care? *School Social Work Journal, 26*(1), 15–29.

Altshuler, S. J. (2003). From barriers to successful collaboration: Public schools and child welfare working together. *Social Work, 48*(1), 52–63.

American Psychiatric Association. (2000). *Diagnostic and statistical manual of mental disorders: Text revision* (4th ed.). Washington, DC: Author.

Ayasse, R. H. (1995). Addressing the needs of foster children: The Foster Youth Services Program. *Social Work in Education, 17*, 207–216.

Bein, A. M. (1999). School social worker involvement in mentoring programs. *Social Work in Education, 21*, 120–128.

Benedict, M. I., & Zuravin, S. (1996). *Foster children grown up: Social, educational, economic and personal outcomes. Final report*, submitted to: DHHS, ACF, Children's Bureau, Grant No. 90-CW-1076. Washington, D.C.: Clearinghouse on Child Abuse and Neglect.

Benedict, M. I., Zuravin, S., & Stallings, R. Y. (1996). Adult functioning of children who lived in kin versus nonrelative family foster homes. *Child Welfare, 75*, 529–549.

Berrick, J. D. (2006). Neighborhood-based foster care: A critical examination of location-based placement criteria. *Social Service Review, 80*(4), 569–583.

Berrick, J. D., Barth, R. P., & Needell, B. (1994). A comparison of kinship foster homes and foster family homes: Implications for kinship foster care as family preservation. *Children and Youth Services Review, 16*, 33–63.

Bilson, A. (Ed.) (2004). *Evidence-based practice and social work: International research and policy perspectives.* London: Whiting & Birch.

Blome, W. (1997). What happens to foster kids: Educational experiences of a random sample of foster care youth and a matched group of non-foster care youth. *Child and Adolescent Social Work, 14*, 41–53.

Burley, M., & Halpern, M. (2001). *Educational attainment of foster youth: Achievement and graduation outcomes for children in state care.* Washington State Institute for Public Policy, Doc. No: 01-11-3901. Retrieved September 12, 20007, from http://www.inpathways.net/edattainfy.pdf

Canning, R. (1974). School experiences of foster children. *Child Welfare, 53*, 582–586.

Cheung, S. Y., & Heath, A. (1994). After care: The education and occupation of adults who have been in care. *Oxford Review of Education, 20*, 361–374.

Clausen, J. M., Landsverk, J., Ganger, W., Chadwick, D., & Litrownik, A. (1998). Mental health problems of children in foster care. *Journal of Child and Family Studies, 7*, 283–296.

Cook, R. J. (1994). Are we helping foster care youth prepare for their future? *Children and Youth Services Review, 16*, 213–229.

Courtney, M., & Dworsky, A. (2006). Early outcomes for young adults transitioning from out-of-home care in the USA. *Child and Family Social Work, 11,* 209–219.

Courtney, M., Piliavin, I., Grogan-Kaylor, A., & Nesmith, A. (2001). Foster youth transitions to adulthood: A longitudinal view of youth leaving care. *Child Welfare, 80*, 685–716.

Dubowitz, H., Feigelman, S., & Zuravin, S. (1993). A profile of kinship care. *Child Welfare, 72*, 153–69.

Dupper, D. R., & Evans, S. (1996). From Band-Aids and putting out fires to prevention: School social work practice approaches for the new century. *Social Work in Education, 18*, 187–192.

Durlak, J. A. (1995). *School-Based prevention programs for children and adolescents*. Newbury Park: Sage.

Eckenrode, J., Rowe, E., Laird, M., & Brathwaite, J. (1995). Mobility as a mediator of the effects of child maltreatment on academic performance. *Child Development, 66*, 1130–1142.

Evans, L. D. (2004). Academic achievement of students in foster care: Impeded or improved? *Psychology in the Schools, 41*(5), 527–535.

Fanshel, D., & Shinn, E. B. (1978). *Children in foster care*. New York: Columbia University Press.

Fox, M., & Arcuri, K. (1980). Cognitive and academic functioning in foster children. *Child Welfare, 59*, 491–496.

Gambrill, E. (1999). Evidence-based practice: An alternative to authority-based practice. *Families in Society, 80,* 341–350.

Gambrill, E. (2003). Evidence-based practice: Sea change or the emperor's new clothes? *Journal of Social Work Education, 39*, 3–23.

Gambrill, E. (2006). Evidence-based practice and policy: Choices ahead. *Research on Social Work Practice, 16,* 338–357.

Geenen, S., & Powers L. E. (2006). Are we ignoring youth with disabilities in foster care: An examination of their school performance. *Social Work, 51*(3), 233–241.

Goerge, R. M., VanVoorhis, J., Grant, S., Casey, K., & Robinson, M. (1992). Special-education experiences of foster children: An empirical study. *Child Welfare, 71*, 419–437.

Halfon, N., Berkowitz, G., & Klee, L. (1992). Mental health service utilization by children in foster care in California. *Pediatrics, 89*, 1238–1244.

Heath, A. F., Colton, M. J., & Aldgate, J. (1994). Failure to escape: A longitudinal study of foster children's educational attainment. *British Journal of Social Work, 24*, 241–260.

Heflinger, C. A., Simpkins, C. G., & Combs-Orme. T. (2000). Using the CBCL to determine the clinical status of children in state custody. *Children and Youth Services Review, 21*, 55–73.

Hughes, D. A. (1999). Adopting children with attachment problems. *Child Welfare, 78*, 541–560.

Jackson, S. (1988). Education and children in care. *Adoption and Fostering, 12*(4), 6–10.

Jonson-Reid, M., Kim, J., Barolak, M, Citerman, B., Laudel, C., Essma, A., Fezzi, N., Green, D., Kontak, D., Mueller, N., & Thomas, C. (2007). Maltreated children in schools: The interface of school social work and child welfare. *Children & Schools, 29*(3), 182–191.

Kerman, B., Wildfire, J., & Barth, R. P. (2002). Outcomes for young adults who experienced foster care. *Children and Youth Services Review, 24*, 79–104.

Kortenkamp, K., & Ehrle, J. (2002). *The well-being of children involved with the child welfare system: A national overview.* Washington, D.C.: The Urban Institute. Assessing the New Federalism Policy Brief, Series B, No. B-43.

Kurtz, P. D. (1988). Social work services to parents: Essential to pupils at risk. *Urban Education, 22*(4), 444–457.

Kurtz, P. D., & Barth, R. P. (1989). Parent involvement: Cornerstone of school social work practice. *Social Work, 34*, 407–413.

Le Prohn, N. (1994). The role of the kinship foster parent: A comparison of the role conceptions of relative and non-relative foster parents. *Children and Youth Services Review, 16*, 65–84.

Manly, J. T., Kim, J. E., Rogosch, F. A., & Cicchetti, D. (2001). Dimensions of child maltreatment and children's adjustment: Contributions of developmental timing and subtype. *Development and Psychopathology, 13*(4), 759–782.

Martin, P. Y., & Jackson, S. (2002). Educational success for children in public care: Advice from a group of high achievers. *Child and Family Social Work, 7,* 121–130.

McIntyre, A. E., & Keesler, T. Y. (1986). Psychological disorders among foster children. *Journal of Clinical Child Psychology, 15*, 297–303.

McNaught, K. (2005). *Mythbusting: Breaking down confidentiality and decision-making barriers to meet the education needs of children in foster care.* American Bar Association: Author. Retrieved on September 26, 2007, from http://www.abanet.org/child/education/mythbusting2.pdf

Mech, E. V. (1983). Out-of-home placement rates. *Social Services Review, 57*, 657–667.

No Child Left Behind Act of 2001, PL 107-110.

Orme, J. G., & Buehler, C. (2001). Foster family characteristics and behavioral and emotional problems of foster children: A narrative review. *Family Relations, 50*(1), 3–15.

Outland-Mitchell, C., & Anderson, R. J. (Fall, 1992). Involving parents of at risk children in the educational process: A literature review. *School Social Work Journal, 17*, 17–24.

Pecora, P. J., Williams, J., Kessler, R. C., Hiripi, E., O'Brien, K., Emerson, J., Herrick, M. A., & Torres, D. (2006). Assessing the educational achievements of adults who were formerly placed in family foster care. *Child and Family Social Work, 11,* 220–231.

Pilowsky, D. (1995). Psychopathology among children placed in family foster care. *Psychiatric Services, 46*, 906–910.

Pine, G. J., & Hilliard, A. G. (1990). Rx for racism: Imperatives for America's schools. *Phi Delta Kappan*, 593–600.

Proctor, E., & Rosen, A. (Eds.) (2003). *Developing practice guidelines for social work interventions: Issues, methods, and research agenda.* New York: Columbia University Press.

Rhodes, J. E., Haight, W. L., & Briggs, E. C. (1999). The influence of mentoring on the peer relationships of foster youth in relative and nonrelative care. *Journal of Research on Adolescence, 9*(2), 185–201.

Rittner, B., & Sacks, A. (1995). Children in protective services: The missing educational link for children in kinship networks. *Social Work in Education, 17*, 7–17.

Runyan, D. K., & Gould, C. L. (1985). Foster care for child maltreatment. II. Impact on school performance. *Pediatrics, 76*, 841–47.

Sawyer, R. J., & Dubowitz, H. (1994). School performance of children in kinship care. *Child Abuse and Neglect, 18*, 587–597.

Smucker, K. S., Kauffman, J. M., & Ball, D. W. (1996). School-related problems of special education foster-care students with emotional or behavioral disorders; A comparison to other groups. *Journal of Emotional and Behavioral Disorders, 4*(1), 30–39.

Stein, M. (1994). Leaving care, education and career trajectories. *Oxford Review of Education, 20*, 361–374.

Stein, E., Evans, B., Mazumdar, R., & Rae-Grant, N. (1996). The mental health of children in foster care: A comparison with community and clinical samples. *Canadian Journal of Psychiatry, 41*, 385–391.

Stone, S., D'Andrade, A., & Austin, M. (2007). Educational services for children in foster care: Common and contrasting perspectives of child welfare and education stakeholders. *Journal of Public Child Welfare, 1*(2), 53–70.

Tate, S. C. (2001). The academic experiences of African American males in an urban Midwest foster care system. *Journal of Social Studies Research, 25*(2), 36–46.

U.S. Department of Health and Human Services, Administration for Children and Families. (2003a). *National Survey of Child and Adolescent Well-Being, One Year in Foster Care; Executive Summary*. Retrieved April 4, 2005, from http://www.acf.hhs.gov/programs/opre/abuse_neglect/nscaw/reports/exesum_nscaw/exsum_nscaw.pdf

U.S. Department of Health and Human Services, Administration for Children and Families. (2003b). *National Survey of Child and Adolescent Well-Being, One Year in Foster Care; Wave 1 Data Analysis Report*. Retrieved April 4, 2005, from http://www.acf.hhs.gov/programs/opre/abuse_neglect/nscaw/reports/nscaw_oyfc/oyfc_report.pdf

Vinnerljung, B., Oman M., & Gunnarson, T. (2005). Educational attainments of former child welfare clients—a Swedish national cohort study. *International Journal of Social Work, 14*, 265–276.

Walker, T. G. (1994). Educating children in the public care: A strategic approach. *Oxford Review of Education, 20*, 339–47.

Wolkind, S., & Rutter, M. (1973). Children who have been "in care": An epidemiological study. *Journal of Child Psychology and Psychiatry, 14*, 97–105.

Zetlin, A. G. (2006). The experiences of foster children and youth in special education. *Journal of Intellectual and Developmental Disabilities, 31*(3), 161–165.

Zetlin, A. G., & Weinberg, L. A. (2004). Understanding the plight of foster youth and improving their educational opportunities. *Child Abuse & Neglect, 28*, 917–923.

Zetlin, A. G., Weinberg, L. A., & Luderer, J. (2004). Problems and solutions to improving education services for children in foster care. *Preventing School Failure, 45*(1), 1–7.

Zetlin, A. G., Weinberg, L. A., & Kimm, C. (2003). Are the educational needs of children in foster care being addressed? *Children & Schools, 25*, 105–119.

Zima, B. T., Bussing, R., Freeman, S., Yang, X., Belin, T. R., & Forness, S. R. (2000). Behavior problems, academic skill delays and school failure among school-aged children in foster care: Their relationship to placement characteristics. *Journal of Child and Family Studies, 9*(1), 87–103.

37

Attendance and Truancy: Assessment, Prevention, and Intervention Strategies for School Social Workers

Erin Gleason Leyba

Carol Rippey Massat

University of Illinois at Chicago

- Why Schools Need and Want to Prevent Truancy
- Risk Factors Associated with Truancy
- Multisystemic Assessment of Truancy Issues
- Evidence Based Interventions: Tiers 1, 2, and 3
- Case Examples

From the beginning of the field of school social work in 1906, attendance has remained an issue of concern for the profession (Abbott & Breckinridge, 1917). Social workers, as attendance officers, studied the social ills of the community—poverty, ill health, and lack of secure family income, and their effects on attendance (Allen-Meares, 2004). This chapter addresses the importance of school attendance, risk factors related to truancy, multisystemic elements of truancy, and evidence-based school social work truancy interventions.

School social work involvement in attendance began as part of a national movement to require children to attend school. Compulsory school attendance laws became well established in all U.S. schools at the beginning of the twentieth century, and by 1918 all states had compulsory school attendance laws. These laws transformed the nature of U.S. schools from elitist institutions for the privileged to inclusive institutions that involve all children and teenagers. The laws reflected the prevailing beliefs that education is a necessary preparation for citizenship, a protection from premature involvement with employment, and an essential prerequisite to success in life. All fifty states now have laws requiring attendance, though states vary regarding details related to ages, vaccinations, acceptable equivalents of education, homeschooling, sanctions, and other regulations. Compulsory attendance laws apply unless parents can demonstrate that their child is getting an education elsewhere that meets the same standards as those of the public school, such as through homeschooling (Derezinski, 2004; Fischer & Sorenson, 1996). A 1972 Supreme Court ruling (*Wisconsin v. Yoder*) established another exception when it decided that Wisconsin could not require Amish parents to send their children to school beyond the eighth grade.

WHY SCHOOLS NEED AND WANT TO PREVENT TRUANCY

Law and education policies cause schools to want and need to prevent truancy and improve attendance. State financial aid to school districts is based, in part, on student attendance figures (Gehring, 2004). Regular school attendance has obvious links to factors related to student success, such as academic achievement, graduation rates, and standardized test scores. The federal No Child Left Behind Act (NCLB) requires schools and districts to improve academic performance or face sanctions. Attendance rates are often a factor in determining adequate yearly progress, and if benchmarks are not met, schools may be closed (Gehring, 2004).

Every state, locality, and school district has its own set of laws and guidelines regarding truancy. It is important for school social workers to understand these laws in order to best work with students, parents, and schools. Social workers may access truancy guidelines in their school district's handbook, the state board of education Web site, the professional literature, or public databases (Teasley, 2004).

Existing school data may not accurately reflect the severity of attendance issues. An average daily attendance rate in a district, perhaps reaching 90 percent, could hide 30 percent of the students missing a month of school annually. While a few districts have good attendance, more have a severe truancy problem (Levy & Henry, 2007). The normally high attendance rates of six elementary grades may be weighed against poor attendance at the middle and high school level. Large numbers of high school dropouts lower the enrollment base and can hide mass absences. Furthermore, the 90 percent figure does not mean that the same 10 percent of children are out all the time. It could mean that 30 percent are chronically absent, only on different days (Levy & Henry, 2007).

RISK FACTORS ASSOCIATED WITH TRUANCY

Attendance and Academic Achievement

Attendance is clearly linked to student academic achievement. A number of studies have linked attendance to grade point averages in elementary school students (Heberling & Shaffer, 1995; Winkler, 1993; Yunker, 1967). Others have found a similar relationship among older students (Ackerman & Byock, 1989; Strickland, 1998). Roby (2004) found a positive relationship between attendance and student achievement in grades 4, 6, 9, and 12, with the relationship being the strongest in the ninth grade. Of course, many other factors influence academic achievement, and in some cases, a sense of failure in school or lack of hope may lead to absenteeism, rather than absenteeism causing academic failure. Whatever the direction of causality, if students are not in class, they do not have the opportunity to learn what is being offered. If school failure leads to absenteeism, then those absences will contribute to a vicious cycle of dwindling academic gains and reduced school engagement.

Attendance and Social Development

Truancy can interrupt students' social development by isolating them from peers and adults (McCluskey, Bynum, & Patchin, 2004). Previous friendships can dissipate, and students may be left with few opportunities to socialize (MacDonald & Marsh, 2004). If students eventually drop out of school, it may be more difficult for them to secure stable, well-paying jobs with potential for advancement because they lack skills or qualifications (McCluskey et al., 2004). Though truancy is rarely cited as a direct cause or effect of antisocial behaviors, it is significantly associated with behaviors that may lead to negative personal outcomes (Teasley, 2004). For example, truancy has been found to be a better predictor than grade point average for all drug use behaviors among middle and high school students (Hallfors et al., 2002). In their study of 2,078 14- to 16-year-old youth in London, Best and colleagues found that excessive drinking is also related to truancy (Best, Manning, Gossop, Gross & Strang, 2006). Truancy is associated with drug use (Hallfors et al., 2002; Schroeder, 1993; Soldz, Huyser, & Dorsey, 2003), running away (Man, 2000), academic failure and school dropout (McCluskey et al., 2004), high school senior drinking and driving (O'Malley & Johnston, 1999), and smoking (Tomori, Zalar, Kores Plesnicar, Ziherl, & Stergar, 2001).

Rational Choice

While truancy is associated with a number of negative outcomes, research suggests that truancy is not a personal deficit, but a student's solution to adapt to personal circumstances. Guare and Cooper (2003) argue that students, as rational decision-makers, are like clients or consumers, in that they decide whether to "buy" units of education or to reject them. Students perform a cost-benefit analysis based on factors such as the importance of the day's lesson related to grades, their excitement or boredom with the curriculum and pedagogy, and the punishment they might receive if they are caught skipping school. The law, however, defines this behavior as truancy and, in this sense, truancy, rather than simply an individual symptom, becomes a function of school officials' and the school community's definition of the situation (Carl, Pawlak, & Dorn, 1982) and willingness to enforce this definition. Thus, truancy intervention involves addressing programs and systems as well as intervening with truants as individuals.

MULTISYSTEMIC ASSESSMENT OF TRUANCY ISSUES

A comprehensive assessment of truancy is essential. Historically, truancy assessment has been approached from the sole angle of "what's wrong with the student or the parent," rather than understanding the impact of multiple systems (Harvey, 2003). Strengths-based, comprehensive assessment includes an understanding of individual, family, peer, academic, school, socioeconomic, cultural and linguistic, and community issues that affect students' attendance behavior. It should include an evaluation of the risk factors that contribute to truancy and the strengths and protective factors that work to prevent it (Teasley, 2004). Assessment could include interviews, reports from significant others, self-monitoring, and behavioral observations about social relationships, extracurricular activities, and rational choice considerations. It could also include an understanding of cultural and economic issues, mental health and health issues, academic ability, school engagement, and both positive and negative attitudes about school.

Individual Assessment

On the individual level, school social workers may examine the functions that are served by nonattendance (Lauchlan, 2003). A social worker may choose to complete a formal functional behavior analysis (see chapter 22) to organize and document this information. According to Kearney and Silverman (1990, in Laughlan, 2003) and Kearney (2007), there are four main functions of nonattendance by students.

1. Students may be trying to avoid the experience of severe anxiety or fearfulness related to attending school. Examples include: fear of a school bathroom, fear of taking an exam, or anxiety about a certain class period.
2. Students may be trying to avoid anxious or scary social situations. For example, they may be harassed by a bully, be socially isolated, or have problems with teachers. Students may be seeking attention or reducing a feeling of separation anxiety.

3. Students may be staying home to take care of a sick or incapacitated parent or sibling, may get special attention at home, or may get attention for an illness that does not exist.
4. Students may be enjoying a rewarding experience that nonattendance may bring. For example, students may get to spend time with their friends, watch TV, or sleep late.

Discovering the specific function served by nonattendance should guide the development of a behavior intervention plan. The plan should help the student achieve the functions and payoffs served by nonattendance, but through appropriate means. For example, if a student is using nonattendance to pursue attention from parents, an intervention plan could include strategies for parents to interact with the student by having dinner together, asking about the student's school day, or doing recreational activities together. If a student skips school in an effort to avoid feeling isolated in school, then the intervention plan could involve introducing the student to a club of interest, inviting the student to join a small social work group, or pairing the student with welcoming peers for classroom projects.

A functional behavioral analysis also identifies the antecedents and the consequences of behavior. Examples of antecedents that occur before skipping school are: staying up late the night before, an announcement of a test in class the day before, something more immediate, such as a panic attack on the way to school, or a frightening incident outside of the school doors. Safety issues in neighborhoods and gang turf concerns could make travel to school difficult or dangerous. In some Chicago neighborhoods, children on the way to school have been shot, and parents have organized to form safety chains to escort children to school.

The consequences of either attending or missing school also influence behavior. If students find that they experience rewards, such as enjoyable activities, or are able to avoid aversive activities, they may change their behavior. Contingency contracting and rewards are far more effective than punishment (Carl et al., 1982), but they must be individualized. Changing the antecedents and consequences of nonattendance can also be an effective way to create an effective intervention plan tailored to unique circumstances.

Social, Psychological, and Physical Issues. Given the developmental importance of peers in adolescent life, the social domain has an immense effect on student choices. Students may feel a sense of belonging to a subculture that protests formal education, or they may worry that they may be excluded from friendship groups if they do not skip school with friends (MacDonald & Marsh, 2004). Students may have difficulty standing up to peer pressure to skip school (Guare & Cooper, 2003). They may be victims of a range of bullying behaviors from name-calling to persistent victimization. They may have conflicts with or be embarrassed around peers or staff members. They may be socially isolated. Margolin (2007) points out that although nonaggressive, socially isolated and rejected students are at high risk, few interventions for this population are reported in the literature. She reports that school social workers working with isolated and rejected students have found that provision of a mentor, positive reinforcement, individual counseling, and linkage to a school job were the most effective interventions.

On the other hand, students develop attachments to friendship groups that support a commitment to school (MacDonald & Marsh, 2004). Students may also feel particularly connected to certain school staff members, and these relationships can act as protective factors.

Students with health and mental health problems are at significantly greater risk of academic failure and absenteeism (Needham, Crosnoe, & Muller, 2004). According to the U.S. Department of Education (2001), 50 percent of children with serious emotional disturbances will drop out of school, as compared to 30 percent of all children with disabilities. Because drug use has been found to be a predictor of recent truancy (Henry, 2007), truancy programming may be integrated with Student Assistance Programs (SAPs) or other interventions that address student drug and alcohol issues (Ferrer-Wreder, Stattin, Lorente, Tubman, & Adamson, 2004; Maynard-Moody, 1994).

School phobia or school refusal is one significant mental health–related cause of nonattendance. School phobia is correlated with a number of mental health conditions, including anxiety disorders, mood disorders, disruptive behavior disorders, learning disorders, and substance abuse. Criteria for diagnosing school refusal include:

1. Severe emotional distress about attending school; may include anxiety, temper tantrums, depression, or somatic symptoms.
2. Parents are aware of the absence; the child often tries to persuade parents to allow him or her to stay home.
3. There is an absence of significant antisocial behavior.
4. During school hours, child usually stays home because it is considered a safe and secure environment.
5. Child expresses willingness to do schoolwork and complies with completing work at home. (Fremont, 2003, p. 1555)

Cases of school phobia call for a referral for a multidimensional assessment that examines both physical and mental health (Rettig & Crawford, 2000). Intervention may include family sessions or the introduction of cognitive behavioral strategies.

In all truancy situations, school social workers should gauge the prevalence of grief, loss, family transitions, stressors, teen pregnancy or parenting issues, abuse, and trauma. Experiences of loss and family transitions can be elicited by interviews with the child and the family in an unstructured format that permits children and their families to reveal sensitive information.

Academic Ability and Engagement. To fully understand causes for truancy, school social workers should assess students' academic abilities, engagement, and attitudes toward school. Teachers can provide this information as well as academic files, special education documents or plans, or standardized test scores. Do students see school as boring or pointless, or do they enjoy it? Do students feel intellectually challenged? Do they feel overwhelmed by academic expectations? What parts of the day do they look forward to or dread the most? What parts of the day are most calming or anxiety provoking? Henry (2007) found that students who get mostly As are least likely to be truant, whereas students who get mostly D's or below are most likely to be truant. Some students may feel alienated in classes in which they cannot keep up (Passmore, 2003). Attitudes about school's relevance and instrumental value are also important. In their qualitative study of eighty-eight young people in northeast England in 1999–2001, MacDonald and Marsh (2004) found that explanations for persistent truancy "related, in part, to powerful, (sub)cultural critiques of orthodox claims about the instrumental relevance of education" (p. 143).

Family Assessment and Intervention

Attendance is an issue that, perhaps more than any other, requires a balanced partnership between the family and the school. Constable and Lee (2004) note, "Families cannot educate their children in a complex modern society without the assistance of schools, and schools cannot educate without the cooperation of families" (p. 224). A home visit can serve to assess contextual factors, parent-child communication and interaction patterns (Lauchlan, 2003), understanding of truancy laws, and methods of discipline that may affect attendance (Teasley, 2004). Home visits are also a way of reaching out to families and creating a bridge between the home and the school. How engaged is the parent in the student's schooling? How do the parents feel about education and attendance? Children whose parents had positive school experiences tend to have more positive educational outcomes (Ferrer-Wreder et al., 2004).

School Assessment

School and classroom climate are critical to engaging students in school. A welcoming and warm climate is more likely to keep students engaged and attending than a chillier one. School policies, programs, climate, incentives, and interventions are all important. An understanding of whole-school class-cutting patterns is also useful. How many students arrive at school in the morning and then cut classes or cut the same periods, courses, or teachers regularly (Guare & Cooper, 2003)? School social workers should listen to school staff to understand how teachers' perceptions and teacher-student interactions influence attendance patterns (Lauchlan, 2003).

Availability of Extracurricular Activities in the School. Henry (2007) found that one predictor of recent truancy was having large amounts of unsupervised time after school. On the other hand, there is a positive relationship between extracurricular activities and academic achievement, including school attendance for the broader school population (Fletcher, Nickerson, & Wright, 2003; Jordan & Nettles, 2000) and for economically disadvantaged, ethnically diverse students (Prelow & Loukas, 2003; Reis, Colbert, & Hebert, 2005), and foster children (Shin, 2003). These findings are important since a response to school nonattendance has been to restrict participation in extracurricular activities. Also, the current emphasis on test scores has led to threats to funding for school-based extracurricular activities. Extracurricular activities, sports, clubs, or other after-school programs may maintain connections to school, reconnect students to school, or provide a means of motivating students to maintain regular attendance.

Economic and environmental issues. Students encounter economic, or other environmental obstacles that affect school attendance and achievement (McMahon, Browning, & Rose-Colley, 2001). Cultural and linguistic factors are important. What is the fit between the culture of the school and that of ethnic minority students (Teasley, 2004)?

Economic issues such as homelessness and economic opportunities may affect attendance. Homelessness is associated with high mobility of students, and high student mobility is associated with reduced academic achievement. Despite the McKinney-Vento Homeless Assistance Act, which requires schools to serve homeless students, schools often (illegally) fail to open their doors to students who cannot document a within-district address.

Economic issues related to attendance should be raised. Do students usually go to college? Where do most students get jobs if they drop out of school? Do students' work schedules affect attendance? MacDonald and Marsh (2004) suggest that if there is a historical abundance of decent working-class jobs, then the importance of a traditional education may be undermined. Or if even high-achieving students can only get minimum wage jobs, then do students really believe school can help them succeed?

EVIDENCE BASED INTERVENTIONS: TIERS 1, 2, AND 3

Strengths, protective factors, needs, and resources that were identified in the assessment process should clearly guide the choice of intervention program (Lauchlan, 2003). Interventions that affect multiple systems (individuals, peers, academics, families, communities) and have a strong base in the research evidence are likely to have longer-lasting effects (Teasley, 2004). Multiyear programs that integrate family and school initiatives and address a broad range of issues are more likely to produce significant behavioral change. In order to result in meaningful change, programs must be of sufficient duration and intensity, must be linked to structural changes, and must be reinforced by all staff (Ferrer-Wreder et al., 2004). Students themselves should be involved in both individual and systemic change efforts (Guare & Cooper, 2003). The following interventions have been reviewed and analyzed in relation to the evidence of their effectiveness.

Tier One: Broad Intervention Strategies

Punishment. Punishments, such as detention time, in-school suspension, additional assignments, prohibition of participation in extracurricular activities, removal of work-release privileges, lowered class participation grades (Wisconsin Legislative Audit Bureau [WLAB], 2000), and prohibition of driving (Viadero, 2004), are popular responses to truancy. Sanctions for parents have included fines, court proceedings, and prosecution. Such measures have little research backing (Judd, 2004). Courts often take too long to see attendance cases, so their interventions are not effective (Reid, 2003c). Critics of punitive measures for truancy argue that punishment unfairly puts schools in the police and prosecution business, assumes a deficit model, ignores environmental issues, and treats the symptoms rather than the causes of truancy (Guare & Cooper, 2003). Punishment can act to further isolate students who are already isolated.

From Prevention to Intervention: Policy Development and School Climate. Schools may respond to truancy through policy development, through programs that target school climate and school conditions, or through programs that focus on helping individual students who are truant. Prevention and policy development can impact a broader part of the problem than a focus on individual truants (Dupper & Evans, 1996; Ferrer-Wreder et al., 2004). Prevention and intervention programs should be integrated. Too often schools have fragmented services and distinct initiatives (Passmore, 2003). Reid (2004) writes, "What really matters is having an effective long-term attendance strategy in place which is consistent, facilitates monitoring, and acts both as a deterrent and, at the same time, in a positive, inclusive, and therapeutic manner" (p. 72). Carl, Pawlak, and Dorn's (1982) review of effective attendance policies and procedures found some agreement that:

1. Parents should be alerted to their children's absenteeism.
2. Parent notification should begin at least with the third absence.
3. Parent and school cooperation in intervention is essential.
4. Consistent limits, enforcement, and record keeping on the part of administration and teachers are essential.

Parent education is helpful to make sure that parents understand their legal responsibilities to make children attend school (Reid, 2003c). Attendance and truancy policies should be clearly explained, written in a handbook, updated annually, and well publicized (Guare & Cooper, 2003; Reid, 2003c). Epstein and Sheldon (2002) found that workshops on attendance were associated with increases in average daily attendance, but they suggest that workshops be specifically related to attendance policies, procedures, and consequences.

In high schools there has been some support for the use of a block schedule rather than an hourly schedule to prevent students from skipping classes. Also, an open-campus policy that allows students to leave during their lunch period can contribute to truancy because students may be tardy or not return after lunch (WLAB, 2000).

School social workers can work to help create a positive school climate that may improve attendance (Guare & Cooper, 2003, p. 74). They can advocate for teaching methods that are participative, exciting, active, communal, collaborative, and meaning constructing (Guare & Cooper, 2003; LeCornu & Collins, 2004). Developing supportive learning environments that improve student self-confidence and combat social exclusion helps students to stay engaged. Knowing that teachers care about them is also crucially important to student engagement (Guare & Cooper, 2003; LeCornu & Collins, 2004). When a student is missing from class, teachers should ask, "Has anyone seen Cathy or Keith today?" (Guare & Cooper, 2003, p. 83). Students need to be consistently made aware that their attendance matters (Reid, 2003c). The most effective programs use contingency management. Recognizing and rewarding students for improved attendance may motivate students to attend school more regularly (Epstein & Sheldon, 2002). Schools should focus on improved and good attendance, not just perfect attendance (Colorado Foundation for Families and Children, n.d.).

Long-Term Strategic School-wide Prevention and Intervention. A whole-school strategic prevention approach, with evaluation over multiple years, may help reduce truancy (McCluskey et al., 2004; Reid, 2004). Such a plan is likely to work best when the idea is chosen and initiated by school staff out of a need-based response to a chronic attendance problem (Reid, 2003a). Since this type of approach is dependent on the consistent participation of all school staff members (Reid, 2003a), school social workers are in a good position to initiate, advocate for, and be key players in its development. Research has shown that the earlier the intervention, the more likely it is to prevent nonattendance (Reid, 2003c; Reid, 2004). Because 35–36 percent of all students' truancy and persistent attendance problems start in primary school, and the "trigger" point for truancy is normally between ages seven and thirteen, it makes sense to intervene in these early years (Reid, 2003a; Reid, 2003b). Staff training, gradual and progressive growth, parent communication, ownership, and clear messages are also critically important to program success (Reid, 2004). The plan is dependent on consistently collecting data during elementary school years and transferring it to secondary schools (Reid, 2004). This information allows for early identification and provides a baseline for evaluation (Reid, 2004).

One example of such a program, outlined by Reid (2004), involves identifying students based on level of risk factors related to truancy. This program's tier 1 intervention involves efforts to prevent the general student population from developing attendance problems; its tier 2 intervention targets at-risk students to prevent serious absentee issues; and its tier 3 intervention, the most intensive level of intervention, is used for persistent nonattenders and utilizes a multidisciplinary team including social workers, teachers, special education supervisors, tutors, or other staff members. The team invites the parents and student in for a meeting, reviews relevant information, tries to determine the reasons for nonattendance, and develops an action plan.

Tier Two: Intervention for At-Risk Students

There are many different interventions that school social workers can use to address students at risk of truancy problems. Some of these follow.

Academic Adjustments. Students who have continuously failed at academic tasks have likely developed negative expectations and a sense of incompetence (Ferrer-Wreder et al., 2004). To return to school, they need academic intervention with frequent opportunities to regain their sense of competence when they have opportunities to succeed and strengthen academic skills.

Mentoring and Tutoring Programs. Student mentoring and tutoring programs may decrease truancy by helping students to reconnect both academically and socially. A program involving 2,500 learning mentors and 1,000 learning support units gave help on-site to students with behavior issues across England. This resulted in a 2.3 percent drop in truancy rates (Passmore, 2003). Successful tutoring programs make academic tasks more enjoyable; build confidence; provide support; show students that people care about them; and reinforce cooperation, teamwork, and on-task behavior. They also give students time to practice resilience skills such as planning, goal setting, self monitoring, and problem solving. Tutoring is especially appropriate for helping students who are at risk of academic failure. For peer-led programs to be successful, they need to have clear program aims and objectives, a good fit between project design and intervention efforts, adequate training of peer leaders, and well-specified interpersonal boundaries (Ferrer-Wreder et al., 2004). One mentoring program tested by DeSocio and colleagues was based on the expectation that a strong teacher-student mentoring relationship could improve adolescents' self-regulatory skills, academic aspirations, and motivation for self-development (DeSocio, VanCura, Nelson, Hewitt, Kitzman, & Cole, 2007). In the program, a mentor teacher was linked with five, at-risk students. The goal was for teachers to build a relationship with each student assigned to them. Teachers sought out students each day, followed up with them if they were absent, provided regular times for one-on-one student check-ins, and encouraged students' special interests. Mentor teachers also facilitated two after-school tutoring sessions per week and helped advocate for students with other teachers. The mentor program was supported by an orientation training for mentors, three hours of compensation per week for each mentor, group support meetings for mentors, small grants for individual student interests (i.e. money to pay for art classes), and a full-time school-based project coordinator. It also involved parent interventions and enrollment of students in the school-based health clinic to overcome health obstacles. Although findings were somewhat limited by a small sample size, students in the intervention group were significantly more likely to remain in school and complete the school year than those in the control group (DeSocio et al., 2007)

Parent Partnerships and Education. School social workers have an important role in promoting parent-school partnerships. These partnerships include general parent involvement in school, communication, outreach, and education. Schools may contact parents about truancy through meetings, letters, or phone calls. A strong effort to contact parents personally may act as a deterrent to truancy (WLAB, 2000). In addition, phone calls made by a person who knows the student or family well (i.e., homeroom teacher) may be more effective at preventing truancy than contact by an anonymous person or a phone recording (Colorado Foundation for Families and Children, n.d.). Reid (2004) emphasizes that the tone of the contact, including language and method of presentation used, is important. Schools need to get parents on their side to collaboratively solve truancy problems. If schools are defensive or punitive, parents are unlikely to want to collaborate (Reid, 2004). Giving parents the name and telephone number of an officially designated school staff member who can discuss attendance may also improve attendance (Epstein & Sheldon, 2002). School social workers can help ensure that communication efforts accommodate families who may have difficulty understanding the language, reading, or receiving mail. They must help parents understand truancy regulations, legalities, and potential consequences.

Children and youths with serious emotional disorders are at high risk of school absence. When parents of these children were highly involved in planning they felt more empowered. However, this level of parental involvement was perceived as the exception, with most parents reporting dissatisfaction and frustration in their partnerships with schools regarding educational planning. Despite the importance of parental involvement for all aspects of school life, Jivanjee, Kruzich, Friesen, and Robinson (2007) found that the educational planning process for children with serious emotional disorders (SED) rarely takes into account family needs and circumstances, their values and their culture. School social workers can work at helping these and all parents as partners in educational planning.

Programming. Alternative curricula, alternative schools, vocational/technical schools, specialized schools, and after-school programs may help some at-risk students to stay in school (Epstein & Sheldon, 2002; Reid, 2003c). In England, over 50 percent of 219 education social workers surveyed felt that more alternative or vocational curricula was the best solution to truancy problems (Reid, 2006). Teen pregnancy or parenting accommodations may also be needed. Students who find it difficult to make progress in one school sometimes do better in a different learning environment (Reid, 2003c).

Student Engagement and Relevance. Educational relevance is critically linked to attendance (Reid, 2003c). Engaging students in relevant, culturally appropriate (Guare & Cooper, 2003), participatory curricula through effective teaching methods is another way to combat truancy. School social workers can challenge practices, expectations, and discipline that have an adverse effect on culturally and economically diverse students. They can advocate for greater multiculturalism and diversity, and thus greater inclusion (Dupper & Evans, 1996; Teasley, 2004). One relationship-building program called "Check and Connect" increased rates of attendance and student engagement (Lehr, Sinclair & Christenson, 2004). In "Check and Connect," a monitor, who is "a cross between a case manager, mentor, problem solver, coach, and advocate" (Lehr et al., p. 284), works with students, families, and teachers over several years. The monitor "checks" and records indicators of students' school engagement/withdrawal (including attendance, tardies, detentions, suspensions, behavior referrals, and academic performance) daily over a period of at least two years. The monitor "connects" by providing basic and individualized interventions to students. The basic intervention, provided by the monitor to all students, involves an introduction to the program and a deliberate, regular (often weekly) conversation with each student about the student's progress and the importance of staying in school, and a review/practice of problem-solving strategies. The monitor also works with families and implements individualized interventions, such as helping with transportation, referring the family to a needed resource, or engaging the student in an extracurricular activity (Lehr et al., 2004).

Community involvement and partnership practices. When the community gets behind the schools in attendance issues, the results can be impressive. One project called Safety and Health through Action and Responsibility for Education (SHARE) developed grassroots assessment and intervention in its community (McMahon et al., 2001) over four years. The project involved priority goal-setting, coordination of community services, door-to-door distribution/collection of a needs and assets survey (in which 70 percent of the population was interviewed), and community meetings. A task force to address the needs of at-risk students in the county was made up of health-care providers, school district representatives, parents, clergy, social service agencies, and local government officials. The project resulted in a 75 percent decrease in truancy. Involving the community in partnership can also help to increase daily attendance (Epstein & Sheldon, 2002). Houston, Texas, hosted a "reach out to dropouts day." This was a city-wide effort where 100 volunteers knocked on the doors of 800 students who hadn't shown up to school in the first two weeks of classes (Axtman, 2004). Existing community-based programs, which include truancy prevention and intervention strategies, such as wraparound services, can prevent out-of-school placement.

Tier Three: Interventions for Chronically Truant Students

Transitions back to school. It is advisable to get the student to return to school as soon as possible, because the longer the student is out of school, the more difficult it may be to get him or her back (Lauchlan, 2003). School social workers should pay special attention to details related to helping chronically truant students return to school. To ensure a smooth transition, the school social worker should attempt to alleviate student concerns related to academics, peers, teachers, and other issues (Blagg, 1987; Reid, 2004).

Social connections. To prevent truancy or to reengage truant students, school social workers may help students to connect with a positive peer group and with school staff. By including students in social work groups, referring them to appropriate clubs or activities, or helping them make friends in other ways, social workers can help students to feel more comfortable and confident. Reynolds (cited in Carl et al., 1982) describes a buddy system, used in combination with positive social and material reinforcement, which contributed to a marked improvement in attendance of thirty chronically truant junior high school students. Students, who were reliable attenders and resided in the same vicinity as the truants or who had access to a telephone, were voluntarily paired with their chronically absent counterparts. The buddies were instructed to make contact with each other daily, either by telephone or by meeting at the bus stop. A motivator party for the program's participants was held prior to the implementation of the buddy system. Throughout the following six weeks, the pair's mutual attendance was greeted with a smile sticker placed upon an attendance chart, which was maintained by a counselor aide. At the end of the six-week period all pairs demonstrating increased attendance, were rewarded with music, picnics, and pizza parties.

Cognitive behavioral interventions. For students who refuse school because of anxiety, cognitive behavioral techniques can be helpful. The school social worker can work with students on relaxation training, self-talk (replacing negative messages with positive ones), and exposure (incremental experience with the anxiety-provoking situation) (Lauchlan, 2003).

Student education and social skills training. Educating students about certain behaviors and lifestyle choices to help them make informed decisions can be helpful, but only if it is one part of a more comprehensive program (Ferrer-Wreder et al., 2004). Because many students do not attend school because of anxiety or social difficulties, training students in social skills can be an appropriate truancy intervention (Lauchlan, 2003). School social workers can help students identify social situations that produce negative feelings and help them to practice how to cope in those situations (Lauchlan, 2003). Another approach to skills training is "life competence promotion," which involves teaching a broad set of skills that promote positive adaptation to life challenges. In order to change behavior, skills teaching should include a combination of generic skills and focused applications (i.e., role-plays or real-life practice opportunities) (Ferrer-Wreder et al., 2004; see chapter 33).

Curriculum. In a qualitative research study on a faith-based alternative education program designed to reengage truant students, Sinha (2007) found that students attended the faith-based school an average of three days per week. This was an increase in attendance when compared to their home schools. The faith-based school integrated core academics, a unit-based curriculum, training in specific skills, small class sizes, and teen recreation lounges. Students also commented that they enjoyed the individualized attention and felt respected by and cared for by the teachers. They felt as if they could form friendships and reported that there was less fighting at the faith-based, alternative program (Sinha, 2007).

Home visits and home-school contracting. In an exploratory study, Epstein and Sheldon (2002) found that when school staff made home visits, they reported decreases in the percentage of students who were chronically absent. Constable (1970) did a study of Home and School Visitors in the Philadelphia schools working with chronic truants. He found that in a largely bureaucratized service, when the Home and School Visitor knew the student well enough to give a description of him or her, it significantly predicted a return to school after the home visits. Kearney and Albano (2000; in Lauchlan, 2003) suggest that home-school linked contracting may be used with students to outline clear expectations for attendance linked with rewards.

Parent education and training. Parent education regarding reintegration strategies after a period of significant absence is also helpful (Reid, 2003c). Parent training related to truancy may also be useful in helping parents work together as a team, manage behavior, give clear expectations, and follow through with consequences (Lauchlan, 2003).

School-police partnerships. Innovative, nonpunitive school-police partnerships may help to improve attendance. In the Truant Recovery program implemented in Richmond, California, police agencies transport suspected truants to attendance offices and contact their parents/guardians for in-person meetings (White, Fyfe, Campbell, & Goldkamp, 2001). The program utilizes a Student Attendance Review Board that reviews habitual truancy cases, and a Suspension Alternative Class that allows for students suspended for truancy to remain in school. Here the teacher interacts with truants to discuss any underlying problems, arranges for the truants' homework to be brought in so they do not fall behind, and provides additional academic work. The primary aim of the program is "to return truants to school as soon as possible." Students who participated in the Truant Recovery program got into trouble less often and skipped school less often but continued to struggle academically (White et al., 2001). In a review of the history and role of police-school collaborations, Patterson (2007) notes that such collaborations require an understanding of what problems actually exist, selection of effective, evidence-based strategies, enlistment of all potential stakeholders (including community agencies) in the collaboration, and involving the students.

CASE EXAMPLES

The following case examples are based on composite experiences with children and youth in school settings.

> The high school is large, with 4,000 students, and few opportunities for students to be noticed. It had taken a punitive approach to absenteeism. More than ten absences result in failure of a class, and additional absences result in arrest and jailing of parents. The community is a lower-middle-class community with some opportunities for employment in fast-food restaurants and retail stores. The library is small and scarcely used. No community groups have taken up the issue of improving school attendance.
>
> Tonya is a white 15-year-old from a working-class family. In the past year, her attendance became a problem, so that, based on her high number of absences, she was in danger of school failure and disciplinary action. Ms. Fletcher, the school social worker, met with Tonya to discuss her absences. Tonya had little interest in school; rather she enjoyed spending time at the mall, watching TV, and seeing friends. She didn't like walking to school in the morning, especially in bad weather. She had few friends and no extracurricular activities at school, and she wasn't doing well in her classes. In a home visit with Tonya's parents, Ms. Fletcher met two hardworking, busy people who work long hours every day and, leaving for work quite early, were unable to ensure that Tonya got to school in the morning. They were concerned and wanted to work with the school to "get Tonya back on track." They had felt forced to write notes for her, since they had heard that they could be jailed if their daughter had too many unexcused absences. Both dropped out of high school before graduation, but they were employed and doing well. They wondered if Tonya would be better off working than in school.
>
> Ms. Fletcher began by developing a working partnership with Tonya and her parents around her attendance. They developed a plan to take Tonya to a friend's house in the morning, so that another parent could drive Tonya to school. Ms. Fletcher intervened with Tonya's teachers and asked them all to greet her warmly, by name, whenever she was in class, and to note and appreciate her presence in class. Tonya was asked to report to the school social worker's office every morning that she was in school, when she would receive a sticker on a chart. After earning ten stickers, she got to go out to lunch at a fast-food restaurant of her choice with the school social worker. Ms. Fletcher

> and Tonya explored some of Tonya's interests and discovered that she enjoyed volleyball. She signed up for the volleyball team. Ms. Fletcher also reached out to the community, sought out key community stakeholders, and advocated for them to develop a community-based program to encourage school attendance. Tonya's attendance gradually improved, and her grades were better after one semester.

In this example, the school social worker engaged both the child and the family in school. Although there were obstacles to this engagement, the interventions attempted in the school did not require major time on the part of the teachers or the social worker, and they did result in Tonya's reengagement in the school.

Attendance problems often represent trends and patterns that need to be effectively addressed at a broader level through community-school-family partnerships.

> The Hometown Schools are in a suburb of a major city. Mr. Blaine, school social worker, has noticed that in the middle school absences and tardies increased over the past year, while student grades decreased. There was no illness sweeping the school to explain this trend. Mr. Blaine brought together a task group to address the problem. It included school staff, the other school social worker, parents, two students, the principal, and the police liaison. The task group decided to conduct a needs assessment to evaluate the needs of the school and community and to identify strategies or programs that might improve student attendance and involved key community leaders in the process. The group found several models of strategies for improving attendance. They surveyed the community to determine which model would be the best fit for the community and decided to adopt a "Reach Out to Dropouts" day and make it ongoing. They combined this with efforts to change the school climate to more fully engage students. They applied for a grant to fund more in-school services, including a Student-Assistance program, to address drug, alcohol, and mental health needs of students. This developed into a community mentoring program for at-risk students. After one year, they had not yet received funding to implement all of their ideas, but a significant increase in attendance had taken place.

School districts have a compelling interest for students to achieve academically, graduate, and perform well on standardized tests, all of which require regular attendance. Attendance is vital for students' social development and personal growth, future career opportunities, and economic survival. Attendance can also act as a protective factor to resist antisocial behaviors such as drug abuse, running away, and criminal activity. Finally, schools may face legal sanctions, get less financial aid from states, or have their schools closed if students do not attend.

School social workers should understand their distinct role on the multidisciplinary team. They are in a unique position to apply a comprehensive multisystemic, strengths-based approach to truancy issues. Their understanding of students in their environments needs to guide their interventions. Focused on risk and protective factors of individuals in their broader peer, family, and community environments, assessments may involve observations, interviews, team meetings, home visits, parent contact, questionnaires, policy review, academic review, or other actions. Punishment strategies, though prevalent, have little research support and can further isolate at-risk students. A variety of interventions have shown promise in preventing and intervening in truancy, including: academic adjustments; tutoring and mentoring; cognitive behavioral strategies; student education and skills training; parent partnerships, education, and training; policy changes; programming; student engagement strategies; strategic long-term whole-school approaches; and community partnerships.

References

Abbot, E., & Breckinridge, S. (1917). *Truancy and non-attendance in the Chicago schools: A study of the social aspects of compulsory education and child labor legislation of Illinois*. Chicago: University of Chicago Press.

Ackerman, S. P., & Byock, G. J. (1989). *Evaluation of the 1988 freshman summer program and transfer summer program, phase II.* Los Angeles: University of Los Angeles.

Allen-Meares, P. (2004). *Social work services in schools (4th ed.)*. Needham Heights, MA: Allyn and Bacon.

Axtman, K. (2004). Knock, knock: It's Houston's new truancy gambit. *Christian Science Monitor, 96*(194), 3.

Best, D., Manning, V., Gossop, M., Gross, S., & Strang, J. (2006). Excessive drinking and other problem behaviours among 14–16 year old schoolchildren. *Addictive Behaviors, 31*(8), 1424–1435.

Blagg, N. (1987). *School phobia and its intervention*. London: Croom Helm.

Brown v. Board of Education of Topeka, KS, 347 U.S. 483 (1954)

Carl, M. L., Pawlak, E. J., & Dorn, D. M. (1982). Research on truancy. In R. T. Constable & J. P. Flynn (Eds.), *School social work: Practice and research perspectives* (pp. 164–180). Chicago: The Dorsey Press.

Colorado Foundation for Families and Children. (n.d.). *10 things a school can do to improve attendance*. Retrieved February 28, 2005, from http://www.truancy prevention.org/attendance.html

Constable, R. (1970). *The home and school visitor and the recidivist, non-attendant school child: An exploration of certain dimensions of a relationship and their association with outcome*. Dissertation completed in partial fulfillment of the Doctor of Social Work degree, University of Pennsylvania. Ann Arbor, MI: University Microfilms.

Constable, R., & Lee, D. B. (2004). *Social work with families*. Chicago: Lyceum Books.

Council of Chief State School Officers [CCSSO]. (2001). *Key state education policies on K–12 education 2000*. Education Commission of the States "Clearinghouse Notes," August, 1997; California Department of Education, Safe Schools and Violence Prevention Office, School Attendance Review Boards. Retrieved February 16, 2005, from http://nces.ed.gov//programs/digest/d03/tables/dt151.asp

Derezinski, T. (2004). School attendance. In P. Allen-Meares (Ed.), *Social work services in schools* (4th ed., pp. 95–118). Boston: Allyn & Bacon.

DeSocio, J., VanCura, M., Nelson, L. A., Hewitt, G., Kitzman, H., & Cole, R. (2007). Engaging truant adolescents: Results from a multifaceted intervention pilot. *Preventing School Failure, 51*(3), 3–9.

Dupper, D. R., & Evans, S. (1996). From Band-Aids and putting out fires to prevention: School social work practice approaches for the new century. *Social Work in Education, 18*(3), 187–192.

Epstein, J. L., & Sheldon, S. B. (2002). Present and accounted for: Improving student attendance through family and community involvement. *Journal of Educational Research, 95*(5), 308–320.

Ferrer-Wreder, L., Stattin, H., Lorente, C. C., Tubman, J. G., & Adamson, L. (2004). *Successful prevention and youth development programs across borders*. New York: Kluwer Academic/Plenum Publishers.

Fischer, L., & Sorenson, G. P. (1996). *School law for counselors, psychologists, and social workers*. White Plains, NY: Longman.

Fletcher, A. C., Nickerson, P., & Wright, K. L. (2003). Structured leisure activities in middle childhood: Links to well-being. *Journal of Community Psychology, 31*(6), 641–659.

Fremont, W. P. (2003). School refusal in children and adolescents. *American Family Physician, 68*(8), 1555–1560.

Gehring, J. (2004). Districts tackling truancy with new zeal. *Education Week, 24*(4), 1–2.

Guare, R. E., & Cooper, B. S. (2003). *Truancy revisited: Students as school consumers*. Lanham, MD: Scarecrow Press, Inc.

Hallfors, D., Vevea, J. L., Iritani, B., Cho, H., Khatapoush, S., & Saxe, L. (2002). Truancy, grade point average, and sexual activity: A meta-analysis of risk indicators for youth substance abuse. *Journal of School Health, 72*(5), 205–211.

Harvey, A. D. (2003). Truancy again—and again. *Education Journal, 69*, 17.

Heberling, K., & Shaffer, D. V. (1995). School attendance and grade point averages of regular education and learning disabled students in elementary schools. *Research Report, 8*.

Henry, K. (2007). Who's skipping school: Characteristics of truants in 8th and 10th grade. *Journal of School Health,* 77(1), 29–35.

Jivanjee, P., Kruzich, J. M., Friesen, B. J., & Robinson, A. (2007). Family perceptions of participation in educational planning for children receiving mental health services. *School Social Work Journal, 32*(1), 75–92.

Jordan, W. J., & Nettles, S. M. (2000). How students invest their time outside of school: Effects on school-related outcomes. *Social Psychology of Education, 3*, 217–243.

Judd, J. (2004, April 2). Maths for mechanics might tempt truants. *The Times Educational Supplement*, p. 21.

Kearney, C. A. (2007). Forms and functions of school refusal behavior in youth: An empirical analysis of absenteeism severity. *Journal of Child Psychology & Psychiatry, 48*(1), 53–61.

Kearney, C. A., & Albano, A. M. (2000). *When children refuse school: A cognitive behavioral therapy approach.* Boulder, CO: Graywind.

Kearney, C., & Silverman, W. K. (1990). A preliminary analysis of a functional model of assessment and treatment for school refusal behavior. *Behavior Modification. 14*(3), 340–366.

Lauchlan, F. (2003). Responding to chronic non-attendance: A review of intervention approaches. *Educational Psychology in Practice, 19*(2), 133–146.

LeCornu, R., & Collins, J. (2004). Re-emphasizing the role of affect in learning and teaching. *Pastoral Care in Education, 22*(4), 27–33.

Lehr, C. A., Sinclair, M. F., & Christenson, S. L. (2004). Addressing student engagement and truancy prevention during the elementary school years: A replication study of the Check & Connect model. *Journal of Education for Students Placed at Risk, 9*(3).

Levy, H. O., & Henry, K. (2007). Mistaking attendance. Opinion article in the *New York Times*, September 2, 2007, accessed 2 September 2007 from www.nytimes.com/2007/9/02/opinion/02levy-1.html?th&emc=th

MacDonald, R., & Marsh, J. (2004). Missing school: Educational engagement, youth transitions, and social exclusion. *Youth & Society, 36*(2), 143–162.

Man, A. F. De. (2000). Predictors of adolescent running away behavior. *Social Behavior & Personality: An International Journal, 28*(3), 261–267.

Margolin, S. (2007). Non-aggressive isolated and rejected students: School social work interventions to help them. *School Social Work Journal, 32*(1), 46–66.

Maynard-Moody, C. (1994). Wraparound services for at-risk youths in rural schools. *Social Work in Education, 16*(3), 187–192.

McCluskey, C. P., Bynum, T. S., & Patchin, J. W. (2004). Reducing chronic absenteeism: An assessment of an early truancy initiative. *Crime & Delinquency, 50*(2), 214–234.

McKinney-Vento Homeless Assistance Act 42 USC 11301.

McMahon, B., Browning, S., & Rose-Colley, M. (2001). A school-community partnership for at-risk students in Pennsylvania. *Journal of School Health, 71*(2), 53–55.

Needham, B. L., Crosnoe, R., & Muller, C. (2004). Academic failure in secondary school: The inter-related role of health problems and educational context. *Social Problems, 51*(4), 569–586.

No Child Left Behind Act of 2001. P. L. 107-110.

O'Malley, P. M., & Johnston, L. D. (1999). Drinking and driving among U.S. high school seniors, 1984–1997. *American Journal of Public Health, 89*(5), 678–684.

Passmore, B. (2003, January 17). Playing the blame game with truants. *The Times Educational Supplement*, p. 24.

Patterson, G. (2007). The role of police officers in elementary and secondary schools: Implications for police-school social work collaboration. *School Social Work Journal, 31*(2), 82–100.

Prelow, H. M., & Loukas, A. (2003). The role of resource, protective, and risk factors on academic achievement-related outcomes of economically disadvantaged Latino youth. *Journal of Community Psychology, 31*(5), 513–529.

Reid, K. (2003a). A strategic approach to tackling school absenteeism and truancy: The PSCC scheme. *Educational Studies, 29*(4), 351–371.

Reid, K. (2003b). Strategic approaches to tackling school absenteeism and truancy: The traffic lights (TL) scheme. *Educational Review, 55*(3), 305–321.

Reid, K. (2003c). The search for solutions to truancy and other forms of school absenteeism. *Pastoral Care in Education, 21*(1), 3–9.

Reid, K. (2004). A long-term strategic approach to tackling truancy and absenteeism from schools: the SSTG scheme. *British Journal of Guidance & Counseling, 32*(1), 57–74.

Reid, K. (2006).The views of education social workers on the management of truancy and other forms of non-attendance. *Research in Education, 75,* 40–96.

Reis, S. M., Colbert, R. D., & Hebert, T. P. (2005). Understanding resilience in diverse, talented students in an urban high school. *Roeper Review, 27*(2), 110–121.

Rettig, M., & Crawford, J. (2000). Getting past the fear of going to school. *The Education Digest, 65*(9), 54–58.

Roby, D. E. (2004). Research on school attendance and school achievement: A study of Ohio schools. *Educational Research Quarterly, 28*(1), 3–14.

Schroeder, K. (1993). Student drug use. *Education Digest, 59*(4), 75.

Shin, S. H. (2003). Building evidence to promote educational competence of youth in foster care. *Child Welfare, 82*(5), 615–632.

Sinha, J. W. (2007). Youth at risk for truancy detour into a faith-based education program: Their perceptions of the program and its impact. *Research on Social Work Practice, 17*(2), 246–257.

Soldz, S., Huyser, D. J., & Dorsey, E. (2003).The cigar as a drug delivery device: Youth use of blunts. *Addiction, 98*(10), 1379–1386.

Strickland, V. P. (1998). *Attendance and grade point average: A study.* (Report No. SP 038 147). Chicago: Chicago Public Schools. (ERIC Document Reproduction Service No. ED423224).

Teasley, M. L. (2004). Absenteeism and truancy: Risk, protection, and best practice implications for school social workers. *Children & Schools, 26*(2), 117–128.

Tomori, M., Zalar, B., Kores Plesnicar, B., Ziherl, S., & Stergar, E. (2001). Smoking in relation to psychosocial risk factors in adolescents. *European Child & Adolescent Psychiatry, 10*(2), 143–150.

U.S. Department of Commerce, Bureau of the Census, Current Population Survey (CPS), unpublished tabulations; and U.S. Department of Education, National Center for Education Statistics. (2001). *Dropout rates in the United States, 2001.* Retrieved February 16, 2005, from http://nces.ed.gov/pubs2005/dropout2001/tab_fig.asp

U.S. Department of Education Office of Special Education Programs. (2001). *Twenty-third annual report to Congress on the implementation of the Individuals with Disabilities Education Act: Results.* Washington, DC: Author.

Viadero, D. (2004). Minnesota governor to link driver's licenses, truancy. *Education Week, 24*(3), 26.

White, M. D., Fyfe, J. F., Campbell, S. P., & Goldkamp, J. S. (2001). The school-police partnership: Identifying at-risk youth through a truant recovery program. *Evaluation Review, 25*(5), 507–532.

Winkler, D. F. (1993). *Working status and student performance.* Hickory, North Carolina: Lenoire College.

Wisconsin v. Yoder 406 U.S. 205 (1972).

Wisconsin Legislative Audit Bureau [WLAB]. (2000). Truancy reduction efforts: A best practices review. *Journal of State Government, 73*(4), 13–15.

Yunker, J. A. (1967). Pre–high school group guidance for potential dropouts and non-college bound students. *Research Report, 39.*

38

Bullying and Peer Sexual Harassment in Schools

Susan Fineran
University of Southern Maine

Shirley McDonald
University of Illinois at Chicago

Robert Constable
Loyola University Chicago

- Legal Distinctions between Bullying and Sexual Harassment
- Prevalence of Bullying and Peer Sexual Harassment in U.S. Schools
- Bullying
- Peer Sexual Harassment
- Responses to Bullying and Sexual Harassment

This chapter defines bullying and sexual harassment and reviews the research on both topics. There are growing concerns that bullying and peer sexual harassment interfere with and inhibit personal development, prevent learning, and make the school into a hostile environment for many pupils. Experience as victim or perpetrator can negatively affect a student's life through adulthood. Each experience of bullying or sexual harassment needs to be understood as a complex set of transactions, not simply involving a victim and perpetrator, but also involving peers, parents, teachers, and the general school environment. Assessment and intervention need to respond to this complexity, and social workers who are able to clearly identify the problems associated with bullying and peer sexual harassment strengthen their positions as advocates for improved school environments.

LEGAL DISTINCTIONS BETWEEN BULLYING AND SEXUAL HARASSMENT

Although both bullying and sexual harassment are serious problems in schools, there are legal distinctions between them. It is important to understand these legal distinctions because, although bullying is considered to be antisocial, aggressive behavior that is linked to criminal conduct (Nansel et al., 2001), it is not illegal according to federal law. Sexual harassment however, is defined in the U.S. as a part of civil rights law (Title IX of the 1972 Education Amendments Act), where it is viewed as a form of discrimination. The following definitions clarify the legal meanings of these two terms:

> Bullying and/or intimidation of others includes any aggressive or negative gesture, or written, verbal, or physical act that *places another student in reasonable fear of harm* to his or her person or property, or that has the effect of *insulting* or *demeaning* any student in such a way as to *disrupt* or *interfere* with *the school's educational mission*, or the education of any student. Bullying most often will occur when a student asserts *physical or psychological power* over, or is cruel to, another student perceived to be weaker. Such behavior may include but is not limited to pushing, hitting, threatening, name-calling, or other physical or verbal conduct of a belittling or browbeating nature. (Zuehl, Dillon, Schilling, & Oltmanns, 2002, n.p., emphasis added)

In 1997, the U.S. Department of Education defined sexual harassment in schools as:

> . . . unwelcome sexual advances, requests for sexual favors, and other verbal, nonverbal, or physical conduct of a sexual nature by an employee, by another student, or by a third party, that is sufficiently severe, persistent, or pervasive to limit a student's ability to participate in or benefit from an education program or activity, or to create a hostile or abusive educational environment. (U.S. Department of Education, 1997, p. 12038)

The distinction between bullying and sexual harassment is important, because a child who identifies a behavior as bullying does not have the same protections as a child who calls the same behaviors sexual harassment. The following 2002 Vermont case illustrates the potential significance of this distinction.

> A parent filed a complaint against the St. Johnsbury School District claiming the district failed to protect her son from bullies on the bus and in homeroom who sexually harassed him with taunts about being gay. The parent subsequently sued the school district under a new Vermont anti-bullying state law, and,

> ultimately, a jury sided with the school. Because this case was litigated in state court under a new anti-bullying law, federal civil rights laws although accessible, were not invoked. Had the parent pursued this as a civil rights case in a federal court the outcome most likely would have been in favor of the son. (Stein, 2003)

Two concerns have arisen about the potential treatment of sexual harassment as bullying. One concern is that state laws do not offer the same protection as federal civil rights laws, and a failure to identify a case as one of sexual harassment, rather than bullying, could lead to a failure to provide all possible protections to victims (Stein, 2003). A second potential drawback to the failure to identify sexual harassment and to call sexual harassment bullying is the potential personalization of the behavior to particular students, whether bully or victim, thus pathologizing them as individuals. This perspective deflects the problem away from being a school climate issue that the school has responsibility to solve under Title IX, to an issue in which individual students are to blame for their behaviors. Under Title IX a school system can be held responsible when school personnel knowingly allow a "hostile environment" (*Bruneau v. South Kortright (NY) Central School District*, 1996). Thus, legally, schools are responsible for the actions of both their employees and their students in regard to sexual harassment, but when the allegation is bullying it is, legally, more likely that the responsibility will revert to the individuals involved.

PREVALENCE OF BULLYING AND PEER SEXUAL HARASSMENT IN U.S. SCHOOLS

Three national studies of bullying and sexual harassment provide statistics regarding these behaviors in U.S. schools. The National Institute of Child Health and Human Development (Nansel et al., 2001) found that one-third of children in grades 6 through 10 are directly involved in bullying, with 10 percent as bullies, 13 percent as victims and 6 percent as both. The frequency of bullying was higher among 6th-8th grade students than among 9th-10th graders. The United States Department of Education School Crime Supplement to the National Crime Victimization Survey (2003) reported that in 2001, 8 percent of middle and high school students were bullied (9 percent males, 7 percent females). Grade level made a difference, with 14 percent of 6th graders, 9 percent of 9th graders, and 2 percent of 12th graders reporting bullying in school. Twenty-five to 29 percent of elementary school principals and 43 percent of middle school principals reported bullying as a problem

The American Association of University Women (AAUW) conducted two national studies of sexual harassment in U.S. schools in 1993 and 2001. Both had similar results, reporting that 81 percent of students experienced some form of sexual harassment during their school years. Fifty-nine percent were harassed occasionally, and 27 percent were targeted often (2001). Additionally, 54 percent of students said they sexually harassed someone during their school years. Similar to bullying, grade level made a difference; but in contrast to bullying, sexual harassment increases with age, with 55 percent of 8-9th graders and 61 percent of 10-11th graders reporting that they had been physically sexually harassed at school. Girls experienced higher frequency of harassment in both grade categories.

BULLYING

Bullying has been well studied. Research on bullying covers the etiology of bullying, differential assessment of bullies, and outcomes for bullies. There have been many attempts in the literature to define the developmental problems that lead to bullying behavior. Bullies have more psychiatric symptoms than others (Kumpulainen, Raesaenen, & Henttonen, 1999). Nansel et al. (2001) stated that these youths suffer from insecurity, anxiety, depression, loneliness, unhappiness, physical and mental symptoms, and low self-esteem. Curtner-Smith (2000) suggested that bullying is learned from influential role models in the social environment of the child. Bullying is a significant indicator of risk for mental disorders in adolescence (Kaltiala-Heino, Pilla, Ruan, Simmons-Morton, & Scheidt, 2000). Parental maltreatment, both emotional and physical, physical discipline, and bullying in the home contribute to the prediction of bullying (Duncan, 1999; Smith & Myron-Wilson, 1998; Smith & Shu, 2000), and children from larger families are more likely to bully (Eslea & Smith, 2000).

Although the literature portrays a dim view of bullies, the picture is worse for the victims of bullying. A history of being victimized (being teased, hearing rumors spread about oneself, being or feeling deliberately excluded, experiencing violence or threats of violence) is associated with subsequent development of anxiety and depression in adolescence (Bond, Carlin, Thomas, Rubin, & Patton, 2001). Victims have a lower level of social acceptance than their peers (Haynie et al., 2001) and more serious mental and physical health problems and fewer support systems than others (Duncan, 1999; Rigby, 2000; Nansel et al. (2001). Finally, victimization is related to a greater incidence of suicidal ideation in young people (Carney, 2000; Rigby & Slee, 1999).

Victims of bullying do not always respond by suffering in silence. There is increasing concern about how these victims may express their frustrations and act them out in the school setting. McGee and DeBernardo (1999) studied sixteen students who committed homicide in the schools and found fourteen of them to be bully victims. A study by Klein (2006) highlights the roles that bullying and sexual harassment played in school shootings. Many of the school shooters had been ostracized by peers, weathered homophobic attacks for months, and formulated revenge schemes. These students chose to retaliate against teachers, classmates, and the school, perhaps in a generalized rage against the school for not providing some protection to them. School was a dangerous place for them, but also a required place. Although not justified, their dilemma may have resulted in retaliatory violence.

Differential Assessment of Students Who Bully

Effective intervention planning calls for detailed assessment. A number of studies make a distinction between the bullies who are impulsive as a condition of an attention deficit disorder, and those who are more calculating. Arsenio and Lemerise (2001) argued that there are hot-blooded and cold-blooded bullies, concluding that the intervention and treatment strategies for school social workers should be differentiated on the basis of this differential assessment. Acting-out children who may be driven by attention deficit hyperactivity disorder (Wolke, Woods, Blomfield, & Karstadt, 2000) are referred to by Arsenio and Lemerise (2001) as the hot-blooded bullies. Treating this type of student strictly as a behavior problem (i.e., without taking ADHD into account) may have serious consequences.

There are also a number of studies that conclude that bullies may be students who are very competent socially. They seem socially skilled, have a high level of self-esteem, and give the impression of being more aloof and detached emotionally from others. These are identified by Arsenio and Lemerise (2001) as the cold-blooded bullies, and they are the most challenging to work with. Sutton, Smith, and Swettenham (1999) concluded that such bullies are likely to be cold, manipulative, and highly skilled in social situations and may pose a higher risk to the safety of other children. They also have significantly higher levels of self-esteem than their classmates (Salmivalli, Kaukiainen, Kaistaniemi, & Kirsti, 1999). Failure to deal with this type of bully as a discipline problem will likely encourage further bullying behavior. The first task of any intervention with this category of bully is the need to develop some motivation for change. The second task is to get the family involved in the intervention plan (Hoover & Oliver, 1996).

Outcomes for Children who Bully

The long-term prediction for bullies is not good. Research shows bullying is a strong predictor of juvenile delinquency and community violence (Baldry and Farrington, 2000; Colvin, Tobin, Beard, Hagan, and Sprague,1998). The most striking conclusions have been drawn from the work of Olweus (1993) who found that former bullies were four times more likely to engage in criminal behavior. At the age of 24, 60 percent of former bullies in his study had one or more criminal convictions, and 35 percent of this sample had three or more convictions. Bullying is learned early in life. We must seek earlier identification and treatment.

PEER SEXUAL HARASSMENT

In contrast to the bullying research, sexual harassment research does not have detailed descriptions of harassers and victims and has been framed as more of an environmental issue located within schools. Students may be victimized by harassment or perpetrate it, but the behaviors are viewed as creating a hostile environment within the school rather than as negative individual personality traits.

The AAUW report, *Hostile Hallways*, first conducted in 1993 and repeated in 2001 lists twelve sexually harassing behaviors:

1. Made sexual comments, jokes, gestures, or looks;
2. Showed, gave, or left sexual pictures, photographs, illustrations, messages, or notes;
3. Wrote sexual messages or graffiti about you on bathroom walls etc.;
4. Spread sexual rumors;
5. Said you were gay or lesbian;
6. Spied on you as you dressed or showered at school;
7. Flashed or mooned you;
8. Touched, grabbed, or pinched you in a sexual way;
9. Pulled at your clothing in a sexual way;
10. Blocked your way or cornered you in a sexual way;
11. Forced you to kiss him or her;
12. Forced you to do something sexual, other than kissing.

In the AAUW study, four out of five students reported being sexually harassed and of those harassed, 85 percent stated it was by a peer. The 1993 study was the first to document a high level of sexual harassment experienced by boys as well as girls. In the 2001 study, 83 percent of the girls and 79 percent of the boys reported being sexually harassed by a current or former student at school. Fifty-seven percent of all boys and 50 percent of all girls surveyed in the 2001 study admitted that they have sexually harassed someone in the school setting. Of the students in the 1993 AAUW study who said that they had sexually harassed someone in the school setting, 94 percent claimed they themselves had been harassed (98 percent of girls and 92 percent of boys). Additional findings from the AAUW (2001) and the Connecticut Permanent Commission on the Status of Women (PCSW) (1995) studies found that students who experience sexual harassment reported more school absence, lowered concentration, and less class participation. These studies also reported physical symptoms including sleep disturbance and appetite changes. Students reported feeling angry, upset, and threatened by sexual harassment, all of which contributed to lowered self-esteem and confidence (Fineran & Bennett, 1999; PCSW, 1995; Strauss & Espeland, 1992; Stein, Marshall, & Tropp, 1993).

A 1995 study in a public high school conducted by the Permanent Commission on the Status of Women (PCSW) found that 35 percent of events of sexual harassment were perpetrated by a schoolmate the student knew casually. Nine percent were perpetrated by a schoolmate the student did not know. Twelve percent were perpetrated by students who were boyfriends or girlfriends. Fifty percent of the boys and 75 percent of the girls reported being upset by the experience of sexual harassment at school. The victims reported that 75 percent of the perpetrators were male and 25 percent were female.

Same-sex Sexual Harassment

A certain amount of sexual harassment is same-sex harassment. In the AAUW (2001) study, 18 percent of girls reported being sexually harassed by other girls, while 45 percent of the boys reported being harassed by other boys. Overall, 16 percent of the students admitted targeting students of the same sex. The negative implications of this become clearer when related to the AAUW (1993) findings. Eighty-six percent of all students surveyed stated that being labeled as "gay" or "lesbian" created the most distress for them. For boys, this finding was particularly severe. The report stated "no other type of harassment, including actual physical abuse, provoked a reaction this strong among boys" (p. 20). Trigg and Wittenstrom (1996) state, "boys were most disturbed by behaviors that threatened their masculinity, such as being called homosexual or being sexually harassed by other boys" (p. 59). They found that the only harassing behavior that boys experienced at a higher rate than girls was being called gay.

In a study of 712 high school students, Fineran (2001, 2002) found that sexual minority students experienced sexual harassment more frequently than heterosexual students. Sexual minority students and heterosexual girls reported being significantly more upset and threatened by peer sexual harassment victimization. In addition, sexual minority students were physically assaulted more frequently than heterosexual students. Gruber and Fineran (2007) conducted a study on middle and high school students that examined sexual orientation, bullying, and sexual harassment. They found that lesbian middle school girls were more apt to experience ridicule (bullying) and sexual harassment than their heterosexual classmates. Among high school students, lesbians experienced more sexual harassment than their heterosexual peers.

Shakeshaft et al. (1995) in their research on peer harassment found that adolescent girls and boys are harassed in different ways, but the central issue for both was whether they conformed to gender stereotypes. Three types of students reported more harassment than did others: girls viewed by peers as being physically well developed and pretty, girls who were considered unattractive and not dressing stylishly, and boys who did not fit a stereotypic macho male image. Klein (2006) in an examination of school shootings theorizes that 'gay bashing' is a related aspect of normalized masculinity, where . . . "boys identified as homosexual as well as boys perceived as 'feminine' or 'weak' by others, but self-identified as heterosexual, are victims of unrelenting peer abuse" (p. 152).

Legal Issues in Sexual Harassment

Legislation and Regulations. Much of our understanding of sexual harassment in the schools has evolved from court decisions involving the workplace and Title VII of the Civil Rights Act of 1964. In general, the interpretation of what constitutes sexual harassment in the educational setting has followed the concepts developed under employment discrimination law. Title VII of the Civil Rights Act of 1964 (42 U.S.C. § 2000e-2(a)) provides the principal framework prohibiting discrimination on the basis of race, color, religion, national origin, and sex. This legislation defines peer sexual harassment as a sex discrimination issue (Fineran & Bennett, 1998). In 1980 the Equal Employment Opportunity Commission (EEOC) issued a definition of sexual harassment, including specific guidelines to prohibit it. Six years later, the U.S. Supreme Court further defined two categories of sexual harassment: ***quid pro quo*** and ***hostile environment.*** The Office of Civil Rights (OCR), which oversees the enforcement of Title IX, restates these definitions in the 1997 release of *Sexual Harassment Guidance* (U.S. Department of Education, 1997). Written expressly for schools, *Guidance* defines quid pro quo and hostile environment as follows:

> Quid pro quo harassment occurs when a school employee explicitly or implicitly conditions a student's participation in an education program or activity or bases an educational decision on the student's submission to unwelcome sexual advances, requests for sexual favors, or other verbal, nonverbal, or physical conduct of a sexual nature. Quid pro quo harassment is equally unlawful whether the student resists and suffers the threatened harm or submits and thus avoids the threatened harm.
>
> Hostile environment harassment, which includes unwelcome sexual advances, requests for sexual favors, and other verbal, nonverbal, or physical conduct of a sexual nature by an employee, by another student, or by a third party, is behavior that is sufficiently severe, persistent, or pervasive to limit a student's ability to participate in or benefit from an education program or activity, or to create a hostile or abusive educational environment. (p. 12038)

It is the hostile environment definition that addresses peer sexual harassment, based on part three of the EEOC (2001) guidelines that holds employers responsible for the actions of their employees. In education this definition has been expanded to include a school's responsibility for the actions of both its employees and students.

> A school will be liable under Title IX if its students sexually harass other students if (1) a hostile environment exists in the school's programs or activities; (2) the school knows or should have known of the harassment; and (3) the school fails to take immediate and appropriate corrective action. . . . A school's failure to respond to the existence of a hostile environment within its own programs or activities permits an atmosphere of sexual discrimination to permeate the educational program and results in discrimination prohibited by Title IX. (U.S. Department of Education, 1997, pp. 12039–12040)

Title IX requires that an institution receiving federal funds provide an environment free of discrimination and sexual harassment and directs educational institutions to maintain a grievance procedure that allows for prompt and equitable resolution of all sex discrimination including sexual harassment. Thus, a person experiencing sexual harassment may pursue the following alternatives: filing a grievance under Title IX within the school system, filing a complaint with the regional Office for Civil Rights of the U.S. Department of Education, or suing in court for damages. Title IX does not make a school responsible for the actions of harassing students but rather for its own discrimination in failing to correct the situation once the school has been given notice.

Schools have been held accountable by Title VII and Title IX for over 30 years, and since 2000 the number of cases of sexual harassment filed by students has steadily increased. The U.S. Department of Education recorded 11 sexual harassment complaints (including adult to student) by elementary and high school students in 1991 and twenty-five by college students. For the years 2000 to July 31, 2007, the combined number of complaints equaled 679 for elementary or secondary schools and 350 for post secondary schools (D. Campbell, Office for Civil Rights, personal communication, August 3, 2007). Complaints now average approximately ninety per year for elementary/secondary schools and fifty for post secondary schools.

Case Law. Court decisions have indicated that schools and school personnel who knowingly fail to respond to harmful conditions, such as peer sexual harassment, are made responsible and can be legally liable. This amounts to a right to a safe school environment and is a strong motivator for schools to respond appropriately to needs for safety.

A landmark case decided by the Supreme Court in 1992, *Franklin v. Gwinnett County (GA) Public Schools,* made it clear that students who suffer sexual harassment and other forms of sex discrimination may seek monetary damages from their school districts and school officials for violation of their civil rights. Prior to this time damages were not included in the compensation awards, so elementary, junior high, and high schools had little incentive to address this issue.

In 1999, a Supreme Court decision concerning student-to-student sexual harassment, *Davis v. Monroe County Board of Education* (1994) found that schools are to be held responsible for student-to-student sexual harassment when the schools have been informed of the offending behaviors. The Court also ruled that schools would be liable for monetary damages "only if they were 'deliberately indifferent' to information about 'severe, pervasive, and objectively' offensive harassment among students (Walsh, 1994, p. 10). In the state of New York, a 6th-grade girl was taunted with sexual comments and physically abused by boys in her class (*Bruneau v. South Kortright (NY) Central School District,* 1996). She filed charges under Title IX and recovered compensatory damages, punitive damages, and attorney fees. The school district was found liable because teachers and administrators knew of the assaults but took no action (Jones, 1994).

Many cases filed by students have involved sexual harassment of males by other males, and lawsuits have been dismissed because of the ambiguity of prior court decisions. In Utah, a sexual harassment lawsuit (*Seamons v. Snow,* 1994) filed by a male high school football player against his male teammates "was dismissed on the grounds that the boy failed to prove that he had been a victim of any concerted discriminatory effort" (Stein, 1999, p. 38).

In two separate yet similar cases, one filed in California and the other in Massachusetts, two girls were harassed by female schoolmates. Both girls experienced sexual taunts, graffiti, and rumors of the girls' alleged sexual behavior with boys. In both cases the school had been notified of the sexual harassment but had not responded. In fact, the California school had decided that sexual harassment could only occur between students of the opposite sex. The Office for Civil Rights, which heard both of these cases, concluded that there had been "pervasive, persistent, and severe sexual harassment in violation of Title IX and that the school districts had inadequate grievance procedures for prompt and equitable resolution of complaints of sexual harassment" (Stein, 1995, p. 157).

Nabozny v. Podlesny (1996) concerned a gay male student who was harassed for four years. During this time he was called names, struck, spat on, and subjected to a mock rape. He brought suit under the equal protection clause, prevailed, and received substantial damages. The court ruled that the school was unjustified in allowing its students to assault another student based on sexual orientation. He was entitled to an equivalent level of protection under 42 U.S.C. § 1983 claiming violation of his 14th Amendment rights (*Nabozny v. Podlesny,* 1996).

These cases of same-sex sexual harassment if litigated today would most likely have positive outcomes owing to the landmark Supreme Court decision, *Oncale v. Sundowner Offshore Services* (1998) that defined same-sex sexual harassment as actionable. Bringing suit under the 14th Amendment is another venue that students (and adults) can pursue, although after the

Oncale decision, the issue of same-sex sexual harassment should be clearer under Title VII, thus providing direction for Title IX cases.

RESPONSES TO BULLYING AND SEXUAL HARASSMENT

Policies will not work unless they reverberate with the culture of the school. A culture of violence, intimidation, and retaliation needs to be changed. This is a most complex and difficult task. Many schools have developed sexual harassment policies and procedures that legislate behavior and are more reactive than proactive. This approach places the burden directly on the student to file a complaint and face the response. Stein (1995) pointed out that arbitrary rules can be problematic. One school district banned all physical touching because of numerous complaints from female students about being sexually assaulted by a football player. Lee, Croninger, Linn, and Chen (1996) pointed out that it is difficult to think that a policy of punishing the perpetrator and protecting the victim will be effective in eliminating (peer) sexual harassment in schools. The victim-perpetrator model breaks down when the majority of students are both perpetrator and victim (AAUW, 1993; Fineran & Bennett, 1998). Using the school as a courthouse with a jury of one's peers may also be questionable (Stein, 1995). Blaming the victim by "popular vote" can have perverse effects. A popular student accused of sexual harassment could paradoxically gain status as a victim, whereas the student who points the finger becomes the accuser and is blamed for provoking the behavior.

Although schools want to offer support to students affected by bullying and sexual harassment, the realities of a victim-perpetrator relationship complicate the situation enormously. This fact poses clinical and policy dilemmas. It would be easy to say that social workers need to provide support groups for victims or perpetrators, and in many circumstances this would be appropriate. However, some students who are victims may be retaliating or perpetrating in self-defense, and other students who are perpetrating may find themselves being victimized. Furthermore, the focus on the victim-perpetrator relationship alone has the effect of shifting the focus away from the normative culture of the school, which may implicitly permit, or even demand, interpersonal violence and retaliation.

One of the main complaints from students experiencing bullying and sexual harassment is that it occurs in front of school personnel who do nothing to stop it, and in these cases inaction supports interpersonal violence (AAUW, 1993, 2001; Stein, et al., 1993; Permanent Commission [Connecticut] on the Status of Women [PCSW],1995). Teachers may be hesitant to intervene unless they are sure that consequences for the behavior are in place and will be enforced. A more direct course, recommended in the best-practices guide *Early Warning, Timely Response* (Dwyer, Osher, & Warger et al., 1998), is for anyone in the school community who is present when students are being harassed or intimidated to intervene. Social workers would work closely with teachers and support them in providing immediate intervention when they observe bullying and sexual harassment. Students are encouraged to move away from their role as "participant observer," to band together and warn or report their peers when they see harassment. As civil rights attorney Catherine McKinnon (1979) suggested, the unnamed should not be taken for the nonexistent. Students and teachers should be encouraged to name bullying and sexual harassment and not accept it as "normal adolescent behavior."

Some policy approaches to the problem are bound to be ineffective because they do not address the basic issues, which are issues of moral and ethical solidarity. Denial of the existence of the problem, or its suppression, will not work. Neither will purely formal changes in the school's discipline code or grievance procedures. What Lee et al. (1996) identified as the ethical approach has a much broader and deeper focus. Shared values and ethical or moral concepts that bind members together as a community are most important. From Valerie E. Lee and her colleagues' perspective, sexual harassment is a sign of the failure of existing organizations to instill ethical coherence and integrity in their members. Schools need to take responsibility for teaching the basic tenets of respect for others, for self, and for a moral community. Lee and colleagues supported a cultural theory approach utilizing the ethical dimensions where "more discussion of basic democratic values" is encouraged and "moral and ethical questions are hotly debated" (p. 409). Stein and Sjostrom (1994) believed that sexual harassment needs to be considered a matter of social injustice and that schools should promote democratic principles.

Bullying and sexual harassment are both significant problems in schools, and public policies to address these issues have emerged both through legislation and case law. School social workers have opportunities to intervene to address these issues in schools today. The following chapter describes the development of safe and responsive schools, and the approaches in schools to address prevention and intervention with bullying, sexual harassment, and other forms of interpersonal violence.

References

American Association of University Women Educational Foundation. (1992). *How schools shortchange girls*. Washington, DC: Wellesley College Center for Research on Women.

American Association of University Women Educational Foundation. (1993). *Hostile hallways: The AAUW survey on sexual harassment in America's schools* (Research Rep. No. 923012). Washington, DC: Harris/Scholastic Research.

American Association of University Women Educational Foundation. (2001). *Hostile hallways: Bullying, teasing and sexual harassment in school*. Washington, DC: Author.

Arsenio, W. F., & Lemerise, E. A. (2001). Varieties of childhood bullying: Values, emotion processes, and social competence. *Social Development, 10*(1), 59–73.

Baldry, A. C., & Farrington, D. P. (2000). Bullies and delinquents: Personal characteristics and parental styles. *Journal of Community and Applied Social Psychology, 10*(1), 17–31.

Bond, L., Carlin, J. B., Thomas, L., Rubin, K., & Patton, G. (2001). Does bullying cause emotional problems? A prospective study of young teenagers. *British Medical Journal, 323*, 480–484.

Bruneau v. South Kortright Central School District, 935 F. Supp.162 (N.D.N.Y. 1996).

Carney, J. V. (2000). Bullied to death: Perceptions of peer abuse and suicidal behavior during adolescence. *School Psychology International, 21*(2), 213–223.

Title VII, Civil Rights Act of 1964, 42 U.S.C. § 2000e (1994).

Colvin, G, Tobin, T., Beard, K., Hagan, S., & Sprague, J. (1998). The school bully: Assessing the problem, developing interventions, and future research directions. *Journal of Behavioral Education, 8*(3), 293–319.

Connecticut Permanent Commission on the Status of Women. (PCSW). (1995). *In our own backyard: Sexual harassment in Connecticut's public high schools.* Hartford, CT: Author.

Curtner-Smith, M. E. (2000). Mechanisms by which family processes contribute to school-age boy's bullying. *Child Study Journal, 30*(3), 169–186.

Davis v. Monroe County Board of Education, 74 F. 3rd 1186 (11th cir. 1996).

Duncan, R. D. (1999). Peer and sibling aggression: An investigation of intra- and extra-familial bullying. *Journal of Interpersonal Violence, 14*(8), 871–886.

Dwyer, K., Osher, D., Warger, C., Bear, G., Haynes, N., Knoff, H., et al. (1998). *Early warning, timely response: A guide to safe schools*. The referenced edition. Washington, DC: American Institutes for Research.

Title IX, Education Amendments Act of 1972. Federal Register, Part II Department of Education. 45, 30955–30965.

Equal Employment Opportunity Commission. (2001). *Revised sexual harassment guidance: Harassment of students by school employees, other students or third parties*. Retrieved Jan. 6, 2008 from http://www.ed.gov/about/offices/list/ocr/docs/shguide.html

Eslea, M., & Smith, P. K. (2000). Pupil and parent attitudes toward bullying in primary schools. *European Journal of Psychology of Education, 15*(2), 207–219.

Fineran, S. (2001). Sexual minority students and peer sexual harassment in high school. *Journal of School Social Work, 11*(2), 50–69.

Fineran, S. (2002). Sexual harassment between same-sex peers: The intersection of mental health, homophobia, and sexual violence in schools. *Social Work, 47*(1), 65–74.

Fineran, S., & Bennett, L. W. (1998). Teenage peer sexual harassment: Implications for social work practice in education. *Social Work, 43*, 55–64.

Fineran, S., & Bennett, L. W. (1999). Gender and power issues of peer sexual harassment among teenagers. *Journal of Interpersonal Violence, 14*, 626–641.

Franklin v. Gwinnett Cty. Public Schools, 911 F.2d 617 (CA11 1990).

Gruber, J. E., & Fineran, S. (2007). The impact of bullying and sexual harassment on middle and high school girls. *Violence Against Women, 13*(6), 627–643.

Haynie, D. L., Hansel, T., Eitel, P., Crump, A. D., Saylor, K., Yu, K., et al. (2001). Bullies, victims, and bully/victims: Distinct groups of at-risk youth. *Journal of Early Adolescence, 21*(1), 29–49.

Hoover, J. H., & Oliver, R. (1996). *The bullying prevention handbook: A guide for principals, teachers and counselors*. Bloomington, IN: National Educational Service Press.

Jones, M. M. (1994). Student sues school for sexual harassment by other students. *Lawyer's Weekly USA, 94,* 12–13.

Kaltiala-Heino, R., Pilla, M., Ruan, W. J., Simmons-Morton, B., & Scheidt, P. (2000). Bullying at school: An indicator of adolescents at risk for mental disorders. *Journal of Adolescence, 23*(6), 661–674.

Klein, J. (2006). An invisible problem: Everyday violence against girls in schools. *Theoretical Criminology, 10*(2), 147–177.

Kumpulainen, K., Raesaenen, E., & Henttonen, I. (1999). Children involved in bullying: Psychological disturbance and the persistence of the involvement. *Child Abuse and Neglect, 23*(12), 1253–1262.

Lee, V. E., Croninger, R. G., Linn, E., & Chen, X. (1996). The culture of sexual harassment in secondary schools. *American Educational Research Journal, 33*(2), 383–417.

MacKinnon, C. A. (1979). *Sexual harassment of working women*. New Haven, CT: Yale University Press.

McGee, J., & DeBernardo, C. R. (1999, May/June). The classroom avenger: A behavioral profile of school shootings. *The Forensic Examiner, 8,* 16–18.

Nabozny v. Podlesny, 92 F 3d 446 (7th cir. 1996).

Nansel, T. R., Overpeck, M., Pilla, R. S., Ruan, W. J., Simmons-Morton, B., & Scheidt, P. (2001). Bullying behaviors among US youth: Prevalence and association with psychosocial adjustment. *Journal of the American Medical Association, 285*(16), 2094–2100.

Olweus, D. (1993). Bullying at school: What we know and what we can do. Cambridge, MA: Blackwell Press.

Oncale v. Sundowner Offshore Services, Inc., 523 U.S. 75 (1998).

Rigby, K. (2000). Effects of peer victimization in schools and perceived social support on adolescent well-being. *Journal of Adolescence, 23*(1), 57–68.

Rigby, K., & Slee, P. (1999). Suicidal ideation among adolescent school children, involvement in bully-victim problems, and perceived social support. *Suicide and Life-Threatening Behavior, 29*(2), 119–130.

Salmivalli, C., Kaukiainen, A., Kaistaniemi, L., & Kirsti, M. J. (1999). Self-evaluated self-esteem, peer-evaluated self-esteem, and defensive egotism as predictors of adolescents' participation in bullying situations. *Personality and Social Psychology Bulletin, 25*(10), 1268–1278.

Seamons v. Snow, 864 F. Supp. 1111 (D. Utah, 1994).

Shakeshaft, C., Barber, E., Hergenrother, M. A., Johnson, Y. M., Mandel, L., & Sawyer, J. (1995). Peer harassment in schools. *Journal for a Just and Caring Education, 1*(1), 30–44.

Smith, P. K., & Myron-Wilson, R. (1998). Parenting and school bullying. *Clinical Child Psychology and Psychiatry, 3*(3), 405–417.

Smith, P. K., & Shu, S. (2000). What good schools can do about bullying: Findings from a survey in English schools after a decade of research and action. *Childhood: A Global Journal of Child Research, 7*(2), 193–212.

Stein, N. (1995). Sexual harassment in K–12 schools: The public performance of gendered violence. The *Harvard Educational Review, Special Issue on Violence and Youth, 65*(2), 145–162.

Stein, N. (1999). *Classrooms & courtrooms: Facing sexual harassment in K–12 schools*. New York: Teachers College Press.

Stein, N. (2003). Bullying or sexual harassment? The missing discourse of rights in an era of zero tolerance. *Arizona Law Review*, *45*, 783–799.

Stein, N., Marshall, N. L., & Tropp, L. R. (1993). *Secrets in public: Sexual harassment in our schools.* Wellesley, MA: Wellesley College Center for Research on Women.

Stein, N., & Sjostrom, L. (1994). *Flirting or hurting? A teacher's guide on student to student sexual harassment in schools.* Washington, DC: National Education Association.

Strauss, S., & Espeland, P. (1992). *Sexual harassment and teens*. Minneapolis, MN: Free Spirit.

Sutton, J., Smith, P. K., & Swettenham, J. (1999). Social cognition and bullying: Social inadequacy or skilled manipulation? *British Journal of Developmental Psychology, 17*(3), 435–450.

Trigg, M., & Wittenstrom, K. (1996). That's the way the world goes: Sexual harassment and New Jersey teenagers. (Special Issue: Sexual Harassment). *Initiatives, 57*(2), 55–65.

U.S. Department of Education. (1997). *Sexual harassment guidance 1997*. Washington: Author. Retrieved January 6, 2008 from http://www.ed.gov/about/offices/list/ocr/docs/sexhar01.html

Walsh, M. (1994, Oct. 19). Harassment suit rejected. *Education Week*, *14*(7), 10.

Wolke, D., Woods, S., Blomfield, L., & Karstadt, L. (2000). The association between direct and relational bullying and behavior problems among primary school children. *Journal of Child Psychology & Psychiatry & Related Disciplines, 41*(8), 989–1002.

Zuehl, J. J., Dillon, E., Schilling, J. L., & Oltmanns, J. K. (2002, January 26). Student discipline issues. In J. C. Franczek & P. C. Sullivan (Eds.), *Attorneys at Law eighth annual school law conference*. Unpublished paper.

39

Developing Safe, Responsive, and Respectful School Communities: Pathways to Intervention

Shirley McDonald
University of Illinois at Chicago

Robert Constable
Loyola University Chicago

Anthony Moriarty
Olympia Fields, IL

- A Context for School Policy and Practice
- Tier 1: Systemic Change
- Tier 2: Targeting At-Risk Students
- Peer Mediation
- Tier 3: Students Chronically and Intensely At-risk
- Restorative Justice in Hong Kong Schools

There are mounting concerns throughout the world regarding school safety. This chapter is focused on planning for school safety, and responding to risks and hazards within the school community. The school social worker builds on the school community's resolution (expressed in policies and programs) that each school must be a safe place. A climate of civility is dependent on the ability of the school community to anticipate potential problems and to plan for a collective, differentiated and healing response. The skills demanded in this process involve direct practice, policy development, and research. Because they involve the practitioner facilitating the complex work of a system, they are a test of our school social work practice model.

Sophisticated, evidence-based, policy and practice interventions, focused on the whole school's response to problems of interpersonal violence, have been emerging with solid research backing (Astor, Benbenishty & Meyer, 2004; Astor, Meyer, Benbenishty, Marachi, & Rosemond, 2005; Dwyer, Osher, & Warger, 1998; National Institutes of Health, 2005). These fit well into the emergent role of the school social worker. Within the context of school policies that demand safe, nonthreatening, nonharmful behavior in the school, school social workers work with victims and perpetrators of interpersonal violence and their families. Through needs assessments, mediation, conflict resolution systems, restorative justice, and safety and crisis plans, school social workers take part with others in the formulation of school policies and development of programs. Centrally involved in the school community, they are often the first to know about a problem. They have been trained to interpret the meanings of interpersonal behavior and to work with others to find respectful solutions. In so doing they draw on their skills of collaboration; consultation; individual, group, and family intervention; social skills education; crisis intervention; conflict resolution; and development of mediation systems.

A CONTEXT FOR SCHOOL POLICY AND PRACTICE

Federal initiatives to promote safe schools began in the United States in 1986 with the Drug-Free Schools and Community Act (20 U.S.C 4601), reauthorized in 1994 as the Safe and Drug-Free Schools and Communities Act (20 U.S.C. 7101), and then included in PL 107-110, the No Child Left Behind Act (NCLB). By 1998 schools were required to conduct needs assessments regarding drugs and violence, establish measurable goals, implement research-based approaches, and assess progress (see discussion in chapter 6). At the same time, in the wake of a number of well-publicized incidents of school violence, the federal departments of Education (DOE) and of Justice, by presidential request, jointly disseminated an evidence-based, best-practices manual on safety in schools. These federal policy initiatives were accompanied by considerable corresponding activity at state education agency (SEA) policy and legislative levels. State laws, policies, and SEA consultants began to mandate a similar model for practice and policy at the local (LEA) school-community level. These mandates, an example being the 2001 Illinois Safe and Responsive Schools Act, can best be understood in the light of the national discussion of best practices and policy development. The focus for concern broadened from bullying to include all students at risk for aggressive behavior:

> The school board, in consultation with the parent-teacher advisory committee and other community-based organizations, must include provisions in the student discipline policy *to address students who have demonstrated behaviors that put them at risk for aggressive behavior*, including without limitation, bullying, as defined in the policy. These provisions must include *procedures for notifying* parents or legal guardians, and *early intervention* procedures based upon available community-based and district resources. (Illinois Safe and Responsive Schools Act, emphasis added).

There is now widespread acceptance and agreement on a balanced and effective approach to preventing violence that includes a variety of efforts addressing physical safety, educational practices, and programs that support the social, emotional, and behavioral needs of students (National Consortium of School Violence Prevention Researchers and Practitioners, 2006).

Early Warning, Timely Response

The DOE best-practices manual, *Early Warning, Timely Response: A Guide to Safe Schools* (Dwyer, Osher, & Hoffman, 2000; Dwyer, et al., 1998) had been sent in 1998 to every school district in the nation. It quickly became the basis for the whole-school approach to prevention and intervention. The term "violence" included a broad range of troubling behaviors and emotions shown by students: serious aggression, physical attacks, suicide, dangerous use of drugs, and other dangerous interpersonal behaviors. Schools needed to create a safe, trustworthy, and respectful environment. The concept of a *responsive*, rather than reactive, school would shift the emphasis from individual students to civility in the school as a whole, and from reactive intervention to prevention. All staff, parents, students, and community members needed to develop an awareness of problem behavior, what they could do to counteract it, and how they could reinforce and reward positive behavior. The school would affirm that a basic principle underlying membership in the school community is that persons respect each other, their rights, and their dignity and can trust each other. When students place others at risk, the school must decide what process is necessary for them to be reintroduced to the school community. The school community by setting clear standards would help individual students to function effectively within a more actively safe, responsive, and normative environment. The social worker, who is often the member of the school community most aware of interpersonal violence and its effects, would assist school administrators and board in the development and implementation of school policies.

However, an effective response would not be a rigid one. Zero-tolerance policies, initially focused on firearms and later extended to drugs, have not in themselves been successful (Astor et al., 2005; National Institutes of Health, 2005). Rigid enforcement of such policies, for example, the failure to distinguish plastic squirt guns from the real thing, is not an appropriate response. In such situations students are likely to hold the school administration in contempt, thus undercutting the supportive school environment necessary to reduce the likelihood of violent behavior (Black, 2004; Mulvey & Cauffman, 2001).

Effective best practices for professionals working with problems of interpersonal violence emphasize: 1) the development of a responsive school community, 2) development of early intervention capacities of school team members and teachers, 3) functional assessment of dangerous conditions, 4) positive interaction training, and 5) early, coordinated, multifaceted intervention with students in need (Dwyer et al., 1998). Building on the determination of the school community that school be a safe place for vulnerable young people, the school district needs to develop policies that recognize the problem and put its resources behind the effort to create a safe environment for each school. This demands a mapping of the safety problem in that particular school community and the use of that information to develop the community's appropriate response to a potentially violent situation (Astor et al., 2004). School social workers can then find a variety of roles for themselves within this broader commitment of the school: These include:

- Contributing to school policy development;
- Developing conflict resolution, mediation, and grievance procedures;
- Making functional assessments of contexts that incite violence;
- Consulting with teachers and administrators;
- Developing the capacity of staff, and others as appropriate, to intervene effectively in potential conflict situations;
- Working with groups in school and in the community;
- Working with victims and perpetrators of interpersonal violence;
- Coordinating services in the community and resources in the school;
- Developing responsive referral and intervention systems; and
- Intervening in the situation as early as possible. (Dwyer et al., 1998).

Characteristics of Safe and Responsive Schools

The key is the school climate of civility and responsiveness. The DOE manual identified thirteen research-based characteristics of schools that foster learning, safety, and socially appropriate behaviors. Effective prevention, intervention, and crisis response strategies operate best in school communities that:

1. Focus on academic achievement.
2. Involve families in meaningful ways.
3. Develop links to the community.

4. Emphasize positive relationships among students and staff.
5. Discuss safety issues openly.
6. Treat students with equal respect.
7. Create ways for students to share their concerns.
8. Help children feel safe in expressing their feelings.
9. Have in place a system for referring children who are suspected of being neglected or abused.
10. Offer extended day programs for children.
11. Promote good citizenship and character.
12. Identify problems and assess progress toward solutions.
13. Support students in making the transition to adult life and the workplace. (Dwyer, Osher, Warger, et al., 1998, p. 6)

Each of these qualities of the safe and responsive school community involves a set of collaborative tasks for all members of the community. Although the school administrator carries primary responsibility for what goes on in the building, the social worker, working in the thick of the issues where the school is most vulnerable, will most likely be heavily involved in this work.

The manual (Dwyer, Osher, Warger, et al., 1998), and later the National Consortium of School Violence Prevention Researchers and Practitioners (the Consortium) (2006) recommended a three-tier approach to thinking about tasks and methods. Intervention could take place at the tier 1 *universal* level (school-wide), tier 2 *targeted* level (for at-risk students), and the tier 3 *intensive* level (for the most chronically and intensely at risk students). This approach has become standard in any discussion of comprehensive, school-based support programs and of outcome-oriented, strengths based service delivery approaches, such as Response to Intervention (RtI) (see chapters 27 and 22):

◆ *Tier One, universal (school-wide).* These are instructional and psychosocial supports so that all students succeed academically and behaviorally and learn cultural competence and respect for diversity. Elementary schools teach students to solve problems and to stop and think before acting. The expected long-term effect of this intervention would be the reduction of harassing behaviors in high school (Batsche & Knoff, 1994).

◆ *Tier Two, targeted (for at-risk students).* This involves more intensive intervention for students at risk for troubling outcomes. An example would be providing a program that provides a long-term, reliable, and positive relationship with an adult mentor. Responsive schools can provide an opportunity that allows children to feel safe in discussing their personal concerns about friends, intimidation, and stress. Responsive schools can help children feel respected and comfortable with being themselves, whether or not they fit the mold of the average student.

◆ *Tier Three (for the most chronically and intensely at-risk students). Intensive* intervention provides individualized and intensive support for students with the highest level of need (Dwyer et al., 2000).

TIER 1: SYSTEMIC CHANGE

Planning is the key to a safe and responsive school community (Dwyer, Osher, Warger, et al., 1998). This would include training for the entire school to become appropriately responsive. Schools develop prevention plans, response teams, and safety plans. Similar to crisis teams, the core prevention and response team consists of an administrator, a pupil services representative, teacher and parent representatives, a school board member, and others from the school community. An effective written violence prevention plan includes discussion of early warning signs of problems, effective prevention practices the school community is undertaking, and intervention strategies. These strategies must include early interventions for students at risk and more intensive, individualized interventions for students with severe behavioral problems or mental health needs. A part of the violence prevention plan is a crisis intervention plan that includes multiple contingency plans to be used in the aftermath of a crisis (Dwyer, Osher, Warger, et al., 1998).

School responsiveness involves the entire school community. Prevention often is a process of developing and changing the basic school culture. Programs such as Positive Behavioral Intervention Systems (PBIS) and Peace Builders are examples of programs that are school-wide, aimed at just such issues, and that develop a support network for help in educating staff and parents about the program.

Mark Mattaini (2001a) and the Peace Power Working Group (2001b) have developed systematic, evidence-based strategies for schools to construct alternative organizational cultures of nonviolence and noncoercive action. The PEACEPOWER and Peace-Builders programs, inculcating proven strategies and certain Native American customs and beliefs, institutionalize practices within the school of:

- Systematic recognition of contributions and successes. Among the practices would be recognition notes, recognition circles, group incentives, and celebrations of success.
- Development of a culture of acting with respect. Among the practices would be "put-ups, not put-downs," respectful discipline procedures, bullying prevention programs, and empathy training.
- Building community through shared power. Among the practices would be councils and working groups to improve school climate, service projects and service learning, family-school partnership programs, and family-school governance structures.

- Making peace. Among the practices would be conferencing to resolve school conflicts and discipline issues, peer mediation, and healing circles. (Mattaini, 2001a, p. 442–443)

Ron Astor's review of effective school-wide intervention programs reveals seven general characteristics, which can be individualized through needs assessment to the particular situation of a school community (Astor et al., 2005; 2004). Such programs:

1. Raise the awareness and responsibility of students, teachers and parents regarding the types of violence in their schools.
2. Create clear guidelines and rules for the school community.
3. Target the various social systems in the school and clearly communicate to the entire school community procedures to be followed before, during, and after violent events.
4. Focus on getting school staff, students, and parents involved in the program.
5. Fit easily into the normal flow and mission of the school.
6. Use faculty, staff, and parents in the school setting to plan, implement, and sustain the program.
7. Increase monitoring and supervision in nonclassroom areas. (Astor et al., 2005)

Such approaches, aimed at building appropriate connections with families, with peers, and within the school community (Smith & Sandhu, 2004), are natural to school social work practice.

Administrative Challenges

School social workers work closely with their administrators and the core prevention and response team. The administrator and the team should oversee the preparation and implementation of the plans and ensure that every member of the school community takes ownership of them.

Few, if any, schools exist without problems in the general area of interpersonal violence as defined above. On the other hand, the mantra of many superintendents and school board members to their principals is that "good administrators do not have problem children in their schools." If an administrator has problems in his or her school, it is often interpreted that the job is not getting done, and that it is time to look for a more qualified administrator. The principal is thus encouraged to give the impression that the school is free of such vexing problems or to minimize them. However, effective administrators are, first and foremost, honest. They must have the courage and support of others to stand up to the sweeping problems of systemic denial that adversely impact many schools.

The first step in developing an effective intervention program may be to develop an anonymous student and teacher survey of the nature and incidence of the problem in the district and in each school (Olweus, 2001). A survey gives a better picture of the problem as experienced in different schools and among different age groups and confronts denial that such a problem exists at all. The next step is for the school board to develop parallel policies that prohibit peer sexual harassment and bullying. Implementation guidelines for these policies need to be included in the administrative procedures and in the student handbook. Budget priorities should reflect a commitment to doing something about an identified problem. A cadre of staff needs to be identified and developed to provide the leadership for a school-wide commitment to work on the problem of interpersonal violence. Staff development and staff awareness training are key to an effective anti-harassment policy. Despite a predictable concern that some teachers may not see the problem's relation to education, effective teaching and learning cannot occur in a hostile environment. There needs to be commitment to a plan.

A *discipline plan* identifies what behaviors are unacceptable. Rules need to be clear, broad-based, and fair. Disciplinary procedures need to be developed collectively by members of the total educational community. They need to be communicated clearly to all parties and followed consistently by everyone. In particular, the disciplinary policy should include a code of conduct, specific rules and consequences that can accommodate student differences on a case-by-case basis when necessary. Negative consequences need to be combined with positive strategies for teaching socially appropriate behaviors. It should include anti-harassment and anti-violence policies and due process rights. The school community should participate in the development of these rules and thus have ownership of them. Peer mediation and conflict resolution would provide student-controlled means of working out some problems and promote a climate of nonviolence.

An effective *safety plan* includes a discussion of early warning signs of potentially violent behavior, prevention practices, and intervention strategies adopted by the school community. A *crisis response plan* needs to reference a wide range of possibilities. Crises can be natural disasters, tragic accidents, suicides, intruders, gang and other violence spilling over into the school, contagious diseases, or losses of members of the school community (see chapter 34). Crises have the potential to overwhelm and shut down the school decision-making process when it is most needed, and shatter any belief that school is a safe place. They have long-term effects on education and children's development. Responses call for immediate planned action, good communication, and differentiation of roles between members of a crisis team and others. Team members and others need to divide responsibilities in advance. Some will deal with individual students and teachers in crisis; others with a victim's family and the community; still others with community resources, agencies, police, hospitals, or the news media. The school social worker has an important role on the team. The crisis plan spells out contingencies and responses as much as possible, even to the point of advance checklists of things to do and people to contact. The team not only plans what to do when violence strikes, but it also ensures that students and staff know what to do.

Students and staff feel secure when there is a well-conceived plan. Everyone understands what to do or whom to ask for instructions. Of course, no one can fully anticipate a particular crisis, but developing some common understandings paves the way to working effectively as a team and a functional school community if something does happen. The plan also needs to include a redundancy component in case a major team member is part of the crisis. Once a plan, however well conceived, is formulated, it needs to be kept up to date. Team members and circumstances change every school year. Moreover, beyond an immediate response to a crisis, it is important to take into account the long-term healing that often needs to take place when something tragic or threatening happens (Dwyer et al., 1998). The crisis response plan can be combined with the safety plan in a school-wide *violence prevention and response plan*.

When policies and plans are developed, the next challenge is their consistent enforcement. Zero tolerance, as a policy, needs to be a reasonable, consistent, and fair response to acts of student misconduct in the school. Such a policy does not mean a rigid reaction to all infringements as equally punishable. A plastic, yellow dinosaur-shaped squirt gun is not a weapon, though it may be inappropriate at school. Even-handed enforcement and proportionality form the essence of a good zero-tolerance policy. Many schools in trouble have good rules; what is lacking is agreement on reasonable enforcement. All staff must come to agreement that a real act of misbehavior, observed but ignored, is an act affirmed. If there are clear rules governing peer harassment in the school, they will be most effective with a total commitment to their being uniformly and fairly enforced.

Disciplining of staff is a very difficult administrative responsibility. Administration is responsible for getting all staff on board. There should be no tolerance of any staff person who ignores the responsibility to follow policies and procedures in place for curbing interpersonal violence. Compliance is no longer an option; it is the law. However, staff need sufficient training and skill development to intervene appropriately and effectively in bullying and harassing behavior. In-service education and consultation on emergent situations are particularly important. Much harassing behavior may well be overlooked because staff simply does not know what to do.

It is important to keep the broader community involved through the whole process: developing agreement regarding policies, planning, training, and testing out interventions for consistency and effectiveness. Parents, as well as students and staff, should have some say in the process. The more broad-based participation the social worker and others can develop, the greater will be the resulting ownership and support for the program.

Once the program is in place, a confidential reporting system must be developed and refined, and an administrator must be assigned to the role of compliance officer. All complaints go through this system and must be taken seriously and in confidence. Although it is beyond the scope of this chapter to address training for the compliance officer, this position is a necessary piece of the program and most state boards of education, and in some cases regional educational offices, can provide such training and guidance.

Finally, the greatest challenge to the school administrator may well be that of developing a creative strategy to reduce repeated and continuous intimidation and harassment once it has been identified. In cases such as these, involving serious behavior problems, traditional school discipline, including suspension, detention, and other punitive measures will not work well. An effective intervention must primarily seek to prevent recurrence of any misbehavior. One approach that has met with considerable success is the Confluence model developed at Homewood-Flossmoor Community High School and other area schools in Illinois (Moriarty, 2002). Rather than responding to events with rigid and punitive policies and procedures, the approach focuses on teaching new behaviors and using individually developed curriculum materials as a prerequisite for suspended students to return to a regular school program. The program provides the opportunity for the school social worker to play an active role working with the behavior of students who harass and intimidate.

TIER 2: TARGETING AT-RISK STUDENTS

The National Institutes of Health (NIH) best-practices report, *Preventing Violence and Related Health-Risking Social Behaviors in Adolescents*, was produced by an independent panel of experts, reviewing systematically the existing evidence on the prevention and treatment of adolescent violence (National Institutes of Health, 2005). Problems of adolescent violence were seen as a *continuum* of risk factors for violence. Interventions that could reduce the prevalence of the risk could reduce the possibility that the outcome (violence) itself would take place. For example, competent parenting skills such as monitoring, consistent discipline, and supportiveness could reduce the likelihood of children engaging in more violent, antisocial behaviors. Pointing out that family, neighborhood, and community were key factors in protecting against or generating antisocial behavior, the report went on to discuss two effective programs dealing with youth at high risk for violence, and their families. These were *functional family therapy* (Sexton & Alexander, 2003) and *multisystemic therapy* (Sheidow, Henggeler, & Schoenwald, 2003). Both are community- and family-based prevention and intervention programs, and both are compatible with the way social workers work with families (Constable & Lee, 2004; also see chapter 29). Positive results (reductions in recidivism, violent crime arrests, and out-of-home placements of children) were sustained in both programs over four years, using external replications and random clinical trials (RCTs). Six other similar programs, including brief, strategic family therapy, were also found to be effective, although only using internal RCTs. These programs are geared to foster competence and skill development in the adolescent and in the surrounding systems. Core components of effective programs would strengthen:

- Parent effectiveness (communication style, behavior management, goal setting, problem solving, and monitoring);
- Individual coping on the part of the child/adolescent (impulse control, anger management, decreased risk taking, communication skills);
- Academic achievement (school readiness, organization skills, good learning habits, reading);
- Peer relations (conversational and other social skills); and
- The social climate of schools (classroom and playground management, parent-teacher collaboration).

These appear to be most effective when adapted to differing developmental levels of their clientele and the differing circumstances of ethnic communities. Many of the interventions were long-term, often lasting a year and sometimes much longer. They worked intensively with their clientele and involved multimodal and multicontextual approaches. Therapists often had low caseloads (4–6) and were available to the family, when needed. Other programs that were coercive, that focused on only one intervention, or that limited themselves to scare tactics, lectures, and toughness strategies, were unsuccessful.

Programs such as conflict resolution and mediation, build on a whole-school commitment that school be a safe environment for everyone, giving at-risk student groups an acceptable positive milieu for working out problems.

Conflict Resolution and Mediation

A discipline plan that identifies and sets consequences for interpersonal violence will create the need for conflict resolution, mediation, and grievance procedures. Mediation procedures reinforce norms that apply to everyone and avoid making faculty alone responsible for norm development and enforcement. They are crucial for a whole-school approach to the development of civility. School social workers currently are creating and coordinating mediation programs that enable the maintenance of a respectful and civil environment. By implication these programs reinforce norms of respect for others.

Conflict resolution needs to be part of a larger plan and school commitment. Alone it cannot be expected to produce a safe school (Astor et al., 2005). Conflict resolution/mediation training can teach students skills and help them to take personal responsibility for developing peaceful and productive relationships; teaching such life skills serves them well as students and later as adults. The school climate is enhanced when students resolve their own personal problems, and a language of respect is developed when people in the school disagree with civility (South Suburban Peer Network, 1993). Thus, conflict need not be avoided. Rather than being something dangerous and a personal threat, conflict can become an opportunity for positive changes when the skills are at hand to resolve the conflict in a creative and lasting way (Moriarty & McDonald, 1991). Some school districts have instituted system-wide training in conflict resolution skills. Some have a formal program, such as specially trained teams of student-mediators or conflict resolvers. These specially trained students are often identified as a team and have regular meetings. In schools that have such teams, there is likely to be a set policy regarding which types of problems are appropriate for referral to mediation. Other districts do some training with all students, but also train a cadre of students who are available for more difficult situations. When emotions are running high, or when there seems to be an imbalance in power, the team would ensure that each party to the dispute is respectful to the other. Younger students may wear special vests on playgrounds and in lunchrooms or during special functions where students are not being closely supervised, to identify them as mediators. Some schools have students identified in each classroom as the designated conflict resolvers. They may hold dispute-resolution sessions in the classroom, ideally in an area somewhat removed from the rest of the class. In all cases, the school must have a way to oversee the referral process and the mediation session so that conflict resolvers and mediators are at all times protected from serious problems or risks.

Conflict Resolution: Skills and Process. The actual process of conflict resolution has several components: identification of the problem using specific language, brainstorming possible solutions, agreeing on a solution, and confirming intent by all parties to make the resolution work:

1. First, students need to learn to identify problems. They must specify problems, avoid general terms and "fuzzy" language (Moriarty, 1992), and then prioritize the problems according to the level of seriousness or, in some cases, according to the level of likelihood of the problem being resolved. Again, learning and using these skills will serve the student in many ways. To learn this skill at a useful level students need to be able to state the present problem as specifically as possible and then identify the most troublesome parts of the problem. At this point, it is important to help all disputants put in words what they feel they want to achieve from an agreement, if they are able to reach one. This is crucial if each disputant is going to be able to accept the outcome as fair. This process usually involves several components:
   - The students need to reconfirm that desire for a solution.
   - They wish this solution to occur within a problem-solving process.
   - The process may involve compromising on some points.

2. Next, it is important for the students to determine what their position is regarding the ideal resolution of the problem, and then, what the bottom line is, that is, what is not negotiable (Fishe, Ury, & Patton, 1991). The students learn that it is better to argue from a bargaining position that has some maneuverability.

3. The next skill (students find this difficult) is to stay focused on the important issues, that is, not get sidetracked. When people get into arguments, they normally have a sense of being threatened, and when this threat becomes too great, it is very common for the disputant to divert the argument by introducing extraneous information or additional complaints not directly related to the argument. In training the mediation team role-plays are probably the most effective tool for demonstrating and practicing the skill of staying with core concerns.

4. Control of emotions is a skill that needs to be emphasized during the actual resolution process. It can be difficult, especially for younger students, but coaching students as they practice can quickly help them see how much emotional control may often operate to their advantage if the real goal is resolution of the dispute.

A formalized problem-solving process. Students need to accept and learn a formalized process of problem solving to keep them on track to the endpoint of reaching an agreement. Problem solving is both a natural and a formal process. Most people are accustomed to going through a process of looking at a few options before making even small day-to-day decisions; a few options are considered and all but one ruled out. This becomes this person's decision about taking action or beginning an activity. The process works well if conflicting emotions are not significantly involved, or if the stakes are not very high. As the outcome of a decision increases in importance, however, emotions are more likely to come into play, complicating the ability to think clearly and creatively. The process and the routine use of formal operations in thinking patterns then becomes more important in the resolution of the problem. Teaching a formal method of problem solving gives students tools to use throughout their lives when they find themselves under pressure. These are steps to the problem-solving process:

1. Identify the specific problem needing resolution.
2. Brainstorm potential solutions without criticizing any suggestions, including some that may initially seem frivolous—all ideas are acceptable.
3. Discuss the positives and negatives of each possible solution that may have some potential.
4. Agree on one solution that has the most potential for satisfying both parties to the dispute, and that has the greatest potential of succeeding.

5. Agree on a timeline for trying the solution, usually a few days to a week. Even if it does not seem to be working very well at first; stay with the proposed solution to give it a chance for success.
6. Evaluate whether the solution is meeting the needs of each disputant in resolving the identified and agreed-on problem, or whether some modifications need to be made or a new solution proposed.

Once the potential solution has been agreed upon, the disputants and anyone helping to guide them through the process should congratulate each other on a successful outcome of the dispute. Older students will often shake hands as a sign of agreement. There should also be an agreement not to talk about the situation or the issues with outside parties or the students who act as mediators once the mediation or conflict resolution is complete, so that confidentiality is respected. It is understood that different mediators or adult counselors will hear any further problems associated with this dispute.

Skill Building for Conflict Resolution. A number of discrete skills are critical in learning the process of conflict resolution. These can be taught, coached, reinforced, and supported by the social worker. Mutual ability to interpret emotional expression allows accurate communication to occur (Fast, 1970). Students need to be able to explore mutually advantageous ways to defuse aggressive responses and to resolve underlying problems before they escalate to physical assault. They need to learn empathy for another person's responses and points of view, even if they disagree. A person in conflict needs to learn to identify his or her feelings, and at the same time to be able to have sufficient empathic sensitivity to others' feelings through attention to their words, facial expression, tone of voice, body posture, and body language. Once students show competence in the communication of feelings, the next step is expressing accurately how one feels, and communicating such feelings with nonpejorative language, such as "I messages" (Gordon, 1975). This gives the disputant the proper language and format to describe how he or she feels when the other disputant behaves in certain ways. This process has three parts:

1. State the behavior that affects you.
2. State the feeling that this behavior creates in you.
3. State the effect of the behavior on you (your feeling reaction).

Using this formula, the following "I message" might be created: "When you ignore me I feel worried because I am concerned that you may not like me anymore." This nonaccusing language may allow enough communication to occur so each disputant may experience how the other is feeling.

Not all people have natural listening skills, certainly not all young people. Unfortunately, these skills are seldom taught or even effectively modeled. People may hear words without comprehending the intended meaning. The child's game of telephone, where a circle of children attempt to pass a message successfully around the circle without the message being changed, illustrates the reality that messages are frequently distorted. Seldom does the message stay intact around the circle. Real listening skills can lead to dialogue designed to "check out" the meaning of what was stated. "Could you be more specific?" "Could you say that in another way?" "Let me tell you what I think I just heard you say, and correct me if I am wrong."

Staying with one subject is also difficult for some children. They may be distracted by something said previously, or by their own thoughts. Phrases such as "How does that relate to . . . (the original theme)?" reconnect the conversation to the stated problem to be solved. At the same time, validating the student's new area of concern is also important, so that he or she does not feel belittled or marginalized. Children can learn to reassure others that they will return to the new topic once the current topic is resolved.

Role-playing assists the development of good listening skills. The skill needs first to be taught and modeled by the instructor. Making up scenarios for role-plays is an enjoyable and useful exercise, which personalizes the activity for students. For younger children, the use of puppets may be helpful to begin a dialogue leading to role-plays. Keeping the dialogue focused on the subject is essential to the process, and staying on task can be confounded by emotionality. It will be helpful to coach children to avoid negative self-talk, that is, to avoid statements one thinks silently, such as, "I'm getting nervous" or "I hope he still (likes me) (doesn't get angrier) (doesn't tell my friends)," etc. To counteract negative self-talk, children can be encouraged to repeat phrases to themselves, such as "Keep it up" or "Did I make that point clearly?" Being their own coaches through the use of positive, constructive self-talk statements is another powerful skill that will serve them well throughout their lives.

PEER MEDIATION

Peer mediation provides a structured format for addressing problems that have a disruptive and negative effect on students' daily lives. Students, able to resolve disagreements with dignity, are more able to pursue meaningful activity in school and are less likely to experience feelings of estrangement or alienation from the school culture and the school system. We have found that students who experience a personal sense of empowerment tend to demonstrate a greater capacity to assume responsibility for their own behavior and welfare than those who do not feel empowered.

Rich East High School

Peer Mediation began in the spring of 1988 at Rich East High School in Park Forest, Illinois and continues to this day. This program has been well accepted by students for its success assisting students to resolve interpersonal conflicts with others.

The Selection Process. The project was initiated in a two-day workshop for the students selected to serve as mediators. These students had to be those who would be sought out by others in times of personal difficulty, rather than those who had identified leadership characteristics resulting from academic, athletic, or social talent. They had to have clout with their peers. Such clout in a school has two relevant definitions: first, it means influence or pull; and second, it implies power or muscle. Deans and counselors were asked to recommend students they believed were sufficiently influential and whom they believed possessed clout. Surprisingly, the deans and the counselors largely recommended the same students, despite the seemingly vague definition of this criterion. The selected students may have not been well known to each other because they were the effective leaders of their separate social groups. All ten of the original nominees agreed to participate in the project. This level of agreement was a surprise to the project planners, who expected some students to decline to participate—however, the level of participation correlates with the characteristics of the students selected. When the general concept of the program was explained, all the students appeared to recognize the program to be a valuable contribution to the school, as well as an opportunity for personal growth.

It soon was clear that students with identifiable clout came from a wide range of social and educational strata in the high school. They did not emerge more frequently from any one particular group. These students defied generalization. They were dissimilar in every category except that of age. Race, gender, grade-point average, extracurricular participation, and regular and special education defined no common characteristics. Some had problems themselves that had brought them to the deans' offices earlier in high school. Others were relatively unknown to the administrative staff.

Mediation Training. Mediation training is an inherently efficient process because it redirects and builds on talents indigenous student leaders may already have demonstrated, especially in peer relationships. Once students are selected for mediation training, the process of refining these preexisting skills begins. A degree of structure is imposed and indigenous leadership skills are shaped. Teaching new skills turned out not to have been a major focus of training, since these students readily learn the fundamental interpersonal communication skills essential to the mediation process. Training tailors skills students have brought with them to the job of conflict resolution. In the training process these skills are defined, identified, and sanctioned by the school as valuable and important. They are put to work for the greater good of the school community and the mediators themselves.

The Orientation Process. This group of fledgling mediators was given an orientation to the process of mediation and a series of structured steps to follow in the actual mediation process. Emphasis was placed on creating the proper atmosphere, personal demeanor, the structuring of the physical setting, and the preliminary remarks made by the mediators. Ensuring confidence and respect in the process by starting out with a well-delivered opening statement was seen as critical to the success of the experience. Consequently, time was spent helping each student develop the opening statement, make introductions, establish ground rules, and explain the process of mediation and rules of decorum. It also was essential that these content areas be explained in language compatible with each mediator's personal style.

Opening Statements. Several elements are necessary in an appropriate opening statement. First, mediators need to structure a win-win environment. The disputants are told clearly that no one comes out of mediation a loser. This stimulates student interest and also lets them know early on that they are being provided a face-saving opportunity. Second, the principle of confidentiality is defined, and its application to the mediation process is clearly established. Third, it is emphasized during the training sessions that a commitment to neutrality needs to be made clear in the opening statement. This is important for two reasons. The students in dispute need to know that the mediators are not going to take sides. It is also important for the protection of the mediators to reinforce the fact that mediators will have no involvement with the problem or its solution outside of the mediation session, including any follow-up. Future concerns will be handled by whomever the administration designates to monitor compliance.

Finally, rules of order need to be introduced in the opening statement. The mediator requires appropriate decorum and specifically states what is and what is not appropriate behavior. In the pilot project, the mediators quickly realized that full control of the mediation session is most effectively accomplished by insisting that all conversation be directed to and through the mediator. This style, although allowing each of the disputants to listen to the other's story, establishes equality and fairness in the disputants' opportunities to present their positions and helps prevent interruptions.

Interpersonal Skills. Disputes brought to mediation often are not thoroughly understood by the disputants. Mediation trainers need to discuss the concepts of secondary or hidden agendas. These ideas were readily grasped by the mediators, as were double-bind messages, reflective listening skills, and the general techniques of good therapeutic style, including the withholding of judgment, neutrality, the use of "I" messages, and confidentiality. The students' affinity for these concepts seemed to be a natural byproduct of their preexisting leadership abilities.

The skill-building component of the training focused on sharpening communication skills to serve the specific goals of the mediation process. The most effective mediators are those who are especially good at the use of reflective statements and those able to quickly ferret out hidden agendas. Reflective statements convey to the disputants that their issues are understood; the discovery of hidden agendas brings into focus why the disputants are clinging to their conflictual issues. The process transcends the angry and rigid presenting of positions and guides the students to their real agendas.

In short, the mediators are learning basic techniques essential to good therapeutic intervention, and they come to appreciate and respect the power of good communication skills.

Issues Brought to the Table. Conflicts presented might involve interpersonal relationships, space violations, and possession of property. Some issues are relatively minor, others potentially catastrophic. The significant point is that the students in dispute are themselves involved in developing the agreement that resolves the dispute. A follow-up component is intended to monitor students' compliance with the terms of the agreement, but this must be done by someone on staff, and not a mediator. Once the dispute is settled and the agreement written and signed by all, and congratulations given for a job well done, the mediators' work is done (other than to continue to maintain confidentiality indefinitely).

Teamwork and Consultation. The classroom group comprises dynamics that can be harnessed to build a peaceful and productive environment—or that can go badly for many students. Teachers have little exposure to applications of group-dynamics concepts in their professional education. There has been a growing awareness of the classroom dynamics of bullying (i.e., that victimization processes in the classroom itself could make some students vulnerable to bullying). Siris & Osterman (2004) discuss ways teachers can counter this in the classroom by supporting potential victims' competency, autonomy, and sense of belonging through their teaching, through their assisting these students to achieve and through their influence on class norms. A group of teachers, who worked together to try this in their teaching, were able to see clear evidence of success in the potential victims they elected to assist, but also recognized in themselves a new sense of confidence that they could in fact reduce the incidence of peer harassment, both by structuring a climate where students would not be excluded and by addressing the very different psychological needs of their students (Siris & Osterman, 2004). Teachers are beginning to show an interest in developing their role in this direction and to recognize that social workers have much to offer them. Assisting teachers in dealing with situations of interpersonal violence in their classrooms, gym, hallways, and other school settings demands a more developed consultative role, together with some possible group facilitation of teachers' problem-solving efforts.

TIER 3: STUDENTS CHRONICALLY OR INTENSELY AT-RISK

Assessment and Early Warning Signs

Tier 3 interventions are directed toward the most chronically and intensely at-risk students. Early warning signs of behaviors that could lead to violence would demand a further assessment. One needs to look for unsafe relationships and unsafe situations in the school. Children who become violent to self and others often are those who already feel themselves rejected and psychologically victimized (Guerra, Huessman, Tolan, Van Acker, & Eron, 1995). Children who exhibit aggressive behavior, if not provided support, may continue a progressive developmental pattern toward severe aggression or violence (Dwyer, Osher, Warger, et al., 1998; Olweus, 1980; Walker, Colvin, & Ramsey, 1995). Meaningful connections with an adult however can reduce the possibilities for violence (Dwyer, Osher, Warger, et al., 1998). *Early Warning, Timely Response: A Guide to safe Schools* lists a number of research-based behavioral warning signs of potential violence for those who are "most alienated from the school community (Dwyer, Osher, Warger, et al., 1998, p. 6–12)." These may not necessarily predict violence, but they denote worrisome situations, of particular concern if an increase in these indicators is observed:

- Social withdrawal,
- Isolation, rejection by peers,
- Feelings of being a victim,
- Lowered interest in school and reduced academic performance,
- Becoming a victim of violence,
- Patterns of uncontrolled anger,
- Intimidating and bullying behaviors,
- History of violent and aggressive behavior,
- Intolerance of differences and prejudicial attitudes,
- Gang affiliation,
- Use of firearms,
- Making serious threats of violence, and
- Limited access to supportive adults.

The implication of the discussion is that to lessen the possibility of serious violent episodes, there needs to be both a focus on vulnerable students and the creation and maintenance of civility within the school community. According to the National Consortium of School Violence Prevention Researchers and Practitioners (2006) "Schools need to reach out to build positive connections to marginalized students, showing concern for them and fostering avenues of meaningful involvement. (n.p.)

School social workers can work directly with students individually or in groups that have become involved in bullying or harassment incidents. They may develop positive interaction or social skills groups. They may work with victims to help them deal with their loss of self-efficacy and allay the certain damage. Such victims may need help to restore their normal, but damaged, assertiveness and feelings about their gender and emergent sexuality. Social workers may work with perpetrators to develop the skills to return to a civil and respectful environment. Social workers may deal with groups to help the group feel safe again or may help teachers to do this. Given the context of a school community determined to be safe, and the concern for the bullies, the victims, and the families involved in these destructive transactions, all of the direct intervention methods discussed in this book are applicable.

Restorative Justice. Bullying is a particular concern in Asian schools. Eizaburo Yamashita (2007), president, School Social Work Association of Japan, comments that a reason for bullying in Japan can be the possession of a distinct trait—the best or worst academic achiever, an excellent athlete or a very poor one, a teacher's favorite or disliked, very rich or very poor, etc. Vulnerability to bullying drives the child to stay away from school and carries with it a risk of suicide. For this reason there is particular interest in restorative justice approaches, which provide opportunities for the victim, the offender, their families, and representatives of the school community as well as the greater community to come together, air feelings, and work together to find solutions. Yamashita has been particularly influenced by approaches developed by Wanda Van De Hey (undated), a school social worker in Oshkosh, Wisconsin.

Van De Hey uses a restorative justice philosophy as the heart of a whole-school approach. According to her, it has had a great "impact on the culture of our building. It is how we solve problems. It is how we do business. Even staff meetings happen in a circle and involve everyone. A quote from one of the teachers illustrates the power of a restorative environment, 'I am passionate about the restorative justice philosophy and feel that it has helped me to become a better teacher and person.' Our school T-shirts say, 'Do the right thing because it is the right thing to do.' Emphasis is placed on respect for all persons, property and the environment (Van De Hey, 2007)."

Van De Hey uses *Circle Conferences* to involve everyone affected by a conflict, whether students, family, staff, or community members, in rectifying it. First an environment safe for everyone is developed. This involves attentive listening, no put-downs, mutual respect, confidentiality, and the right to pass. The facilitator makes a summary statement about what happened and what we are here to discuss. Frequently this is put in rather general terms, such as, "There has been a great deal of conflict between these students, and we are here to talk about how people are treating each other and what needs to happen to repair the harm and solve this problem" (Van De Hey, 2007). She comments on this process: "I've learned with middle schoolers it can take all day to get to the bottom of who did what and who started it (Van De Hey, 2007)."

Then the group addresses some of the following questions, typically:

- Who do you think has been impacted by this situation?
- What are your personal feelings about what has happened?
- What do you think needs to happen to repair the harm?
- What are you personally willing to do to repair the harm?

It is not uncommon for students, and especially those who have been best friends, to experience conflict. The circle conference allows students and their parents to have an opportunity to talk about hurt and angry feelings and restore the relationships that have been damaged. In cases of bullying behavior it can be extremely helpful for family members to hear about the situation from various perspectives. It is important for offenders to take responsibility for their actions and to hear about the impact they have had on others. Otherwise, problems that are not fully dealt with resurface over and over. Punishment frequently results in anger. The goal is to change behavior and teach students how to solve problems, rather than to create anger.

RESTORATIVE JUSTICE IN HONG KONG SCHOOLS

Dr. Dennis Sing-Wing Wong is a practicing school social worker, an associate professor at the City University of Hong Kong, and Chairman of the Centre for Restoration of Human Relationships in Hong Kong, China. Concerned about the high level of physical violence, extortion bullying, and gang activity in the Hong Kong Schools (higher than with comparable populations in the U.S and the U.K. (Wong, 2004), he has been developing a restorative justice model to deal with the complexities of the problem. In Hong Kong he found many of the same problems noted in this chapter's discussion of bullying and school violence. The zero-tolerance attitude of the police as well as the use of harsh punishment were not effective. They were bully-focused, blame-driven and only led to cycles of revenge on others (Wong, 2004). Restorative practices were compatible with Chinese culture, which emphasizes collective values and restoration of interpersonal harmony. The meaning of the term *he shi lao* represents a village elder playing the role of facilitator or mediator to rebuild a harmonious relationship between two parties, sometimes at the expense of individual rights. The goals of the process, restoring human relationships and achieving a healing effect, go beyond the dispute settlement functions of mediation. On the other hand, recent Chinese experiences of informal systems replacing formal law left people distrustful and fearful of the use of any informal systems to resolve conflicts (Wong, 2005a, 2005b)—they would perceive them as arbitrary and unfair (Wong, 2005a). Informal practices would not substitute for law, but be based in law. Dr. Wong, himself having had experiences of bullying as he was growing up, faced an uphill struggle in developing comprehensive restorative justice programs treating bullying and interpersonal violence in the Hong Kong schools. The following description briefly outlines his development of a comprehensive, antibullying strategy, using our division of work into tiers 1, 2, and 3.

Tier 1. Bullying and triad gang membership are serious problems in Hong Kong. People had accepted bullying as a normal rite of passage that everyone would have to go through. They minimized it as small conflicts between peers: "Boys will be boys." Police would respond with harsh punishment. Schools were heavily focused on academics with very little time to deal with anything else. Dr Wong developed a long-term, comprehensive antibullying strategy, directed to the Hong Kong schools and to the broader community. Built upon cooperation among all parties in the school, his program includes a wide range of activities such as peer mediation, formal curricula in antibullying strategies, anger management, and safe schools and peace education as a way to prevent physical bullying (Wong, 2004). Using press releases and media and school appearances, he raised public awareness of the problem. He particularly focused on teachers, social workers, and parents, wanting them to take the problem seriously and respond appropriately to it. Wong published research on the problem and other countries' responses. He developed the Centre for Restoration of Human Relationships and trained staff to do tier 2 and tier 3 interventions, and provided training to teachers and parents, and taught students social skills and emotional control. The schools began to respond to bullying, contacting the parents of the children involved and developing policies. Staff development for teachers, counselors, and social workers in responding to bullying took place. All students received life education around conflict resolution and restorative justice (Wong, 2006). Peace education (21 hours) was developed for all secondary school first-, second-, and third-year students. The program for all students consisted of four major parts: self-understanding, emotional control, problem-solving skills, and interpersonal communication skills (Wong, 2004).

Tier 2. A whole-school restorative process was developed. This involves:

- A clear set of policies highlighting restorative strategies and procedures for dealing with bullying and other problems. Bullies had to restore healthy relationships with their surrounding communities and the people they offended;
- The policy would be made known to all parties;
- Teachers, social workers, or counselors, and parents, should be trained to use restorative practices in handling students conflicts and misbehaviors;
- Students would be involved in conflict resolution;
- Students would be provided with a life-education curriculum with emphasis on skills training, conflict resolution, and restorative justice;
- The whole-school approach would start with the principal and school management committee signing a protocol against bullying. There would be staff development, social skills training for bullies and assertiveness training for victims, talks for parents, and workshops for parents of bullies or victims. School social workers, counselors, and senior students would get mediation skills training (Wong, 2006).

Dr. Wong and his staff make use of small-group sessions and meetings involving students in conflict resolution. Their evidence-based approaches aimed for social skills development, the development of resilience and protective factors (i.e., good parental monitoring, fair reward and punishment practices, rational parent-child or teacher-student communication, use of forgiveness, and a strong sense of interdependency between child and parents or students and teachers) (Wong, 2004).

Tier 3. Formal mediation between victims and offenders is a very important component of the work at the school level. Social skills training for bullies involved understanding individual differences, experiencing exclusion and the surrounding feelings, developing and showing empathy, discussion of bullying incidents, the victims" and their families' feelings, restoring relationships, anger management and use of new phrases to communicate. Victims receive assertiveness training around human rights and their rights, facing challenges and self protection, strong posture and movements, appropriate verbal and nonverbal expressions, use of "I" messages, developing friendship with mentors, and developing self confidence by expressing feelings and thinking.

There is an elaborate sequence of pre-meeting preparation, facilitation of the conference itself, and post-conference follow up (Wong, 2005a, 2005b). Both bullies and victims and their families would be individually prepared for a meeting with each other aimed at:

- Bullies understanding the feelings of victims and realizing what they did was wrong;
- Victims expressing their feelings and becoming assertive to face the situation during the conference;
- Bullies having a sense of regret, apologizing and offering (usually monetary) compensation;
- An agreement that bullies would not be labeled after the meeting. Victims can let things go and move on;
- A relationship between both and with their families can be rebalanced and restored. (Wong, 2005a, 2005b)

For most pupils, especially adolescents, the school experience is critical to their personal development and readiness to become part of the adult world. Peer sexual harassment, intimidation, and bullying of any kind interferes with and inhibits this important developmental process. Social workers who are able to clearly identify the problems associated with peer sexual harassment and bullying strengthen their positions as advocates for improved school environments. They assess hostile school environments as a serious social problem with negative mental health and legal ramifications. In the past, peer harassment has been viewed as just "teasing" or "good natured fun." This "typical behavior" needs to be reframed as behavior that hurts everyone in the educational setting and perpetuates discrimination against students who are vulnerable or who do not fit the current social model for appearance or behavior. The school needs to become a moral community. As in the Oshkosh, Wisconsin, middle school, its members can strive to "Do the right thing because it's the right thing to do."

References

Astor, R. A., Benbenishty, R., & Meyer, H. A. (2004). Monitoring and mapping student victimization in schools. *Theory into Practice, 43*(1), 39–49.

Astor, R. A., Meyer, H. A., Benbenishty, R., Marachi, R., & Rosemond, M. (2005). School safety interventions: Best practices and programs. *Children & Schools, 27*(1), 17–32.

Batsche, G. M., & Knoff, H. M. (1994). Bullies and their victims: Understanding a pervasive problem in the schools. *School Psychology Review, 23*, 165–74.

Black, S. (2004). Beyond zero tolerance: Schools don't need extreme policies to be safe and secure. *American School Board Journal.* Retrieved September 14, 2004, from http://www.asbj.com/current/research.html

Constable, R. T., & Lee, D. B. (2004). *Social work with families: Content and process*. Chicago: Lyceum Books.

Drug-Free Schools and Community Act, 20 U.S.C 4601 (1989).

Dwyer, K., Osher, D., & Hoffman, C. C. (2000). Creating responsive schools: Contextualizing early warning, timely response. *Exceptional Children, 66*(3), 347–365.

Dwyer, K., Osher, D., & Warger, C. (1998). *Early warning, timely response: A guide to safe schools*. Washington, DC: U.S. Department of Education. Available at http://www.air.dc.org/cecp/guide

Dwyer, K., Osher, D., Warger, C., Bear, G., Haynes, N., Knoff, H., et al. (1998). *Early warning, timely response: A guide to safe schools*: The referenced edition. Washington, DC: American Institutes for Research.

Fast, J. (1970). *Body language*. New York: Pocket Books.

Fishe, R., Ury, W., & Patton, B. (1991). *Getting to yes*. New York: Penguin Books.

Gordon, T. (1975). *Parental effectiveness training*. New York: Bantam Books.

Guerra, N. G., Huessman, L. R., Tolan, P. H., Van Acker, R., & Eron, L. D. (1995). Stressful events and individual beliefs as correlates of economic disadvantage and aggression among urban children. *Journal of Counseling and Clinical Psychology, 63*, 518–528.

Illinois Safe and Responsive Schools Act, PA 92-0260. 105 ILCS 5/10-20.14: Student Discipline Policies (2001).

Mattaini, M. (2001a). Constructing cultures of non-violence: The Peace Power! strategy. *Education and Treatment of Children, 24*(4), 430–447.

Mattaini, M., & Peace Power Working Group. (2001b). *Peace Power for adolescents: Strategies for a culture of non-violence*. Washington, DC: National Association of Social Workers.

Moriarty, A. (1992). *Training guide.* (Mimeograph). Park Forest, IL: Author.

Moriarty, A. R. (2002). *Managing kids: Direct answers for tricky issues*. CASE/CCBD Mini-library series on safe, effective and drug free schools. Arlington, VA: Council for Exceptional Children Press.

Moriarty, A., & McDonald, S. (1991). Theoretical dimensions of school-based mediation. *Social Work in Education, 13*(3), 176–184.

Mulvey, E. P., & Cauffman, E. (2001). The inherent limits of predicting school violence. *American Psychologist, 56*, 797–802.

National Consortium of School Violence Prevention Researchers and Practitioners (NCSVPRP) (2006) *Fall, 2006 School Shootings Position Statement*. October 27, 2006, Author. Reproduced in *SSWA Bell*, November 2006.

National Institutes of Health. (2005, January 18). *State of the Science Conference Statement: Preventing violence and related health-risking social behaviors in adolescents* (October 13–15, 2004). Retrieved February 24, 2005, from http://consensus.nih.gov.

No Child Left Behind Act of 2001, PL 107–110.

Olweus, D. (1980). Familial and temperamental determinants in aggressive behavior in adolescent boys: A causal analysis. *Developmental Psychology, 16*, 644–660.

Olweus, D. (2001). Peer harassment: A critical analysis and some important issues. In J. Juvonen & S. Graham (Eds.), *Peer harassment in school: The plight of the vulnerable and victimized* (pp. 3–20). New York: Guilford.

Safe and Drug-Free Schools and Communities Act, 20 U.S.C. 7101.

Sexton, T. L., & Alexander, J. F. (2003). Functional family therapy: A mature clinical model for working with at-risk adolescents and their families. In T. L Sexton, G. R. Weeks, & M. S Robbins (Eds.), *Handbook of family therapy* (pp. 323–350). New York, Brunner-Routledge.

Sheidow, A. J., Henggeler, S. W., & Schoenwald, S. K. (2003). Multisystemic therapy. In T. L Sexton, G. R Weeks, & M. S Robbins (Eds.), Handbook of family therapy (pp. 303–322). New York: Brunner-Routledge.

Siris, K., & Osterman, K. (2004). Interrupting the cycle of bullying and victimization in the elementary classroom. *Phi Delta Kappan, 86*(4), 288–291.

Smith, D. C., & Sandhu, D. S. (2004). Toward a positive perspective on violence protection in schools: Building connections. *Journal of Counseling and Development, 82*, 287–293.

South Suburban Peer Network. (1993). Susan Tantillo & Frank DuBois. Steering Committee Coordinators, Homewood-Flossmoor High School, Flossmoor, IL.

Van De Hey, W. (2007). Personal communication to Robert Constable, November 6, 2007.

Van De Hey, W. (undated). *Restorative justice in school communities: An alternative that is fair, constructive and inclusive.* Cited in M. Huxtable (Ed.), *Electronic Newsletter.* August, accessed August 26, 2007 at http://internationalnetwork-schoolsocialwork.htmlplanet.com. Also in http:www.oshkosh.k12.wi.us/aboutus/restorative.cfm (accessed October 23, 2007).

Walker, H. M., Colvin, G., & Ramsey, E. (1995). *Antisocial behavior in school: Strategies and best practices.* Pacific Grove, CA: Brooks/Cole.

Wong, D. S. W. (2004). School bullying and tackling strategies in Hong Kong. *International Journal of Offender Therapy and Comparative Criminology, 48*(5), 537–553.

Wong, D. S. W. (2005a). *School bullying and tackling strategies.* Hong Kong: Centre for Restoration of Human Relationships.

Wong, D. S. W. (2005b). *Restorative justice for juveniles in Hong Kong: Reflections of a practitioner.* Paper presented at the Sixth International Conference on Conferencing, Circles and Other Restorative Practices. Penrith, Australia, 3 March 2005.

Wong, D. S. W. (2006). *Managing school bullying: Factors contributing to the success of practicing restorative justice in Hong Kong.* Paper presented at the National Symposium for School Social Work and Counseling, Singapore, June 21–22.

Yamashita, E. (2007). *Bullying and restorative justice: For the development of school social work in Japan.* Retrieved August 26, 2007, from http://internationalnetwork-schoolsocialwork.htmlplanet.com

Appendix A
School Social Workers and Confidentiality

Position Statement of the School Social Work Association of America

Adopted March 15, 2001

Standards of practice for school social workers require that "adequate safeguards for the privacy and confidentiality of information" be maintained.[1,2] Confidentiality is an underlying principle of school social work and is essential to the establishment of an atmosphere of confidence and trust between professionals and the individuals they serve.

Information is communicated to school social workers by students and families with the expectation that these communications will remain confidential. An assurance of confidentiality promotes the free disclosure of information necessary for effective treatment.

ETHICAL AND LEGAL RESPONSIBILITIES

Direct Services

Providing services to students in the school setting requires a careful balance between legal and ethical responsibilities. School social workers must be conversant with federal, state, and local laws and policies governing confidentiality. School social workers must follow the guidelines established by the state and school district in which they work, recognizing that these guidelines may differ from those governing private practice.

---

1. Standard 14, *NASW Standards for School Social Work Services,* June 1992.
2. *NASW Commission on Education Position Statement: The social worker and confidentiality.*

Most states recognize that communications between social worker and client are privileged[3]; however, this privilege is not absolute. School social workers as members of a team of professionals may be confronted with situations where disclosure of information is critical to providing assistance to the student and family. It is the school social worker's obligation to obtain informed consent, i.e., explain the limitations on confidentiality to the student and family, prior to service delivery.

Information should be shared with other school personnel only on a need-to-know basis and only for compelling professional reasons. Prior to sharing confidential information, school social workers should evaluate the responsibility to and the welfare of the student. The responsibility to maintain confidentiality also must be weighed against the responsibility to the family and the school community. However, the focus should always be on what is best for the student.

School social workers must be conversant with affirmative reporting requirements. All states now require school professionals to report suspected cases of child abuse and neglect. School social workers should be aware of school board policies and should ensure that such policies safeguard confidentiality of the reporting individual.

School social workers should familiarize themselves with school board policies and state and local laws governing reporting requirements for students who are HIV-positive or have AIDS. School social workers should also be aware of state statutes providing confidentiality to minor students who seek treatment for sexually transmitted diseases, information about and access to birth control, and pregnancy-related health care and counseling.

Therapists, including social workers, are under an affirmative duty to warn if there is clear and present danger to the student or another identified individual.[4] The social worker must warn any individual threatened by the student and must take steps to ensure the safety of a student who threatens suicide.

In all instances, school social workers must weigh the consequences of sharing information and must assume responsibility for their decisions.

Written Material

School social workers must be conversant with federal, state, and local laws and policies regarding confidentiality of and access to education records. Education records are all records which contain information

---

3. Privileged communications are statements made by persons in a protected relationship, which are legally protected from disclosure on the witness stand. The privilege is exercised by the client and the extent of the privilege is governed by state statutes. H. C. Black, *Black's Law Dictionary,* Fifth Edition (1979).

4. *Tarasoff v. Regents of the Univ. of Calif.,* 17 Cal. 3d 425, 1551 P.2d 334 (1976).

directly related to a student and which are maintained by the educational agency or institution.[5] Parents have the right to inspect and review education records. Social workers' personal notes kept for use by only those individuals are not considered education records and are confidential.

School social workers should inform students and parents that information gathered under the individualized education program (IEP) process may be shared with all members of the IEP team. The team, which includes other school personnel and the parents, may use the social history compiled by the school social worker in making decisions about the student's educational program and placement.[6]

Documents maintained on a computer become education records if shared orally with another staff person. Sole possession records maintained on a computer are not considered part of the education record and are confidential. School social workers should also be aware that other staff members or computer technicians may have access to school-owned equipment. Saving sole possession records to an individual diskette and securing that diskette may provide greater assurance of confidentiality.

Confidential records should be transmitted by facsimile only when absolutely necessary. Such reports should include a notation indicating that the material is confidential and is for professional use by only the designated recipient. The notation also should indicate that review, dissemination, distribution, or copying of the facsimile is prohibited.

CONCLUSION

The school social worker must carefully weigh the decision whether to preserve the confidentiality of information or share the information, using the best interests of the student as a guide. Those decisions must be informed by federal, state, and local laws and policies, as well as the professional ethics of the school social worker.

---

5. *The Family Education Rights and Privacy Act* (FERPA), 20 U.S.C. § 1232g; *Individuals with Disabilities Education Act* (IDEA), 20 U.S.C. § 1400 (1997).

6. IDEA § 1412(a)(4).

Appendix B
School Social Work Personal Safety Guidelines

School Social Work Association of America

- Personal Safety
- Guidelines When Providing Transportation Assistance on the Job

PERSONAL SAFETY

Incidents reported in local and national media have brought a heightened awareness of violence and the potential for victimization in school and community environments. School social work has a long history of conducting community outreach activities to students, families, and resource providers. Thus, personal safety issues are of increasing concern to school social workers and their administrators.

The School Social Work Association of America offers the following personal safety precautions as preventive measures to assist school social workers and other educational personnel in avoiding problems and increasing their awareness of actions promoting personal safety. Guidelines cannot be constructed to address every conceivable situation, therefore school social workers are urged to rely on individual and professional judgment as the best assurance for promoting personal safety in any situation

Before You Leave

- Always inform a responsible school employee, such as an administrator or secretary, of your destination(s) and anticipated time of return. Maintain and leave a readily accessible schedule including names, addresses, and telephone numbers (if available) where you can be reached.

- Leave a complete and detailed itinerary with your office.
- Confirm appointments ahead of time to remind the person you are about to visit.
- Obtain clear directions to your destination and keep current city and county maps in your car.
- Research and utilize the safest route. If you get lost, do not make it obvious. Be very discreet and careful when asking directions.
- Conduct visits with another school staff member when you have reason to believe that personal safety may be at risk.
- Arrange for the school to maintain your car license plate number and description it you use your vehicle for conducting community contacts.
- Carry a preprogrammed cellular telephone with you if at all possible and set your quick dial options to include 911.
- Request nearby police surveillance if you think a significant degree of risk may be present.

Walking

The immediate surroundings hold a wealth of obvious and subtle clues to an observant individual. Traveling on foot in a new or less frequented environment can, in and of itself, cause a person to feel less comfortable.

- Be actively aware of your surroundings.
- Always appear confident and purposeful.
- Carry keys and money in a pocket rather than in a purse or wallet.
- Ignore individual(s) who verbally harass you and immediately distance yourself from them.
- Turn around and make it obvious to anyone you sense following you that you are aware of their presence. Immediately move to a less isolated area where other people are present.
- Call your office to announce a safe arrival at each destination, if possible.

Driving

Traveling in a vehicle can provide a false sense of security especially when you are driving in a new or less frequented environment. It is even more important to practice safe driving habits under these conditions.

- Drive with the doors locked and the windows closed, whenever practical. Lock doors prior to leaving school property.
- Keep wallets, purse, and any other valuables out of view.
- Remain in your vehicle if someone "bumps" you from behind. Motion to the other driver to follow you to a police station.
- Park in open areas, routinely check for suspicious persons in the area before exiting your vehicle, and always lock all doors as you exit.
- Call your office to announce a safe arrival at each destination, if possible.

- Be prepared to unlock the driver's door by placing the car key firmly in your hand prior to returning to your vehicle.
- Look underneath your vehicle while approaching it. Walk around the exterior of your vehicle checking both the front and rear seats for intruders before entering. Lock the doors prior to departing.

Assessing Danger

School social workers are trained to be sensitive to and aware of the social dynamics of various social situations. Trust your instincts and apply this skill in unfamiliar or new situations.

- Avoid locations and buildings that appear unsafe. Those that are dark, isolated, and obstructed or where individuals are loitering and/or disorderly should not be entered.
- Avoid family-owned or neighborhood dogs. Ask the family to put their pet in another room or ask to keep the pet leashed.
- Identify yourself readily as a school employee conducting school business. Offer your school business card or identification card.
- Avoid moralizing, resorting to blame, and/or presenting ultimatums. State your purpose clearly. Always leave an "out" for the other individual(s).
- Share information in a respectful, sensitive manner. As a school employee, you are a guest in their environment. Remember that many individuals and families you work with are experiencing considerable emotional stress and that you may be relaying information which will increase their level of stress.
- When encountering a parent or other person who appears under the influence of alcohol or other drugs, advise the individual(s) that you will contact them at another time and leave your school business card and/or telephone number. Try to remain between the exit and the individual.
- Be especially cautious when contacting individuals who have a previous known history of violent or criminal behavior. Strongly consider interacting by telephone, in a public location (such as a mall, coffee shop, or place of employment), and/or asking another school staff person to accompany you. Where possible, sit between the client and the exit doorway.
- Do not enter a known drug house. When an emergency arises at school, such as a sick or injured student, school employees should attempt to conduct the necessary interactions/notifications by telephone. When telephone access is not available, the school system should have a policy delineating proper procedures to follow.
- Reschedule your business when you find yourself in a potentially unprofessional and/or compromising situation. For example, persons are not fully clothed or when confidentiality cannot be ensured.

- Listen and observe attentively when encountering an individual who states and/or indicates that you are unwelcome. Do not argue or insist on a visit.

Working with Agitated Persons

The following behaviors can help in calming a distraught and/or agitated individual during your interactions.

- Remain calm and observant. Attend to reducing your own fears and stay in control of your emotions.
- Be aware of your body language and personal space needs of the client. Agitated or potentially violent persons should not have their personal space threatened or violated. Even if your intentions are good, moving closer may raise the person's level of anxiety. Being closer than 2–3 feet, even in nonthreatening situations, is generally uncomfortable.
- Request the upset individual be seated or remain seated. Locate yourself between the person and the exit doorway, and at eye level with the agitated individual.
- Have your cell phone easily accessible in case you need to call 911.
- Speak clearly and directly regarding your intended reason for interacting with the agitated individual. Avoid language which could in any way be construed as argumentative, demanding, or demeaning. Do not touch the agitated individual.
- Speak clearly and respectfully, utilizing a low, calming tone of voice. Ask the distraught individual to speak clearly and at a normal pace so that he/she can be understood. Do not patronize the individual.
- When the level of agitation becomes personally threatening, focus the remainder of the interaction on the immediate problem. Alter your original agenda as needed.
- Listen attentively and respectfully, allowing the distressed individual to talk. Clearly communicate that your desire is to help the person solve problem(s) which are upsetting them.
- Terminate your interactions if the distraught individual remains in an agitated state or becomes increasingly agitated, uncooperative, verbally abusive, threatening, or displays a weapon. Exit promptly if any such circumstance arises and immediately report the situation to your supervisor and/or school security personnel, and local law enforcement when needed.

If You Are Victimized

Experience dictates that it is extremely unlikely that a school employee will be victimized while conducting official school business. In the unlikely event that you are victimized or threatened you should act quickly to do the following:

- Access emergency medical services when necessary.
- Report the incident to local low enforcement and your supervisor and/or school security personnel.
- Document the incident thoroughly, including the interactions, time, place, and individual(s) involved as soon as possible. Complete written documentation is essential for accurate recall and any potential law enforcement action.

GUIDELINES WHEN PROVIDING TRANSPORTATION ASSISTANCE ON THE JOB

At times, transporting students and/or families by car has been an expected and encouraged school social work service. Unfortunately in today's climate of litigation, transporting students can put the school social worker in jeopardy. SSWAA believes school social workers need to be aware of possible legal ramifications and make an informed decision before agreeing to transport students and/or families as a part of school employment. SSWAA recommends the following steps be taken by school social workers who provide occasional transportation assistance for students and others.

If providing transportation is expected on the job, then:

- Child and parent transportation expectations should be addressed in job descriptions and in collective bargaining agreements (when applicable). The purpose is to protect the school social worker.
- The LEA should provide liability insurance specifically covering employee transportation of students and others. School social workers should periodically review their district's policy.
- School social workers should contact their personal auto insurance carrier to determine the extent of liability coverage for accidents which may occur when providing transportation while on the job.
- If the school social worker has professional liability insurance through the employer or by individual purchase, a statement regarding transportation liability coverage should be obtained from that insurance provider.

If providing transportation is not expected on the job, then:

- School social workers should check with the employing LEA to find out if providing transportation violates any LEA rule, regulation, policy, or practice.
- School social workers should contact their personal auto insurance carrier to determine the extent of liability coverage for accidents which may occur when providing transportation while on the job.

Index

Page numbers followed by *f, n,* or *t* refer to figures, notes, or tables respectively.

Abbott, Edith, 15
Academic achievement, children's mental health and, 467
Academic skills, 626
Acanfora v. Board of Education (1974), 311
Accountability, promoting collegial, 241
Accountability checks, 327
Acculturation, 347–348
Activities
  assessing, 45–46
  communicating, 45
  evaluating, 45
  planning, 45
  relating, 45
Adaptive behavior
  assessment measures for, 442–446
  assessment of, 437–439
  clinical judgment in assessment of, 446–448
  common assessment measures for, 439–446, 440t
  common screening measures of, 440t, 441–442
  determining limitations in, 435
  environment and, 436–437
  as function of age, 436
  as function of cultural expectations, 436
  qualifications of social workers for assessing, 434
  reasons for screenings of, 432
Adaptive behavior assessment, 422–427, 437–439. *See also* Assessment
  formal, 422–427, 431
  informal, 422, 431
  measures for, 442–446
  qualifications of social workers for, 434
  reasons for, 432–433
Adaptive Behavior Assessment System— Second edition (ABS-II), 443
Adaptive Behavior Evaluation Scale— Revised (ABES-R2), 443–444
Adaptive Behavior Inventory (ABI), 443
Adaptive Behavior Scales (ABS), 442
Adaptive skills, categories of, 435
ADHD. *See* Attention deficit hyperactivity disorder (ADHD)
Administrators, 77
Advocacy, 353
  policy, 162–163
Affectional structure, 182
African American children. *See also* Minority children
  freedom schools, 297
  post-civil war schooling of, 292–293
  pre-civil war schooling of, 291–292
  school segregation and, 294–298
African Americans
  education and, 303
  racism and, 303–304
Age, adaptive behavior as function of, 36
Agents of change, school social workers as, 163–164
Ages & Stages Questionnaire (ASQ), 441
Alderson, John, 20
Alexander v. Holmes County Board of Education (1969), 297
Alternative placements, continuum of, 365–366
Amber Tatro et al. v. Irving (Tx.) Independent School District et al., 266n28
American Association of Visiting Teachers, 14–15
American Association on Intellectual & Development Disabilities (AAIDD), 432
Analytic competencies, 161
Anger management, 671
Annual goals, 512–513

Anxiety, 644
  heightened, 644
Anxiety disorders, 484–486
  Internet resources for, 489
  post-traumatic stress disorder, 485–486
  separation anxiety, 485–486
Arlington Central School District Board of Education v. Pearl Murphy, 271–272
Asperger's disorder, 482–483
Assertion skills, 627
Assessment, 6. *See also* Adaptive behavior assessment
  Case Study, 415–422
  of classroom learning environments, 326
  cultural, 354
  decision making and, 409
  defined, 25
  family, school attendance and, 698
  functional behavior, 427–429
  imaginization for, 187–189
  individual, school attendance and, 695–698
  of learning environments, 410–414
  for least restrictive environment, 362–363
  of maladaptive behaviors, 437
  measures of, for adaptive behavior, 442–446
  of mental health disorders, 468–469
  observation and, 411–412
  process of, 329–332
  qualitative, 325
  resources, 337
  school, attendance and, 698–699
  for school and vulnerable families, 562
  school social work, 325–326
  in school social work, 322–323
  Social Developmental, 422
  strengths-based, 409–410
  systems, 350–354
Attendance, school, 692–693. *See also* Truancy
  academic achievement and, 694
  creating positive school climate for improving, 701
  evidence based interventions, 699–709
  family assessment and, 698
  individual assessment and, 695–698
  rational choice and, 694–695
  school assessment and, 698–699
  social development and, 694
Attention, units of. *See* Units of attention
Attention deficit hyperactivity disorder (ADHD), 475–478
  Internet resources for, 488
  interventions, 476–477t
  The Journey for, 668–669
  screening measures for children and adolescents, 479t
Autism, 482
Avoidance, purposeful, 643

Bartlett, Harriet, 18
The Battelle Developmental Inventory—Second edition—Screener (BDI-2S), 441
Bayley Scales of Infant Development (Bayley III), 444
Beck Youth Inventories, 614
Behavioral consultation, 386
Behavioral Intervention Plans (BIPs), 495–497
Behavior Education Program (BEP), 670–671
Behaviors, 219
Beliefs and opinions, 219
Benchmarks, 514–515
Bennett, Robert Lafollette, 309
Bilingual education, 312–315
Bilingual Education Act, 312–314
Bipolar disorder, 480–481
Bisexual students. *See* Gay, lesbian, bisexual or transgender (GLBT) students
Black codes, 294
Board of Education of Oklahoma City v. Dowell, 304
Boston, Massachusetts, 13
Boundaries, professional, 328
Brokered service networks, 170
Brooks-Gunn, Jeanne, 146
Brown v. Board of Education of Topeka (1954), 12, 156, 295–296, 344
Bruneau v. South Kortright (NY) Central School District (1996), 722
Budgets, school, as research tool, 146–246
The Bulletin (journal), 15, 17
Bullying, 122, 713–714
  in Asian schools, 747
  defined, 714
  differential assessment for, 717
  outcomes for children who engage in, 717–718
  prevalence of, 715–716
  research on, 716
  responses to, 723–724
  sexual harassment *vs.*, 714–715
  victims of, 716–717
Bureaupathologies, 179
Burlington School Committee v. Department of Education, 272–273, 273n40

Campbell Collaboration, 141
Case identification, 327
Case law, 82–83
Case management, 581–583
  approaches to, 582t
Case Study Assessment (CSA), 415–422, 497
Casework in schools, rethinking, 19
Centralization, 180
Challenging Horizons Program, 669–670
Change, managing organizational, 189–190
Change agents, school social workers as, 163–164
Chapman, Samuel, 292–293
Characteristics, 219
Charter schools, 131–132
Chicago, Illinois, 13
Child abuse
  disclosing confidential information and, 104
  in United States, 120–121
Child Abuse Prevention and Treatment Act (CAPTA) (1974), 103–104
Child and adolescent community mental health services (CAMHS) (New Zealand), 403–404
Childhood poverty, 117–118
Children involved with child welfare
  educational needs of, 675–677
  interventions for, 678–687
  social and emotional needs of, 675
Children's Behavior Checklist, 614
Children unable to benefit from education, 265–267
Children with disabilities
  coping with, 569–571
  court cases affecting, 167
  defined, 260
  educational rights of, 166–169, 255–257
  families and, 569–571
  least restrictive environments for, 267–268
  placement procedures for, 268
  practice model of, 8–9
  related services for, 261–262
  required school services for, 264–267
  role of local school systems and, 259–260
  social work services for, 260–261
  special education for, 261
  special education systems for, 258–259
  suspending or expelling, 268–270
  suspension or expulsion from school and, 268–270
Child welfare system. *See also* Children involved with child welfare
  collaboration between schools and, 677–678
  schools and, 674
Circle conferences, 747–748
Circle diagrams, 181
Civil Rights, Office of, 310
Civil Rights Act (1866), 295
Civil Rights Case (1883), 295
Classroom group dynamics, 410–411
Classroom learning environments, assessment of, 326
Classroom observation. *See also* Observation
  event sampling, 458–460, 459f
  of multiple students, 460–461, 461t
  overview of, 452–454
  Sanders classroom observation form, 454–458, 455f
  of teacher-pupil interactions, 461–462
Clients, 76, 77
  determining, confidentiality and, 99–101
Climate, organizational, 41
Clinical consultation, 80, 384
Clinical judgment, in assessment of adaptive behavior, 446–448
Clinical model, of school social work, 20
Clinical school social work, 6–8
Clinical social work, case study, 536–540
Clovis Unified School District v. California of Admin. Hearing, 265n19
Coalition building, 164
Cobb, Charlie, 297
Cochrane Collaboration, 141
Code of Ethics, NASW, 74, 97–98. *See also* National Association of Social Workers (NASW)
  clinical consultants and, 80
  compelling professional reasons and, 101–103
  confidentiality and, 97–98
  disclosure without prior consent and, 80
  flaws of, 76, 78
  preamble to, 156
  privileged information and, 87
Coercive power, 182
Collaboration, 376–380
  challenges of, 377–378
  community, 380
  competencies, 379
  defined, 377
  family-centered, 379–380

guidelines for building effective, 378–379
interagency, 379
interprofessional, 379
between schools and child welfare, 677–678
Collaborative decision making, 327
Collaborative research, 237
Collaborative teams, 327
Colleagues, 77
Collier, John, 308–309
Comer, James, 553
Commission on Education, NASW, confidentiality and, 98–99
Communication
of activities, 45
improving, for children involved with child welfare, 680–681
intrateam, 327
protection of privileged, 87
Communication structure, 182
Community, as unit of attention, 543–544
Community collaboration, 380
Community profiles, 352
Community school model, of school social work, 20
Compelling professional reasons, Code of Ethics and, 101–103
Competence core value, 74
Competencies, for policy practice
analytic, 161
interactional, 161
political, 161
value clarification, 161
Complex prevention initiatives, 170
Compliance skills, 626
Comprehensive Children's Mental Health Services Program, 466
Conduct disorders, 483–484
Challenging Horizons Program for, 669–670
Internet resources for, 489
Kids Together, 670
Confidentiality
African American parents and, 71
checklist, 91
Code of Ethics and, 97–98
Commission on Education and, 98
dangerous situations and, 103–105
decision-making procedures and principles for, 73–86
determining clients and, 99–101
Latina mothers and, 71
laws about, 86–89
professionalism *vs.,* 102–103
release of information forms and, 108–109
schools and, 72
School Social Work Association of America and, 98–99
school social workers and, 753–755
Conflict resolution
for safe schools, 738–742
skill building for, 741–742
skills and process of, 739–741
Congress of Racial Equality, 296
Connors' Rating Scales-Revised, 614
Consent, disclosure without, consequences of, 111–112
Consequentialists, 73
Constitution, U.S.
Fifteenth Amendment, 292, 293–294
Fourteenth Amendment, 292, 293–294, 298
Thirteenth Amendment, 292, 293–294
Consultation, 376–377
behavioral, 385–386
case example for multiple models, 394–395
challenges, 389–390
clinical, 384
consultee-centered case, 391
defined, 380, 381
education and training, 383–384
knowledge base of, 380–383
mental health, 385
models, 383–387
New Zealand case example of, 403–407
organizational, 387
phases of, 387–389
preferential, 369–370
process of, 329–332
program, 386
role of federal government, 381–382
school social work practice and, 380
seeking, 80–83
teamwork and, 329
Consultee-centered case consultation, 391
Continuum of alternative placements, 365–366
Contracting, private, 132
Cooper v. Aaron (1958), 296
Coping behaviors, 36–37
defined, 32–33
Core values, of social work, 74
Costin, Lela, 19, 115
school-community-pupil relations model of, 20
Council of Federated Organizations, 296
Counts and rates, 219

Courses of action, identifying, 79
Crises. *See also* Trauma
assistance to teachers and, 654
community healing for, 658–659
community meetings for, 655–656
consultation for, 654
critical incident stress debriefing for, 653
defined, 647
levels of, 647–648
media and, 65
ongoing support groups for, 653–654
ongoing tracking and review of, 654–655
on-scene interventions for, 649
practice model of, 8
rumor control mechanisms for, 656
scope of school responses to, 652
screening of victims, 653
student notification and, 651
support services for, 651–652
teachers' meetings and, 650–651
Crisis intervention, 647
Crisis plans, 648–649
Crisis response plans, 735
Crisis teams, 647–648
activation of, 650
Critical incident stress debriefing (CISD), 653
Cueing, 668
Culbert, Jane, 14
Cultural assessment, 354
Cultural awareness, adaptive behavior assessment and, 436
Cultural competence, 340–341
through perspective building, 342–346
Cultural exchange, 347–348
Culturally competent school social work practice, 340–342
framework for, 348–350
planning effective service delivery in, 358–360
skills of, 355–358
Culture
defined, 184
organizational, 184–185

Dangerous clients, 83–84
Dangerous situations, confidentiality and, 103–105
Data analysis, for needs assessment, 226–228
Databases, 248
Data sources/resources, for needs assessment, 223–224
federal government, 230–231
nonprofit, 231–232
private, 231–232
state government, 230
Davis v. Monroe County Board of Education (1999), 122, 722
Decentralization, 180
Decision-making structures, 182
Decisions
procedure and principles for, 73–86
Decisions, enacting, 85–86
De facto segregation, 299
De jure segregation, 294–295, 299, 344
Demographics, of United States, 117–118
Deontologists, 74
Depression, 478–480
Desegregation, 295–296
Desires, 219
Developmental disabilities, defined, 435
Developmental learning objectives, 502, 503–508t
Diagnostic and Statistical Manual IV Text Revision (DSM-IV-TR), 469–470
advantages and limitations in using, 469–470
Dignity and worth of person core value, 74
Dilemmas, analyzing, 76–79
Discipline plans, 735
Disclosure
necessary, 109–111
students' reactions to violation of privileged, 84
without consent, consequences of, 111–112
Disclosure without prior consent, Code of Ethics and, 80
Dissociation, 643–644
Distress, predictors of, 644–646
Diversity, 4
in United States, 343–346
Dix, Dorothea, 466
Documents, education, confidentiality and, 753–755
Dropout rates, in United States, 123
Dryfoos, Joy G., 171
Du Bois, W. E. B., 293
Due process hearings, 271–272, 272–273
Duty to warn or protect, 105
harmful acts and, 105–106
imminent violence and, 106–107
physical violence and, 105–106
Dysfunctional structure, 180

Early intervention services
defined, 278
statewide system requirements for, 278–284

Ecological perspective, 35
Ecological systems approach, 21–22
Ecology, 35
Education
  local initiatives in, 131–133
  purposes of, 5–6
Education and training consultation, 383–384
Education for All Handicapped Children Act, 166, 255
The Education of the Negro Prior to 1861 (Woodson), 291–292
Education systems, student preparation and, 115–116
Effectiveness
  efficacy *vs.*, 51
  intervention, 56–61
Efficacy, effectiveness *vs.*, 51
Elementary and Secondary Education Act (ESEA) (2001), 126–128
E-mails, for policy advocacy, 162–163
Empowerment, 284
  school-based family, 586–593
English Language Learners Act, 314
Environments. *See also* Least restrictive environment (LRE)
  adaptive behavior and, 436–437
  learning, 410–414
  matching persons with, 39–41
  quality of impinging, 34
Equal Educational Opportunities Act (1974), 298
  bilingual education and, 313
Ethical principles, 74–75
Ethical principles screen, 75t
Ethical thinkers, 74
Ethics
  law and, 86–89 (*See also* Code of Ethics, NASW)
  school social workers and, 753–755
Ethnography, 354–355
Evaluating activities, 45
Event sampling, recording, 458–460, 459f
Evidence-based interventions, school social work practice and, 62–63
Evidence-based practice (EBP), 547–548, 679
  components of, 140
  defined, 470
  evidence of effectiveness of, 145–147
  with groups, 610–611
  group work and, 596–597
  Internet resources for, 489
  principles governing transparent, 144–145
  process, 472f
  in school social work, 141–147
  school social workers' use of, 470–475
Excel, tips for using, 226–227
Expectations, 38
Expertise
  clinical consultation, 80–81
  legal advice, 81
  seeking outside, 80–83
  types of, 80
Expertise power, 182
Eyes on the Prize: The Fighting Back Years, 296

Families
  children with disabilities and, 569–571
  development of children and, 3
  effects of school reforms on, 173
  necessary arrangement of relations between schools and, 554–556
  respecting relational structure of, 566–569
  role of school social workers with, 559–573
  school as community of, 551–554
  school-based empowerment of, 586–593
  school social work practice with, 550–551
  with severe caregiving demands, case example, 571–573
  as unit of attention, 542
  vulnerable, 556
  vulnerable, assessment of, 542
Family assessment, 354–355
Family-centered collaboration, 379–380
Family-centered social work practice, 284–287
Family centers, 170–171
Family Educational Rights and Privacy Act (FERPA) (1974), 81–82
  education records and, 109
Family processes, 557–558
Family resilience, 558
Family resource centers, 133, 591
Family systems perspective, schooling and, 559–561
FAPE. *See* Free and appropriate public education (FAPE)
Federal government resources, 230–231
Fifteenth Amendment, 292, 293–294
Focus groups, 224, 225
Foreseeable harm, 81
Formal adaptive behavior, 422–427, 431
Formal adaptive behavior assessment, 422–427
Formalization, 178–180

Formal structure
  defined, 178
  of organizations, 178–181
Foster care, children living in, 674–675. *See also* Children involved with child welfare
Foster Youth Services Program, 681–682
Fourteenth Amendment, 292, 293–294, 298
Franklin v. Gwinnet County (GA) Public Schools (1992), 721
Free and appropriate public education (FAPE), 255, 257, 515n2
Freedmen's Bureau, 292
Freedom schools, 297
Freedom Summer Project, 296–297
Full-service schools, 133
  philosophy of, 171
Functional behavior assessment, 427–429
Functional behavior objectives, 501–502
Functional family therapy, 737
Functional structures, 180
Funding, school, funding for, 129–130

GAS. *See* Goal attainment scaling (GAS)
Gay, lesbian, bisexual or transgender (GLBT) students
  sexual harassment and, 123
  suicide risk with, 123, 487–488
Gender discrimination, educational policy and, 309–311
General education
  assessment in, 331–332
  outcome-oriented, strengths-based service delivery approach for, 332–334
  partnerships with parents and, 553
General education teachers, needs of, for LRE, 367–369
Generic knowledge, 15–16
GLBT students. *See* Gay, lesbian, bisexual or transgender (GLBT) students
Goal attainment scaling (GAS), 502, 508t, 615
Goals
  annual, 512–513
  monitoring group, 611–616
  monitoring individual, 611–613
  process of setting, 501–508
  quantitative measurements of, 613–615
Go Grrrls program, 632, 633t
Gold standard of research, 147
Goose, Rev. Thomas, 292
Gordon, William E., 18, 22
GRADES test, 209–211
Green v. County School Board of New Kent County (1968), 296
Grief, trauma *vs.*, 646–647
Griffin v. County School Board of Prince Edward County (1964), 296
Group composition, 599
Group interventions, evidence of effectiveness of, 145–146
Groups. *See also* Social skills groups
  evidence-based practice with, 610–611
  goal setting in, 612–613
  methods for monitoring, 616–618
  monitoring goals of, 611–616
  monitoring processes of, 616, 618
Group structure, 598, 600
Group work, 595–596
  evaluation and, 601–602
  evidence-based practice and, 596–597
  monitoring outcomes of, 618
  planning for, 597–602
  practice model of, 9
  pre-group interviews, 602
  session content and, 600–601
  stages of, 602–608

Hamline School, Chicago, 166
Hampton Normal and Agriculture Institute, 292–293
Harm, 80–81
Harmful acts, duty to warn or protect and, 105–106
Hartford, Connecticut, 13
Head Start, 124, 553
Health Insurance Portability and Accountability Act (HIPAA) (1996), 81, 82
Helping processes, common factors of effective, 147
Homeless children and youths, in United States, 118
Home visits, 566–569
  truancy and, 706
Hong Kong schools, restorative justice in, 748–751
Honig v. Doe, 266n24, 268, 269n32
Horizontal complexity, 181
Hudson Scales, 614
Hyperarousal, 644

IEPs. *See* Individualized education programs (IEPs)
Imaginization, 187–189

Imminent harm, 81
minors and, 107–108
Impartial due process hearing, 271
Impinging environments, 37–39
matching persons with, 39–41
quality of, 34
Implementation, of decisions, 85–86
Importance of human relationships, core value, 74
Inclusion, 4. *See also* Least restrictive environment (LRE)
history of, 11–12
least restrictive environment and, 363–365
preparations for, of new student, 370–371
principle of, 257
promoting, in research, 239–243
Indian Education Act (1972), 309
Indian Reorganization Act (1934), 309
Individual differences, respect for, 12
Individualized education program (IEP) teams. *See also* Teams
defined, 508–509
placement decisions and, 370
Individualized education programs (IEPs), 258, 495, 497–501
attaining, 509–510
confidential information and, 110
defined, 262–264
hypothetical case study, 510–512
IDEA 2004 and, 126
involving children in, 515–517
Individualized family service plans (IFSPs), 275, 280–281, 495, 517–520
expected outcomes, 519
service coordination, 519–520
Individualized interventions, 336
Individuals with Disabilities Education Improvement Act (IDEA) (2004), 124–126, 140, 169, 255–256, 258–259, 270
analysis of, 276–278
individualized education programs and, 126
infants and toddlers at risk of disabilities and, 276–278
Part B services, 275
Part C, 274–276
screenings of adaptive behavior and, 432
Infants and toddlers with or at risk for disabilities, 283–284
developing best practice models for, 284–287
Informal adaptive behavior assessment, 422, 431
Informal structures, 182–184
affectional, 182
communication, 182
decision-making, 182
factors contribution to development and maintenance of, 183
functions of, 183–184
mapping, 183
power, 182
In-person, 226
In re Grossman (1974), 311
Instructional integration, 367
Instrumental values, 43
Integration
instructional, 367
social, 367
temporal, 366–367
Integrity core value, 74
Intellectual disability, defined, 434–435
Interactional competencies, 161
Interagency agreements, 581
Interagency collaboration, 379
Internet resources, 65–66
for ADHD, 488
for anxiety disorders, 489
for conduct disorders, 489
for evidence-based practice, 489
for mood disorders, 488
for PDD, 489
Interprofessional, 379
Interventions, 334
effectiveness of, 56
evidence-based, 62–63
findings, 56–57
individualized, 336
positive behavioral, 334–335
response to, 335–337
targeted, 336
Tier 1 (universal), 525–526
Tier 2 (targeted) interventions, 526–527
Tier 3 (individualized), 528–529
universal, 336
Interviews, key informant, 224–225
Intrateam communication, 327
Involvement, promoting, in research, 239–243
IQ testing, 307–308

Jaffee v. Redmond (1996), 86
Jim Crow laws, 294
The Journey, 668–669

Judgment
clinical, in assessment of adaptive behavior, 446–448
social work and, 44
Judicial review, 272–273
Justice core value, 74

Kattan v. District of Columbia, 266n27
Kennedy Report (1969), 309
Key informant interviews, 224–225
Kids Together, 670
Knowledge
defined, 44
in needs assessment, 219
Know yourself step, of decisionmaking, 73–76

Larry P. v. Wilson Riles (1984), 307
Lau v. Nichols (1974), 313
Laws, 38–39. *See also* Policies
Learning environments,
assessment of, 410–414
dynamics of, 410–411
LEAs. *See* Local education agencies (LEAs)
Least restrictive environment (LRE)
assessment for, 362–363
for children with disabilities, 267–268
defined, 363
inclusion and, 363–365
needs of general education teachers for, 367–369
preparations for inclusion of new student for, 370–371
transition planning, 372–374
types of integration and, 366–367
Least restrictive environment mandate, 258
Legal advice, 81
Legitimate educational interests, 81–82
Legitimate suspicion, defined, 678
Lesbian students. *See* Gay, lesbian, bisexual or transgender (GLBT) students
Letters, for policy advocacy, 162–163
Levine, Art, 165
Liaison Education Adolescent Project (LEAP), 404–405
Local education agencies (LEAs), 128
children with disabilities and, 259–260
homeless children and, 311–312
individualized education programs and, 126
NCLB and, 127
Local initiatives, in education, 131–133
charter schools, 131–132
private contracting, 132
school-linked services, 132–133
voucher programs, 132
Locality development, 380
LRE. *See* Least restrictive environment (LRE)

Mailed surveys, 225
Maladaptive behaviors, assessment of, 437
Manchester Teaching Service, 681–682
Mandated achievement testing, 5
Mandated reporters, 678
Marcus, Grace, 15–16
Max M. V. Thompson, 265n16
McKinney-Vento Homeless Assistance Act (1987), 311
Media, crises and, 655
Mediation, 271
peer, 742–745
for safe schools, 738
training, 743
Medicaid, 133–134
"Melting pot" metaphor, 345–346
Mental health
children's, academic achievement and, 467
school social work and, 464–466
Mental health consultation, 385
model, for school social workers, 390–394
New Zealand case example of, 403–407
Mental health disorders
anxiety disorders, 484–486
assessment of, 468–469
attention deficit hyperactivity disorder, 475–478
conduct disorders, 483–484
mood disorders, 478–481
pervasive development disorder (PDD), 481–483
in U.S. children, 119
Mental health policies, school social work and, 466–467
Mental health services, role of school social worker in, 467–468
Mental Measurements Yearbook (Geisinger, Spies, Carlson, & Blake), 426
Mental retardation, 434
Mentoring programs, for truancy, 702–703
Meredith v. Jefferson County Board of Education, 299, 305
Meriam Report (1926), 308–309

Mesosystems, school community, 353
Milford Conference Report, 15
Miliken v. Bradley (1974), 299
Mills v. Board of Education of the District of Columbia (1972), 167–168
Minimum possible information, 109–111
Minority children. *See also* African American children; Sexual minorities
  achievement gap of, 305–306
  Native American children, 308–309
  overrepresentation of, in special education, 306–307
  racism and, 303–304
  standardized tests and, 307–308
Minors, imminent harm and, 107–108
Missouri v. Jenkins, 304
Monitoring the Future project (University of Michigan), 119
Montgomery, Louise, 13, 166
Mood disorders, 478–481
  bipolar disorder, 480–481
  depression, 478–480
  Internet resources for, 488
Moral citizenship, 74
Moral conundrums, ethical-legal typology of, 88–89
Morgan, Gareth, 187
Moses, Bob, 297
Mrs. B. v. Milford Board of Education, 265n17
Multicultural education, connecting to unrecognized constituencies of, 238–239
Multicultural resources, developing, 237–238
Multidimensional Self-Concept Scale, 614
Multidisciplinary problem-solving teams, 326–327
Multidisciplinary team, in special education, 330–331
Multisystemic therapy, 737

Nabozny v. Podlesny (1996), 122, 311, 722
Narrative therapy, 284
National Advisory Council on Indian Education, 309
National Association for the Advancement of Colored People (NAACP), 296
National Association of Social Workers (NASW), 17. *See also* Code of Ethics, NASW
National Association of Visiting Teachers, 14
National Center for Culturally Responsive Educational Systems, 307
National Council on Indian Opportunity, 309
National Court Appointed Special Advocates (CASA), 683
National Institute of Mental Health (NIMH), 466
National Institutes of Health Review, 61–62
National Mental Health Act (1946), 466
National Quality Forum, 64
Native American children, educational policy and, 308–309
Needs assessment, 25
  data analysis for, 226–228
  data sources and resources for, 223–224, 229–232
  defined, 217–218
  implementing, 222–226
  planning, 219–222
  reasons for conducting, 218–219
  reporting findings of, 228–229
  of school community, 323–326
Needs identification, 327
Networks
  of service organizations, 42–43
  social, 42
New York City, 13
New Zealand, case example of school and mental health agency collaboration in, 403–407
No Child Left Behind Act (NCLB) (2001), 115, 127, 140
  "highly qualified" school personnel and, 328
  minority children and, 306
  research stipulations of, 235
  testing goals of, 677
  as vehicle for school reform, 164–165
Nonattendance, school. *See* Attendance, school
Nondiscriminatory evaluation, principle of, 256
North Carolina Board of Education v. Swann (1971), 298

Objectives
  annual, 512–513
  process of setting, 501–508
  short-term, 514–515
Observation, 224. *See also* Classroom observation
  assessment and, 411–412
  family assessment and, 355
Occupational, 435
Office of Civil Rights, 310

Oncale v. Sundowner Offshore Services (1998), 722–723
100 Black Men of America program, 684
One-stop shopping centers, 133
Oppenheimer, Julius, 14
Optical scanning, 227–228
Organizational charts, 181
Organizational climate, 41
Organizational consultation, 387
Organizational culture
  school as, 184–185
  taking actions about, 187
  understanding, 185–187
Organizations
  climate of, 41
  communication and, 41
  formal structure of, 178–181
  imaginization for assessing, 187–189
  informal structure of, 182–184
  managing change in, 189–190
  networks of service, 42–43
  people-processing and people-changing perspectives of, 177–178
  understanding, 41–42
Outcome categories, 36–37
Outcome-driven education, 4
Outcome-oriented, strengths-based service delivery approach for, 332–334
Outcome-oriented practice, 143–145
Outcomes
  defining, 55–56
  future directions for quality of, 63–65
Outcome studies, review of, 1998-2007, 57–61, 58–60t

Papcoda v. Connecticut, 265n17
Parental involvement, developing, 553
Parent and student participation, principle of, 257
Parent education, for truancy, 700–701
Parent participation, 123
Parents
  dimensions of interactions with children and, 146
  effectiveness of schools and, 146
  expectations of, 552
  participation of, 553–554
  partnerships with, 552–553
Parents' Evaluation of Developmental Status (PEDS), 441
Parents in Action on Special Education v. Hannon (1980), 308
Parents Involved v. Seattle School District, 299, 304
Parks v. Pavkovic, 265n20, 266n24
Part B services, IDEA 2004, 275
Part C, IDEA 2004, 274–276
  continuing impact of, 287–289
Partnerships
  with communities and multiple organizations, 284
  between home and schools, 552–553
Paternalism, 78
PDD. *See* Pervasive development disorder (PDD)
Peace-Builders program, 733–734
PEACEPOWER, 733–734
Peer mediation, 742–745
Peer-pairing, 670
Peer relationship skills, 625–626
Peer sexual harassment, 718–723
Pennsylvania Association of Retarded Children (PARC) v. Commonwealth of Pennsylvania (1971), 167
People-changing perspectives, of organizations, 177–178
People-processing perspectives, of organizations, 177–178
Personal safety guidelines, for school social workers, 757–761
Personal values, 43, 73–74
Pervasive development disorder (PDD), 481–483
  Asperger's disorder, 482–483
  autism, 482
  Internet resources for, 489
Phobia, school, 697
Phone surveys, 225–226
Physical health, of U.S. children, 118–119
Physical violence, duty to warn or protect and, 105–106
Placement decisions, process of, 370
Placement procedures
  defined, 268
  for least restrictive environments, 267–268
Placements, continuum of alternative, 365–366
Planning activities, 45
Plessy v. Ferguson (1896), 295
Policies, 38–39. *See also* Laws
  defined, 194–196
Policy analysis, 196
  elements of, 197–198
  of hypothetical school system's policy, 198–215
  presentation of, 216

Policy practice, 178
in action, 162–163
competencies for, 161
components of, 160
practice model of, 10–11
school social worker skills needed for, 161
school social worker's role in, 157–159
skills of, 159–162
tasks of, 160
Policy-related practice, 178
Policy sensitive practice, 178
Political competencies, 161
Poole, Florence, 15–16
Positive behavioral interventions and supports (PBIS), 334–335, 665–668
Post-traumatic reactions, common types of, 642–644
Post-traumatic stress disorder (PTSD), 485–486, 641
Postvention, 649
Potential danger, 83
Poverty
childhood, 117–118
risks for children and, 557
in United States, 117–118
Power, types of, 182
Power structure, 182
Practical skills, 435
Practice guidelines, 148
Pratt, Henry, 308
Pre-experimental designs (PEDs), 617–618
Preferential interventions, 326, 414–415
Prescreening Developmental Questionnaire—Second edition (PDQ-II), 442
Prevention programs, for truancy, 700
Primary values, 43–44
Problem-solving teams, least restrictive environment and, 367–369
Procedural due process, principle of, 257
Professional boundaries, 328
Professionalism, confidentiality *vs.,* 102–103
Professional values, 43, 73–74
rules governing, 77–78
Program consultation, 386
Program development, 327
Psychotherapy, children with disabilities and, 265
Psychotherapy notes, HIPAA protection of, 82
PTSD. *See* Post-traumatic stress disorder (PTSD)
Public school children, demographics of, 4
Punishments, for truancy, 700
Pupils. *See* Students
Purposeful avoidance, 643

Qualitative measurements, of goals, 615–616
Quality of impinging environment, 34
Quantitative measurements, of goals, 613–615

Racial discrimination, 294
Racism, African Americans and, 303–304
Random clinical trials, 147
Rapid-assessment instruments (RAIs), 614
Rational choice, school attendance and, 694–695
Record keeping, 89–91
Records, education, confidentiality and, 753–755
Re-experiencing, 642–643
Referent power, 182
Reflection, in decision-making process, 86
Regular Education Initiative, 167
Related services, defined, 261
Relating activities, 45
Relativists, 74
Release of information forms, 108–109
Research
applications of school-based, 236–238
collaborative, 237
connecting to unrecognized constituencies and, 238–239
dialogue between school social work practice and, 147–148
economics of, 146–147
gold standard of, 147
guidelines for starting, 243–245
improving home-school-community partnerships and, 239
low-cost, straightforward methods for, 245–251
promoting inclusion and involvement in, 239–243
school-based practitioners and, 233–235
in schools, 235–236
Research studies, evaluating, 52–55
Resegregation, 304–305
Resilience, 54
of children, 551–552, 557
of families, 558
Resolution sessions, 270–271
Resource development, challenges of, 579–581
Resources, 37
developing multicultural, 237–238
Response-to-Intervention model of services, 433f

Response-to-Intervention (RtI), 335–337
approaches to, 523–524
defined, 522
evidence base for, 529–530
focus of, 523
levels of intervention, 523
models, 523
overview of, 522–523
process of, 525–529
public policy and, 524–525
Responsive schools. *See* Safe and responsive schools
Restorative justice, 747–748
in Hong Kong schools, 748–751
Reward power, 182
Rhoades, Charles, 309
Risk, 54
Roberts v. City of Boston, 295
Rochester, New York, 13–14
Role development, 26
Roles, defined, 6
Rowley case, 264–265
RTI. *See* Response-to-Intervention model of services
Rumor control mechanisms, 656

Safe and Drug-Free Schools and Communities Program (SDFSC), 466
Safe and Drug-Free Schools and Community Act (SDFSCA) (1986), 466
principles of, 466–467
Safe and responsive schools
characteristics of, 731–733
Tier 1 interventions for, 732–737
Tier 2 interventions for, 732, 737–745
Tier 3 interventions for, 732, 745–748
Safety, school, 728–729
effective best practices for, 731
federal initiatives for, 729
state initiatives for, 729–730
timely responses and, 730–731
Safety plans, 735
Same-sex sexual harassment, 719–720
San Antonio Independent School District v. Rodriguez (1973), 129
Sanders classroom observation form, 454–458, 455f
SAS (Statistical Analysis System), 226
Satisfaction reports, 615
Scales of Independent Behavior—Revised (SIB-R), 444–445
Scanning, optical, 227–228
Schaffer v. Weast (2005), 271
School-based family empowerment, 586–593
School-based services
implications of, for social workers, 172
models of, 169–171
School change model, of school social work, 20
School climate, creating positive, for improving attendance, 701
School community context, for school social work, 23–24
School finance, 128–129
School funding, 129–130
discrepancies in, 130–131
legal remedies for, 131
School-linked services, 132–133
School program, as unit of attention, 541–542
School reforms, 164–166
effects of, on families, 73
implications of, for school social workers, 171–173
locally based, 166
Schools
assessing, 188–189
case example of New Zealand mental health collaboration in, 403–407
child welfare system and, 674
clinical social work in, case study, 536–540
collaboration between child welfare and, 677–678
as community of families, 551–554
development of children and, 3–4
full-service, philosophy of, 171
group work research in, 145–146
literature on effective, 146
managing change in, 189–190
necessary arrangement of relations between families and, 554–556
as organizational culture, 184–185
parents and effectiveness of, 146
partnerships between home and, 552–553
people-processing and people-changing perspectives of, 177–178
research in, 235–236
social development and, 4
social work services in, 260–261
transagency teams in, 583–584
School safety, 121–123
School social work. *See also* School social work practice; Social work
Alderson's models of, 20
assessment in, 322–323
beginning of specialization period in, 18–19
beginnings of, 12–13

broadening approaches to, 20–22
centralization period of, 17
characteristic focus of, 39f
clinical and environmental interventions in, 21, 21f
consultation and, 380
contexts of, 23–25
Culbert's definition of, 12
emergent issues for, 22–23
emergent role of, 22–23
evidence-based practice in, 141–147
evidence of effectiveness of, 145–147
factors affecting contemporary, 133–134
with families, foundations principles for, 55–61
functions of, 20
historical analysis of, 11–23
mental health and, 464–466
mental health policies and, 466–467
models of, 6–11
outcome-based practice and, 50
purposes of, 5–6
rationale for, 15–16
rethinking casework in, 19
role of, in education process, 3–4
school community context for, 23–24
society context of, 24–25
specific *vs.* generic practice, 15–16
theory development issues for, 148–149

School social work as person-environment transaction, 18
School social work assessment, 325–326
School Social Work Association of America (SSWAA), confidentiality and, 98–99
School social work consultants, challenges for, 389–390
School social workers, 6. *See also* Social workers
as change agents, 163–164
clientele of, 23
confidentiality and, 72–73
confidentiality decision-making procedures and principles for, 73–86
contributions of, 31f
disclosure dilemmas facing, 96–97
ethical responsibilities of, 753–755
evaluating effectiveness of, 50–51
focus of, 6
guidelines when providing on the job transportation assistance, 761
implications of reform movements for, 171–173
Internet resources for, 65–66
legal responsibilities of, 753–755
mandated reporter role of, 678
marginalized children and, 3–4
mental health consultation for, 390–394
personal safety guidelines for, 757–761
policy advocacy and, 162–163
policy and, 193–194
policy practice in action, 162–163
policy practice role of, 157–159
in policy space, 196–197
preferences of, 46–47
role development and, 26, 535
role of, in mental health services, 467–468
role of, in education process, 5
role of, with families, 559–573
social worker-learner role of, 346–347
tasks of, 25
traumatic events and, 640
truancy and, 699–709
use of evidence-based practice process, 470–475
use of people-processing and people-changing perspectives of, 177–178

School social work practice. *See also* School social work; Social work practice
culturally competent, 340–342
dialogue between research and, 147–148
evidence-based interventions and, 62–63
with families, 550–551
with families, case example of, 563–566

Scientific values, 43
Screening measures
for adaptive behavior, 441–442
for attention deficit hyperactivity disorder, 479t
for depression in children and adolescents, 479t

Seamons. v. Snow (1994), 722
SEAs. *See* State education agencies (SEAs)
Segregation, 294–295
de facto, 299
de jure, 294–295, 299, 344
in North, 298–299
resegregation and, 304–305

Self-determination, 78
Self-management skills, 626
Separation anxiety, 485–486
Serious harm, 80–81
Service coordination, 281–282
Service core value, 74
Service delivery, planning effective, 358–360

Sex discrimination, educational policy and, 309–311
Sexual harassment, 122–123, 713–714
bullying *vs.*, 714–715
case law, 721–723
defined, 714
legal issues in, 720–723
legislation and regulations, 720–721
peer, 718–723
prevalence of, 715–716
responses to, 723–724
same-sex, 719–720
Sexual minorities, educational policy and, 311
Sharecropping, 294–295
Sheff v. O'Neill (1996), 299
Short-term objectives, 514–515
Shy children, group work for, 597–602
Single-system designs (SSDs), 617
Skills. *See also* Social skills
occupational, 435
of policy practice, 159–162
practical, 435
school social worker, for policy practice, 161
social, 435
Social constructionism, 284
Social development
schools and, 4
truancy and, 694
Social Developmental Study (SDS), 415–422. *See also* Case Study Assessment (CSA)
Social integration, 367
Social interaction model, of school social work practice, 20
Social justice, 341–342
Social networks, 42
Social planning, 380
Social situations, constructing realistic, 627–628
Social skills, 435. *See also* Skills
classroom approaches, 634
common focus areas for training in, 630–632, 631t
conceptualizing, 622–623
defined, 622
Go Grrrls program, 632, 633t
guidelines for teaching, 628–630
training, 621–622
types of, for healthy development, 625–627
Social skills groups. *See also* Groups
evidence base for, 623
group composition for, 623–624
program goals for, 624
refining selected skills, 625
selecting skills for, 624–625
Social work. *See also* School social work
activities of, 45–46
clinical, case study, 536–540
core values of, 74
future of, 44
judgment and, 44
Social work activities, 45–46
purpose of, 36
Social workers. *See also* School social workers
characteristic focus of, 32–35
infants and toddlers with or at risk for disabilities and, 283–284
personal *vs.* professional values of, 73–74
as resource developers, 593–594
Social worker-student relationships, laws addressing, 81–82
Social work knowledge, 35–36
Social work practice. *See also* School social work practice
family-centered, 284–287
incorporating expanding knowledge base into, 51–55
Social work services, for children with disabilities, 260–261, 264–265
Social work values, 12, 13t
Society context, for school social work, 24–25
Solution-focused therapeutic interventions, 671–672
Southern Christian Leadership Council, 296
Special education
assessment process for, 330
defined, 261
multidisciplinary teamwork in, 330–331
outcome-oriented, strengths-based service delivery approach for, 332–334
overrepresentation of minority children in, 306–307
partnerships with parents and, 553
team process in, 329
Special education system, process of, 258–259
Special needs children. *See* Children with disabilities
Specific knowledge, 15–16
SPSS (Statistical Package for Social Sciences), 226
Stakeholders, 76, 100–101
Standardization, 179–180
Standardized measurements, for goals, 614

Standardized tests, minority children and, 307–308
Standard of care, 83–84
Standards for School Social Work Services (NASW), 63–64
State Children's Health Insurance Program (SCHIP), 118–119
State education agencies (SEAs), 5, 128
  NCLB and, 127
  team member roles and relations, 328
State government resources, 230
Statement of needed special education and related services, 500
Strengths-based assessment, 409–410
Strengths-based perspective, 495
  examples of, 496t
Strengths-based practice, 284
Student Nonviolent Coordinating Committee, 296
Students
  practice model of consultation and placement of, 9
  as unit of attention, 542–543
Substance abuse, 119
Substance Abuse and Mental Health Services Administration (SAMHSA), 466
Suicide, 486–488
  reducing contagion of, 656–658
Surveys
  of groups, 615
  in-person, 226
  mailed, 225
  phone, 225–226
Suspension, children with disabilities and, 268–270
Swan v. Charlotte-Mecklenburg Board of Education (1971), 298
Systems assessment, 350–354

Tarasoff v. Regents of the University of California (1976), 82–83, 104–105
Targeted interventions, 336
Targets, practice, 35
Teacher-pupil interactions, observing, 461–462
Teams. *See also* Individualized education program (IEP) teams
  crisis, 647–648
  individualized education program (IEP), 370
  problem-solving, LRE and, 369–370
  professional boundaries and, 328
Teamwork, 326–329
  process of, 329–332
Teen sex and pregnancy, in U.S., 119–120
Telephone calls, for policy advocacy, 163
Temporal integration, 366–367
Testimony, for policy advocacy, 163
Theme interference, 393–394
Theory development issues, for school social work, 148–149
Thirteenth Amendment, 292, 293–294
Tier 1 (universal) interventions, 525–526, 666
  for children involved with child welfare, 679–682
  for safe and responsive schools, 732–737
  for school attendance, 700–702
Tier 2 (targeted) interventions, 526–527, 666–668, 682–685
  for safe and responsive schools, 732, 737–745
  for school attendance, 701–705
Tier 3 (individualized) interventions, 528–529, 666, 685–687
  for safe and responsive schools, 733, 745–748
  for school attendance, 705–709
Timothy W. and Cynthia W. v. Rochester, N. H., School District, 266n2, 266n21
Title VII-B (McKinney-Vento Homeless Assistance Act), 311
Title IX (1972 Education Amendments), 309–311
Tonya K. v. Chicago Public Schools et al., 272n39
Transactions, 35
  defined, 32
  matching person and environment in, 39–41
Transactions Individuals Environment (TIE), 34f, 36
Transagency teams, 583–584
Transcultural perspective, 356
Transference problems, 393
Transgender students. *See* Gay, lesbian, bisexual or transgender (GLBT) students
Transition plan goals, attaining, 509–510
Transition planning, 372–374
Transition services, 500
Transportation assistance, guidelines when providing on the job, 761
Trauma. *See also* Crises
  grief *vs.*, 646–647
  Type I *vs.* Type II, 641–642
Traumatic events, 639–640
  defined, 640–641
  school social workers and, 640

Traumatic stressors, 640–641
Trends in International Mathematics and Science Study (TIMSS), 116
Truancy. *See also* Attendance, school
  case example, 707–708
  long-term whole-school strategic approach, 700–702
  multisystemic assessment of, 695–699
  policy development for, 700–701
  punishments for, 700
  reasons school need and want to prevent, 693
  risk factors associated with, 694–695
  "trigger" point for, 701
Trust, increasing, 680
Tuskegee Normal and Industrial Institute, 293
Tutoring programs, for truancy, 702–703
Type I traumas, 641–642
Type II traumas, 641–642

Ultimate values, 43, 44
Unaccompanied youth, 311
United States
  child abuse and neglect in, 120–121
  demographics of, 116–117
  diversity and, 343–346
  dropout rates in, 123
  homeless children and youths in, 118
  mental health disorders in children in, 119
  physical health of children in, 118–119
  population diversity of, 117
  poverty in, 117–118
  student preparation and schools, 115–116
  substance abuse among students in, 119
Units of attention, 6
  choosing, 562–563
  community as, 543–544
  family as, 542
  process of working with different, 544–547
  pupil as, 542–543
  school program as, 541–542
  school social work roles and, 540–541
Universal interventions, 336

Valeria v. Davis (2002), 312
Value clarification competencies, 161
Values
  defined, 44
  in social work, 12, 13t
  types of, 43–44
Vander Malle v. Ambach, 265n17
Vertical complexity, 181
Vineland Adaptive Behavior Scales (VABS), 445–446
Violence
  early warning signals of, 746
  imminent, duty to warn or protect and, 106–107
  physical, duty to warn or protect and, 105–106
  in schools, 121–123
  youth, 121–123
Violence prevention
  practice model of, 9–10
  response plans and, 736
Visiting teachers, 13–14
Vocational Rehabilitation Act (1973), 168–169
Voucher programs, 132
Vulnerable families, 556
  assessment between school and, 562
Vulnerable populations, schools and, 302–303

Walsh, Froma, 558
Washington, Booker T., 293
Weschsler Intelligence Scale for Children, 308
Weschsler Intelligence Scale for Children—Revised, 308
Williams v. Mississippi (1898), 295
Winkelman v. Parma City School District, 272
Women's Education Association, 13
Woodson, Carter, 291–292, 293, 295
Wraparound planning, 584–586
  steps for, 587–590t

Youth violence, 121–123

Zelman v. Simmons-Harris (2002), 132
Zero reject, principle of, 256
Zero-tolerance policies, 730–731, 736